Also by Pico Iyer

Video Night in Kathmandu

THE LADY AND

THE MONK

THE
LADY
AND
THE
MONK

Four Seasons in Kyoto

PICO
IYER

THE BODLEY HEAD · LONDON

First published in Great Britain 1991
© Pico Iyer 1991
The Bodley Head, 20 Vauxhall Bridge Road,
London SW1V 2SA

Pico Iyer has asserted his right under the Copyright,
Designs and Patents Act 1988 to be identified
as the author of this work

Owing to limitations of space, all
acknowledgments of permission to use
previously published material
may be found on page 339.

A CIP catalogue record for this book
is available from the British Library

ISBN 0-370-31722-X

Printed in Great Britain by
Mackays of Chatham PLC

*For
Michael Hofmann,
and my friend
Hiroko*

Acknowledgments

Like any foreigner in Japan, I suspect, I encountered more kindness and consideration than I had ever found elsewhere, and certainly much more than I deserved. The two to whom this book is dedicated exemplify that spirit in more ways than I can articulate.

I also, however, owe especial thanks to Mari Gotō, who not only taught me a great deal about her country, but endured my gaucheries—and my Japanese—with angelic patience. Somehow, in the midst of an inordinately busy schedule, she took time out to answer all my endless questions and to conduct tireless researches on my behalf. In the process, she taught me by example about much of the sweetness, attentiveness, and thoughtfulness that are so remarkable in Japan.

While I was in Kyoto two of my kindest guardian angels were Barbara Stein and Naohiko Iwasa, who not only opened their home and hearts to me, but also provided me with tea and warmth and friendly conversation even as I was depriving them of their study and their peace. I consider myself very fortunate, too, to have been introduced to Yūko Yuasa, an exemplar of all that is most elegant in Japan and most civilized in any place. Many of the most beautiful parts of Kyoto, like many of the finer points of Japan, I would never have seen had it not been for her; she opened windows for me as well as doors.

I profited greatly from the conversations I enjoyed in Kyoto with Tyrrell O'Neill and Andrew Hartley, among many others, and hope they do not feel let down by what I have produced; Eric Gower was my smiling *sensei* on all things Japanese, a model of how to live in Japan without losing a sense of humor or proportion. Back home, I was, as ever, buoyed and uplifted beyond measure by Kristin McCloy and Mark Muro, who read what I was scribbling with extraordinary sympathy and care, at once cheering me on and holding me to the very highest standards; Steve Carlson, with his genius for conversation, got me to say things I didn't know I knew; and the late Kilian Coster provided me, and many others, with a model of fairness and calm. I am very grateful too to Charles Elliott at Knopf, and Elizabeth Grossman, for all their help in actually seeing my words into print: in the former, I enjoyed the rare luxury of an editor who not only showed exceptional insight and understanding in training a searchlight on my prose, but was even able to correct my Japanese misspellings.

All the time I was living in Kyoto, nobody could quite understand how I was supporting myself while simply reading old poems, wandering around temples, and doing as I pleased. I would not have understood either had I not known *Time*, whose editors continue to find ways of sustaining me even as I go off in stranger and stranger directions. Without them, and the forgiving cooperation of their Tokyo Bureau, I could not even have gone to Japan.

Finally, all the time I was at home, and away, I was kept upright by my long-suffering mother, who reconciled herself with typical patience to a son who always chose to live in the most inconvenient of places, and without a word of complaint, collected my mail, deposited my checks, and looked after my well-being—showing that grace, no more than kindness, is hardly peculiar to Japan.

All that a man has to say or do that can
possibly concern mankind is in some shape
or other to tell the story of his love —
and to sing; and if he is fortunate and
keeps alive, he will be forever in love.

— THOREAU

AUTUMN

1

THE FIRST TIME I ever set foot in Japan, I was on my way to Southeast Asia. Japan Air Lines was putting me up for the night, not far from Narita Airport, and after stumbling out into a silver late afternoon, I was taken to a high-rise hotel set in the midst of rice paddies. After a brief, disjointed sleep, I woke up early on an October morning, clear, with a faint touch of approaching winter. I still had a few hours to spare before my connecting flight, so I decided to take a bus into the local town. Narita could not be a very distinctive place, I thought, as the Japanese equivalent of Inglewood or Heathrow. Yet I was surprised to find a touch of Alpine charm in the quiet of the autumn morning. A high mountain clarity sharpened the October air, and the streets were brisk with a mountain tidiness.

As I began to walk along the narrow lanes, I felt, in fact, as if I were walking through a gallery of still lifes. Everything looked exactly the way it was supposed to look, polished to a sheen, and motionless. Shoes were lined up along the entrances to tiny houses. Low tables sat, just so, on impeccably brushed tatami mats. Coffee-shop windows gazed out upon vistas of rocks and running water. A clatter of kettles rattled outside a silent teahouse.

Then, turning through some wooden gates, I found myself inside Narita Temple. Everything, here too, was held in a state of windless calm. An old man sat on a wooden bench, alone. A swan flapped noisily, and then set graceful sail. A baby, pouched on her mother's back, cast huge eyes up towards the sky. Black and gold swished past, the rustling robes of two young monks.

A gong began to sound, and a column of thin smoke rose high in the clear air.

And then, walking round a corner, I came of a sudden upon a flutter of activity, a cluster of schoolchildren scattered this way and that around the quiet paths, hunched over the ground at strange angles like a flock of odd birds. No more than six years old, perhaps, these curious little creatures were dressed all alike in tidy uniforms: pink and blue hats, white skirts and shorts, sporty white socks. Occasionally, one of them would find what he was looking for—a bean, apparently, or some kind of acorn—and toss it into a cellophane bag, then hurry off in search of more. Otherwise, they all remained so deep in concentration, and so inviolate, that none of them seemed to notice me as they crouched along the tree-shaded path, silent and intent. Around them, in the freshly minted morning, was the coming autumn's faint chill of regret.

And somehow the self-contained quiet of the children, and the elegiac softness in the air—the whole rapt stillness of the scene—took me back, in a flash, to faraway mornings on October days in England, when the Oxford Parks were pungent with the smell of burning leaves and crisp with the crackle of leaves underfoot. For the first time in twenty years, I was back in a duffel coat, futureless and blithe, running through a faintly sunny morning to throw bread to the swans in the lake, then hurrying home for tea in the darkening afternoon. Called back through the years to distant childhood, I was back, too, in the blue intensity of knowing nothing but the present moment.

There were many features of Japan that might have reminded me of England: the small villages set amidst rich green hills, all scaled with a cozy modesty; the self-enclosure of an island apart from the world, not open to sea and light, as tropical islands are, but huddled in upon itself, an attic place of gray and cold; a sense of polite aloofness, a coolness enforced by courtesies and a language built on shadows; even the sense of immovable hierarchy that made both countries seem like giant Old Boys

Clubs, where nobody worked in college because the name of the college alone was enough to decide every future. But none of that could explain the urgency of a Wordsworthian moment on a mild October morning, in a place I had never seen before. And the moment stayed inside me like the tolling of a bell.

That first fleeting taste of Japan felt like the answer to some unspoken question. For through whatever curious affinities propel us towards people or places we have never met, I had always been powerfully drawn towards Japan. Ever since boyhood, I had only to glimpse a Hokusai print of peasants huddled under driving rain, or to enter the cold beauty of a Kawabata novel, to feel a shock of penetrating recognition. For years, the mere mention of an "inn," or "snow country," or even a "prefecture," had sent a shiver through me, and a chill. And though I knew almost nothing about Japan and had never had the chance to study it, I felt mysteriously close to the place, and closest of all when I read its poems—the rainy-night lyrics of Japanese women, the clear-water haiku of itinerant Zen monks. From afar, Japan felt like an unacknowledged home.

The next year, I happened to return to Japan, for a slightly longer stay. This time I was there with my mother, on a brief sight-seeing tour, and as soon as we arrived, we found ourselves propelled through the modern nation in all its bullet-trained efficiency. For four days, we glided through uniform hotels, in and out of tour buses, through one fluorescent coffee shop after another. At night, I went out alone into the streets and lost myself in the clangor of their amusement-arcade surfaces, the crash of white signs, bright lights, neon colors—a toyland gone berserk with an intensity that could not have been further from the lyrical land I imagined. Yet even here, in the midst of commotion, images would occasionally bob up and pull me down below the surface of myself: just a picture, perhaps, of a girl alone beside a rain-streaked window; or a monk all in black, alone with his begging bowl, head bowed, in the midst of shopping crowds.

One evening, I wandered through the ancient geisha quarter of Kyoto as night began to fall over the houses, and life to stir within them. The crooked, narrow streets were secret in the dusk, but still I could catch snatches from within: laughter from some inner passage, figures outlined in an upstairs window, the whitened face of an apprentice geisha slipping like a ghost into a waiting taxi.

By the time the street led out onto a busy road, it was dark, and I could just make out, in front of me, the entrance to a park. Inside the giant *torii* gates, I found myself amidst a carnival of lights like nothing I had ever seen, or dreamed, before. Families were gathered by the side of a pond, ringed by lanterns, and lamplit stalls were set along their paths. A surge of people were marching up a path, and as I hurried after them, the way led through the darkness and into another, broader path, framed on both sides by lanterns. The lights, red and white, bobbed ahead of us, up another slope, and then along a further path, until, of a sudden, the path gave way to a kind of plateau. Around me, families ducked under lanterns or darted into shrines to have their fortunes told, inscribed in sweeping calligraphy on wooden blocks. Above me, lights danced across the hill like fireflies.

As I began to climb, the noise fell away, and the crowds started to thin out. Soon I was far above the town, alone in a world of lanterns. For on this, the Night of a Thousand Lanterns, lights had been placed beside every grave, to lead departed spirits back to Buddha. And I, somehow, without knowing it, had found my way alone into an ancient graveyard. For many minutes I stood there, in the company of ghosts and shivering lights.

When finally I made my way back down, and into the festive

streets, the spell did not shatter, but only gained texture and animation. Round businessmen in loosened ties went reeling arm in arm amidst the weaving lights, and gaggles of giggling girls shuffled behind, fluent in their best kimono. The tea-houses along the Kamo River were strung with lights this summer night, and large parties were gathered on their wooden terraces, set on stilts above the moonlit water. Along the darkened riverbank, lovers sat side by side, spaced out at regular intervals, as self-contained as in some *tableau vivant.* I had passed through a looking glass and into a world of dreams.

That second trip was enough to decide me: it was time to put my visions of Japan to the test. At home, these days, one heard constantly about the zany forms of modern Japan, the double standards of its political system, the strategies of its companies, all the craft of the collective rising sun of economic power that seemed to be the capital of the future tense; but the private Japan, and the emotional Japan—the lunar Japan, in a sense, that I had found in the poems of women and monks—was increasingly hard to glimpse. If this imaginative Japan existed only in my mind, I wanted to know that soon, and so be free of the illusion forever; yet if there were truly moments in Japan that took me back to a home as distantly recalled as the house in which I was born, I wanted to know that too. Residing six thousand miles away, I could only remain as distracted as when one tries and tries to recover the rest of some half-remembered melody.

In Japan, moreover, I wanted to put another daydream to the test: the vision I had always cherished of living simply and alone, in some foreign land, unknown. A life alone was the closest thing to faith I knew, and a life of Thoreauvian quiet seemed most practicable abroad. Japan, besides, seemed the ideal site for such an exercise in solitude, not only because its polished courtesies kept the foreigner out as surely as its closed doors, but also because its social forms were as unfathomable to me, and as alien, as the woods round Walden Pond.

In the fall of 1987, therefore, as a kind of dare to myself, I bought a ticket for Japan. I took nothing more than a little money that I had saved: no plans, no contacts, no places to live. In my suitcase I had a few essentials, and copies of Emerson, Wilde, and Thoreau; in my head, the name of a temple, a few phrases I had learned from a Buddhist priest in Santa Barbara, and a schedule of the festivals by which the Japanese measure their seasons. On September 22 — the first official day of autumn, a new-moon night with an eclipse of the sun, and, as it happened, the day on which the aging Emperor underwent an internal bypass operation that threatened the central symbol of the land — I took off for Japan.

2

So it was that one day later, I found myself standing in Kyoto, two cases in my hand, outside a tiny temple in the rain. A shaven-headed monk, an albino as it happened, with vague eyes and a face like baby's milk, appeared before me, smiling. "Do you speak English?" I asked him, in Japanese. *Litteru,* he replied, and so I asked once more. "One night, three thousand, five hundred," he said. "Free breakfast." Then he pointed to a courtyard behind him, crowded with bicycles, motorbikes, and mopeds. "My hobby," he explained.

That, it seemed, was the end of the conversation, of small talk and of big. Eyes bulging, the pale monk motioned to a pair of slippers, then led me through a maze of gleaming corridors, past a tidy rock garden, across an altar room equipped with gong and elegant calligraphy, and into another tiny room. A room was all it was—a bare rectangle of tatami mats bordered by sliding screens. Pulling out a mattress that was standing in the corner, he nodded in my direction, and I collapsed.

Later, many hours later, when I awoke, the world was dark. I looked around, but there was no way of telling whether it was night or day. On every side of me was a sliding door: one that gave onto another tiny, empty space; another that led into the darkened shrine, spectral now in the gloom; a third that proved to be nothing but a wall; and a fourth that, when I slid it open, afforded me a glimpse of the garden behind and, rising high above it, the silhouette of a five-story pagoda, the moon a torn fingernail in the sky.

Fumbling my way through the dark, I stumbled through the

shrine and out into the entrance hall, and then into the narrow street. Everything, here too, was hushed. Temple roofs and spires haunted the brownish sky. Banners fluttered from the wooden eaves of teahouses. The darkness was pricked by nothing save white lanterns and the blue-and-white badges of American Express.

I walked along the empty lane in a dream of strange displacement. No other pedestrians walked these midnight streets; no cars purred through the ghosted dark. Only occasionally could I catch the distant murmurs of some secret entertainment. Then, as the first speckles of rain began prickling my arms, I hurried back into the temple. All night long, the rain pattered down on wooden roofs, and I, now sleeping, now awake, sat alone in the darkened shrine, not really knowing where I was.

The next morning, when I got up and made my way uncertainly out to the altar room, the monk bustled up to greet me. The first item on the agenda was a guided tour. And the first stop on the tour was what appeared to be the only piece of decoration in the place: a framed photograph of himself, seated atop a tricycle, looking astonished, a bobble hat on his shaven head and a Mickey Mouse shirt under his alabaster face. "This me," he explained. "I am Buddhist monk." Then, in the same provisional tone, he proceeded to recite the American sites he had seen—"San Francisco, Los Angeles, Monument Valley, Grand Canyon, San Antonio, El Paso, New Orleans, Washington, Philadelphia, New York, Buffalo." Then he led me to a low table, overlooking the temple garden, and vanished.

A few minutes later, my bewilderment now almost mirroring his own, he hurried in again and laid down before me a black lacquer tray filled with elegant little bowls of vegetables, fruit, pickles, and rice; later, a toaster, some bread, and a thermos of hot water for my tea. Then he disappeared again.

I was just beginning to enjoy the feast, looking out upon the green and silver stillness, when suddenly his astonished-looking face appeared again, speeding through the garden atop a motorized contraption. He rode up to the room where I was sitting, looked astonished some more, waved like a queen, and then roared away again in a minicloud of smoke. The next thing I knew, he was at my door, on foot this time, peering in with a hesitant smile. "Tricycle," he said, pointing at the offending instrument, Mickey and Minnie grinning on its license plate. With that, he disappeared.

My second day, as I sat in the alcove looking out onto the other garden—a stream, a wooden bridge, a stone lantern, and, beyond, Yasaka Pagoda rising through the trees—the second, and only other, monk of the temple, an older man, with the breathless, frightened voice of a perennially bullied schoolboy issuing from a spherical wrestler's body, padded over to me. He spoke even less English than his colleague, but that did not seem to matter, since his was not a verbal medium. Huffing and puffing, but without a word, he sat down beside me and pulled out six sheaves of snapshots: himself (wide-eyed) in front of the Taj Mahal; himself (bemused) on a bridge above the Thames; himself (bewildered) on l'Île de la Cité; himself (perplexed) on the steps of the Piazza di Spagna; and himself with a variety of other scenic wonders. Then, show complete, he trudged away again.

A eunuch and an albino: the monks with whom I was living were the strangest-looking pair that ever I had seen, and a cynic, no doubt, would have had no trouble explaining why they had turned their backs on the world before the world could turn its back on them. Yet they were an eminently kindly pair, and peaceable, and I began in time to think of them as good companions. Every morning, as I took my seat in front of the rock garden, they laid before me a four-course breakfast, and every morning—with a thoughtfulness and precision I could imagine only in Japan—they gave me something different. Every evening, when I went out, I found them squashed together on the floor, at a tiny table in a tiny room, drinking beer before some TV ball game. "Catch you later," the albino monk would call out after me, waving his bottle merrily in my direction, chalky white legs protruding from tomato-red shorts.

The area where I had settled down was, by happy chance, one of the last remaining pilgrims' districts in Japan, an ancient neighborhood of geisha houses and incense stores built in the shadow of the city's most famous temple, Kiyomizu, the Temple of Pure Water. Wooden boards still marked the places Bashō had admired, and monks still bathed in the ice-cold Sound of Feathers waterfall above. My own street, as it happened, was still a center of the *mizu-shōbai*, or "water trade" (of women), and also the place where the widow of the city's fiercest shogun, Toyotomi Hideyoshi, had retired, on her husband's death, and built a villa and a temple. In the temple, I had read, *yama-nekko*, or "mountain lion," geisha had entertained at parties for the monks, and even now the elegant characters on the lanterns denoted the names of the women who worked within.

Thus the whole area was preserved as carefully as a museum treasure. My local café was a rock-garden teahouse, sliding blond-wood screens opening out onto a clean geometry of wood and water; the neighborhood stores were polished galleries selling sea-blue Kiyomizu pots, silken fans, and woodblock prints, all silvered with the sound of water music; and my next-door neighbor was a forty-foot statue of the goddess Kannon, majestic against the mapled hills.

Few places in Japan were as self-consciously Japanese as Kyoto, the romantic, templed city that had been the capital for a thousand years and even now was faithfully preserved as a kind of shrine, an antique, the country's Greatest Living National Treasure. Almost 100,000 tourists (mostly Japanese) came here every day to pay their respects to the "City of Peace and Harmonious Safety," and the city, accustomed to their worship, handed itself over to them like a collection of gift-wrapped slides — even the place mats at the local McDonald's (which had once set a world record for serving two million burgers in a single day) were maps of the city's lyrical conceits, locating the temple whose floorboards sang like nightingales and the rock garden that traced the pattern of infinity.

Yet even the efficiency of its charm could hardly diminish the city's beauty. My first Sunday morning in Kyoto, I hurried out of the temple at first light and climbed the steep cobbled paths that lead up to Kiyomizu. Taking the wrong path without knowing it, and passing through a side temple, I slipped out into a rock garden. A woman, mistaking me for a VIP, came out with a gold-and-indigo tray bearing a cup of green tea. The maples before us climbed towards the blue. Everywhere was a silence calm as prayer.

Minutes later, I was walking through the teeming basement of a department store, overflowing with more fruit, more pickles, more high-tech gadgets than I could easily take in; sorbet houses and wineshops, noodle joints and macaroni parlors, melon outlets and chocolate-makers. I bought an ice cream from a girl, and she wrapped it in a bag with a smart gold twizzle around the neck, put that bag in a larger, foam bag, complete with two blocks of ice to keep the whole from melting, and wrapped it all in the stylish black-and-gold bag of her company; I went to temples and was handed entrance tickets that looked like watercolor prints; I walked into a park again, in the cloudless exaltation of a perfect Sunday morning, and could scarcely believe that I had stumbled upon such a flawless world. To partake of the gleaming splendors of the *depāto* and to sip green-tea floats in teahouses; to find moonlit prints in convenience stores and damascene earrings in coffee shops: it shook me out of words.

It sometimes seemed, in fact, in those early days, as if all Japan were at once charging into the future with record-breaking speed, and moving as slowly as a glacier; both sedative and stimulant, a riddle of surface and depth.

And so, in time, the days in the temple began to find a rhythm of their own, and I to set my watch by the pattern of their calm. Every morning at 6 a.m., the sound of the tolling gong and the husky rumble of chanted sutras, broken by the silver tinkle of a bell. Then the patter of receding footsteps. Sweet incense seeping under the screen, making the space all holy. Then breakfast in first light, beside the garden, and random walks through lemon-scented mornings, rainbow banners fluttering above the wooden shops. At noon, the elder monk would take his dog, Kodo, for a walk and then, regal in black robes, clap his hands above the pond, summoning the carp to lunch. A little later, the temple was silent again, and the tidy pairs of slippers outside one room, and the squeak of a TV hostess, told me that the monks were eating.

At night, when the city was asleep, I took to slipping out of the place to make phone calls to my employers in Rockefeller Center (New York offices were open from midnight to 8 a.m. Kyoto time). And only then, as I stood in a squat green phone booth, plastered all over with trim stickers advertising topless girls—a novel kind of convenience shopping—did I see the other, shadow side of Japan begin to emerge: the derelicts with wild hair, the crazy-eyed vagrants and disheveled beggars, venturing out into the pedestrian arcades or huddled together under department store eaves, tidy in their way and self-contained, as if, in some part of themselves still good Japanese, they were determined not to intrude upon the world around them. Watching these denizens of the underworld—all but invisible except in the city center and late at night—I recalled that such a one, six centuries before, had gone on to found Daitokuji, the Temple of Great Virtue.

* * *

By day, though, the temple was mostly deserted: just me, the two monks, and their dog. Sometimes, on the wall above the toilet, another visitor appeared, a vile, pale-green lizard, with eyes like raisins on the top of his head. And one bright morning, after I had finished breakfast, I met the only other member of the household, a laborer who came each day to make the gardens perfect. As soon as I returned the gardener's smile, he came on over and shook my hand in the glassy autumn sunshine. "Are you wealthy?" he began. A little taken aback, I did what I had been told to do in every meeting with a Japanese male: handed him my business card. This he scrutinized as if it were Linear B.

"My hobby is making money," he went on, and then, before I could get him wrong, interjected, "Is joke!" I see, I thought, a joke. Then the conversation took a literary turn.

"Have you read Milton? And Shakespeare? How about Nietzsche, Kant?"

"Sometimes," I said. "Have you practiced English with many foreigners?"

"Oh no." He waved his hands at me. "I very embarrassed. I cannot. Especially girls. I very, very shy."

This, I thought, was familiar enough terrain. "So you like American girls?"

"At first." He paused. "But gradually, no."

"They are not *shizukana*," I tried.

He nodded happily. "Not modest."

"You must be working hard today."

"Not so hard. One hour I talking monks. Now Grand Sumō tournament. Monks love Sumō very much; every day they watch. Three hour." Yet another surprising arrow to their quiver!

The other unexpected feature of the temple was that it was ringed, in large part, by the gaudy purple blocks and curtained parking lots of love hotels. This was, of course, in a way, quite apt:

monks and women had always been close in Japanese literature —
had, in fact, been the main purveyors of classical Japanese
literature — and Gion itself, the name of the "flower district"
here, was also the name of a famous temple. Professional women
had long been known as "Daruma" (after Bodhidharma, the
first patriarch of Zen) because, like legless Daruma dolls, they
tumbled as soon as they were touched, and then bounced back.
And "dark willows, bright flowers" — a Zen metaphor for the
Buddha nature — had long been a euphemism for the pleasure
quarters, or so I had learned from a scroll I had seen in
Santa Barbara, by the eighteenth-century Zen monk Gakkō,
suggesting that Daruma could as easily be found in a brothel as
in a temple. Even one of the most famous episodes in Bashō
had found the wandering monk and a disciple in an inn, spending the night next to two concubines and their elderly consort.
The next morning, the girls, on a pilgrimage to Ise, had expressed
their wish to travel with the monks, and Bashō, regretfully, had
demurred:

> At the same inn
> Play women too were sleeping,
> Bush clover and the moon.

Nonetheless, it came as something of a shock to me, on the
night of the harvest moon, to return to the temple to find two
pairs of delicate white pumps resting neatly in the yard of
motorbikes. I wondered whether the monks were entertaining,
but I could hear no whispers in the dark, no rustling behind
doors. Next morning, I stumbled off my mattress at the sound
of dawn prayers, as usual, and wandered into the breakfast
room, to find two young Japanese girls — perfectly composed, of
course, and tidily dressed, even at this extremely godly hour —
standing in the garden, while the elder monk fussed all about
them. Then, with a gallantry I had not expected of him, he
effected an introduction of sorts, led us to the low table, and

presented us all with a full, five-course Japanese breakfast. A little awkwardly, we sat around the table, the two girls exchanging giggles and dainty jokes, then shy smiles and painful pleasantries. They asked me a question, and then giggled. I returned the favor, and there was more giggling. Their giggles came close to hysteria when they looked across the table to see the foreigner flapping around wildly with his chopsticks, and losing, by a technical knockout, to a piece of sushi. Then, just as fun was at its maddest, up roared the albino, astride his motorized tricycle and giving us all his Empress wave. With that, he zipped away. We were only just beginning to catch our breath after this unexpected command performance when suddenly he materialized again, pale legs pumping furiously as he pedaled through the delicate garden on a baby-blue tricycle, Donald Duck chuckling on its mudguard. The girls clapped their hands in delight and giggled some more, and the monk, flushed with his success, gave another majestic wave and pedaled off again.

The idea of living in a temple while stealing out after midnight to make contact with New York appealed to my sense of incongruity, and I felt open and uncluttered in my empty room. But I could tell that it would be an encumbrance to continue staying there, not least because my after-midnight telephone calls disturbed the monks' early nights as surely as their dawn prayers disturbed my early mornings. Besides, the main purpose of monasticism, I thought, was to help one build a shrine within, so strong that time and place were immaterial. I decided, therefore, to find myself a basic, functional room and to keep the temple as my secret hideaway.

When I told the monks that I was leaving, there was a great commotion. The albino asked me, again and again, if I could not stay but a single night more, and the gardener, with whom I had grown accustomed to having daily chats, announced that I was the first foreigner he had ever met who was "reserved, polite, and modest" (an encomium that his own politeness doubtless prompted him to deliver to every foreigner he met). The elderly monk invited me into his chamber for a final cup of tea, and only the lizard seemed unmoved.

3

ON ONE OF MY first days in Kyoto, a poet from Boulder, whom I met by chance in the Speakeasy "American-Style Coffee Shop," urged me to go, that very evening, to a once-a-month happening called the Kyoto Connection. On my way there, in the bus, a frizzy-haired potter from Santa Cruz sat down next to me and told me that she was going there too. Five minutes later, we found ourselves in a quiet Londonish square, in front of a murky little dive with blackened windows on which was inscribed: "Studio Varié: Le Chat qui Fume."

Inside was a small stage in front of a bar, and lots of smoky little tables at which were seated a ragtag group of Bohos: foreigners with shaven heads, foreigners in dreadlocks, shiny-faced Japanese men with ponytails, and bright-eyed Japanese girls. Two girls came in and joined us at our table—friends of Siobhan's, I gathered—dressed in scarves, with kohl around their eyes and hennaed hair and bangles. One, with a ring in her nose, was just back from Tibet; the other, wearing a yin-yang necklace and maroon Nepali trousers, was settled now in Angola. The first talked about "the full moon on the terraces of Lhasa," the other about "the powerful kind of energies in Luanda." An emcee got on the stage, an Aussie with a thick black beard—a former Rajneeshee, I was told, from Tasmania—and announced that this was to be the "Peter Tosh Memorial Evening." A Japanese "salaryman" in his middle years strolled in and sat down at our table, whispering to me urgently, "Please help me. I want to meet foreign girls." And then the show began.

The first group was a quartet singing "Blowin' in the Wind" in Japanese, and soon they were followed by another Japanese group, a trio of young students with soft high voices and angel harmonies, singing, "It never rains in southern California," and then, "I'm proud to be an Okie from Muskogee," and then, in words I could scarcely recognize, "Good morning, America, how are you? Say, don't you know me, I'm your native son. . . ." Next up was a local bluegrass sextet delivering "Tennessee Homesick Blues," and I began to wonder whether people here sang songs only if they had American place names in their titles.

Then the foreign acts began: satirical stanzas, shouted out in confrontational Beat fashion, that began, "I am a clump of cottage cheese"; poems about Mao, poems with allusions to Godard, and—inevitably—love poems about persimmons wet with summer dew ("Well, she liked it," huffed the bearded American poet when the audience began to jeer). A Japanese girl got up, holding a white rose, and sang a plaintive ancient melody, *"Hamabeno Uta,"* by Narita Tamezo.

> *In the morning on the beach I walk around, remembering.*
> *The sound of wind, the shape of clouds, the surf, the color*
> *of the shell;*
> *In the evening, my lover wanders on the beach,*
> *Remembering the waves come up, go down;*
> *Moonlight, starlight.*

As I was taking all this in, my eye happened to catch that of the quiet foreigner beside me. He was a shy-looking fellow in plaid shirt and scuffed gray corduroys, sitting by himself and doodling in a sketchbook. Seeing me watching him, he explained that he was an artist, and came from San Francisco, and had lived here on and off for fifteen years, learning to paint in the traditional Zen *sumi-e* tradition. Before that, Mark went on, he had been a student in Santa Barbara, and when I told him my name, he told me that he had taken a course in Spinoza from a Mrs. Iyer—my mother—and we were off, busily exchanging names in common while, around us, a potbellied character in glasses, so overcome with emotion—or something like it—by the Philip Glass variations being played by a Japanese waiter on a Chinese harp, got up and began swaying to the music, rolling his hands around like a Balinese nymph, and various others started humming "Om" or sat back rocking on their chairs, eyes closed.

Four hours later, sometime after midnight, the show was over, and a mix of strange spirits spilled out into the half-lit lanes: a ponytailed imp from New York, whose claim to fame was painting the patriarchs of Zen with Marty Feldman faces; a girl from Minnesota who was married to a Japanese flamenco dancer; a slightly unsteady Japanese woman, whose American husband had been the translator of some of Japan's most famous love poems; a vivacious Japanese girl seemingly on the lookout for foreigners ("I live in Gion"—pretty giggle—"you know, the entertainment area?"); and two hearty beer-swilling German students, one bespectacled, besweatered, and apparently keen to hear more about Gion, the other long-haired and leather-jacketed, with a blasé look that suggested that he, with his rock-star looks, had already found a local girlfriend.

Meanwhile, the diligent salaryman kept sidling up to one foreign girl after another, whispering something in each one's ear and then standing erect and nodding solemnly as he got the bad news, receiving each rejection like a gift.

A few nights later, as I shuffled through the business cards I had collected at the gathering, I noticed, to my surprise, that the street on which Mark was living had the same name as my own. Japanese streets are notoriously as straight as their sentiments and as easy to follow as their sentences. But still, I thought, this was a lead worth following. Going to the nearest phone booth, I gave him a call.

Two minutes later, I was seated in Mark's creaky old Japanese-style house — the very Santa Cruz vision of what a Zen painter's house should be, its central paper lantern reflected in the window twice over, twin moons, as we sat cross-legged on cushions at a low, worm-eaten table.

The old room was rigorously spare and clean: just a few cassettes in a wooden cigar box, a collection of brushes in a tin, and, on the wall, some paintings of Zen themes and a nude. From next door came the steady, monotonous chanting of a Buddhist woman; from the rafters, the scuttling of rats. Putting on some tea, Mark told me a little of how he had come here.

He had grown up, he said, in San Francisco, surrounded by artifacts from Japan, brought over by his aunt and uncle, and fascinated by the stories they had told him of the land where they once lived. Yet he had never really had any contact with the island until his senior year in college, in Santa Barbara. "And then this man called Shibayama came over from Kyoto. Only for a week. But somehow — it was one of those things — everywhere I went that week, I kept running into him." He shook his head at the memory. "He was this really amazing guy, the head abbot of Nanzenji: gentle, but very direct. I'd never met anyone like him before."

This was '69, and having survived the student riots, Mark had taken off with a blackjack dealer from Nepal, across the Overland Trail — through Turkey, Iran, and Afghanistan — and ended up living with a Tibetan family in Kathmandu. But as he'd settled down there and begun to take the measure of his trip, and to read deeper in the book of Shibayama's that he'd been carrying around with him, he began to feel "that there must be some reason for my meeting him. So that really confirmed my sense that I ought to come over to Kyoto to study with him."

By then, however, he was beginning to run out of money, so he went back to the West Coast, started saving up again, and finally, three years after that first meeting, made it to Kyoto. "My first day here, I went over to see the *rōshi*, and his first question was what I wanted to do over here. Jeez, I had no idea! But I'd done some sculpting in Santa Barbara, and Shibayama's interpreter and assistant—this really amazing woman called Miss Kudo, whom I'd met in California—had suggested that I mention my interest in painting as well. So I did, and he instantly said, 'Oh, I have this friend who's a painter. Let me introduce you.' And so, the very next day, I was introduced to Jikihara-sensei, who's one of the top *sumi-e* painters in the country. He didn't speak any English and I didn't have any Japanese, but we got on without any problems. And when I told Shibayama that I was also interested in Zen, he sent me to a temple—Antaiji— and as soon as I arrived there, I ran into an American monk, who found me a place to live with another student of Zen.

"So anyway, my first few days here, everything pretty much fell into place, and I met all these people who were going to have a big influence on my life—Shibayama-roshi, and my teacher, who's still my teacher now and probably the main force determining the course of my life, and these two Zen students who are still in many ways my closest friends. Fairly soon there were also these two friends I knew from Santa Barbara, who came over to become monks." A quiet smile. "Just kind of karma, I guess.

"Two years later, after I'd settled into an artists' village in the mountains—and into the rhythms of my new discipline—the *rōshi* died. On the day of his funeral, there was a thin drizzle, really thin. A line of pilgrims stretched all the way from the main hall to the next subtemple. And all of them were carrying bells. I still remember the sound of their bells ringing in the drizzle. A little later, Miss Kudo died too."

Handing me a gift before I left—a friend's homemade map to the city's secret places—Mark invited me to come with him next day on a walk through some of the nearby temples. By the time I arrived, early on another blazing morning, the sun was flooding through his wood-framed windows. Pulling the screen door closed behind him—he never locked his door, he said—he led me down a maze of alleyways and towards the eastern hills. As we walked, I asked him a little more about the practice of Zen.

He had never been a monk himself, Mark explained, but he had stayed in a temple sometimes and had attended monthly sessions of *sesshin*—five days of almost uninterrupted meditation, even in the unheated monasteries in the depths of December. Many of his closest friends were monks, and though his teacher too was not a formal Zen master, he had a temple of his own on an island near Osaka. And though Mark took care not to say it, I could quickly tell that Zen had given him a discipline and a focus: in the cycle of vagrancy and stillness by which he led his life—now spending two years in Kyoto, now taking off for Grenada or Mexico or California for a while, then returning again to Kyoto; in his devotion to his teacher, with whom he had lived for two years as a personal attendant; and, most important, in his training in an art that was, of course, a training in a life.

Though many of Mark's friends had left their temples by now, that was mostly, he implied, because they had reached a stage at which the temples would not leave them. Many of them, he said, had wearied of the worldly aspects of the monastic life—the politicking, the emphasis on sheer willpower, the need for subservience, the stress on hierarchy: all the qualities, in short, that could make temples seem just like any other affluent, rule-bound Japanese company. Yet the temples had given them a certain intensity, a sense of discipline, that stayed with them even now.

We walked past a temple graveyard—newly cut flowers at the base of many headstones, and candies still fresh in their eighty-yen wrappers—and Mark pointed out how such rites were the source of many of the temple's riches: a single headstone here cost twenty thousand dollars. Recently, in fact, the temples had made headlines by refusing to pay taxes to the city and threatening to close their gates to visitors—thus paralyzing the city's most lucrative tourist attractions—unless they were granted an exemption. This much, I knew, was in keeping with Kyoto's history: spiritual and temporal powers had always clashed as often as they had conspired here. If the purity of religion had occasionally touched and elevated the *daimyō,* the chicanery of realpolitik had more often lowered and implicated the monks, who had famously become warriors and libertines and even moneylenders. Poems regularly punned on the closeness between *sen* (a kind of money) and Zen.

"You'll also notice," he went on, as we mounted a steep hill, framed by orange *torii* gates, "how the Buddhist temples here are always dark and somber; black. People associate them with death. And usually they come to them only for funerals—or as tourist sites. The Shinto shrines, by comparison, are always red and orange—these really bright and happy colors—and that's where people come for marriages and New Year's Day and other festivals."

Nowadays, of course, he continued, Zen had much more appeal for foreigners than for Japanese (who generally entered monasteries only if they had to take over a family temple): this despite—or maybe because of—the fact that outsiders had a great deal to give up before they could even enter the front portals of Zen, and the surrendering of self and cerebration clearly came less easily to us than to many Japanese. "I remember this one Zen teacher told me, soon after I arrived, that the appeal of Zen to many foreigners was like a mountain wrapped in mist. Much of what the Westerners saw was just the beautiful mist; but as soon as they began really doing Zen, they found that its essence was the mountain: hard rock."

And so we wandered on, past quiet mothers wheeling prams, and age-spotted men pulling yapping dogs; past schoolgirls shuffling their slow way home along canals, and coffee shops where women sat alone, the autumn moon above them in the blue.

Finally, our path meandered into the Tetsugaku-no-michi, or

Philosopher's Path, a narrow, tree-shaded walkway along the base of the eastern hills, beside a slow canal. Above us, a thick camouflage of trees carpeted the slopes, broken, now and then, by the severe spire of some temple; on the other side, pink coffee shops and teddy-bear boutiques rested placid above the bustle of the city. I noticed the Bobby Soxer pizza and spaghetti house, and the Atelier café, run, so I'd heard, by a former mistress of the novelist Tanizaki; I noticed too, amidst the trees, the small temple of Anrakuji, where once—in one of the most famous of all Kyoto's scandals—two of an Emperor's favorite concubines had stopped to hear two priests, and been so bewitched by them (or by their message) that they had chosen to forsake the court and join the temple as nuns. Upon hearing of this defection, the enraged Emperor had sentenced both Anraku and the other monk to death.

We stopped in a café, owned by a *samurai* actor, and as we walked on, were given salted plum tea by two chirpy salesgirls. Farther on, inside a shrine almost Chinese in its solemnity, with stone lions perched on either side of its imposing orange entrance, Mark pointed out a small statue covered with a scarlet bib and surrounded by knickknacks—stuffed animals, frilly shirts, flowers, and piles of stones. Jizō, he explained, was the patron saint of children and of travelers (very apt, I thought, since every child is a born adventurer and every traveler a born-again child). These offerings, in fact, were remembrances of *mizugo*, or "water children"—children who had died young or been stillborn or, in most cases, aborted. "Is that a sign of real sorrow or just a kind of ritual?" I asked, assuming, as always, that the Japanese were not like other people (the same assumption that so enrages us when the Japanese apply it to us). "Well," said Mark quietly, "I've known a number of women here who've had abortions, and they're always really affected by them." Having lived here for fifteen years, Mark was clearly well accustomed to dealing with wide-eyed romantics from abroad.

Finally, we arrived at the sprawling compound of Nanzenji—

Shibayama's temple—and stopped in a small room to drink green tea, the dark, red-carpet chamber lit up by a rush of silver down the rocks it faced. In the rooms that followed, we saw stylized paintings of white cranes and prowling tigers on gold-lacquer screens, and then the famous rock garden designed by Kobori Enshu ("Approach a great painting," he had written, "as you would a great prince"). I noticed how the pines and maples on the hill behind, faintly red and orange and green, blended seamlessly into the pattern of raked gravel, Nature consenting to become a part of art. "This was the first painting I ever did," Mark explained. "The 'Leaping Tiger Garden.' The first time I visited my teacher, he just gave me three sheets of paper and said, 'Come back in a week with three paintings.' I did. And when I showed them to him, he just redid them himself—right on top of my drawings!" His quiet voice caught fire. "And I was breathless. The vitality he gave to the scene! The stones had real power, tension. He caught the sound of the water, the softness of the hills behind. He made the whole place come alive!"

Then, as we wandered back into the streets, watching two models set up for a TV ad, Mark asked me with a quiet smile if I thought I might find a Japanese girlfriend.

"Oh no," I replied easily enough. "I've come here mostly to live alone; and besides, I don't think any Japanese girls are likely to have much time for me."

"Well," he said with a penetrating glance, "it would have to be an exceptional girl. But that's the only kind that you would want."

That night, Mark introduced me to two of his closest friends, Shelley, a funny, warmhearted lawyer from Brooklyn, and her husband, Kazuo, trim in his jeans, with close-cropped hair and glasses, a teacher of animal sciences at Kyoto University, the most high-powered site of higher learning in the country. Over mounds of curry, a "Positive Thinking" tape reproducing the lap and hiss of the ocean behind us, Mark and Shelley reminisced a little about the folklore of the foreigners (or *gaijin*) here: of *gaijin* who had been directed to the vet when sick, of *gaijin* who, after three years in a firm, were still listed in the company directory as "Mr. Foreigner," of *gaijin* who had been made to sign confessions if ever they were late in renewing their Alien Registration forms.

Kazuo, meanwhile, sat silent in his chair.

"How was your summer?" Mark asked him.

"I was in the temple," he said tersely. For three whole months, he went on, he had been up Mount Hiei, the famous sacred mountain in the northeast of the city, training to be a Tendai Buddhist monk. For the first month, he had had to get up at five every morning, take a cold shower, and then climb the mountain to collect pure water from a well. In their second month, the apprentice monks had had to get up at two and do the same, while praying three or four times every day. The food was sparse, and the days were cold and hard. But that was only the first stage. Those who were serious would have to complete another course, lasting three full years — sweeping leaves for six hours a day — and then another, for five years, and then, if they were ready, they could try the famous thousand-day circuit, the "Great Marathon" around the mandala mountain and in and out of the city, in which they would have to run, in handmade straw sandals, fifty miles a day for one hundred days at a stretch, year after year, until they had done the equivalent of running around the world. Part of their training involved going nine days without food or water or rest, watched around the clock by two monitor monks. Many of them lost weight, fell ill. Some even died. Any who failed to complete a single part of the course felt obliged to slash their own throats. But those who survived, anointed as "Living Buddhas," took on the unearthly glow of souls that had almost passed through death; during their nine-day fasts, they grew so sensitive that they could hear ash falling from an incense stick, smell food being prepared many miles away.

For years, I recalled, women had not even been allowed on the three-thousand-temple mountain. Now, though, Kazuo told me, a woman was actually trying the thousand-day course—a woman, in fact, from Santa Barbara.

I asked him why he was putting himself through all this. He looked very gloomy. "My mother's father and uncle have a temple," he explained. "I am the only male who can carry on the succession. So I must become a monk."

4

WHEN I ABANDONED the temple, I moved across town into a tiny four-and-a-half-tatami room in an undistinguished modern guesthouse near the base of the eastern hills. The name of the house was I.S.E. (though not, alas, in honor of the great sacred shrine of Japan), and the district into which it was tucked, as tidy as a paperback in one of the area's crowded bookstore shelves, was called Nishifukunokawa-chō, or Western Happy River Neighborhood. It was a quiet area, of sleepy dogs tethered to their red-roofed villas, and elderly ladies in kimono, with thinning hair and backs so stooped they walked almost parallel to the ground. Outside my room, in a lane too narrow even for cars, I could hear the sounds of a drowsy world: the cries of playing children, the occasional scuffling of a cat, the patient, insistent tinkle of some conscientious student trying and trying to get a piano melody correct.

My new home was a simple enough space, appointed only with a desk, a heater, a cold-water tap, a hot plate, and a futon; in the corridors were two toilets, a phone, and two showers to be shared among the house's fifteen residents. Outside, the props were no less simple. Every morning, at eight-twenty exactly, there came a high, tinkling cry of "Okā-san!" (Mother!) from the tiny lane, and soon thereafter, a procession of quiet, tidy children on their way to school, faces well scrubbed and hair shining, animal-faced satchels on their backs. At noon, an autumn silence along the streets: old women leading their grandchildren by the hand, in shuffling steps, to local grocery stores and flower shops. In midafternoon, young mothers carried their tiny, silent, wide-eyed charges home from school on the backs of shiny bicycles; and then, after dark, on the other side of town, there came the counterprocession of the night—the hostesses of the "floating world" slipping out of taxis at five minutes to eight, shoving change into the drivers' white-gloved hands, and wiggling, in black leather skirts and high heels, down the neon-blazing alleyways.

It was, indeed, almost entirely a world of women and children that I found myself inhabiting in Kyoto. Not being part of the working world, I had no contact with the gray-suited office worker, the bowing interpreter, the straphanging commuter, that form so much of our image of corporate Japan. Japanese men, who were generally captive to the office from eight until eight each day, and then sequestered in their closed-door bars until they went home to sleep, were almost entirely absent from the world I saw. So whenever I was in temples or coffee shops or movies, I found myself, apart from monks, most often amidst groups of young girls, all frightened gravity and giggles, or tidy matrons. And whenever I was downtown, I moved among troops of postcard-perfect young women, the picture of impassive chic in their expensive Dior dresses, lustrous hair waterfalling down their downturned heads as they marched in well-pressed battalions from one shop to the next. In public at least, in their official demeanor, Japanese girls seemed to conform not only to a model but to a peculiarly uninflected model: with their ritual giggles and the mechanical bird song of their voices, they looked to me like public-address systems on two legs.

The sweetest of all the Kyoto scenes, though, took place right outside my window. For every morning, round about nine, the small area in front of my guesthouse filled up with two or three young mothers, prettily lipsticked, and trendy in their denim jackets, together with their tiny charges. And every day until five, six days a week, I would find them there, the neatly dressed mothers looking on with infinite patience while their quiet toddlers bumped around on tricycles or waddled about the courtyard with an air of grave purpose. I never saw any of the children shout, or squawk, or throw a tantrum, and I never saw any of the mothers lose her smiling equanimity: both parties formed a tableau of contentment. In New York, the near-absence of children had struck me as a denaturing almost, and in California, the sense of endless possibility that was the state's greatest hope seemed all but a curse in the hands of its young. But here, wherever I looked, I found images of madonna-and-child, in a world that seemed so settled that it almost cast no shadow. Even Pierre Loti—I read in my first few days in Kyoto—while writing off nearly all Japan as a giant playpen, had grumpily admitted, "It was the only thing that I really liked about this country: the babies and the manner in which they are understood."

Five minutes to the east of me in my new home was a temple, where I began to go on hazy mornings when the grayness seeped inside me and my mind would not engage. Sitting in its spacious silences, the tree-thick hills rising beside me towards the blue, a tolling gong behind me, I was brought into focus by the details: an old monk brush, brush, brushing a pathway clean; a young girl seated on the temple platform, as clear as the pond before her; another stone Jizō littered with the offerings of disappointed mothers; a sitting Buddha imparting a peace so strong it felt like wisdom. The temples in Kyoto, around the eastern hills, took one literally out of the world, leading one up through narrow flights of stairs between the pines, away from the rush and clamor of the everyday. Yet one could never forget the world entirely. Floating up from below came the sound, plangent and forlorn, of a garbage collector's truck playing its melancholy song.

Five minutes to the west of me was a blast of pachinko parlors, convenience stores, and shopping malls more modern than anything I had ever seen at home. Walking the shopping streets in Japan, I felt as if I were wandering through some children's wonder-world of indulgences, soothed by jingling Muzak and singsong reassurances. My local video store, whenever I entered, greeted me with a robot's voice that cried, "Welcome!" and, later, "Thank you very much!"; my local supermarket, after piping in chirpy messages all day, serenaded its customers when it closed each night with an unbearably mournful rendition of "Auld Lang Syne." And the dizzying *depātos* —compact boxes within the great gift-wrapped box that was the modern country— not only glittered with accessories and video screens, hallways of food in the basements, and twenty or more restaurants on the top floor, but even provided whole rooftop amusement worlds, not playgrounds but entire Playlands, sprawling cities in the sky offering views of the hills and the temples on one side and, on the other, a dazzling array of robots, panda trains, goldfish tanks, mechanical raccoons, and Ferris wheels.

Sometimes, in fact, it seemed as if all Japan were a kind of tinkling dollhouse, with props from around the world reconstituted in shops that were peddling foreign dreams. In my neighborhood alone, I found the Ergo Bibamus restaurant, Notre Quotidien Pain (just a couple of blocks from Our Daily Bread), and La Casa Felice—nearly all of them filled with Kyoto Valley Girls who wore warm-up jackets with legends such as *"Style vivant: nous nous aimons et nous vivons"* and who tended, I gathered, to do *arubaito* (part-time work) in order to pay for their *vacances*. Not far away were the Café-Bar Selfish, the Café Post-Coitus, and the Ringo coffee shop, which had Beatles posters plastering the walls, nonstop videos of the mop-tops jamming, menus designed like copies of *The White Album*, and even an ad soliciting members for the Ringo Stars American football team. Yet every time I went into one of these imported theme spaces, be it the Shalom restaurant (all its signs in Hebrew and English), or the Moghul (advertised by a bowing subcontinental cutout in a turban), or the Mozart coffee shop (which specialized in Sacher torte), I was met by exactly the same scene: a team of flawlessly polite Japanese women on both sides of the counter, playing their parts impeccably amidst the exotic stage sets.

Along the cosmopolitan streets, moreover, it often felt as if every need was somehow taken care of and every person treated as a VIP (in the formula phrases of the PA system, customers were given the honorific suffix generally reserved for gods and rulers). On one of my first extended trips downtown, I found exquisite French pastries, orange *givrés*, Lata Mangeshkar tapes almost impossible to find outside India, the entire inventory of New and Lingwood, haberdasher of my youth. Whole liveried ranks of servants came literally running out to serve me, gold buttons gleaming, each time I slouched, in torn jeans, into a large hotel to use the rest room. And where even the affluent in New York could sometimes feel like prisoners, with cockroaches in their sinks and garbage outside their doors, even the poor here, I sometimes thought, could feel like dignitaries, each purchase wrapped for them like priceless treasure.

That Japan was colonizing the future with its ingenious conveniences was already, of course, a universal given; yet still I was startled to find waitresses taking their orders with computers; washbasins at the exits of Kentucky Fried Chicken parlors; special machines in my tiny local laundromat for dry-cleaning sweaters or washing old sneakers. And it was not just that the Japanese had designed telephone cards to get around the inconvenience of stuffing coins into a slot, but that they had made their inventions artful, decorating the cards with images of rock gardens or Hokusai mountains, of cartoon characters or the Golden Gate Bridge, of sumo stars and teen idols, and even — I later learned — of oneself or one's loved ones. And one could buy these conveniences in the streets, from machines, or in stores, laid out in little bags to keep them magnetized. The perfect world, gift-wrapped.

Nor was a single speck of time or space to be wasted. Banks

provided magazines so that one's waiting time would be well spent, coffee shops were as well equipped with video games and diversions as amusement parks, and Sony was in the process of perfecting a portable VCR that executives could use while waiting for traffic lights to change. Even the tiny, unvisited alleyways around my house were pressed into service for the larger good, crowded with ranks of vending machines: vending machines for noodles, soup, and every kind of fruit juice; vending machines for cans of tea and coffee and cocoa, with every permutation of milk and sugar, so hot one could hardly hold them; vending machines for tickets to movies or temples or zoos, with additional machines for giving change. There were vending machines for batteries and beer, huge bottles of sake and cartons of milk, and even—should one suddenly get the urge after midnight, without a twenty-four-hour convenience store in sight—for hard-core pornography, their little windows crammed with thirty-one skin mags, six X-rated videotapes, and eight inscrutable sex aids.

To find such appurtenances in a quiet family neighborhood— row after row of dimpled teenagers posed in positions of compliant ease under (English-language) titles such as *Dick, Deep Special,* and *Mad Sex* —dramatized most graphically this society's difference from our own. Yet whether these shots of innocence in transit—cherry blossoms in the flesh, in a sense— were an incitement to perversity or a defusing of it, I could not begin to tell. Certainly, in a city where I never saw couples even holding hands, and where the streets felt cleansed of every sexual threat, I suspected that public impulses were as separated from social ones as the "floating world" was from the family home. So perhaps these magazines, with their secular cult of the virgin, served only to encourage sex in the head, catering to that famously sentimental Japanese Romanticism that prefers the idea of a thing, its memory or promise, to the thing itself. And if sometimes I felt I was living inside a gallery of antique canvases, sometimes I felt I was living in a world of vending machines, shining sentinels humming through all the quiet lanes in the dark.

My first social engagement in Japan came one windy evening when Mark invited me to a meeting of Amnesty International — less for the meeting itself, he suggested, than in order to meet a friend of his, an uncommonly cultured and philanthropic woman who had lived for many years in England and was head now of the local group. Ready to try anything, I strapped on a helmet, and on a chill night full of stars, through a whipping wind, we rode his Honda through a maze of twisting little lanes up to an elegant old house. Inside, the walls were lined with musty, arcane volumes that had an attic air to them, and after making voluntary donations at the entrance, we were ushered up to a comfortable room where various Japanese, mostly young, were seated on the floor.

"*Dōzo, dōzo,*" cried a man as soon as he saw us, jumping up to usher us to a couple of chairs placed near its front.

Typical, I thought: foreigners were given the best seats in the house (a sign of Japanese graciousness) and, in the same act, were segregated from all locals (a sign of Japanese prudence). My suspicions were only confirmed when, a couple of minutes later, two other foreigners — a tweedy, very distinguished-looking couple from Massachusetts — were ushered to the front. "*Gaijin* ghetto," muttered the old gentleman as he took his place, looking every bit the retired foreign service officer in his gray slacks, Ivy League jacket, neat red tie, and faultlessly aristocratic bearing.

Good Lord, I thought, what on earth could have brought these New England patricians to this shaggy little gathering of student radicals? Were they CIA? Or worse? And then, in a flash, all my impudent questions were dispelled, as Mark's friend Etsuko swept in, greeting the man as she passed with a dainty "Good evening, Reverend Farnsworth."

Behind her came the guests of honor, a family of three Argen-
tines eager to describe their torture at the hands of the military
government. The father was a gaunt, long-faced man in his late
thirties, who looked the part of a workers' hero, a Latin Walesa
in his denim jacket and jeans; his wife was a plump madonna
type, dressed all in black, with thick raven hair that fell to her
waist; and their perky little son, twinkling impishly at every
Japanese girl he passed, was now an eleven-year-old sixth-grader.

Etsuko delivered a brief introduction to the audience, in
Japanese, and then, looking over in my direction, asked sweetly,
in her bell-like English, "Shall we begin?"

Nobody else said anything, so I replied, "Oh, yes." Maybe this
was her way of acknowledging me?

And then the man began speaking, delivering a sentence or
two of introduction, in the rough Argentine Spanish that turns
yo into *zho* and *vas* into *vasch*. There was silence. The man
looked at me. Etsuko looked at me. Thirty pairs of Japanese eyes
looked at me. I looked at everyone else. And then, with a
sinking heart, as the silence deepened, I realized what was going
on: mine was not, it seemed, just a foreigner's place of honor—it
was the translator's chair. Apparently, my Spanish-sounding
name and vaguely Hispanic looks had been enough to have
procured for me, unbeknownst to me, the job of interpreting
from Spanish, a language I had never learned, to Japanese, a
language Francis Xavier himself had considered the work of the
devil. My only qualification for the task, I thought bitterly, was
that I was probably the only person in the room who spoke
neither Spanish nor Japanese.

Glumly, I leaned forward, thirty pairs of Japanese eyes following me as I did so.

The tortured man looked back at me. "Do you speak Spanish?"
he asked under his breath, in almost unintelligible Spanish.

"Not really. I'm not Spanish, you see; I'm Indian."

"I see," he said, looking gloomier than ever. "Okay."

"But if you speak very slowly and simply, I can probably follow."

"Okay," he said, looking very much as if he had come seven thousand miles in vain.

And so I began. "It was like a movie," I found myself saying. "He put a gun at my head, and said, 'Juan Carlos, you are a dead man.' Then they put handcuffs on me and threw me under a blanket in the car." Etsuko duly relayed this information to the goggle-eyed audience, and the narrative went on. "I will not go into the methods of torture they employed, but they laughed and joked at me, and I remembered that there was a school of torture in Argentina, a school for the members of the death squads." On and on the torture ran, and all I could do was try desperately to tell the difference between *cabeza*, which means "head," and *cerveza*, which means "beer," between *esposas* meaning "handcuffs" and *esposas* meaning "wives." Only a couple of weeks earlier, in the temple, I had read Scott Spencer's *Waking the Dead*, about a family of Chilean refugees led around by radical groups to meetings such as this one. Now, as I tried not to say, "They tied me up in wives and wrapped a blindfold around my beer," I felt as if I myself were waking the dead.

"When I was released from prison, I was of two minds," I went on, morosely. "I was happy at the prospect of seeing my wife and son, my only child. But I was very sad at the thought of all the dear friends I was leaving behind. The Mothers of the Plaza de Mayo have embarked on something very dangerous and difficult, spontaneously forming their group. Some of them have themselves disappeared."

As the terrible litany ran on, I found more and more that the Japanese words that always deserted me when I needed them were now the only words I could remember. When I had arrived in Japan, fresh from Cuba, I had often found myself saying *Sí* or *Permiso* to frightened-looking Japanese who looked more alarmed with every syllable. Now, however, I found myself saying, *"Hai, hai"* to the anguished Argentinians and *"Ah sō, desu ka?"* to their heartfelt explanations of the "Dirty War." *Tabun* in Japanese means *tal vez* in Spanish, I kept telling myself, *casa* means "house" in Spanish and "umbrella" in Japanese. Meanwhile, Reverend Farnsworth was squirming in his seat and muttering imprecations each time I uttered the words "liberation theology," and the Japanese on the floor were looking increasingly unhappy and perplexed. Finally, the narrative ended.

Before I could catch my breath, however, the audience, eager to hear more about these alien horrors, started firing questions at the long-suffering Argentinians. "Were there any Japanese among the detainees?" "Do you know of any Japanese who have disappeared?" "Are there Japanese among the prisoners still in jail?" all of which I deftly turned into Spanish sentences about wives and umbrellas.

Then, out of nowhere, a Japanese man in the audience, unable to wait for the interminable process of translating Japanese into English and then into Spanish and back again, suddenly spoke directly to the family, in Spanish. "Do you know this friend of mine," he began, "who disappeared? I lived in Argentina for many years, and I know all that you are describing." Madre de Dios, I thought, my mind on anything but the *desaparecidos*: here was a man who was perfectly equipped to translate from Spanish directly into Japanese, and vice versa. I was off the hook!

Which only shows how little I understood Japan. "*¡No, no, me olvidado de todo!*" the man cried out, with enviable fluency, when it was suggested he serve as translator. "*¡No me acuerdo de nada!*" And try as I might, I saw that there was no way at all of persuading him to speak a tongue in which he might possibly, just possibly, in the space of several paragraphs, make a single tiny error. And so I went back to my horrible task, stumbling through more accounts of torments made scarcely more pleasant by the dawning realization, as the Argentine speaker interrupted my translations and the whole family fell into animated debate about which parts I was distorting most, that the main speaker knew more English than I did Spanish; that his wife, who had sat through it all with a look of great pain, spoke both languages well; and that their son, who was enrolled in a Manhattan junior high school, was fluently bilingual. "And so I say to you, my friends," Juan Carlos said through me, my unhappy look a fair translation of his own, "that your efficiency and discipline and unity have turned this country into the third-strongest power in the world. Just think what you could do if you worked on behalf of human rights!"

Later that night, Mark and I went to a *yakitori* house nearby for dinner. Just as I happened to look around, in the midst of our conversation, the young Japanese man next to me caught my eye. "Excuse me," he began. "May I talk English with you?"

"Of course," I said, more than grateful to be back in my own tongue.

"What country do you come from? How long are you in Japan? How do you find Japan?" Trying to find answers compatible with these phrasebook questions, I felt as if I were being worked on by a student doctor eager to practice his still-unformed skills.

"I saw the American movie *2010*," he went on, though whether in a spirit of bonhomie or bewilderment I could not tell. "I could understand the computer — Hal. No problem. But I could not understand the human beings."

"Really?" I said, not sure how to take this.

"But she" — he pointed to his glumly chic young consort — "she is student of English literature."

Ah, I thought, my years of study were not in vain.

"What courses are you taking?" I began.

"One course," she said haltingly, and with some apparent pain. "It is in Henry James." I registered surprise that they would be given the most byzantine of English stylists to begin with. "And," she went on with a bulldozer determination, "in other course, we study nineteenth literature."

"Nineteenth century?"

She nodded unhappily, her eyes never once leaving her bowl.

"Dickens, for example?"

"Not Dickens," she said with some authority. "Dickens is twentieth. We do Swift."

Ah, I thought: the inscrutable Orient.

"Don't worry," said Mark consolingly as we made our way home. "You'll soon find ways of getting out of that. Everyone does, sooner or later."

Back in his house, while making some tea, Mark put on an old tape of Ry Cooder: lazy, sunlit songs about the border.

"Nice album," I remarked.

"Yeah. It's funny! This was the very same tape that Ray had with him while he was living in the monastery. Did I tell you about Ray? No? Well, anyway, Ray was this huge, king-size guy from Dallas, who came over to join the Peace Corps in the Philippines and somehow ended up as a Zen monk over in Daitokuji. And somehow, he had this deal worked out whereby he kept a motorbike outside the monastery walls, together with his cowboy boots and leather jacket. And every few weeks, he would steal out to visit his girlfriend. Or occasionally he'd come over to my house. And every time he came, whatever time it was, it was always party time, because this was the only chance he was going to get. Jeez, he was something! He just had this incredible energy, which living in the monastery only intensified. And the monks couldn't come down on him so long as he made it back before morning prayers at four a.m.

"Well, he had the stamina to keep this up—slipping in just before four a.m. every time he left—for months. But one day, on New Year's Day, he left when he shouldn't have, and the head monk, who had never much liked him in the first place, seized the opportunity to get back at him, and told him that he would have to go back to the beginning of the course—become a training monk again! After seven years in the place! So he put all his things in a wheelbarrow and rolled them out of the monastery gates. And he went off to his girlfriend's house and spent a month with her. And of course, after seven years in the temple, he was totally defenseless — totally unprepared to live in a regular domestic situation — and she just sliced through him, completely ate him up."

He paused. "It's funny; many of the so-called Zen masters in America have the same problems — with money or sex or alcohol. Anyway, Ray decided to go off to Berkeley to write. He'd been corresponding with Anaïs Nin from the temple, and she'd given him some really good contacts in the Bay Area. So he had a book of poems published — by a press in Santa Barbara, in fact — and he was going really strong until an old girlfriend from high school came over and dragged him back to Texas. So suddenly he ended up in this clean suburban town where everyone thought he talked funny and nobody could begin to understand what he'd been through. He got a few odd jobs and tried to write a novel. But pretty soon, his relationship fell apart, and he did too. The trouble was, poor guy, he just wasn't ready for the world. The monastery had prepared him for everything *except* the world. Last thing I heard, he was a bouncer in a reggae bar."

5

As autumn began to draw on in Kyoto—and the first touches of color to grace the eastern hills—Mark invited me one day to attend a special private initiation ceremony. A longtime friend of his, now a head priest at Tōfukuji, one of the Five Great Temples of Kyoto, was about to ascend to a new rank, the youngest Zen master in Japan to attain such a position. It was a closed ceremony, of course, but Mark had been invited, as a friend, and he thought that I might be interested too. Certainly, it sounded like a rare opportunity to see a little behind the enigmatic transparencies of Zen, if only to the next layer of its public face. So when the day arrived, I dusted off my best jacket and tie, put on a black motorcycle helmet, and, thoroughly incongruous, popped onto the back of Mark's Honda. Whizzing through the crowded streets, we veered along a maze of narrow lanes and ended up at last outside the temple compound, all abustle in the brilliant morning.

By the time we arrived, sober parishioners in their best suits were already heading under purple banners into the temple, along with monks who looked like giant bats, black robes billowing out around them. "That's Soto-san," Mark whispered as one such figure hurried past. "I knew him in California." In the glorious sunshine, the thickly forested hills that rose above a plunging gorge were glowing almost, and the maples, through which the sunlight streamed, were just beginning to turn. In the shadeless gravel courtyards of the temple, monks were scattering this way and that, some of them in special orange-and-black raiment, some waving tidy scarlet flags. Inside one of the temple's

Buddhas, I once read, the beautiful poetess Ono no Komachi had secretly stashed her love letters.

Slipping off our shoes at the entrance to the monastery, we followed a shaven-headed monk (from California) into an antechamber and there were offered tea. This, I gathered, was the *gaijin*'s corner: it included a middle-aged American student of Zen with his teenage Filipina bride; another eager-eyed American; and a New York woman with granny glasses who handled words as if they were thorny roses. Beside her, and next to me, sat a seamlessly elegant Japanese lady in a flowing dress, who apparently found it incumbent on her to make conversation with me. Where did I come from? she began hesitantly. How long had I been here? What was I doing in Japan?

At that moment, bells began tolling, and we were led off again, in our little group, around a rock garden and over the famous hanging causeway and along a wide stone pathway to the great *zendō*, a celebrated National Treasure usually closed to the public. There, under a dragon-writhing roof, the ceremony commenced. Drums sounded sonorously as the monks walked in, one by one, in purple and orange robes, with orange sashes and pointed Chinese shoes. A screeching came from within, and the *rōshi* himself appeared, followed by a long, muttered wailing that sounded like a coyote's howl. A monk waved a bamboo whisk above us all, extending a skinny, but commanding, hand in each of the main directions. The solemnity was broken, in our corner, as the Filipina, giggling brightly, asked if we knew where the rest room was. Four men blew on bamboo flutes, piercing, mellifluous, and sad.

Outside once again in the radiant morning, men in dark suits, women in kimono, stood on the Tsuten Bridge, bowing with the ceremonious elegance of characters from *The Makioka Sisters*. One woman glittered like a brooch in a blue-and-golden sari and metallic blue fingernails, her temple dancer's features sharp under kohl-ringed eyes. Old men in grave suits sat on Coca-

Cola benches, reclining in the autumn sun like ageless school friends of the Emperor.

When we returned to our places in the monastery, we found beside every seat an elegant purple carrier bag with golden lettering, loaded high with gifts; in front of each setting, two wooden boxes on a tray, stuffed with every kind of delicacy; and—since there was no way that anyone could begin to eat all this—another elegant bag, and a stylish lavender cloth, or *furoshiki*, in which to pack the boxes and take them home.

Again I found myself next to the decorous Japanese woman. Again the obligatory questions began. Who was my favorite musician? What was my age? How did I like Kyoto? Apparently, my answers were the right ones—she, too, was thirty and liked Bruce Springsteen and felt that Kyoto was "little magic town"—and so, as we munched our inexplicable food, she ventured a little further. "Sunday, my daughter little have birthday party. Please come here my house." Sure, I replied, game for anything, and she wrote down meticulously the name of a train station and then her telephone number. "Please you come. Maybe two o'clock, begin." "Thank you very much," I said, and then, with a mother's brisk efficiency, she whipped out my *furoshiki*, packed my food away into my boxes, wrapped the boxes in the lavender cloth, and handed it all back to me as if it were her gift.

Later, back home, I peeled back layer after layer of the elegant cloth. Simply opening the temple's treasure was an almost sensual experience. Caskets of Japanese cake sat inside, and bottles of expensive sake; a poem in flowing calligraphic script, written by the *rōshi* himself, and a screen on which to mount it; and, of course, the purple cloth, touched now with the lady's perfume.

Five days later, I was spending all morning writing on Ruth Prawer Jhabvala, my mind on the follies of credulity, when suddenly I remembered the woman's birthday party. It had been a fairly casual invitation, I thought, with no meaning attached to it, but I felt that courtesy alone suggested I attend. "You never know what to expect with these things," Mark had advised me, but I felt pretty sure that children's birthday parties must be something of a universal: fifteen or twenty kids careening around, amidst a mess of many-colored balloons and party hats, alternately laughing and screaming, while mothers stood by the kitchen, enforcing order and swapping gossip. So I packed the bear that I had bought as a ceremonial offering, and timed my arrival to be a safe forty-five minutes late. That way, I thought, I could slip into the background and easily make my escape.

When I arrived at the station written down by the mother, I walked out into the street and found myself inside a honeycomb of unmarked alleyways. Streets forked this way and that on every side of the diverging railway tracks. Narrow lanes led off into the distance. Signs were nonexistent. I looked for the nearest phone.

"Moshi-moshi," came an excited voice at the other end, up to its neck, I assumed, in children and chaos.

"Moshi-moshi. This is Pico Iyer." There was a silence. "The man you met in Tōfukuji Temple?"

"Ah, hallo. How are you? What place you now?"

"I'm not sure. I'm just outside the station."

"What name street?"

"I don't know. I came down the stairs, and I'm standing outside a coffee shop called U.C.C."

"U.C.C.?" she repeated, incredulous.

"Oh, I'm sorry. That's the name of the coffee they're advertising. Anyway, I'm near the stairs."

"Stairs?" She giggled nervously. There was a long silence. "You come here my house?"

"Oh, I'm sorry. I thought it was your daughter's birthday party."

"I think maybe you no come. Now three o'clock."

"Oh, I'm very sorry."

"Please you wait station. I come."

Two minutes later, a small and pretty figure bounced up to

me, long hair tumbling over her shoulders, a bright turquoise scarf over her black shirt, and leg warmers covering her acid-washed jeans. I was not quite sure who this was, but I assumed it must be the funky teenage sister of the woman I had met at the temple, maybe ten years younger than that elegant matron with the severely swept-back hair and the long brown dress. As she flashed me a dazzling smile, though, I recognized the look, and the soft, melodious voice—and realized that this was the same woman, remade now in a different role. She led me down the station stairs and, breathless, filled me in on the plans.

"Other person little telephone my house. They little late. Maybe five o'clock."

"Oh fine. Well, if it's easier, I can come back then?"

She looked at me, confused. "You no want come my house?"

"Either's fine really. Whatever's easiest."

"You not want come *ima* now my house?"

"Sure—if it's no trouble."

"Maybe other person come five o'clock. Maybe six. Are you okay?"

"Oh yes. No problem."

She led me through a sliding door, and I found myself inside a compact modern flat. The main room was utterly silent. It had the look and feel of a teenage girl's bedroom. On the walls were two posters of the teen-idol pop group a-ha (a latter-day Osmond family from Norway, so far as I could tell) and one of Sting, in all his open-shirted glory. Album covers of Sting hung from the doors, and more beefcake posters of a sultry-eyed a-ha. From the ceiling, an upside-down sea otter chuckled down at me, and all along the gleaming bank of high-tech stereo and video equipment that were the room's main decoration were stickers from Tokyo Disneyland. The teenage artifacts sang out strangely in the quiet of the room on this sleepy afternoon.

"Please you sit," offered Sachiko-san, motioning me towards her small paisley sofa. "You like Sting?"

I felt I could hardly admit that I found him one of the more disagreeable creatures on the planet. "Oh yes." With that, she gave me a pretty smile of delight, pressed a few buttons on the stack of gleaming black consoles, and disappeared. I sat alone in the silent, empty room and listened to the maestro sing dirges about Quentin Crisp and Pinochet.

A few minutes later, Sachiko-san reappeared, bearing two cups of Twining's tea on a tray (I recalled that I had mentioned, *en passant*, at the temple that I preferred English tea to Japanese). She sat down beside me and smiled shyly.

"You seem to like the West," I began.

She nodded gravely. "My brother go Kansas City study. Three year. My mother very sad, many time say, 'Don't go!' But then he send picture from your country, always biggg smile! America, he say, little animal country. He think he living movie world— little Disneyland cartoon. But he much much want return."

"So he's here now?"

"Now Switzerland. Jung Institute. You know this place?"

"Oh yes. Have you visited him there?"

"I like." She paused. "But now I am mother part. Japanese system, man visit other country, very easy. But woman must always stay Japan." A long pause. "Very sad."

A difficult silence fell. Then she brightened up. "But my son now little learning English. He want go Switzerland. He much love Matterhorn. T.G.V."

"Really?"

At that moment, the record finished, so she popped up and stepped over to the tower of video monitors, laser videos, and speaker systems. "You like Chris Lay?"

"I'm sorry, I don't know him."

Her brow creased up in confusion. "You not know Chris Lay?"

"No."

"Please you try."

At this, she put on another record, a very, very slow love song, delivered by a husky, infinitely gentle male voice, about a lovers' parting. We listened in silence to the slow, heartfelt ballad, with its drawn-out, wrenching climax: "I'll always love you . . . September Blue."

There was silence.

"Very nice song," I said brightly, hoping to lighten things up.

"You like? Please one more time." She bounced up again, pressed a button, and again, in silence, in the empty room, we sat side by side on her couch, listening to the husky, heartrending strains of the teary love song.

When it was finished, Sachiko-san jumped up again. "I write word," she announced proudly, and then pulled down from the wall a computer printout on which was typed, " 'September Blue' by Chris Rea," and all the words in English.

> I'll be all right, though I may cry,
> The tears that flow, they always dry,
> It's just that I would rather be,
> With you now. . . .
>
> And every time I see that star,
> I will say a prayer for you,
> Now and forever,
> September Blue.

"You have a computer too?"

"My husband buy."

"Is he here?" I looked around. Now it was my turn to be confused.

"Not here. He cannot holiday. Every day, much much work."

"Sunday too?"

"Sunday too. Every day, he come home twelve o'clock."

A long silence.

"Your country same?"

"No, not really."

At this point, two small heads suddenly peered around the screen door: one belonging to a boy of about seven and the other to a five-year-old moppet. "Ah, please," said Sachiko-san, smiling happily. "Please you see. This my son, Hiroshi. This Yuki."

They stood in silent shyness at the door.

"And today's her birthday?"

"No. Today no birthday. Two day before."

"I see," I said, though of course I didn't.

Both children stared at me in neat decorum, at once intrigued and, I assumed, faintly unsettled by this funny-looking foreigner. Then their mother invited them to sit down, and the four of us sat in silence in the small room, presided over by rock stars, and listened again to the slow and emotional ballad, with its air of tender intimacy. "I'll always love you . . . September Blue."

The song was just starting up again when Sachiko-san vanished into the kitchen. I looked at the children. The children looked at me. Chris Rea murmured his love. Then Sachiko-san emerged again, bearing a beautiful cake, with fresh strawberries and melon slices — the ultimate Japanese luxury — pieced around the message O-tanjōbi Omedetō (Happy Birthday). Lighting the five candles, she went over to the system, turned off "September Blue," and turned off all the lights. Then, flashing a smile of encouragement at me, by the light of five flickering candles, she began singing, in quavering, high-pitched English, "Happy birthday to you . . ." I joined in, and her son did too, three wobbly voices in a plaintive refrain in a room lit by candles. When we finished, the birthday girl blew out all the candles, and we were left again in the dark. I felt Sachiko-san stirring beside me, and then the lights came on again, and she brought us all orange juice to enjoy with our cake, and Chris Rea began to sing of love once more.

I liked Sachiko-san very much — she seemed unusually warm and openhearted, as well as demure and chic in the approved Japanese fashion — and her sleek-haired, almond-eyed, utterly quiet children were entirely irresistible. My sense that mothers and children were the two great blessings of Japan was only getting confirmation. But still, I thought, this was a rather sad and awkward way to celebrate a fifth birthday, and I could not help shuffling a little in embarrassment as we sat there in a silence broken only by the song and my occasional mutterings of *"Yuki-chan, O-tanjōbi omedetō!"*

Then, suddenly, I remembered the bear that I had brought for Yuki and withdrew it from my bag. And Yuki, in delight, bundled off and brought back a rabbit, a koala, a fluffy bear called Pooh, and even an orange raccoon. Delighted in turn, I inquired after their particulars and then, pointing to the Tokyo Disneyland stickers on the front of the stereo system, mentioned how much I enjoyed the place, and the children scurried off to show me their photos of their visit. Paging through the album, I pointed to photos of Yuki and asked if she was Mickey, pointed to Mickey and asked if that was Goofy, pointed to her mother and asked if it was her father, and the next thing I knew, the little girl's sides were shaking with laughter, and she was beginning to tickle me, and I was retaliating with the aid of a bear, and Hiroshi was making a counterattack with a rabbit, and all of us were making mayhem.

A few moments later, the children were pulling me out, one by each arm, into the street to play ball, and we were bouncing a tennis ball back and forth while Sachiko-san kept throwing her long hair back and saying, "Oh, I'm sorry. Children very happy. I'm so sorry. Are you okay?" And then Hiroshi decided that I must see his school, and all of us marched off to the shrine of the Meiji Emperor nearby, and then to the shrine of General Nogi, to play hide-and-seek, and soon the children were racing off to bring me sprigs of flowers, and Hiroshi was feeling bold enough to tell me the name of his best friend, which I ritually mispronounced, and his mother was smiling anxiously, and clicking away with her camera, and saying, "You tired? I'm very sorry. I'm so sorry," and Yuki was clinging to my hand, and we were all running races up and down the darkening lanes.

By the time night had fallen, all four of us were back home, and Yuki was clambering all over me, giggling helplessly as I pointed to pictures in her new Richard Scarry book, of hippos in aprons and rabbits playing golf. "*Tanuki wa doko deshō ka?*" (Where is the raccoon?), I kept asking. "*Kono dōbutsu wa tanuki deshō ka?*" (This animal here, is it a raccoon?) As one whose Japanese was strongest when it came to animal words, I realized that this was a conversational opportunity not to be missed. And Hiroshi was driving his trains all over my stomach, and Yuki was bouncing her flattened orange raccoon up and down on my chest, and Sachiko-san, as if in proof of Ruth Benedict's claims about the blurring of apology and gratitude in Japan, was saying, "Thank you. Sorry. Thank you. I'm so sorry."

And then I threw still more oil on the fire by teaching all three of them the English word "raccoon" and telling them how much I had always been taken by the *tanuki,* the mischievous masked figure, half badger and half raccoon, who stood outside most sake bars, advertising in his potbelly the Dionysian pleasures of the open road. All the while, Sachiko-san kept asking me, doubtfully, "You like raccoon? Really? True you like raccoon?" and I kept saying, "*Hai, hai!*" until she told me that the Japanese, as a rule, were not very fond of him: the raccoon was the rival to the fox, the other malefic trickster said to disguise itself as a beautiful woman to bring down innocent priests. Undeterred, I recounted how the Germans called them *Waschbär* and explained how they were famous in California for making raids on carp ponds.

And that night, when I got home, I was so caught up in the spirit of the day that I sat down on my futon, imagining Yuki by my side, and wrote out a story for the children about a princess trapped in a castle by a jealous father, and the two raccoons, gallant, resourceful, and speaking in couplets, who spirit her away to a new life of freedom.

6

As I began to settle down in my new home, I began, very slowly, to make my way, in translation, through some of the great works of Japanese literature. And as I did so, I was struck again and again by how much Japanese writing was touched with a decidedly feminine lilt and fragrance, a kind of delicacy and a lyricism that I associated, however unfairly, with the female principle. This softness was apparent not just in the watercolor wistfulness of Japanese poems, but also in the very themes and moods that enveloped them—loneliness, abandonment, romance. This was, perhaps, as much a reflection of my own tastes as of anything, and in men like Mishima, or the modern-minded Abe and Ōe, there were, of course, some towering exceptions. Yet still it seemed to me that much of Japanese writing, right down to such near contemporaries as Tanizaki and Kawabata, was devoted to the private world, a Jane Austen stage of domestic passions. The world of state, the striving of the office and the marketplace, the realm of public affairs—all these were scarcely glimpsed amidst the quiet, unworldly dramas of the soul. Even gangsters, at their deaths, wrote poems to the seasons.

Historically, of course, there were good reasons for this. For one thing, the Japanese syllabary, though invented by a Buddhist priest, had originally been used almost exclusively by women—to such an extent that it had become known as "woman's hand"; and while men had been confined to the public, official script of Chinese, women had all but invented Japanese poetry. As a result, perhaps, early Japanese poetry was all love poetry (where its model in China dealt more often with friendship). And by the tenth and eleventh centuries, and the great cultural flowering of the Heian period, the Japanese alphabet was so much a woman's domain that men actually pretended to be women if they wanted to use the native script, and even fit themselves into the conventions and emotions of women.

> By and by I'll come
> he said and so I waited
> patiently but I
> saw only the moon of the longest month
> in the dawn sky.

That plaintive love poem was written by a Buddhist priest.

Many of these verses, clearly, were as ritualized as thank-you notes, especially in a culture where writing poems was as *de rigueur* as dancing might be in other courts; clearly, too, in a society whose public life was close to formal pageant, it was only in private, behind closed doors, that people began to seem interesting to themselves. Yet whatever the reasons — or the qualifications — poetry and femininity seemed almost interchangeable in Japan, as they would never be in the literature of Chaucer, Milton, and Johnson, say; and every modern scholar seemed to agree with Kenneth Rexroth in saying that the Heian period was "certainly the greatest period of women's writing in the history of any literature."

Certainly, too, as I began reading *The Pillow Book* of Sei Shōnagon, one of the two great testaments of the Heian court, I felt that much of its charm, as with Lady Murasaki's *Genji*, lay in its girlishness, its womanly refinement, its sensitivity to nature, and to the lights and shades of relationships. Here was the poetry of the paper screen — of delicate walls and sliding panels, of shadows and suspicions, of secrecy and stealth.

Yet all this was also of a piece with Sei's extreme fastidiousness about the observation of ritual courtesies, a kind of hypersensitivity that amounted, in the end, to snobbery. Obsessed with impressions and reputations, with what was and was not "cricket," Sei revealed herself as something of a stickler for protocol, even when it came to matters of the heart. Everything to do with the common folk she found contemptible; everything to do with the Emperor or Empress—even their bad moods—she found a source of great delight. And in her habit of anatomizing emotions and cataloguing poetic sights as if even the motions of the heart were finite, she betrayed something of the stylized reflexiveness of a society in which not only gestures but feelings themselves were prescribed; one of the "Rare Things" she exalted was "a person who was in no way eccentric or imperfect," and one of the "Embarrassing Things" was "to hear one's servants making merry." One could almost hear the lady-in-waiting at Buckingham Palace saying, "But really, my dear. It's simply not done."

Thus Sei's delicacy in responding to Nature turned into a kind of pedantry when she dealt with human nature; she read people as if they were gardens and as if both should be raked into the same kind of impersonal perfection. And in her fussiness regarding the proper associations of blossoms, the emotional effects of the moon, and the etiquette of the morning-after letter, one could see how love of beauty in such a world might often mean no more than the beautiful gowns worn by aristocrats in Florence or Versailles. The elegance we ascribed to Japanese souls belonged sometimes only to their tastes; Sei, in a sense, had designer views.

I was more taken aback, though, to find this same preoccupation with niceties, and with the right way of doing things, in the other great classic of the *zuihitsu*, or "follow the brush," form of collected sayings, the *Essays of Idleness* of the fourteenth-century monk Kenkō. The title, with its distinctly Thoreauvian air, promised typically serene meditations on silence, solitude, and impermanence, and all these it did indeed provide; the monk did much to enunciate the aesthetic of Japanese Romanticism, explaining why it was better to dream of the moon than actually to see it, and how longing was better than love. Yet in between were reflections on women ("devious but stupid"), interviews with backgammon champions ("You should never play to win, but so as not to lose"), lists of "Things Which Seem in Poor Taste" ("A man should avoid displaying deep familiarity with any subject"), and descriptions of "seven kinds of persons [who] make bad friends." The monk wrote about his frissons of pleasure when passing an unknown woman on a night of moon viewing, and the protocol of making love; how "lamplight makes a beautiful face seem even more beautiful," and "beautiful hair, of all things in a woman, is most likely to catch a man's eye." Most unexpected of all, at least to me, were the priest's anxious obsessiveness with appearances ("A man should be trained in such a way that no woman will ever laugh at him"), and his strongly worded snipes about lower-class men and other "insufferable" or "disagreeable" types ("It is unattractive when people get in a society which is not their habitual one"). If the lady-in-waiting occasionally wrote with the exalted purity of a monk, the monk often wrote with the sharp-tongued worldliness of a lady-in-waiting.

At times, in fact, it became hard to tell the two of them apart. Sei wrote that one of the "Unutterable Things" was "snow on the houses of the common people. This is especially regrettable when the moonlight shines down on it." Kenkō echoed her almost to a fault. "Even moonlight when it shines into the quiet domicile of a person of taste is more affecting than elsewhere." Sei flaunted her irreverence by mischievously declaring, "A preacher should be good-looking . . . an ugly preacher may well be the source of sin"; the monk returned the favor by writing, "A man may excel at everything else, but if he has no taste for lovemaking, one feels something terribly inadequate about him." Both of them, weighing fashion against tradition, seemed—even more than their counterparts elsewhere—to be writing almost impersonally. And yet the effect was ravishing. That, in fact, was the confounding paradox of this land of pragmatic romantics:

If you find something beautiful, it seemed to say, why not simply reproduce it and reproduce it *ad infinitum* (even if it was a woman or a poem or a gesture)? If you've found something pleasing, why ever deviate from the norm? And what answer could one provide when the finished product shone with such an enameled perfection?

It did not take me long, in the autumn afternoons, to find that whenever I tried to find any particular place in Kyoto—to locate, that is, a specific site on a map—I ended up wandering around in circles, through riddles of dead-end lanes, thoroughly defeated by the maze of Japanese planning. There was, I thought, a metaphor in this: one could not plan epiphanies any more than one could plan surprise visits from one's friends. Expectations would only defeat themselves. So as the days went on, I tried to keep as open as I could, waiting to see what kind of things found me.

One day, I was just walking home down the narrow lane, when suddenly I was hailed by a strapping, red-faced fellow with a mat of straw-blond hair. "Excuse me, mate, d'you live near here?" He pointed to an ad for my guesthouse. "Yes, I do." "Would you mind if I tagged along and took a bit of a look at it?" "Not at all." Bob, I quickly discovered, was a former professional Aussie-rules football player and sometime engineer who had recently moved here from Surfers Paradise. I would not have believed that such a place existed, with so immodest a name, except that the previous day I had met a man in my very own house who also came from "Surfers" (the Santa Barbara of Australia, so it would seem). Bob was something of a larrikin—he still walked eight hours a day, he said, to keep himself in shape—and as he eagerly accepted my offer of a cup of tea, I began to see that he was more in need of company than a room. But still he struck me as a friendly fellow, in the Aussie way, and he seemed to have a genuine wish to do well. "Thing with the

Japanese is," he declared, "they're a clever group of bastards. Found out how to be hard the nice way. I've been living in the youth hostel over in Osaka"—he made it sound like an Irish pub—"two months now. Way I see it, you get here for a year, learn a bit of the culture, give yourself a chance to crack the language. Jesus, I'm learning more English than my students— grammar, y'know, and all that bullshit! Way I see it, you've got to know something if you know nothing." (The Zen of Surfers Paradise, so it would seem.) "Not like a chapter from a book, but in a real sense. Mind's a tough bastard to control.

"I'm also interested in Asian girls," he went on disarmingly, "as a possible partner for life. Went over to the Philippines a couple of times, for a month or so, looked it over. Nice girls, if you know what I mean. But psychologically—naw! I mean, you want to have a chat now and then, if you know what I mean. A lot of my friends over in Queensland, they have these Filipina brides. But they're just simpleminded guys; as long as they've got someone to take care of them and have sex with a lot, they're as happy as pigs in shit, if you'll pardon my French.

"See, the way I look at it"—Bob apparently did a lot of looking—"you've got up here" (he put his hand parallel to his head) "all these incredibly obnoxious, dominating, demanding American and Australian women—you might think this is sour grapes, but it's not; it's just a statement of fact—and you've got down here" (he put his hand at heart—or was it breast?—level), "down here, you've got all these really feminine Asian girls, and sexual too; I mean sex not just for sex but for other things too. Way I figure it, it's easier to bring these girls up than the other ones down, the ones who are busy saying, 'You guys have had it good for a thousand years, now it's our turn to take over.' So you raise the girl, and you're raised yourself."

I wasn't entirely persuaded by his logic, but I kept my ideas to myself, and Bob brought his Sunday sermon to a rousing climax. "Nice to talk to you, mate," he said, extending his hand, and headed off for more of his eight hours walking.

* * *

The East, of course, had always been filled with Bobs, with Western men seeking Asian wives, as well as Asian wisdom, and not always troubling to distinguish between the two. Romance and religion had long constituted the double lure of the Orient, and in recent years, the confusion of the two had grown even more intense as the presence of U.S. troops on the continent—in Japan, then Korea, then Vietnam and the Philippines—had turned every war zone into a kind of erogenous zone, leaving more and more Westerners smitten with Buddhism, and with the other graceful attractions of the East.

In Kyoto, however, the division was especially vexed. Here, after all, was a city built on an imperial grid, yet curlicued with scented gardens and pretty floral canals. Here was a city still inscribed with the bloody feuds conducted in its hooded temples and dark castles, yet a city that was now a repository of all the country's female arts. Kyoto today was the center of kimono and flower arrangement and geisha; of lacquerwork, paper umbrellas, and fans. Even the Kyoto dialect was famously a girls' tongue, best suited to a high, melodious delivery, in which *arigatō* became *okini*, and *wakaranai, wakarahen.* "Every city has its sex," Kazantzakis had pronounced unequivocally. "This one [Kyoto] is all female."

Thus the "City of Purple Hills and Crystal Streams" had always been defined, for the foreign world at least, by the monks who lived in the hills and the women who dwelt along the streams. The two great mountains surrounding the city were known as the "Mount of Wisdom" and the "Mountain of the Cave of Love." The mountains themselves were supposed to carry the male energy of yang; the rivers, yin. Yet the division had never been as clear as its designers would have liked. For temples had famously been used as trysting places, and Buddhist storytellers had sometimes doubled as prostitutes. Paintings had shown Daruma dressed in courtesan's clothes, and vice versa. Even today the classic postcards of the city showed fledgling geisha standing, coquettish, outside temples. And for foreigners, who came to Japan in search of "a good life" and "the good life" and were not always able—especially in a country whose language has no articles—to tell one from the other, the dialectic was especially bewildering. I was probably typical, having long been drawn to the aesthetic and the religious elements in Japan, and wishfully hoping that the two were one and the same (the Japanese made a religion of pure beauty). Even the latest of the Western poets to settle in Kyoto, Brad Leithauser, had taken as the epigraph for his novel about the city Shakespeare's sonnet 144, the classic statement of the conflict between two loves, one heavenly and the other of the earth.

I was just musing on all this when Mark, as he had promised, gave me the book of poems by his friend Ray Coffin, a book whose very title, *Poetry for Crazy Cowboys and Zen Monks*, announced the same dialectic (one poem was even entitled "Ode to Narcissus and Goldman"). He had gone East, the American monk had written, in search of "some simple, sound horizons" and had found them in Japan—in his memories of Texas. As for Zen's immersion in the moment, its sense of immediacy and intensity, he had found that mostly with his girlfriend, in their unsanctioned kind of moving meditation. His love nights, he wrote, were "rich, gusty and full of the ever-fleeting NOW."

The stay in the temple, in fact, seemed to have made him only more Texan—because more himself—and his poems read like old Dylan songs set to an irregular Zen beat. They hymned faraway girls, Mexican bars, "the sweet easy drone of a steel guitar on a summer night"—all the pleasures, I assumed, that had grown more piquant for him as they grew more distant. And so the dialogue gained force and fire, the cowboy on his bike, in handmade Nocona boots, chafing at the monk, head bowed in meditation. Sometimes the monk disciplined the cowboy, sometimes the cowboy liberated the monk. And finally the unlikely duet concluded with "Cowboy sun Monk moon friendship—A total eclipse."

The very next day, I was reading Zen poems in my room when a call came for me on the guesthouse telephone. A call? I thought. Whom did I know in Japan? I answered it and heard a high, breathless female voice. "Hallo. My name is Sachiko Morishita." I could almost hear the phrasebook flapping in the background. "Thank you very much coming here my house. I'm sorry. Children very happy. Very fun. I'm sorry. Thank you very much." Amidst a confusion of girlish giggles and long pauses, I slowly dug out her meaning: in return for my playing with her children, Sachiko-san was offering now to show me around Nanzenji. Like every Japanese citizen, she apparently had a schedule as precisely organized as that of any head of state, what with going to her part-time job, taking her children to school, collecting her children from school, taking her children to swimming lessons, ballet lessons, piano lessons, and English classes, doing her aerobics, paying duty visits to her parents and her in-laws, and preparing her husband's food, bed, and bath each night. Still, she said, she could be free for a couple of hours on Wednesday morning. Sensing both her loneliness and her openness, I did not have the heart to tell her that Nanzenji was one temple I had seen already.

A couple of days later, when I arrived at the Heian Shrine, I found her waiting for me eagerly, a tiny figure of casual chic in a thick U.S. Army jacket with a Sting sticker on one pocket, hands shyly crossed behind her back, and bouncing on the soles of her feet. Exchanging greetings in languages neither of us could really understand, we began wandering together through the sleepy backstreets of Kyoto. Ambling into a garden, we found an arrangement of rocks and water, and Sachiko-san backed away when she saw the gliding carp below. In the street, a dog strained at its leash, and again she started, moving quickly to the other side. But her sheltered smallness was most apparent in her enthusiasms. "Last night," she said, "I go Chris Lay concert. Osaka Festival Hall. Very beautiful concert. 'September Blue' encore. I very, very excited. All day I cannot eat. Stomach big problem. Heart cannot control. Very beautiful day." The epiphanies of her world seemed almost sadder than her trials.

As she fell into a pregnant, thoughtful silence, I tried to lighten the mood by telling her that I'd been so invigorated by her daughter's party that I'd written a story for her children, about two heroic raccoons.

Having learned this new word just the previous week, she tried it out with glee. "Raccoon story?"

"Yes," I answered with some pride.

"You write raccoon story?"

"Yes."

She frowned. "You job, raccoon story writer?"

Some things, it seemed, got hopelessly lost in translation.

And so we wandered on, down drowsy lanes, past noodle shops and china *tanuki*, to Nanzenji, and there, on the platform overlooking the Leaping Tiger Garden, we sat side by side, looking out upon the maples, as I had done with Mark two weeks before. There was, as Mark had noted at the temple ceremony, a curious kind of intimacy that Sachiko-san established — she seemed to draw a net around one as if to shut out the rest of the world. And as she explained the symbols of Zen to me in the giddy autumn sunshine, I caught snatches of her perfume, saw silver bracelets jangling on her tiny wrists, realized that her eyes — finely folded and alight — were the first Japanese eyes I had ever really seen. Sometimes, in the sun, I saw the red lights in her hair, hair she fastened on one side with a mother-of-pearl comb and let fall free across her shoulder on the other.

Sachiko-san's influence was soft and subtle as a mild spring breeze, yet still I could feel the warmth in that breeze, and as we walked back into town, I could sense her straying closeness. This strange, unlooked-for intimacy was only formalized when, as we walked along the Kamo River, I suddenly saw a familiar figure on his bicycle. The last time I had seen Billy, a former U.S. Army man, he had been hanging out with two other foreigners, eyeing Japanese girls over their beers. I tried as hard as I could not to see him, but Billy was quick to see me—or at least my companion.

"Hey," he said, turning round, getting off his bike, and walking back towards us. "I can see you're settling down quite nicely." He looked her up and down. "You seem to be doing really well."

"In a way."

"Great. Looks like you're doing real good." He gave me a conspirator's grin.

"How are things going with you?" I said, eager to change the subject.

"Aw, pretty good. All my students tell me I look like Randy Bass—you know, the slugger for the Tigers?" He flashed Sachiko-san an engaging grin. I refrained from telling him that this was more a reflection on his students than on him, since the Japanese apparently thought that every bearded foreigner looked like Randy Bass. I had heard one portly white journalist likened to Michael Jackson.

"So anyway," he said, "bring her along to a Halloween party we're having." Then, after a final inspection, he got back on his bike. "Costume required!" he called back as he began cycling away.

"Can I come as an Indian?" I shouted after him.

"Sure," he called back. "I'm going as a *gaijin*!"

"Very nice man," Sachiko-san giggled sweetly as we went on our way. "I like you friend. Very kind, very warm."

"Oh, sure," I muttered sullenly.

At the Montessori kindergarten, Yuki proudly showed me her agility on the swings. Then, through shifting sunlight, all three of us made our slow way to a sushi restaurant. "I wonder if it'll rain," I said, looking up at the sky.

"Old Japanese people say, '*Onna-no kokoro, aki-no sora,*'" said Sachiko-san, shooting me a sidelong glance (The autumn sky is like a woman's heart). "Your country same?"

Ten minutes later, little Yuki was seated in front of a mountain of eight empty sushi bowls, while I, incriminatingly, had nothing to show but one. Sensing my unease (I had yet to make my peace with sushi), Sachiko-san suggested that it was time for them to leave. Outside, in the street, the clouds were turning to sun again. "Like woman's heart," she said, and looked at me again.

7

ONE REASON I had always been interested in Zen was my sense that for people like myself, trained in abstraction, Zen could serve as the ideal tonic. For Zen, as I understood it, was about slicing with a clean sword through all the Gordian knots invented by the mind, plunging through all specious dualities— east and west, here and there, coming and going—to get to some core so urgent that its truth could not be doubted. The best lesson that Zen could teach—though it was, of course, something of a paradox to say or even think it—was to go beyond a kind of thinking that was nothing more than agonizing, and simply act. In that sense, Zen reminded me of Johnson's famous refutation of Berkeley by kicking a stone. It was unanswerable as pain.

This training had particular appeal for me, perhaps, because I had often thought that the mind was, quite literally, a devil's advocate, an agent of diabolical sophistry that could argue any point and its opposite with equal conviction; an imp that delighted in self-contradiction and yet, though full of sound and fury, ultimately signified nothing. None of the truest things in life—like love or faith—was arrived at by thinking; indeed, one could almost define the things that mattered as the ones that came as suddenly as thunder. Too often, I thought, the rational faculty tended only to rationalize, and the intellect served only to put one in two minds, torn apart by second thoughts. In that sense, God could be said to be nothing but the act of faith itself. Religion lay in the leap and not the destination. And Zen was as much as anything a refutation of doubt itself; a transcendence of the whole either/or sensibility that makes up all our temporizing. Instead of temporizing, as Thoreau might have said, why do we not eternize?

In all these ways, Zen seemed the natural product of a culture that has little time for philosophical speculation but stresses instead the merits of ritual, rigor, and repetition. The directness of Zen appeared to reflect the utilitarian concreteness of modern Japan, where people seemed rarely to dwell on suffering or to give themselves to close self-study. Zen, after all, was about whole-heartedness—or, at least, whole-mindedness. Strictly speaking, I knew, both Shintoism and Jodo Buddhism, the other great faiths of Japan, were equally free of doctrine and scripture, and, moreover, Zen had been invented by an Indian monk in China. The first Zen temples were active in Korea before the teaching had ever come across the Tsushima Strait to Japan. Yet still the finest achievements of the discipline today were associated with Japan, not least because the qualities sought out by Zen—spareness, self-discipline, precision—seemed closest to those of Japan. Did Zen help to create the features of Japan, or did Japan help to form the distinctive qualities of Zen—it was a question as old in its way, and unending, as the famous Zen conundrum "What was your face before you were born?" Whatever the answer, I thought, if Zen had not existed, the Japanese would have had to invent it.

Talking to Mark, though, and to Kazuo, had already brought me a little closer to earth. Besides, I knew that coming to Japan hoping to find a world guided by the stern and gentle precepts of Buddhism was as misguided as going to America hoping to find a society graced at every turn by Christianity (but America was shaped and strengthened by Christian writers, one could almost hear a visitor saying—Jonathan Edwards, Emily Dickinson, T. S. Eliot: how could modern America be so forgetful of its inheritance?). I realized, too, that the very qualities that made Zen so attractive to me were also the ones that made it so alien. Most of all, I suspected that if the Japanese really did have a religion, it was very likely one that outsiders like myself would not be able to recognize if we saw it, since it would probably have more to do with rituals than with texts. That religion could have a shifting relation to morality; that religious affiliations could be taken off or put on again as easily as costumes; that the Japanese could partake of what Rexroth had called "a secular mysticism, which sees experience as its own transcendence" — that religion, in short, could be capricious and practical as love, that other celebrated act of nondenominational faith, was something we Santa Barbarians found hard to understand.

I got a glimpse of this one day when Mark and I came across a Zen student from New York, who was all marshmallowy softness. ("And what are *you* doing in Japan?" she cooed. "A journalist? Oh, how *wonderful!*") As we walked away, Mark, usually so gentle, could hardly contain his impatience. "Jeez," he began, shaking his head, "that's the kind of stuff the Zen guys can't stand! Because they know what it's really like — how tough and rigid and down-to-earth it is: waking up at three a.m. in the winter and sweeping leaves in the rain and going begging in the snow. Yet these Zen students are always coming over from America and putting on this weird, goody-goody kind of sweetness. And the Zen guys know that has nothing to do with it."

As he talked, I could see how right he was, yet also, perhaps, how protective of the Zen he knew. The hardest part of this discipline, like any other, must be to free oneself from a notion of what it was to protect.

Because I was interested in this aspect of Japan, Mark invited me one day to come and meet his best friend, an American who had lived in a temple for a while but now devoted most of his energy to his wife and children, while teaching English, translating Japanese, and spending long hours reading or playing the piano.

The next thing I knew, we were seated inside Joe's house and some frenzied Dennis Hopper madness was exploding on every side of us. *Ghostbusters* was blasting out of the video set, and some throaty jazz was thrumming out of the stereo system. Joe's four-year-old son was somersaulting across a tiny room jammed with "Hello Koala" bags and a tank of fish, while his three-year-old daughter was scampering around on all fours like a dog. The master of the household was blowing up balloons as fast as Mark could draw feet on them, and his nine-month-old baby was scattering toys and juice on the floor and feeding at the breast of a mother who was muttering something in Japanese. "She wants to know if Ringo Starr is homosexual," said her husband, setting up a chessboard for the two of us, and then the phone began to trill. He picked it up. "A hundred fifty thousand? Listen—what's your problem, man? If I say it, you can believe it. Yeah, all right, one forty-five thousand. Jesus fuck, I don't believe this, man. One forty thousand," and then he slammed down the phone and picked it up again. "Listen, Umeda-san, we really had a great time last night," and then, "Oh shit, man. I just dialed the number of the same guy I was talking to. Wrote down his number, man, and then dialed it again. He must have thought I was crazy or somethin', callin' about a piano and then me thankin' him for dinner. . . ."

Joe looked over at us, his unshaven face cracking, and began laughing. His laugh got started like an aging Plymouth on a winter's day, until he was chortling and chuckling infectiously. His unorthodox directness was hitting me like a slap in the face. But I could see that it was the most Zen-like quality about him and, if nothing else, he was very much his own man. Cackling, uncombed, talking with the crazy intensity of someone forever under some foreign influence, he put on another tape, and as *The Neverending Story* went on neverendingly, he began telling me about Japan. "Like my students, man. One time, I had to teach them the meaning of the words 'necessary,' 'useless,' and 'useful.' So I asked them to rate all their subjects in one of these categories. And you know the one all of them—one hundred

percent of them—listed as 'necessary'? Sports, man! Fuckin'
sports! And the one that every single one of them listed as
'useless'? Religious education! Except for one guy, who put
it as 'useful.' But everyone else laughed at him and said it
was because he was a Christian. Weird, man, fuckin' weird.
But I thought about it, and it makes sense. Not just because
sports makes them healthy. But it instills in them this sense
of the team. And it makes them competitive. And in most ways,
this is a very competitive society. The place is like a pyramid,
man; the whole place is a fuckin' pyramid. And the one subject
you *never* mention to them is politics. *Never*, man. Makes them
go dead. It's like in the U.S., if you had a class on Byzantine
Church doctrine or somethin'—they don't care about it. They
don't know anything about it. It's not their concern. It just
makes them dead. Not a single fuckin' political science department in the entire country. No one here gives a damn about
politics.

"There are two myths that the Japanese have about themselves.
One is that they're a small country. They ain't small, man.
France and Spain are the only countries in Europe that are
bigger. And look at the fuckin' population, man. Sometimes I
get out an atlas and say to them, 'How many people in Denmark,
man? Five fuckin' million.' And they say, '*Ah sō?*' This country
ain't small, man. Look at a map. And they think that this is an
old country. It ain't old. Ask any Japanese high school graduate
to read somethin' before 1868. He can't do it, man. They have
no connection with their literature. In the old days, before
Meiji, they didn't have this Emperor-worship thing. One old
Emperor was just this nothin' guy who had to sell his own
calligraphy to keep goin'. But then in Meiji they built a new
nation and trained people to think a certain way. Education
didn't mean broadening horizons. It just meant learning to be a
part of society. And hey, man, if they decide to bring back
Emperor-worship, you better have short hair, man." Joe's eyes
were wild now. "And you better get new clothes. And you

better not talk in the street. No fooling around with those guys, man. You watch what you're doin'."

Joe was certainly giving me a crash course in one-pointedness—and in the frustrations of a longtime resident. The next thing I knew, he was flinging down before me a box that featured a floppy-eared rabbit above the legend "I Am Somebunny Special." Inside was a novel, flawlessly typed, called *Tree-Planting in America,* by someone from Little Lake, Michigan, who was, Joe said, just some penniless guy living in a cabin without a toilet, electricity, or running water. "I knew this guy way back—in Massachusetts. We were buildin' a *zendō* together. But he never talked about Zen. Never. Or writing. Then, last summer, he gave me this manuscript. I read it by kerosene lamp in his cabin, man, and I was gettin' more and more excited. This is a true book, man. At fifteen, this guy tried to be a painter. Then at eighteen, he decided to be a writer. By twenty-two, he had all the skills, he says—more than he's got now—but he hadn't anything to say. So he put it aside for twenty years. Now, he says, he's got somethin' to say, so he writes this, supporting himself by slayin' deer. That's integrity, man. He didn't want to make money out of his writing; he just wanted to make art. He's starving to do it, doesn't have any friends. He's kind of like Kundera, I think—it's funny, but it makes you think."

Integrity at any cost, I thought; a rigor of dissent. "D'you like Jim Harrison?" I asked, casting around in my mind for any other Zen-minded writer who came from Michigan.

"Sure. I read *Warlock* and some other book by him. Better than Saul Blow or John Updick. Man, I can't stand those guys. Best place I ever found for buying books was Taiwan, man—I'd go into this store, buy five books, read 'em, and sell 'em back to the guy the next week. I remember two books I got there. One was *The Big Sleep.* The other was by this guy called Ben Garcia, and I'm ashamed now that I gave it back. Ben Garcia, I'll always remember the name." He shook his head at the memory. "You could tell his wasn't a learned style or anything, but this guy had truth! It was a true book, man, a true book. About this Mexican who lived with the Indians. I remember its beginning: 'I've got a ranch, wife, and kids, but for seventy years I feel like I'm living in a coffin. Ranching, making money—none of it means a thing.' That's how it starts, man. Only book he ever wrote. True book, man, fuckin' true book.

"Taiwanese, though, they only like food. When I asked my students what they wanted for their birthday, they'd just say, 'Food,' man. That's why you'll find a Chinese restaurant anywhere you go. Anywhere in the world, man, you go and you'll find a Chinese restaurant—even Grenada, or Huehuetenango."

Noticing his four-year-old son careening like a dervish around the room, Joe suddenly told him to stop. Abruptly, the boy sat down where he was, cupped his hands, and folded his legs in a perfect lotus posture. Eyes closed, he fell into a silent meditation.

"Man, I was reading Charlie Chaplin's autobiography the other day," Joe started up again. "Chaplin, man, the only guy I know who started out life with no ideals—just tryin' to survive— and then he got famous and started havin' ideals. Great, man. Fuckin' great!" And then there was more, about R. K. Narayan and *Travels with My Aunt,* about the infighting of monasteries and piano techniques, about bilingualism and the chess game that lay finished in one corner. And finally, it began to rain, pittering and pattering on all the flimsy roofs and walls.

"*Shito-shito,*" said Joe softly. "And *goro-goro* for thunder. *Zā-zā* for heavy rain. *Pica-pica* for starlight. You don't have words for these things. Just sounds, man, perfect sounds."

And I thought how well you could always hear rain here, on wooden walls and roofs, in every Japanese poem and home.

8

As the October days eased on, Autumn stole like a thief into Kyoto, in one fluent succession of days so calm they took my breath away. Wandering through the buoyant days, I felt I had never known autumn before, not even in New England. For the mild and milky afternoons were graced with a distinctly Japanese touch, unintrusive in its effects, and hesitant, and still. The reticence gave dimension to the beauty.

Sometimes it rained, but when it did, it truly poured; other times, everything was a radiance of blue. The weather here was rarely indifferent, rarely caught in the bleary in-betweens of England; whatever the inflection, it usually seemed unqualified, and the days often passed with a kind of metronomic regularity, of sun and rain and sun and rain and shine. Sometimes the rain came down steadily, relentlessly, with an unlifting persistence that blurred the world for days; other times, mornings dawned crisper and clearer than any I could remember outside the Himalayas in winter. Occasionally, the two extremes would alternate on a single day, but still, even then, the pattern never wavered: either rapturous or foul.

Besides, Kyoto was lovely in the mist — the air rising clear above the hills, the dogs barking in the hillside temples. The singing cries of children rang out in the ringing air, and everything was green and cleansed. Kyoto back streets were lovely too, on shiny afternoons after days of heavy rain: the tangerine trees in bloom, and monks on slow-moving bicycles, and ladies bent over rain-washed alleyways, rearranging flowers. The Heian Shrine was all patterns of sunlight and reflections in the water:

girls crouched meditative over ponds; orange gates solemn under
blazing autumn skies.

Autumn, moreover, was beginning to be observed in every
corner of Kyoto, as a religion might be, but in a place where
religions were often both secular and consumerist. Coffee shops
now were advertising "Autumn ice cream sundaes," and vending
machines, like towel-bearing waiters, were changing their offerings from cold to hot. One trendy boutique had chalked a new
slogan on its window: "Autumn is the season to do pretty things
for you." And at Koshien Stadium, where the local baseball
team, the Hanshin Tigers, was playing its last game of the
season, the air was thick with elegy. Before the game began, the
great star of the Tigers, the huge and gentle Oklahoma farmboy
Randy Bass, got up on the rostrum, bowed all round, and
stepped down again. Then he got up on the rostrum, bowed all
round, and came down. Then he got up . . . eleven times in all,
while Bass flags fluttered everywhere and a little boy next to
me, in a flowing white happi coat with "R. Bass" on its back,
looked on in wonder. After the game ended, every member of
the team came out onto the field and bowed in unison to the
fans. For fifteen minutes, not a supporter left the stadium. All of
them—all of us—stood to attention, singing every last verse of
the sober, martial Tiger fight song, in one massed, mournful
choir. Here, I thought, was a team in last place, thirty-six games
out of first place, which had lost two games out of every three
for more than six months—yet still its faithful were rising to give
it this heartfelt show of support. *Sayōnara*s were hosannas here.

A few days later, on another brilliant morning, the trees beginning to turn under skies that were blue and puffy white, I went
to see one of the three great occasions of the Kyoto year, the
Jidai Matsuri, or Festival of the Ages, in the Imperial Palace.

When I arrived, an hour or so before the procession was to begin, the performers were relaxing backstage, on the lawns of the spacious compound. Little girls whose ghost-white faces and twisted hairdos reproduced the high elegance of Sei Shōnagon and Murasaki sat erect in priceless kimono under trees. Old wooden carriages stood at rest on gravel walkways, forgotten props from some period movie. Wrinkled men in fierce warriors' dress glared for cameras in the shadeless courtyards. Incarnations of great figures from the city's past, the performers were as shiny as the apple-polished day around them.

And as the parade began, one stately procession of spirits walking and breathing through the high-rise town—*daimyō* and *samurai*, courtiers and geisha, caparisoned and costumed, and fighters all in armor, watched in respectful silence by the crowds—I could not help but think of the last such celebration I had seen, just two months before I arrived in Japan: Carnival in Havana. It was an absurd comparison, I knew, yet the difference was as striking as between real life and art. For Cuba, however circumscribed by government edict and reduced by poverty, was still one pulsing, writhing explosion of lust and liquor, of bikinied girls and wriggling dragons and foot-high paper cups of beer foaming over beside the seaside Malecón. Here, by contrast, all was grave formality. Boys in black walked two by two, in synchronized steps, playing pipes; ancients regal on slow-stepping horses passed in noiseless dignity across the gravel; girls as stately as Heian courtiers glided with phantom steps through coffee-shop streets. The audience was as silent as a congregation. Everything, timed to the moment, was as rigid as a catechism.

All festivals, of course, are acts of collective myth-making, chances for a nation to advertise its idealized image of itself. In Cuba, for all the privations, that meant abandon, gaiety, and bacchanal; here, it meant mellifluous order, solemnity, and grace. In Cuba, one could feel the effusions of a passionate, rhetorical people able and eager to give themselves over to the sentiments they voiced so recklessly; here, the effect was one of strange, almost awestruck, disengagement. It seemed as if the Japanese were almost paying homage to the fact of ritual itself—and to the religion of Japan—so that the ceremony became pageant, and the festival a kind of memorial service.

Before the day was out, however, this, like most of my generalities about Japan, found its refutation in the country's other side, the side that came out after dark—in this case, in the mysterious Fire Festival held that very night in the village of Kurama, in the hills to the north. I had heard for days how terrible the crowds would be, so I took pains to leave home early, arriving at the train station just as the late-afternoon sun was turning faces to gold and catching the firelights in hair. This was the magic hour of the Kyoto autumn, the last hour of light in the waning days: the hills silhouetted with a shocking clarity, the sky a burnished strip of gold and silver.

The minute the train drew into the station, the whole huge crowd piled in until we were packed as tightly as nuts in a bag of Japanese sweets. I bumped against rows of silky hair, was shoved into pockets of expensive perfume, buried myself in a new Springsteen tape. Through all the crush, the Japanese remained unfailingly calm, some of them even sleeping where they stood.

As soon as we arrived at the village, the crowds piled out again and into a steep, narrow main street, so thick with bodies that one could scarcely move. A smell of bonfires redolent of Guy Fawkes Night, on a blazing, chill November evening in England, the details of the world smoothed down now in the dark. Lanterns all about, and the shadows of hills, and ashes spitting into the night like fireflies in some Peter Brook production. Along the tiny, toylike streets, the crowds expectant, a loudspeaker conferring on everything an air of panic and authority.

Finding no room amidst the crowds even now, four hours before the festival was due to begin, I started to climb up the hill, away from the town, up towards Kurama Temple, towering solemn above the crowds. There I sat, and walked about, hands stuffed into pockets, and waited. I waited some more. The night grew chilly, with a winter snap to it. Still there was nothing to see but crowds. I watched a pair of German boys attach themselves to three smiling "office ladies" and smiled to myself as the Germans, new to the country, took the shy giggles and polite questions for encouragement and began sliding hands behind backs, as the girls, smiling sweetly, edged away. I listened for a while to the Springsteen tape, rented today, the very day of its release, from a neighborhood store. I watched a teahouse high above the street, where VIPs were sedately taking dinner in a perfect Tokugawa tableau of high elegance. I nibbled on corn chips, stamped up and down in the cold, began to wish I'd never come.

And then, of a sudden, there came a quickened intensity, and then a roar, and a flash of fire, and a rush of boys, naked save for loincloths, arms lifted in the dark, streaking furiously through the winter streets, bearing torches, shouting, "*Sareyā, sareyō,*" eyes blazing. It was like nothing I had ever seen in Japan: wild, pagan, full of danger. The torches played crazy games on the faces they passed, and the shouters raced to the shrine like intoxicants, faces lit up by their torches. Pointing their torches to the middle, they started building a huge fire. Flames licked the air, torches began to waver, the crowd let out a gasp. Sparks were flying this way and that, policemen were roaring through megaphones, the whole crowd, pressed as closely as in some rock concert, was shaking and wobbling as one. Shouting "*Sareyā, sareyō,*" the men in loincloths, bodies glistening in the night, poured more heat onto the fire, the flames racing up in the sky above them, their eyes alight. I could feel the danger in the air, sense the pull of some ancient force. I could feel an electrical crackle in the air.

All night the fires raged, subsiding shortly before dawn.

A couple of days later, I found myself walking along a broad avenue in the sunshine with Siobhan, the potter I had met from

Santa Cruz. "For a long time, you know, I used to repress this thing about being a witch," she began, as we walked past groups of horn-rimmed students, remarkable only in their normalcy. "When I was young, you know, I was always afraid of all that stuff about devils; I believed that knowing anything about them was a form of possession. And then one day, Pam, who I knew from Connecticut—but she's in Santa Cruz now—came up to me and said, 'You're a witch, you know.'

"And at first I just said, 'No, no, I'm not.' But she could tell. And she had her own coven. And then one night I saw my dead mother in a dream, and I could just tell she was in a very different place, but a good place. And that's when I accepted being a witch."

Siobhan smiled, and the day smiled with her.

"Anyway, now I'm in this really comfortable place in the countryside, and everything's cool. Except that my Japanese roommate—she's really into Stendhal and is going to France next year—has fallen in love with this young German boy who lives with us. Fell in love with him just for the way he washes the dishes. Plus, of course," she said, eyes flashing, "there's the whole Christmas cake thing. Keiko's twenty-six."

"Christmas cake?"

"You know. For girls." I must have looked perplexed. "You don't know about it? Maybe it's something they only tell girls. Anyway, it's this system they have over here; they even use the word, in Japanese, *Kurisumasu kēki*. You know how on the twenty-third of December a Christmas cake is supposed to be fresh and worth investing in, but by the twenty-fourth it's getting kind of old? And after the twenty-fifth, it's starting to get stale and no one wants it. Well, that's how they think of women over here. Twenty-three is a good age to get one. Twenty-four is a little close to the deadline. And after twenty-five, forget it!"

"Which is why girls over the age of twenty-five often make a beeline for foreigners—that's their only chance of getting married?"

"Exactly!"

As soon as I heard this, many things began to fall into place. For my initial sense that every foreign male here found some demure but passionate Japanese companion to dance attention on him had only been strengthened by some of the characters I had met in Kyoto. Everywhere I turned, I seemed to run into men who were in a kind of spell here, having not only met girls but dream girls who were the embodiment of everything they wanted in a woman. Lifelong bachelors began talking about marriage; newlywed husbands could not stop extolling the goddesses they had married; hardened Lotharios found themselves disarmed by girls whose innocence was touched by a hint of guiltless sensuality.

And though most Japanese women, I assumed, would still unquestioningly follow their prescribed course towards a Japanese husband, there was, by all accounts, a minority — and an increasingly large minority — who would do anything possible to find a foreign boyfriend, if only for a while, in order to get a taste, firsthand, of the glamorous foreign world they had seen on their TV screens. In the discos of Tokyo and Osaka, foreign men were currently as fashionable as Chanel shirts or Louis Vuitton bags, trendy accessories to be shown off to one's friends. But even in less cosmopolitan Kyoto, foreigners were still agents of escape — like the crickets kept by Kawabata's Kyoto girl Chieko, inhabiting "a separate realm, an enchanted land ... filled with fine wine and delicious food from both land and sea." The Japanese looked on foreigners, I sometimes thought, with the same awestruck condescension that we might bring to heavy-metal rock stars, secretly convinced that they are, at heart, somewhat vulgar and barbarous, yet undeniably seduced by the fact that they belong to a flashy, semimythic world of money, fame, and glamour. We look down our noses at Jon Bon Jovi, but invited to meet him, we jump at the chance.

In Kyoto, however, the attraction of opposites was especially strong, not least because this most conservative of cities, in one of the most traditional of all societies, attracted—indeed, because of its traditionalism attracted—some of the freest and most radical of visitors from abroad, the hiders and seekers, the rebels and dropouts who did not fit in, or did not want to fit in, at home. And Japanese girls had long been the subject of romantic fantasies of our own in the West. Pierre Loti had hired his Mademoiselle Chrysanthème as soon as he laid anchor in Japan; the Santa Barbaran Rexroth had found his Muse in a mysterious Japanese woman poet who lived in the shadow of a Kyoto temple. Even Lafcadio Hearn, who had done so much to bring Japanese Buddhism to the West, had declared that "the most wonderful aesthetic products of Japan are not its ivories, nor its bronzes, nor its porcelains, nor its swords, nor any of its marvels in metal and lacquer—but its women." And even today, the *Japan Handbook*, the standard guidebook used by most young foreigners in Japan, devoted an entire section to "Sex," informing its readers, with guidebook authority, that Japanese women were "orgasmic," longed to be swept off their feet, and "[expected] you to be an aggressor and in the old-fashioned sense to make [them]"—an alarming suggestion, I thought, in the hands of men looking for "a possible partner for life."

Besides, the pairing of Western men and Eastern women was as natural as the partnership of sun and moon. Everyone falls in love with what he cannot begin to understand. And the other man's heart is always greener.

9

ONE SUNNY MORNING, I was huddled over some proofs in my room when suddenly a call came for me. It was Sachiko-san again—now, she said, on her way to the zoo, together with her children and Sandy, the American woman with granny glasses I had met at the temple ceremony, and her children too. Would I like to join them? This, I thought, was too good an opportunity to be missed (to show off eleven of the twelve words I knew in Japanese), so I readily accepted, and an hour later, when I approached the giant *torii* gate that bestraddles one of Kyoto's central streets—making it fit for ceremonial processions—I found all six of them in picnic mood. Inside the zoo, we duly inspected the raccoons, the tiger, and the California seals, and I felt more than ever like the only adult male of the human species inside this shop-window collection of stylish young mothers and glossy-haired silent children. I half expected a sign to be hung around my neck identifying the rare, and undomesticated, *Homo subcontinentus*.

When it came time for Sandy and her children to go home, I half expected that Sachiko-san would go with them. But no, she said, her children had asked whether they might possibly come and see my room—their first chance, I assumed, to visit that close cousin of the zoo, the *gaijin* guesthouse. So together we ambled through the sunstruck streets, the children teetering on walls and scuffling after acorns, while Sachiko-san's apologies tumbled out unstoppably.

When finally we arrived at my house, the children apparently found all the excitement they had anticipated. "*Okā-san, okā-san, mitte!*" cried Hiroshi, pointing in horrified astonishment at the American-sized shoes lined up at the foot of the stairs. "Mother, mother, look at the shoes!" The footsteps of the yeti would, I thought, have been no more remarkable to him. His mother, for her part, showed just how much of a mother she was — and how Japanese — by bending down to tidy up the shoes that the foreigners had left so higgledy-piggledy, arranging them all in a neat, color-coordinated row. Upstairs, when I opened the door to my room, the children's eyes grew even wider as they took in the pile of proofs scattered messily across my desk (convincing Sachiko-san, no doubt, that my job was not that of a raccoon story writer but a proofreader).

"You like story?" she asked me, taming her children with one hand as she spoke.

"Oh yes," I said, "very much."

And so, as her children careened around the room, she began telling me an elaborate old Japanese folktale — the oldest surviving story in the land — about a princess, Kaguya-hime, who had come to live with an old bamboo-cutter and his wife but then at last had been obliged to leave them and return to her home, in the Palace of the Moon. When Sachiko-san finished the story, I was startled to see, her eyes were bright with tears.

There was a long and awkward pause.

"Maybe we little go home?" she said. Taking the hint, I offered to walk them back to the station, and as the four of us wandered through the crowded streets in the dusk, I suddenly remembered to remind the children of the new word I had taught them just a week before. At that, the day broke open like a smashed window, and the children, thrilled with their new discovery, began reeling through the crooked lanes, crying, "Raccoon car! Raccoon bus! Raccoon shop!" while I, spurring them on shamelessly, shouted, "Raccoon coffee shop! Raccoon cinema! Raccoon plane!" and all the while Sachiko-san serenely continued recounting ancient Japanese folktales that left her again and again in tears.

The Japanese were famous, I knew, for their delight in *lacrimae rerum* and for finding beauty mostly in sadness; indeed, it was often noted that their word for "love" and their word for "grief" are homonyms—and almost synonyms too—in a culture that seems to love grief, of the wistful kind, and to grieve for love. So I was hardly surprised to learn that most of their stories were sad and that all of them ended in parting. Parting was the definition of sweet sorrow here. Yet still I was taken aback by this curious flash of intimacy: Sachiko-san sinking deep into her sadness, while her children pranced gaily through the gathering dark, shouting out their new mantra with the zeal of proselytes. "Raccoon train! Raccoon street! Raccoon temple!"

Making plans with Sachiko-san was always, I had found, an uncertain business, not least because whenever she called me, both of us would engage in a polite, but ruthless, tug-of-war as to which should be the medium of confusion. Both of us were determined to speak the language we didn't know (she to practice her English and I to try out my Japanese), and so, very often, we ended up communicating in a kind of jangled bilingual hybrid in which nothing was lost except meaning.

Whenever we tried to fix meetings, therefore—she confusing "Tuesday" and "Thursday," I mixing up *ka-yōbi* (Tuesday) with *kinyō-bi* (Friday), she routinely transposing "yesterday" and "tomorrow"—the result was madness. "Where would you like to meet?" I would ask her, in Japanese, and she would reply, in English, "You want to come here my house?" in a tone that suggested more apprehension than delight. She would say she was free at two, and I would arrive, for a brief encounter, only to learn that she was free for two hours. I would say that I was leaving for three days, and she would assume I was leaving on the third. That first day, when she had casually invited me to drop in on her daughter's birthday party at around two and I had casually dropped in at two forty-five, only to find that there was no party at all and I was forty-five minutes late, increasingly seemed an augury of all that was to come.

Once we met, of course, the craziness would only accelerate. For one thing, Sachiko-san was as unabashed and unruly in her embrace of English as most of her compatriots were reticent and shy. Where they would typically refuse to utter a single sentence unless they could deliver it perfectly, she was happy to plunge ahead without a second thought for grammar, scattering meanings and ambiguities as she went. Plurals were made singular, articles were dropped, verbs were rarely inflected, and word order was exploded – often, in fact, she seemed effectively to be making Japanese sentences with a few English words thrown in. Often, moreover, to vex the misunderstandings further, she spoke both languages at once, as if reading simultaneously from both columns of a phrasebook: "*Demo* but where are you *ima* now?" she sometimes asked, hardly stopping to bother about the fact that *demo* means "but" and *ima*, "now." Other times, she suddenly came up with an affirmative "Sí!" suggesting that somehow or other she had got hold of a French or Spanish phrasebook instead of an English one. Often, too, I could see in her sentences the scorch marks of an all-too-hasty trip through the dictionary: "Is America very high?" she asked me (since *takai* in Japanese means both "expensive" and "high"), or, to more alarming effect, "The bullet train is always very early" (since *hayai* in Japanese means "early" as well as "fast"). Sometimes, when she said something like "I have this happy feeling touch," I could tell that she had whizzed through a list of synonyms fatally unseparated (in her mind at least) by a comma.

I, of course, was hardly better, turning Japanese nouns into adjectives, using feminine forms for myself, and sometimes just deploying English words, with random vowels hopefully stuck in at the end, foolishly confident in the belief that Japan had incorporated an enormous number of English terms (*Hamu to tōsto, kudasai!*). Having picked up most of my Japanese from a businessmen's handbook and bilingual editions of poetry – a fitting combination, I had thought at the time—I was able to deliver nothing but sentences like "Please give your secretary the autumn moon."

To complicate matters even further, Sachiko-san, in the classic Japanese manner, contrived to make everything as ambiguous, as circumspect, as consensual as possible—even in English. If ever she wanted to use the English word for *itsumo*, which I had been taught meant "always," she always said, "usually," so as to soften the assertion and allow for the exception that might one day prove the rule (leading to such statements as "Usually, the first day of the year is January one"). And where we would say yes, she always said *tabun*, or "maybe." When once she told me that Yuki was sick, I replied, with empty assurance, "I'm sure she'll be better soon." "*Tabun*," she replied. "Maybe." "No, really," I insisted, "I'm sure there's no problem." "Maybe," she replied, all caution. The effect was one of instant melancholy, though really she must have been as sure as I that all would be okay. And of course, every adjective that was less than entirely positive—and much else besides—was qualified with a *chotto*, meaning "little," so that Frankenstein became "a little strange," and traveling to the moon "a little difficult."

Much of this, clearly, was as much an act of courtesy as of caution, and not so different, really, from the reflexive softenings in which I too had once been trained in England. Always prefer a rhetorical question to a bald assertion ("Might it not be easier perhaps to try this road?"). Never disagree outright ("I'm not absolutely sure that's true"), and sometimes soften the dissent further, with—what else?—a rhetorical question ("It's so hard to know for certain, don't you find?"). If absolutely forced to say no, say anything other than "no," diluting every term in the sentence ("I'm very sorry, but I'm afraid it might be just a little difficult"). None of these were lies, as such, only stratagems for easing the social machinery.

Thus the intricacies of Japanese protocol were compounded by those of my own English training, and both were made nonsensical by the relentless exchange of gibberish. Whenever I said anything that made her happy, she assumed I was being polite, and whenever she replied, I assumed this was mere Japanese indirectness. So I would say, "Do you want to have some coffee?" and she would answer, "Okay. Do you want some coffee?" and I would have to say, *Iie, kekkō desu* ("No, thank you, I'm fine as I am"), and both of us would end up exactly where we had started.

"Should we meet on Tuesday?" I asked her. Sachiko-san gave me a smile. "No problem! Yesterday, Thursday, okay!"

Nonetheless, we did occasionally manage to meet, at almost the same time and place, and one day I found myself sitting with her in a shrine, on a bare wooden step, the light coming through the ginkgo trees as we waited for Yuki's English lesson to conclude. Carried away with excitement for my latest enthusiasm, I asked her if she preferred Mishima or Tanizaki.

"All Japanese writer, I like," she replied. "But my favorite is little foreigner man. His name Hess-e."

"Hermann Hesse?"

She nodded solemnly. "I much like this man. *Siddoharuta. Narushisu and Gōrudoman*. And *Petā Kamejindo*. When I little high school size, I all reading."

"But that's incredible," I said, pulling out of my bag the book I was reading at the moment, in this city of artists and anchorites, *Narziss and Goldmund*.

She, too, looked taken aback. "You read this book?"

"Yes! It was my favorite when I was a boy."

"Maybe you your country reading, I, too, same time!"

"Yes. And did you know that Hesse was a close friend of Jung, whom your brother is studying? And that he lived in Switzerland, where your brother lives? When I was in high school, this book was the only common link between my boarding school in England and California, where I went home in the holidays!"

She shook her head in amazement. "Also, I like Emily Brontë. You know *Storm on Hill*?"

"*Wuthering Heights*?"

"Maybe."

"That's one of my favorites too."

Minutes later, we were seated on a bench in the flowering gardens of the Imperial Palace, while three hundred school-children sat in rows on the gravel before us, patiently listening to a pep talk from their teachers. Sending her daughter off to play amidst the trees, where she set about making a pretty brocade of leaves (Japanese children had a remarkable gift, I noticed, for playing with flowers; their training in Nature awareness started early), Sachiko-san started telling me the story of the "North Wind's Daughter," an endearing children's story about a bear and his sorrow, made all the more engaging by her ideogrammatic delivery.

"Bear live in house. Mother, father, grandma, all die. All brother, sister, die — hunting! Bear very sad in his heart. But he has much pride; he never not cry. He think music very happy sound, then he little make sign, 'Please. I need Music Teacher. I have money.'

"Then much banging on door, very big noise. Man in blue there. He have trumpet. Then he play music. Sun shine, and set. Bear very happy. Then very sad in his heart. He try trumpet — but sound very bad sound. Then he blow much much, break tooth. He say man, 'Please you teach me.' Man say, 'You cannot play. You tooth break. Please you give me blueberry pie.' Bear give him pie, but in his heart very sad.

"Then blue woman come here his house, North Wind. She has violin. She play violin, very beautiful sound, little silver staircase sound. Sun shine, and set. Bear in his heart very happy. He try violin. But very bad music. He very sad. Very cold. Woman say, 'Please look your icebox. Please give me pineapple pie.' He give.

"Then much banging his door. Very pretty child there, North

Wind daughter. She blue! Bear sad. He has no food in freezer.
But girl say, 'Please you close eye. Please you count.' Bear try,
then open eye: hot cakes and chair! Bear very happy. Then girl
say, 'Please you close eye. Please you count.' Bear try, then open
eye. Then bear very sad. She not there. She gone. But he still
have music, and many beautiful memory."

"Happy ending?"

"Yes," she laughed sweetly, her voice like running water, and
with that, she took her daughter home.

One delicate autumn day a few days later—the sky now gray,
now blue, always like a woman's uncertain heart, a light drizzle
falling, and then subsiding, and falling once more—I met Sachiko
outside an Indonesian store, for a trip to Kurama. She was, as
ever, girlishly dressed, her hair falling thickly over one side of
her face, held back on the other by a black comb with a
red-stone heart in its middle; the tongues of her black sneakers
hanging out from under lime-green legwarmers.

As we traveled towards the hillside village, she set down her
backpack beside her on the train and began telling me excitedly
about her friend Sandy, and how it was Sandy who had
first introduced her to Zen, Sandy who had first taken her
to a temple, Sandy who had first encouraged her to try *zazen*
meditation. "I Japanese," she said softly. "But I not know my
country before. Sandy my teacher." More than that, she said,
it was Sandy who had shown her another way of life and given
her the confidence to try new things. Sandy, supporting two
children alone in a foreign country and at the same time
embarked on a full-length course of Zen studies, had shown
her that it was possible, even for a woman, to have a strong
heart.

Now, she went on, Sandy was planning to send her children
back to America for high school. "I dream, maybe Hiroshi go
your country, Sandy's son together. You see this movie *Stand by*

Me?" I nodded. "Very beautiful movie. I want give my son this life. I dream, he little *Stand by Me* world feeling." And what about her husband's view on all this? An embarrassed giggle. "I don't know. Little difficult. But I much dream children go other country." She paused, deep in thought. "But I also want children have Zen spirit inside, Japanese feeling." I asked her to explain. "Example—you and Sandy, *zazen* very difficult. Japanese people, *zazen* very easy. I want my children have this spirit."

"But if your children go away, they may grow distant. Maybe never talk to you. Maybe forget all Japanese things. Wouldn't that make you sad?"

"*Tabun.* Maybe."

"It's very difficult, I think."

And so we get off the train, and climb from shrine to shrine, scattered across the steep hills of Kurama, and the rain now drizzles down, now stops again, and the two of us huddle under her umbrella, sweaters brushing, her hair almost falling on my arm. "*Ai to ai gasa,*" I say, thinking of the phrase I had read in a Yosano Akiko poem, describing two people sharing a single umbrella. "Maybe," she says, with a lilting laugh, and we climb some more, the hills before us resplendent now, and then still higher, in the gentle rain, till we are sitting on a log.

In front of us, the trees are blazing. "I like color now," she says, pensive. "Later, I not so like. More sad. Leaves die. Many thing change." And then, carried away by the view, perhaps, she recalls the only other time she has come to this hill. Kurama is only a few miles north of Kyoto, a thirty-minute train ride. But Sachiko has not been here for fifteen years, and all that time, she says, she has longed to return. "I so happy," she whispers, as if in the presence of the sacred. "I so excited. Thank you. Thank you very much. I very happy. Very fun. Before I coming here, little teenage size, together three best friend. We climbing mountain, I very afraid, because I thinking snake. Much laughing, many joke. Very fun. My friend's names, Junko, Sumiko, and Michiko. But Osaka now. Very busy, marry ladies."

We walk down again, through the drizzle and the mist, then up slippery paths, between the trees. "I much love Kurama," she says quietly, as if in thought. "Sometimes I ask husband come here; he say, 'You always want play. I very busy. I cannot.' And come here together children, very difficult. Soon tired. Thank you very much, come here this place with me."

This is all rather sad. She tells me of her adventures, and the smallness of it all makes me sad again: how, when she was a little girl, she went with her cousin and brother and aunt to a cinema, and her aunt allowed her to go and see *The Sound of Music* alone. "I very scared. All dark. Many person there. But then, film begin, I soon forget. I much love. I dream I Julie Andrews." She also describes reading about Genghis Khan. "I dream I trip together Genghis Khan. I many trip in my heart, many adventure. But only in my heart." She tells me how once, last year, for the first time ever, she went alone to Osaka, forty minutes away, to see the Norwegian teenybopper group a-ha in concert, and then, exhilarated by this event, went again that same week to another of their concerts, in Kobe, with her son and her cousin, all three of them sharing a room in a luxury hotel. The night she spent in the hotel, the trip to the coffee shop after the concert, the way she had chanced to see the lead singer's parents in the coffee shop and then to meet the star himself in an elevator — all live on in her as what seems almost the brightest moment in her life. "I very lucky. I very excited. I dream, maybe next summer, I go this hotel again. See other a-ha concert."

And when she says, more than once, "I live in Kyoto all life; you come here only one month, but you know more place, very well," I feel again, with a pang, a sense of the tightly drawn limits of a Japanese woman's life, like the autumn paths vanishing in mist around us. For I could see that she was saying something more than the usual "Tourists know more of towns than their residents ever do," and I could catch a glimpse of the astonishing circumscription of her life. Even while her brother had been to

Kansas City to study for three years and was now in his third year of pursuing Jung in Switzerland, she had never really been outside Kyoto. She now worked two mornings a week in a doctor's office, but it was the same place where she had worked during junior high school and high school, in vacations, just around the corner from her parents' house. Her cousin, a kind of surrogate sister, sometimes worked in the same place. Her own house was in the next neighborhood down, within walking distance of her parents-in-law's house. And her mother still called her every night, to see how she was doing.

Every year, she said, her husband got three or four days of holiday, and the trips the family took together on these breaks—to the sea once, and once to Tokyo Disneyland—still lived within them as peak experiences. Even a trip such as the one today, for a few hours to a suburb, seemed a rare and unforgettable adventure.

"Please tell me your adventure," she begins to say. "Please tell me other country. I want imagine all place," but I don't know where to begin, or how to convey them to someone who has never been in a plane, and what cloak-and-dagger episodes in Cuba, or nights in the Thai jungle, will mean to one who has scarcely left Kyoto.

"I dream you life-style," she goes on, as if sensing my unease. "You are bird, you go everywhere in world, very easy. I all life living only Kyoto. So I dream I go together you. I have many, many dream in my heart. But I not have strong heart. You very different."

"Maybe. I was lucky that I got used to going to school by plane when I was nine."

"You very lucky. I afraid other country. Because I thinking, maybe I go away, my mother ill, maybe die. If I come back, maybe no mother here." Her mother, she explains, developed very serious allergies—because, it seemed, of the new atmospheric conditions in Japan. (All this I found increasingly hard to follow, in part because Sachiko used "allergy" to mean "age"—

she regularly referred to the "Heian allergy," and when she was talking about "war allergy," I honestly didn't know if it was a medical or a historical point she was making. I, of course, was no better, confusing *sabishii* with *subarashii*, and so, in trying to say, "Your husband must be lonely," invariably coming out with, "Your husband is wonderful. Just fantastic," which left her frowning in confusion more than ever.)

"When I little children size, my mother many times in hospital. And Grandma too. And when my brother in Kansas City, my grandma die. He never say goodbye. She see my husband, she think he my brother. Very sad time. So I always dream in heart. Because many sad thing happen. But dream stay in heart." This seemed a sorrowful way to approach the universe, though eminently pragmatic. Yet she held to it staunchly. "Maybe tomorrow I have accident. I die. So I always keep dream." That was lovely, elegant, Sachiko: Sachiko, in her teenager's high-tops, keeping a picture of Sting in her wallet and sometimes losing sleep over him—a thirty-year-old girl with daydreams.

All this gets us onto what is fast becoming a recurrent theme in our talks, the competing merits of the Japanese and the American family systems. I, of course, argue heartily for the Japanese.

"It makes me so happy to see mothers and children playing together here, or going to temples together, and movies, and coffee shops. In America, mothers and daughters are often strangers. People do not know their parents, let alone their grandparents. Sometimes, in California, parents just fly around, with very young girlfriends or boyfriends, and leave their children with lots of money but no love." (My sense of America, in Japan, was getting as simplistic and stereotyped as my sense of Japan had been in America.) "So fifteen-year-old girls have babies and drive cars, and have money, many boyfriends, and lots of drugs."

"Maybe. But in your country, I think, children have strong heart. Do anything, very easy. Here in Japan, no strong heart.

Even grown-up person, very weak!" I think she means that they lack adventure, recklessness, and freedom, and in all that I suppose she is right, and not only because twelve Japanese CEOs have literally collapsed this year under the pressures of a strong yen. And she, of course, as a foreigner, sees only the pro ledger in America, while I, over here, stress only the con— though when I am in America, I find myself bringing back to American friends an outsider's sense of their country's ever-green hopefulness.

And as we continue walking, a few other people trudge past us up the hill, elders most of them, with sticks, the men in berets and raincoats, the women in print dresses, occasionally looking back through the curtain of fine drizzle at the strange sight of a pretty young Japanese girl with a shifty Indian male. Sachiko, however, seems lost in another world.

"What is your blood type?" she suddenly asks, eyes flashing into mine.

"I don't know."

"True?"

"True."

"Whyyy?" she squeals, in the tone of a high school girl seeking a rock star's autograph.

"I don't know. In my country, people aren't concerned about blood types."

"But maybe you have accident. Go hospital."

"I don't know."

"Really? True??"

"Really. Foreigners think it's strange that the Japanese are so interested in blood types."

"Really? *Hontō ni?*"

"Yes." I am beginning to feel I am letting her down in some way, so I quickly ask if she is interested in the Chinese calendar, or astrology. All this, though, is frightful to try to translate, and when Sachiko says that she is the sign of the "ship" and I say, "Ah yes, you mean the waves," she looks very agitated. "No, no waves! Ship!" Now it's my turn to look startled. What is going on here? "The Water Bearer?" "No." "The Fish?" "No. Ship!" She is sounding adamant. Then, suddenly, I recall that Aries is the ram. (Thank God, I think, for all those years in California!) "Oh—sheep! You are the sheep sign." "Yes. Ship."

And then, of a sudden, she plops down on a bench, and draws out from her backpack a Japanese edition of Hesse, and shows me the stories she likes, and repeats how he had struck a chord in her when young. "When I little high school size, I much much like. But Goldmund, not so like. When I twenty, it not so touch my heart, not same feeling. Now thirty, maybe different feeling. Which you like?"

"I don't know. That's why I'm reading it again now. When I was young, I liked Goldmund. Then, later, I understood Narziss a little better. For a long time, I spent one month living like Goldmund, traveling around the world, and one month like Narziss, leading a monk's life at home. Now I'm trying both at the same time, to see which one is better."

Somehow the world has misted over as we talk, and time and space are gone: the world, I think, begins and ends on this small bench. And as we sit there, sometimes with her dainty pink umbrella unfurled, sometimes not, I pointing to the yellow trees, or the blue in the sky, and saying, *"Onna-no kokoro, Kurama-no tenki"* (The weather in Kurama is like a woman's heart), I can see her perfect white teeth when she laughs, the mole above her lips, a wisp of hair across her forehead, another fine strand that slips into her ear. She bends over to look at the magazine in my hands, and her hair falls all about me.

"You tell parent about girlfriend?" she says, looking up.

"Well, for many years, I haven't had—or wanted—a girlfriend."

"So what am I?" A long silence. "I man?" She giggles girlishly, and I don't know where that puts us: our discourse is soft and blurred as autumn rain.

"I think you're a very beautiful lady," I say, looking down at my outstretched legs like a bashful schoolboy. "Your husband is a very lucky man."

"I not so think. I bad wife."

And then, seizing the closeness in the air, she tries to formulate more complex thoughts. "I very happy. Today, time stop. Thank you very much, coming here this place together me. I only know you short time, but you best friend feeling. I think I know you long time. I no afraid, no weak heart. You foreigner man, but I alone together you, very easy. I think maybe you very busy man. But talking very easy. I very fun, thank you." All of this is a little heartbreaking, I think, together on a bench on a misty autumn day, and she so excited to see me after only two weeks of acquaintance.

Standing up, we start walking slowly down the hill, through faint drizzle, talking of her closeness to her mother, and the poems of Yosano Akiko. And as we leave the hill of temples behind us, she turns and bows towards the shrine, pressing her palms together and closing her eyes very tight.

That evening, I read Yosano Akiko late into the night and try to recall the short *tanka* Sachiko had recited to me on the hill. But I know only that it begins with *kimi,* the intimate form of "you," as so many of Akiko's poems do. Falling asleep over the book, I awaken with a start in the dead of night, imagining that I am holding her by the hand and saying, "Sachiko-san, I'm sorry to disturb you. I know you have a husband, and I'm very sorry, but..."

And later in the night, I think of the two of us under her pink umbrella, and flip hurriedly through the book in search of the phrase *"ai to ai gasa."* When I find it, my heart seems almost to stop: it is, it seems, a classic image of intimacy, and one of the most famous figures in Japan for lovers.

10

As I went back and forth between my walks with Sachiko and my talks with the Zen-minded foreigners, I was beginning to pick up a little more Japanese by immersing myself in a bilingual edition of Yosano Akiko's almost unbearably sensuous poems, *Midaregami* (Tangled Hair). Voluptuous and rich as full-bodied peaches, her *tanka* presented a world quite different from the one I had found in the haiku of the monks: hers, indeed, was the world of the temple as seen from the other side, by a young girl loitering at its gates, provoking the monks with her come-hither boldness:

> *You have yet to touch*
> *This soft flesh*
> *This throbbing blood —*
> *Are you not lonely,*
> *Explainer of the Way?*

In the rich nights, I sank deep into Akiko's delectable tremors; in the bright afternoons, I steadied myself with the clear-water verses of Ryōkan:

> *If your hermitage is deep in the mountains,*
> *Surely the moon, flowers and maples*
> *Will become your friends.*

Certainly, the more I read of Ryōkan, the more I found myself thoroughly won over by this gentle eccentric spirit, wild brother to Thoreau, who lived all alone in the mountains for most of his life, as good as his poetic word. Yet as much as he savored his loneliness, the friendly old monk seemed never to forget that solitude can only be as strong as the compassion it releases. All his life, according to the folk legends, he drank sake, danced freely in the villages nearby, spent his days playing hide-and-seek with children or stopping for a game of marbles with some geisha.

It was, in fact, his sense of warm mischief that rescued Ryōkan from sanctity and that seemed to make him as much at home with the world as with the universal. ("The great man," wrote Emerson, "is he who in the midst of the crowds keeps with perfect sweetness the independence of solitude.") Ryōkan's truth, he confessed, with typical simplicity, was "not that I do not wish to associate with men. But living alone I have the Better Way" (in almost perfect anticipation of the celebrated Romantic credo of his contemporary Byron: "I love not man the less, but Nature more"). Yet it seemed only fitting that the light of his last years was the twenty-nine-year-old nun who fell in love with him and tended the sixty-nine-year-old monk in his final four years and then for another four decades after his death. It was she, in fact, who brought out the first collection of his poems — not, she said, as a work of art but rather as a testament to his life. The two terms in any case dissolved in his work.

> *What is the heart of this old monk like?*
> *A gentle wind*
> *Beneath the vast sky.*

One day, legend has it, a famous scholar from Tokyo came to visit the old monk. Ever hospitable, Ryōkan asked his guest to wait for a minute, while he went down to the village to buy sake. Minutes passed, and more minutes passed, the distinguished guest kept waiting, but still there was no sign of Ryōkan. Finally, after more than three hours, the man went out to look for his host — only to find him sitting on the ground just outside, gazing at the moon. "Isn't it beautiful?" Ryōkan asked his guest. "Yes. But what about the sake?" "Oh yes, the sake. I'd quite forgotten about it."

This was, of course, a classic Zen tale of absentmindedness, in the highest sense of the word: the mind was absent to the world—but only because it was taken up with something higher. Who, I thought, could resist the figure of this fun-loving monk who took the official name of Great Fool and wrote about his daily life, his walks with the local children, his love?

Yet who, I also thought, could withstand Akiko's sumptuous lyrics, with their almost palpable musk of sensuality, more subtly delicious than any poems I knew, except, perhaps, for the quatrains of Rumi? A kind of overpowering perfume suffused her lines, humid with the pressures of spring rain.

> O this heaviness of spring,
> Surrounding
> Maiden and priest,
> From her shoulders a lock of hair
> Over the sutra.

And her central image of "tangled hair" suggested all the wildness and abandon that the Japanese generally kept so strictly under wraps (not least, perhaps, because their word for "hair" was a homonym of their word for "god"). Hair, for the Japanese, was a way of keeping perfection all about one, and hair, in the Heian period, had been the focus of an attention "so overwhelming," in Ivan Morris's words, "as to seem almost obsessive." Even a millennium ago, Japanese women had prided themselves on their long, straight, glossy hair, making up the deficiencies of nature with their art. Yet Akiko, locked up by her father in her bedroom as a girl, had broken out to write some of the most rebellious verses ever heard in Japan, throwing her hair—and everything around it—into disarray. All her sympathies she had given, subversively, to the women who had traditionally been regarded as mere playthings, and even to such celebrated outlaws as the young shopkeeper's daughter who had been executed for burning down her family house in order to be closer to the priest she loved. Akiko had even committed the heresy of outdoing her poet husband, himself the son of a priest. In her explosive poems, hair was nearly always loose and tangled, as far as possible from the shaven clarity of the monk.

> *Pale handsome priest,*
> *Can you not see*
> *The girl lost in dreams*
> *By the tree of pink blossoms*
> *This spring evening?*

And so I read on, across the parallel texts, lady tempting monk, monk renouncing lady.

The first time Sachiko invited me to her house for dinner, I was taken aback, and touched, to come in to find that she was playing a Bruce Springsteen tape (in honor, no doubt, of my stray comment at the temple). Sitting me down at her small round table, she brought out a four-course dinner of all the favorites I had mentioned in passing—a salad lit up by strawberries, a dish of corn, potato croquettes, and Earl Gray tea. On her piano sat a spray of gold and violet flowers. "Every room need little flower," she explained, as gracious as a Heian courtier. "Every day I find new flower. I think person, then I choose flower. This flower you!" The whole room, in short—like Sachiko herself—had been remade for the occasion.

After dinner, she glided through the next act of what seemed as efficient a plan of hospitality as at some geisha house. Inviting me to sit down on her couch, she drew out a guitar and started singing, in a strong, high voice, a series of bluegrass-flavored songs, all of them sounding like "Red River Valley," yet all, she said, made famous by the Carter Family (yet another all-American institution I had never heard of till I came to Japan). Then she broke into some Japanese folk songs, their melancholy tales of broken love carried by the lilting softness of her voice. As with so many things in Japan, female singing seemed to be done to formula, and yet it was a lovely formula, guaranteed to please. The songs rang out in the quiet room, as fresh as the flowers, and as sweet.

This song, she explained, was about lanterns floating down a river at night, each of them carrying a spirit of the dead, yet seeming, to the children along the bank, nothing more than an exciting play of lights. "This song little same my father sing in war," she declared. "But feeling, little different. This more spring light feeling—*Subaru*," though here, I gathered, she meant not the car but the constellations for which it had been named.

And as she sang, I was struck again at how the Japanese, shy as they generally are—perhaps, indeed, because they are shy— tend to be professional performers at home, almost as if they feel obliged to shower guests with accomplishments as well as other kinds of gifts. I, by contrast, would rather do anything than perform on cue, though on this occasion, sensing an unspoken request, I glumly sat down at her piano and tried to bang out some half-remembered Beethoven and Bach.

Later, just before I left, I pointed out the yin-yang symbol on the blue scarf she was wearing round her neck. Surprising me yet again, Sachiko put her hands behind her hair, unknotted the scarf, and handed it over to me as a gift. I turned it around in my hands, the cloth smothered in her perfume. It was a dizzying experience, and heady: the scarf in my hands, her fragrance all about.

By now, I felt, I could understand a little more the nature of Sachiko's quiet urgency, her sense of impatience in pushing against the limits of her tightly reined life. At thirty, she had clearly spent her last, perhaps her best, seven years in absolute thrall to her family—or, more precisely, to the dictates of her society. She had, I was sure, played all the roles demanded of her with typical efficiency, and yet by obediently following a schedule imposed on her from without, she had also, I felt, cut herself short somehow, allowing herself to be propelled precipitously through the roles of perfect fiancée, perfect wife, and perfect mother, without ever really having fully worked out other parts of herself. Even now, therefore, something of her youth still lodged inside her, like a slide stuck in a projector, jamming all the images that followed and threatening to blow up the whole system.

This sense of missing the boat was, I suspected, particularly vexing in a society where the boat always, but always, left on time (a feeling I was already coming to know when racing to a bus stop at 10:12 a.m., knowing that there was no chance—absolutely no chance in this relentlessly punctual land—that the 10:10 a.m. bus had not left already). In Japan, stages in life seemed as rigorously demarcated as the hours of the day: just as people changed kimono or bracelets with the seasons, just as restaurants served different kinds of rice, or tea, according to the time of year—customs that we, not imprisoned by them, could afford to find enchanting—so Japanese people had to change roles and identity on cue, with the seasons of their lives.

Age, therefore, was always stressed in Japan as much as it was downplayed in the U.S. (where, in California at least, a sixteen-year-old girl often looked so much older than her age, and her forty-year-old mother so much younger, that mother and daughter truly did end up looking like sisters, as the soap ads promised). One reason Japanese generally asked one another, as soon as they were introduced, "How old are you?" was station—a thirty-year-old was expected to defer to someone thirty-five and to have priority over someone twenty-five. But it was also, and relatedly, to give, and enforce, a sense of identity. Just as Sachiko's life was set up so that she gave her mornings to herself, her afternoons to her children, her evenings to her parents, and her nights to her husband, so the stages of a woman's life seemed all but scheduled in advance: 0–5 for shiny bowl cuts and indulgence; 6–18 for ponytails and the blue-and-white sailor-suits of school; 19–24 for bangs, high fashion, and a stint in an office; 25–45 for child raising in jeans and pretty sweaters; and the years that followed for sober matronhood in perms, a return to the workplace, perhaps, and, at last, a rounding of the cycle in the licensed second childhood of old age. The *Kurisumasu kēki* phenomenon was only the most flagrant example of a system that propelled its people into stages as forcibly as commuters into train compartments.

There was, in fact, a prescribed look, a kind of uniform, for every stage. So although the old cliché about all Japanese looking alike was clearly absurd, there was some truth in saying that all Japanese of a certain position or age—all nine-year-old schoolgirls, say, or forty-five-year-old executives—were encouraged to look, or at least dress, alike by a society that wanted them to conform to an anonymous model, to become generic, in a sense. A sense of interchangeable identity not only helped to enforce unity; it also made one parent's daughter seem almost like another's, and thus enforced a larger sense of duty. So when Sachiko talked of her "mother part" and "wife part" and "daughter part," she caught nicely, if inadvertently, the absoluteness of the way in which people here were both parts and partitions—and parts, in fact, were inflexibly partitioned.

But now, with the years fast slipping away from her, and her children both in school, I could see how avidly Sachiko was grasping after her receding youth, having matured to a point where at last she could appreciate the freedom that she was no longer allowed to have. I could also see how this longing was tied up with all things Western, as if she could not find an authorized Japanese precedent for being a thirty-year-old teenager. This side of her, then, came out through foreign contact mostly— in her giddy excitement at hearing about Phil Collins, or her high school girl's absorption in reading every last detail of Michael J. Fox's life in the Japanese equivalent of *Tiger Beat*. And part of this whole desperate last stand against conformity clearly included the befriending of *gaijin*, not only because the foreign world was associated with the young, the new, the trendy—and, more to the point, the reckless and the self-indulgent—but also because the foreign world was, apart from her posters and her daydreams (and akin to them too, perhaps), her only alternative to reality. Foreigners meant freedom in a land where freedom itself was largely foreign.

So I could see one reason why she was so active in cultivating me, even if it was a reason, perhaps, that had never consciously occurred to her. One of the first things I was learning in Japan was how easily shrewdness and shelteredness could go hand in hand. When Sachiko lent me a tape, I could see that she was doing so partly in order to ensure that I would have to see her again (to give it back), and when she invited me to dinner, she was binding me up in a debt I would surely feel an obligation to repay. Yet even the subtlest and most elaborate of her emotional gambits were in pursuit of ends that seemed in themselves disarmingly innocent.

Meanwhile, as I fell deeper and deeper into such thoughts, I kept meeting foreigners who could not stop singing of their conquests. One softspoken American told me how he had fallen in love with a girl just by watching the way she sharpened his pencil. Another told me how, upon arrival, he'd been given an option on his best friend's house, his bike, and even his girlfriend. I ran one day into an old friend—from Santa Barbara, of course—a sweet if slightly scatterbrained soul, who had always seemed girlproof, so lost was he in Mahayana meditations and herbal teas. Now, though, he said, after thirty-nine years without ever really having had a girlfriend, he was on the brink of marriage—to a woman he'd met only six weeks before. She was, of course, thirty-eight, and she'd even told him that if he didn't marry her, he could at least, please, give her a baby. I shuddered at the consequences.

Another day, after meeting another shy foreigner, who instantly began telling me about the love letters he had received from his students and how little they meant to him—really, how little—I asked Mark what he thought of these relationships.

"I would imagine," I said, "that a Japanese woman would make a very good wife, if only because she has so precise a sense of what it means to be a perfect wife, and a perfect daughter-in-law, and a perfect mother."

"Sure," said Mark, with the sharp, smiling glance I knew so well by now, "and a precise sense of what it means to be a perfect husband." In his experience, he said, the marriages often worked out well when a Japanese girl was matched with a flighty or irresponsible foreign man, in part because Japanese women were well trained at housebreaking men and, like the heroines in Shakespeare's comedies, were often bright and agile enough to bring their ne'er-do-well partners to heel. But the marriages that brought more sensitive, and passive, kinds of foreign men together with Japanese girls often seemed to founder. Because, of course, the kind of Japanese woman who was interested in a foreign man was, by definition, a radical, independent-minded and ready for adventure; while the kind of man who was drawn to Japan was often a more retiring sort, in flight from the perceived aggressiveness of the West. So the girl, who wanted some wild, macho, Harley-throttling pop-star type, ended up, very often, with a man who had come to Japan specifically to escape the wild, macho, Harley-throttling pop culture of America; and he, drawn to Bashō or Murasaki, ended up with a girl who was trying to transcend the compliant surfaces enforced by Japanese convention. She wanted to see the world; he wanted just to settle down. Thus the woman ended up complaining that her partner was not wild enough, and the man that the girl was too wild; she, eager for the wrong man, found herself saddled with an unworldly Mr. Right, and he, hoping for a poem, ended up with a would-be rock song. The only thing they had in common was that both were taken with a dream.

A few days later, Mark handed me a copy of Isaac Bashevis Singer's *Spinoza of Market Street* and told me to read the title story. Previously, in my ignorance, I had always scorned Singer, imagining him somehow to be an elderly taste. But as I began reading, I could see why Mark had given the book to me, and why now, with an unforced aptness that seemed a kind of gift in him. For "The Spinoza of Market Street" was shot through not only with Singer's customary sense of wry wonder but also with a kind of worldly uplift, an exaltation in the face of earthly things, that I had not expected. At its conclusion, a man, all his life a hermitic philosopher, gets up from his marriage bed and looks at the moon and realizes that marriage has gone against all his reason and philosophy, and yet has somehow redeemed him beyond reason (and without reason), with a logic all its own — a moment as moving and transcendent as the same scene, more chillingly evoked, in the new Springsteen song I had been listening to in Kurama. Springsteen's faith was, of course, very different in texture from that of Singer's Spinoza-lover — it was a rougher thing, of the open road and big cars, not philosophy and books — but still it came to much the same thing: both characters had given up what they held dearest, the very basis of their lives — their *premises* — for a woman, and then had found in her a kind of saving grace. They had opened themselves up and, in the opening, found a transformation. In the pretty pun of C. S. Lewis, they had been "surprised by joy."

Increasingly, then, as I went on reading Singer, I began to see that the great project of this closet pantheist was, quite literally, to build a rainbow bridge between heaven and earth. Again and again, his robust tales turned around men who wished to renounce the world in favor of some unearthly, abstract love — a devotion to scholarship, or even God — and then, of a sudden, found themselves confronted with the presence of something less lofty that seemed to betray a higher source; again and again, his people were divided, their eyes on the heavens and their hands on earth. And invariably, Singer resolved the issue by showing that earthly love could be just the manifestation of heavenly love; that it revealed to us a radiance and a beauty that were otherwise concealed; that this was all we could know of heaven here on earth, and all we would need to know. "The more we know of particular things," Spinoza had written, "the more we know of God."

11

THE FOLLOWING WEEK, I met Sachiko early one morning and we set off together on another expedition: to Nara. Whenever she had the choice, I saw, she loved to go not to places she had never seen but to ones she already knew. Our trips, I sensed, were journeys as much into remembrance as freedom; and in visiting the places she had not seen since college, Sachiko was visiting, I sensed, the parts of herself she had not known since before her children and her marriage.

On the train through the countryside, I took out a fading twelve-year-old copy of Joni Mitchell's *Blue* and said that in the West, at least, such songs were very popular with girls. The sadness of the songs appealed to them, I went on; the complexities of boyfriends lost and babies missed, and lonely nights in lonely rooms. Perhaps it was not so different from Japan? Sachiko was silent as I told her this, but her face looked puzzled. "I think people in your country very, very strong," she said at last, reiterating her favorite theme. "Woman too, very tough." "In some ways," I said, reiterating my favorite theme, "American women are often as tough as men. They work in offices and hold good jobs." "But," she tried, "when they go home, they all alone, very sad?" "Exactly! And that's when they listen to Joni Mitchell and dream of boyfriend or child." I dealt in stereotypes, I knew, in laughable cartoons, but I felt that nuances would only get lost between us and that I could not overdramatize for her the gulf between the world she knew and the one that she imagined.

When we got off the train, I realized that I was in for another surprise: we were not, it seemed, going to Nara at all, but rather to the nearby town of Asuka, the ancient city where Buddhism had arrived in Japan thirteen hundred years before and subject of some of the most haunting of old love poems:

> *The mists rise over*
> *the still pools at Asuka.*
> *Memory does not*
> *Pass away so easily.*

Outside the tiny country station, the obligatory schoolchildren were lined up, scores of them, seated in rows in which they listened to the instructions shouted at them through megaphones: one movable feast of unified young humanity. But mostly, the villages and fields were quiet as we wandered along the lanes and up a hill, walking over rice paddies, and lost, for the most part, in our talk. The sun came out and disappeared; a mist rose above the mountains; the sky was slivers of blue in a gray porcelain bowl.

As we meandered along the quiet paths, Sachiko bent down to trace the flowers with her fingers, teaching me their names, and what they represented. This one, she said, was the cosmos, the harbinger of winter, this one the "orchid" (she knew the English word because it was the favorite flower of Morten, lead singer of a-ha). This one was her grandmother's favorite; this one, she said, was me.

We walked through quiet lanes of little huts, and she motioned to a stream swishing through a ditch. *Seseragi,* she explained. I stopped for a moment and realized of course she was right: the silence was made musical by the gurgle of the water. This time to herself, she said, was very special, "very fragile, like grass" (and now it was my turn to look confused, having forgotten her tendency to say *r* for *l*). "Very fragile time," she said again, ruminative. "These days I always hold in my heart." She paused for a moment on a bridge and looked into the running brook below. And I sensed that this chance to wander without plan called her back to something long hidden within herself like a temple bell.

Then, recollecting herself, she led me over more country hills, and as we walked, I taught her the English words I chanced to use—"innocent," "delicate," and "subtle." She looked up at me with searching eyes. "You teach me what is in my heart?"

I chose to evade that, and asked instead if she was hungry. "I forget," she said dreamily. "Time stop. My stomach hungry, but my heart very full."

And so we straggled on some more, and later, in a village, stopped in a tiny shack for "Fox Noodles" and "*Tanuki* Noodles," and then walked out, across the random fields. She told me how her nickname since girlhood had been "Hime," or Princess, and how she dreamed now of going to spend a night with her best friend, Keiko, in Osaka, only a few minutes away from Kyoto, provided she could get her husband's permission. And gradually, as the hours passed, the day began to ease open, as if some catch had been unclasped. And as the sun began to set, our talk grew gradually more close. "Sunset time very beautiful," she mused quietly, "but sad. Because children stop play, and I cook dinner, and all things finish. You are bird, I woman. You are hawk; you have strong heart, do anything, very easy. But I cannot. Then I only dream. Please you bring me world." She paused, in a temple, in front of a painting of a monk seated before a ball of fire. "This time dream time."

Then, in the train going home, as she looked out on the darkening fields, I tried to cheer her up by telling her a story I had dreamed up as a boy, and as I did so, I realized, with a start, that somehow, without my intending it, this tale of white birds bringing dreams across the sea, above a silver "moon path," was more apt—and more Japanese—than ever I had known. Even the raccoon story I had made up for her children, with its theme of a rescued princess, and the provision of dreams, did not seem quite so innocent anymore. And yet, I realized now, there too, I had inadvertently gone Japanese by including two heroes instead of one, and so, somehow, providing a denouement that concluded not in marriage but in parting.

Finally, in the failing light, turning from the window, she summoned up all her English in a brave attempt to tie up the day. "Thank you very much. You give my heart much imagination, much feeling. Thank you very much. I very, very fun. This magic time for me. When I little children size, I many times visit Grandma house. I dream very different life. But soon wake up: same me, same everything. Today I wake up, I feel new me. First time, I learn this feeling. Now I wake up—same bear with North Wind daughter. I think I bear, I have new heart."

That night, back in Kyoto, I walked into Mark's room to find a middle-aged woman listening to a Grateful Dead tape and looking up at me with a stare of unnerving intensity—a capable New England matron by the looks of her, in sensible brown sweater and Seven Sisters skirt. "Hello," she announced, "I'm Emily. I'm a pagan." At that, Mark appeared from out of his crooked staircase, and the three of us found a cab, cowboys running around on a tiny pay-TV in front of us, spouting Japanese. As we weaved through the festive lights and crowds downtown, an ad on the screen showed a teardrop, silver, and a necklace on bare skin.

In the waiting express train, as we took our seats, Emily chattered away about the religious impulse and her belief in Seth and about a new image of the Goddess that should be associated not just with Kali but with the spirit of Fertility. Around us, Osaka sparkled like a jewel box in the dark: sapphire and emerald neon making dream patterns on the buildings, bright lights gleaming in the fresh-washed night. Off in the distance the shadowed, silent mountains, and a full moon rippling through the river below.

Getting out of the train, forty minutes later, we walked along moving stairways, up escalators, through corridors of signs, and out into a narrow lane of jangled colors. Under a bridge, across a tunnel of lights, stood an illuminated dome called Studebaker's. Inside was quite a scene: a blond American deejay was flinging his hands about at the front of a room and spinning oldies— "California Girls," "Twist and Shout," "Return to Sender"—while four female customers in front of him, all in expensive, primary-color dresses, hair falling down their backs in identical styles, stood in a perfect row on the dance floor and went through elaborate steps, in perfect sync, to every song, a different step for every song, following the lead of the fast-talking deejay, never stopping, never sweating, just rolling their hands or twisting their hips or punching the air, impassive, song after song after unrelenting song. The whole place was done up in bright, Beach Blanket Bingo colors, pinks and Cadillac reds, and the waitresses, in perky ponytails, red miniskirts, and Laguna Beach sunglasses, danced as they went around the room, hold-ing trays and jumping onto tables every now and then to do the twist, while the waiters, also sunglassed and fresh-faced, leapt onto the bar and strummed crazily away on unplugged guitars in a pantomime of fun, all of it meant to replicate some squeaky-clean, synthetic movie image of Redondo Beach in '64.

The tables were filled with businessmen and their pretty paid companions, the former apparently exulting in this walk on the American wild side, the latter smiling whenever required to do so. When asked to dance, they headed out onto the floor, in orderly groups, and, lining up in rows, serious as workers doing morning calisthenics, set about duplicating the deejay's every move. Here an arm to the right, there a finger in the air. The energy and the unity of the place were breathtaking. Below me, the four topettes were still boogying on cue, not one of their silky hairs out of place, not a trace of fatigue on their bright, unsmiling faces. They exchanged no looks or words or gestures as they danced, and when one of them went to the ladies' room, the others kept on dancing, leaving a blank space in the line for the missing girl to fill as soon as she returned. These girls, I assumed, must come here every night and go religiously through their motions. They did straight-faced surfing moves on "Surfin' Safari," broke into a conga line for a Sam Cooke song, clapped through "Locomotion." Behind them, everyone else was equally punctilious, waving their hands about every time the deejay waved his hands about, bending their knees every time the deejay bent his knees, mimicking berserkness whenever the deejay went berserk, and some foreigner at my table, a Buddhist businessman from Staten Island, was shouting, exultant, "This place is perfect! Just perfect for Japan! Everyone in lines. And following the American leader!"

Emily the pagan and a hippie girl, meanwhile, were arguing furiously about the nature of the fifties and the conformity of hippies, and around us the bouncy waitresses continued wriggling on cue, tireless as cheerleaders, and the four chic "office ladies" jived, expressionless, through Motown moves. An Iraqi sailor from Basra sat alone at the next table, nursing his drink and shyly clicking away with his Instamatic. Several gray-suited American businessmen were led in by their eager-to-please Japanese hosts, and looked as if they would very much have liked to be elsewhere. Two goofy salarymen in their fifties got onto the dance floor with two American escorts, absurdly tall and elegant girls who must have been pulling down three hundred dollars apiece just for teetering over their dates.

All the while, Elvis and the Supremes and Ritchie Valens kept blasting on, and the guests on the dance floor went manic on cue, dipping their knees to "409" and hopping up and down to "Jump" and banging their fists together on "Hand Jive," as an old copy of *The Dancing Wu Li Masters* was passed around our table. Then, out of nowhere, the deejay spotted our group of aging foreigners. "Hey," he said, pointing a trigger finger over at us, "this one is just for you!" And on came the one and only Top 40 hit from the Grateful Dead.

* * *

Two days later, at Arashiyama, along the western hills of town, everything was erased in the holiday sunshine. Boats meandering across a sunlit lake; teenage girls in kimono extracting disposable cameras from gold-lamé bags; bright crowds thronging across the Togetsu Bridge as in almost every Hiroshige print I had ever seen. Old men leading their grandchildren to stalls along the riverbank and coming away with ice creams or strange sweetmeats; ladies in kimono arranging themselves like flowers in a small, exquisite garden; families flocking in patterns through the bright, still air, as quiet as the trees around them.

It was, in fact, as much the people as the leaves that made the Japanese autumn: seated on low red-cloth tables under a canopy of colors, sipping tea and sitting silent, their talk, when it came, as soft as running water. The Japanese autumn was never wild or febrile, as in other tree-filled lands, but diffidently spectacular in its tidy, daily miracles, the air as mild as spring. And the people who came to inspect the scene were miraculously quiet, as hushed as viewers at some play. Having beautifully civilized Nature, made it orderly and trim, they fit themselves into its rhythms without ever making a sound. So even when there were crowds of people, as today, they were all so modest and self-possessed — and so fluently disappeared into the whole — that the purity of the scene remained unsmudged. At times like this, the observation of the seasons seemed akin, almost, to a playing of the national anthem; a solemn, silent act of faith.

12

As more and more experiences began to crowd in on me in Kyoto, and my once empty room began to fill up with more and more presences, I was finding it harder and harder to keep clear. I had ended up, so it seemed, in a whirlpool of paradoxes, such as the one about what a sadist should do to a masochist. What does a would-be solitary do in the company of other solitaries—the very people, in other words, whose company he most enjoys? How does a Thoreauvian respond to a society of antisocial Thoreauvians? Was not keeping oneself open just a way of dodging all commitments?

And as my days in my new home began to turn into weeks, and my discoveries into day-to-day occurrences, I found, inevitably, that I was beginning to domesticate the dream, to know my way around the marvel and superimpose upon the map of Kyoto's streets my own particular homemade grid: this was the restaurant where I could find the most delicious *chai,* made by a Japanese woman who was a devotee of Sri Chinmoy, and this the coffee shop that had the best "morning service" (not, as it happened, a religious rite but a toast-and-coffee special); this was the bus that took me to the smoky jazz bar where polite longhairs served up baked potatoes mysteriously attended by slices of lemon and chopsticks, this the one that took me to the latest issues of *Sports Illustrated;* this was the temple where I did tai chi on early Sunday mornings, and this the one where schoolgirls never came.

Often, moreover, as a resident, I did not have to go out to find Kyoto, for Kyoto was all too ready to come in to find me. One day, I was sitting inside my room, deep in Peter Matthiessen, when there came a knock upon my door. Outside, in the corridor, stood an elegant, gray-bearded man in a suit, accompanied by a sweet-smiling popette. They looked like the host and hostess of some morning talk show.

We bowed in all directions at once, and the man quickly pursued his objective. "What country do you come from?"

"England," I said (hastily riffling through alternatives).

Digging into his briefcase, he presented me with a brochure advising me not to fret; God had guaranteed happiness for us all. This made me happy. Then he followed up his advantage. Would I like a Bible?

No, thank you, I told him in a Japanese that apparently afforded him some pain. I had been to a Christian school in England and had had ample opportunity to read the Bible there. Looking unhappy, he bowed. I bowed. The girl bowed. I bowed again. Then there was more bowing all round, and the threat moved off to another room.

Two nights later, I was just hurrying home through the rain, a hot box of Kentucky Fried Chicken in my hands, when suddenly a boy loomed out of an alleyway before me. He asked me a few questions, and I, assuming he wished to try out his English on me, grimly replied in ungracious Japanese. Then he asked if he could bless me. This did not seem like an offer to refuse. Dutifully, I put down my box of two legs and a thigh (original flavor) and stood before him in the drizzle. Putting his hands together in prayer, he asked me to do the same. Then, eyes tightly closed, he recited three times something along the lines of "Oh, please, great spirit, bless this *gaijin*, thank you." Then he asked me to cradle my hands in front of my stomach and close my eyes for two or three moments while he did some extra petitioning for my soul. This I did, in the midst of the rain, my chicken growing colder and wetter by the minute. Finally, he gave me permission to open my eyes, and *kuriingu* complete, I was free to go home with my soggy dinner.

The next day, therefore, when a man in the laundromat turned around and started to engage me in conversation, I was all set to close my eyes and get a few extra credits in the heavens—until I realized that he really did just wish to tell me about his honeymoon in Disneyland. A little later, though, when I went into Shakey's with an American student of Zen, a waiter hurried up to us, blocking our way and motioning for us to leave. The place was full of happy diners at the time, conspicuously consuming their corn-and-pineapple pies, while a voice on the public-address system declared, "This is Mr. Tender Juicy Chicken, a spokesman for Shakey's..." When we tried to move closer to the salad bar, however, the employee panicked, shaking his head furiously. "But we only want to eat some salad." "Salad?" He looked thunderstruck. "We're only here to eat." "Eat?" He stole a terrified glance at the copy of *Time* I was carrying, with its cover shot of Arafat. Apparently, he had thought that these foreigners had come here to convert defenseless pizza-eaters to some messianic figure in a kaffiyeh.

Mostly, though, I was free to wander around alone, in the company of the autumn. The smell of fresh-baked bread on the Philosopher's Path, on a shining afternoon, and the solemn tolling of a gong across a wall. A flash of gold on the wrist of a temple maiden. Men with jackets on their arms swaggering past in loosened ties, practicing English sentences: "When you are middle-aged, you must take care." A girl in Porsche sunglasses and blazing scarlet trousers trying out "Where do you come from?" Middle-aged gentlemen standing rigid as statues while harassed photographers waved them back into the sun.

Stopping off one morning in Shisendō, the Temple of the Poet Hermits, I sat on the veranda, looking out onto the garden. A lady, very beautiful, her face the faint pink of pearl, came and sat down by my side. A light, light rain began to fall, so light that I had to strain my eyes to see it and knew that it was raining only because the bark on the trees was growing browner. Another Comme des Garçons girl came in and slid down on the floor beside me, her head on her cashmered shoulder, as she looked out at the dreamy rain. Occasionally, a drop trickled down from the rafters. The leaves were scarlet, green, and burgundy. The drizzle was softer than a silk still life.

A little later, I gave Sachiko a call, and we arranged to go to Kobe, the shining, broad-avenued port that had always been, of all Japanese places, the one that was closest in spirit to a foreign town. As always when we met, the day was all sunshine and light drizzle. But the rains began to lift as we got onto the Kobe train, and by the time we arrived, the sky was blue above the silver sea.

Drifting along through the huge antiseptic spaces of Kobe's lonely de Chirico streets, we chatted leisurely about Bjorn Borg and Victor Hugo, Holden Caulfield (whom she loved) and Jacky Chan (whom she admired for his "child's eye"). Then, coming upon a bench, she suddenly sat down and began fishing out presents from her knapsack, handing them over to me in sequence: a pretty drawing, in crayons, of the story I had told her ("I'm sorry. In my heart, very beautiful, but paper not so good"); then a sheaf of autumn photos—yellow light streaming through the ginkgo trees, and maples rusted against the blue; then, out of nowhere, a monkey-decorated telephone card (a woman's gift, I thought, and a Japanese woman's gift, obliging me to call her).

Making our way towards the port, we looked out at the ocean liners, black in the chromium light, and sitting down on a log, the wind blustering all about us, we fell into our usual patter, she telling me how America was the land of the free, I telling her how much of what I saw in America was loneliness. And every time I ventured some generality that even she could not assent to—that the Japanese were close to their parents, say, or that thirty-year-old Japanese had the hearts, very often, of fifteen-year-olds (where in America it was often the reverse), or that

Japanese women half expected their men to take on mistresses—
she simply nodded and answered sagely, "Case by case." A
gentler putting-in-place I could scarcely imagine.

Then, through the wide boulevards of the town, we walked
up Tor Road, up into the hills of Kitano, and the small cobbled
streets of the foreigners' quarter. Surrounded by white stucco
villas scattered along the winding roads, the sea below, the sky
all blue above, I could easily imagine myself in the canyons of
North Hollywood. Across the street, as if by design, the name of
the ice cream store was Santa Barbara.

And so we drifted in and out of foreign dreams: in a Peter
Rabbit store, she wound up a music box and put it to my ear—I
heard "As Time Goes By" and then a song she identified for me,
whispering, as "Lili Marleen"; at the English House, commemo-
rating a foreign way of life, she lingered in the pretty flowered
bedroom, gazing at it dreamily and talking of Emily Brontë.
Wandering along past restaurants called Lac d'Annecy and Café
Chinois, she asked me what Rob Lowe was like and why I did
not think that Cyndi Lauper was cute. As we talked, I taught
her a few new words: "soul" and "clear" and "fascination."

Then, when least I expected it, I looked up to see that we
were standing outside a restaurant called Wang Thai, the only
Thai restaurant in this part of Japan, and something I had
despaired of ever finding. This, too, seemed an augury, a present
from the fates, and so, without a pause, I bustled poor Sachiko
in and ordered her a spicy chicken soup. Soon she was daintily
choking over her bowl, while trying, with typical courtesy, to
find something positive to say.

Once she had laid the poisonous broth aside, and the second
course arrived, she tucked her fork, delicately held between two
fingers, into the rice and offered brightly, "I like Kali." I was
wondering what kind of demon I had roused within her to get
this demure lady to champion the goddess of destruction—a
less useful figure, I recalled, than the spirit of Fertility—when
she repeated, with more heat, "Kali, I like very much," motioning

to her plate, and I realized that it was only the curry she was extolling.

Yet for all these customary hazards, Sachiko seemed to be drawing closer as the meal went on, and towards the end, as she leaned towards me, oblivious suddenly of the stylish *Ramayana* murals all around us and the dreamy Thai pop music on the system, I realized that she was working around to some confession. Still, it was, as always, a little hard for me to follow what exactly she was saying. "With you," she began, "I have clear heart. I talk my heart, very easy. But I very shy." She smiled and hid her face in her napkin, and it was harder still to guess what she was trying to convey; I could tell it was important only by the diffidence with which she brought it forth. "When I meet husband, I little teenage size, nineteen. First time I together man. We talking bluegrass music — very easy, very fun. I expect soon marry. Before many times, I talking brother. Very close feeling. But his wife soon little sad, maybe little jealous. So long time, I not talking him. But now my heart very different. With you, talking very easy, very fun. You have clear heart. No dust on your mirror." She stopped again, and I held my breath. "I have two heart," she continued slowly. "I like children very much. I like you. But different. With you is dream world." I was getting a little confused at all this. "You have found young heart in me," she said. I said that I sensed as much but I did not know if her two hearts were in collision or in sync.

"I very shy," she went on. "But I say true. If not good, please you say. I not want bad."

"I'm really happy to be with you."

"Really?" She sounded incredulous.

"Yes, really. Thank you for your friendship."

"You're welcome," she said with a bright light, tilting her head on her shoulder and flashing me her prettiest smile. "My pleasure" — she tried out the phrase I had taught her.

Thus we struggled on through a curious discussion. Her wavering, heartfelt nonconfession seemed to mark the crossing of some threshold, and now, of a sudden, she opened up with a flood of foreign images. She imagined my mother in a deep-blue sari, with a golden border, she said, and she would wear a sari for me on my birthday, even though she did not own one. She had always dreamed of India. She liked above all Thai reds.

"Art, you mean?"

"No. Red!"

Then she went on to tell me a Inoue Yasushi story about a man who quit his country to seek out the moon in Tibet, and I reciprocated by telling her about my readings in the Zen traveler and poet Issa. And so we wandered out into the Californian hills, past girls in "SANTA BARBARA: High Fashion Dreaming" shirts, along chic cobbled streets, a theme-park vision of gentrified Victoriana, with Sherlock Holmes alleyways and olde England streetlamps. This shiny local version of foggy London was called "romantic Kobe," she informed me. "Many, many Japanese woman like come here this place." "For shopping?" "Also for romance!"

We sat down on a wall, and in the minutes before twilight, she laid her head upon my shoulder. I could feel her perfume all around me, and as we watched the clouds catching the last of the light on the city below, she sighed, and a chill came into the air. I had never seen eyes shaped like hers before, with ocher eye shadow and folded lids, and when she looked up at me, I felt a shudder. "Time stop," she said. "Why clock not stop moving?"

Then, smiling, she took my hand in hers, and hanging on to my arm, a skipping girl again, she walked me back to town.

At the station, as we waited for the train, she pulled out a scarf and tied it round my neck. Then, as we got in, taking seats by the window, I could feel her sadness building as we rode back into town. Squashed together in the crowded compartment, I improvised a story for her then, a story of a lady and a monk, and when I got to the end, I saw her eyes fill with tears. She looked down, embarrassed, and hid her face in my jacket. "I'm sorry. I very sad. Sun set. And train go back Kyoto. I understand your story. Very sad." "But Japanese people like sad stories?" "Yes," she said. "Maybe you catch true Japanese heart."

Then, brightening abruptly—as if she had quite literally taken a grip on her errant self—she looked up smiling and offered me a pastry she had bought from a German bakery. "This baker's name is the German word for 'friendliness,'" I said, trying to lighten the atmosphere. She beamed. "You two kind bird. Hawk—and owl. You give me much input. Thank you." And as the train drew slowly into Kyoto station, she covered my hand with hers. "Now," she said, "I little catch bird."

There was once a beautiful lady who lived in a village near the ancient city of Kyoto with her husband. One day in late summer, as the crickets began to fall silent, the man fell ill; and by the coming of the autumn, the woman could see that he was almost gone. All night, she sat patiently by his side, tending to his needs and listening for his breath; and as the light came up, she felt his heart, and knew that he was gone.

She loved him still, she knew, but the woman was too strong to let her own life wither. So, each day, in her black kimono, through flurries of falling leaves, she went back to the local temple, to lay scarlet flowers on his grave.

Now it happened that the guardian of this temple was a monk who had inherited it from his father in his youth. Seasons had passed, and the monk had grown sturdy in his faith; impervious to the world, his mind was fixed on Buddha. Yet when a member of the village died, it fell to this monk to perform all the rites for sending the soul on its way. So when the young lady came each day with scarlet flowers to the temple, he sat beside her and told her of the Buddha's teaching, she in her black kimono, he in his black-and-golden robes.

As time went on, the woman began to return more and more often to the temple, and the monk, though lost in meditation, could not so easily keep his mind in focus; even in the meditation hall, he could see a flash of red, could hear the rustle of kimono. The forty-ninth day of the husband's death came and went, but still the woman kept returning, as if she could not put the memory away. And even when he said his sutras, the monk found that his mind was filled with the image of the long-haired woman in the garden, red flowers in her hand.

One day, as the first bite of winter chilled the air, the monk decided that he must barricade himself against such distractions and recover the strength of his faith. He caught her fragrance in the hall, he sensed the lady everywhere. But all day long he kept his face turned towards the wall. And when at last he returned to his room that night, he found a single red flower laid outside his door.

And so it continued each day for a week: not once did he open his eyes to his visitor, but each night, when he returned to his room, he found a flower by his door. When his teacher, a head abbot from Kyoto, came to visit, he saw all that was happening, but he knew that there was nothing he could do: the monk would have to face this challenge by himself.

Finally, one cold and brilliant day, the monk decided to wait in his room to watch for the lady's visit. He saw her arrive at dawn, shivering in the winter chill, and even as he recited his sutras, he saw her waiting there all day, eyes smarting in the cold. As he watched her standing there, the monk felt shaken out of words: here, he thought, was a purity and singleness even truer than that he gave to Buddha. Here, in fact, was the meaning of devotion. As darkness fell upon the garden, and the woman got up to leave, he suddenly called out to her.

"Please wait," he said. "I saw you standing here all day, hardly moving save for cold. Please drink some sake before you leave."

When she saw him, the woman turned pale, till her face was ghostly white; but as he pulled back his screen, she slipped off her sandals and entered the incense-filled space. Sitting together on the tatami, they watched the full moon rise above the eastern hills.

That night was the coldest of the year, but neither the monk nor the lady knew it. And when the monk went to prayers at dawn, his bare feet tingled on the frost.

That morning, when the woman returned to the temple, the monk was nowhere to be seen. And so it was for many days, she returning to the chilling temple garden, red flowers in her hand, and he alone in his chamber, silently aflame. Finally, when she arrived one morning, the lady found a white flower placed outside the monk's door, inside of it a letter.

"You have given me," the letter began, "all the warmth and color of the world. I want to keep my image of you as clear as running water. Please take this flower as a memory of our friendship. And know that, though we should not meet again, it is you I always think of."

The woman took the letter and the flower, and the monk never heard from her again. But next morning, when he rose to say his sutras, there, on his doorstep, was a red flower, and a black kimono, scented with her fragrance, and the first faint touch of spring.

And as the leaves began to fall, I really did begin to feel that something was flowering in Sachiko, as if—though I feared to say it—she really was a kind of sleeping beauty awakened by romance, or at least its distant shadow. And for all her composure and supercompetence as a mother, for all her chic and self-possession, I could tell that hers was a heart more than ready to take flight and soar out of her control. And even though I had often been abroad, and often been faced, therefore, with the issue of what to do with foreign dreams, whether to try to encourage fantasies of abroad, or simply damp them down, I still had no sense of how much she was interested in making her visions reality, or whether, as a good Japanese, she was content simply to maintain another world that she could visit in imagination.

At times, in fact, I wondered whether, in encouraging her to express her dreams of flight, I was falling prey to the temptation I had already noticed in some of the more softhearted of the foreigners in Japan: the urge to give the Japanese a glimpse of the world on the other side. When she had attended her first tea ceremony, Siobhan had told me, she had found herself, this radical feminist pagan from the Haight, surrounded by elegantly prim young housewives-in-the-making, getting their training in all the ladylike arts. The school play, she could not help but notice on a nearby bulletin board, was *Cinderella*. And seeing all of them preparing for a life of simple self-denial, she had started inviting some of what she called "the good girls" back to her hippie commune, to get a taste of forbidden freedom. Later, she said, she had heard them excitedly telling their friends about their "wild night of sin."

I wondered, too, whether in encouraging Sachiko to indulge all the hopes that Japan so strenuously teaches its children to suppress, or to enjoy only in specific, and very circumscribed, conditions, I was schooling her in desires she could never fully realize. Encouraging people to realize their potential was an especially dangerous occupation in a country that taught them to fulfill their duty instead.

Most of all, I wondered how deep the ambiguities between us really reached. For even in the same tongue, we were rarely speaking the same language. To begin with, of course, she was married, and I did not know what exactly that betokened—especially in a culture where marriage was often nothing more than separation by another name. Much of the time, Sachiko functioned as if she had no family at all, using her society's sense of extended ties to find parents or friends to baby-sit for her, and tuning out her marriage as if it were just a distant radio station. It was almost as if being a mother and a wife was a role to her, and thus a self she could shrug off as easily as her mother's clothes or voice; she seemed, in fact, less fettered—or more resourceful about slipping free of fetters—than most single people that I knew at home.

She, in turn, of course, knew little of foreign codes of friendship and how to translate them into terms she knew. So every time she said, "My children little want see you," I did not know to what extent that meant that it was she who wanted to see me. And every time I replied, "I want to see your children," I did not know if that just meant that I wanted to see her. And even though traveling had schooled me, I had thought, in the seven types of ambiguity, and more, I still had to admit that Sachiko was the end of the line in this field, the state of the art: for Japan itself was firmly based on people's not saying what they meant and on the accompanying assumption that what was meant was rarely what was said. And women in particular were encouraged—even trained—to project an air of charming acquiescence that suggested everything and meant nothing. In a land where language itself was a force of separation as much as communion, where foreigners were invariably treated as symbolic carriers of abroad, and where everything was turned into soft focus—surrounded by an all-embracing vagueness—it all added up to the most troubling of riddles.

13

As AUTUMN DEEPENED, bringing with it new intensities, I took myself off one morning to Nara. After listening, in silence, to my story of the lady and the monk, Mark had lent me a tape of Laurens Van der Post delivering a lecture on the unlikely, even unpromising, subject of "The Unwritten Literature of the Bushmen." And as I got on the train, crowded now with tidy, festive families, old couples going on temple tours, a young monk shyly turning his face from tourist cameras, and packs of schoolgirls on their way to Dreamland (the modern amusement park that was now the most popular attraction in the ancient capital), I turned on the tape and fell into the rhythms of the old Dutch farmer's swelling, bardic cadences. Birds, he was saying, in every kind of folklore, stood for the world of the heavens, emissaries from above. Birds were messengers from the gods bringing inspiration to earthbound men. That was why among the American Indians, and the tribes of Africa too, chiefs traditionally wore crowns of feathers, as if their heads were flocks of inspirations. That was also why Plato called the mind a cage of birds.

I thought of this as we rolled through the countryside, and of my own story about birds, and of how Sachiko always referred to me as a winged ambassador from abroad. I thought of how much I wanted to share this thought with her, so sonorously phrased, by a disciple of her brother's guru, Jung, and how strange it was that stories and images that had come to me unbidden seemed much more pointed than I knew. And as the train rolled into Nara, I was jolted from my daydreams by the

Buddhist capital itself, where a local department store was offering a cup of gold-flaked coffee for more than three hundred dollars, and posters of Madonna fluttered from the souvenir stalls.

Inside the famous Deer Park, though, one was back inside a more changeless Japan. Families were enjoying picnics on the grass, deer grazing at their sides as in the Oxford college where I had cavorted as a boy. Ladies strolled through galleries of red, papers held up to their ashen faces to shield them from the sun. A group of smiling elders sauntered through a reception line of blazing orange trees, the sun catching the copper in the women's hair, the men framed by an extravagance of gold. Now and then, the tolling of a distant bell summoned us back, so it seemed, to a higher time and self.

Making my way up to a temple terrace, I leaned on a railing and watched the blue hills in the distance, half shrouded now in wood smoke. Coins clattered in the collection box behind me, and an old woman grabbed the clump of white and red and orange ropes and rang and rang and rang the temple bell. An aged couple asked me to take their picture, framed against the falling leaves. Around us, the sun came down with the cleansing intensity of mountain light.

In Nara, I saw a shrine with statues of moonlight and sunlight, three thousand lanterns bobbing above the moss. Across town in the Hall of Dreams, I visited the famous Korean Bodhisattva, salvaged, like so much else here, by the visiting American Ernest Fenollosa. Outside the Great Buddha, commanding the largest wooden building in the world, I saw a wandering mendicant, a mountain monk, in white robes and straw sandals, standing stock-still, swathed in a curious mix of animal skins and bells, muttering shamanic chants.

In Nara, the temples were more hidden than in Kyoto, left to themselves, with room to breathe. To get to them, one had to change trains twice, at sleepy country stations, walk for many minutes through crooked, nameless lanes, ascend unforgiving flights of steps; one had, in short, to earn the temples, and travel away from the workaday world—and self. A visit here could only be a pilgrimage.

Later, returning in the falling light to Kyoto, I descended once more into Van der Post as he spun out Bushmen tales of how a man had spent his whole life pursuing the reflection of a bird he had once seen, and only grabbed a feather on the day he died; and another of how a man had caught the goddess of the moon, but then, through looking in a casket full of starlight and seeing nothing, had lost her too. By the time the train pulled into Kyoto Station, I was lost in the world of the storyteller's flights and, loath to hurry home, began to walk through narrow lanterned streets and along the Kamo River, lit by a trailing series of red lights.

As I walked, past houses lit up by a brilliant moon, I thought how much the Japanese were a people of the moon, the central image of the first Japanese story I had ever heard. And though they traced their lineage to the Goddess of the Sun, the sun was mostly used now to describe the modern or the public world—the Sun Plaza American-style convenience store, the Sunflower Hotel, and rows of Sunny cars were all five minutes from my home. The moon, by contrast, was the part they kept jealously to themselves. In their hearts, I thought, the Japanese were still a people of the Rising Moon. And just as I was dwelling on this, and recalling how Kyoto itself had once been known as "Moon Capital," I turned on the tape again and—out of nowhere—heard Van der Post talking about how the moon in Japan was always three times larger than in any other place and how the Japanese had a deep affinity with the moon, renewing themselves, after earthquakes or wars, as cyclically as the moon.

The moon, I recalled, was the one possession that even monks did not renounce. When he lost his house in a fire, the Zen poet Masahide wrote, he found occasion for new hope: he now enjoyed a better view of the rising moon.

* * *

When next I visited Sachiko's home, for dinner, she sat me down and put on a tape of *Howard the Duck*. Gloomily I surveyed Duck magazines, Duck TV shows, and a host of lame Duck jokes. "I much love George Lucas," she averred. "Spielberg too. They have very innocent child heart. Coppola little different feeling; he more big brother heart. You see this movie *Goonies*?"

I shook my head no.

"*Gremlins*?"

"I'm sorry, no." She looked disappointed. "But I do like Kurosawa."

She now looked very grave. "Japanese person not so like this man," she said. "Foreigner person like, no problem. But Japanese not so like. Little show-biz feeling."

The next thing I knew, though, she had slipped into her other, deeper self, drawing out her guitar and breaking into a series of piercing, lovely lullabies. I could see her eyes as she sang begin to glitter at their corners; I could hear a quaver as she hit the high notes. She sang another wistful ballad, then, about a man looking at the pressed flowers that his lover had left for him, and again, as she sang, her eyes filled with tears. *Monoganashii*, she explained, the beauty of what's fleeting.

In terms of everything I knew, things were fast becoming more and more slippery and strange. When I gave her a couple of poems I had written for her in Nara, she looked up at me with a kind of melting intensity and said, "Me too." And when she showed me an album of her wedding photos, and I admired the loveliest one of all, of the bride in a white veil, caught in golden light, she simply peeled it out and handed it over to me. Now, I felt, I was not only gate-crashing her marriage but actually taking possession of her memories.

Whenever I tried to ask her about her husband, though, or his family, she never said anything except, "My husband very good man, but weak heart." If ever I tried to get anything more out of her, she just laughed it off, and said, "*Chotto muzukashii*"

(It's a little difficult). Her husband, in the telling, was nothing more than a kind of spectral, distant authority figure on the margins of her life, spoken of in the terms that people in a large company might reserve for the CEO. So I never really got a sense of his features, his preferences, his self; he was just a kind of shadowy bogeyman who, like many a Japanese man, dutifully did "family service" on his one day off a week, filled up his spare hours with jigsaw puzzles, and was too scared of foreigners ever to meet me or any of his wife's other foreign friends.

Then, finally, seemingly heavy with emotion, she tried to put into words why we should not meet in Kyoto. "I'm sorry," she began, "my heart much change," and I got ready for a brush-off—a prudent one, I thought, in the circumstances, and one in which I almost wanted to assent. "Before, talking very fun, very easy. But now . . ." she went on, and I did not have a clue in what direction her heart had changed, when this had happened (since past tense and perfect were elided in her English), and whether she now felt closer than before or more distant.

I was also beginning to realize how treacherous it was to venture into a foreign language if one could not measure the shadows of the words one used. When I had told her, in Asuka, *"Jennifer Beals ga suki-desu. Anata mo"* (I like Jennifer Beals— and I like you), I had been pleased to find a way of conveying affection and yet, I thought, a perfect distance. But later I looked up *suki* and found that I had delivered an almost naked protestation of love. Often, too, I would use the particle *ga*, never remembering that it could be both nominative and accusative. And both of us, in other ways, were forever confusing subject with object. So she would say, "You help me," and it was a long time before I realized that she meant, "I'll help you" (and not just because one good turn deserved another). Thus both of us ended up like children in the dark, flinging around pronouns at random till it was utterly unclear who was meant to be doing what to whom. When we got to sentences like "I'll call your house," the ambiguities became positively disabling.

Worse still, of course, matters of causation were invariably scrambled and Humpty-Dumptified, since the Japanese put their "because" in the opposite place from where we do. Thus I, in essaying "I like you because you are kind," would come out with the equivalent of "You are kind because I like you," and she would look back at me, frowning more than ever. Noticing that she still tended to use the Japanese word *dakara* in every sentence, even when speaking English, I thought I was doing her a favor by teaching her "therefore." But this only vexed the chaos further. "I little sad, therefore you are leaving," she said, and I recalled — too late! — that *dakara* could mean "because" as well as "therefore." And she often used "yes" where we say "no" ("You're not cold?" "Yes!").

And just as Sachiko, I could tell, became franker and bolder — more direct — when she was speaking English, shedding her inhibitions in translation, so I began to see that I too was probably more daring, more intimate, more reckless with myself, when I ventured into Japanese, throwing around terms I had found in Rexroth's love poems without ever really knowing the nuances they carried. Meanwhile, of course, nearly all her shadings were lost to me, and I felt sorry for her having to box her feelings into the few adjectives she knew, throwing heavy terms over subtle, fleeting nuances — like the loose and flabby U.S. Army jacket she wore over her tiny body. Once, when I had to leave her house ten minutes early, she said, "I very sad," and another time, when I simply called her up, she said, "I very happy" — and I began to think her unusually sensitive, or else prone to bold and violent extremes, when really she was reflecting nothing but the paucity of her English vocabulary, all the more frustrating, I imagined, for one accustomed to a language that so finely distinguished between melancholy and mournfulness, wistfulness and sorrow. Talking in a language not one's own was like walking on one leg; when two people did it together, it was like a three-legged waltz.

Yet in the end, the fact that we were both speaking in this

pared-down diction made us both, I felt, somewhat gentler, more courteous, and more vulnerable than we would have been otherwise, returning us to a state of innocence. In speaking a simplified English, we were presenting simpler and clearer accounts of ourselves, edited down, with the rough spots filtered out. Reduced to essentials, in fact, and bare declarative sentences dominated by basic adjectives, we ended up speaking with a little of the clenched, suggestive clarity, the clean simplicity, of Japanese poetry. And since she spoke always in images, and I tended to mirror her speech, our conversations grew more and more lyrical, and more so still, since the Japanese words I had learned, I had largely learned from the poems of Yosano Akiko.

I knew very well that this kind of lyricism was offhand, and almost second nature in this country, and that it reflected in part just Sachiko's limited command of English; I knew, too, that this kind of phrasing, which sounded so poetic to me, could often be formulaic in a land where people thought in images (Saikaku had once composed 23,500 *renga*, or linked verses, in a single day; even the future prime minister had composed 2,000 haiku). I noticed too how every English metaphor I explained to her—"raining cats and dogs," being "the apple of my eye"—struck her as ineffably poetic. Yet still I could not easily resist the sustained delicacy of the terms she used and the sense of moment, as well as depth, she brought to every meeting. Her emotions seemed as exquisitely worn as her seasonal bracelets or earrings, and the words she used had a kind of otherworldly, romantic Zen flavor—or, at least, a sense of clarity and calm that seemed to cut to the heart of Zen and to the very notion of depth in Japan. She made our friendship seem a sacrament.

And all the while, the brilliant blue-sky afternoons kept coming, day after day as clear as road reflectors, and the hills of Kyoto began to blaze with reds, the trees along the canals to light up like gold. And on these shining days of autumn, the sky shifting from milky white to blue, the trees a rhapsody of colors, I felt the brightness of the Japanese autumn was like nothing I had ever seen before: such hope and stillness in the air. Tingling mornings in shiny coffee shops, dazzled afternoons among the white-robed priests: singing Handel days of rapture and precision.

14

As AUTUMN DREW towards an end, I found myself returning one day with Sachiko to Kobe, and on the train, as we sat side by side, she reached up and unclasped, for the first time ever, her mother-of-pearl comb, letting her hair fall in a rush down the right side of her face. The suddenly loosened sensuality hit me like a shock. "This year," she said, "Autumn more more beautiful. I see beautiful color, and many flower, and cosmos flower, little messenger of winter. But sometimes I sad. I thinking moon soon full, then small again; my heart little same. Now full. But future, I don't know. Maybe very empty." In response, I told her Van der Post's story of how the moon renewed itself.

She nodded slowly, with determination. "I want build strong heart. Please you help. I want very strong, so when you go, I not so sad. Sometimes I little fragile" (she had learned the word from a Sting album). "But now I more confidence. Before, I say, 'Be careful! He bird! He stay in Japan only one year.' But now heart control, very difficult. I open window and you give me sunshine." She smiled at me warmly. "Santa Barbara sunshine."

Already, I could tell, she was savoring the poignancy our walks would have in memory, smoothed down and elegized by its sepia tints. Already she was composing—and relishing—her reminiscences. And yet, with half her mind, wondering whether a happy Western ending might not be better than a melancholy Japanese one.

In Kobe itself, city of foreign romance, we made our way, in the blithe blue morning, to the silent modernist spaces of Port

Island, walking through avenues of glass. When once she saw a piece of litter on the spotless walkway—the first blemish I could remember seeing in two months in Japan—she could not hide her shame. "I'm very sorry," she said, bending down to snatch it up. "This place very dirty. Japan not so clean place." I could not explain to her that it was far and away the cleanest place I had ever seen, and so we went on talking, and walking, amidst the glinting high-rises and Californian plazas of this spacey world, the stores called Printemps and Los Abrigados and Orso. She asked me which of Vivaldi's Four Seasons I liked, and told me how much she loved Goethe's *Faust*, which she had read three times. Once, she explained, she had been fascinated with the Tarot too, but then had chosen to put it aside, after foretelling some uncomfortably dark truths about her cousin. She went on—though Paul Kennedy had yet to hit the best-seller list in Japan—that every country had to go through its cycle of power, as Egypt, Greece, India, China, England, France, and America had done. "Now Japan Number One," I said, and she was bemused. "Soon," she replied, as all Japanese did, "Korea more more strong." Whether this was fatalism or a spur to greater effort, the Japanese seemed alone in the world in assuming they were about to be overtaken.

Later, as we walked, she talked about her love of "macaroni Westerns" and explained how Diana Ross had changed her look to appeal to whites; and then, of a sudden, how she had won a school oratory contest with her heartfelt account of the Hiroshima bombing, which had left her aunt sterile.

At times, I realized, it was easy to interpret too much—as well as too little—from the way she had to fashion elaborate English packages, wrapped up in images, analogies, and parallels, to get her meaning across to me. Yet still Sachiko's words rang out like music after the more familiar Californian diction of "coping" and "sharing" and "parenting." I was falling in love, in a sense, with the fairy tales she made of even the smallest of our encounters—"If you not here, then flower not open," or "Where your white horse? I think you prince"; she not only quoted but lived out the ancient poems I had always sought.

Then, walking into the Portopia Hotel, we came, unexpectedly, upon what resembled a Japanese production of *Gatsby*: the whole yawning lobby was taken up with men in black ties and tuxedos, girls with Isadora Duncan hats above black flappers' dresses.

"Is there some kind of marriage going on?"

"No marriage," she said soberly. "These lady little hostess feeling. Not real people."

"But this is a hotel. And these men seem to belong to some company."

"This Japanese system," she went on. "If company have party, many hostess here. Wife must always stay in home. If man introduce wife, very terrible feeling. Then company give little hostess."

"But isn't this very expensive?"

"Very expensive," she said solemnly, stealing a glance over at a hostess as she might at a gangster's Rolls-Royce. "Night-world person, very sad eye," she whispered, with a faint tremble that suggested she would like to turn to other things. "Please we go upstairs?"

Upstairs, in the coffee shop, she was a bouncing girl again, excitedly explaining how this was the very hotel where she had stayed a year before, stealing away from her husband for the first time ever and buying an a-ha ticket for several times the forty-dollar price, and then, after the concert, coming by chance upon her heartthrob Morten. The moment still glowed inside her like first love. When she had met him, she said, in the elevator, she had given him a present: What did I think it was? Flowers? No. A ring? No. A record? No, a book. Oh, Inoue Yasushi? No, a book about Zen. Because, she explained, she had read that he was a devout man who had almost become a priest. And this book was the best way for a foreigner to get to the heart, the very soul, of her country.

Just as I was about to wonder about her judgment, though, she took me, as ever, by surprise. "But I not want visit this man's house in London," she went on. "On stage, I look him, very easy, very fun. But in his life, I not want talk. I think he not remember me. Maybe he never read book. He not know my name. But not important. I always keep him in my heart." The quintessential Japanese balance, I thought: to surrender all of yourself to an illusion, and yet somewhere, in some part of yourself, to know all the while that it is an illusion.

Meanwhile, Sachiko was meandering again into an account of her life and telling me about her fear of the sea, and how a carp would suddenly bob up and pull her down, down into its mysterious depths, where it was bottomless and dark. The sky was all right, she said, because it could not exert such a pull on her, and the jungle was okay, though she feared its central darkness. She told me, too, how Madonna was traveling with a fourteen-year-old boy, because of her conviction that in an earlier life, she had been a boy who died at fourteen.

"Madonna is like an elephant," I said facetiously.

"Very different," she answered quietly, and grave. "She jaguar. Very beautiful, very dangerous, man-eating jaguar."

I, for my part, told her about malls in California, and Valley Girls, about gay waiters, and husbands who did the cooking. All this she seemed to find remarkable. "Why? Whattt? True??" I told her that trains were not invariably on time in America, and she could not even digest this kind of aberration. "Why? How? Not possible, I think." "Well," I began, Reaganesque in my evasions, "sometimes they are broken." "Really? *Hontō ni?* Why? How possible?" "Well, maybe it is an old train and not perfect." "Why? How?" She frowned uncertainty back at me. "I not understand!"

Later, as the afternoon went on, I taught her some new words—"clever," "bright," and "precious." "Thank you for a precious day," she dutifully sang back to me. And when the sun got ready to set, I could see the sadness in her eyes. "This day," she said slowly as we took our seats on the train, "I open door of heart. Then put memory inside. Then close."

"Like a safety box?"

She nodded sadly. "Safe box. And when I have 'myself time,' then I open and look."

She paused again, falling silent as we drew towards Kyoto. "Sometimes I want wing, fly away."

"For a day or two?"

Nodding solemnly, she smiled in shame.

Meanwhile, my occasional dabbling in Zen straggled on. Often, I asked Mark directly about the Zen experience, but more often he gave me glimpses of it when I did not ask. Left to his own devices, he rarely seemed to talk about either his painting or his training. There was, in a sense, no seam in him: cut him in any place, and he was the same. His doctrine was his being as surely as his being was his doctrine.

When I asked him about this reticence one day, he said quietly, "That's my teacher. He believes that the first thing you must do is get yourself together as a person. The painting's really just an act of discovery; it's so direct that it becomes a way of seeing yourself. So, in *sumi-e,* there's really no difference between the state of your mind and the state of your art. My teacher, for example, has two altars in his house — one devoted to Shibayama and one to Bashō: the abbot and the artist. And he has his own temple on Awajishima. But for him, I think, his painting is a form of meditation." He fell silent. "Usually, I wouldn't use that kind of word around foreigners, because they haven't got a very deep sense of meditation. They think it just means mindlessness, emptying out."

"Whereas in fact it means mindfulness?"

"Yeah. And emptying out, but with awareness. It's hard to understand unless you've done some sitting. Some of these guys, they're just incredible. I remember one group of monks that did *zazen* for forty-nine straight days after their head monk died. I was amazed, but when I thought about it, it really wasn't so strange. Their teacher just believed that *zazen* was the only truth and that was the way to go."

In *sumi-e*, he said, as in haiku or in any Zen training, the aim was to develop a discipline so sure and a spirit so true that one could afford to be utterly spontaneous; to get into such a state of deliberateness that as soon as one put pen to paper, one would produce something powerful and true (like Shakespeare, perhaps, never blotting a line). Thus a *sumi-e* painting should be quick and direct as an ax cutting wood (akin, I thought, to Shelley's definition of poetry as "a sword of lightning, ever unsheathed"). Instantaneous in its execution, a *sumi-e* painting should catch the moment before it fled; and let the moment speak, unclouded by hesitations or revisions. And though this sounded strange to me at first, I recalled how, whenever I had tried to record dreams, I had had to transcribe the instant before the moment fled, without thinking or even realizing I was writing. If I waited even a minute, the mood was gone and the images would fade; if I waited any longer, it would soon be impossible even to remember that I had ever had a dream.

The most eloquent aspect of Mark's explanation, though, was simply his example; he lived Zen a good deal more than he talked about it—indeed, one sign of this was that he spoke very little at all, and then only with a slow, and prudent, settledness. And whether this was the cause of his feeling for Japan, or its effect—or, more likely, both—he seemed to know exactly where he stood, and so had found the self and life he wanted.

As I read deeper in the Zen poets, I soon stumbled upon Ikkyū, the fifteenth-century sword-wielding monk of Daitokuji, who had entered a temple at the age of six and gone on to express his contempt for the corrupt monasteries of his time in famously controversial poems. Like the Sixth Dalai Lama, in his way,

Ikkyū had been a patron—and a laureate—of the local taverns, and of the pretty girls he had found therein; and like his Tibetan counterpart, or John Donne in our own tradition, he had deliberately conflated the terms of earthly love with those of devotion to the Absolute. The very name he gave himself, "Crazy Cloud," had played subversively on the fact that "cloud water" was a traditional term for monks, who wandered without trace, yet "cloud rain" was a conventional idiom for the act of love. His image of the "red thread" ran through the austere surroundings of his poems as shockingly as the scarlet peonies of Akiko. And in his refusal to kowtow to convention, the maverick monk had turned every certainty on its head: whores, he said, could be like ideal monks—since they inhabited the ideal Zen state of "no mind"—while monks, in selling themselves for gold brocade, were scarcely different from whores. Many of his verses trembled with this ambiguity. One couplet, taken one way, was translated as "Making distinctions between good and evil, the monk's skill lies in knowing the essential condition of the Buddha and the Devil"; taken another way, it meant: "That girl is no good, this one will do; the monk's skill is in having the appetite of a devilish Buddha."

So the Zen practice of dissolving all distinctions was taken to its most unsettling extreme in Ikkyū's "wild fox" Zen, and the lingering sense that Zen addressed every problem except that of men and women was confounded by the unorthodox monk who explicitly sang of his love for girls, and their private places:

> *A beautiful woman, cloud-rain, love's deep river.*
> *Up in the pavilion, the girl and the old monk sing.*
> *I find inspiration in embraces and kisses;*
> *I don't feel at all that I'm casting my body in flames.*

A couple of days later, she called my guesthouse again, beginning, as ever, with phrasebook propriety—"Hello, my name is Sachiko Morishita"—and then, almost instantly, leaping into a tone of whispered intimacy, her voice, as ever, like that of an awestruck worshiper. "Today I write poem about wind. I much like wind. Very free feeling. When I children size, I every day talking wind. Now too. Last night," she went on softly, with her air of explorer's wonder, "I little wake up four o'clock. I want see star."

In response, I began to tell her about the light nights I had seen just a few months earlier in Iceland, and she replied that she knew this *thema* very well and, in fact, that she had seen the movie *White Nights* and it had changed her life. "I see this movie, I much much love. Much cry. Then I see Mikhail Baryshnikov, Osaka Festival Hall. *Giselle.* First time ballet. No words, only music—but verrry beautiful. I more more cry. Then I see Gregory Hines, Osaka Kintetsu Hall. I have best seat, I shake hand. After, I take Yuki classical ballet class. Before, she three years old, she learn modern dance; now, two month ago, she start classical ballet. So"—she giggled sweetly—"this movie little change Yuki life."

All this brought home to me again how strongly the quaint Victorian notion of feminine accomplishments still held in Japan, and perhaps especially in Kyoto, and how often women here still seemed to belong in some polite and proper Austen drawing room. Here was a fairly typical young woman—a normal, middle-class woman of limited means and opportunities—who routinely drew, wrote poems, made kimono, painted watercolors, played the koto, sang foreign folksongs with guitar, could hammer out a couple of melodies on the piano, played the banjo, was an expert at aerobics, knew *kendō* and kung fu, and was mistress of all the other traditional arts—serving tea and sewing, acupuncture and *ikebana*; her five-year-old daughter, no less typical, was already cultivating Chopin on the piano and learning to dance *Giselle.* And as in an Austen world, women lived so much in the parlor that even the slightest encounter with the world outside had the capacity to thrill or shock.

The next thing I knew, though, Gregory Hines had set her off on other tangents, and she was asking me what I thought of the movie *Soul Man*. After I gave a suitably evasive reply, she said, abruptly, "Sometimes, I think, we talk telepathy."

"Telepathy?"

"Sometimes I alone, I talking you, and then I hear you talking. Please we always have telepathy?"

"Sure," I said, though, as ever, I had not a clue to what I was assenting.

"Please you wait," she said, and a few seconds later, I heard a music-box lullaby over the phone. Then her soft sigh. "Usually, this style, many time, I think not good."

"I understand," I said, though really I didn't.

"Usually not so fun."

"That's okay," I assured her, assuming that she was trying to keep me at a distance. I could imagine the strain of trying to shuttle between lives, across a gap as wide as the Pacific.

"Now sun set, and I together children. Very different life. Big heart control, little difficult." I took this at first to mean "damage control," as it did, but then I saw that she meant something more.

"This year," she went on, "autumn more more beautiful. But I look leave, then I think, next year, you gone."

That night, I had a whole series of bad dreams: that someone was advancing on me with a gun, that I felt a paralyzing chill, which stopped me from moving, that I was looking for a man called Wisdom but stumbled onto Wimbledon instead. All night the dreams spun on, about oversleeping, about missing something, about threat.

15

AND JUST AS it is common to hear how, when one is in love, anything one sees reminds one of that love—our feelings remake the world in a secular equivalent of the faith that sees the hand of God in everything—so I began to find that when one is thinking on a theme, everything seems to reflect on it. Suddenly, everything I saw or read, in this girlish city of temples, seemed to take me back to the theme of the lady and the monk.

When Sachiko gave me a translation of Inoue Yasushi's *Roof Tile of Tempyō* to answer some of my questions about the spread of Buddhism to Japan, I found myself again inside the same struggle, of doing and being, and the same question, of whether the products of a life could be its absolution. Inoue was no more analytical than any other Japanese writer, and his pale, ink-wash style refused to deviate from narrative. Yet still, with its tale of Japanese monks devoting their lives to protecting and transcribing Buddhist scripture, his story set up an array of troubling questions. What avails monastic aspirations when, as Mark had said, religious geniuses were born and not made? Could not renouncing the world be a form of self-indulgence? Was not monasticism, in the end, as much an act of cowardice as courage?

Then I picked up a copy of *The Slave* by Singer, and again the theme that impressed itself on me was the same. As the hero, Jacob, tried and tried to parse the Song of Songs, to unriddle the relation of spirit and sense, and the presence of murderers and whores in a God-created world, he was tugged at by Lilith, who was, in some sense, a Polish version of a *tanuki*, going abroad at night to lure men to their doom. In the end, Singer concluded, "everything comes from God—including lust." There was a point to everything, and everything justified itself; we could doubt it, or fail to understand it, but still it continued to exist, indifferent to our uncertainty, and we could do nothing but accept it.

I was just musing on these issues—the lady at the temple gates—when I met a former monk called Rick, and when I talked to Rick, the image became even more poignant simply because Rick was so clearly torn by it, and living with its legacy. Rick's story, as Mark had explained it to me, was at once remarkable and perhaps archetypal. Trained as a conservatory student at Oberlin, he had suddenly abandoned family and career and come to Kyoto to serve as a monk. For seven years he had lived in Daitokuji—Ikkyū's temple—together with his best friend, Ray. But like his meditation mate, he had never managed entirely to break with the world, and like Ray, he had often stolen out at night to visit a girl. And when his girlfriend had borne him a baby—as had happened to Ikkyū's principal disciple—Rick had felt obliged to quit the temple to join her. With nothing in his hands, he had walked out of the place and across town to where his girlfriend lived, together with his nine-month-old daughter. But the temple, of course, had prepared him for everything except living with a woman, and soon thereafter they had ended up having terrible, screaming, plate-throwing fights. Finally, he had left her—only to find himself totally isolated: his girl, now his wife, enraged that he had left her as a fallen woman, in charge, moreover, of a half-caste child; the monastic community outraged at his defection; and all the foreign community gathered in one clucking chorus to condemn a man—a monk, no less—for seducing a Japanese lady and then abandoning her. The final, implausible climax had come when Rick's wife and his abbot had actually joined together in their disapproval and, bound tight by a common adversary, had become partners of a sort. Rick, meanwhile, had fled to Kobe, and then to a run-down hotel in New York City, and at last to San Francisco.

When I met him, Rick, now working for a computer company in the Bay Area, was returning, on a business trip, to the city he had left in disgrace seven years before. As we drove through the country lanes, the mountains sharp in winter light, he simply kept repeating, *"Natsukashii!"* (It's nostalgic), and I could sense that it was too intense and charged a homecoming for him to begin to articulate.

We went to an Indian restaurant in the countryside — I was no longer surprised to find so many Japanese hippies here, or so many of them experts in reproducing the subcontinent — and as we sat, drinking *chai* and munching hot cashews while an Indian woman sang *ghazals* on the sound system and people drifted in and out of the red-and-yellow mirrored curtains, I was almost mesmerized by Rick's quiet intensity. He was always right there, this short fellow with the bald egghead and the shambling simian gait, now in his late thirties: his eyes arresting, his voice softly purring, all of him buzzing with a quiet fire. Even here, talking in a disheveled restaurant about the tricks of self-presentation, he blazed.

Rick was full of good stories about his years in the monastery: about sitting for ten days before the temple gates in order to gain admission; about covering his face with a wicker hat and going on his daily rounds of begging through the red-light area (where his American friend from Stanford was living, as the first non-Japanese geisha); about learning to sweep the maple leaves into a circle, because Zen teachers believed that if you could sweep them into a perfect circle, without bending down, it meant that your mind was as whole and fluid as a circle. And though this sounded strange to me, I could understand the way Zen worked by thinking of the calm I sometimes felt in washing dishes, and the pleasure of seeing a once filthy plate shine.

"Growing up in Ohio must have hardened you a little to the Kyoto winter."

"Shit, no," he replied. "Not in the monastery. I had to stand out there in the cold, before dawn, in bare feet, shivering. It's hard, man; you don't know how hard it is. In summer, you sweat; in winter, you shiver. Every day in the monastery you're facing some kind of pain. And those old monks are killers, man; they really whack you with those sticks!"

"What took you to the monastery?"

"Well, I was learning to be a professional trumpet player. And then I began reading some books on Zen. And one day, on acid, I read Daisetz Suzuki to see how it measured up, and it was an awesome experience — a kind of awakening, almost — and it reminded me of that line from the mystic Heinrich Suso: 'I felt like a vase that had contained a precious ointment and now all that remained was the perfume.' So I sold all my trumpets and stuff, and came over. Went into training for the monastery.

"After I left the place, I found this amazingly elegant woman in Kobe. But her father was really uptight, hired a private detective and shit to follow me everywhere. So I went back home and became an interpreter in the Catskills" — the Catskills! — "working with this monk, a Living National Treasure, who had unified an entire sect of Zen for the first time in its history, and then, just as suddenly, left the temple. He just stripped his robes and spent three years going from temple to temple, challenging monks with koans and then, when he beat them at their own game, stripping them of their robes, and tearing them up to be used as diapers."

Later, we sat around Mark's low table, under the bamboo lantern, and Rick played the *shakuhachi* bamboo flute — Ikkyū's instrument — with a kind of piercing intensity that sounded like the voice of Zen itself.

The next night, we went to a party together, and it turned out that the host, a complete stranger, was someone with whom Rick had shared a writing class in Vermont many years before — someone, indeed, who had come to Kyoto largely as a result of hearing Rick's haunted memories of temple life. As the evening wore on, the former monk took to washing dishes, and again I saw his spotlessness and the simple severity of his monastic discipline. Later, when we walked out into the street and piled into a cab, Rick began talking again, hypnotically. "I'm thirty-nine now, but I really feel as young as ever. Shit—God, I don't know why I'm using that word so much; must be because I'm near the monastery again. Anyway, I feel all my life is ahead of me. Sure, I feel more aches and pains than I did fifteen years ago, but basically I feel as young as ever. There's this guy called Stephen Chang, a doctor in law, in medicine, from Chinese universities, master of tai chi, acupuncture, all this stuff, and he has this book called *The Tao of Sex*. In the West, you see, we've got all fixated on the orgasm. Usually, you go for that, and, bang, it's over—with the woman usually not quite satisfied and the man totally exhausted." What was this ex-monk talking about? "But this thing is all about conserving male seed, male energy. So you don't bother about orgasm but use this energy for higher things, send it to the sixth *chakra* or wherever."

"And you've been using this?" The taxi was whizzing past pachinko parlors, video arcades, coffee shops—all the high gloss of a Kyoto winter night. And the former monk, as taut as a violin string, kept talking about girls.

The very next day, I experienced a strange kind of inversion of my encounter with Rick when I met a group of foreigners at a Thanksgiving party. None of them had any connection with Zen, yet for all of them, everything they did, it seemed, was a meditation. I talked to a flighty California girl who worked in collage. "For me, tea is a kind of meditation." Beside her sat her husband, a bearded Bay Area writer. "Yeah, the thing about kite flying is, it's a sort of meditation." Even as the Zen monk was mastering the tongue of Don Juan, these wanderers seemed to be talking the language of Zen.

"I've been studying tea for three years," the woman went on. "See, the thing about it is that it combines calligraphy, lacquerwork, scrolls, flower arranging, all the rules about bowing and manners. So everything's right there; tea's like a compilation of all the Japanese arts."

"But to a typically uninitiated viewer, it's a little hard to see the subtleties."

"Sure, but they're *incredible.* Believe me, they are *amazing.* Like, in pouring the tea, you've got to curl your finger into this exact shape" — she curved it prettily — "which is meant to be the exact shape of the moon two days after it's new. No way you can do the second-day moon, no way you can do the fourth. You've got to make it the third. And there's a different tea, not just for every season and every month, but for every week! So you have to have this amazing concentration — like aikido too."

"Do you enjoy it?"

"Yeah. But I kind of think it's time to quit. The truth is, the longer you do it, the more you see what you're supposed to be doing. You get more self-conscious, more uptight — more Japanese, I guess. I remember one day I had been doing tea for two hours, and then I was arranging a flower, while looking out a window. Nobody could see me. Nobody! But this lady came up to me and told me I was sitting wrong. I felt like saying to her, 'Fuck it! Who cares how I'm sitting if nobody's here?' But you can't do that. So I had to sit the right way, and there's no way I can sit the wrong way again. I've got to be self-conscious even when I'm fucking sitting down! When I first came here, I was just like this kind of happy idiot, stumbling over everything: a real bull in a china shop. But the more sensitive I became to the Japanese, the more self-conscious I had to become. I think I'm burned out."

Another person at the party, a quiet-minded teacher who had lived for years as an editor in San Francisco, tried to explain to me what had drawn him here. "All my friends in the Bay Area thought I was completely crazy. 'What do you know about

Kyoto?' they kept saying. 'What makes you want to go there?' 'I dunno,' I'd say. And I'd look in the papers and see things like 'Moon Viewing in Oakland Botanical Gardens,' and I'd go along to that, and my friends would say, 'Why? How come? What's the point?' And I'd go, 'I dunno.' It's just like this mountain I kept on seeing, and I had to go there. So then I came. I gave myself a year to stay, with an option on another year. And I knew nothing about the place—*nothing*—when I came over; I thought it was just a small town.

"I got a job teaching at a university, and there was this girl who worked in the office there. Anyway, one day, she sent me a card about a play I had produced. I went back to California for ten weeks. And when I came back, I just answered her card. That was in April. In May, we went on a date. In October, we began living together. By February, we were married. Now she's expecting. It was just one of those things, you know—I thought I was going to leave after one year, and there was this girl saying 'You're not going to leave.' Now, of course, I think that *she* was the mountain I had been seeing all that time."

Two days later, Mark and I went for Thanksgiving dinner to his friend Etsuko's house, a fairy-tale mansion in the Japanese context, its intercom-activated gate leading into a garden softly lit with lanterns, its large wooden doors giving onto an exquisitely appointed living room—a museum in miniature—lined with Chinese scrolls and ancient Javanese puppets and books about the art world, in Japanese and English. Bach was floating through the room on a Deutsche Grammophon compact disc, and for appetizers, our hostess placed before us a couple of almond and horseradish wafers.

Etsuko's situation was more or less typical, so it seemed. Her husband lived in Tokyo, roughly three hundred miles away, and she saw him only occasionally, on weekends, if at all (in all the years he'd known her, Mark had talked to her husband only once, very briefly, on the phone). She, meanwhile, devoted most of her energy to raising her teenage daughter. But what time and attention she had left over, she threw into a flurry of activities, setting up charitable organizations, helping to run an English-language magazine for visitors, representing her husband's family at social ceremonies and conferences, and, for the most part, running intercultural institutions aimed at introducing Japan to foreigners and vice versa. Having spent almost half her life abroad, she sought now to act as a kind of ambassador from each world to the other, trying to repair diplomatic relations which were always frail as china.

Serving us the sweetest grapefruit juice I had ever tasted, in cut-glass tumblers, she patiently fielded my questions, explaining how the Japanese had different colors for each wind, as well as for every season, telling me the different words for moonlight on the water, spelling out the name of the insect that was virtually synonymous with dusk. Many of these words, she explained, were suffused with a sense of nostalgia, harking back to the age of Asuka and the versatile Nukata no Okimi, once Empress of Japan; and only then did I realize that on the day Sachiko had taken me to Asuka, she had in fact been introducing me to a woman's sanctuary, a private, forgotten place charged with the memory of this famous poetess.

Then, with a graceful bow, Etsuko ushered us into her dining room, ringed with beautifully arranged blue cups and a gallery of china plates. She served up chrysanthemums in tiny blue bowls, and fine, rare mushrooms; then, in honor of the day, a huge Thanksgiving turkey; and then, for dessert, sustaining the seasonal motif, a delicate sweet shaped like a chrysanthemum. Over tea—made from a host of Fortnum's selections, with a separate china cup to keep the water hot—I learned a little more about this unlikely housewife, professional gerontologist, and former student at Edinburgh, who could speak, without strain, about *quattrocento* churches in Florence, Mozart pieces (identified by Köchel number), and the early writings of Fosco

Maraini. She was going to Tuscany soon, she went on, to see various chapels whose art reminded her of a certain style of Chinese painting—"blasphemous though that doubtless is." She spoke, in French, of her studies at the Sorbonne, of the three years she had spent in Kathmandu, of Keats's "Ode to Autumn." She described the latest holdings in the Musée d'Orsay. And I, many fathoms out of my depth and amazed to see someone move in this almost Jamesian aura of refinement, realized anew how, whatever role the Japanese played, they played it so well and took it to such a pitch of excellence that one could never wish to see the part played again. A Beatles freak here was a freak to end all freaks, with five hundred albums in his collection; a gardener was a wholehearted purist who gave all his life to developing a single perfect flower; and a woman of culture was so accomplished at her role that she made her counterparts anywhere else seem puny by comparison. The Japanese played themselves as Gielgud, Hamlet.

A few days later, as the month drew to its end, I awoke at dawn to find my window all fogged over: the first hard frost of winter. Longing to share the moment with someone—I had not experienced winter for three years now—I hurried out into the mild invigoration of the morning to visit Mark. It was a joy undiminished to awaken in the cloudless blue and see the mountains sharp in the distance, to feel the briskness of a winter morning in the sun. The whole world felt uplifted and refreshed: the narrow lanes alive with oranges, old women chattering away below the muted sun, and everywhere a sense of purpose.

My only disappointment, I told Mark as I came into his house, was that I would not be able to see the *hatsu-yuki*, or first snowfall of the year. I would be leaving Kyoto the following day, not to return for a month, and I knew that I would miss the winter's first moment of silent transformation.

The next day, my last day in Kyoto, Sachiko came to my room again, bringing with her a book by A. A. Milne and a textbook for an English lesson. I led her up to my tiny space, and there, in the winter dark, I tried to teach her again the words that she might need. We sat on cushions on the tatami, the dark room lit by the glowing orange bar of my single-element heater. Often, in explaining the terms of my own language to her, I felt as if I were explaining them to myself. As I began, slowly, to speak English as a second language, my own tongue came to seem as new to me, and mysterious, as Japanese.

Patiently, sometimes frowning over the words and muttering, "*Muzukashii!*" sometimes giggling away the difficulty, she stumbled through a text about fishermen in Holland. When we were through, she looked at me, there was a long silence, and I stood up in the darkening room to make some tea.

As she wandered round the tiny space, inspecting the *gaijin* in his native habitat, I tried to divert her with some questions. I held up a Christmas card. "Ah, Monet!" she cried. Then a postcard I had bought in a museum. "Rodin!" Then a paperback I had found downtown, in Sony Plaza. "Paddington Bear!"

After the kettle had boiled, I put down two mugs on the table and knelt down on the tatami to show her some earrings I had bought for my mother. She leaned forward till her hair was tickling my face. In the winter darkness of the tiny room, the fire glowing, I brushed back her hair, felt her lips touch mine, her body shaking as if electrified.

Later, we walked along the river in the dusk. Turning, we saw the eastern hills, thick with orange trees, glowing in the dying light. Then, sitting down beside the red-lit river, she sang me a melody from *The Sound of Music*—"Something Good"—about Maria's escape from her abbey, in a quavering, high, but steady voice. "When I little children size," she said, "this song my favorite. But I never think I find this feeling. I think I cannot. I always 'lost lady.' Now I feel this song more more. Thank you very much."

There was a long, charged silence on the riverbank. "Autumn now ending," she said, as we watched the last light leave the hills. And that night, it snowed.

WINTER

Our old older, Our new newer,
Our kind kinder —
Welcome to Japan.

—THE SIGN OF MAKITA POWER
TOOLS, GREETING ARRIVALS
IN OSAKA AIRPORT

IT WAS THE SMELLS that hit me first: smells of cooking, smells of rotting, smells of people being people – all the smells I had not smelled for months in exquisitely deodorized Japan, where only pleasant fragrances are permitted: the lemon scent of air freshener, the costly glamour of French perfume, an occasional hint of incense. The minute I set foot in Taiwan, I was assaulted by smells, sultry, piquant, and strange: assaulted, too, by spitters and shouters, by offers, importunities, cries of "Why you no buy? Best price for you!" Waiters dropped plates on my table as if they were hot (which they never were), men whispered, "Dollar, dollar," crowds pushed and shoved and squawked. There was the sudden shock of car crashes in the light-dizzy streets, of winking cabbies, of women in blinding pantsuits who caught my eye and held it.

Three days later, landing in Southeast Asia, I felt again, in a rush, all the things I had been missing in Japan, not so much the roughness now as the spiced softness, the seduction of kerosene lamps and unlit back lanes, the lure of night-market meals and clove-scented villages; thronged festivals, black markets, a flash of white smiles among the trees. The whole whirl of tropical sensations hit me like a fever dream: the darkness full of spirits, and whisper-soft girls in off-the-shoulder dresses; the sound of gonged instruments in the night. None of the hard, purposeful austerity of Japan, but stronger, darker forces in the hot tropic air; here again one was in the realm of the subconscious.

My very first night in Thailand, I found myself standing on the Golden Mount, talking about water buffaloes with an irresistible shaven-headed twelve-year-old monk in saffron robes and sandals, as together we watched the full moon rise above the diamond capital; half an hour later, in the midst of crowds, I was being befriended by two sidelong-glancing, strangely affable transsexuals. Even the Japanese department stores here, all video smarts and squeaky-clean announcements, were lit up from within by a blast of Thai warmth and laughing dishevelment; and even aseptic Singapore, an aspirant Japan, seemed ripe with the promise of adventure, a veritable Marrakesh after Kyoto, with its unkempt bands of ricksha men, shirts cracked open to their hairless chests, and sharp-faced, lipsticked hookers, brazen in their scarlet shirts. Suddenly, the imagination was given something rough to chew on, a world unedited.

At times, of course, I grew so enamored of my thesis that everything confirmed it: how dowdy were the Chinese, I thought, looking at a group of revelers, gawking clumsily, in my Taipei hotel; how different from the elegant self-possession of the Japanese. And then the people began to speak, and their language — of course — was Japanese.

Yet still, I had hardly left Japan before I could better see how the Japanese regard all the world outside as barbarous and crude, undeveloped in every sense of the word, and terrifying too. So sheltered had my life become in Kyoto — so sanitized of danger or alarm — that I had all but forgotten that another world existed; and now it was a shock to enter a stage where tempers were lost, things went wrong, the surface snapped. And if even I felt this, after only ten weeks in Japan, how much more unnerved must a Japanese be, suddenly propelled out of his cozy home and into a world of disruption and threat. Mother Japan prepared its children only, and ideally, for Japan.

Coming from Kyoto — quasi-Japanese myself now — I found myself at sea abroad, forgetting to leave tips, reluctant to jaywalk across empty streets, recoiling like a child whenever men approached me on the streets with offers of hotels. I stood outside taxicabs, waiting for their doors to open automatically, and then, once inside, fell into broken conversations—how many children do you have, how many hours do you work?—in Japanese. When once, returning home, I put my shoes on inside my room, I felt as surreptitious, as sacrilegious almost, as if I had worn a Walkman into church.

Abroad, as unguarded as a Japanese now, I left my things unattended and my room unlocked, and wandered round with $170 in my pocket (Japan was, perhaps, curing me a little of materialism, though not in the way expected). Whenever I bumped into someone in the street, I said, reflexively, "*Sumimasen,*" and when I returned to California, I startled teenage shopgirls with my earnest *Sō, sō, sō*s. On my way home from Los Angeles Airport, a Mexican in a gas station rushed up to me in relief—a compatriot, so he thought—and pressed me in Spanish for details on the way to Calexico. "*Hai, hai*"—I nodded briskly—"*Demo kochira wa...*" and looked back to see the poor man terrified.

After Japan, even Harrods looked a little déclassé, and when I bought a cup of tea at the Singapore Hilton for $2.20, I could not believe the bargain. I was Japanese enough now to shiver when I saw a man kiss his girlfriend in a Bangkok restaurant. And at home, in California, I felt Japanese enough to appreciate, for the first time ever, the lavender blush of hibiscus in the mild December days and the piercing clarity of Venus in the denim sky. Japanese too, I could see now, for the first time ever, the true beauties of California: long hours and long horizons.

But I felt a little closer to Japan now in some deeper sense as well, in affiliation as well as habit. Whenever I saw groups of JAL-packaged tourists being herded through the Grand Palace in Bangkok, or pairs of frightened-looking girls in khaki shorts, deep in sidewalk negotiations with some local con man, I felt, mysteriously, a pang of sympathy and kinship; abroad, the Japanese looked so lost to the world, so far from the reassurances to which they were accustomed. They looked to me as vulnerable as shy teenagers alone, in a corner, at their first real cocktail party—not just afraid and disoriented, but anxious to combat self-pity. And whenever foreigners fell into the usual litany ("But the Japanese are so strange, so neurotic, so hard to get close to"), I found myself rushing to their defense: "But they're so innocent, so thoughtful, and so kind." Taken on any terms other than their own, the Japanese did, to be sure, seem tough negotiators, industrial spies, and torturers of whales, playing life to win; but now I was able to see them a little more from the other side, in terms of which everything they did made perfect sense and the world they produced was hard to improve upon. In a sense, in fact, it was that very perfection that removed them further from the world at large (as a concert pianist has that much less in common with a garage band) and made the world at large seem that much more menacing and dark. Watching the Japanese circling around Asia in a kind of see-no-evil, speak-no-evil, hear-no-evil spell, taking in everything with polite enthusiasm, screening out disease and dirt—exemplary guests as well as hosts, as good at receiving pleasure as at giving it—my heart went out to a culture bound, and perhaps determined, to be misunderstood.

Abroad, in fact, it was even clearer that Japan was taking over the role of America in the fifties. In Japan itself, it was easy to see its affinities with the Eisenhower era, in its nuclear families with their clean suburban homes, placid and a touch complacent; its identically dressed commuters on their trains, men in gray flannel suits dreaming of golfing holidays; its almost science fictive world of gadgets and consumer goods and a conformity so absolute that it gave rise to the intertwined notions of the affluent society, the organization man, and the lonely crowd (and, in response, of Ginsberg howling poems in Kyoto streets). Abroad, however, the likenesses were even easier to see. For with the dawning of the Japanese Empire, the "Ugly American" of thirty years ago was fast being replaced by a new focus for the world's envies and fears. Now it was the Japanese who were traveling around the globe in groups, like conquering armies on the march, dressed in Hawaiian shirts and Bermuda shorts, cameras slung around their necks, marveling at how everything was smaller— and better—at home. Now it was Japan that seemed the role model—and the hated archrival—of many developing countries, even such unforgiving former colonies as Korea. Now it was Japan, indeed, that seemed the Land of Opportunity, and to Japan that foreigners came in search of new lives for themselves, and new identities, in a land of promise and abundance—in search, in fact, of the American Dream. And now it was America that seemed the funky, disorganized, low-budget slice of exotica that the Japanese delighted in inspecting whenever they wanted a taste of primitive wildness. Whenever I visited expensive hotels (or expensive countries, like Bhutan), nearly all the tourists I saw were groups of wealthy, retired Westerners and youthful Japanese. It seemed a natural pairing.

It was only when I returned to the world at large, moreover, that I realized how far away I had been in Kyoto. It was not just that Japan occupied a different kind of universe, which rarely made contact with our own; but, more, that this island was—by choice as much as circumstance—psychically as well as physically removed from the world at large. The analogy here was not so much with Gulliver as with Alice; in Japan, one felt as if the world had been turned upside down and inside out, all its values and assumptions turned on their heads—as if, one might say, the force of gravity had been so radically altered that one had ended up on another planet. It sometimes seemed—and Japan liked to make it seem—as if Japan had a different epicenter from the rest of the world, as if, indeed, all the rest of the world inhabited a Copernican, and Japan a Ptolemaic, universe;

and so, where much of the rest of the world traditionally looked to America as its center, Japan looked only to Japan. America might be a fashion accessory, a collectible, a sign of imported glamour; but it was not the end-point of most aspirations here. America was an alternative to Gucci, not to *Bushidō* or Emperor-worship or Japan.

Besides, Japan's strength was only growing as America's declined. It was morning in America, but in most parts of Asia, especially in Tokyo, it was already the next evening. And the notion of a Japanese takeover was gaining an almost literal significance as the Japanese bought up hotels and companies and entire downtowns; the sluggers of the major leagues, the diamonds of Tiffany's, the canvases of Van Gogh. Even Monet's "Soleil Levant" had been spirited away, by *yakuza*, or gangsters, to Japan (the Rising Sun itself was going East). Meanwhile, all the news from America was bad: AIDS, crack, Irangate; an aging president, a collapsed economy, a clergy double-crossing itself with scandal. And my sense that America was beginning to look more and more like an underdeveloped country next to Japan was only eerily confirmed when, my first night back in California, a thunderstorm began to shake my hillside house, rattling the windows and pounding the walls all night, like the ghost of a monsoon, until, of a sudden, we were plunged into darkness, powerless for twenty hours while the wind howled all about.

Ambushing Japan from afar, I was better able to see what I liked about it. Bangkok, for example, bustling by day and dazzling by night, alive to business and to pleasure, struck me as the ultimate urban intoxication; yet it also seemed to encourage the abandoning of vision for mere fantasy. It was hard to imagine reading there, or thinking, or leading any kind of life that would engage the deepest part of one. The place invited one to surrender to reality, not to lead a life so much as to be led by one. And where people came to Japan, very often, to pursue something, they came to Bangkok—or Bali, or Sri Lanka, I suspected—not to do so. Thus spicy, sultry, vivacious Bangkok sent me back with renewed affection for Japan. Thailand, I thought, was the girl at the edge of the temple, beckoning one away with a smile.

2

I HAD NOT EVEN set foot in Kyoto on my way back to Japan before enlightenment and seduction—and the intertwining of the two—were all about me once again. On the plane back from L.A., I found myself next to a glamorous young Korean who was all fluttered eyelashes and whispered invitations, until I exposed her, in midflight, as a Mormon practicing her missionary positions. And when the plane got stranded in Seoul, I found myself sharing a room with a tree planter from Sonoma County, who was, he said, on his way to India to spend twelve hours a day, for one hundred eighty days, meditating in a cell. I said hello to him, and he raised his hands in prayer and said, "I'm so grateful to meet you, sir"; the airline representative gave us vouchers for our break-fasts, and he said, "I'm so very grateful for your gift, ma'am." I asked him how his flight had been, and he smiled, beatific. "At first," he began, "I couldn't sleep because I was next to these two kids, and they were crying. It was beautiful that they had to cry"—he smiled forgivingly again—"but it made it kind of hard to sleep." Then he addressed his spiritual life. "I used to be into this guru thing, Rajneesh and all that stuff. But I suffered a lot of alienation. Now I just want to find this quietness inside of me, and be of service to humanity. After a while, you know, when you're meditating, you just get into this state, and all your sexual energy disappears." A fit antidote to Rajneesh, I surmised.

"Sure," he said, looking out upon the sleek neon blocks of Seoul. "Meditation and relationships—those are the ways to do it, I guess." He thought a little more. "Relationships, I guess, are the fastest way."

That night, I had strange dreams of Kyoto: of huge boulevards and people sitting in the streets; of standing on large intersections late at night, not knowing where I was, and groups of Japanese terrifying me in their clowns' costumes, painted red faces dreamlike in the dark.

My first night back in Kyoto, the city was indeed a dream to me again, as I wandered through its dizzy streets, in and out of weaving crowds, past megaphone voices and floodlit stalls, a fairy world of Pierrot faces. A surge of kimonos everywhere, streaming through the reeling lanes, in and out of noodle stalls, snapping up octopus pancakes and New Year's tofu, features all invisible in the dark, then shockingly lit up by passing lanterns. Shadows gliding through the temple corridors, billowing white banners above their hooded entrances; figures collecting fires from a central roaring blaze; and then, at midnight, the great bronze bell of Chion-in, tolling and tolling in the new Year of the Dragon.

Jet-lagged on New Year's Day itself, I arose before dawn and hurried out into the phantom streets, where the dark blue was beginning to clear above the lowering mountains and silver the city's canals. All the commotion was gone now, and all noise vanished: just unlit lanterns in the street, deserted stalls, silence and debris. A few students observing the year's first sunrise; a girl in blue kimono and white stole, hugging herself in the dawn, condensation escaping like a whisper from her lips.

Inside the Heian Shrine, the new world was just beginning to stir. White-robed priests in conical black hats stood under orange pillars, ceremonious in the cold-breath morning. A gray-suited man bowed before an altar, the young light shining off the polished wood around him. A flock of white priests, unearthly in the early light, shuffled in slow processional along the corridors, sticks of incense held in front of them. Smoke rising off the dying fires like communal breath in the dawn.

Later, very slowly, the open courtyard began to fill up, patient as a painter's canvas: women in flowered kimono, snow-white fur stoles around pale necks, clopping on wooden clogs across the sunlit gravel, the sun spreading warmth across the yawning space; worshipers tossing coins into boxes, clapping their hands and, eyes closed, murmuring the year's first prayers; then receding again into the day's perfection. In the shining winter light, families took up positions on low wooden tables spread with indigo and scarlet cloths; lovers lingered round sun-dappled streams; pedigree ladies led pedigree cats in warm leather jackets across the shrine. A gong, slow and solemn, tolled and tolled, and little girls with flowers in their hair joined hands with beaming fathers in flowing black kimono.

Walking home, through the sun, flowers placed on doorsteps and futons draped over balconies, I felt as if I had landed in some matter-of-fact utopia. The high cries of children playing hopscotch in the lane. Householders polishing their bikes in the quiet sun, unloading furniture from houses, silently hosing cars. The rites of everyday life polished till they shone like glass. In Kyoto, every day felt like New Year's Day, so deft were the Japanese at remaking themselves each day. For a foreigner at least, able to enjoy all the conveniences of this world without having to pay the price in terms of obligation, there was a sense of airy weightlessness to life here that seemed to suspend harsh realities. Coming back to the sharpened air of Kyoto after a few weeks away, I felt as clean as a small town after heavy rains subside.

Later that morning, New Year's cards were hand-delivered to everyone in the land, and I found myself with a bouquet of lyric offerings: from Sachiko, a pretty snowdrop, inscribed with her own calligraphy, above a printed message that said, "She has a floral word meaning 'a solace' "; from the Buddhist priest who had taught me executive's Japanese in California, a hand-drawn cartoon of two happy alligators, one bestriding a pair of scales, the other cradling a baby, a soccer ball between them, and the greeting "Happy Rew Year" (*rew* —or, more properly, *ryū* —means "dragon"); from Mark, a *sumi-e* dragon, all Buddhist power and coiled strength; and from an American businessman in Tokyo, a photograph of himself.

A letter had also arrived from Nagoya, home to no one I knew, and when I tore it open, I found a long and penetrating inquiry from one of the giggling girls with whom I had shared breakfast at the temple in my first days in Kyoto, asking me whether I thought the Japanese were superficial.

Next day, I awoke at first light and buried myself again in Ryōkan, reserving his words for moments when the morning was new and the early light gilded the houses of my lane, painting gold stripes across the corrugated iron. Later, after the day was smudged, and encumbered with emotion, it was never quite so easy to retreat into his silent hut within the woods. Now, on a cloudless, high, and Zen-blue morning, I drank strong tea and read through the old monk's verses, while Van Morrison sang "She Gave Me Religion" in the Quaker's room next door.

That afternoon, as the New Year's holiday went on, I made my ritual visit to Sachiko's home in Peach Tree Mountain. She greeted me at the door in soft-lined winter kimono, orange with the delicate outline of plum blossoms, a red ribbon wound around her tied-up hair, and snow-white, split-toed socks around her feet. Motioning me to her couch, she served New Year's cakes, made in the temple by her children, then drew out an antique koto from its cover and played a winter melody. I watched her in the quiet afternoon—surrounded by two VCRs, a laser-disc player, a tape deck, a TV, two speakers, and a

framed portrait of her children with the abbot of Tōfukuji—
bent over her ancient instrument, the winter sun streaming
through the wavering curtains at her back.

A little later, Yuki and Hiroshi clambered in to show me their
first paintings of the year, and then, taking themselves quietly
into a corner, began playing the traditional New Year's game of
Hyakunin-Isshū, a version of Snap that used one hundred classic poems instead of cards. Already, I noticed, they were
absorbing, from their mother, the whole standard repertory of
Japanese gestures and emotions, the way children in America
might be taught the reflexes of "Please" and "Thank you." Yuki,
in particular, was already as demure as a courtier, handing me
gifts with exactly the right intonation of *Hai dōzo!* (the equivalent of *Bitte!*), singing back *Arigatō!* to every greeting, sitting
entirely upright, and silent, on the train. Already too, I noticed,
the children were naming all their animals after TV characters,
where we, perhaps, would be likelier to give them names of our
own devising (Japanese training in received dreams began early).
Then, after handing me New Year's gifts of origami raccoons,
the children padded off to bed, and Sachiko shuffled round to
serve apple tea, a tiny, antique figure in her small-stepping
socks and kimono.

Yawning a little as she pulled out her guitar, I mentioned that
it was still 4 a.m. for me, California time, and she, duly solemn,
replied, "Only monk awake time. You California monk, maybe?"

"Maybe," I replied, thinking how appropriate it sounded: a
Californian monk, lay acolyte of indiscipline.

Then, with the air of reverence that attended so many of her
movements, she handed over a photo album, a fluffy Pekingese
on its cover, a red rose on its head, and the printed message
"URBAN DREAM. Everyone has a precious memory with one's
heart. Whether it is a small memory, for you it must be a world
of wonderful dream. Place your dream in 'Urban Dream.'"
Inside, mementos of the winter: temples under snow, canals all
white, a new world covered and uncovered.

Seeing her at home again, I noticed how much younger she was in English, freed from Japanese assumptions, and able therefore to claim another self, for which her mother tongue seemed to have no terms. "Why is Mummy waving her hands?" Yuki had cried over dinner. In Japanese, I gathered, Sachiko never spoke with her hands.

3

WINTER MADE EVERYONE a kind of monk in Japan, bringing out a streak of worldly asceticism that was never far from the
surface in this land of spartan epicures. It was not so much that
the weather was punishing; indeed, it was cold only indoors.
Yet even the affluent here, in the world's most advanced society,
lived often, it seemed, in conditions that we would regard as
neoprimitive, in miniature, half-furnished houses, with out-
door toilets, and flimsy walls, and an absence of all central
heating. Their homes, very often, seemed as scaled down as
their hopes.

Again, this suggested to me how public dress here was almost
a form of public address. In public, people presented themselves in highly expensive clothes and shiny, late-model, lily-
white cars; behind closed doors, they lived like paupers almost.
The whole society, it sometimes seemed, schooled its people in
denial even as it indulged them — as any parent might — allowing
them to believe that they could find any kind of cake or good or
service, at any time of day, yet reminding them that they could
not hope to gain a more intangible kind of license. And winter
seemed to enforce the lesson, bringing a penitential strain to the
rites of self-negation.

Even the Emperor, as a boy, had been made to stand out
under an ice-cold waterfall, in dead of winter, for fifteen minutes
each day, without complaining or even permitting himself a
grimace. And even Sachiko, jeans-wearing, Tom Cruise–loving
Sachiko, observed her own monastic rites: each day, she told
me, in winter or summer, come rain or shine, she got up at

dawn and took a shower in freezing-cold water, crying out chants to the gods to ensure good health and fortune for her family.

The more time I spent with Sachiko, as the winter went on, the more ease and lightness we found together. I knew by now the mischievous glint in her eye whenever I teased her about pachinko parlors, and the speeding grace with which she flung her clothes into drawers as rapidly as she tossed her words into English sentences. I knew by heart now her bright smile and her photogenic grin; the way she'd let out a child's cry of delight—*Haitta!* —every time she sank a ball at pool, and the way she'd whisper, a co-conspirator, as she bent down to stroke the cats we met in the temple. I knew by now the way that, after a single glass of cider, she would careen down the street, arms extended like a plane. When I grew sleepy on a train, she sang me traditional Japanese lullabies, and whenever I thanked her, she'd flash back, with a lilting laugh, "You're welcome!" She made my name new with the inexplicable high softness that she gave to it.

Through Sachiko, I was coming to see more clearly the Japanese way of glee, less famous than their gift for grieving. When I told her one day, after she had been talking and talking, *"Sumimasen. Kekkō desu"* (Thank you very much, I think I've had enough), she burst into peals of such wild laughter at my overformal Japanese that I began laughing too, in embarrassed perplexity. And often, she was so happy that she began, quite literally, to bounce on the soles of her feet. As soon as I began to anatomize her charms, I realized I was falling deeper than I knew.

Usually, though, her main gift was surprise, and when she visited my room one day in early winter, she flung open her bag and brought out one wonder after another: an indigo pot of yellow flowers, wrapped in a bright yellow ribbon; a guitar that she asked me to keep and that, unasked, she began to strum, hair streaming down one side of her face as she belted out the sad folk songs she'd sung to her dying grandmother; and, finally, a brand-new Walkman. Silently, as if performing some ceremony, she handed over to me a second pair of earphones, and once she'd pressed a pink button, I found myself listening to the gruff, romantic tones of Georges Moustaki, crooning, "Ah, je ne suis jamais seul, avec ma solitude . . ."

The irony of listening with her to this classic psalm to solitude was almost too much for me. Sachiko, though, responded less to its meaning than to its gauzy atmosphere.

As soon as the song was over, she solemnly took off the earphones. "When I little high school size, this song my favorite."

"You mean you liked Georges Moustaki when you were sixteen?" With Sachiko, I often sounded foolishly incredulous.

"I like," she nodded smilingly.

"But he's really obscure. The only people I know who listen to him are lovesick seventeen-year-old European girls and English schoolgirls just back from their first romantic summer on the Continent."

"Me too. I listen this song, then much, much dream. When I little high school size, I also many dream. I dream movie star." She enunciated the syllables of a name I could not follow, then burst into a Hindi melody.

"No! Surely you weren't listening to this stuff too?"

"I listen," she insisted, adamant. "True! I many many picture in my room. Indian movie on TV, one week, one time! I meet Indian person in my parents' cigarette shop—they come here, Fushimi Inari Shrine. When I junior high school size, I play princess. Ali Baba and the Forty Thieves!"

Good Lord, I thought: this girl was more cosmopolitan than Isabelle Adjani. The next thing I knew, her eye had fallen on my copy of Antony and Cleopatra, which I was rereading as a handbook to the East, and its ambiguous charms.

"Ah, very beautiful story!"

"You know it?"

"I see movie! Four times! You know Jack Wild?"

"Jack Wild?" I hadn't heard that name in more than a decade. "You mean the teenage boy who played the Artful Dodger in *Oliver!*?"

"Ping-pong," she sang back in the happy affirmative of a TV quiz show ("yes" seemed a word of acquiescence more than of affirmation for the Japanese). "And *Melody* too." I thought back to a film I had seen when I was fifteen, at the same time I was reading *Narziss and Goldmund*, being serenaded by Georges Moustaki, and losing my heart to Olivia Hussey's Juliet. Somehow, I seemed to have more in common with this Kyoto lady, enjoying the same things at the same time, than with most of my contemporaries in England or California.

"Do many Japanese people like Jack Wild?"

"Many, many like," she replied. "I before, Jack Wild Fan Club. I see this man one time in Heian Shrine!"

Egad, I thought, almost ready for anything now, and she bubbled on to express her devotion to Alain Delon and Catherine Deneuve, and her love for Baudelaire. When I asked after Marcello Mastroianni, she nodded with delight.

"What does this mean?" I said, pointing to the red stone in the middle of her comb, with dancing figures all around it.

She sang back the melody of "Over the Rainbow." So then we were off on that subject too, exchanging reminiscences of ancient movies, and she was telling me, excitedly, "When I little children size, only two times my father take me movie. '*Hundred One Dog*' and *War and Peace*. I much love Audrey Hepburn!" (Everyone in Japan seemed to love Audrey Hepburn, for her Japanese demureness and air of gamine innocence.) In some respects, indeed, Sachiko's tastes were strictly programmed by her culture (nearly all Japanese seemed to have cosmopolitan tastes, but nearly always they were the same tastes: Chopin, Baroque music, the Impressionists; Somerset Maugham, O. Henry, and the Beatles. In that sense, they were all somewhat received tastes, as ours are, no doubt, for Mishima or Itami). But Sachiko, as we kept on talking, often broke the rules: she liked

Monet, she said, but preferred Millais; she liked Maugham, but got more out of de Maupassant. She even hotly expressed her love for Hemingway, and Steinbeck's *"Angry Grapes,"* as well as his *"Red and Green"* (I could hardly carp, I thought, if she really had read Stendhal). When it came to names at least, and surface responses, there seemed no limit to her range. Trying to find some weakness in her repertoire, I chided her about her indifference to baseball; she promptly assured me that she did indeed like Sadaharu Oh, the foremost star of the Yomiuri Giants, but was not so fond of his celebrated teammate.

"Nagashima very good player," she pronounced judiciously. "But I think not so good man. He has child's heart. Little same Mozart!"

"Mozart!" For a moment, I was taken aback by a comparison that seemed to owe more to *Amadeus* than to the shadowed Requiem. Then I recovered. "But Mozart's childishness was essential to his art; if he hadn't had that kind of heart, he couldn't have produced such sunny music."

Silently, she accepted this. "He have many dream. And very beautiful life. You know Jung? This man Jung say dream come true. Then I very happy."

I clumsily replied that so far as I knew, Jung was addressing the mysteries of the subconscious more than the whimsical daydreams of rock fans. And Sachiko, listening to her newly pedantic friend, took it all in philosophically. But still I could feel something in me breaking, and it was the sound of certain illusions about Japan.

When next I met Sachiko, outside a temple one frosty morning, the city all tingling and refreshed, I was terribly worn out; I had hardly slept all night for dreams, the worst of them featuring her (transfigured, by strange dream logic, into a beautiful nineteen-year-old cousin of mine in Delhi) arriving at my room one day to find three half-wanted friends there, all of whom refused to leave. After I recounted the dream to Sachiko, who took such portents seriously—Kyoto women, after all, were famous for listening to their dreams ever since the Heian period, and besides, Sachiko's brother had introduced her to the work of various Jungians—she nodded gravely. "I much worry this dream," she said.

Nonetheless, we walked together through lanes bulging with china raccoons, one of them, with impish eyes, dressed in the habit of a nun, and back in my room, I set about helping her through a passage of English, trying to teach her the meanings of "mischievous" and "brave" and "clumsy."

"I not so good study," she said, after stumbling repeatedly over "clumsy." "You think my grammar very bad?"

"Not at all."

"My friend say, she talking phone, foreigner person, her grammar very bad. He not see her, then he think maybe she little black. If I bad grammar, other person think I black?"

"No, no, don't worry," I reassured her.

Sachiko still looked glum, however, her attitude to English summarized in her furrowed brow.

"I not so like study. I little guilt feeling."

I looked up, startled.

"Please don't worry," she said appeasingly. "Other person teach me this word, 'guilt.'" She tried it on again for size.

Just then there came a furious knocking at my door. Who on earth could it be, I thought, visiting me at breakfast time on a freezing winter morning? As soon as I opened up, a familiar figure extended a huge smile and a hand. "Oh, hallo! Awfully good to see you again. Hope I'm not disturbing you. Very good to meet, actually. Very good indeed!" In the last ten years I had seen Matthew only once, and never even heard from him. But now he bundled in as naturally as if he were living down the street.

"Very good timing, actually; awfully nice to see you! Oh, terribly sorry to interrupt," he said, smiling over at Sachiko, and talking in the speeded-up regimental voice that I remembered so well. "Had some friends in Italy, actually, kept telling me about this place Kyoto. Then, few days ago, got your Christmas card. Thought it was a sign, perhaps, a karmic hint. Thought maybe I should come over here and try some high seriousness; austerity and all that. Rio, Bangkok, Italy—all terribly fun, of course, but really what's the point? Thought I might come over here, get some Buddhism. Get back on the spiritual track." He flashed another reassuring smile at Sachiko, and she smiled dumbly back. For as long as I had known him, Matthew had been wandering the globe in search of the perfect place, or the perfect girl, and if ever he found one, he decided he ought to have been looking for the other.

"Very nice city, actually, awfully charming!" he went on, throwing a sheaf of tourist pamphlets onto the tatami and flopping down, with a thump, on a cushion. "Really think this might be the right place for me. Looking for a place to stay, actually, just for a month or two."

"But how long have you been here?"

"Let's see." He looked at his watch. "Ten o'clock now. Got into the Miyako at about eleven, then went round the entertainment quarter, got some bumf from the Tourist Information Center. Not quite myself yet, I suppose." He certainly did seem even more revved up than usual. "Twenty-eight-hour flight, actually. Milano to Zurich. Then Paris. Then Anchorage, and Tokyo. Then Osaka. Took a taxi over here." It sounded like a précis of his life.

"Awfully sorry. Won't be a moment." He smiled warmly over at Sachiko again. "Wonder if I could just ask you a couple of questions?" He scattered the brochures around some more and started frowning over them. Sachiko, meanwhile, looked simply thunderstruck. Then, suddenly remembering his social obligations, he looked up again and began firing questions over at her, causing her to blink furiously and look plaintively over to me for help. Thus the three of us embarked on an utterly unnecessary conversation in which I deftly translated from English into English and then back again.

"Are your parents alive?" he began abruptly.

Sachiko looked over at me, frowning.

"Your parents are in Kyoto?" I tried.

"In Kyoto!" she said, looking over at him with a delighted smile. "Please you meet!"

"Oh yes, yes, love to," laughed Matthew in embarrassment, and then there came another yawning silence.

Now Sachiko attacked the issue at hand. "What country you living?"

"Italy, actually," said Matthew in his telegraphic way. "Living in a hill town—very charming, actually—just north of Milano."

Sachiko looked terrified. "Hill?"

"Yes, yes." Matthew gave her an encouraging smile.

"You live in hill?"

"Not quite. You see . . ."

"But my friend say, Italian man very dangerous. She standing street, man come here. He say, 'Please you come together me, hotel.'"

Matthew looked at me, perplexed.

"She means that her friend got propositioned by a man in Italy."

"Oh yes, yes, quite." Matthew beamed back. "Awfully embarrassing. Must be terribly careful. Very roguish types all round. Can't trust them at all."

Sachiko smiled in incomprehension.

"You very good smell," she assured him. Taken aback, Matthew began sniffing around at his clothes.

"No, no. She means you have a good smile."

"Oh yes, yes, of course," he said, showing off his "smell."

Then, as abruptly as he had appeared, he bounced up and began clambering down the stairs again and wriggling and wiggling his way into his shoes.

At this, Sachiko tried to put the whole uncanny encounter

into words. "You little bad people," she suddenly offered. "I think you little bad!"

"Oh, really? Very true, very true," he said, smiling with his lawyer's politesse and looking at me as if all his worst fears had been confirmed.

"She means that you are the thing with feathers, always flying from one place to the next."

"Oh yes, a bird, quite so! Absolutely right! Couldn't think of a better way of putting it," he burbled, waving cheerfully and bumping into the door as he walked, half backward, down the lane, in search of a place to stay.

Sachiko looked back at me, shaken. "Your dream true!"

Though Matthew still seemed about as steady as a pendulum, there was never any doubting his charm, or the worthiness of his intentions: the only trouble was that his intentions were so varied and so versatile that he never knew which one he was pursuing. His genius for confusion had only been compounded by the fortune he had inherited, tying him up in golden knots. Still I was delighted to see him again, and by the time we met up two days later, he seemed already to have taken the measure of his new home.

"Went to the Philosopher's Path yesterday," he shot out at 78 rpm as we walked, in thick coats, through the coldest Sunday of the year. "Little quaint, don't you think? All these dainty tea shops and pink boutiques? Rather surprised, actually, to see a place called the English House on the road of contemplation!"

"A little twee, perhaps?"

"Exactly! Absolutely! So glad there's someone here who knows exactly what I mean! Rather like some kind of retirement home back in England."

"Well, that's probably a good description of many things here. It's like a retirement home for everyone. Everything's as cozy and comforting as possible, designed to soothe and coddle.

That's partly why the Japanese are so thrown off by foreigners: they don't know how to make us happy."

"My inn, actually, feels rather like a hospital."

"Well, everything's got to be streamlined here, and sterilized," I went on, sententious, after three months here a self-professed Japan hand. "And a customer is always treated to the same rather overpolite solicitude usually accorded a terminal patient."

This did little to raise Matthew's spirits, and as we wandered through the temples along the eastern hills, I watched him get his first taste of what it was like to be a mascot and a superstar: a foreigner in Japan. As we strolled up to the main hall of the head temple of Jōdo Buddhism, an old man bustled up to us and, without introduction, declared haltingly, "I was once in America. Two month," then padded away. ("Funny," said Matthew, "he didn't look very American.") A little farther in, a gaggle of kimonoed girls, hiding their mouths with their hands, asked if they could have their pictures taken with this exotic creature with blue eyes and brown hair, in an expensive Italian coat. When Matthew, ever gallant, extended his hand towards one, four photographers crowded round to record the immortal moment. In Shōren-in, a whole traveling company of middle-aged sightseers hailed us beside a carp pond and had us stand poker-faced with them in a team photo, as proud as if they'd captured a koala and a hippo in the same frame. We played our part in the pantomime with silent acquiescence.

A little later, walking through the temple garden, Matthew suddenly looked up, bewildered. "Is this supposed to be tranquil, or is it meaningful?"

"Well," I said, accustomed to these abrupt gunshots of sincerity, "I think the two are meant to be the same. The only meaning is the quiet you find within."

"Oh yes, yes, of course," he said, correcting himself quickly. "No either/or in Zen."

4

ONE OF THE MOST famous of all Zen stories, sometimes ascribed to Hakuin, tells of the lovely young girl, unmarried though pregnant, who is asked by an angry community to identify the father of her child. Spitefully, she points her finger at an old Zen monk long renowned for his purity. When confronted with the charge, the old monk simply replies, "Is that so?" and accepts responsibility for the child.

Many years pass, and the old monk diligently raises the child as if it were his own. His name is discredited now, his person derided. Then, abruptly, the girl confesses to her parents that she'd lied before—the monk had had nothing to do with her. Mortified, the family rushes to the monk to make amends, and tell him of the terrible error. In response, the monk simply replies, "Is that so?"

As winter deepened, and I continued reading, the theme of the lady and the monk continued to pursue me everywhere, and everywhere I turned, I found new variations on the theme. It was there in Kabuki, in the celebrated legend of Kiyohime, a typical Japanese demon-woman who grows so obsessed with a monk that finally, in her fervor, she turns into a serpent and scourges him. It was there in Nō, in the classic work *Izutsu*, about a monk meeting a woman at a well and the two of them transporting themselves back into the love story that had once unfolded there. It was there in fiction, in Naka Kansuke's novel *Inu*, about a monk renowned for his unbending purity who grows so infatuated with a woman that he becomes demented, turning her into a dog, and himself too; and, again and again, it was there in folklore, as in Lafcadio Hearn's shocking "Force of Karma," about a handsome monk so unsettled by temptation that he throws himself before a train.

That monks could be licentious—a satire on themselves—was hardly surprising or unique; Chaucer had written the book on that for us. And it seemed only natural that the Japanese boulevardiers of the eighteenth century should sing the virtues of tarts in the form reserved for Buddhist parables: prostitutes, after all, were called "singing nuns," and the term *saihō jorō*, or "Shimabara tart," slipped nicely into its complementary opposite, *saihō jōdo*, or Buddhist Pure Land of the West. Sukenobu's *ukiyo-e* picture book *Steeped in the Indigo River* could also be translated as *Sex at the First Encounter*. And a monk's solitary musings on the impermanence of life could easily merge into a woman's lonely complaints about the impermanence of love. If Saikaku's definitive courtesan, the Woman Who Lived for Love, retired into a convent (ambiguously known as the Hermitage of Voluptuousness), and Genji found his ten-year-old playmate in a religious retreat in the mountains, monks were meanwhile scurrying in the opposite direction. As the old slur had it, "Never offer a night's lodging to a holy man unless you want your daughter raped."

What was more surprising, though, was that sometimes the woman's virtue could be stronger than the monk's, that, in a sense, the woman could become an agent of belief and a gateway to a heaven not only seen in earthly terms. In the story of Gyoren Kwannon, a lovely girl, by virtue of her loveliness, entices people to the sutras; and Kawabata's *House of the Sleeping Beauties* was only the most famous example of a story in which girls of easy virtue were taken to be emblems of a higher purity. "Religion is not to go to God by forsaking the world," the monk Sōen Shaku had written, "but by finding him in it."

Mostly, then, the two impulses lay tangled together as a passionate couple, as troublingly intertwined as in the lyrics of Emily Dickinson or Madonna.

> *I fell in love with the Lord Buddha*
> *when I kiss his chill lips sacrilegiously*
> *my heart swoons.*

Belief itself, as in Graham Greene, could be the highest version of romance.

The next time I ran into a gathering of monks was when I went one night into Mark's house, to find Mark himself seated in a corner, deep inside his painting, while the one-pointed Joe was sitting at the wooden table, drinking beer and listening to a tape of a mandolin player from the streets of San Francisco. The screens were all pulled in tight in the early-winter dark, to give a sense of warmth and close enfoldedness (with their sliding screens and panels, Japanese rooms were as malleable as their selves). A kettle was steaming and puffing atop the kerosene heater.

The minute I pulled back the front screen behind me, Joe fixed me with a penetrating stare.

"You know Ted Williams the ballplayer?"

"Sure."

"I read someplace where the reason he could hit so well was he could slow the ball down. His fuckin' concentration, man, it was so good, he could make the ball come slowly. That's what I do when I'm playin' the piano. It goes slow, man, real slow."

"Or chess?"

"Sure. It's like goin' into a trance, man. Only thing is, you gotta do it alone. All movements, man—fuckin' Moonies. I remember this one time, these guys from the temple were doin' *takahatsu*—daily beggin', y'know—outside my window, doing that weird kind of chanting of theirs. It was like seven in the morning, man—on a Sunday!—and I was tryin' to get some sleep. And I was in this tiny old room, with a leak in the ceiling, and I had this bucket of water by my bed. So I picked it up, and I opened the window and ..."

Joe began chuckling, and I braced myself for another strong dose of unorthodoxy. "Those monks, man, they can really put the sake away. Only people drink more than they do are the geisha. On New Year's Eve, man, you just see these senior guys grabbin' some monk and pourin' sake into him till he's spewin' the stuff up. Other times, man, they go, like once a month, on their day off, down to Tōji—you know, the strip joint south of Kyoto Station—and all these girls, they come up to the front of the stage and say, 'Hai dōzo.' Come and get it."

Again I was taken aback, and again I realized that Joe was dispensing Zen wisdom in a purer form than any textbook: the need to slow things down, to speak your mind, to shake up lazy assumptions. Going to the famous Kyoto strip joint was still, after all, known as "going to see Kannon" (the Goddess of Mercy); and Mishima's *Temple of the Golden Pavilion* had largely dealt with Kyoto monks' visits to the red-light district. I was just about to ask Joe something about whiskey priests when Rick, the onetime monk, came in, just returned from San Francisco. Today, for the first time in seven years, he had seen his wife again, his teacher, and his daughter. Now, on his way back from the encounter, he looked overwhelmed, as if the occasion had taken him so deep he could not easily bob back to the surface.

"How was your daughter?"

"Great, just great," he said, a long way off now from *The Tao of Sex*. "She's really pretty." His eyes were shy now, self-denying. "Not, like, model pretty, but she's beautiful to me." He told us how he had talked to her about "Für Elise" and how the two of them had just sat there alone, for the first time in their lives. Later, he said, someone or other had come in and taken a picture of them—"some monk, or the abbot's wife, or someone, I don't know. I was just so moved, I couldn't focus on a thing."

Then, unable to put words to his feelings, Rick picked up his bamboo flute, made for him by his teacher, and played along with the Billie Holliday melodies seeping through the room, summoning all the feelings that he could not voice.

"The only thing you need, man," Joe piped up, as soon as he was finished, no more respectful of his friend's sentiments than of any other doctrine, "is more rests. Like Mozart, man. That guy, man, was a genius, a fuckin' genius. All the music he made was in the pauses. Everything in the symphonies depends on rests. A fuckin' genius, man, and at thirty-six he died, and they put him into the ground and covered him with lime. Death, man, it's a bummer." He looked around at us and chuckled, and, as ever, I felt that what he was getting at was a little less obvious than it seemed. "That's why you gotta have a baby in the house. Baby's a real good thing to have in the house. Like right now, Sammy's nine months old. He's gonna be grown up. So we've got to get a baby in the house." This was the way he operated: to start with some truism and then, like a jazz musician, to work improvisations around it, turning it round and round like a stone, till it began to throw off unexpected lights. "Man, you gotta have a baby in the house. Like my wife—if she wants to go out and hustle all day in the rat race, she can have it! She's welcome to it. I can just stay home and watch my children grow. Makin' money's the least interesting part of life; I'd rather be at home, man, playin' with my kids. You know why? Because a baby, man, he's just seen the light! He's just sittin' there, and he's light! I pat him on the head, and I'm touchin' light. You know *The Tibetan Book of the Dead*? It's all in there. Why babies are light."

"That's also why Shelley used to accost babies in the street," I broke in, "and cross-question them about life in the hereafter. He wanted to get a first-person account of what it was like in heaven."

"Jesus fuck," said Joe, shaking his head and grinning broadly to himself. "I wish I believed that, I really do. I really wish I believed that was true."

And I remembered how the demon Mara, when he was trying to tempt the Buddha, having failed to bring him down with discontent or desire, unleashed his strongest weapon: love.

Whenever I wandered the winter streets alone, though, Kyoto still aroused in me a surge of unaccountable elation: even in winter, the skies were unreasonably blue, and the days had a bright, invigorating chill that seemed to admit of no despair. In Japan, there was truly a sense of a culture calmly on the rise, in possession of itself and buoyant, and the mild air itself felt cleansed of cynicism and decay. Nothing was left to age here (much as the conservation-minded foreigner might have wished there to be); everything felt newly minted as a nickel. Other countries—my trip had reminded me—might seduce or assault or implicate one with the challenge of an outstretched hand; the influence of Japan, by contrast, was soft as a sheet drawn over one's body.

I knew, of course, that it was dangerously easy for a foreigner, who enjoyed a kind of *carte blanche* in living outside the system, to endorse a world in which men dragged themselves off from 6 a.m. to 11 p.m. six days a week, while women were condemned to a kind of emotional exile. I knew, too, that the lightness of being here could be unbearable—an evasion or a denial—and that Japan's optimism was willed, sometimes, or no deeper than its sugar-coated surfaces, its pink-ribboned girls quite literally trying to make their eyes as wide as possible. (When she asked her students to find three adjectives to describe themselves, a longtime foreign teacher told me, she had had to ban the use of "cheerful," or else every girl in class would use it.)

Yet still, I thought, it took a certain courage to be positive, and it was always easier to negate than to affirm. The fact that they had been trained always to see the good, and to expect the same in others, might make the Japanese vulnerable abroad, but at home it worked as a kind of self-fulfilling prophecy. And the smiles might be all artifice, but better false smiles, I thought, on the level of daily routine, than honest rudeness. Within its strict limits, and on paper at least, the Japanese seemed to have created a kind of child's utopia of clean surfaces and safe pleasures. One reason Kyoto took me back to England was that it took me back to childhood, and to its sense of protected calm.

My one problem, in fact, with Japan was that it sometimes seemed so free of problems. That was one reason, I often thought, why these people, so famously considerate in the domestic realm, appeared so notoriously indifferent to refugees, or war victims, or to the demands of the world at large. In its way, Japan had constructed such an orderly, friction-free society that its young, at least, free of the Occupation, could not easily grasp the details of a world of pain and privation — the real world, in short. Human rights and suffering made little sense in this shiny, wound-up society where both were either taken for granted or denied (even the beggars here seemed mannerly and sane, while cripples were ritually shipped off, in many cases, to the Philippines). This removal from all pain gave Japan at times the air of a wealthy, well-intentioned dowager, alone in the comfort of her home, and responding, without malice, to stories of need elsewhere with an airy "Let them eat cake!"

Besides, pretense could have its virtues. I thought back to the line in the Singer story "A Piece of Advice" I had read a few months before: "If you are not happy, act the happy man. Happiness will come later. If you are in despair, act as though you believe. Faith will come afterwards." Certainly, belief in the virtue of Japan could be as self-validating as any other leap of faith; egotism itself almost seemed collective here. And only a little later, when I returned to Kenkō, the fourteenth-century monk who wrote with a duchess's fastidiousness, I found again the perfect defense of pretense. "If you run through the streets saying you imitate a lunatic," wrote the monk, "you are in fact a lunatic. If you kill a man saying you imitate a criminal, you are a criminal yourself. By the same token, a horse that imitates a champion thoroughbred may be classed as a thoroughbred, and the man who imitates Shun belongs to Shun's company. A man who studies wisdom, even insincerely, should be called wise." And, I thought, a society that keeps telling itself it's unified is on the way at least to being what it says.

5

ONE DAY a little later, the phone in my guesthouse trilled, and I happened to be the one to pick it up. *"Moshi-moshi."* *"Moshi-moshi?"* *"Hai! Moshi-moshi."* Through the inevitable tangle of *Moshi-moshi*s that followed, I could make out a flustered middle-aged female voice. *"Moshi-moshi?"* *"Hai, hai, moshi-moshi,"* I replied, and then she started up again, in English. "My name is Tsukimoto. I want foreigner person for job. . . ."

"No," I replied with careful patience, accustomed by now to such requests. "I do not want to teach English. But there may be other people in this house who do."

"No, no," she said. "Movie. We need character in movie. We need foreigner character. Why *you* not come along? We give you three thousand yen, interview fee."

Twenty-five dollars, I thought: that would be the first yen I ever earned. "What kind of movie?"

"GI. Occupation movie. Why you not come? Three thousand yen for one hour."

Two days later, I arrived, as arranged, at the Takashimaya department store downtown. Tsukimoto's face, when she saw me, was not a picture of joy: apparently the *gaijin* who sounded so English on the phone was in fact a small and scrawny Indian. Loss of face seemed imminent.

Nonetheless, she took me in with harried stoicism and, gathering together a circle of twelve specimens of foreign manhood, bustled us all into a fleet of waiting taxis. Twenty minutes later, our convoy pulled into Eigamura — Movie Village — the Universal Studios of Japan. A little man hurried up to us and led our ragtag group into a dingy little room, Tsukimoto bustling along behind. In her wake came a clutch of harassed-looking teenage assistants and the director, a smoothly grinning dandy in bomber jacket, muffler, and Yves Saint Laurent glasses.

The picture of worldly urbanity, thick gray hair flopping over designer glasses, he let a few words escape through his ingratiating smile. There was silence. Tsukimoto stared at him in terror. There was more silence.

"He said the movie's name is *Nikutai-no Mon,*" a shy sociology student from New Zealand finally piped up. "That means 'Gate of Flesh.'"

The director purred a little more.

Looking around at the blank faces, the New Zealander gamely took the bit between his teeth. "Apparently, the film is about the Americans in Japan after World War II," he continued, mumbling under his spectacles, locks of brown hair falling across his face. "It features GIs, prostitutes, *yakuza.*" The director fired out a few more mellifluous sentences. The New Zealander, looking down at the table, condemned now to translate, gamely soldiered on. "Some of it is very brutal. It will require people to get hit very hard." The director, smiling all round, rattled off some more. "Also, it does not portray Americans in a very favorable light. If that bothers you, please say so. And"—the poor shy fellow was now muttering through his hair in embarrassment—"there will be some carnal scenes."

There were titters all round.

This was too much for Tsukimoto. Firmly stepping forward, she handed out a few sheets of paper to a handful of foreign men—the largest in the room—and asked them each to read out the first sentence. One after another, the foreigners intoned the opening line: "From border to border, from coast to coast, here comes the Happy Cowboy!"

"Wait a minute," someone cried. "Japan has no borders!"

"Maybe 'From island to island, from coast to coast,' would be better?"

"No. The thing doesn't make sense anyway. Who in hell's the Happy Cowboy when he's at home?"

At this point, Tsukimoto quickly interceded once again.

"Please stand up!" she barked, sensing that things were not going well. "You must be seventy inches high!"

All of us got up, and I cast an eye over my rivals: an aging Brit, who had recently starred in another sexploitation movie, thanks to an earlier Tsukimoto casting call; a phlegmatic, *tanuki*-bellied Israeli with a walrus mustache and a look of deepest sorrow; a sour, balding American in a green down jacket, who looked like a graduate student on his way to the stacks; an improbably beautiful blond German in a leather jacket, who resembled a West Hollywood waiter; and a six-foot-four-inch Larry Bird look-alike from Lafayette, Indiana, whose main qualification for becoming an English teacher in Japan had been selling Dove Bars outside Trump Tower. There were short *gaijin*, fat *gaijin*, tall *gaijin*; thin *gaijin*, dark *gaijin*, squat *gaijin*. Every kind of *gaijin*, in fact, except the type likely to belong to the Eighty-second Airborne.

As Tsukimoto anxiously surveyed the talent before her, questions began to fly.

"What kind of picture is this?" "What sort of person do you need?" "What scenes will we get to do?"

"Well," said the New Zealander—now, unwittingly, the official spokesman for the film-makers—"he did say it was pretty brutal!"

"Yes, yes," said Tsukimoto excitedly. "We need man for lape."

There was a startled silence.

"Yes, yes, we need lape scene. Very important lape."

Several comments, few of them pious, escaped from the thirteen assembled males.

"We don't know how to rape—Japanese girls are so willing," smirked a handsome Austrian in a brown leather jacket. "If you want a rapist, look no further," cooed a South American. "How are you going to measure us up?" "Don't worry about that!

You're not going to get to do the rape. You're going to get to *be* raped!"

Again the flustered Tsukimoto burst in.

"You have experience?" she said, earnestly turning on a small, round New Yorker well known in Kyoto as a serious student of *kyōgen* drama. "You have done before?"

"Experience as a rapist?"

"Yes, yes. Lape scene need lape experience. Very important."

At that, the director clearly tired of the whole song-and-dance routine and pointed a brisk finger at the five men in the room with beards and three others who were plump. The lucky eight were led off to a separate room to demonstrate their skills as rapists, and the rest of us were left, as it were, on the cutting-room floor.

Tsukimoto, however, was eager to give solace. "They have bad-side atmosphere," she told us kindly. "Very bad-side. They look like lape men."

This was not altogether reassuring. I was sorely tempted to confess to Tsukimoto that I did in fact have just the kind of experience she wanted: my only other major motion picture role had featured an unhappy impersonation of a Mexican military cadet in a tragically overlooked horror movie, *Evilspeak*, about a trio of wild boars that attack naked girls in the shower while the former child star of *Gentle Ben* networks with the devil on his computer. My auditioners then had been a pair of bikinied Californians whom memory conveniently recalled as Cindy and Candy, and who stretched themselves out on poolside deck chairs and languorously fingered anyone willing to get a military-length haircut.

Before I could make this known to my employer, however, the would-be rapists were led back in again, the Pyrrhic winner the paunchy *kyōgen* actor, now looking more than a little molested himself. "I guess I just looked the scuzziest," he averred modestly as the runners-up barreled in, slapping him on the shoulder like Miss Universe contestants in reverse. "I don't know how my wife and her family are going to take this!"

Tsukimoto, however, was in no mood for small talk. "This lape we need very badly," she assured us once more. "Lape very important with this movie."

A little later, in the taxis heading home, as people began to discuss the hazards of trying to simulate rape, even for $250 a day, the New Zealander turned his sociologist's eye on the experience. "That's the way it is with movies here," he began, earnest as a lecturer already. "All their B movies are set in the Occupation, and they always have the GIs as these hulking murderers and rapists. That's the way it always is." (Just as American movies filmed in Japan, I thought, always involve the *yakuza*.) "But I suppose it does make a certain kind of sense. A lot of the foreigners here, they aren't here to do any teaching. They just like to fool around." He was hitting his stride now. "Like I know this one guy who rides every day on this special train full of college girls waiting to be picked up. And this other one who goes to discos all the time and kept up four girls at a time—until he got the clap. And I heard about this one bloke from Zaire—you know, black, really scary and fascinating to these people—who had them lined up outside his door and took care of six of them a day. At first when you come here, your ego gets a real massage. Then you realize that they're just saying the same thing to everyone. It's a dangerous psychology."

Certainly, I could see by now how the Land of the Rising Sun could be the ruin of many a poor boy—not least because being taken as an exotic, or a demigod, was one of the hardest states to abandon.

The movie call, however, had a particular aptness for me. For often, with Sachiko, I felt as if I were responding to a similar kind of summons, auditioning to play the part of a freewheeling foreigner in the long-running romantic picture she'd been screening in her mind. Often, in fact, I got the sense that she was trying to squeeze out of our times together every last pretty or haunting image she'd ever taken in from movies or songs or ballets, as if this were her first, and perhaps last, chance to experience all the sensations that she'd always heard about. Marriage she clearly regarded as a businesslike proposition—a matter of domestic deals and daily accounts in which emotions were as irrelevant as love songs in a résumé; now, though, suddenly, she had a chance to walk across a bridge of dreams, as the Heian courtiers had it, and find all the sensations she kept so neatly in her head, of "First Love" and "True Love" and even "Lost Love." Sachiko, like many Japanese perhaps, was an uppercase Romantic, with an innocence that idealized experience and turned it into a reflection of itself.

No less than her words, then, her gestures summoned all the props of high and courtly romance: the hankie smothered with perfume that she gave me to keep in my pocket, the love songs with which she serenaded me, her constant plea to make contact with her by looking at the moon. And already, I could tell, she was developing her inner photographs, turning our times together into pretty, plaintive images—*memento amori*—that she could look back on as a trip to a foreign country. Sometimes she seemed almost to be inspecting her feelings like an enraptured tourist, never troubled by a sense that "perfect" and "true" need be incompatible.

Thus every aspect of our friendship was efficiently made to correspond to something from her pool of dream images, rather like the New Year's game in which people matched the opening of ancient poems with the close. One weekend she went with her family to Nagasaki, and came back excitedly telling me how she had seen there Rembrandt's "Face of Christ." "This picture little same you eye!" she announced. I had hardly had time to savor this rare compliment, however, before she was also telling me that the raccoons in the zoo had my eye too (and, presumably, that of Christ). My voice, she said, was "little same Michael Jackson," and my spirit, "little Baryshnikov feeling." Whatever face I presented she managed to match with some counterpart in her anthology of ready-made images—mysterious Indian, history-steeped Brit, fun-loving Californian, romantic loner, wandering writer, sometime monk. Partly, I could see, this was just a way of crossing the language, and the culture, gap, finding a common frame of reference, and partly, too, a reflection of the fact that we were obliged to speak in metaphors and images (and she variously represented me as a penguin, a bear, an owl, a raccoon, and a mole—she, too, it seemed, knew more animal words than adjectives). Partly, perhaps, she could only apprehend a foreigner—and romance—through the imported images she'd consumed, just as I could see her only through the keyhole of ancient Japanese love poems. But partly, too, I could see, with a pang, how keen she was to remove our lives from the everyday world, to lift them to some timeless, fairy-tale realm, immutable, imperishable, and immune from unhappy realities. Realism was reserved for what she did at home (where she wore different clothes, spoke a different language, and used a different voice); our time was "dream time."

Thus boundaries began to blur, and the fact that our friendship was described in terms of movies led her more and more to see movies as a reflection of our friendship. The first time I took her to the cinema, to see the Ken Russell extravaganza *Mahler*, she filed out of the auditorium in tears. "This movie little same you-me feeling," she said, too deeply affected, almost, to speak. Insofar as Mahler had, as I had seen it, been portrayed as a cruel and egotistical tyrant given only to abuse of his women, this was not, I thought, a happy parallel. But Sachiko, true to her vision, had somehow succeeded in screening out all the negativity and taking away nothing but reassurances. "First time, I many, many movie understand," she whispered, awestruck.

And sure enough, when she saw *Out of Africa*, she found it so close a reflection of our relationship that she was moved to tears too. *9½ Weeks* made her think of our "cherry blossom love." Even *Fright Night* left her stunned. "I little see this movie," she whispered to me, breathless, "I think of you." I began to hope she'd never see *In the Realm of the Senses*.

Songs, too, were a receptacle for all the powerful emotions she had never had the chance to experience in real life, and after every other one, I found her in tears. When I played her Springsteen's "Independence Day," I was touched and pleased to see that she was all choked up when it finished, a reflection, I thought, of how closely she identified with its character's yearning for freedom, and an escape from the cycles in which his parents were trapped; my pleasure was dimmed a little, however, when I saw that Aerosmith also moved her to tears, and Michael Jackson's synthetic version of "I Can't Stop Loving You." Her feelings were so strong, and her opportunities for releasing them so limited, that they came out in torrents, poured into the unlikeliest of vessels. One of them was me.

In the midst of winter, I accompanied her one chilly night to Osaka to see Bryan Adams in concert. The minute he came out on stage, Sachiko began dancing, and so she continued, eyes flashing, smile unfailing, through song after song after hard-driving song, her energy never flagging. When Adams took a brief break, she turned to me and suddenly recited an unearthly poem from the *Manyōshū*, the famous eighth-century anthology of lyrics; eyes shining, with a lingering intensity whose depth I could not fathom, she told me that she now knew all the delicate sadness of a lovesick maiden at her window. Then, when the concert ended, and we streamed out amidst packs of cheerful teenage girls, she suddenly, in a rush of exhilaration, burst into the choral section of Beethoven's Ninth Symphony, in Japanese, as we headed off for dinner at the nearest Dunkin' Donuts.

Occasionally, I could see, the transposition of the movie world and reality played havoc with her mind. When, a little later, she saw *Another Country* on TV (a great favorite in Japan, thanks to its endless shots of pretty young English boys swapping daisies and sonnets against a backdrop of quaint historical buildings), she rang me up in a frenzy of confusion.

"This your high school?"

"Yes," I said.

"Then you little spy man? My mother say maybe you spy."

"No, no, Sachiko, I'm not a spy."

"And you not gay?"

"Gay?"

"Then why you go this gay school? Why you not same *Stand by Me*?"

I'm sorry, I felt like saying; not all of us can come to maturity in Steven Spielberg's imagination.

Usually, though, her wish for seeing our lives as gauzy art, a permanent monument to evanescence, made for scenes as artfully composed as postcards, and dreamy, gentle Sachiko was as expert at spinning dream images as at producing gift-wrapped memories: she, looking over the Kamo River, eyes shining in the dark; she, in plum kimono, plucking the koto in front of billowing curtains; she, holding her breath and closing her eyes tight as she stood before the Buddha. Coming to Japan in search of romance, I found myself now a protagonist in someone else's dream, and found, too, that the favor was returned.

"This dream?" she often said, and the only answer I could find was yes.

6

ONE DAY, thrilled to learn that the fabled Shigeyamas, the first family of *kyōgen* comedy, were bringing a whole program based upon raccoons to town, I bought two tickets and dragged poor Matthew off to inspect this curious spectacle. Ready to try anything in his quest for he did not know what, Matthew had already started attending aerobics classes with Sachiko, flopping up and down amidst rows of grinning, fiendishly energetic housewives; accepted an offer from the matronly owner of his inn to accompany her on a pilgrimage to Tokyo Disneyland; and sat through an eight-hour session of Sumō.

None of this, though, has prepared him for a raccoon theatrical festival. Soon after we take our seats, I, in the spirit of a West End theatergoer, bundle off to purchase a bag of Green Tea candy. Inside is a sachet full of blue and white micromarbles, designed to keep the candy fresh. Matthew, however, is not accustomed to such tricks of Japanese ingenuity. He peers down dubiously at the bag. "Sugar, do you think, perhaps?" he begins, breaking open the bag and shaking a few of the baubles into his hand. "Some kind of exotic confectionery?" he goes on, tossing them all into his mouth and beginning to crunch appreciatively. "Very strange, actually," comes his first report. "No taste at all. Really rather strange. Can't taste a thing!" He tries to bite into one. "Awfully strange! Must be glass!"

In a flourish of fellow feeling, I, too, pop a few of the marbles into my mouth. Matthew is right: there is no taste. They are, in fact, without a shadow of a doubt, glass. I spit them out. Matthew, however, continues chewing, as serene as a cow in pasture.

On stage, a curtain is rising on a striking blue-and-golden lacquer set, five musicians sitting stock-still, in indigo and gray. One of them begins a piercing, dissonant melody on a flute. The others pound drums. An old man walks onto the stage and goes through a strange, slow dance, flinging his sleeved arms out like wings and emitting occasional strangled grunts. We sit back in gloom: the whole thing, clearly — and understandably — is to be in Japanese.

Next to us, two schoolchildren crane forward with the attentiveness of critics, recording the pathos on a Sony. The unearthly sounds continue, redolent, to our philistine ears, of nothing but John Cleese.

Then, like an Indian raga, the invocation suddenly gains momentum, picks up speed, gathers an almost mesmerizing intensity — and is over. We sit back exhausted, and to celebrate our release, purchase two ice creams from an aisle-patrolling lady while Matthew looks about.

He is still muttering something earnest about George Romero's *Night of the Living Dead* when the curtain ascends once more, and, the lights still on, we watch a raccoon masquerade as a teakettle.

"Very primitive," Matthew shoots out in a staccato whisper, settling back in his seat with a copy of *What's on in Kyoto.* "Very strange."

Then, of a sudden, he sits up sharply. "Think it is glass, actually! Can feel it in my throat! Rather bizarre, actually!" The comedy on stage has nothing on this.

Meanwhile, the audience breaks into uncontrollable hysteria as a servant is surprised by the kettle-impersonating raccoon. Matthew is looking less and less enraptured. Then "The Miraculous Teakettle" gives way to "The *Tanuki*'s Belly Drum" and a classic fairy tale of a raccoon dressed as a nun trying to outfox a hunter by delivering a sermon on the iniquity of taking the life of any sentient being. Matthew looks positively sick by now. Then at last the *tanuki* passes round a bottle of sake and brings all the loose ends together in a cheerful, transformative dance.

Matthew looks over unhappily. "Childlike, don't you think? Terribly immature, really."

"Maybe. But just imagine a typical Japanese businessman going to the theater in London and ending up at *No Sex Please, We're British* or a Christmas pantomime—especially if he can't speak English. Not really very different." As the instigator of this expedition, perhaps, I have good reason to defend what really feels like a reproach to dilettantishness and a reminder of just how culture-bound we are.

Afterwards, less than satisfied by the entertainment so far, Matthew expresses his keenness to sample Kyoto's nightlife. I, having always assumed this to be a closed shop, know nowhere to go except the prescribed foreigner's haunts. At a noisy dive called the Earth Bar, we munch on cucumbers in plum sauce, cold Korean tofu, and white mushrooms cooked in butter, while drunken laughter and reggae music rise up from along the crowded wooden benches on which sit jostling multicultural couples. On a blackboard, obscene graffiti has been scrawled—to import an air of foreign aggressiveness, perhaps—demeaning Jesus with various four-letter words and culminating in the unexpected declaration: "Get your shit together: everybody must get stoned." In a culture where exactly 6.1 ounces of cocaine was confiscated in all of 1988 and swear words are famously nonexistent, this strikes me as a curious motto.

Matthew looks up and down the smoke-filled room mournfully, then tells me what is bothering him.

"It's not that one has to understand other people," he begins plaintively, "but one does want to be understood. I'm fascinated by the Japanese. But I have the feeling they're not at all fascinated by me."

"I think they're just shy, or afraid, or too embarrassed to express themselves in a language whose codes they haven't mastered," I opine. "It's just as if you were to run into Bruce

Springsteen or Robert De Niro in a restaurant; you might be too shy to go up to them. And even if you did, you might not know what to say. They seem to belong to another realm."

"Yes, yes," he says impatiently. "But where are all the girls who idolize Sting and ought to see that I'm the closest they'll ever get to him?"

"All around. You just don't recognize them because you're looking too hard."

"But somehow the charm doesn't work here. In Brazil, in Italy, in Thailand, I never had any trouble meeting people. But this place is like another planet. I mean, people stare at me in the street as if I were a kind of animal." He looks puzzled, and my heart goes out to him. "Actually, I suppose it's all rather good. Awfully good, actually. Terribly liberating." He doesn't sound convinced.

"But why should they want to be friends, Matthew? Why should they make the effort to cross the culture gap? It's not as if we have that much to offer them, scarcely speaking their language and ignorant of their culture. When I'm at home, I certainly don't go out of my way to befriend the Hmong, say, or the Japanese, especially if they can't even speak my language."

"Yes, yes, suppose you're right," he says, gloomier than ever.

"Remember, too," I go on remorselessly, "that we're seeing them in the one context—speaking English—where they're liable to seem most ungraceful and ill at ease. And yet we bridle when they mock—or even when they compliment—our Japanese. Complaining that Japan is closed seems as beside the point as a Japanese complaining that America is open."

"I know," he continues sadly. "But I still feel like the man who fell to earth."

Outside again, we thread our way across quiet canals in the dark, the winter silence broken only by the cracked importunities of husky streetwalkers with the voices of old men. Around us, amidst the reeling neon, hostesses in tight makeup and cocktail dresses are wriggling out of the entrances of clubs, bowing their customers into taxis, arranged like nodding dolls on the sidewalk. Weaving through the water-world, Matthew suddenly looms up before a gaggle of startled-faced girls. "Hallo! Any of you interested in a Merchant Taylors' man?" Often, I think, it is his genuine charm that makes his unacknowledged sadness all the deeper.

In Pub Africa, a kind of social club for the foreign dispossessed, five or six lonely *gaijin* men are seated around a semicircular table in front of a giant video screen, munching tiny pizzas. In booths around the darkened room, clutches of Japanese girls, maybe three or four in every giggling party, nervously look around them, drinking in the air of foreign danger and looking up occasionally to where Suzanne Vega is sitting on a video-jukebox stoop, singing about child abuse. Unable to catch the Japanese, I hear only the usual litanies of *gaijin* talk. "The Japanese are really obsessed with keeping themselves apart! Hypocritical bastards!" "My students are really a pain! They're just too damned shy to speak English!" "I can't believe how narrow these people are, how superficial!" On and on go the conversations—condolences in disguise—delivered, I think, with something of the overwrought intensity of a teenager spurned, trying and trying to understand why the object of his affection won't return it and replaying all their arguments in his head ("She said I didn't talk. But I did talk. Look at her! And why all the time . . . "). "You know the Japanese word for 'different' is the same as their word for 'wrong'?" I hear someone say. Does that mean that the Japanese are wrong? I wonder. Just because they're different? Sometimes the fabled ethnocentrism of Japan seems more than matched by that of many foreigners in Japan.

As we stuff coins into the jukebox, pressing numbers so haphazardly that, suddenly, a Japanese teen idol appears on the screen before us, Parker, a friendly Southern boy from my guesthouse, appears at our side. "I need a girlfriend," he begins, after shaking hands with Matthew. "I just broke off. I had a Japanese girlfriend for two months, then I found out that she'd had a boyfriend all the time." Determined to find a partner in

Japan, Parker has effectively ensured that he can never find one; his insistent trying seems only to confound itself, and the girls he does meet see only a man in search of girls. Thus he ends up like a kitten with a ball of string; the more he tries to untangle himself, the more tied up he becomes.

As Parker heads off into the night, an Australian hippie, shaking his long, heavy-metal hair out of his granny-glassed eyes, leans back in his chair and extends a hand to Matthew. "Scuse me, mate. I'm Brad. Just got here, and I'm lost. All my ideas of the place were erased as soon as I got off the airplane." "If you look for anything here," declares Matthew, wise now after a couple of weeks, "you won't find it. But if you don't look for it, you'll find it. Somewhat paradoxical, I suppose."

With that, we dutifully proceed on our hegira, passing strip clubs, sake bars, and weeping willows, peering in on a "live house" (with a "Snobbery Connection" badge on its window), where four boys in pink tuxedoes and black bow ties are singing "La Bamba" in the original. The main other spot on the *gaijin* map—the only other night stop more or less colonized by aliens—is Rub-a-Dub, a wall-to-wall reggae joint that encourages cross-cultural communication by squeezing people into so small a space that they are obliged to sit in one another's laps. This is too much for Matthew, though, who now feels let down by both traditional Japanese culture and the foreign imports. By now, he's getting desperate.

Finally, we find ourselves in front of a glittering eight-story building along the canal, as slim and elegant as a giant Parker pen in the Kyoto night. Lights wink and glitter up and down the spine of the Imagium, a pleasure dome situated somewhere east of *Blade Runner* in the year 2040. Outside the glowing block is a board of shiny panels advertising the names of the boîtes inside this sybarite's Tomorrowland.

"Which shall we try?" asks Matthew, determined to break through Kyoto's panels of glass screens.

"Well, I don't think one can really go to any," I offer timidly.

"It's not like Thailand here." Above us, the building towers, enigmatic and reproachful as the mysterious block in 2001. "Most of these places are Members Clubs, and the ones that aren't are by invitation only. They're virtually closed to foreigners."

"Oh no, not at all," he says, and off we go. Up and up and up the silent elevator glides, through the winter night, up to the very peak of the thin wall of lights, and then it begins to come down, one floor at a time. At each stop we peer out into some postmodernist dream chamber: Hip to Be True, Nostalgia Space Was, the Pleaisure Dome. Finally, at a "café club" called Is It a Crime?, we step out into a dark chamber done up in soft indigo and sapphire neon. Inside, in the funeral hush of some rich gangster's nightspot, an unnaturally pretty girl in a slim white dress to offset her long black hair leads us, bowing, into the club. Within, four waitresses, all in black or white, are arranged next to pillars like counters in Go. One of them steps forward and leads us to a small round table, black-and-white chopsticks placed atop a black marble surface. Behind the bar, three more color-coordinated girls, long black tresses against sheer white dresses, strike fashion-model poses, showing off their profiles. One of them shakes up a drink, white arms flashing teasingly above the sleek black counter. A girl in black stands against a pillar, ramrod straight and motionless; across from her, another unmoving girl, all in white. Men in expensive dark suits sit beside the cash register, whispering.

Matthew turns his Milano eyes around the darkened room, one silent capsule of blinding white and black. "No good at all," he pronounces. "It'd look terrible in the daytime. All *maya*, really, all an illusion. Just animated mannequins."

"Animated?"

"Yes! Like in a cartoon! All here to impress. No heart. Just for show! What time is it?"

I look at my watch and realize that here, on my first night inside the circles of the pleasure quarter, I have swallowed a kind of lethe; the night feels as weightless as some Armani ad.

The Japanese seem to use their dreams less as stimulants than tranquilizers; like the death chambers in *Soylent Green,* almost — convenient, soundproofed ways to ease oneself away from time and space.

The girls in black and white rearrange themselves, their dresses knotted loosely in the back.

"Do you think we should get the bill?" Matthew says at last, another vision closed to him. A girl delicately lays the paper on the table, and he consults it with horror: two glasses of iced oolong tea — more ice than tea — cost thirty-five dollars. "Is it a crime?" he huffs. "Yes!" The beautiful hostess in white bows winningly and presses the elevator button for us. Then, as the door closes, she bows again, very deeply, and the hushed style sample disappears from view.

7

ONE DAY I got a call from Sachiko, even more breathless than usual.

"You know passport?" she gasped at the other end.

"Yes."

"I have!" she exclaimed. "I get. Husband not know."

"Your first time?"

"First time passport!" she announced. "I little go office, Osaka. Then many many question answer. Now I have! Please I show you!"

"Yes, please. *Demo ima tottemo isogashii desu.*"

"*Ima* now? You little busy?"

"*Hai!* Yes! Why? Are you free now?"

"*Tabun* maybe."

"*Demo* today is very beautiful day."

"*Tabun* maybe." Our conversations, as ever, were strange affairs, shards of different languages flung across distances we couldn't gauge.

A few hours later, though, with a speed and efficiency I was coming to see as characteristic, Sachiko arrived at my room, proudly bearing her new possession, very likely the first Japanese passport she'd ever seen, let alone owned. And already—for between the intention and the action there fell no shadow here—she was working on a larger plan.

"I much reading newspaper. Then maybe I little try tour-conductor course, Osaka! I not so strong, maybe little difficult. But I want try. I want little wing."

"You'll go to Osaka every day?"

"One week, two times! Maybe I go five o'clock, come back ten o'clock."

"And what about your children?"

"I find baby-sitter. Many, many baby-sitter. I not want mother know. If know, biggg problem!"

Before, when she had said, "I little jealous, you job," I had thought, in my vanity, that she resented my work for keeping me away from her; only now did I realize that what she had really meant was that she, too, wanted a job, and a self of her own. Looking over at her bright-eyed resolve, I could not help but wish to cheer her on.

"Usual Japanese person believe, *akirameru* life better," she went on. "You know this word?"

I flipped through my tiny dictionary and found it: "resignation."

"But I not so want this life. I want dream! My mother all life very lonely," she went on. "My father very good man, but not so good husband. Always tired. Sometimes little angry. They not so close feeling. I not want this same, my mother's life." Her mother, I inferred, had been obliged to fill up her emotional life with poems and temples and flowers, and it was precisely the absence of any real companionship that had made her so close to her daughter and, in a sense, so dependent on her. Now, I imagined, it would not be easy for her to watch her daughter seeking out the freedom that she herself had always lacked — and, in the process, depriving her of her only confidante.

"But, Sachiko, this will be very difficult."

"I know." She smiled back with determination. "But I little thinking *Gone With the Wind*. You know last scene? Tomorrow bring new world. I little hoping my life same."

That afternoon, she asked me to go with her to Osaka to visit the office where she would be taking her classes. As we chugged along through mile after mile of factories and featureless suburban housing, she gradually turned more philosophical.

"All life," she began, looking out the window at the offices, "I think, woman very weak."

"But in Japan, don't you think that the women are often stronger than the men?"

She nodded gravely. "They must! If not so strong, then little big problem! But woman try man's life, very difficult. Woman very lonely life—only thinking—very difficult. Woman need Nature!"

As usual, I had no idea whether she meant this in some spiritual or elemental sense—that women were in constant touch with moon and tides and cycles of the earth—or whether it was a more social meaning she intended (that in this perfectly organized society of distribution of labor, their job was to raise children and nurture the men who were money-earning boys). Yet still I could catch her mood, even when the meaning vanished.

Then, ruminative once more, she went on, "Man world, woman world, very different. Woman live in feeling world, man in reason world." This was standard enough. "Man do baby-making ceremony, body only, very easy. Woman have two part: body and heart." All this, I thought, was not so unusual. But then, as ever, she took me by surprise. "Man go away, woman heart very easy. But body much much miss him."

"Wait," I said. "You mean the other way round? Body adjusts, but heart misses him?"

She shook her head firmly. "Heart no problem! Heart have many memory. But body much need him."

This in itself I had not expected, though the notion that memory could appease the mind was familiar to me from every classic Japanese love poem I had ever read. Then she extended her metaphor to Japan. "I think all Japan two side: one very strong side, man side. Like Emperor. Many thing happen, he do nothing. You know *Bushidō*? Little *samurai* feeling! Other part, woman heart, see many thing, but little fragile. Not so strong. Very sad." Stoicism and sensitivity, I thought; self-discipline and self-pity. That might almost be the warp and woof of this practical, lyrical land of down-to-earth aesthetes and self-denying pleasure-lovers.

Arriving in Osaka, we walked among the early plum blossoms and, in the brooding shadow of Osaka Castle, wandered through a long avenue of pink and white flowering trees, chilled by the stiff February breeze. She stood stock-still and closed her eyes, imprinting the memory on her mind. By now, I was coming to know the alphabet of Sachiko's smallest gestures: the way she'd whisper, as if in church, "Thank you very much, give me dream"; the way she'd turn down her eyes at moments that moved her, demure as a medieval maiden; the air of transported breathlessness that made her greet each moment like an explorer coming for the first time on the Taj Mahal.

"Japanese person say, *hidamari,*" she explained, pointing to a small patch of sunlight along the otherwise cold stone of a nearby shrine. In the dark of the Kyoto winter, Sachiko was my *hidamari.*

One cold, bright Sunday in early February, I awoke in the chill blue dawn, flakes of snow swirling across the sky in drifts, and, breath condensing, hurried across town to the chilly silence of Tōfukuji. Sachiko had offered to take me to one of the *rōshi*'s early-morning *zazen* sessions for the public — the Buddhist equivalent of a Sunday service — and by seven o'clock on this freezing morning, I found myself in a large, spotless hall, with perhaps fifty other people, all but Sachiko and myself elderly patrons of the temple. Four monks, baleful in black robes, stood silent sentry at the far end of the room, holding wooden sticks upright above their shoulders. All of us were instructed to take off our watches. Then there was absolute silence. Nothing but the early singing of the birds.

For a while, as the *zazen* began, I entered the darkness and felt cleansed. Time and space and self were lost. Then, inevitably, the monkey mind began to frolic. Eyes still shut, I heard the almost silent padding of the monks, as they trod on patrol, step by step, down the line. Occasionally, the silence was cracked by the sound of a stick thwacking some sluggard—two sharp, swift blows on one side, two more on the other. Soon, the sound of hits took on a regular beat. I held my breath as if to disappear when I heard the footsteps approach; then, as they receded, I relaxed again, my mind still full of unsolicited distractions.

Half opening my eye—a child playing hooky—I saw old people in their seventies bowing before the policing monks, asking to be cudgeled. The monk stepped before them with his stave. Then the miscreant laid his head on the ground, right hand clutching his chest to prevent his shoulder from being separated. The stick rang down on him. Then, changing hands, the meditator exposed the other shoulder and was whacked again. He bowed his gratitude, and the monk moved on, feet lobster red in the February cold.

As the minutes seeped on, meandering and ponderous, I felt my sense of stillness intensifying, as if I were gaining weight and depth; but then again my mind began to buzz like a cicada-crowded glade, with thoughts, recollections, plans, worries about punishment, anxieties over the form, questions about the purpose of the exercise. My legs began to ache, and I grew desperate to stir—to move my legs, to go to the bathroom, to steal a glimpse of Sachiko beside me, to do anything at all. The whole exercise began to seem like just another Japanese hardening of the will, an act of mindless discipline. How did everyone else know the proper way to bow? What if I, the only foreigner and the only newcomer here, inadvertently violated some sacrament? Where were these people going in the dark?

Finally, the darkness lifted, as looked-for as the dawn on a night when one cannot sleep. The parishioners lined up in rows before the feet of the *rōshi*, and the *rōshi* delivered a ninety-minute *teishō*, or talk, on the Five Buddhist Precepts—a shorter and simpler version, as it happened, of the Ten Commandments. "Do not kill. Do not steal. Do not lie. Do not commit adultery.

Do not drink." When he was finished, the four lieutenant monks served tea and cakes, and questions were asked. Then we issued forth, out into the tingling air.

One reason, I began to realize, as the winter deepened, why I was following Matthew's progress with something more than mere sympathy and amusement was that he seemed to me the perfect advertisement for Zen: with his lawyer's determination to do anything but follow his instincts, and the congenital self-contradiction that resulted, he was himself like the sound of one hand clapping. Yet the very equivocation and restlessness that made it so important for him to come to Zen was precisely what made it impossible for him to get to Zen. As Mark once put it, citing the old Zen parable, "He's searching for the ox while riding on the ox."

One blue late afternoon, drifts of snow coming languidly down along the narrow streets, leaves blowing over the slow-moving canal, we met up in the Afternoon Tea coffee shop downtown. Pink Floyd was seeping out of the sound system, and Matthew, when I arrived, was deep in a book on Zen— in part, it seemed, in the hope that it might attract some stranger into conversation. Many a foreigner came here ostensibly to study Buddhism but in fact to find a partner; if he failed to find a girl, he'd leave, complaining about the lack of Buddhism.

By the time we wandered out, night had already fallen. Tiny lanterns had come on along the doorways of the ancient tea-houses lining the narrow canal, and above them, their upper rooms glowed quietly, as quaint, in the falling snow, as in some child's paperweight. Down and down came the flakes, all about us, silent and mild, "with the stately solemnity," in Mishima's phrase, "of an ordered ritual," and as we crunched along the newly fallen white, we could see diners in rows along the upper windows and red lanterns reflected in the water, a winter scene of old stone bridges and weeping willows, silent as a photograph.

More and more convinced – and alarmed – that he was being locked out of the real Japan and that his time was running out, Matthew was determined now to break through Kyoto's walls at any cost. In the slim-waisted street of Pontochō, in the geisha quarter, he knocked on one locked door after another and finally, finding one open, jumped breezily into the entrance hall, calling, "Hallo? Hallo? Anybody home?" A frightened grandmother appeared before us, bowing.

"Oh, hello," he greeted her with all his London suavity. "Awfully nice to meet you. Do hope we're not intruding. Could we come in, please, take a look?" He pointed into the inner sanctum. This, however, was too much for the lady. Violently shaking her head no, she made a cross with her arms and brandished it in front of us as she might with a vampire. We headed back out into the gently falling snow.

Matthew, however, was in no mood to be thwarted. Every time we passed an open alcove, he charged in, greeting the blinking proprietress with reckless good cheer and shooting out such a flood of accelerating pleasantries that even I could scarcely follow. At last, we passed the Pinky Pinkum, as private and barred a place as all the rest. Without a moment's hesitation, Matthew led me in, and together we began hopping around, stork-legged, in the entrance hall, removing our thick shoes.

There were only six seats in the Pinky Pinkum, and four of them were occupied – three by besuited businessmen and the fourth by a professional-looking lady in her early forties. One of the men was squeezing a microphone between his fingers, singing some ineffably sorrowful old ballad while video images of white-maned horses galloped, in slow motion, across the wall. A young girl slithered around gracefully from behind the bar, got down on her knees, and, bowing at our feet, welcomed us in. Then she showed us to the bar, barely two feet away, where a pretty young boy stood at attention.

Matthew was exultant. "Yes, yes," he cried excitedly. "This is it! Absolutely the same as the Japanese bars in Thailand! Video, singing, the whole thing! Quite charming, actually!" Newly invigorated, he ordered a whiskey, and a Coke for me. Meanwhile, the microphone was slowly passed along, precious as an Olympic torch, from one person to the next. Song followed heartrending song. Before long, the microphone had arrived at Matthew's neighbor. He crooned a dirge.

"Very good indeed! Awfully good, actually! Better than La Scala," cried Matthew, beaming over at him, ever friendly. "Excellent! Really excellent!" The man stared back at him, perplexed, and then, very slowly, realizing that the praise was genuine, beamed back. The next thing we knew, the microphone was suddenly passing into Matthew's hands, and the businessmen were bustling about to find a list of English songs: "Yesterday," "Take Me Home, Country Roads," "Green Green Grass of Home," "Love Me Tender."

"Oh no, no, couldn't, I really couldn't," he smiled back at them, unaware, as yet, that in this country foreigners, like performing seals, were often expected to sing, quite literally, for their supper. "Awfully nice of you, very kind, actually," he went on, "but really I can't." The microphone passed down in the opposite direction.

The first businessman received it and started unburdening his sorrow in a deep bass again, and then his neighbor, and then the woman, and soon the place was rocking. All of us were clapping along, the businessmen were delivering wrenching threnodies, and Matthew was slapping his neighbor on the back and smiling at him with an almost hysterical infectiousness. Just at this tender moment of cross-cultural communication, the bartenderess suddenly took up the mike and broke into sweet song. Matthew gazed up at her adoringly. "Will you marry me?" he asked, as she belted out some plangent ballad about a young girl's errant marriage.

"Absolutely wonderful," he confided under his breath. "The

real Japan! Maybe we should go before the moment fades. How much do you think it'll be?"

"Thirty-five dollars, maybe," I answered, trying to soften the blow.

"Oh, very good. Awfully good value, actually. Very good deal: native culture and all that."

Then the pretty hostess—his fiancée manqué—handed us the bill: sixty dollars for a whiskey and a Coke. Matthew stared at it unhappily.

I refrained from reminding him that we had, in a sense, gotten off lightly: the traditional teahouses of Gion were famous for their expensiveness—that was one of their traditions, in fact, and that was part of the attraction for the Japanese, who came here exclusively to pay $330 for a single drink, with a bowl of special nuts. Matthew, though, was in no mood for consolation. Jet-propelled, he charged out of the place and started marching through the falling snow. "Noodle shop, noodle shop," he shouted mirthlessly as we walked down the canal, past the soundless, lit-up teahouses. "Noodles! That's what the evening calls for!"

Finally, we retreated to the relative safety of a Mexican restaurant, and over enchiladas, Matthew started discussing the competing merits of the high life and the higher life.

9:00 p.m.: "Really think I ought to make a go of it here."

9:15 p.m.: "Actually, if it doesn't feel right, why force it?"

9:30 p.m.: "But if I leave now, I'll feel I've failed."

9:45 p.m.: "Really, though, Thailand's so much more pleasant. If you're not comfortable, how can you grow?"

And on and on, et cetera, et cetera, *und so weiter,* for two hours or more: Thailand was seductive, so he ought to go there; Thailand was seductive, and therefore to be avoided. Japan was hard, so it was eminently good for him; Japan was hard, so it was not for him at all. He really wanted to try to find a home; he really ought to let a home find him. Unable to accept anything less than everything, he ended up with nothing, reminding me, often, of a man who has waited for so long to take a plunge into cold water that his legs at last have gone dead on him.

"Thing is, I've got all the time and money, really want to be of service. Really ought to find how I can be of use. Could be a lawyer, I suppose, but that's so corrupt. Should become a monk, maybe, but really takes a lot of discipline. Suppose I could go back to college, but then I'm not doing anyone any good at all. Could become a teacher here, but it doesn't feel quite right."

Finally, I could take no more. "Look," I said. "The more time you spend wondering what you're going to do for others, the less time you spend doing anything at all. And the more you keep looking for a perfect answer, the less likely you are to find one. Stop second-guessing your own emotions, and do something."

Captive to my own mind now, I started babbling on, determined to try to shake him out of subjunctives and optatives, into simple declaratives.

"But what about understanding?" asked Matthew, a little plaintively. "Isn't that any good?"

"What good has understanding ever done you? When has understanding ever brought you happiness or goodness or peace? It's useless; it's got nothing to do with anything! The mind's an obstacle; it teaches you only what you never need to know. Just be decisive, single-pointed. Make a choice — any choice at all — and you'll be happier."

Matthew nodded gloomily, as startled as I was to hear this sudden burst of bromides. He didn't know, I suspected, that one reason for the vehemence was that I was talking to myself. One reason I got so impatient with Matthew was that I saw so much of him in me.

Sachiko, meanwhile, still and always had an unrivaled capacity for touching me, her gestures were so thoughtful. For my birthday, she asked if she could take me out to dinner. When I arrived at

City Hall, at the time we'd arranged to meet, I found her standing there, waiting patiently in the cold, in a red and golden sari—as she had promised several months before; with it, under kohl-rimmed eyes, a thick mink stole and black high heels. She looked like a Rajput princess. Handing me a rose of the most delicate lavender, she began clopping along the street, not with her usual easy fluency but with precise, clear-stepping elegance.

"Please," she said. "I want give you present. We go Osaka?"

Together, we rode the train through the winter afternoon. She opened up her Paddington datebook (which came here with a space for listing one's "Tax Accountant's Number") and pointed at the paw mark on the day, symbol of a national holiday: my birthday, she reminded me, was the same as that of the Japanese Empire. I explained to her about Tibet, and the Tibetan New Year that I was going off to celebrate the next day, and she, nodding solemnly, said, "All life there, very severe! All life, I think, little *sesshin*."

Later, when we got to Umeda Station, she led me through the crowds to the Hilton Hotel, and up, up, up in the elevator to the sixth-floor Photo Studio. Around us, clutches of apprehensive wedding parties stood around gravely, waiting to have their moment immortalized. I looked on in surprise as Sachiko fell into animated chatter with the startled-looking lady at the desk (not accustomed, I suspected, to seeing a Japanese girl in a sari asking for a wedding picture alone). Then, eyes alight, she handed over $160 for two formal portraits of herself.

"But, Sachiko," I protested, bursting in. "That's enough to buy an air ticket to Thailand! Surely you can use this money better!"

"Please," she said, putting a finger to her lips. "Please don't worry, Pico! I want give you something you always keep together. Photo never change; you take many place, always happy memory. Later, you old man, maybe you little look this photo, time stop; you always remember this time. In photo, I always very young, maybe little beautiful."

"But, Sachiko, it's so expensive. You don't have that much money!"

"Please stop. This very cheap price, I give you all-life present. I not so rich, not so special. I cannot give you many thing. Then I want give you dream!"

I didn't know what to say.

Later, on a night of pale light and water and mist, I told her, with regret, that I had never seen Kyoto in its full winter dress, steeples blanketed with snow, temples covered in white. The next morning, when I awoke, the flakes were coming down in long silent flurries, falling soundlessly upon gray roofs and canals, falling down upon dark temples and back streets, leaving scant trace of the buildings, making no sound as it made the city new.

With that, another cycle seemed to end, the drifts smoothing out all imperfections and presenting me with a world reborn. I looked around at the other presents I had received: the photo from Sachiko, together with an elegant, high-tech case of writing implements and a temple charm; a merry Falstaffian *tanuki* from the Brooklyn lawyer Shelley, wrapped in paper scattered with red and green cherries and inscribed with cheery cherry quatrains: "To make you happy, my pretty many cherries / I wrote you a netter my dear cherry / We play on the garden our hand are touch / We take each other and run away."

And, from Mark, a beautiful *sumi-e* drawing of a Buddha, still and depthless, found in meditation.

SPRING

Spring rain
In our sedan chair
Your soft whisper.

—THE ZEN POET BUSON

1

ON THE NIGHT I returned from my trip to see the Dalai Lama, only hours after I stepped off the plane, I got a call from Sachiko, more softly urgent than ever, begging me, through snuffled tears, to meet her now, please, anywhere, even though it was almost midnight. I hurried over to the coffee shop she mentioned, and felt a pang of fondness as I saw her standing there, her small figure patient in the dark. Smiling bravely through her tears, she led me inside, still sniffling, and ordered "milk tea" for us both, then flung herself sobbing into my lap.

"Sachiko, Sachiko, what's wrong?"

She sat up, brushing the tears from her face. "I little see movie, *Mannequin.*" This in itself did not seem cause for sorrow. "No, no," she went on. "You not understand! I plan go together Sandy, Canadian man. But Sandy, many plan change, all cancel! Then I go together Canadian man! Very good movie, I very fun. But then he attack me!"

"What do you mean?"

She shook her head, inarticulate with grief.

"What exactly did he do, Sachiko?" I persisted, typically crass. "I don't understand."

"He try kiss me," she finally got out. "First time, my life! Japanese man very gentle, very kind. But foreigner man so different. I very shock." She gulped down sniffles and sobs. "Foreigner person very dangerous!" In all her life, she had told me in the autumn—and it was easy to believe her—she had only ever kissed her husband. And in a life so empty of event, even the smallest upset could seem like devastation.

"Don't worry, Sachiko," I reassured her with spurious fluency. "Not all foreign men are terrible. Two kinds come to Japan: some wanting much money, many girls; some who truly want to understand the Japanese heart." She looked at me solemnly, swallowing back her tears, attentive as a chastened child, but I could tell that theories wouldn't help, and I could tell that she was already beginning to feel the terrors of straying far from native ground.

Back in Kyoto now, I settled back into myself as into a hot *sentō* bath, feeling invigorated by the city, and cleaned out. Sitting at my sun-washed desk in the quiet days, I returned to familiar observances: the punctual singing cry, each morning, of the little girl calling to her mother; the midmorning walk of the hobbled old lady with hair the color of smokers' teeth to the coin laundry down the street; the afternoon tinkle of trilling piano melodies; the lonely, melancholy sound of country ballads from the Chinese laundry shop drifting through the narrow lanes at night.

In the weeks I had been away, my neighborhood had, on its surface, transformed itself: a two-story concrete block with the look of an ice cream sandwich towered now above the grandma-and-pa grocery stores, and in the next alley down, a gleaming new health food store was trying to attract new customers. A card dealer from Reno—and, before that, Santa Barbara—had moved into my guesthouse, as well as a tall, brittle businessman from Harvard, who stalked up and down the corridors, in two-tone shirts and three-piece suits, howling, "Blow, winds, blow."

The coordinates of my own Kyoto, however, remained unchanged. When I went to the copy shop, the cackling, clown-faced proprietor was so delighted to see me—her most faithful, and I sometimes suspected her only, customer—that she even effected an introduction to her growling familiar, a lumpy, sad-eyed dog called Goro, thirteen years old now and half blind.

The matron at the photo shop demurely murmured "Pico-san," as soon as I walked in, and chuckled happily as she tried once more to turn my name into phonetic Japanese characters. And the three girls at the post office, though looking up in alarm from their abacuses when they saw me enter, were sufficiently worldly now to deal with a letter to Brunei Daressalam, to know that American Samoa (despite its zip code) had little to do with America, and to handle a parcel to a person whose surname I didn't know. When I rang up the Tourist Information Center to ask who had won Miss Universe, the girls who worked there not only surprised me with the answer but, after a giggling conference, asked if I approved.

So much of my Kyoto life caught up now in these unprepossessing associations, and, by now, so much of myself. Giving up the world, I thought, was easy; renouncing the Rolls-Royce or Rolex I had never wanted in the first place was no harder than going on the wagon for a teetotaler. But giving up my world—the specific feelings and mementos that seemed the fabric of my being—was altogether different. On that form of attachment, though, as on every other, Zen was singularly uncompromising: memories could be as possessive, and as wasting, as sapphires, or lusts, or hopes.

Though I had been four months in Japan now, it still seemed, often, as if I had landed, with an unseemly bump, on some unworldly star. Whenever I walked down the street to my local convenience store, the Familiar, I felt as if I were walking into a surrealist's collage. On the wall of my lane, a sign informed me, pleasantly:

> This is my STYLE.
> The city is a 24-hour stage where we act out a life
> that is lively, free, and convenient. Be it day or
> night, we go out at any time to wherever we like,

looking for something new. This scooter is just right for a life-style.

—CITY MOTORBIKE

Around me were fresh-faced, bespectacled boys in warm-up jackets that said "Neo-Blood," shy teenage girls whose coats said "Dental Democracy."

Inside the store itself, where a Japanese Springsteen was delivering a Muzak version of the Boss's "Brilliant Disguise," I bought some Chips Company potato chips, their box announcing, disarmingly, "We are the nicest friends in all the world." As a happy-voiced announcer on the PA system advised us all to enjoy our stay in the store, I went over to buy a Clean Life Please dustcloth. "FACILE for your clean life," this helpful rag declared. "You grow to be beautiful in a pleasant and unforgettable mood." Nearby, goods were clamoring to reassure me: My Green Life utensils, Enjoy and Laundry cloths, hand soaps for "creating your dreamy life." Sometimes the objects here seemed almost more animated than the people.

As I headed home, newly befriended and more beautiful, in a pleasant and unforgettable mood, past the machine that offered Drink Paradise and Your Joyful Drink, I glimpsed a pink cushion embroidered with renditions of a cartoon cat. On it, entitled Fleçon Chat, was an atmospheric scene:

> There's a tranquil mood all over Montparnasse in the afternoon. The only sound is the gay chattering of Lyceenne and her mates. A persian cat with a beautifully silky hair hunches down gracefully near the window. She looks a little like a lady putting on airs. Her fascinating blue eyes! What a brilliant, happy afternoon, as if we're in the world of Baudelaire's poetry.

These sunny, baffling sentiments were everywhere in Japan— on T-shirts, carrier bags, and photo albums—rhyming, in their way, with the relentlessly chirpy voices that serenaded one on elevators, buses, and trains; it did not take a Roland Barthes to identify Japan as an Empire of Signs. These snippets of nonsense poetry were also, of course, the first and easiest target of most foreigners in Japan, since they were often almost the only signs in English, and absurd: creamers called Creep, Noise snacks that came in different colors, pet cases known as Effem (whether in honor of the fairer sex or high-frequency radio, it was hard to tell). Every newly arrived foreigner could become an instant sociologist when faced with this cascade of automatic writing, not stopping to think, perhaps, how often we may spray paint our T-shirts with elegant-looking Japanese characters that mean nothing to us, or something worse.

Nonetheless, it was hard not to notice how often certain words recurred in these slogans and contrived to create a certain atmosphere. Multimillion-dollar ad campaigns were no more random here than in America, and it was clearly no coincidence that they chose again and again to return to "dreams" and "feelings," to metaphors of community and gentleness, to imported notions of freedom and society. ("Coke is it," the slogan nearly everywhere else in the world, became, in Japan, the moodier, and more involving, "I feel Coke.") So too, it was hard to overlook how many of the T-shirts spoke of "clubs" and "tribes" and "circles," and how often kiosks or clubs or signs invoked the first person plural (Let's Archery or the Let's grocery store). Even packs of cigarettes announced themselves as "An Encounter with Tenderness," and Toyota and Honda gave their domestically sold models unusually soft and feminine names. Sometimes, in fact, the Dada fragments seemed almost to be inventories of cherished values, as in the Roget's exuberance of the ad for Nescafé's Excellent Coffee:

> It's happiness people loving casual time caring
> friendly tasty everyday relaxing cosiness fun inti-
> mate heart open likeable and togetherness. It's

warmth heart embracing pure gentle comradeship
you us family sharing sociable aroma liveliness
tenderness smiling easy and yours.

Occasionally, too, they let out the other side of Japan: a group
of S & M kiddies on motorbikes, fierce-eyed and demented,
with hostile scowls, under the legend: "Though They're Hot-
Blooded, Hard-Nosed and Crazy, Really They Act According to
Their Principles. It's a Purple Story at Midnight." Rebellion
made user-friendly; just another fashion statement.

Most often, though, the Japanese brought their poetic touch
to English and created out of the imported sounds a haunting
kind of synesthetic beauty, with an air of lulling, melancholy
mystery; often, the buzzwords came together to create a kind of
Pop Art haiku, rainswept and misty as a video.

SMOKE ON THE PURPLE TOWN

When time is softly
Veiled in a flower of black
tea, what dreams are your dreams?

ran an ad under a picture of a Picasso-like fellow enshrouded in
fog on a Dantean New York street, under the warning: "All
worldly things are transitory."

In the same magazine, another set of images again turned
rough surfaces into poems:

BEYOND THE MEMORY OF MAN

my sepia memory
blurred with tears. I long
for it so much now.

These dreamy flights of inspired lyricism could work on one
strangely, composed as they were not of words but associations:
syllables used as moods, as ideograms. I came in time to find my
imagination expanded by my Clean Mail writing paper, subtitled

"Sound of Waves," or the monochrome photo album entitled Les Étoiles Brillantes (its subtitle sketching a Japanese ideal: "The wind whispers softly, the sun shines brightly all around, the flowers radiate joyfulness. Here the animals live cheerfully in peaceful co-operation"). Even the paper on my individually wrapped Fine Raisin Cookies declared, "Beautiful things are beyond time. Woman's history never ceases to yearn for beauty."

This poppy poetry was, in spite of itself, Japanese, I thought: in some sense, it meant nothing, and yet—in the Japanese way—it substituted atmosphere for meaning and so caught the aroma of a feeling. Meaning or its absence hardly mattered; there was no more point in belaboring a meaning here than in trying to pin one down in a photo or a *tanka*. Instead of analysis, one should simply surrender; surrender to the lovely, strange trompe l'oeil:

> *City streets at dawn*
> *A soft mist*
> *Fire on the mountainside.*

Downtown Kyoto was strange to me in different ways, for as I came to know the central covered mall, I registered a curious discrepancy. There were two parallel aisles in the arcade, both of them typical strips of buzzing lights, cartoon faces, fast-food joints, and the occasional porno store. One, though, was always in the usual Japanese state of perpetual quiet rush hour, crammed with uniformed schoolgirls, sleek ladies of the water trade, and beribboned office ladies; the other was as lonely as a ghost town.

One day, as we wandered through the mall together, I asked Mark about this. Well, he said, one of the streets, Teramachi, or the Street of Temples, had long been a place of religious sites and graveyards, razed now by the mallifying city. But Kyotoites still tended to shun it as much as they did the areas of the untouchables, or any haunted house: they did not relish the sensation of walking on the bones of their ancestors. So the whole strip was generally empty, save for its Buddhist shops.

Certainly, the longer I stayed in Kyoto, the more I discovered how many spirits still lingered in its byways and back alleyways, and how much, even now, an animistic strain still haunted this sleek and secular society. For all the futuristic finish of the city's ways and surfaces, it had never fully relinquished its wilder pagan past. The Japanese still slept in certain directions that they deemed auspicious, and left food out on their doorsteps to appease the fox spirits; in the countryside, where houses lacked air-conditioning, people still told one another ghost stories to keep each other cool in summer. Sea spray was said to be the heads of shipwrecked ghosts, and a winter exorcism was still conducted near my home. One foreigner I knew lived rent-free in a huge old house that no Japanese would enter because it was said to be haunted; even a seven-hundred-dollar Shinto priest had failed to clean it out.

I noted too, as time went on, how often Sachiko referred to God, and how much he resembled the stern Calvinist dispenser of the West. If clouds began to gather on a day we met, she'd grow quiet, very often, and say, a little ruminatively, "God little give this day. Maybe he want punish me." When I told her that I had had a chilling dream of her turning hard and brittle, she startled me by explaining, "You me very close. Then maybe God little jealous." Most often, though, she would interpret—or describe, at least—every happy development in her life as a gift from heaven. "I get very good Benny Goodman ticket," she said once. "Maybe God give me!" "I don't think so," I replied, a little churlishly. "I think God has bigger things to think about."

I knew, though, that I was being less than fair or understanding. For God was clearly one of the terms that got most thoroughly misplaced in translation (with singular and plural fatally blurred, and Sachiko, perhaps, translating her beliefs into words I'd understand), and however much she seemed to be conflating Christian images with Shinto superstitions in the rites she performed in Buddhist temples, she was clearly committing herself to something more than form or ritual. Whenever we passed a Buddha, she would stop and close her eyes, her palms pressed tightly together. And whatever the communication taking place, it clearly involved some exchange of feelings so intense that I stood back so as not to trespass on it. It reminded me at times of Niels Bohr's answer to the people who said that he could not truly believe in the lucky charm he kept on his wall. Of course not, he said, but it was said that it brought you luck even if you did not believe in it.

When harassed, Sachiko still took herself to the daphne-scented quiet of the temples. And when she had done *kendō* fencing at dawn, she said, or when she listened to the *rōshi* speak, or when she went alone to Eikandō, she fell into a place so still, it sounded like a higher self. It was not so much, perhaps, that her feeling for Zen betrayed a Zen spirit as that both her feeling and Zen betrayed a common source still deeper in the Japanese heart, a natural sympathy for purity and peace.

At the same time, in Sachiko, I was beginning to see a plaintive sense of guilt that made again a mockery of the sociologists' explanations of how the cultures of the East have a sense of "shame" and not of "guilt." Again and again, when we were together, she said darkly, "I very bad daughter. I very bad mother. I bad wife," and though some of this may only have been a ritual disclaimer, some, I could sense, really did prey on her. For a while, I had wondered whether perhaps she had a secret life that was the subtext of these self-reproaches. But in time, I realized that she didn't, and that her sense of insufficiency stemmed only from the fact that she longed now and then to be away from her children, chose on occasion to go out without telling her mother, craved sometimes a little time for herself. In Japan, of course, that was tantamount to heresy—if everyone started indulging herself in this way, the whole system would collapse. Self-interest must be communal.

Sachiko, then, was tyrannized by the cult of perfection here.

But more than that, I could see that she was haunted by the fear of failing other expectations, which were something more than social: she felt discomfort at her knowledge that her mother's death might be a source of relief as well as sorrow; guilt at the fact that she could not wholeheartedly embrace the notion of unquestioning self-sacrifice; unease at her sense that her dreams—or, more exactly, her wish to realize them—were a violation of the code in which she had been trained. She sensed that she was a traitor to Japan's values, and she knew that excommunication here was, quite literally, a fate worse than death (since death at least involved the preservation of honor).

Yet all these feelings had another, surprising twist, to me at least: for insofar as she felt any unease about our being together, it was clearly because she saw it as a betrayal, not of her husband but of her mother. Her husband, she often implied, was no more affected by her doings than a big boss might be; her emotional life had little to do with the practical setup of her marriage, and he, in any case, had little interest in her life. But her mother was the one she saw as conscience, confidante, and caretaker of her better self. It was her mother who checked in on her daily, closely assessed her performance as a mother, and told her often—this highly capable and efficient thirty-year-old mother of two—that she should not go out in the rain or venture outside after dark. It was her mother who exerted the gentlest kind of emotional blackmail, in large part because it was her mother who had always been her one and closest friend. And so her mother had become, in a sense, an instrument for her sense of religion, until her religion itself came to seem a reflection of her mother: both were symbols of a higher law that held her to moral standards.

Thus the qualities she responded to in the Buddha, she said, were his calm smile and "sweet eyes"—like those of a mother; and the reason she listened to the *rōshi* was that he tended to his followers as a mother to her flock; and her favorite statue in Kyoto was the Buddha at Eikandō looking over his shoulder to check on his disciple, an emblem of maternal solicitude and love. Motherhood was, of course, her constant frame of reference—her job, in a sense—and therefore the keyhole through which she saw the world; yet it was also something more, as if the mother were as integral to her notion of religion as a father is to ours. "Please you show me picture your mother?" she often asked, with even more urgency than the people from whom I had heard the same request in such matriarchies as Cuba and the Philippines.

It was, I supposed, only natural, in strictly partitioned Japan, where mothers have complete control of home and family, and fathers take all responsibility for work, that images of compassion and conscience be invariably associated with the mother. Doi Takeo's claim that *amae,* or the feeling of indulged passivity a baby feels at its mother's breast, was a sensation peculiarly important to Japan—the emotional heart of Japan, in fact—was all but a cliché now. Yet it also confirmed my sense of how closely the sense of motherland here reflected—and paralleled—the sense of motherhood. When she had got married, Sachiko told me, it had been as fearful an act to her as exile; and her mother, really, was her clearest embodiment of Japan, with her reverence for the Emperor, her love of ancient poems, her fidelity to all the antique customs. Conversely, of course, society itself here smothered its children like an overprotective mother, winding them up in a net of social securities that was all but impossible to escape. And when venturing out of their motherland and into the world at large, the Japanese really did seem often like chicks jumping out of their nests into a *terra* that was all *incognita.* Japan was a mother, mother was Japan: the two great nurturing deities converged.

Even Ryōkan, I recalled, the high priest of unorthodox self-sufficiency, had returned, in his mind, to the two still points of worship:

> The island of Sado,
> Morning and evening I often see it in my dreams,
> Together with the gentle face of my mother.

2

ONE DAY, before the cherries came to town, I jumped into a bullet train—the perfect emblem of Japan, all noiseless speed and purpose, the world flashing by in a series of well-framed tableaux, all comforts brought to one in an air-conditioned space—and went to Nagasaki. All day I walked along its gently sloping hills, down an avenue of temples fringed by palm trees and cactus, through quiet streets lit up by kindergarten cries. Whether as cause, or effect, of its historical position as the one Japanese port mostly open to the world, the city had a looseness, and an ease, I hadn't found in Kyoto, a freedom from care that let dogs run around unleashed and taxi drivers go ungloved.

In the evening, I found a room in a tiny traditional inn, which doubled as a shell museum, and drew myself a deep hot bath. Just as I was settling into it, however, there came a frantic knocking at my door; it was one of the matrons of the inn, desperately summoning me downstairs. There, she pointed to the phone, dangling off its hook, and as I picked it up, stared at by the matron and a goggle-eyed accomplice, all of us surrounded by tanks of tropical fish, I heard a fact-checker in New York asking me whether the Thai name of Bangkok could be translated as "village of wild olive groves."

Since the answer (it could) had to be faxed off immediately to New York, I took the two ladies out of their misery by taking myself out of their hostel and setting off down the silent, empty streets. Then, after giving my fax to the largest hotel in town, I slipped into the nearest restaurant I could find: a basement dive called Caveau. Inside, amidst the clinking of glasses and the makeshift incense of smoke rings, I saw, to my surprise, one whole table of jolly young Japanese toasting two foreigners: a bearded, ruddy engineer, from Boston, I learned from eavesdropping, and a bewildered, fresh-faced Englishman. Every time either of them spoke, there rose up a great roar of approval, as the other diners clinked glasses and doubled over in loud mirth. I, taken aback, took a small booth in the corner and ordered pizza.

Before long, however, and inevitably, a couple of the *gaijin* groupies leaned over and invited me to join the party. I soon found myself in what seemed a kind of heretic clan, a secret society gathered in this underground haunt to imbibe and celebrate the values of abroad. All five Japanese at the table had the lit-up, fervent look of eager revolutionaries. One of them, a thirty-eight-year-old businessman, in pressed white shirt and black tie, a graduate in economics from Nagasaki University, leaned over woozily, extended a hand, and said, "Bullshit. I am happy to meet you." Another, a stocky young character, flop-topped and flip-tongued, announced over the general roar, "My name is Shinji. You can call me Jason.

"Very strange Japanese guy, hey," he went on, surveying the scene around us. "Wild and crazy guy!"

"Are you a student?"

"Naw. I was in Waseda University, one year. Then I drop out. This stuff is bullshit! One hundred forty thousand dollars for one year doctor's school!"

Shinji presented himself, in fact, as a perfect inversion of the Japanese ideal. Instead of defining himself by his professional affiliation, he refused to admit to any job; instead of observing the same routine every day, he claimed that he spent most of his time just zigzagging around the country; and instead of pledging his life to family, community, and Japan, he seemed to dream only of escape. I could not tell whether he was ashamed of his job (as a glorified delivery boy, perhaps) or proud of it (as a smuggler of sorts?), but I could see that his main interest was to observe Japan through foreign eyes.

Later, as the party began to disperse in a cloud of happy *Fuck yous* and bleary toasts, Shinji showed again how eager he was to be an American by inviting me to hit the town with him the following night, the first such invitation I had ever received from a Japanese male (most of whom, in any case, had no nights at their disposal). The next day, he called me in the shell museum to assure me he was coming—even the rebels in Japan seemed inalienably Japanese—and then, on the stroke of seven, appeared on my doorstep. Diligent as a tour guide, he began driving me through the winding hills of Nagasaki, until we reached a lookout point, a classic lovers' view of the muzzy lights of the city, as romantic from here as Loti's city, with the great liners out at sea transporting their cargo of lights. A view of possibility, a vision of flight.

As we wound our way back down again, Shinji started to cross-question me.

"Who is your favorite musician?"

"Do you know Jackson Browne?"

His eyes widened. "My favorite!" he exclaimed in astonishment.

Somewhat taken aback, I wrung his hand in delight.

"Actually, I also like Bruce Springsteen."

His eyes brightened. "My favorite!"

Remarkable, I thought: we seemed to have exactly the same tastes.

"You like Dire Straits?"

"Very much."

"My favorite!" he exclaimed, in mock astonishment.

Clearly, "favorite" was as elastic a term here as "best friend"; and however much "Jason" was keen to leave Japan, the Japanese wish to harmonize had clearly not left him.

"What about David Lindley?" I asked, trying to make my choices a little more obscure.

"Sure! My favorite!"

Then, just as credibility was beginning to snap, he added, "I have a tape, very special tape, David Lindley live, together Clarence Clemons!"

Swinging into a parking place, Shinji announced, with his chuckling air of boyish bonhomie, "Now I introduce you Nagasaki restaurant."

"Excellent."

We made our way through a generic mall, all dizzy lights and giggly girls, and into a McDonald's.

"Cheeseburger, cheeseburger!" he cried, doubling over in laughter.

Together we trooped upstairs and found a table under a cartoon landscape. Later, as we munched our fries, Shinji outlined his worldview.

"All Japanese like blond hair, blue eye, green eye, pale skin. To us is very beautiful. I don't like." Around him, McDonald's was a clatter of trays and conveyor-belt fun. "Japanese people do not know other country. Not interesting. Japanese people think all Americans open, friendly. 'Hi.' Some are. Some not so friendly. Many Americans do not like *Saturday Night Live* because it makes many jokes about the Jews, many jokes about the Irish. The Jews are not like other Americans. They have a too strange mind. Too strange!"

He let out a raucous whoop. They're not the only ones, I thought.

"I meet an American Jew one time—too strange! The Koreans here are the same as the Jews in America. The Japanese are very unfair to Koreans. Why? You know that eighty percent of pachinko parlor owners are Korean? Pachinko parlor owners very rich! Japanese people know about England and America. But they know nothing about Asia. But we are part of Asia!"

He was sounding more and more like a Kyoto *gaijin*.

"English people, too much snob—their nose in air! I have friend, his father friend Attenborough. But English people, French people, very gentle." He meant, I saw, as Sachiko did, "gentle" as in *gentil*, the back-derivation of "gentleman." "Canadian man too.

"Which movie you like? My favorite John Belushi. And Jack Nicholson! Cheeseburger, cheeseburger!"

Then, with typical abruptness, Shinji lowered his voice and spread a softer kind of subversion. He was reading now a "secret history" of the war—precisely the kind of book, I realized, that foreigners loved to read here. It explained how FDR was aware of Pearl Harbor in advance, and went on to outline all Japan's atrocities and cover-ups. "Same *Last Emperor* movie," he whispered, brandishing his heresy. "You like Miami Dolphins?"

"Sure."

"My favorite!"

Then, as we got ready to go, Shinji cast his eye over all the bright Formica tables, where chic college girls were sitting primly over Happy Meals and Corn Potage Soups. "All of them," he intoned, making his face cartoonish, "pay much high money for clothes. But here"—he pointed to his head—"empty!"

The next thing I knew, he was whizzing me back through the mall, and occasionally dancing up to groups of female passersby, like De Niro in *New York, New York.*

"You want to see my home?"

"Okay," I said, and again we were driving through quiet streets into a silent neighborhood.

"Why you so kind?" asked Shinji, not for the first time. My kindness, I knew, had extended so far to nothing more than accepting his hospitality, but I heard the same question from Sachiko too, and knew that it reflected not just empty pleasantry or routine inquiry: the Japanese really were anxious to know what was expected of them in return, and what kind of emotional debt they were running up.

Credit ratings uncertain, we parked along a canal and, slipping between wooden homes, stole into a house, and up a staircase, past his sleeping father. Shinji's room, not unexpectedly, was a perfect replica of Western undergraduate chaos, one skewed pile of tangled sheets and tapes and books and empty cartons of Kentucky Fried Chicken. Above the bed smiled a semi-life-size Shiseido girl.

"My parents are divorced," Shinji announced, as if to certify his status as a crazy, messed-up Western kid.

In one respect, though, his room was typically Japanese. For the main item that commanded attention here was the high-tech HQ, one long black switchboard console of CD, VCR, TV, stereo system, and Bose speakers, lined up on a shelf as carefully as a shrine might be in an Indian household. And Shinji's record collection was like nothing I had ever seen before, big enough to stock a record store: hundreds upon hundreds upon hundreds of albums, all kept in clean, transparent sleeves, arranged by genre and alphabet, across shelf after shelf—soul, jazz, country, female vocalist, psychedelic, British Invasion, punk, L.A. session band, art rock, soft rock, surf rock.

"Cheeseburger, cheeseburger!" he cried again.

I looked up from all the albums, dazed.

"You know cheeseburger?"

"Sure! I eat them all the time!"

"Cheeseburger very funny," Shinji pronounced. The Japanese word for "funny" had the same double meaning as our own, I recalled. Then he flipped on a tape of Bill Murray and Chevy Chase doing some "cheeseburger" routine on an old segment of *Saturday Night Live*: *samurai* humor took on new meaning here.

"You like all these kinds of music?" I went on.

"Right now, my favorite the Mersey Sound," he said, shutting off the "cheeseburger" routine. "Gerry and the Pacemakers! Herman's Hermits! The Dave Clark Five! You know Manfred Mann?" I nodded. "My favorite!"

"Do your friends like this too?"

"Naw." He mimicked disgust. "Japanese like only two kind music: Japanese pop and top hits, MTV style. They do not know Dave Clark Five, Sam Cooke."

"You have Sam Cooke?" I said, perking up.

"Only six," he apologized, pulling them out from the S section of Soul, rarities unavailable in the U.S. for years, complete with paisley-tone liner notes by "Hugo and Luigi" and cover versions of classics like "Blowin' in the Wind."

"Kinks?"

"Only three."

"Dead?"

He looked back, stunned. "My favorite! 'Playing in the Band.' I am sixties person. Hippie. But Japanese people only like eighties."

"You should come to Kyoto."

And so the interrogation went on, through Elvis Costello, and King Crimson albums I hadn't seen since my teens, and even such arcana as Pete Sinfield. More surprising to me, Shinji wasn't just a collector; he actually knew the records well and had all the right rock-critic views on them. "Carly Simon has same face Mick Jagger! New Springsteen record *mā-mā* [so-so]. Some of it, like 'Nebraska,' some very big sound. I think Mark Knopfler's teacher, Ry Cooder. My favorite Ry Cooder song is Hawaii one. He great! But not like money. Many star, too much money! Too much rich! MTV, videos, producer. Much money spoil people. Look Jackson Browne: first three albums very good, then too much money! Diane Lane same. She has old woman's face. And Daryl Hannah—she *baka* [stupid]! Nothing in her head." Such was the predicament of a Japanese dissident, I thought: little to rebel against save MTV and Daryl Hannah.

Then he flipped open a box of tapes and pulled out a rare David Lindley bootleg.

"This is for me?"

"Sure," he said.

As I looked it over, Shinji strolled over to the chest of drawers, reached for a bottle, and slapped on some aftershave. I stared with new intensity at his albums, eager not to know what was going on; Shinji began cleaning his teeth. I looked around for reassurances, and steadied myself with two framed photos of his girlfriend. Then, just as I was excavating some prehistoric Neil Young, Shinji started running his electric Norelco over his face. Now, I thought, I knew how a girl felt when her host started prettying himself up.

Suddenly, just as I was sinking into the Dead's "Mama Tried," he jumped up and said, "Let's go." I looked at my watch and realized that it was eleven-twenty; to cover my options, I had told him that I had to be back at the shell museum by eleven-thirty.

Driving back through hushed and rainswept streets, he suddenly asked, "Yesterday, what will you do?"

Another piece of surrealism, I thought, till I remembered Sachiko's similar confusion.

"Tomorrow, do you mean?"

"Sure."

"I think I'll leave," I said, to be on the safe side. "Do you like Richard Thompson?"

"Sure! My favorite! Fairport Convention!"

"With Sandy Denny."

"Hey, you like folk? Pentangle, Steeleye Span, Lindesfarne. You know 'Led Zeppelin IV'?"

"Led Zeppelin?"

"Sure. Sandy Denny make guest appearance. Now dead."

Then, his slaphappy exuberance not subsiding for a moment, he continued, "What kind of dream you have tonight? Wet dream?"

"No. Very dry."

"About exams?"

"Maybe. And the Emperor."

That, I thought, should keep him quiet. But only briefly. "How about I share your bed?"

This, it seemed, was taking his love of the foreign a little far. "No, thank you."

"Why?"

"I'd rather be alone, thank you. Good night."

"Good night," he said, politely dropping me off at the entrance to the inn and waving a cheerful textbook goodbye.

3

BACK HOME in Kyoto, the late-March days eased by in one seamless flow of blue epiphanies: the first touch of spring was bringing a refreshed brilliance to the heavens, and mild afternoons of loosened shirts and hopes. I drank tea with a slice of orange and ate melon sorbet in a coffee shop whose window announced, unexpectedly, "I'd like to eat with you and gaze into your eyes while we talk of UFOs," and I went to a university rock concert where a couple of blue- and pink-suited emcees exchanged TV patter while mop-haired singers in dark glasses leaped up and down on stage in a frenzy of punk nihilism, jerking themselves around with borrowed fury while a guitarist played solos with his teeth; I read articles about this year's Miss Universe contestant from Japan ("Michiko Sakaguai enjoys flower arrangement, playing the electronic organ, and golf") and translated Latin tags from Iris Murdoch—it was always Iris Murdoch here, among the matrons and the *literati*—for an overzealous professor of English literature who felt he could not understand her without knowing the meaning of these phrases. I caught a glimpse of the Grammy Awards on Mark's TV and felt as if I'd stumbled onto hidden treasure.

In Kyoto indeed, as anywhere abroad, I was recovering a kind of innocence, as time slowed down, and space opened up, and everything seemed new, even—especially—the things I knew from home. Going to the movies only once every two months, I found myself curiously spellbound: I went to *Fatal Attraction* (equipped here with a happy—or, at least, less savage—ending) and gasped at its most standard of manipulations; I saw *Benji:*

The Hunted in a darkened cinema and was intensely moved by the otherworldly self-sacrifice of its eponymous hero—a kind of four-legged Bodhisattva—until I noticed that the only other person in the theater, a frazzled-looking salaryman, was slumped over in his seat and breathing very deeply.

Being abroad, in a place still strange to me, senses sharpened, and ready to be transformed, was like being a child again—or being in love. I found myself speaking more slowly, more deliberately, here, as I delivered simple sentences in Japanese, or in an English that a Japanese might understand. Instead of trying to make phrases, or impressive sentences, I was concerned only with making sense. In speaking around a foreign language, indeed, I was forced to rethink myself, to gather my thoughts in a state of preparedness and then translate them into clarity; to speak, in fact, with a little of the lucency of Zen.

The elegant Etsuko, meanwhile, was diligently trying to give me a taste of the other side of Japan, the fine-tuned, closed-door world of the upper-class matron. One day she invited me to a meeting of a special cultural group that she had formed to bring Japanese people (mostly women) together with foreigners, the better to get to know one another, and Japan.

When I arrived, in a smart modern salon in the fashionable area of Shimogamo, I found myself in a room bright with the chatter of dapper ladies in their early forties, trendily turned out in leather skirts and cashmere sweaters. This, it seemed, must be the Kyoto equivalent of what Embassy wives do at the club, except that here one found an air of sophistication more rarefied than even the dinner party rites of English country houses. As soon as I entered, a group of ladies descended on me, all smiles and English phrases extended as daintily as *hors d'oeuvres*, and I was divested of a small donation, ticked off a list, given a name tag, and handed a program. A Mr. Ono, it seemed, a local graduate student, had planned the day's activities in an exhortatory spirit: "Let's get on this special train leading to a galaxy of cosmic symphony."

Looking around anxiously, I saw that I was the youngest person here by a decade or two, the only vagrant and the only male, save for an extremely rumpled old German professor in a dark-gray suit and an air of Schopenhauer gloom, his mood apparently not improved by being identified on his name tag as "Rols" (his wife, more cryptically still, was labeled "Bal"). Depositing myself down next to Rols and Bal, I was well embarked on lugubrious chitchat when suddenly Mr. Ono called the meeting to order. His subject, he said, was play, and its meaning. His particular expertise was in the giant swing to be found in downtown Bangkok, and his belief that play admitted us to the same sense of liberating ecstasy as religion. Rols slumped back in his chair, the chirpy bird ladies craned forward, lipsticked faces alert, pretty skirts tidy against bended knees.

Then, leaping up, Mr. Ono started playing *Jonkenpun* (or paper/scissors/stone) with himself and scribbled some marks up on an impromptu screen. The Embassy wives murmured a collective "ooh," heads delicately balanced on fists. Rols, however, looked a long way from catharsis. Then, unexpectedly, Mr. Ono darted around the room, handing out pieces of string. Please could we make cat's cradles? he urged. Doing so, we felt, in some cases, little of the liberating ecstasy of religion.

Then we adjourned for lunch,. an exquisite affair of persimmons, strawberries, kiwifruit, salad, and pizza. Daintily, the Embassy wives picked at their pizza with chopsticks. I, circulating inwards more than out, ambushed a couple of them and made a bid for cultural understanding. One of them professed a breathless concern for the stories of Somerset Maugham, the other was reading *Les Misérables* in the original.

Then Mr. Ono, a serious-looking fellow with spectacles above his broad young face, and a jacket and tie, strode back into the room with a cello, accompanied by another student, carrying a flute. A sweet-looking girl in black velvet dress and sheer white stockings—recently escaped, it seemed, from some heart-shaped Victorian locket—sat down at the piano and, pedaling with stockinged feet, unraveled a rippling melody. Mr. Ono, closing his eyes with feeling, started bowing his cello in a series of plaintive duets by Elgar, Saint-Saëns, and one "T. Ono." Then, half collapsing from his exertions, the versatile hero sank into a chair, and we were treated to lilting piano and flute duets.

Then, just as all seemed lost, suddenly a revived Mr. Ono burst into song, a ditty written by himself, no less, ineffably plaintive in its commemoration of lonely bicycles and vanished youth. Finally, the tireless trio tore into a sonata by Handel and, in response to cries of "Encore!" from the enraptured women, yet another Handel trio.

Sitting in the sunlit room on this bright afternoon, a spotless tatami chamber beside me, and perky doctors' wives, conversant to a woman with Paris and New York, while a Masterpiece Theatre heroine played the piano in an Emily Brontë dress, I felt I had landed in a salon fashioned only from the imagination. And at the end, two pretty sprites, maybe nine years old each and fresh from *The Faerie Queene,* padded in, and shyly presented roses to each of the performers. Then—of course—it was photo time again (turning life into memorial art), and a departure from this Sei Shōnagon circle, back into the world.

As winter began to lift, Sachiko began to find new ways for us to spend time together. One day, as we were walking through a temple, she asked me, as if casually, "You eat every day in restaurant?" And then, a little later, "Where you wash clothes?" I answered her directly, and only later saw her drift. "Why you not come here my house, eat dinner? Why you not give me dirty clothes? I have machine; no problem." That was how the system worked: when her friend Hideko's six-month-old baby was in hospital, Sachiko visited him every day. The next week, she announced with delight, Hideko was obliged to baby-sit for her.

One could no more say that this was "calculating" or "guileless" than one could say that turquoise was either green or blue; Sachiko's instincts were so shaded, I could not put a name to them.

One day, while I was writing, the phone in my guesthouse kept ringing and ringing. Picking it up at last, I heard Sachiko's soft excitedness. "I'm so sorry call you house! I know you working! But before you say you much like orange cake. I find! Now I very close your house. Please I come here your room, give cake?"

I could hardly say no, and when she arrived, she quickly preempted all protests. "I'm so sorry," she began. "I very bad, I know. You need work. But I much want give you this cake. Maybe you eat, then work very easy." A few days later, it was some chocolate she had bought, and then a button she was eager to sew on, and then the tatami that she wished to clean. And though I could tell she was holding me hostage with kindness, I could also tell that she truly did do her thinking with her heart, and that it was as natural for her to seek out opportunities for kindness as to exercise a kind of emotional usury. Every time she visited, by now, she brought some flowers, to match the day and mood, and then, unable to wait, started fishing out other offerings from her bag. "I little give you present, are you okay?" she usually began, phrasing her question with such mischievous charm that it was all but rhetorical. "You not guilty? Is okay?" And then she pulled out a pillow, or a washcloth, or a sea otter key ring. "You hear this, you little think I here," she said beautifully, hanging a dangle of wind chimes outside my room one day. But that night, they tinkled all night long, and their lovely silver music kept me up till dawn.

Before very long, as I looked around my room, I realized that Sachiko was colonizing me more subtly than Japan had ever done Taiwan; and the bare room that I had set up as my secular monk's cell now had more and more of a domestic aspect. Her claims on me were everywhere: in the long-birded "Wonder

Worker" mugs she'd given me (no random gift, of course — she saw me as a bird, and a long-beaked one at that); in the guitar she'd propped against the wall, a constant reminder of her presence; in the spray of flowers on my desk and the "Bear" blanket on my floor. Taking me over with her gifts, she was remaking my room, and me, and each time she said, "Please you take," she managed to take over a little more ground.

Sachiko was also, almost unnoticed, installing herself in my life and putting her fingerprints even on the parts she couldn't see. She was courting my mother now with birthday cards, the more engaging because they were so transparently sincere, and when I mentioned, in passing, a seven-year-old boy I greatly admired, in California, she instantly came back with "Yuki send this boy little letter, are you okay? He little new friend, no problem?" The next thing I knew, I was ferrying drawings and photos between this infant Pyramus and Thisbe, and Sachiko, pointing out all they had in common — Montessori schooling, a love of ships, and "Sesame Street" — had acquired a new contact abroad, and a new claim on my California life.

Yet all this she achieved without ever making a demand on me or ever abandoning her natural grace; she had surrounded me with her presence, while scarcely seeming to move. And I could hardly blame her for wanting to stake a claim on her elusive new friend and seeking some guarantees in return for all her risks. "You little same cherry blossom," she said one day. "Long time I waiting. Then you come back, I very happy. My life very beautiful. Then you must go again." It was true, I knew, and there was nothing I could say.

It was also natural, I thought, that she try to lure out of hiding a foreigner who was almost Japanese in his evasiveness and self-containment. "Strong heart," she was finding, could be an antonym to "soft" as well as "weak." Soon she was beginning to tell me, pointedly, of the new dress she had bought for going out, of how her husband was taking her to a piano bar, or of how the American monk at Tōfukuji could speak to her in fluent Japanese.

"One man," she said one day, "Canadian man, very warm, very kind, he say he give me English lesson. Very cheap. No problem."

"Look," I said, rising to the bait. "I'll give you English lessons free, okay?"

"Really?" she said, delightedly, drawing out her datebook to fix a time. "Two times, one week, we meet, no problem?"

One night, not long thereafter, she suddenly called my house, her voice strangely coiled, and when I called her back from the street—not wanting to tie up the guesthouse phone—and cheerily sang out, *"O-genki desu ka?"* (Are you well?), she said, "I'm fine. Not so fine." A long pause. "Not fine."

"Sick?"

"Maybe. Little problem in heart."

I didn't know exactly what this meant.

"I ask you many questions, are you okay?"

"Okay," I said, though the night was dark and cold, and faces kept appearing at the phone booth, looking in.

"Why you no angry if I have other foreigner friend?"

"Anger no good. I cannot control your heart."

"Whyyy?"

"It is your heart, your choice. Anger doesn't help."

"But you sad?"

"Maybe." I was certainly turning Japanese. "But I think it's fair: if I do bad thing, then bad things happen to me."

"Please we meet," she said urgently, more or less telling me that I had failed.

Twenty minutes later, on an unseasonably chilly night, we met outside the hooded gate of Chion-in, ghostly now in the late-winter dark, and walked amidst the stone carcasses of temples, cold and silent in the night, returned now to all their grave antiquity.

Shivering in the chill, her voice choked up, she began to talk. "Today my heart little *muzukashii* feeling. I feel little dynamite in heart." She laughed gaily at the new word she'd learned, but I knew it was her social laugh.

"I'm sorry if I helped you put it there," I said.

"No, no," she said, as she always did when I apologized (the Japanese seemed to use "no" mostly to shrug off apologies or thanks, almost never to contradict or repudiate). Her voice then took on an unaccustomed hardness, a steeliness I had heard only when she was speaking Japanese. Her words came out with the condensation of her breath.

"If my marriage broken, what you think?"

"I'd be sad."

"Why sad?"

"Because I think your husband is a very good man." Anything I could say now would only incriminate me. "He takes good care of you and your children."

"Why you not happy?"

"Well, for example, if your brother goes away, you cannot stop him. But still you feel very close to him." Everything I said was only digging me in deeper.

"But what you do if I say *sayōnara*? If I find other foreigner friend, what you say?"

Blowing out cold air as we walked side by side along the deserted temples, the street all hushed around us, I got every answer wrong. "I would be disappointed," I said, "but I would accept that you had good reasons for it, or that larger forces were at work. I would be sad, but I would accept that I could not change your heart, or life."

"I think maybe I wait long time for you," she said.

She was correct, I knew, though I did not know what was the right thing to do.

Then, suddenly, eyes flashing in the dark, she said, in an eerie and unearthly tone, "I'm very bad. I little devil. I fox-woman." Her face in the dark was distant and haunted. "I little ghost. Old Japanese story: ghost visit man many many times, many very happy time together. But man's friends much worry. His face more weak, more pale. Ghost eating his heart."

She could hardly have given more eloquent expression to all my unspoken fears. I knew all too much about the Japanese fox-woman, who was said to possess innocent ladies and make them wild. I had seen the Lady Macbeth figure in Kurosawa movies, I had read about the avenging fury of Lady Rokujō in *Genji*. It hardly mattered that "fox possession" now was said to have been taken over by "TV possession"; ghosts in Japan were nearly always said to be jealous women driven by unburied grievances.

The next thing I knew, though, all the force had gone out of her, and she was crumpling down, sobbing (or laughing) as she said, through sniffles, "I'm so sorry. I'm very bad. I'm very sorry! Japanese woman very difficult. Face very soft, but inside very hard. I little fox feeling, I'm so sorry!"

"Maybe you are an Inari fox," I said to comfort her, reminding her that her hometown was the center of Japan's most famous fox shrine.

"I have two face," she went on. "Two side me."

And then she broke into tears, the condensation coming out of her mouth in gasps, on the silent, deserted avenue of stone temples.

4

WHEN THE CHERRY BLOSSOMS came to town, it was a punctual miracle, as well rehearsed and perfect as all the other events on the city's calendar. For weeks now, the preparations had continued: paper blossoms had been fluttering off the lampposts of the major downtown stores, and newspapers had run elaborate charts giving notice of the cherries' busy schedule. Mild Seven cigarettes had brought out their latest seasonal packs — all cherry trees and geisha — and *depāto* shopgirls had changed into their vernal clothes. Everything had re-dressed itself to show the blossoms off to advantage. And the trees themselves stood perfectly placed, as efficiently blocked out as seasoned actresses, arranged in such a way and so strictly trained that they were guaranteed to ravish.

So when the blossoms came at last, they mocked all jadedness with their otherworldly beauty, as stunning as a stage set by a heavenly designer. A blaze of lustrous pink above the city's canals, more dizzy and intense than any words could find, a shock of fluffy, fluttery pink frothing above the city roads. Pink-framed branches outlined against the faultless blue, branches drooping prettily above the pink-reflecting water.

All the people of Kyoto were well trained too, in amending themselves to the whims of the seasons, and so they streamed out on boundless Sunday afternoons and arranged themselves in well-framed pictures with the blossoms: old couples standing under sure-shot branches, young girls clad in the colors of spring, in peach skirts or apricot kimono, delicately fading into the retiring pinks, men in dark suits, stiffening their shoulders;

the colors framing all of them as sharp as any dream. The Philosopher's Path was one foaming avenue of pink now, and couples meandered through long trellised tunnels of the blossoms, sundappled in the blue; along the Kamo River, lovers sat silent under the blessing of weeping canopies of pink; and on Mount Hiei, a cable car ride up the sacred slope through a psychedelic tunnel of overhanging pinkness left me reeling with its Day-Glo brightness.

It was not long, however, before I found that I was, quite literally, allergic to the photogenic images of evanescence, and soon enough, my nose was stuffed and my nights stretched out through labyrinths of headached dreams. But where previously, in such fever states, I had found myself going round and around all night the Mondrian maze of the Paris metro, now, in my delirium, my mind shuffled and reshuffled the names of Japanese companies: Sony, Matsushita, Mitsubishi.

My conscious mind was turned round, too, by all the well-prepared grace of the season. Was beauty beauty if it could be mass-produced on cue? Why not, I thought: a ballet or an opera or a symphony was performed again and again, yet each time was transformed by the interpreter, and interpreted again in the mind of every listener. Could there be paint-by-number miracles? Did assembly-line epiphanies make sense? Sometimes, in Japan, the seasons were so formulaically displayed and so formulaically enjoyed that one was tempted to eliminate the active voice altogether: just to say that sake was drunk, blossoms were observed, and merriment was had.

And when the blossoms began to fall, breezed down through the sunlight by a passing gust of wind, or by a fleeting rain, there was a silent, rushing snowstorm of pink, fluent, soft, and noiseless, down upon the ground, the water, the pink-kimonoed ladies. After the rains, dead blossoms carpeted the earth and blanketed the rivers, leaving the trees half nude, their branches outlined black against the cloudless blue.

* * *

"Marriages are such an efficient system in Japan," a friend of mine called Michiko explained to me one day. "The woman makes up a résumé list—it usually consists of tea, flower arranging, and a couple of more up-to-date skills, like tennis or *chansons*, to show that she is a *mōga* (or modern girl). For the man, it's mostly a matter of what car he drives and how much money he earns. Then the marriage broker puts them together, and they're wed." Supply matched to demand; a minimum of risks and a pooling of resources. It was no wonder that marriages here came almost supplied with money-back guarantees.

After the wedding, things were no less sensibly pragmatic—he devoted his time to making money, and she to disbursing it; he took care of practical support, and she emotional. Formally, the woman was treated as a mere dependent (and the -ko suffix used for most women's names here literally meant "child"); behind closed doors, however, the positions were tidily reversed: the woman treated her husband like a baby, putting him to bed each night, giving him his allowance once a week, and sending him off each morning with a box lunch. Thus each party was allowed to be active in some worlds, passive in others, parent and child at once. The only complication came when feelings jammed up the system. (Kawabata's Chieko, asked if she has feelings, calmly explains, "It seems to cause trouble when one has too many.") It was no wonder that Japan enjoyed the highest marriage rate in the world (more than 98 percent of women found a mate).

"But I don't think Japanese women resent their marriages," Michiko went on, "however much they may regret them. They know how to make the most of them, and they know how to turn them to advantage. In some ways, I think, they're much freer than many American women." Freer? "At least they do not live vicariously through their husbands. They function pretty much independently of their husbands. If you go to a party here, you'll find that the women hardly ever talk about their husbands. They define themselves in different ways. In some ways, they're more able to lead a separate life. That's why they tend not to get divorces. In any case, even if they do seek divorces, they rarely get the children — or any alimony." It was no wonder, then, that as recently as her parents' generation, exactly one Japanese marriage in every thousand ended in divorce.

Michiko herself, though, was far from free of the system. Now thirty-four, she had been brought up and educated in America and worked now for an American company, even though she was entirely Japanese. (Talking to me, she seemed a regally tall, highly sophisticated, poised international businesswoman; the minute she addressed a Japanese, though, she became the very picture of a demure, deferential Japanese girl, all yielding softness and ritual self-denial.) Her mother, she told me, kept asking her and asking her why she did not have a husband. Her father spent all his spare time looking around for a potential son-in-law. And though they had lived for most of their lives abroad, her parents still could not get over the fact that their daughter was working for a company — and, worse still, a foreign company. By having a job, she was writing herself out of the collective script.

A little later, as the cherries began to fall, I decided to return for a while to the temple where I had first stayed, to see how much it had changed, and how much I had. On a fresh young morning, the narrow lanes of pilgrims' shops quiet save for strollers, the trees in gorgeous flower — all the city stirring now with the first tremors of rebirth — I went again to the ancient part of town, where the seasons were marked as a millennium before. April had brought a gentleness to the air, after the gray tumult and anxiety of March; there was a sense of healing in the mild, warm days, and of convalescence.

As soon as I entered the front courtyard, full of motorbikes, the albino monk hurried out to greet me and, his astonished face more astonished than ever, invited me in for some tea. Donning slippers, I padded after him to the tiny TV room, scarcely big enough for three, where the head monk was sitting, legs splayed out in front of him, clicking over channels with a remote-control device. The Nietzsche-loving gardener was summoned too, to greet the returning prodigal, and I, feeling obliged to respond somehow, settled down, cross-legged, at their small square table and began to talk of Sumō.

Apparently, however, some intonation was off a half note, for the head monk, nodding gravely at everything I said, responded with a vigorous lecture on male-female relations in India—he had been to the Taj Mahal, he reminded me—and, after every phrase, turned to me for confirmation of the marvels he described. I, by now accustomed to lusty participation in conversations I couldn't begin to follow, nodded too, and said, with conviction, "That's really so!" whenever I sensed he was asking a question, and "Is that so?" whenever it seemed that he had made a statement.

The proprieties observed, the albino then led me back into the room I had occupied many lives ago, and through the long afternoon, I savored the temple's luxuries of silence and open space. In the night, the outlined figure of the shaven-headed older monk shuffling through the blackened antechamber and letting out a startled, high-pitched cry upon discovering me, alone in the dark, looking out on the distant pagoda. In the dawn, my small bare room slatted with light, and the song of birds. In the chill first light, when some places look exhausted, and others seem reborn, Kyoto seemed always a miracle of early-morning hopes.

As I wandered in the days through the neighboring streets, I could begin to see how Kyoto had lost by now a little of its imagined purity to me, the simple clarity of myth; had become, in fact, so much a part of me that I could see it no more clearly than the back on which my shirt was hanging. The shops along the lanes seemed a little gaudy now, and no longer so uplifting—a sign, perhaps, that I was spoiled more than they were—and now it was the brassy American songs on their sound systems I noticed and not the lovely geometry of their goods. Kyoto was no longer a magic lantern to me; more an album of photographs, thick with associations, particularized, and domesticated. A certain hazy preciousness had been lost, on both sides, and in both senses of the word.

Yet in return, a certain specificity had been gained, a sense of detail that gave flesh and fiber to the dream. And as I walked through the drowsy streets one late afternoon to Maruyama Park, lost in thought, I looked up idly and, suddenly, lost all breath: the huge central weeping cherry tree in the park, its richly flowering branches drooping almost to the ground, was spotlit now, a blaze of burning pink against the dark-blue sky. I had seen this shot a hundred times before, in pictures and posters and books, but now, coming upon it unexpectedly, a royal elegance of blue and pink, I felt as if transported from the world.

In the shadow of the famous tree, revelers were seated in rows on blankets, eating bean cakes in the shape of cherry blossoms, strumming guitars, and bawling drunkenly as the sky turned pink behind the mountains. Shutters snapped, men in expensive suits put on their smiles, drooping girls made peace signs for the camera. And then, as darkness fell, torches came on along the waterways, their golden lights flickering in the pond. Suddenly, now, the park was a blaze of colors: navy blue and gold, a flash of pink, the black hills darkening in the distance.

In that instant I knew that Kyoto had installed itself inside me much deeper than mere fancy. No other place I knew took me back so far or deep, to what seemed like a better time and self. And as I wandered back in the dying light, lit up with a sense of rapture and of calm, I remembered the line of the poet Shinsho: "No matter what road I'm traveling, I'm going home."

5

As SPRING WENT ON, Sachiko and I still found ourselves often trading metaphors over the phone, exchanging complex feelings in pieces small enough to throw, and catch, I at a little open booth, on an empty, narrow alleyway, in the dark, she in the small room that sometimes seemed an almost unbearably wistful compound of her dreams.

"I want only dream time together you. You are from other world. I want see and learn this other world. But I cannot join. My heart very tiny—little fragile, like grass on windy day."

"But dream world only not so good," I replied, reflecting her English back to her. "If I were talking to Yuki, I could tell her stories, because she is a child. But you are not a child. I want to help you if you have problems. Dream time only not so good." I realized that I must be sounding bizarrely like Richard Chamberlain addressing the aborigines in *The Last Wave*.

"Then your heart change?"

"Not change. But sometimes tired. I feel I am on a beach, waving, calling out, 'Sachiko,' but you are on a far boat and cannot hear me. I want to help, but if you cannot see or hear me, I cannot give you food or medicine."

"I little moon feeling, then you cannot reach?"

"Yes. And I cannot give an answer to your problem. I can only give you a quiet time, a relaxed time, the chance to forget your problems so that you will be more strong to conquer them. It's like going from South Kyoto to North: you cannot run all the time—you must sometimes walk, sometimes stop in a coffee shop for food. The coffee shop does not get you closer to North Kyoto, but you need it to arrive there. You cannot always run."

"You say true. But if I much cry, have much tear in eye, then I cannot see star, or beautiful thing. Only cloud."

To that I could say nothing in return.

Towards the end of spring, I made my first official trip to the water world, the fabled entertainment quarter, of Kyoto. So segregated was the demimonde from the daylight world that walls had once been erected to separate it as firmly from the temples nearby as, in Japan, one self is shut off from another (if you are relaxing, relax without scruple, goes the logic, and if you are working, work without distraction). The area was also largely closed to nonmembers, as Matthew and I had discovered. Now, though, a local businessman was eager to take his son—on his way to Santa Barbara—out for a farewell night on the town, together with his son's English-language teacher. Eager to make a grand show of his hospitality, he begged the teacher to bring along some friends, and I found myself invited as an expert on Santa Barbara, together with the ubiquitous New Zealander, here, yet again, to translate risqué Japanese quips into proper English terms.

Our group met in the coffee shop of a large hotel—the two other foreigners, father and son, and two attendant girls, giggling and bebanged, and decorously attached to son and teacher.

"How much does a Corvette cost in California?" was the departing student's first question to me.

"Oh, I don't know," I said, ready to aim high. "Maybe forty thousand dollars."

"Phew!" The boy whistled through his teeth. "Incredible!"

"Expensive, right?"

"Expensive? No. Very cheap! I can buy two!" The father beamed down his blessing on Junior's ambitions. Then we went out into the streets of Shimabara, the ancient pleasure quarters, built around a willow tree, symbol of transience for both monk and courtesan. Piling into taxis, we headed off to the father's regular bar, in Gion.

Inside, the decor was meant to reproduce a French salon — plush sofas and love seats, a big grand piano, tall, heavily made-up vamps in short dresses, slinking around with iron smiles of uninterest. Hard-faced, hard-mannered, and hard-boiled, they glided about like tropical fish, objects of brightly colored weirdness. One of them sat down and played "As Time Goes By" on the piano, another placed herself beside a baby-faced guy in a perm and white shoes, and smiled at him through clenched teeth. ("Look," muttered the New Zealander to me, through his own clenched teeth, "if you utter the Japanese word for that guy, we're finished!") Elsewhere, at another table, a handsome man in an expensive gray suit sat back while another woman, tall and cool as the drink she served, languidly lit his cigarette.

Truly, I thought, this was a shadow world in the Japanese setting, inverting all the laws and expectations of the daytime world, with everything reversed as in a negative. No reticence here, but boldness; no giggles, but hard smiles; not men in control, but women. It was, again, a form of Japanese pragmatism at work: if one had to find some relief or release, then one went to a special pleasure world in which certain ease could be found without danger of explosion or confusion. Debauchery on cue, a licensed kind of licentiousness. Safe sex might almost be a redundancy here.

The only exception to this Mardi Gras reversal was a young girl who sat down at our table and, perky as a university student, told us that she was doing this only as *arubaito*, or part-time work; the other ladies at the table laughed encouragingly and stared at her with hatred. In fact, she went on with engaging guilelessness, she was still taking classes. Tonight, Cinderella-like, she had to be home by twelve. This, as it happened, she continued sweetly, was her nineteenth birthday. The other girls cackled some more, their laughs like broken glass. For all I knew, hers was a role too, perfectly designed to offset the others, on this, her hundredth nineteenth birthday of the year.

All around, the ladies kept on slinking in and out, clouds of costly French perfume receding and approaching, whiskey glasses filling up, plates of cheese appearing on the table, fed to customers by hand. The English teacher did a brief stint on the piano, and in the giddy applause that followed, the father began talking to him casually, offering jokes and, parenthetically, a job worth two thousand dollars a month. The giggles and the backchat continued, glasses were clinked, a melon was filled with brandy. The teenage girl opined, "I want to learn English," one of her colleagues adding, "I want to visit other country." Beady-eyed, the company man threw in a couple of extra clauses to his offer. Then the mama-san sidled up to join our table, a small, hard bird, dressed all in white, with a soft, sweet face and gambler's eyes.

The night eased on, whiskey and tinkling laughter, and tinny melodies on the piano, and soon—most eerily of all—I noticed that I could no longer tell the difference between the professional hostesses and the "respectable" girls at our table: both giggled too much at every comment, were promiscuous with flatteries ("Oh, you're so clever! And your Japanese is so good!"), and picked their way through English with sweet determination, dishing out an impersonal sweetness. All Japan, it sometimes seemed, came on like a hostess—sleekly appareled, full of automatic charm, and dedicated exclusively to your happiness, as if her life—or livelihood—depended on it. Yet all Japan also seemed like a mother to its own. And with classic neatness, the Japanese had always kept its women and its feelings separate: one for heart and one for hearth, one to take care of the man in the world, one to take care of him at home. The divisions were airtight. Geisha traditionally were supposed to have no home, while wives were known as *okusan*, or "persons of the interior." Geisha traditionally were not allowed to carry money, while women were deputed to handle all household finances. Geisha were not supposed to marry, while wives were desexualized by the husbands who called them "Mother." The Japanese were accomplished technicians of the heart.

Through Sachiko, meanwhile, I was beginning to see a little more of the other side of the female equation here: the young mothers I had so admired on arrival. Her best friend, Keiko, was an acupuncturist (like her father) and, like her father, a Communist; but her main activity seemed to be romance. "She little Meryl Streep feeling," Sachiko had explained. "Japanese man much love this style." And certainly, with her short bangs and whitened face, Keiko was the kind of Kyoto beauty that Japanese men adored. Her main outlet now, though, I found, was American football: by attaching herself to the Kyoto University Gangsters — as team herbalist — she had stolen into a world where she was the only woman among fifty fresh-faced boys (and vulnerable boys at that: when I attended a game between the Gangsters and the Kansai University Fighters, the shaven-headed linemen, the occasional postinterception jigs, the squeaky pom-pom girls shouting "Dee-fense!" "First down!" and "Go go" — all in English — could almost have belonged to a California high school; but after the game, when I visited the locker room, the defeated *samurai* fighters were slumped amidst their pads like exhausted warriors, red-eyed, or sniffling, so choked up that they could not even speak).

Now, I gathered, Keiko lived with the twenty-one-year-old manager, her four-year-old daughter, and her ball-playing husband, in an arrangement they chose to keep ambiguous.

Hideko, Sachiko's other closest companion, was the opposite extreme — less than ninety pounds, her eyes shy and wide with childlike wonder, she was the very picture of propriety. Smiling sweetly, nearly always silent, carrying herself like a porcelain vessel in her neat skirts and expensive shirts, she was the Platonic incarnation of what a Japanese wife should be, one of those gracefully demure types, as Matthew put it, "who would in England be called a cardigan-and-pearls lady."

At least on the face of it. "She very small lady, very fragile — little flower feeling," Sachiko had told me before introducing her. "Other person think very shy, very quiet. But inside"—her eyes flashed with mischief—"very different! She not have dream. She love money only!"

I took this at first to be an exaggeration, or, at least, one Japanese woman's somewhat cutting appraisal of another. But as I came to know Hideko, I found that Sachiko had not overstated at all: Hideko's main interest really was in money. She had married a doctor—as prudent an investment in Japan as in America—and, by virtue of having no feelings for him, was able to play the perfect doctor's wife. With all the energies and feelings that were left over, she devoted herself to becoming the very model of a high-fashion sophisticate: she played tennis, she went on scuba trips to the Great Barrier Reef, she spent her days buying Italian handbags and French cakes. She memorized all the foreign names she could, and still often boasted, this extremely poised and intelligent young woman, that she had been the only student in her college with a Gucci bag.

When Sachiko told me that Hideko loved living near banks — their presence actually turned her on—I took it as a joke. "Very different," Sachiko told me, shaken. "I thinking little joke, I little laughing. But she very, very serious. Her heart not so open. She not so close husband. Then I little sad." Hideko referred to money by the affectionate diminutive that most people reserved for children or close friends; she even got a corgi (in emulation of Queen Elizabeth II) and gave it a name that was a rhyming-slang homonym for "money." Often, said Sachiko, Hideko told her friends how she was planning to spend her husband's money as soon as he was dead.

There must, of course, have been a deeper side to Hideko

that she did not want to show the world, or even acknowledge to herself, but certainly she played the part of loving money with unfaltering consistency. And though she was much too decorous to speak an English that she had not entirely mastered, she could hardly conceal her excitement when she heard that a foreign millionaire had come to town. So Sachiko effected an introduction to Matthew, and all three of them spent long afternoons together, sitting in coffee shops and watching videos, engaged in discussions I could scarcely begin to imagine. Sometimes, he told me, they would just be sitting in the Café Mozart, munching on Viennese pastries, when Hideko, overcome by the moment, would cry out, genuinely transported, "I'm so happy!"

Sachiko, in turn, seemed equally shaken by Matthew: here was the classic, almost ideal Japanese image of a foreigner — footloose, charming, with homes around the world and debonair Italian clothes — and all she could see in him was his sadness. He was sad, I told her one day, because he did not have a girlfriend, and he could not find a girlfriend because he was sad. She nodded solemnly. "This man only stay Japan very short time," she said. "He have very sad eye. Then I want give him warm heart."

Watching the three of them together, I began to see why Sachiko so exulted in foreign company, almost regardless of the person. Once, at her birthday party, as she bubbled on merrily, tripping over her ungrammatical English with careless delight and laughing with Matthew, Mark, and Sandy, I caught a glimpse of Hideko, in the corner, her eyes very hard: she did everything so perfectly, she was clearly thinking, why could the foreigners whose admiration she so coveted not understand that she was much better than her rough-and-ready friend?

6

ONE DAY, I decided to surprise Sachiko with a message. I knew that she always went to the kindergarten at twelve-fifteen to collect her daughter, so at twelve-ten I stood inconspicuously around the corner from the gate. The other mothers were milling about, stoical, propping their bicycles against trees, tiny babies on their backs, waiting around outside the barred gates. I leaned on a bicycle rack and watched them small-talking in their sensible clothes. Then, with a sudden instinct, I caught sight of her, on the far side of the busy street, her white comb in her hair above the broad expanse of her forehead, where it kept the hair from falling in her eyes. Her mouth was red with unfamiliar lipstick. And her face was a face I had never seen before, hard and clenched and closed. By her side strolled her husband in a sports coat, cheery in his stride, blithely indifferent to his partner, everyone's picture of an amiable paterfamilias.

Suddenly, I saw all the sorrow of her life, caught by surprise in the passing seconds: she so taut and coiled, waiting to release her warmth on anyone who'd take it; he so friendly and impervious, jaunting along merrily by her side. The sight of the two of them—not a couple really, just two people walking down the street together—so shocked me that I left my post and hurried away, catching her eye across four lanes of traffic and seeing the sudden gratitude of her smile as I hurried home, very fast, to await her call.

Although I knew very well that the Japanese made a business, and an art form, of keeping up appearances, reassuring one with smiles and never once letting the mask slip, I was still somewhat astonished at how faultlessly Sachiko could maintain the pose. Through six months together, often for hours at a time, in situations of such closeness that every vulnerability was released, she had never once lost her temper with me, or betrayed any tiredness, or even said anything unkind—except for her one flight of foxishness. It was a kind of training, I supposed—just as some people never drink, or never, however desperate the circumstances, swear—but nonetheless it was unsettling to me how well she could play her part. Her command of her role was so perfect, she knew her lines so fluently, that it sometimes felt as if playing the picture-perfect partner came as naturally to her as being herself.

I knew, of course, that she was being especially tough in her self-censorship so as not to lose her hold on me, and the freedoms I could offer; but this very sense of vulnerability, I thought, would make most people fragile, or edgy, or brittle. That, though, was not the Japanese way: she liked me, therefore she made herself likable to me; she ran her emotions as efficiently as an office manager. Japanese women knew that the best way of attaining their dreams was by becoming dream objects themselves; that was how, like the Canadian Mounties, they always got their man. They told themselves they could not, or should not, get sad or angry or tired, and they did not. One time, when I asked Sachiko why she never lost control, she sounded, this intense and impulsive woman, like logic itself. "You come here Japan very short time. One year. This year very important time my life. Then I want make only happy time: many happy memory and dream."

I knew, too, that in part this was because, from birth, she had been taught that satisfaction came in service; that happiness came from making other people happy. Sachiko was so well trained in pleasing that it came to seem almost a reflex in her: if ever I told her that I liked a dish, a shirt, or even a phrase in a letter, she filed the like away and served it up again and again; when I gushed over a sweater she once gave me, she promptly rushed out and bought another one, identical. Indeed, she stored away my preferences as diligently as a courtesan and did everything she could to procure and accommodate every one of them: one week, after I had given her a tape made up of poems by Keats, Yeats, Marvell, and Shakespeare, she came to my room hoisting a Japanese edition of *The History of English Literature* almost larger than herself. She had already been boning up on the poets I had read to her, she explained, and now was eager to ask about other figures she had run into before. What did I think of Arnold Bennett? She had read one of his books long ago. Did I enjoy Orwell? Which was my favorite work of Somerset Maugham?

In time, too, I noticed how determined she was that we should always be of one mind. Whenever we went to a restaurant, I began to notice, she always ordered what I ordered, even if it was something that almost made her sick. At first I thought this was because she was new to Indian food, or Thai, or Mexican. But in time I came to see that it was simply an unvarying pattern, part of her strenuous desire to please. Soon she was beginning to drink Earl Grey tea, very strong, with milk and sugar, and to school herself in Van Morrison. One of her favorite phrases in English, which she deployed as often as possible, was "Me too!"

When I explained to her one day my boyhood fondness for Paddington Bear — we were contemporaries and had grown up in the same cozy, protected, English middle-class world — she dutifully went off and opened an account with Mitsui Bank, because their mascot, represented on every book and desk, was Paddington. At every opportunity, in fact, she went out of her way to harmonize, to reflect my own tastes back to me. In Japan, I gathered, opposites detracted, and even on the personal level, unity had to be asserted at every step, in every detail — most graphically, to us, in the honeymoon couples who traipse around Waikiki or Surfers Paradise or Anaheim in identically colored shirts, slacks, bags, and even belts, perfectly color-coordinated twins for every day of their trip.

I could find explanations for all this, but still I felt unnerved by Sachiko's unslipping perfection; at times, I began to wonder whether she was not more honest in her words than in her actions. Part of it, I could tell, was her gift—her culture's gift—for always seeing the best in things and always putting the best face on them: not exactly distorting the truth so much as always accentuating the positive. Sachiko saw great beauty in Nature where I saw nothing; but she also saw great beauty in Rob Lowe movies, Steve Perry songs, and her Betty Boop pencil box. She took away from *Stand by Me* the golden vision of boys together, but recalled nothing of the extended mass-vomiting scene. When I told her of someone I knew who had destroyed his whole home by carrying on a twenty-five-year illicit affair, she gasped, enraptured, "Very beautiful story. True love, I think." In return, she implicitly asked me only to give her happy or reassuring news (certain topics were taboo, I could tell, and if ever I brought them up, she would say, "I not so like this *thema*," and filter them out as efficiently as her culture had done with the Rape of Nanking).

It was not, really, that Sachiko was naive; rather that she had been trained to find reassurance everywhere. It always amused me when she extolled her friend Sandy because, she said, Sandy was always smiling, never raised her voice with her children, never let her sadness show; because, in short, Sandy embodied for her all the sweetness, cheerfulness, and self-control that we associate with Japanese women. To me, this was mostly a reflection of Sachiko's own innocence in reading foreign cultures and of her penchant for sifting out only the good and remaking the world in her own happy image. The first principle of Japanese Romanticism seemed to be the culture's Emersonian assumption that it could refashion the world as it chose, and might as well do so, therefore, in a bright and pleasant light.

Yet her unfailing self-command only aggravated the eternal game of she loves me, she loves me not. I often wondered: was I attracted to her because she was so like me, or was she so like me because I was attracted to her? In Japan, this was as vexing a riddle as the chicken and the egg: *dakara* all over again. When it came to shopkeepers, say, I could happily accept that all their kindness was feigned, or functional at least; but when it came to Sachiko, that was less easy to acknowledge.

And then, at last, one night, I got my answer. Just as I was getting ready for sleep, the phone rang in the corridor downstairs, and it was Sachiko, asking me to come across town to her house; when I arrived, I found her sobbing and sobbing, her lavish hair tied up in a scruffy ponytail, her unmade-up face puffy and smeared. As soon as she caught sight of me, she threw herself upon me and buried her head in my chest, her small body heaving, and sobbing, and sobbing, as if with no hope of respite. I could feel her convulsions around me, her fingers tightening round my waist so hard I shook. I leaned back to look at her, but she grabbed me again, digging her fingers into my back, and sobbing, and sobbing, and sobbing.

Finally, motioning me to a chair, she pointed, through tears, at her tiny, worn dictionary, opened up on her "Bunny" table-cloth. I leaned over to where she put her finger under a word: "sacrifice."

"So," I said, as gently as I could, "you think that you must make all the 'sacrifice,' and I don't have to make any?"

Eyelids bruised and tired, she nodded.

"I know; maybe you're right. And you think my life is easy and free but yours is very hard. Because you must make plans, find baby-sitters, give excuses to your mother. While I am alone, and everything's easy. And you have to live with your husband and your children, while I have only myself." A small nod, that of a little girl getting told off.

"I know, Sachiko. I know it's hard for you. Please cry if you like." And she did, flinging herself round me once more. I held her, and looked round—at the otter smiling down at me from the ceiling, at the jigsaw puzzle on the table, at the winking red jewel in her Wizard of Oz comb.

"You can cry," I went on. "That's all right. Don't worry," I mumbled into her hair, and she sobbed, and clung, and shook in my arms. "That's all right. Please don't worry." Her Swiss cuckoo clock struck ten, and at last she sat back and brushed away her tears.

Then, over the little table, in one steady, uninterrupted flow, she came out with the whole story of her life, and all the accumulated sadnesses that had brought her to this lonely, perky room. "Before I always living parents' house, I little prison feeling," she began. "Mother many times sick, father always tired. Grandma die. Dog die. Brother go many place; but I must always help parent. Then first time I meet husband, little rescue feeling. I dream maybe little *Gone With the Wind*.

"But soon true marriage, very terrible feeling! Mother-in-law, father-in-law, more more prison feeling. Husband all day work, never together time. Then I have first child, I more more excited. But children not so help. Soon very tired. I have many dream. But I think I cannot find."

Outside, a train whooshed past, drowning out her words.

"Husband many times promise we little visit my brother, America. But he never do. My husband very kind man but not so strong: usual Japanese situation. He want only usual life, very quiet life. He not have dream."

That, I could see, was his main transgression: he was not, in her telling, a drunk or a tyrant or a philanderer or a crook; just a regular, fallible man captive to his received sense of duty and too small to accept the challenge of change. "He very good man," she went on. "But he much afraid his mother and father. Last year I ask, which you prefer: me or mother? Please you choose. And he choose mother. Then I 'all lost' feeling."

My heart went out to her, and to him too, this fond and dutiful father and husband, clearly decent and agreeable, and

confused now, surely, as he felt his pretty, vivacious wife slipping away from him, but not sure what he could do to reverse it
or what he had done to deserve it. He was only guilty, in a
sense, of innocence; but now, unable to get home before eleven-
thirty six nights a week, and totally exhausted on the seventh—
working all through the night, sometimes, at his parents' shop—he
could not find the time to turn things around. He might wish
that he had more time with his family, but that seemed as
fruitless as wishing he had six legs.

And Sachiko, too, was clearly captive to nothing but her
situation; captive to Japan, in fact. I could see why she wanted
to escape and how difficult it must be to have that hope cen-
tered on another. And as she went on talking, all her heart
came finally tumbling out: how her perfection had indeed been
an act of will; how she had wanted to be flawless lest flaws drive
me away; how she had tried to act out only the best parts of
herself. I had upset her sometimes, and she had smiled; she had
worried, and had laughed.

That night, Sachiko crossed a threshold of sorts, and ever after, I
saw a more relaxed and shifting kind of person: a heart, in fact,
not so different from the ones I knew at home—spontaneous,
scared, willful, and warm. She allowed herself sometimes to get
put out, or jealous, or depressed; she grew more direct in her
requests; she even started ordering her own dishes. I came to
know the feel of her warm tears on my cheek (though if ever
there came a knock on the door, she composed herself instantly
and put on a radiant smile). I came to see her emotional prudence,
always watching the endings of movies first (in order to enjoy
the pleasure of melancholy in advance). I came to recognize her
favorite, self-delighted cry—"I cannot stop. Cannot control. Cannot other! I so sorry!"

Yet even now, with so much to lose, she still responded to
most disappointments more in sorrow than in anger; and I felt

her occasional reproaches the more because they were unvoiced. If ever I did something to upset her, Sachiko's eyes would silently fill with tears, and I felt more strongly rebuked than by any rough obscenity; she was Japanese enough, I thought, to be truly gentle, and to use that gentleness to induce a sense of guilt as well as debt.

Mostly, though, I could never get over how happy she remained, even now. Ardent, dreamy, mischievous, and sweet, she giggled on cider and got up at dawn for *zazen;* practiced kung fu kicks in the temple and spun herself around in her joy. Here she was, I sometimes thought, loosed of all moorings, her parents antagonized, her family all but abandoned, and an unknown future in front of her, and yet, even now, she humbled me with her good nature.

7

ONE DAY, on a clear spring morning, I decided it was time at last to go and stay in a Japanese monastery—not a temple like the one where I had lived on first arriving, but a training center where I could briefly sample the rigors of the monastic life. The natural choice seemed Tōfukuji, where first I had tried *zazen* and where first I had met Sachiko. The largest Rinzai sect monastery in Japan, Tōfukuji was also well known for its cosmopolitan *rōshi*, one of the few Zen masters in Japan willing to take in Western students—even women—and concerned about the state of Zen around the world.

When I arrived at the temple gates, I was met by a young fifth-year monk from California. In the heavy silence of the entrance hall, a would-be monk was kneeling on the polished wooden stairs, head bowed in supplication, maintaining a motionless position that he would have to keep up for two days or more while his petition to enter the temple was ritually refused. Nearby, in a tiny antechamber, another aspirant—at the next stage of the process—was seated alone, in silence, in a position he would have to keep up for five more days before being admitted to the temple. Once inside, each of them would have to spend three years or more in a regimen unswerving as the temple's cedar pillars.

Greeting me in the silence with a bow, the monk led me along the narrow polished corridors of the monastery, a few busy figures robed in black gliding past us. As we went, he explained, in a whisper, all the disciplines that I would have to observe: how I must walk, hands folded across my chest, and how I must bow each time I entered and left the *zendō*; how I must step across the threshold with my left foot first, and how I must line up my sandals, in a perfect row, at the base of the meditation platform. How I must sit, how I must breathe: how I must learn to live deliberately.

He led me to a tiny guest room and asked me to take off my watch. Then, serving tea, he told me a little about his life. At times, when he talked of L.A. and his family, he sounded like a kid again, the twenty-two-year-old college boy he had left behind as soon as he entered the temple; at other times, when he talked of Zen, he acquired a sonorous *gravitas* that made him indisputably my elder. It was a little like being with Sachiko again: when the monk asked about where he could find the best pizza in town—on his one day off each month—he seemed a guileless teenager; when he told me how he wanted to live, I could see why he was the *rōshi*'s prize student.

Then the training began in earnest. In silence we went into a simple medieval chamber, and in silence ate a dinner of vegetables served from wooden buckets. If I wanted more, my guide had explained, I would have to tap my bowl; and after I was finished, I would have to rinse out the bowl with my finger and hot tea, ensuring that not a speck of rice was left. Then I would have to wrap the bowl up, left over right over bottom, in the *furoshiki* that was almost the monk's only possession. They were allowed no books, no keepsakes, no reminders of their lives outside; nothing but their robes, their bowls, and the body-length mats on which they slept face-up.

Our dinner finished, we walked across, in the chill of the darkening afternoon, to the wooden shack where the monks were allowed, once every five days, to take baths. The man preparing the bath today, a bespectacled man in his fifties with a look of frightened bewilderment, was rushing around in panic while the younger monks shouted orders at him. Only a week before, I learned, this man had been a regular salaryman, living with his family at home; then, however, he had learned that he would have to take over his family temple and been obliged to join a monastery. Now, as the junior monk in the place, he was the one the others were obliged to toughen up.

Scrubbed and rinsed clean in the scalding water of the tub, we proceeded to the ancient meditation hall. As the last light of day seeped in through the pulled-back screens, I sat with the monks, erect on the wooden platform, in silence. Occasionally, a monk, standing silent sentry by the door, strode forward and whacked, with his long wooden stick, anyone whose form was slipping—usually the terrified-looking newcomer in spectacles. The other seven sat in motionless *zazen*. Now and then, in the bird-scattered quiet of dusk, the mournful melody of a garbage collector's truck floated up from a nearby street. Occasionally, there was a swish of black robes, a flash of motion, as a monk headed away for *dokusan*, his daily private conference with the *rōshi*.

I too, once, at school, had gone off on evenings such as this for private meetings, and alone with my thoughts—too new to be above this—I thought back in the dark to school in England, so similar to this: the cold showers at dawn, the ascetic bare rooms, the beatings, the daily prayers in five-hundred-year-old chambers. The sense of hierarchy, the all-male rites, the chores, the fears, the longings—all seemed eerily the same. But that kind of school had been preparing its students to take over the world, while this one taught them to renounce it; ruling ourselves, at school, we were made to feel we could rule everything; while here, ruling the self, one was trained to need nothing from the world.

My legs by now were aching, my body was stiff; I waited and waited for the session to end. Finally, with relief, I heard a monk stir, and draw back the screens against the night. In a flash, with movements as quick and precise as in some army drill, the monks whipped out their bedrolls and stood at attention; the poor businessman, wrestling unhappily with his lot and unable to get it all done in five seconds, earned more sharp shouts and rebukes. Then, single file, we walked off to the temple garden, silver in the moonlight.

Nine figures, eerie in black robes, shaven heads shining in the silent dark, sat perfectly erect in the cool night air. When at last I left to sleep, all eight were sitting there, ready to continue through the night.

By three o'clock the next morning, my guide was rustling me awake. Bare feet cold on the wooden planks, we shuffled back into the meditation hall. There, still groggy, I followed the monks to another room, where gongs sounded and sutras were chanted, broken by the silver ringing of a bell. Then we returned to the hall for more *zazen*, screen doors open to the chilling dark as, very slowly, the light began to seep in and the birds to sing.

Hours, many hours later, we took a brief breakfast of gruel and pickled plums. Then we went out into the golden light of morning and began sweeping leaves, the monks working rapidly, in silence, sweeping and sweeping till every last inch was spotless. Above us, the temple's cherry tree blazed against the dawning blue.

Then there was long scrubbing of floors, on all fours, and chopping of wood, a quickly taken snack, and more hard physical labor (a form of moving meditation). In midmorning, the monks donned straw sandals and wicker hats and went into the neighborhood on their daily alms-collecting rounds. Then they returned for more work, more meditation, and, perhaps, at night, a few hours sleep on their mats. To an outsider, the Californian monk had told me, the temple seemed as calm and motionless as a river; inside, however, you got caught up in the rush and intensity of the surging currents. Every day was so full, he said, that there was never a moment of true rest. Did he ever miss the world? I asked. No, he said, touchingly. Nothing but his books.

Before I left the monastery, I went for an audience with the *rōshi*, whose presence I had felt all the time I was in Kyoto, as Mark's longtime friend and Sachiko's steady counselor. Seated in a thick leather chair, a tiny figure in huge orange robes, his windows thrown open to the green and golden quiet of the garden, he looked at me with warm and piercing eyes. He greatly feared for Zen in America, he told me over tea, because everyone there was after instant wisdom. Some people were so intent on *satori*, or instant revelation, that they actually bought books with answers to koan. The Americans did have one advantage over the Japanese, insofar as they were willing to take one day a week off. But as long as one reminded oneself constantly of how much fun one should be having on a holiday, it was not, in the true sense, a "holy day."

The "pride" of Americans, he went on, and their openness to challenges were exemplary; but he worried about their ambition, their love of cerebration. By coming to Zen with their minds, they were all but ensuring their failure at a discipline whose aim, after all, was to short-circuit the mind. "You should not think about the koan," he said, as any Zen master must. "You should become the koan."

During his own training, he explained, his teacher, Shibayama-roshi, had shouted at him constantly, "Be an idiot! Be a fool!" And in time, it had worked. At first, when he had begun, he had always been thinking of his girlfriend and his college pals. For five years, he had not been free of this. Intense meditation, after all, sharpened the very powers of memory that were the main block to meditation. But then, at last, he had learned to live in the moment.

The *rōshi* ended, in the classic Zen manner, with a story. Once upon a time, an old man was trying to explain to his grandson the belief of Jōdo Buddhism that the Pure Land lies in the West. Practical and alert as children are, the little boy had pointed out that if you go west, and farther west, you end up going around the world and back where you first started. Paradise, in short, was all around us, if only we would stop and look.

I, however, incorrigible foreigner, was still lost in books and hoping to bring Zen home to me by reading in Thoreau. For the rough earth of his prose was crisscrossed with the footsteps of Zen poets. Certainly, his ground seemed theirs — and his heaven too!—as if all of them were acolytes living in hermit huts scattered across the slopes of some sacred mountain. With his discursive essays on "Moonlight" and "Autumnal Hints," his retreat into the woods to "transact some private business with the fewest obstacles," and his insistence on living in a society of one, Thoreau seemed to have worked out for himself what was sacred in Japan (where the very character for "Nature" could be read as "self-seeing"); and every Zen wanderer and poet and solitary seemed, in his way, another sojourner in Walden, living off berries in the wood, sustaining himself on natural scriptures, devoting himself to slowness and to idling. Having given up everything, he had nothing to lose—and all the world to gain.

So when I read in Bashō, "My solitude shall be my company, and my poverty my wealth," I felt I was reading again the anarchist of Walden, pursuing his nonviolent revolution of words, remaking the world by reversing its meanings. And when I read in Dōgen, "Why leave behind the seat that exists in your own house and go aimlessly off to the dusty reaches of other lands?" I could almost hear his neighbor in New England declaring, "It is not worth the while to go round the world to count the cats in Zanzibar." And when I read Kamo no Chōmei's "Account of My Hut," singing the praises of a simple life of solitude, I found Thoreau again in the recluse's famous claim that none can know the pleasures of loneliness who has not tasted them himself.

Soon, in fact, the parallels started doubling back on themselves, till the Buddhists almost seemed the Transcendentalists' disciples. When Emerson wrote that "The great gifts are not got by analysis. Everything good is on the highway," he all but enunciated the guiding principle of the wandering Zen monk. And when he wrote, in a poem, "Sleep is not, death is not, who seems to die, lives," he sounded almost like a Buddhist haiku master. Even the Buddha could sound at times like a follower of the Sage of Concord: "Self is the lord of self, who else should be the lord?"

I got the strongest chill, though, when I read in Emerson: "Women, more than all, are the element and kingdom of illusion."

What could be closer to the old Mahayana saying: "Of all the forms of illusion, woman is the most important"?

Just as I was pursuing these connections, Mark, with his unerring gift for reading my thoughts the better to guide them, handed me a volume of Santōka, one of his favorite poets, a monk who was said to have walked 28,000 miles on his path, along the back roads of Japan, in a straw hat, retracing some of Bashō's steps. Though the natural descendant of Bashō and Ryōkan, this solitary figure was a citizen of our century, who sustained his "walking meditation" through all the tumult of the early decades.

Santōka's free-style haiku were a model of the form, so cleansed of ornament and abstraction that they sometimes ended less than ten words after they began; his art seemed to come to him as naturally as breathing. Free of pretension, his poems were free of tension. And in accordance with that spirit, his life was also as clear and simple as running water. His great joy, he said, was "one room, one person, one light, one desk, one bath, and a cup of sake." The only journal he read was his own, and what little extra he had, he gave away. Even the constant sake drinking he did, he did, as he did everything, with all his being.

When I read of Santōka's defection from society and most civil of disobediences—refusing to participate in the preparations for war—I could hear his words echoing round the woods at Walden, and so too, when he wrote, with characteristically bracing simplicity, "To do what I want, and not to do what I don't—this is why I entered such a life." Yet the most striking thing about his wanderings was that they were always in pursuit of something more than self. "My pilgrimage," he wrote beautifully, "is into the depths of the human heart."

A little later, in the spring, Mark and his teacher put on an exhibition together of paintings based on Santōka's poems, Mark translating them into simple images, his *sensei* scrawling the poems, in vigorous calligraphy, round the edges of the shapes. And when I went to the gallery and spent an hour or two with the pictures, slowly, in the silence of the department store, I began to feel I could understand a little, for the first time ever, the power of blank space. How space can live, and draw one in, as silences can speak; and how the Japanese, more than anyone, could charge the emptiness. When Mark drew the lonely figure of Santōka, one felt the space around him, irradiated with his quiet, and when he drew a flower, he drew nothing but its shape. Autumn was merely the faintest outline of a falling leaf. Attention had been brought to such a point that it turned into a kind of meditation.

At the exhibition, I realized, for the first time, why the Japanese were fascinated with *ma,* or space, and how they tried to sustain it inside their crowded homes and lives. They sought to approach life, in a sense, the way one spoke one's language to a foreigner, in a spirit of simplicity, sympathy, and clarity. In Santōka's poems, translated by the side of the paintings, nothing extraneous intrudes.

> *My begging bowl*
> *Accepts the falling leaves.*

Mark's painting of the poem was just a leaf in downward flight.

> *No more houses to beg from,*
> *Clouds on the mountains.*

Mark's painting showed just clouds.

> *All day I say nothing,*
> *The sound of waves.*

The painting caught sound, and nothing more.

The poems themselves, in their clarity and ease, began to open up a space within. One had to tread them slowly, as through snow; and step by patient step, one began to savor the crunch, the texture, the depth.

> *Brightness of the snow*
> *Fills the house with calm.*

Reading very slowly, I began to feel the calm of that, the soothing quiet of the falling snow, remaking the world without a sound. I began to see the warmth of the poem, too, and its freshness; how snow brought silence, and a spaciousness within. The gradual movements of its flight began to slow the mind down, as surely as the tolling of a bell.

> *No path but this one,*
> *Spring snow falling.*

As I wandered round the room, with Sachiko by my side, I began to think how much we need space in those we love, space enough to accommodate growth and possibility. Knowledge must leave room for mystery; intimacy, taken too far, was the death of imagination. Keeping some little distance from her was, I thought, a way of keeping an open space, a silence for the imagination to fill.

"At the same time that we are earnest to explore and learn all things," Thoreau had written, "we require that all things be mysterious and unexplainable."

And as we walked around the paintings, Mark's teacher, eighty-six years old now, but alive with coiled energy, his shaggy gray hair falling bohemian across his face, came into the gallery. Full of energy, he began telling us about his coming trip to China, his various projects, the classes he gave, the books he was working on. Then he spoke warmly of the abbot of Tōfukuji, a friend of his for life.

"*Chotto kibishii,*" said Sachiko of the *rōshi*. "A little strict."

"*Demo yasashii,*" added the painter, smiling. "But gentle too." "Strictness without gentleness is not so good," he went on, "and gentleness without strictness is not so good. Strictness and gentleness together are the best."

8

Sᴀᴄʜɪᴋᴏ's ɢᴏᴏᴅʙʏᴇ, when it came, was as perfectly planned, as exquisitely decorated, as everything else in this land of ceremonies.

One day, towards the end of spring, she invited me and Matthew to join her and Hideko at a tea ceremony. She appeared in the hotel lobby in a radiant blue kimono, hair done up in the style of a Meiji maiden, her steps in pure-white socks and wooden sandals slow and reticent. We watched a woman in a white peacock kimono glide along against the paper screens, flooded now with early-morning sun, and we entered our names with thick brushes in a visitors' book. Then, with a bow, we were ushered into a room full of bowing matrons, all beady-eyed and kimonoed, as used to this as we might be to church. Seated cross-legged, we sipped at our tea, dutifully inspecting the lacquer tea box, inscribed with a scarcely visible tracery of cherry blossoms. "Night cherry," Sachiko whispered under her breath, and the matrons leaned a little closer. "Little *monoganashii* feeling." We inspected a scroll that told of a flower and a butterfly, and, eyes bright, she looked over at me meaningfully as the springtime message was translated.

Matthew, meanwhile, was his usual engaging self, and as the matrons looked at us in wonder, he started pulling at the legs crossed under him, forming a hideous frown and delivering, in loud stage whispers, a moving account of his torments. "Can't understand it. Terribly simple, actually. Legs quite dead. Can't move. Don't know if I'll ever recover!"

"Are you okay?" Sachiko asked anxiously, leaning over me towards him, to extend a hand.

"Oh yes," he said, smiling tightly. "Fine, fine. Just a little stiff. Can't move, you see. Awfully painful, actually. Quite extraordinary."

The pantomime continued, I as ill at ease as Matthew, and the matrons staring over at us with quickened excitement, exchanging happy glances and then looking back at us, in awe; for them, I imagined, hardened veterans of these rites, the presence of two galumphing foreign males, banging against walls, attacking their tea with chopsticks, and pulling at their limbs like pretzels, was doubtless a welcome gust of comic relief in what was otherwise dull routine. "Terribly sorry, awfully embarrassing," Matthew apologized, smiling unhappily back at them. "Not sure, actually, whether I can move!"

"This was something Merchant Taylors' never prepared you for," I whispered back.

"No, quite," he answered, tight-lipped, then erupted into schoolboy chortles.

The tea bowl went round and round for our admiration, we munched at our sweets, scattering crumbs, which we proceeded to fold ineptly in the napkins Sachiko gave us. Then at last it was over. Matthew and I disentangled limbs and got up, legs so dead that I, standing up, reeled and staggered against the paper screen before bowing farewell to the delighted matrons and tiptoeing out to the lobby. Outside, in the soothing sun, Sachiko led our incongruous band to a coffee shop, and as the four of us settled round a circular table, Matthew filled us in on how a two-day trip to Tokyo Disneyland had somehow kept him away for a month. In Tokyo, he explained, he had found everything he wanted: high fashion, neon futurism, even an English-speaking girlfriend. After two weeks, however, of a consuming intensity that had almost frightened him, he had rung her up one day, to find that she had dropped him for a new foreigner.

"Ah, very beautiful story," said Sachiko dreamily. "Little cherry blossom feeling. One-night dream."

"Yes, yes, precisely," said Matthew agreeably, used by now to the Japanese habit of turning even pain into something lovely, and unaware, perhaps, that she was in effect referring to a one-night stand.

After our coffee was finished, Sachiko dispatched the other two into a taxi bound for a department store, and clomped along the wide boulevard by my side, in tiny footsteps. "I come you room?" she asked. "Are you okay? We little buy cake?" and, stopping at a bakery, we made our way through a riddle of sunny streets, back to my room. There, sitting down, she unclasped her earrings and, laying them tidily on my table, took me by surprise.

"Today," she began, "I wear kimono so you always keep very happy memory of me." I could not fathom what she meant. "You give me much dream, much imagination. I want you write many thing, very beautiful memory of Japan. We together time, very happy, many dream. But then, other life, very difficult. I much much thinking in my heart—then little stomach problem. My heart little sick."

She stopped, and I, accustomed both to the solemnity of her feelings and to their sudden turns, held my breath.

"You have very beautiful bird life," she went on. "Very free, very easy. But my life very different. I tiny, I not have wing. I need more *akirameru.*" She stopped and, turning to her crumpled, leather-bound old dictionary, skimmed through the pages and stopped on the word she wanted. "Re-sig-na-tion. Here in Japan, this very important. All person must have this resig—"

"Resignation."

"Re-sig-na-tion. If not have, many problem. Then maybe I must little say goodbye."

Looking back at her, I fumbled for my words. Then, turning to the only piece of paper at hand—the happy orange-and-white bag of the bakery—I sketched a diagram of my heart, and she, a little sadly, nodded over her cake. I then drew another picture, of the three routes open to us.

"Maybe goodbye best," she said. "But please today, you come together my house, play together children?" There was nothing I wanted less to do right now, but I could see that she needed to recast the play, to establish herself again in the mother's role and me as the friend of the family. And so we went back out into the mild spring sun, and on the long train ride across town, I watched her rearrange her self, as I did too, putting on a bright smile and an air of cheerful competence.

Back at home, Yuki and Hiroshi raced out and bounced all over me, pulling me this way and that, and I began roaring at Hiroshi like a bear, and lifting Yuki high into the air while she screamed, and, when they were not looking, wheezing and whistling like an imagined raccoon. Then Yuki careened off to grab her moth-eaten, one-eyed orange raccoon. ("Lasker," explained her mother. "Lasker?" And she sang me the jingle of a TV cartoon, "Rascal Raccoon.") Then the children, well trained already in how to entertain all visitors, changed into their best clothes — Yuki into a pretty frock, Hiroshi donning a red bow tie — and solemnly took turns playing the piano, feet dangling poignantly only halfway to the floor. Then all four of us went back to the Nogi Shrine, in a light spring rain, and played hide-and-seek in the gathering dark, as we had done on the day we met.

In the dying light, Sachiko bought us all cans of milk tea, and while the children played with acorns, the two of us padded around the noiseless shrine, dedicated to the hero of the Russo-Japanese War, the man who had been the Emperor's headmaster and role model. The walkways were deserted now in the rain, the wet ground strewn with petals; the bare branches were black against graying skies.

"Yesterday," she said dreamily, guiding me to her favorite tree, "I lie down this bench, and look at sky. Sky very blue; cherry very pink. Spring wind come down, so soft. I look up, I dream I have little wing. Bird talking, leaves dancing in spring wind."

She pointed out the different trees to me, told me the stories that she shared with them, explained which one was king and which his ladies-in-waiting. "But today," she went on ruminatively, "all cherry fall. Little fox wedding day."

"Half rain, half sun, you mean?"

She nodded, and I could see her in a fox wedding mood herself, caught between conflicting dreams.

In her flat, she cooked a quick dinner and packed the children off to bed. Then, seated at the small table that took up nearly all of the poster-filled room, she told me, eyes shining, about all the hopes she'd ever had, and how they'd disappeared. I looked around at the pictures of a-ha, the grinning sea otter on the ceiling, the framed photo of her children with the abbot of the temple: this was how the Japanese ended things, I thought, avoiding the embarrassment and mess of sudden death with the clean break of a kind of suicide. Everything brought to a ceremonial close, as shapely as a morning-after poem.

When it came time for me to leave, she brought out a scarf and tied it round my neck to keep me from the cold, and then walked, as usual, to the train station, as on the first day that I'd visited. As the train pulled away, I watched her standing alone on the platform, waving and waving till her small figure was finally out of my sight.

SUMMER

Surface is an illusion, but so is depth.

—DAVID HOCKNEY

1

Now that matthew had finally exhausted Tokyo, there was nothing left for him in Japan. Having found the worldly life he'd always craved, he decided that he should, in fact, be seeking out the spiritual life. He doubted what he knew, and then revised his doubts. And the very qualities that attracted many foreigners to Japan—that it left one alone, and therefore free—were for Matthew, I could tell, an ordeal; Japan offered him everything except direction. He felt his own uncertainty mocked by the equable calm and self-containment of Japan. Besides, Japan had little time for agonized self-scrutiny or coffee-house ruminations; speculation and introspection were regarded as indulgences that took one away from the matter at hand. So now, having stuck it out through the darkest days of winter, just as the weather was beginning to clear, he decided to leave.

I was sorry to see him go, my partner in bewilderment, especially since he had no special place to go, and on our last night on the town, I invited him to come along with me to one of the year's last performances of the Miyako Odori, the biannual geisha dance, which had been, for more than a century, the only occasion when the general public could see the most storied and private of entertainers in action. Performed in spring and autumn, when the blossoms were pink and the maple leaves red, the all-woman show was a kind of counter to the all-male performances of Kabuki. And over the years, the show itself had generated almost as many legends as those it represented: most famously the tale of George Morgan, the American millionaire, who had grown so smitten with a young apprentice geisha, or *maiko,* whom he saw onstage that he had embarked on a love affair as famous as those of Mademoiselle Chrysanthème or Okichi-san. Nowadays, however, there was such a shortage of girls willing to enter the old profession that the producers had had to turn to local high school students, and the daughters of loyal patrons, to fill the twenty places.

Seated in the quiet auditorium, having missed the tea ceremony beforehand through our inability to read the tickets, Matthew and I watched scene after scene unfurl with the precise exquisiteness of watercolor prints, in richest indigo and whitest white. A chorus line of *maiko* came prancing, tiny-footed, onto the stage in tidy, decorous rows, bearing crimson leaves of maples or blossoms of the daintiest pink. The geisha, however, who lined the balconies, cradling samisen and letting out screeching cries, were the most terrifying hags I'd ever seen: craggy old harpies, dressed all in black, their unsmiling, berouged faces soured with the lines of scowls. Refugees from some country production of *Macbeth,* they gave new meaning to the notion of a dragon lady. They also put one Japanese romance firmly in its place.

The show, however, unfolded in one shimmering sequence of gossamer backdrops—love stories presented as immortal tableaux, emotions translated into standard, stunning gestures. Then we streamed out into the bright afternoon and began walking along Hanamikōji-dōri, or Flower-Viewing Street, the paper lanterns outside the ancient teahouses painted all with plovers in the dying afternoon. Suddenly, I heard a voice behind me.

"Excuse me, are you Pico?"

I looked around to see a young foreigner, with a bright-eyed woman I took to be his mother.

"Yes."

"I'm John Horton. You may not remember me, but we were on a bus together in Tibet two years ago!"

"Of course," I said, looking at him again. The last time I had

seen John, he had indeed been in a rocking vehicle crowded
with peasants, bouncing across Tibetan plateaus, while his brother
had been stretched out on the back seat, moaning, the simulta-
neous victim of Chinese food, altitude sickness, Chinese airline
service, and the bus itself. At the time, I remembered vividly,
John had been on his way to Kobe; a quick-witted entrepreneur
who'd been in business since his teens, he'd told me he had
heard that Japan was good for quick kills and, better yet, that
Japanese girls were mad for Western men.

"You're living here now?" I asked him.

"Right!"

"Doing business, I assume."

"No, no. My only interest is in Buddhism."

"But the last time we met . . ." and then, seeing his expression,
I let the sentence trail.

"Yeah. My plan is to go to China, learn the language, and
then go to this Vipassana meditation center in Bombay." Japan
had a wonderful knack, I noticed, of awakening foreigners'
interest in every form of Buddhism except the Japanese. Still,
John's conversion had at least been in a relatively positive
direction; most people seemed to come to Japan for Buddhism,
and end up after girls or cash.

"Good luck with your studies," I said, as Matthew and I strolled
away. It was apt, I thought, that Matthew see this before he left,
and I, too, of course; the confusion of interests—of people coming
here for good deeds as well as good times—was everywhere.

The guesthouse in which I lived, in fact, might almost have
been a sociologist's model designed to illustrate the varieties of
romantic experience, made up, as it was, mostly of lonely foreign males and shady, water-world Japanese. The place's noises
alone were a constant register of frustration and fulfillment.
One Belgian girl loudly satisfied herself each day, while the
room next to mine was a veritable laugh track of giggles and
slaps and high-pitched squeals of "Stop! Stop it! Please stop!" in
Japanese.

One night, a man down the corridor began howling and howling, rending the night with obscenities. "Oh god, oh fuck, oh jesus!" he cried. "Oh god, please stop, I can't stand it." Wrenched from my dreams, I lay there in the dark, listening to his terrible wails. "Oh god, oh jesus, oh god, why did I do it?" The shrieks of the damned must sound like this, I thought. "Oh jesus, oh fuck, oh god, how can you do this to me?"

Later, I learned that he had been in great physical pain; his main affliction, though, was loneliness.

Another night, at 3 a.m., I was woken by some banging and knocking on another neighbor's door. A few hours later, I was startled out of sleep again by a clamor of excited whispers in the corridor outside. Opening the door, I found three teenage Japanese girls, no older than fifteen, apparently camped out on the floor. The day went on, but they did not, and every time I came or went, I found them squatting on the floor, next to a pair of his-and-hers Snoopy slippers, laying sustained siege to the quiet, studious Swede who lived next door to me.

For three days, the unlikely pop trio remained there, as patient as a courtly lover outside his sweetheart's balcony, cleaning their teeth at the basin in the corridor, padding, in towels, to the shower, and occasionally finding other foreigners to take them in for the night. When finally Hans returned home from a trip one night, he surveyed the scene and shrugged his leather-jacketed shoulders. "I only meet these girls one time," he said helplessly, "in Pub Africa. I do not understand."

A couple of days later, when I went down to the guesthouse telephone to make a call, Parker, the gracious Southern boy, shyly opened his door and invited me in for a chat. By the time I arrived, he was deep in Hume's *Treatise Concerning Human Understanding*.

He put the book down. "I need a girlfriend—and bad!" he

began disconcertingly, this tall and scholarly lawyer's son whose dream was to go to divinity school. "I haven't had a woman for so long that if I don't find one soon, I'm going to leave." I looked around at his monastic cell: Heidegger, volume after volume of Kierkegaard, *The Principles of Buddhist Psychology.* "Maybe summer will be better. Have you seen all the pregnant women around right now? I'm thinking, if they're pregnant now, summer must be the time when it's all happening." He looked at me pleadingly, with an eager freshman's smile that bespoke the depths of his desperation. Around him were volumes of Rilke and Nietzsche and Zen.

"You like philosophy?"

"Yeah," he says, a frat boy abashed. "Didn't I tell you? I lived in Oxford last year, studying being. And I'm spending a year over here, doing nothingness." There was no apparent irony in his voice. "I really love books. Books and women. If I can't have one, I've got to have the other."

Parker, I recalled, had managed in his nine months here to pick up precisely four words of Japanese—"little," "horny," "sorry," and "cockroach." (I often wondered what kinds of sentences he fashioned with this small but pregnant repertoire—"I'm a little horny cockroach," perhaps—and what effect they had on the girls he was trying to impress.)

"I wish one could be married and still be a monk," he said.

"But that's exactly what they have over here! That's one of the principles of Buddhism in Japan."

"Then why become a monk?"

I, thinking of Sachiko, and my plans of being alone, could give him no answer: all of us, it seemed, found only what we did not crave, and vice versa.

2

ON THE NIGHT of the May moon, the famously hazy spring moon beloved by monks and second in importance only to the harvest moon, I walked with Mark through the local temples in the early warmth. The moonlight magnetized my attention this night, glowing at the edges of my mind—it blazed— and Mark told me the story of the Chinese poet who tried to grab the moon's reflection in the water and drowned. For the Buddhist, the moon was illusion, *maya*, all that was chimerical; yet it was also the Tathagata, a symbol of enlightenment, and of the operations of divinity in the world. The Buddha's mind was said to be like the reflection of moonlight in clear, deep water; and the Buddha himself was said to be as constant as the moon, though sometimes he looked full, sometimes empty, sometimes half shrouded in clouds.

Meandering slowly past the silent, shadowed houses—a wood-block of ancient stillness—I thought again of how the lady and the monk interacted here, as did so many of the riddles of Japan. Was the moon a symbol of some higher beauty, or was it just a pretty earring in the sky? Enlightenment, I recalled read-ing in Dōgen, was "like the moon reflected in the water. There is no disturbance here, and all the moon is reflected in a drop." Sei Shōnagon, though, in certain moods, had taken it for what it was, no more: "At any time, and in any place, I find moonlight very moving."

Mark, then, went on to tell me of the Bashō poem of the clouds that obscured the moon, and as so often with him, I could see how much he had picked up from being around Zen monks and teachers; how he, too, had the gift of keeping one true to oneself, yet always thinking the best of one: a rigorously monitored idealism. I mentioned this to him, and he grasped my meaning quickly.

"The whole idea of a teacher," he said, blue hawk eyes flashing, "is to present a reflective mirror. Not a blank surface, really, but a screen, on which you have to confront yourself. Like the moon on the water, in a way. When you confront a Zen master, what you're really seeing are not his limitations but yours."

"So that if you think he's strict, it's because you're guilty? And if you find him silent, it's because you talk too much?"

"Yeah, I guess. There are many ways to do it. Sometimes they just let you talk yourself into trouble. Or they'll shock you out of your assumptions. Or they'll cut you down. Everything you think you're seeing in him is actually coming from yourself. A saint, I think, is someone who brings out the good in everyone he meets."

"So it's almost as if he's your true nature, in a sense, the better part of you?"

Mark, schooled in silences, said nothing.

A little later, at the beginning of *tsuyu*, or the rainy season, I went to stay with Mark in a temple on Awajishima, the resort island not far from Osaka. The monk who came to greet me at the ferry landing, a puppyish and frisky rock-star fan, thirty years old but still living in the temple that his parents ran, ushered me eagerly into his Toyota Crown, buzzing with bright lights now, a full moon cradled in its skylight and soul music thumping out of its tape system, its dashboard fit for a 747. I pushed a button, and the back seat beneath me began to recline, till I was all but supine, looking out at midnight-blue neon and green, clean bright colors inscribed across the night. Through the sleek, rain-washed streets of the little town we drove, the lights out to sea like ornaments, the big hotels strung along the coast like candles on a birthday cake. Past floodlit courts of tennis, and eerily spotlit swimming pools.

The temple, when we arrived, was a sleeker and more high-tech contraption than any I had seen in Japan. Inside, red lights were humming in the darkness of the entranceway, a panel to control the other lights and the clean white lanterns set atop the bushes. I followed my guide through long brown corridors, shadowing the small, lush garden, and lit so quietly I felt I was trespassing upon a daydream. In a perfect, clean-swept room, we ate strange celery and a rainbow of pickles, followed by ice cream made of strawberry, carrot, and plum. Afterwards, the monk went upstairs and I wandered round this house of marvels. Using the toilet, I found myself in some electric wonder system, with different mechanisms to warm the seat, shoot up hot air, expel a spray of water, and flatter one's behind—do everything, in short, but flush. From upstairs, meanwhile, where the young master of the household was commanding a whole bank of videos, Betamaxes, laser discs, and Bose speakers, I heard the gunshots of a *Rambo* tape, some dialogue from *Flashdance*. Outside, I saw the temple's switchboard lights, as complex as a deejay's console; beyond, the neon of the city, as still as night lights on an airport runway. A silent summer night alive with lights, as if, as Pynchon had written of L.A., one had turned a transistor upside down and opened its back to see the tangle of wires, alive with humming energies.

In the morning, I walked with Mark through the quiet, windless streets of what looked like an English country town, the glowing, twenty-four-carat neon signs and Members Clubs all vanished now in the shiny Sunday calm. Girls in red shirts, pink ribbons in their hair, stepped through polished arcades of smiling bunnies, puzzled pandas, chuckling raccoons. A Wildean photo album in a store said: "TRUTH: Virtue is the beauty of the mind." Schoolgirls, tethering their bikes to trees, whispered excitedly when they saw us, unaccustomed to foreigners, and then, "Brazil? Brazil?" In the local art museum, where Mark was having an exhibition, a grandma, given license to do anything by her age, appeared before us, with an equally ancient friend, in sunhat, giggling at her side. "I am eighty-eight years old," the woman said. "I dreamed of being a lawyer. But when I was young, a woman was not allowed to have a strong position. I pity myself. I am eighty-eight years old now." With that, she bowed and padded off.

On the beach, in the afternoon, the waves were deferential as a waiter, lapping quietly against the shore, a shock of white sails behind them on the blue; in front of me, eight matrons in a perfect row, lined up like birds, surveying the sea, identical in their pretty skirts and sweetly appreciative coos. In the twittering, sultry afternoon, a hot siesta stillness fell upon the town. The long thin lanes resembled alleyways in some sunlit Sardinian town, sleepy in the steamy afternoon. For once, all the country's energy was motionless and mute.

"If you were to believe some of the things you read," Etsuko began, "all of us Japanese are living in some cobwebbed net of obligations, our hands tied by *giri* and *on*. Of course, these elements are there. But to concentrate entirely on them is to produce a kind of caricature, a comic version of us. It's like taking an X ray, which catches the outline of the skeleton but has nothing of the spirit, the humanity. Or"—she paused while a former *maiko* came to deposit a few more mysterious delicacies on the table before us—"or like a bowl of seawater in which one has all the component parts, but they do not cohere to make a whole."

"It's too disembodied, in other words?"

She nodded ruefully.

She had taken me, this rainy-season evening, to one of those celebrated hidden centuries-old Kyoto restaurants where there was no menu and no bill, and there were no customers who could walk in off the street. Few, perhaps, would be induced to do so, in any case, since the entrance was an unassuming one, just a single small banner above an aged wooden gate at the foot of the eastern hills, on one of those narrow-waisted Gion streets that were all white lanterns and stone passageways.

We had walked along a moss path, lanterns jutting this way and that through the garden, to an entrance, where the madam, with the painted face of an old courtesan, in electric-blue kimono, had come out and bowed profusely before us, her head almost reaching to the floor. Given special slippers, we followed a wooden corridor, past rooms full of parties and the phantom forms of young geisha, to a large, empty room, bare save for an alcove in which there was a scroll lit up by a flash of calligraphy and, under it, a slim vase cradling a violet tea flower. New screens and mats had recently been installed to register the summer—they were changed with every month, I gathered— and our own screens gave out onto a trim garden, vibrant green intensified in the early-evening gray. A single tiny hole had been made in the wall so that the moon, coming through, would be shaped as a pretty crescent. The crockery was antique, chosen only for us; the small talk as delicate as china.

On Etsuko's pink kimono was a tracery of rain.

"Is that seasonal?" I asked redundantly.

"Yes, but just a tiny bit off, a few days early. Really, this should be worn in July, with the end of the rainy season. It's like these dishes." She pointed out the pattern of a well, or a whirlpool, on the goodies before us. I recognized the way that every detail had been made to fit the moment, the room itself turned into a seasonal poem. "These, too, should be eaten just a little later in the year, as you know." I did? "And of course, all these foods have water in them." Of course. It was not the first time I realized that Japan was so strictly trained that it took a trained eye to appreciate it.

Etsuko watched approvingly the silent bustle of the woman

bringing in more dishes. "We Japanese ladies have a way of effacing ourselves without losing ourselves," she explained. The woman, with a little bow, stole away from the lanterned room.

"Do you think Japanese women are the strength of Japan?"

"Yes. But we have to keep it a secret," she giggled coyly. "We know how to seem weak. You can see that in our women writers."

"Are there women's presses in Japan?"

She looked surprised. "You have them in America?"

"Oh yes." I went on to explain their assumptions to her.

"But surely that is a poor reflection on women, to be published only in women's presses?" The quiet rebuke stung like a needle. "If they are good, should they not be publishable anywhere?"

Having lived so long abroad, Etsuko regarded her country now, I sometimes felt, as a mother might an errant daughter. And as she tried to bring each culture to a better understanding of the other, she fretted, I could tell, about all the same issues that routinely vexed every foreigner: was it better to leave the people here in their state of happy ignorance, like the dwellers of Plato's cave (surrounded, in this instance, by Platonic forms), or should they be schooled in the facts of life, in the ways of the world, in uncertainty?

In the midst of all this, though, Etsuko was still Japanese enough to dodge every question with a smile, to talk in enigmas, to keep herself mostly to herself. One day a little later, she called me up to tell me that she could not, alas, attend a meeting of her culture club; I was hardly surprised, I replied, since I knew her life was so full of obligations. We talked for a while of *ma*, the Japanese notion of "betweenness," and the space between people, and the summer. Finally, after perhaps twenty minutes of chat, I asked after her father; when last we had met, she had told me, in passing, he was ill. "He died early this morning," she said calmly. "Luckily, I was there at the time. But I have to return to Tokyo tonight for more arrangements and the service."

That was why, I realized, she could not come to the club meeting; but she would never have told me had I not brought it up.

I dream one night I am on the Big Sur coast. The fog is rolling in across the sea, and a strange aircraft above makes me feel as if all the world is moving. I am talking Ryōkan with a hippie there, and we walk across stepping-stones in a quiet lotus pond, where I find, somehow, that everyone is speaking Japanese. The man at the front office, recognizing me, says, "Sachiko is going into fits. You probably don't remember her, but you knew her very well once. Now she doesn't know whether to ask you to dinner or not. I hope you don't mind my ..." "Of course not," I say, startled to find that there is a Sachiko here. The coastline is magical today, high above the surf, and the cedar tubs take me back—far back—to Japan.

3

THE NIGHT I got home, after saying goodbye to Sachiko, I lay awake for most of the dark and silent hours. Outside, the rain was coming down so gently I could scarcely hear it, trickling down pipes, pattering into gutters, tapping as silently on my roof as a mother awakening her child. At times, when I could not sleep, I rose and penned mock-Japanese poems.

> *All night, the rain.*
> *I listen again in the dark*
> *To the sound of footsteps departing.*

And as the daylight came in, I felt that what I wanted most to express to her was admiration: out of habit, I clambered up to my desk and looked up the Japanese word for "respect," though by then, perhaps, the chance to use it was gone, and I felt a little like someone who's holding a winning lottery ticket long after the deadline has passed.

Sachiko's goodbye marked, so it seemed, the ending of a cycle; from now on, I sensed, she would be charting a new life on her own. But as the days went on, I also came to see that she could not so easily hold to her resolve, if only because she needed some external impetus to help her to break free. By now, she was fully embarked on her tour-conductor course, attending classes in Osaka twice a week, committing to memory the niceties of foreign customs and places, taking tests in the logistics of a "bird life." And for the first time ever, I suspected, she had found a field wide enough for her to spread her wings, a forum large enough to accommodate all her diverse energies.

Everywhere one looked in Japan, one saw an identical sorrow: so many women with so much to give, and so little occasion to use it. Nine in every ten women here had completed twelve years of schooling; yet in their brief stays in the office, they were rarely allowed to do anything more than look decorative and make tea. Put the character for "woman" together with the character for "woman" twice, and you got the character for "trouble."

This it was, I assumed, that produced the notorious super-moms, who trained all their formidable powers of will on Junior-chan's success, and this it was that began to explain that other infamous figure of urban folklore, the rapacious landlady, who threw herself on any foreigner with such naked intensity that he was left, very often, shaken, almost terrified, by the vehemence of her unspent passions. If the first cliché of being a foreign male in Japan was finding a faultless dream girl, the second was to find oneself almost consumed by the ravening ardor of these women, who could, if they chose, turn that same unearthly attention, in an instant, on someone else. Regardless of their object, they were as obsessive and Zen-pointed in love as in every other pursuit and brought the same degree of concentration, and full-bodied surrender, to their affections that they might elsewhere bring to their company, or their baseball team, or their religion.

Now, though, for the first time ever, Sachiko seemed to have moved beyond mere diversions—first Zen, then aerobics, then a-ha, then me—to some larger sense of destination. And as she did so, inevitably, she found her whole society arrayed in a vengeful chorus all around her. Her mother had told her that if she continued the course, she would never talk to her again. Her brother, recently returned from Switzerland, had warned her that she was "little balloon. If not usual Japanese-style life, I cannot stay ground." Her Japanese friends were either jealous or disapproving of her for seeking out the free-dom they had so diligently denied themselves. And her husband was sorrowfully bewildered, gallantly giving her a tour-conductor record for her birthday, then silently going off to another woman. Only her father, the longtime adversary whom she affectionately thought of as a child, now became an unlikely ally, secretly urging her to see the world (and asking her if she'd take him with her).

Watching her swimming bravely against the current, I longed to do everything I could to help her. One day, therefore, in early summer, I invited her on a tour of Osaka Airport, only the third time in her thirty-one years she had ever visited this thorough-fare of dreams scarcely an hour from her home. In wonder, when we arrived, she gazed up at all the people moving off to other lands and lives, and tried out the new phrases she had learned. "De-par-ture lounge," she spelled out to herself. "In-ter-national arr-i-val." "CIQ," she proudly informed me (customs/immigration/quarantine). Together we stood before the depar-ture board, and she recited to herself the destinations clicking over, a registry of hopes.

After that, still far from Japan, we traveled to Kobe, the city closest to a foreign place, and nibbled on tacos in a Mexican restaurant, complete with Mexican waitress, *piñatas*, and pon-chos on the wall, then climbed up to a tiny second-story sari shop, with soft sitar music piped through elegant, silk-wrapped chambers, copies of *Vogue* lying beneath framed Kashmiri miniatures. On the way back into town, we stopped inside the English House and posed for photographs in Victorian gear (Japanese tourist sites always had these props on hand, so that one could actually occupy a foreign identity for a moment and have the moment commemorated). "I little crazy?" she asked, more in hope than apprehension. Craziness, I could tell, was the foreign country to which I could admit her.

In some ways, I was discovering, Sachiko seemed to know everything about the world, sampling the products and photo-genic images of different cultures as easily as in some Interna-tional Expo. Yet in some ways, she knew nothing. In geography, as in everything, the Japanese seemed to favor a ruthlessly edited version of the world, converting each country into a collection of gift shop pleasantries and postcard images. The classic example was the TV documentaries in which some pretty young hostess led viewers through a Third World hellhole, either screening out the suffering in search of scenic vistas or treating it as a kind of artificial prop that only increased the quaintness and exoticism. Even the Japanese tourists I ran across abroad seemed not really keen to understand or penetrate other cultures, but content just to collect them, and to snap up a few Taj Mahal souvenirs or pictures of the Eiffel Tower to take back home like trophies. The rest of the world, like Japan itself, they saw mostly through rose-colored lenses or through blinkers.

So when I mentioned Bhutan to Sachiko, she knew every last detail of this picturesque land, where the people, wearing their own versions of kimono, resembled some theme-park recreation of the Muromachi period; Japanese TV had shown a famous documentary on the subject. As for Burma, Central Asia, the caravan stops along the romantic Silk Road, now being featured in every Japanese book and screen, she was all but definitive. Yet when I mentioned Nicaragua, she had never heard of it, and eager only for good news, she, like nearly every Japanese I knew, had never heard of the Cold War, was shocked to learn that Washington and Moscow were ideologically opposed, knew nothing at all about China's difficult reforms.

When I took her later that afternoon to an exhibition of anti-apartheid art, partially sponsored by the tireless *gaijin* crusaders of Kyoto, she was stunned and horrified; incredulous to learn of a place where such discrimination was employed (though to foreign eyes, racism and segregation were scarcely alien to Japan). And as we watched a video of Afrikaners talking about their experiences with the system, Sachiko's eyes filled with tears and she lost all words. On heading out, she asked me if I would take her to *Cry Freedom* and *A World*

Apart, and when I told her that Japanese were considered honorary whites in South Africa, she could scarcely contain her indignation: "Why this system? Not so fair! This system very terrible!"

It amused me to find that I, least politically informed of creatures, was introducing her now to many of the things that Japan so carefully screened out: to inequity, to unexpectedness, even to tipping (though when I tried to explain this habit to her, she looked quite shocked at the notion of institutionalized bribery; "service," in Japan, meant not an extra charge but, in fact, an extra dish or gift that the customer received *gratis* — and in any case, every gift here left the recipient doubly indebted).

Through the world I inhabited too, Sachiko was ending up in situations she had never known before. Slipping into the Western world, as through some Lewis Carroll looking glass, she had entered a world of fun-house inversions and fairy-tale shocks, in which new conventions loomed up at her as suddenly and scarily as the glowing skeletons in the Haunted House to which I took her once, which left her clinging to my arm in a state of happy terror. One day, she called my guesthouse and was answered by the eccentric young gay from Harvard who had somehow grown fascinated with her. *Moshi-moshi*, she called out, uncertainly; *Moshi-moshi*, he replied, recognizing her voice. "I love you." There was, I gathered, a long silence on the other end, and then an uneasy giggle. "No, really," he went on. "I love you. If you weren't already claimed, I'd want you for my own. If you were my girlfriend, I'd never want a boy again."

Four days after the incident, Sachiko was still shaken by the conversation. Everything she considered sacred had been defamed. To talk to a self-professed gay was itself an unnerving novelty for her. But to get a frank admission from him, and to hear from a relative stranger intimacies of the kind she had never heard in public even from her husband — it clearly left the ground beneath her shaking.

Just as often, though, her innocence seemed almost proof

against the world, making the world seem innocent. When I introduced her one day to an English friend, she looked at him with awe as he politely complimented her on the beauties of her town. Then, unable to contain herself any longer, she abruptly said, "Your country very beautiful country. I many time dream this place. Cinderella, many big castle, fairy princess. When I high school size, I always dream this world. Your world little Emily Brontë world."

He burst out laughing and went on rhapsodizing about Japanese teahouses and Sōseki's novels.

But Sachiko was not to be sidetracked, or to be diverted in this rare encounter with an emissary from the land of dreams.

"Japanese person much love your country air. British Airways!" She was proud of her new knowledge.

"British Airways?" he repeated, incredulous, thinking of rock-hard rolls and hockey-stick attendants. "I usually try to go with JAL."

"Japanese person not so like this air. Very cold feeling; little distant."

"But, Sachiko," I butted in, "isn't that how all Japanese service is? Isn't that, in fact, the glory and aim of Japanese service?"

She looked confused.

"We in the West usually like to go Thai Air," I went on, "or Singapore Airlines. Many people think those two are the best in the world."

"Japanese person not so like Thai Air!"

"Why?"

"Bad smell!"

"Bad smell?"

"True! Asian air very bad smell! Japanese person like only British Airway. Cathay Pacific too—but very expensive."

"But, Sachiko, Cathay Pacific is Asian too."

She stood firm. "Japanese person like!"

* * *

She in turn, of course, was introducing me to many things, not least the shallowness of my own reading of Japan. As I went on blathering about Hiroshige or Buson, I realized that it must have sounded as jejune and uninformed to her as typical Japanese raptures about Chopin did to us. And when I told her, proudly, about my visit to the famous geisha show, she was singularly unimpressed. "You know Michael Douglas movie?" "You mean *Fatal Attraction*?" "Ping-pong! This Miyako Odori, little same feeling!"

I got a similar response, once, when I suggested we visit the love shrine at Kiyomizu and make the ritual walk, eyes closed, along a series of twelve stepping-stones, that was the famous highlight of every tourist's visit. Listening to my suggestion, she could hardly contain her mirth. "This little teenage place," she giggled. "Usually only high school person come here this place." It was the same response, I realized, I would have received had I invited a mature thirty-one-year-old New Yorker, and mother of two, to a Coney Island photo booth.

Often, too, as I inflicted on her haiku of my own composition, the effect must have been as jarring to her as hearing a prayer rewritten. And once, eager to show off my command of Japanese wisdom, I quoted to her Bashō's famous, plangent cry of wonder, an epic in three words, *"Matsushima ya / Ah, Matsushima ya / Matsushima ya."* But somehow, in the heat of the moment, I began intoning, *"Matsushita ya / Ah, Matsushita ya ...,"* converting the poet's poignant ode to a moonlit island into a call for the Japanese equivalent of Data General. That same day, she told me excitedly, "My friend give me little foreigner poem. Very beautiful poem. Please you see." And handed over some verses by Leo Buscaglia.

4

GREEN, GREEN, green were the colors of Kyoto in the summer: the dripping green of moss gardens, the thick dark emerald of the pine trees on the temple slopes; the illuminated jade of white-barked bamboo shot through with summer light. Green lichen, green hills, green light. Always the sharpened intensity of solid colors in Japan, so strong they knocked the breath out of one: pink against blue, gold on black, a blaze of reds. And the beauty of a city that measured its year by its blossomings: the coming of plums to Kitano in early winter, the cherries on Mount Hiei in late April, the deepening of moss in the rainy season.

In the early days of summer, with the first suggestion of returning haziness and heat, Kyoto took on a Californian lightness, and the days were motionless and blue. Lazy cumulus days without a trace of wind. Red and blue carp banners drooping from the rooftops, and lazy Bach toccatas in local coffee shops. A Constable world of suspended motion. Then, as the heat came on, a creeping intensity: Sachiko sucking ice cubes in the sultry nights and giving me new wind chimes to keep me cool (as courtiers once had spread silk cloth across the mountains to shield an emperor's eyes from summer glare); shopgirls eating long, fine, pure-white noodles served on ice.

Along the avenue of trees that led to Shimogamo Shrine, weekend painters sat relaxing at their easels above a dry stream, silent on their chairs as they tried to transcribe the intensity of green and blue. Etsuko, meeting me outside the shrine, greeted me with a poem she had just translated:

Ah July,
The rushing stream washed over the stones,
And the stones sparkle.

Then she led me into Kawabata's house, turned this day into a gallery of dreams, lustrous kimono spread out upon their racks like carpets or fine silks, ten-thousand-dollar gowns with fifteen-thousand-dollar *obi*, bearing the faintest tracery of cranes, or phoenixes, across their midnight blue. Farther on, in a room full of windows, we took a traditional meal while a few chattering women tried to set me up in marriage with their daughters.

"I think it is because we are externally so powerless," she later explained, putting the encounter into perspective, "that we Japanese women must be powerful in spirit. And so it comes out in these violent and inverse ways, as in the *hannya.*"

"*Hannya?*"

"You must know this?" I didn't. "It is the recurrent figure in Nō drama and in so many of our stories through the centuries, like *Dōjōji*: the woman who consumes a monk in the fury of her passion. The term, of course, was first created by a monk; it refers to the first word of a very famous sutra. But if you say *hannya* today, most people think instantly of the demon-woman." She smiled. "I think it must be a theme men like, it is repeated so often in our literature."

In the middle of summer, the third great festival of the Kyoto year transformed the city again into a display of scenic back-drops. On the eve of Gion Matsuri, the narrow lanes at the center of town were clogged with thirty-one elaborate, multi-story floats, smothered in treasures and portable shrines, wobbly on their giant wooden wheels. Around them, the ancient houses were open to the street now, floodlit, their living rooms on show like a series of illuminated stage sets.

House after tiny wooden house set up as in some spectral diorama: paintings, lacquer screens, old men playing cards around low tables. Occasionally, a group of naked-chested boys streaking through the lanes, making a strange cacophony as they passed.

The next day, a ten-year-old boy with scarlet lips and whitened face, crowned with a phoenix, led the clanking wooden floats through the central streets of town, past geisha houses and old inns, towards the shrine that towered above the entertainment district. That afternoon, in the same shrine, I visited a special exhibition honoring the famous, centuries-old sweet-makers of the ancient capital. It was, of course, a private show, but somehow Etsuko, in the midst of arranging her father's funeral, had found an invitation for me, at twenty-four hours notice, and, more than that, had given me a letter of introduction inside a card of Oxford, and, in fact, a picture of the very building in which I had once lived. (I thought with shame of how hard it would be for me, in California, to find a picture of *her* college, or whether I would even try.) Inside a special tent, a kimonoed woman, whose family had sweetened the palates of twenty generations of emperors, took me round the display of sweets, laid out on plates like Harry Winston jewels on a velvet cushion, each of them devoted to this year's theme of "New Life." Sweets laid out as teardrop crystals, sweets in watercolor seascapes; sweets alluding to the flower that heralded rebirth, sweets suggesting the imminence of cresting surf. Sweets as shells along the shore, sweets as snakes sloughing off old skins. Sweets that conveyed, with a drop of salt, the heartbreak of new affections. My own guide's display was of Dante and Beatrice, made all of sweets, under the title, in sweet-form, "Vita Nuova."

Poems out of evanescence, old myths turned into candied images. And the next day, all these artifacts, the creation of a year, were gone.

* * *

One night, Sachiko called me up shortly before midnight, her voice as ever soft and breathless. "I want meet."

"Now?"

"I'm so sorry. I want meet."

"Okay. I'll meet you at the market twenty minutes from now."

A little later, she was walking towards me, smiling in the dark. "I'm very sorry," she began, burying her head in my chest. "I need meet. I cannot patient."

Together, we walked through the darkened, narrow streets and into Kurodani Temple. The early-summer moon hung above us, ringed with phosphorescence, capturing the eye. Around us, here and there, lanterns pricked the dark. Beside us, in silence, a fire burned. Below, far below, as on a phantom ship, the quiet shimmer of the city's lights.

As I led her through the towering temple gates, Sachiko suddenly stopped and caught her breath. "My dream," she whispered. "I dream this gate. When I little children size, I dream this place." She looked around in startled wonder. "I not come here this place before. But I feel come here before." A chill went through me, and she shivered. "I little afraid this dream. Dream gate."

Together, in the shadow of the entranceway, we looked up at the temple, grave against the hooded, dark-blue sky. In the distance, a statue of Jizō; my favorite Buddha; the hills full of graves in the dark. A few dogs skulked across the asphalt. The sudden roar of a lone motorcyclist approaching; then a departing hush. Our features scarcely visible in the sacramental dark.

"I remember," she began, almost under her breath, "New Year Day. Very warm night, little same today. I walking in grave, together brother. He say, if we together, very old, we always live together."

I held her, shivering, against the windless night, and together we looked up at the hazy moon of monks. "I dream of sea," she said, "and many star." Above us, the moon was balanced on the branches.

Then I felt her hot whisper in my ear, and saw her lying down, her curved eyes flashing in the dark.

The moon, the mild, warm air; the silent, sleeping dogs.

5

As summer deepened, Buddhism still continued to pursue me much more assiduously than I did it, and the procession of holy men to my guesthouse showed no signs of abating. One day, having narrowly avoided the Jehovah's Witnesses (attractively represented by two young nymphs), I surfaced just in time to get a blessing from another roving evangel, who invited me into the corridor for some *kuriingu* (an alarming sight for a newcomer to the guesthouse, who walked up the stairs, jet-lagged, on only his second day in Japan, to see me and the girl, bowing our heads in the corridor, hands joined in prayer, repeating a mantram together, eyes closed). Soon, in fact, my alertness to the threat was so great that when a man appeared at my room, all politeness, I instantly assured him, "Thank you very much. But I've been blessed many times in recent weeks. That's enough. Thank you!" and closed the door on the half-terrified face of a TV repairman.

Another day, in Osaka Airport, I was wandering around the customs area, waiting for Sachiko, when a man materialized at my side. He extended a hand and then a business card, and told me how much he enjoyed living in Michigan. I was pleased; this was the first Japanese businessman who had ever come up to introduce himself.

Then, however, my new friend began looking around shiftily. Was I alone? Yes, I said, for the moment. The next thing I knew, he was handing me a four-color brochure advertising a meditation institute that looked disarmingly similar to the one founded by Wayne Newton in the latest James Bond movie. The place was Buddhist, he said, handling the word with all the exotic and elegant associations it held for foreigners, and it had many foreign adherents; his life's work would not be complete until I was among their number.

Just then, up raced Sachiko, out of breath, to rescue me again from a Buddhist career.

In Tokyo, a little later, I was looking for a place to stay. "Please try the Hokke Club," a hotelier friend of Sachiko's advised. "It's in Ueno, and I can organize a special foreigner's discount. It's very unusual." "Hokke Club?" I said, wondering whether its associations were with sports or truancy. "No problem. I'll call up right now. How many nights?" "How much?" "Don't worry. Any price okay."

I wondered what I was getting myself into as I went across town towards a hotel that sounded as suspicious as a members-only escort agency: when I arrived, I quickly got the picture. Through the lobby, like crowds from a Cartier-Bresson portrait of Shanghai in the thirties, filed a sea of strange gray families as far as possible from the polished Japanese norm: squinty little boys, skulking fathers, dowdy mothers. Some of them gathered in disorderly groups around the TV. Others, in summer kimono, filed like sci-fi creatures into an elevator. Others shambled through the lobby with the furtive air of *yakuza* or traveling minstrels, people exiled somehow from the promise of Japan. Like the derelicts downtown, or the snake-eating dwarfs I had seen once in a Kyoto freak-show tent, they seemed to belong to some hardscrabble underside of Japan.

When I presented myself to the desk clerks, they led me up in the elevator, through a long corridor, up an emergency staircase, to a bare little room without a washbasin. Breakfast, they said, was compulsory, and would cost ten dollars. No exceptions were made. I did not sleep soundly that night in the Hokke, or Lotus, Club, at the heart of the Tenrikyo sect of Buddhism, one of the "new religions" of Japan, so affluent and powerful that it ran a whole city of its own near Nara.

* * *

In my own essay in Zen idleness, meanwhile, I was beginning to see how hard it was to leave thought alone. Not unlike Matthew, perhaps, I was realizing that I did not have the discipline to meditate, and because I did not meditate, I did not have the discipline. The analysis itself meant more paralysis; reason proved unable to transcend itself. And everywhere I looked, to my chagrin, I found admonishing injunctions: even in the metropolitan prose of Julian Barnes, worldliest of writers, I came across moments that sounded like pure Zen: "Stop the loom, the futile chattering loom of human thought. Stare at the lighted window, and just breathe."

In other ways, though, inevitably, I was also beginning to see that I drew closest to the discipline only when I did not know that I was doing so—in the utter absorption of writing about Sachiko, say, or talking with her sometimes. Happiness came with self-forgetfulness, and it seemed only apt that the Buddhist principle of "right absorption" was translated often as "right rapture." True concentration took one out of time and self, an unacknowledged ecstasy. And if Zen extolled the child as much as any Romantic poet did, that was partly because the child lived fully and intensely in the moment, free of both nostalgia and a sense of future. Only when the mind was not preoccupied could it be fully occupied by something else.

I thought back then to what the abbot of Tōfukuji had said, explaining how even a businessman or journalist had something to gain from a night in a monastery, and a taste of stillness. One had to learn how not to spend time, he had suggested. "When you're hurrying around too quickly," he had said, "there's a part of the world you can't see. If, for example, you're taking a wrong direction in your life, it's only when you stop and look at things clearly that you can revise your direction and take a more proper course. The message of Zen is that in order to find ourselves, we've got to learn to stop." This whole year, now, seemed a lesson of that sort.

As Sachiko came towards the end of her tour-conductor course and the beginning of her dreams of taking off into the dark, the pressures on her grew more and more intense, till it seemed as if she were wandering through a kind of wind tunnel. Often, when I saw her, she seemed alight with her new prospects, quickened and uplifted by her expanded sense of horizon. Just as often, though, I could see how much her struggle to be free could weigh her down.

One day, as she was excitedly telling me about her plans for travel and self-sufficiency, the phone rang, and she picked it up brightly. As the minutes passed, I saw her face fall. "*Chigau, chigau,*" she kept repeating. "No. That's wrong! You don't understand!" Finally, after forty-five minutes of discussion, she put the phone down and flopped into her chair, her spirit broken. "My mother say she want die," she told me, through her tears. "I need stop course. I cannot more. I dream bird life, but I cannot. My dream, child dream. I not bird; I human."

"But, Sachiko, you need a dream if you want to change. If no dream, all your life will be sad."

"This part I know very well," she said sadly. "But I not so strong. I not so have confidence. I see foreigner person, they little giant feeling. Anything do, very easy. But I little scared. My boat very tiny."

She stopped, and brushed her eyes clean. "Middle life best, all person say. But I have problem. I cannot stop. Middle life very easy, I know very well. But I want dream, I want more difficult life. This Japanese system: no dream—no problem."

By now, I could more easily understand why dreams held such a talismanic importance for her. In dreams lay responsibility, in a

very literal sense; in dreams lay her only hope for realizing—
even transcending—herself. Dreams meant carving out a little
imaginative space of one's own—a retreat—in a world as cramped
in time as it was in space; yet the Japanese were more keen to
have dreams entertain them than the other way round. It often
seemed to me, in fact, that all the tinkly amusement-park surfaces and chipper reassurances of the public world here were
almost a way of keeping people quiet; or at least of providing
them with preshrunk pleasures so that they would not seek out
unscheduled dreams of their own—let alone acknowledge any
kind of sadness. Thus all the happy communal rites—from
Disneyland tours to cherry blossom parties—seemed ways of
providing safe, user-friendly forms of organized happiness, satisfaction guaranteed, a little like the bright baubles that a parent
might offer a child to prevent him from crying. This was the
social contract in Japan: forfeit your individuality and you would
receive a life of perfect stability and comfort; give yourself over
to Japan and it would never let you down. It was like a kind of
emotional welfare system: give up your freedom and you would
receive a life so convenient that you'd hardly notice the freedom you'd relinquished.

So when Sachiko went on talking of dreams, I tried to hold
my tongue. For her, every dream was something of a triumph,
and movies like *Rocky III*, which she had seen four times, were
especially liberating tales to one who was struggling to see how
an individual could live apart from the system. She had told me
recently of a friend of hers, a twenty-year-old girl, whose ardor
for a-ha was so intense that she had taken a part-time job and
worked around the clock to save up enough money to see every
single concert on their forthcoming tour of Japan, following
them from Tokyo to Nagasaki to Osaka to Yokohama to Fukuoka
and around. Didn't she think it was sad, I said, that this was the
closest her friend could get to foreign feeling?

"Not sad! This her dream!"

"But isn't it sad that she must have such a dream? It means

her real life is a little empty. She would not need such a dream if she were fully happy. And she would not love a-ha so much if she had a real-life boyfriend."

This reasoning left Sachiko subdued. It was only later that I realized that to downgrade dreams with her was probably as cruel as to quicken them.

The first time that I ever saw Sachiko really bristle, though, was one day when I told her that I'd just gone to see *The Last Emperor.* She had not seen it and, she said, she never wanted to see it, after what her Japanese friends had told her. "Why this movie show many Japanese person do terrible thing? Whyyy? All person crazy in war. Japanese, Korean, your country person — all same!"

"But foreigners get upset that the Japanese pretend that the conquest of Manchuria never happened. It's not the movie the Japanese government wants to cut; it's the documentary footage of what really went on, the same material that is deliberately left out of all your history books. Japan is too proud to admit its mistakes."

Sachiko, though, was not appeased, and much as she longed for images of exotic China, and all the mystery and splendor of the Silk Road, she adamantly refused to see this matchless vision of the Forbidden City. "Why foreigner person not understand Japanese heart?" she went on, somewhat plaintively. "They say Japan very terrible, many killing whale. But whale very special animal, Japanese person believe. Eating whale little religious ceremony. Other animal not same."

Now the box was open, there was no putting a lid on it.

"You see this movie, little three lady, devil?" she continued.

"The Witches of Eastwick?"

"Maybe. Jack Nicholson little devil feeling."

"Right."

"Jack Nicholson little Japanese man feeling?"

"Japanese??"

"I think foreigner person think Japanese man devil."

"No, no, Sachiko, that's not true. Maybe sometimes they see him as a little robotlike." I tried—and failed—to be diplomatic. "But not devil. You can see in Kyoto how many foreigners want to come to Japan. Besides, in America there are so many Chinese, Koreans, Filipinos, Indians, Vietnamese, and Afghans, no one has a very clear sense of the Japanese."

"But my friend say"—this was always the prelude to some Japanese superstition about abroad—"she go many country Europa, many person not so kind for Japanese."

"Not so kind to Europeans either, I expect."

"Really?" But I could tell she didn't believe me.

"Really! Japanese visitors are usually very polite, very gentle, very shy."

"But I read in magazine, foreigner person think Japanese man little devil."

She had also, I remembered now, read in a magazine that Howard the Duck was meant to be a foreign caricature of the Japanese abroad, small, well-dressed, polite, and forever put upon by the humans he was so foolishly parodying.

At moments like this, I could see how hard it would always be for her to break away from Japan, and not only because Japan had never taught her to live without it. For something deeper was going on here than the usual conflict between self and society, or, in the Japanese context, between *giri* and *ninjō* (duty and feeling); something deeper, too, than the familiar double standard that allows us to challenge the criticisms from others that we ourselves feel free to make (I can attack my mother, but you cannot). And as fast as Sachiko sought the foreign way, Japan remained as deeply rooted in her as her family did. Watching her waver between a Western and a Japanese destiny, I began to wonder whether the country itself, determined now to turn "international," as its last divine-born Emperor lingered on his deathbed, would ever be able—or even want—to surrender the beliefs that kept it in a world all its own.

"Japanese need change heart," she said one day, more able now to see her country's limits.

"But then the whole system, which has become the most successful in the world, must change."

She nodded slowly. "Maybe very difficult."

I could see her extending the analogy towards herself.

"Don't worry, Sachiko," I said with glib assurance, not even really persuading myself. "Worry doesn't help; it only clouds or distorts. If you can solve a problem, there's no need to worry; and if you can't, there's nothing gained by worry. Just stay calm, and there's nothing you can't do."

Sachiko took this in, remaining very silent.

6

Through all the time I had been living in Japan, the one force of which I had been most conscious was Time. It was not just that I found myself hoarding moments like a miser, taking time as a measure of freedom and painfully aware that hours, once lost, could never be retrieved; it was also that modern Japan, secular Japan, the Japan that was racing into the future as swiftly and smoothly as a Rolls-Royce, seemed strangely captive to Time. In Kyoto, I sometimes felt as if I were living inside a hall of clocks—the digital counters all around counting down the days till the next great exhibition or the minutes till the next train, the little clocks at the bottom of the TV screens ticking off the breakfast hour during morning shows, the dates dutifully printed on many photographs and even on computer screens; everything became a wake-up call or a keepsake, an attempt to hold time back, or rob the passing minutes of a moment. In that sense, I could see that Sachiko's awestruck, breath-held whisper of "Time stop!" was truly the highest praise that she could give.

It often seemed, in fact, that the greatest of all the forces in Japan was Time, if only because it was the most implacable. Yes, the Japanese could manage Time, better than anyone I knew; yes, they could harmonize themselves with its rhythms and pay homage to it with their rites (a girl becomes a woman on this day, and on this day autumn turns to winter); yes, they could make uncommonly good use of Time. But still, Time could not be controlled, as Space, or Nature, or even Truth, could be.

That was why, I sometimes felt, the Japanese were such

connoisseurs of memory, the faculty that allowed them to pack-age Time and turn the bumpy chaos of successive moments into an elegy as beautiful as art. It was also, perhaps, why they excelled so much at slowness and at speed. Most of all, it began to explain why so much of Japan was set up as a retreat from Time, a way to stay Time, or step out of it. The monastery, where one took off one's watch as soon as one entered, was the purest expression of this; the water-world, where life was inverted with such Bacchanalian precision that women called out "Good morning!" to one another at midnight, was another.

I got my own most vivid taste of this one day when I missed the last train home from Kobe. I could not find a business or city hotel nearby, and even if I could, I knew that it would be painfully expensive. I could not see a capsule hotel. The only alternative, I knew, and the only place as reasonable as a monastery, would be a love hotel.

Off a side street, just under the gleaming boutiques and ethnic chic of Tor Road, I came upon a collection of these brightly decorated dream chambers, recently renamed "fashion hotels," and lined up with the implausible, synthetic neatness of buildings along Main Street in Disneyland. I peered into the Rabbit's Ears Hotel and saw an aging couple shuffle off into the futuristic Charon. But the one that appealed to me the most was the Gatsby Hotel. It had an especially sharp, cream-colored stylishness to it, with sports-car stripes down its middle, and its name, I thought, could only be auspicious. As soon as I ven-tured inside, a robot greeted me with a Japanese cry of "Welcome," and I was faced with a panel of photographs of rooms, some of them illuminated. I pressed the cheapest one that I could find—it looked like a gentrified, modern one-room apartment, a palace by Japanese standards—and an arrow flashed in the hallway above me. I followed it up a bright flight of European-style stairs, past framed Barney's ads, a message in Greek, an article about Christopher Isherwood, an old London playbill, a glossy profile of Natasha Richardson, and a sign that said, "Some of the best-dressed beds will be wearing white linen," all of these West Hollywood artifacts set smartly against the white, white walls. Through the bright, noiseless corridor the arrow kept blinking, silently, at the level of the EXIT signs, leading me on and on and on to a room with a flashing number, whose door swung obligingly open before me. I went in, slipping into a pair of wool-lined sandals at the entrance.

As usual in Japan, the photos had not lied: the room was possibly the cleanest and most stylish suite I had ever seen. Everything was color coordinated in elegant, Art Deco hues of black and gold: black Kleenex boxes, black matchbooks on a gold glass table, black beakers with the gold logo "Gatsby" on them. In the spotlessly clean bathroom, black-and-gold bottles of aftershave, neatly wrapped toothbrushes and combs, black-and-gold-rimmed mirrors; the door on the shower just fuzzy enough to turn movement into the haziest suggestion of movement. In the dining area, a table, a refrigerator, a black kettle for tea. And beside the spacious white bed, on its slightly raised platform, a digital, remote-control switchboard from which one could soften lights, select music, switch on TV or warm the room. One could play video games on TV (explained in a slim black-and-golden book), pen endearments to one's sweetheart (a black-and-golden notebook was provided for such purposes), or enjoy *Rental Wife* on the special hotel channel, in which Yumi, a long-legged nineteen-year-old, lent herself out as a friend to the lonely. Reclining on the bed, in a space as chic as some SoHo café, I felt in command of the world.

Or, better yet, exempted from the world, in a space all my own. Time and the self were ritually annulled in this capsule; all noise and distraction were screened out in this soundproof chamber. There were no windows, really, no maids, no noises from the hall; for once in Japan, there was total privacy and freedom. Not a trace of the world outside the designer fantasy.

I had expected—I had feared—in coming to a love hotel, to find something more rococo or stridently theatrical: a room like a space-age rocket, perhaps, or a caveman's den, some other-worldly setting to accommodate the demand for a holiday from self. But just the insulation, the hushed spotlessness, of this elegant space was fantasy enough; entering it, one stepped into another world. The compact apartment in black and gold was not only the smartest place I had ever stayed in, it was also the most relaxing. And the main decoration in the room, I noticed as I settled in, was a beautifully framed poster announcing "The Still Center of the Turning Worlds (Intensive Seminars in Zen Buddhist meditation with Zen Master Rama)." After giving a brief synopsis of Zen, the black-and-scarlet poster provided an address from which one could procure a book called *Zen for the Computer Age*. It was, all in all, the perfect prop: for when I woke up the next day, and walked out into summer sun, the robot calling "Welcome" as the automatic doors slid closed behind me, I felt as cleansed as if I had been staying in a temple.

I got my final taste of how the Japanese secede from Time when Etsuko invited me, one late summer day, to a traditional tea-house along the Philosopher's Path. Inside a spotless antechamber, we sipped some piquant apple juice, in tiny tumblers, fresh as mountain water. Then we followed a woman in a kimono out into the exquisite garden, one small stone wrapped in black marking the direction. Again we found ourselves inside a wait-ing room — all polished black tables, and a single paper lantern, plover-shaped.

Within the tearoom itself, every detail sang the shifting of the seasons. The poem in the *tokonoma* alcove spoke of hearts resembling the autumn moon. An incense holder reproduced the circle of the harvest moon. The seven autumn grasses poked, haphazardly elegant, out of a long-necked vase. "In tea," said Etsuko softly, "we can get a taste of eternity — if I may use such a term." She giggled self-consciously. "And that is completely separate from our real, quotidian lives. But tea gives us a concentration, and helps us empty ourselves out. By concentrating on the ritual, on all the forms and details, we can clean ourselves out. And then we can return more strongly to our usual lives."

In the distance, I could hear the faintest implication of a koto. The temple bells were beginning to sound along the eastern hills. A faint chill of autumn could be felt now in the air; the moon was dimly outlined in the blue. I wanted, desperately, to escape time now; autumn, and departure, were quickly drawing near.

7

NOT LONG BEFORE I left Japan, I got a chance at last to see Sachiko take her first tremulous steps abroad; my work was sending me to Korea and Australia, and I arranged my schedule in order to be able to meet up with her on foreign soil. It was, as I had expected, a pleasure unalloyed to see her setting foot abroad, so electric with elation, and so high that, as she readily admitted, "My stomach little hurt. Too much excited. Cannot control. Cannot sleep!" Eager to be charmed, ready for delight, she felt herself swept up in such a surge of freedom that, her first day out of Japan, she literally began skipping across her hotel room like a hopscotch-playing schoolgirl.

I felt like skipping, too, at times, so magically did she remake the world with her fresh Miranda eyes. Usually, I could not bear even the mention of discos, but Sachiko was so excited to see these wonder worlds that I took her dancing every night, and saw these gaudy pleasure-domes anew. Once, when I invited her to an expensive French restaurant in Seoul, she was so confused and overwhelmed by the list of delicacies, this smallest and most ladylike of women, that she started ordering one dish from every section of the menu—poultry, meat, and seafood. Later, when I took her to the nightclub area, I could feel her tensing up, as anxious and excited as a girl on her first trip into the big city. That night, back in the hotel, she was so full up, in every sense, that she simply flopped down on her bed and fell asleep in her best clothes.

Often, too, I could see how her buoyancy actually reshaped the world it met. One night, I took her to a country-and-western bar in the red-light district of Seoul, where huge, big-necked GIs straddled bar girls while "Maggie May" and "Smooth Operator" rasped across the system. After we took our seats, a harassed, pretty Korean girl sauntered up to take our order. Sachiko, however, was so disarmed by this kind of place, and so intrigued, that she started asking the girl questions, and with such happy sincerity that the girl in turn responded — and soon the two of them were sitting side by side, chatting away in an unlikely English and telling one another, through shining eyes, their hopes for one another's future. Around them, bargirls squealed over darts, and Asia hands fondled Asian thighs; but all the world was lost to Sachiko and her friend as, earnestly, they exchanged their hearts. When finally we got up to leave, many hours later, the hostess extended a warm hand to each of us, eyes bright.

Whenever we went to a restaurant, Sachiko greeted the waitress with a happy *"Kansahamnida!,"* her first Korean word, and if ever she got a reply in Japanese, she let out a breathless sigh of relief and returned to her native tongue with a happy *"Yokatta!"* (I'm so glad). In sushi bars, she looked on in horror as Japanese businessmen, in golf shirts and crisp pants, picked their teeth and stared into the distance, with an air of lazy ownership, while their local girlfriends slurped down noodles. And when, on her last night in Korea, I took her to a performance of classical dance, she came out shaken, close to tears. "Before, I always thinking Korean person little animal person. Very big voice, very tough, always fighting! Now I'm so sorry! I very embarrassed! I see Korean person have much pride! They make very beautiful dance, very special custom. But I not know. I so sorry!"

In Australia, the first time she had ever seen a non-Asian culture, she felt, not surprisingly, even more transported, as giddy as if she had walked, quite literally, through a screen. "I feel I little living in TV," she reported in quiet wonder, displaced by something more than jet lag as we walked Down Under streets. "This dream world? I sleepy? Maybe soon wake up?" As we sat in a restaurant outside the Opera House, white table-cloths snapping in the lazy sunlight, and the chic young things of Sydney stretching out their golden limbs, she let out a gasp. "This not Kobe movie? This not Nagasaki park? This true? That lady, little same Olivia Hussey feeling! This man, little Hall and Oates! That man, Robert Redford! This true? My life? Why movie not stop?"

Sachiko in Australia was the spirit of delight incarnate, bending down to interview every child she passed, surprising old ladies by asking if they would pose with her in pictures, cross-questioning teenagers about their dreams. She could hardly walk past a single shop without letting out a cry of pleasure and rushing in to look more closely at their unimaginable discounts, and after visiting the beach one day, she felt so light that she simply took off her shoes and scampered barefoot through the Sydney streets. As our plane took off from Brisbane, she gasped with wonder, and sat by the window throughout the flight, peering out into the clouds. She had never seen a green-eyed child before, never heard buskers playing music in the street, never spent a whole day driving. She had never ordered a cocktail before or ridden a horse, been approached by men on the street or visited a noisy pub. Dressing up each night in her very best clothes, she had left the old Sachiko far behind.

"This true not dream?" she asked more than ever, and I did not know what to say.

I noticed, too, as Sachiko rhapsodized about this new world, how familiar her rapture sounded. Every child here, however runty or unexceptional, seemed a "doll"; every person impressed her as "very kind, very warm." Every new street hit her like some otherworldly dream. She sounded, in fact, like me exalting the lanterned lanes of Gion.

And nothing ever fazed her here except the signs of a Japan that she was seeing as if for the first time. She had never noticed before how the Japanese always wore black and white; she had never noticed before how incongruous they looked in their scuba divers' goggles or "Wombat" ties (as incongruous, almost, as big-boned blondes in kimono). She had never, in fact, felt so estranged from the group. Brisbane Airport, she pronounced, was very dirty, "because many many Japanese person here." In Surfers Paradise, as she watched her countrymen moving in tidy hordes to snap up Gucci bags and Cartier watches, she could hardly conceal her shock. "Why they all want same-same? Before, I thinking Japanese person coming Australia very special! But this style person very different. Not so special."

And as we wandered through the latest outpost of the Japanese Empire — a Gold Coast cluttered now with *o-bentō* stalls and koto-Muzaked malls, where couples in "Homey Honeymoon" T-shirts walked along sidewalks thick with signs crying, *"Irasshaimase!"* and koalas advertising prices in yen — Sachiko, in a fit of mischief, tried out the new phrase she had learned in her tour-conductor course.

"I think I want vomit. Please can I have an airsickness bag?"

Later, as the summer drew towards an end, back in Japan, we traveled to the Izu Peninsula, the mountainous resort not far from Tokyo, and soon I found myself sitting at dawn each day in a secluded cedar bath, high above the rushing of a stream, encircled by a ring of tall pines. The mist lifted off the water like a screen behind a stage. At night, in our small room, Sachiko curled a finger behind the shoji screen, making the shadow of an evil-eyed wolf.

After dark, in the distance, we could hear a pagan pounding through the trees, reminiscent of the distant drums in Kawabata's famous "Izu Dancer" story. Lanterns, red and white, were strung across the hillside, like light bulbs in some high school carnival. A long line of grannies circled slowly around a central tower, to the shrill notes of traditional music, flapping their arms around, slow and ceremonious as dying coquettes, as they summoned spirits back to earth, marking the start of the Night of a Thousand Lanterns. Along the edge of the trees, toddlers in indigo *yukata* scooped goldfish out of tanks, while tourists from the city ascended the tower to deliver heartfelt, deep-voiced renditions of melancholy love songs.

Together, Sachiko and I meandered in and out amidst the trees, along the roaring stream, a gauzy summer moon high above us. The music was carried faint to us, and eerie, through the trees.

"I think," she said mistily, "this little Heian Age. Many curtains. Very quiet. Man, woman, not so direct feeling. Japanese person much love poem life."

Emboldened, I told her how much I found of her in *Genji*: in her devotion to flowers, her fondness for cats, a quickness to sorrow that could almost come to self-pity. So much in her reminded me of the spirited, dreamy, quick-witted women of the Heian period, less conventional, perhaps, than their men (if only because they had less to lose), and pledged, as the author of *Sarashina Nikki* had it, "to walk across the bridge of dreams." Sachiko, however, did not seem uplifted by this.

"I not so like *Genji*. Much much baby-making ceremony there."

"But in the Heian period, it sounds so poetic. Lovers together in kimono, looking at the moon, then leaving at dawn with a morning-after poem."

"Maybe," she said. "Maybe very beautiful letter. But all *Genji* little 'sex machine' feeling. Genji little same Rod Stewart. This story little singles-bar style. I not so like." With that, she went into a rapturous tribute to John Denver.

By now, Sachiko and I were bypassing language altogether very often. And though there were parts of me she could not see, and vice versa, they were really, I thought, the parts least worthy of being seen, the verbal and the analytical sides that made up nothing but a captious surface. Not seeing them, in a sense, allowed us to see one another more clearly, just as the bareness of a Japanese room sharpened attention and heightened intensity. The words we could not share left us more room for ourselves.

The Japanese, of course, had long prided themselves on their ability to communicate without words (in part, no doubt, because this served to bind the tribe together and so keep aliens out); in phrases like *ishin-denshin,* they enshrined the Buddhist ideal of speaking through actions more than words. And Sachiko, living her life in subtitles now, and resolving herself into the simplicity of a haiku, was, without trying, teaching me gradually to see a little below the surface and grow more attentive to the small print of the world. Once, when she handed me some chocolates wrapped in a stylish green pouch, I tore open the bag and gobbled them down. Only later did I gather that the present was not, in fact, the candies but the bag. It was the green, she explained, of "little cartoon eating food" (she burst into a rendition of the "Popeye" theme song). And the Japanese word for "spinach," she said, was a homonym for their word for "secret love." Thus, ever since the Heian period, giving someone a present wrapped in a bag of spinach-green had been the most eloquent way of giving him one's heart.

ONE DAY, towards the end of summer, wearing a long red dress to offset the blinding green, and carrying a red silk umbrella against the rain, Etsuko invited me to the fabled rock garden at Ryōanji, its enigmatic stones a natural koan, and one stone omitted so that each visitor could make the meaning something different. Along one side of the Dragon Peace Temple, a washbasin read simply, "I learn to be contented."

As we sat on the platform, in the early drizzle of a hazy afternoon, Etsuko asked if I had been following the news about the Hanshin Tigers. I knew that the summer had not been treating my favorite team well. Japanese champions just two years before, they were now in last place. Their longtime star, Kakefu, or "Mr. Tiger," was said to be contemplating retirement. Taxi drivers squirmed and sucked their teeth whenever I brought up their favorite subject, and Sachiko, in a characteristic burst of impishness, had happily asserted, "This year Tigers not so strong! They not true Tigers; they Hanshin Cats!"

The drama had come to a climax, though, when the son of their leading star, Randy Bass, had developed a brain tumor. Bass, who had led them to the championship, had compiled the most impressive statistics of any American ever to play in Japan; more important, perhaps, he had adjusted philosophically to the Japanese system, not only slugging fifty home runs in a season but bowing when requested to do so, stoically refusing to complain when rival teams conspired to prevent him from breaking Japanese records, and even inspiring a chant that went, "God-Buddha-Bass!" Recently, though, he had flown off to San Francisco to be at his eight-year-old son's bedside. The Tigers had grown restive. Complications had developed, bringing the boy even closer to death. The agreed-upon deadline passed, and still Bass had stayed by his boy. Finally, the team had offered an ultimatum: come back or get fired. Bass had remained with his son, putting family before company. That, to the Tigers, had seemed the ultimate heresy. So, in a kind of strategic suicide, they had fired their Most Valuable Player.

To replace him, they had scouted around for another *gaijin* and, somehow or other, had ended up with a famous malingerer whose indiscipline was so legendary that he had already been jettisoned by both the Yankees and the Angels. (The next foreigner they signed slugged thirty-eight home runs but incurred the wrath of all Japan when caught by a photographer making breakfast for his son, while his wife slept in.) Loss followed loss, of games as well as face.

"Did you hear what happened yesterday?" Etsuko asked me in the quiet of the rock garden, face pale.

"No."

"The general manager of the Tigers jumped to his death from the eighth floor of the New Otani Hotel."

Meanwhile, in lesser ways, the cross-cultural collisions were continuing all around me. Each night, from my room, I could hear the former president of Harvard's Spee Club stalking up and down the corridors, complaining of the "epistemological uncertainty" of a land "where nothing was real," while someone else marveled aloud about how he could earn $250,000 a year here as a translator. A group of thirteen Israelis began camping out in a single room downstairs, part of a circuit of foreigners who lived off the Madonna and Mickey Mouse posters they could sell on the street, making three hundred dollars or more a night. Another newcomer from Santa Barbara appeared, called, as if in some bad movie, "Beach."

Matthew, by now, was living in Thailand, and Siobhan had returned to the Haight with a tall, silent, ponytailed Japanese boy, with whom she had no common language. Etsuko was making plans to take off for California herself—as soon as her daughter was out of school—and write a thesis on folklore and Christianity, picking up the intellectual interests she'd had to keep in storage for so long. And Shinji, the *gaijin*-lover from Nagasaki, had managed somehow to make it to the outside world—Australia—which he now proclaimed to find "very easy, very boring." One day, I got a package from Sydney, and tore it open to find eleven different tapes, all handmade, and carefully labeled, and based on the stray preferences I had expressed in Nagasaki almost six months before; later, another shipment came, and then another. For all his willed rebellion, I gathered, Shinji was as thoughtful and kind as every other Japanese I had met, and as skilled in the ways of obligation: having showered me with presents—David Lindley bootlegs, Amazulu tapes, ancient Buffalo Springfield tapes, and the latest from the Waterboys—he now felt free to ring me up at 6 a.m. and ask for a Burberry coat or information on helicopter licenses, advice for his friend in her college applications or a letter in support of his American visa. And since any favor I did him reduced his emotional credit, as well as the interest he could collect on it, both of us kept trying to outdo the other in kindnesses, in part so as not to have to do them again. It reminded me a little of the "you first; no, you; no, please, I insist" routines that had so charmed me when first I arrived.

No place, of course, is an idyll to its residents, as no man is a prophet in his own household. And foreigners everywhere are more solicitous about the traditions of their adopted homes than natives are (as converts are more zealous, often, than those born into a faith): Asians in America sometimes seemed as intent on keeping up the "American Way" as foreigners in Kyoto were on preserving the ancient capital's streetcars and old wooden houses. Yet still, in Japan, the divisions seemed uncommonly intense, if only because Japan lived at the other extreme from the self-analytical and abstract ways of the West, and was anxious to enforce that distance. The Japanese drove on the right and read their magazines from back to front. They put their verbs at the end of sentences and took their baths at night. Sexually, they "went" where we "came"; emotionally, they smiled where we wept. Even their baggage carousels moved in the opposite direction. Translated into terms we understood, two plus two made five here.

This it was, I suspected, together with the maintenance of a public face that never cracked, that began to account for the unusual violence of so many foreign responses to Japan—the same people who so admired the formality and reticence of the Japanese aesthetic complaining, often, about the formality and reticence of the Japanese people, and the same ones who so bridled at Japanese claims that Japan could be understood only by the Japanese mocking the way the Japanese spoke English. This it was too, perhaps, that helped to explain why foreigners' responses to Japan seemed so uniform and yet so violently divided—in proportion, perhaps, to the gap between public and private. The tourists who came here for two weeks could not stop marveling, often, at the silence of the place; the longtime residents heard only the clatter of pachinko coins, the blare of right-wing megaphones, the syncopated roar of TV baseball crowds. The people who were sightseers here seemed moved, nearly always, by the courtesy and consideration that they found; the residents saw nothing but hypocrisy. And the visitors went home, very often, wishing that the West could be more like Japan; while the residents stayed here, unable to forgive Japan for not being more like the West.

For my own part, I began to realize that every statement I made about Japan applied just as surely in the opposite direction. I might think it odd that Japanese girls covered their mouths whenever they laughed—until I remembered that we were trained to cover our mouths whenever we yawn. I might wince every

time I read dismissive talk of "foreigners" in Japanese novels—
until I thought how we use "Orientals" in our own. I might be
surprised at the formal rites of Japanese courtesy—until I remembered how firmly I had been taught to say "Thank you," even
for gifts I did not like.

The best advice on the subject, though, seemed to come,
appropriately enough, from a baseball player, Ben Oglivie, the
famously literate right fielder for the Milwaukee Brewers, celebrated for reading Plato and Thoreau on the team bus. Now in
his sunset years with the Kintetsu Buffaloes, Oglivie had only
one problem here, a friend of mine who knew him said, and
that was his philosophical bent; while other imported stars took
the money and ran, Oglivie dwelt and dwelt on the challenge of
different cultures. And his conclusion seemed infinitely more
enlightened than that of many thinkers and social critics. "It's
no good coming over here and criticizing the Japanese game,"
he told my friend. "That's like going into someone's house and
criticizing the way he's arranged the furniture. It's his house,
and that's the way he likes it. It's not for the guest to start
changing things around." It took a ballplayer, I realized, to teach
us elementary civility.

The complexities of cultural cross-breeding came home to me
most poignantly, however, when a Japanese friend from California came to visit in Kyoto. In Santa Barbara, Sumi had always
struck me as a typically sweet exemplar of her culture: an
accomplished listener with a computer memory, an earnest,
almost guileless, optimist, and a model of hardworking consideration, holding down eight jobs and taking four courses
while still finding time to design her own cards for birthdays,
Thanksgivings, and Halloweens. Now, though, after three years
away, she found herself as estranged from her homeland as
from an America that conformed less and less to cliché. She was
shocked, she told me after she arrived, to see, for the first time

ever, the sorrow and frustration of this endlessly hustling country. I was shocked to see how she had slipped, without noticing it, from first person to third when talking of the Japanese.

Returning to her small hometown, moreover, Sumi had found herself shunned by all her high school friends, not only because she had made it to the land of which they only dreamed, but also—and especially—because she presented it back to them now as something more complex than a beach poster. They could not forgive her, so it seemed, for importing some reality. She, in turn, having read about Japanese history for the first time abroad, and about Buddhism, could scarcely believe now, or forgive, the distance at which Japan lived from that knowledge, and from the source of its traditions. America, she said, seemed so optimistic, and I, thinking of how I viewed Japan, could only bite my tongue. It was, perhaps, the old half-empty/half-full conundrum; but we are optimists when faced with another culture, and pessimists when faced with our own.

Such confusions were growing more and more common now as more and more Japanese women began going abroad—or joining foreign firms—to gain the possibilities denied to them at home. This, the papers proclaimed, was the *Onna no Jidai*, or Era of Women. And even those who played by the accepted rules seemed far more complex than the smiling pietàs by whom I had been so enchanted when first I had arrived. Through Sachiko now, I was meeting all kinds of women with lives quite as quirky as any in the West—one who did not even know what her husband of ten years did for a living, and another who, in three years of marriage, had never had it consummated; one mild-mannered girl who ran a pyramid-game fraud, and another who patiently waited for the one day a year when she could spend a night together with her married lover. The acupuncturist Keiko, meanwhile, after four months of living with both her husband and her boyfriend, had finally broken down and tried to slash her wrists. Filing for divorce, she had moved back with her parents, who every night received anonymous phone calls from a woman who gave them details of their daughter's infamy.

Only Hideko, the textbook model of a decorous mother and wife, seemed to be keeping up the role of a perfect ōtome fujin (or "automated wife"), and that was because her emotions were so little implicated in the role. Now she was just returned from Australia and could not stop talking about the strip shows she had enjoyed, this prim and tiny lady, every day of her stay. The little girl she led around with her was already a mistress of distances; eyes huge, she hid behind her mother's designer skirts, keeping the world outside at bay.

Just as I was trying to put all these lives into perspective, I chanced to pick up a collection of short stories by Tsushima Yūko, one of the leading women writers in Japan today, and the daughter of the famous novelist Osamu Dazai. And suddenly, racing through her sad and suffocating tales of single mothers dreaming of flight, waiting for the men who invariably walk out on them, I felt I was seeing modern Japan for the first time, the world that all the great male novelists so scrupulously sifted out. Tanizaki and Kawabata loved young women mostly for the use they made of them, pygmalionizing them, treating them as flowers almost, totemizing them as perfect emblems of threatened purity ("It's as if Kinko has no personality of her own, and that's why she seems so extraordinarily feminine," Osamu Dazai himself had written, in the voice of a fictitious schoolgirl). Even contemporary female writers seemed often to embrace the assumptions forced upon them ("A rational woman is as ridiculous," writes Enchi Fumiko, "as a flower held together with wire"). But here in Tsushima's gray and rainy tales of lonely, wasted women exchanging intimacies in coffee shops and love hotels, I felt I was seeing Japan through the other end of the telescope at last: the concrete blocks behind the cherry blossoms.

Most of her stories were set within the moody, blighted landscape of modern industrial Japan, amidst smog-shrouded, look-alike station cafés or lonely, boarded-up seaside resorts where it was always out of season. Always the main character, like Tsushima herself, was a weary single mother, surrounded by her children, hemmed in by her duties, and hostage to her culture's expectations, and always she was dreaming of escape—to the sea, to an inn, to anywhere other than her clangorous apartment. Women alone in the dark, dreaming of the day when they'd grow wings "and everyone would finally realize that she hadn't been just some mother."

The men in her stories were not cads or fiends; just married men in search of pleasure, with other matters on their minds, giving their lovers children, and giving their children presents, so that they would not have to give themselves. They were not so much members of a household as sightseers there. "A man was the sort who'd give you any number of children and then run off when the mood took him"; a father was "a mere shadow in a photograph." The setting of the story, often, was the day after, in an age that did not believe in morning-after poems.

Yet even as she described the transaction as a woman's plight, Tsushima did not, I felt, overlook the reserves of strength that Japanese women kept in private: all her women were living in a transitional age, when the reality of their inherited powerlessness was tempered by the first suggestions of a dawning freedom. In one story, a woman known only, and archetypally, as the "Mother," absently cleans up around her drab room while waiting for her runaway daughter to return. With half her heart, she fears for her only companion; with the other half, she almost envies the girl for laying claim to a freedom that she herself has always been denied. Again and again in the stories, Tsushima alluded to the overgrowth at the side of a garden, the wilderness just beyond the neat suburban parks. Always, around the immaculate public places, there lurked a few "dark tangles along the walls." And it was in these undomesticated spaces, she suggested, that the women were beginning to gather their strength unseen.

9

As SUMMER drew towards an end, Sachiko got ready for her biggest move of all: taking off on a new life of her own. She had finished her Osaka course by now and passed the qualifying test, and she was ready to begin working as an international tour guide. With her monklike swiftness and one-pointedness, she had already mapped out a concrete plan of action: how she would file for divorce, move into a new home with her children, reassume her maiden name, and set up a professional life, leading tours around Asia and Japan. It was hard for me to recall now the Sachiko who, only a few months before, had hardly stepped outside Kyoto.

As she closed in on her dreams, the cavils of her society only mounted and intensified. On a practical level, her friends were extraordinarily generous: when her Walkman broke, Keiko promptly gave her another, and when she started looking around for a home, Hideko promised her an electric range and a VCR. Emotionally, though, they seemed determined to box her into the same narrow compartments to which they had resigned themselves. The best way to express yourself was to efface yourself, they kept reminding her; a woman's strength should come from weakness. Foreigners were dangerous, and so were dreams; a woman should fulfill herself within the family. Speaking her mind, they said, was almost worse than telling lies.

Sometimes, Sachiko seemed exhausted by all this. "Woman's world very complicated," she often told me. "Japanese woman, not so easy heart. Much jealousy there! I want say true. But always say true, soon biggg problem." More often, though, she sped along unstoppably, her air of confidence intact. "Aren't you worried, Sachiko?" I asked her once as she prepared to commit herself to an unknown future. "Worry not so help," she sang out, mirroring my own words back to me. "I not want worry. You know this song? 'Que será será.'"

As I got ready to leave Japan, Sachiko asked me one day for a copy of a photograph I had taken, a thoroughly unremarkable picture of my own long shadow in the eerie light of late afternoon. The last time I visited her home, I noticed the picture on her piano, set in an indigo frame, and suddenly resonant—a way, I guessed, of keeping at least my outline in her life. And before I left her house that day, she gave me, in return, a golden lacquer box decorated with a cosmos flower—to remind me, she said, of the walks that we had taken when the days were bright with flowers.

Autumn this year promised to hold even more elegiac weight than usual, as all Japan, in a sense, was holding its collective breath, waiting for the Emperor to die and a new imperial era to begin. And for me, as I felt the first chill entering the city and saw a whole new generation of foreigners beginning to appear, the season itself seemed to have grown older, as the city had. By now, I felt, I knew Kyoto's moods so well that I could almost tell the time without looking at my watch: how the light lay silver on the river in the sharpened afternoons, how the temples exhaled mist in early light. Autumn seemed much deeper than spring, as sadness is deeper than brief joy, or memory than hope: the age-old Japanese assumption. Sometimes, in the dying days of summer, the beauty of Kyoto was almost hard to bear.

Just as I was packing my final bags, though, Sachiko gave me the finest farewell gift of all: a sense of what the discipline of Zen really meant. For as she readied herself for a new kind of life, living at a tangent to the norm and seeing people turn away from her whenever she told them that she was about to leave her marriage, the only friends who came unfailingly to her assistance, encouraging her to extend herself and disinterestedly offering her all the support she needed, were those she had made through the temple. Sometimes, when her confidence was wavering, she called up Mark for inspiration; sometimes, when she needed to be reminded of how even a woman could have a "strong heart," she turned to Sandy.

Most often, though, when she found herself in need of counsel, she went to see the abbot of Tōfukuji. And he calmly told her that he would give her anything she needed to keep herself and her children in good health. Would two thousand dollars a month be enough? If she wanted more, he said, she only had to ask.

Though Sachiko politely declined the offer — she was determined to do things by herself — the incident gave me a glimpse at last of what all the meditation was about. "The ultimate purpose of Zen," I remembered the *rōshi* telling me, "is not in the going away from the world but in the coming back. Zen is not just a matter of gaining enlightenment; it's a matter of acting in a world of love and compassion."

On the final day of summer, Sachiko took me to Arashiyama to watch the cormorant boats. The night was navy blue and gold when we arrived, a lone torch burning against the dark-blue hills. On the top of the distant mountains sat a round white moon. Along the riverbank, red lanterns shivered in the faint, chill breeze, their echoes wavering red in the reflecting water. A single pagoda, lonely as a plover's cry, jutted up into the heavens. A solitary canoeist pulled himself soundless through the dark.

Far in the distance, car lights glided silent across the Togetsu Bridge; in a teahouse nearby, the upswept coiffure of a geisha flashed briefly in an upstairs window. Occasionally, above the water, a firework shot up into the dark, and then, with a quiet hiss, streamed down in a sad, slow extravagance of gold.

There was a sense of elegy about the river tonight, the smell of spent fireworks, the faintest hint of autumn chill, the happy, clapping songs of summer's final parties.

Cool in her summer kimono, Sachiko led me over the bridge to where the boats knocked against the dock, lanterns along their sides bearing the faint outline of cormorants. Stepping behind her into a boat and steadying myself, I saw the moon shivering in a row of silver lanterns.

Without a sound, our boat set off across the lake, the darkness deepening above the dark-blue hills. The boats, with their crisscrossing lines of lanterns, looked eerie now, and ghostly in the gathering dark, their white globes doubled in the rippling water. From across the water came the dull thud of an oar. The teahouses cast reflections, red and white and blue, across the rippling water.

And so we drifted through the night, approaching, then receding from, the other silent boats. Occasionally, an open cormorant punt came past, torches burning at its prow, scattering sparks across the dark. For a moment, in the torchlight, the aged fishermen's faces were lit up, in a flash of Rembrandt gold, and then, as soon, their wrinkled features and medieval grass-skirt forms vanished again into the dark.

Another boat glided past, ringing with the laughs of company men lined up around a long, low table, served strange delicacies by white-faced geisha. A firework shivered off into the dark, and then came down in a shower of white and gold and pink. The torches singed the water gold. Every now and then, a bird plunged down into the water, emerging with a fish within its beak.

"This place before, I little goodbye ceremony," said Sachiko, face whitened in the dark. Behind her, the lanterned boats were slow and soundless in the night. "I not know this. But he say he want only friend." Her voice trailed off into the dreamy dark. A boat bumped up against us, and the gold reflections blurred and shivered in the water.

Along the bank came the sudden sound of children laughing. A grandfather bent down to light a firework for his toddler, and it veered off into the sky, a shooting, soundless bird, then slowly came back down again. Lovers wandered off into the cicada-buzzing dark. Across the water, the lone canoeist pulled his way in from the shadowed, distant mountains.

"Summer soon finish," she said softly. "Soon weather little cold again. Tonight last summer party." Thoughts turn to autumn, and to separation. In the distance, the sound of ancient folk songs, and of grandmas dancing.

It was only later, after I had left Japan, that I realized that everything had been there that night: the lanterned dark, the moon above the mountains, the dreamlike maiden in kimono. There was the Heian vision I had sought since childhood. And yet, by now, it was so much a part of my life that I had not even seen it till it was gone.

Permissions Acknowledgments

Grateful acknowledgment is made to the following for permission to reprint previously published material:

New Directions Publishing Corporation: Excerpt from poem from *100 Poems from the Japanese*, translated by Kenneth Rexroth, and excerpt from poem from *Women Poets of Japan*, translated by Ikuko Atsumi and Kenneth Rexroth. Reprinted by permission of New Directions Publishing Corporation.

Charles E. Tuttle Co., Inc.: Three poems, #7, #47, #54, from *Tangled Hair* by Akiko Yosano, translated by Sanford Goldstein and Seishi Shinoda. Reprinted by permission of Charles E. Tuttle Co., Inc., Tokyo, Japan.

Warner Chappell Music Limited: Excerpt from "September Blue" by Chris Rea. Copyright ©1987 by Magnet Music Limited. Reprinted by permission of Warner Chappell Music Limited.

Weatherhill, Inc.: Excerpt from poems from *One Robe, One Bowl* by Ryokan, translated by John Stevens, and five haikus from *Santoka* by Santoka, translated by John Stevens. Reprinted by permission of Weatherhill, Inc.

TREASURES OF THE ARMADA

ROBERT STÉNUIT

TREASURES
OF THE
ARMADA

Translated by
Francine Barker

DAVID & CHARLES
NEWTON ABBOT

0 7153 5601 1

Text set in 11 pt. Baskerville
and printed in Great Britain
at The Pitman Press   Bath
for David & Charles (Publishers) Limited
South Devon House   Newton Abbot   Devon

Happiness is a childhood dream
fulfilled in adulthood.

Freud

To dream is easy. To make a dream come true is not easy. A dreamer will not succeed alone. True, he drives the practical people with him toward a goal, but he would never reach that goal if the same practical people were not physically pushing him towards it.

Money, hardware, backbreaking work, enthusiasm, confidence were the things I absolutely needed if I were to succeed in taking back from the sea the treasure of the *Girona*. All these things, a Maecenas has given me. Henri Delauze, the Maecenas has dived many times to 32,000 feet in the French bathyscaph (of which he was 'Chef de Laboratoire'). With the diving systems, the suits, the breathing apparatuses which he and his company have engineered, he has dived down to 1,100 feet. Arriving there took him half of his life, but today under the seven seas his divers are opening a new field to the off-shore oil industry. To achieve just that, Henri Delauze has built the right organisation: COMEX, Compagnie Maritime d'Expertises, originally of Marseilles, now of the whole world. It has become the number one company in the field of deep diving and under-water engineering, and today Henri Delauze, President of COMEX, has thought fit to put back to the service of undersea archeology the tool and the fortune made from his under-sea businesses.

Without the divers of COMEX, without COMEX, without Henri Delauze, there would have been no treasure and no book.

Robert Sténuit

Contents

9

Contents

PART TWO: GOLD UNDER THE SEAWEED

Illustrations

COLOUR

BLACK AND WHITE

Illustrations

Prologue

The galleass rolled from side to side in a welter of foam. Suddenly, looming in the night, 'Breakers ahead!' The first man on his feet leapt to the prow. With one blow of his axe he cut through the ropes that retained the cable. The anchor dropped.

Too late. The watch-keepers, who were desperately trying to heave in, saw a huge black and white mass hurtling towards the ship's side. With a cracking that seemed to herald the end of the world, the *Girona* gutted herself on the rocks, spilling out her cannon, her coffers, her innards. Into the breaking waves she cast one thousand three hundred sick men, many of them too exhausted to struggle.

One thousand three hundred men; including Don Alonzo Martinez de Leiva, Knight of Santiago and Commander of Alcuescar, the bravest captain of them all, favourite of Philip II, and commander designate of the Felicissima Armada, in the event of the death of Medina Sidonia; including sixty sons of the most noble families in all Spain, specially entrusted to Don Alonzo and anxious to serve under none other; including a young hidalgo, whose last thought as he choked on salt water must have sped towards Spain. Before setting out to conquer England, he must have spent his last night ashore with his betrothed. In the morning, his horse was already saddled, when she slipped a ring on his finger, a keepsake, specially commissioned from the best goldsmith. Left and right the swell tossed his body. Crabs and conger eels gnawed away his flesh. The ring slipped from his bony finger, and rolled away, with the contents of his pockets, down into a crevice. Storms heaped sand onto it, lumps of rock and lobster shells, slowly cemented together by the rust from the oxydising cannon balls.

After 400 years, deep in the dust of archives, I reconstructed the story. Under 30 ft of icy water I found the site of the wreck and with four team mates explored every cranny. We broke up the concretion, lifted huge boulders, sifted every grain of sand. Right at the bottom, beside a two escudo piece from Toledo and a few pieces of eight, we found the ring, given, to the music of the lark's song, by that tearful, red-eyed fiancée.

On the boat, the ring shone softly in the Irish sun. Out of all the treasures of the Armada, this is the most beautiful, the most moving. The setting is a tiny hand holding a heart and an open belt clasp. Engraved in the gold, I read these words: '*No tengo mas que dar te.*' 'I have nothing more to give you . . .'

13

From CAMBRIDGE UNIVERSITY PRESS

1 (one) x 306604 : Alperin's : Local Representation Theory

COMPLIMENTARY COPIES / ~~INVOICE TO FOLLOW~~
(delete as applicable).

PART ONE

THE MOST FORTUNATE FLEET

Jehovah blew and they
were scattered.
(Dutch Commemorative Medal)

I

King Philip's Mission

Reverently I placed the ring in a jam pot in the bow of the boat, strapped a fresh cylinder on my back, gripped the mouthpiece between my teeth, and dived again.

A jungle of brown seaweed covers everything, our measuring lines included. But by now I know every rock and every crevice in the chaotic world of the seabed. Winging my way over that dense foliage I can spot them by a slight protuberance, an imperceptible hollow. Just as hurricanes flatten palm trees in Florida, the ceaseless swell of the Atlantic furls and unfurls the sunken forests. The swell is the sea's pulse. We live by its rhythm. To go forward I must wait for a wave to catapult me. When the movement stops I cling to a rock or to a sea tangle hurled suddenly backwards, its fronds flapping in the current like a flag, while the hose from my regulator, pulling against my clenched teeth, vibrates next to my ears. Then, like so many whips, the thongs of seaweed lash back again, and I am hurled once more towards the narrow cleft in the rock that I am heading for.

At the end of my last dive I had to leave a silver coin wedged in the rock. This coin intrigues me. It is not a piece of eight, or four, such as we find everywhere. On the half visible face I manage to make out the unexpected words, HILARITAS UNIVERSA. I have brought a hammer and chisel with me this time. Gripping my legs round a rock to steady myself against the swell, I set to work on the calcareous mass that cements the rocks together. I shift one small stone to get at a larger one. I kick that out of the way. Now, sweeping with one hand, I can stir up the sand at the bottom of the cleft. The swell carries it off in thick clouds and reveals a cannon ball in its rust-coloured matrix. The matrix shatters under my hammer, the water turns black. A taste of iron in my mouth. I lift out the cannon ball. Later on I shall mark its exact position on the plan. At last I can slip my crowbar in through the gap. I push long and hard on it. The boulder moves. I grasp it, straddle it, arch myself, take a deep breath and wait for a good roller. I pull with all my might. The boulder rolls out of its hole.

I pick out the coin and rub it between my thumb and fore-finger. A profile appears—a Roman breastplate, straight nose and forehead, a

17

grave look in the eye, a noble beard. On the reverse the arms of Spain in an oval frame. A Neapolitan silver escudo, hardly blackened. Of course! The *Girona* was part of the squadron of Naples, the capital of the Kingdom of the Two Sicilies. It's the ambitious king, the administrator, the spider king, who, from the depths of his palace of San Lorenzo de Escorial, spun that intricate web with which it was his mission to bind the world. It is Philip II, the Prudent, Defender of the Faith, Suppressor of Heresy, by the grace of God, King of Aragon, Castile, León, King of Sardinia and the Two Sicilies, King of Navarre, of Granada, Toledo, Valencia, Galicia, Majorca, Seville, Cordoba, Corcyra, Murcia, Jaen, the Algarve, Algeciras, Gibraltar, the Canary Islands, the East Indies, the West Indies, the Spanish Main, King of Portugal, of Algarva, Brazil, the Azores, the Cape Verde Islands, Ruler of the Guinea, Angola, Mozambique and India settlements, Governor of Aden, Muscat, Ormuz, Java, the Moluccas, the Philippines, Macao, Archduke of Austria, Duke of Milan, of Limburg, Brabant, Luxembourg, Guelders, Marquis of Antwerp, Count of Hapsburg, Burgundy, Tyrol, Barcelona, Flanders, Artois, Hainault, Namur, Holland, Zeeland and Zutphen, Lord of Biscay, Molina, Overijssel, Tournai, Groningen, Utrecht and Friesland, King of Jerusalem, a defeated King.

Numb with cold, my fingers close on the history of Europe. For years I have pursued it, spending hour upon hour in dusty libraries and archives in Britain, Spain, France, Belgium and Holland. At last I have history literally in my grasp, here, under the sea, in the very place where it was made.

I close my eyes and Philip lives again, the man who, in 1588, after twenty years of intrigue and hesitation, launched against England the most powerful expedition, the largest fleet ever seen, 'because such was the mission he had received from God.'

The sun never set on Philip's empire, and never had so scattered an empire depended to such an extent on supremacy at sea. Each year more gold was mined in America than had existed in the whole of Medieval Europe. Special fleets of armed galleons, the *Platas Flotas*, the plate fleets, carried this annual haul back to Cadiz. Pirates of all nations dreamed about it, and so did the sailors of Her Most Gracious Majesty Queen Elizabeth's Royal Navy. Sometimes they did more than dream. If Philip was going to keep the world in his clutches for himself, if he was going to protect the Spanish trade monopoly with the Americas, to continue unhindered transporting from Peru and Mexico to his own coffers the gold necessary to maintain Christ's Army, there was one last rival still to be swallowed, Elizabeth, who obstinately persisted in putting England and her ships in his way. (See page 25.)

As early as 1568, this divine mission must have begun to take shape in the mind of His Most Catholic Majesty. That year, one of his ships was leaving Spain with an escort of four *zabras*, taking as pay for the Duke of Alba's troops to Flanders, one million gold ducats. The ship had to make an unscheduled stop at Southampton. Elizabeth stole the gold. Unable to pay his men, Alba found himself in an extremely difficult situation. He retaliated by putting an embargo on all the English merchandise he could lay his hands on in Flanders. Elizabeth replied by seizing every Spanish merchant ship in English waters. Spain then seized all English ships in Spanish ports and sent their crews to the galleys. England arrested the Spanish Ambassador. Negotiations went on for years, but Philip never saw a *maravedis* of it again.

His mission was brought to mind again in 1580. For as long as anyone could remember he and the Pope had been financing and arming Irish rebels. Encouraged by the fact that the Earl of Desmond, leader of the latest uprising, had managed to crush the Lord Deputy's troops at Glenmalure, Philip sent over in support a landing force of several hundred Spaniards and Italians. An English army hurried to the spot, took them all prisoners at Smerwick, and strangled them one by one. There was nothing Philip could do. There had been no formal declaration of war. Spoke Spanish, did they, these soldiers? Strange. Where could they have come from? He, in any case, knew nothing about it.

Action became more pressing still in 1583, when Elizabeth expelled Don Bernardino de Mendoza, the Spanish Ambassador in London, certain ministers having accused him of being rather too deeply involved in Throckmorton's plot to kill the Queen. Philip took offence. He threw all the English in Spain into jail, confiscated their property and put a ban on all trade between the two nations.

During a corn shortage in Spain, in 1585, he gave a specific safe conduct to a group of English merchants and invited them to send a fleet of corn ships over to his northern ports in May. The fleet had hardly arrived when one crew threw overboard some Spanish soldiers who attempted to go on board in disguise. Phillip ordered that both ships and cargo be seized and the crews sent to the galleys. But one ship managed to get away, and brought the news to London. It met with an angry reaction. The good faith of the King of Spain was quiestioned.

And during these last fifteen years, English pirates persisted in plaguing Spanish ports and the Spanish fleet with their plundering expeditions, carried out in the Queen's ships, financed by her, by her ministers and by her courtiers. Vigo, the Cape Verde Islands, Cape St Vincent had all been attacked. A certain adventurer, of humble birth, Francis Drake, was waging his own personal war against the most powerful king in the world. He had sacked most of the West Indies ports at least once. He had pillaged San Juan de Ulla, scoured the Gulf of Mexico and brought down Nombre de Dios, helped by some French pirates and a band of runaway black slaves. In the Isthmus of Panama he had seized the annual haul of gold from Peru, on its way by mule from the Pacific to the Atlantic. On his return Drake explained to the Queen that the booty had been acquired through 'exchanges with the natives.' The Queen passed this on to the Spanish Ambassador, who very nearly exploded with rage.

As the *Golden Hind* rounded America in 1580 by the Straits of Magellan, *El Draque*, the dragon, completed the first round-the-world buccaneering trip, at the expense of galleons looted en route and Spanish ports on the Pacific, where he had arrived unexpectedly. The voyage had lasted two years and ten months. Of the five ships that set out four did not return. Nonetheless there were still silks, spices and purloined gold (much of the silver had been thrown overboard before the return journey because it was too bulky), enough to yield a dividend of 4,700 per cent to the shareholders, over and above Drake's own cut and Her Majesty's. And still England and Spain were not at war. When the Spanish Ambassador, in the name of his sovereign the King, thus discomfited and robbed, demanded compensation for his ruined merchants and his murdered subjects, and insisted once again that the man responsible be punished, the Queen hesitated. Once again she reckoned up the share of the fabulous booty that lay in her coffers. After a sumptuous banquet, she dubbed the marauder Sir Francis and appointed him Admiral of her navy. Then, the *pirata luterano*, as the Spaniards called him, again put to sea. After looting on the outward passage various ports in Spain, the Canaries and Puerto Rico, he held San Domingo for ransom and pillaged it, laid siege to Cartagena, set fire to St Augustine in Florida, and returned with two hundred cannon in addition to the usual booty.

Philip's divine mission had become very clear indeed when Elizabeth opened the royal purse and lent ships to Don Antonio, the Prior of Ocrato and illegitimate grandson of Manuel I, who had himself crowned King of Portugal, to the throne of which Philip held title by his first marriage. It had become clearer still when Elizabeth started making overtures to the Sheriff of Morocco, suggesting an alliance with him against Spain, his traditional enemy.

Now, Elizabeth signed a treaty with the Dutch. She had garrisons at Flushing and at Brill, and in 1586 her favourite, Robert Dudley, Earl of Leicester, had landed 5,000 foot and 1,000 horse, paid for out of her own funds, to support the rebel heretics of the Seven Provinces, the northern provinces which no governor had managed to bring into line.

On 8 February 1587, the executioner laid down his axe in the great hall of Fotheringay Castle. He stooped down to grasp the auburn hair, then raised his hand high, crying the customary words 'Long live the Queen'; the crowd had shouted in chorus after him. Only then did the headsman realise that all he held in his hand was a wig and a kerchief. Clotted with blood, the head had rolled to the edge of the scaffold. 'And all could see how worry and anxiety had by her forty-fifth year withered and greyed the queen, who in her lifetime had been counted among the most beautiful women in the world.' The head was that of Mary Stuart, Dowager Queen of France, deposed Queen of Scots, and in Philip's view, legitimate heir to the throne of England. Action was now inescapable.

The execution deeply shocked the whole of Europe. Political etiquette required that kings and princes be assassinated, preferably poisoned. A public beheading at the hands of the common executioner was considered outrageous by the nobility. It made royal princes subject to the common justice of ordinary men.

By Catholic law, the dead queen had every right to the throne. It so happened that, before her martyr's death, she had disowned her Protestant son, James VI of Scotland (who, notwithstanding, later became James I of England) and secretly promised her throne to the direct descendant of the sons of Edward III, His Most Catholic Majesty the King of Spain. She had put her wish in writing and sent copies to Philip, the Pope and the Spanish Ambassador in Paris. It was now up to Philip, the Defender of the Faith, he felt, to carry out the sacred mission of freeing the English people from their Protestant yoke—to take the crown that was rightfully his—or rather, as he promised the Pope, to place it on the head of his daughter Isabella Clara Eugenia.

Philip learned of the execution on 23 March 1587, in a dispatch from his Ambassador in Paris, Count Bernardino de Mendoza. He spent the whole of the following week deep in thought; when he emerged from his study he had made his decision to strike.

2

The Enterprise of England

The Prudent King had drawn up his plan. The Governor of the Spanish Netherlands, Alexander Farnese, Duke of Parma and Piacenza (Spanish documents refer to him variously as Duke, Grand Duke or Prince) was to assemble the army of Flanders at Dunkirk, while at the same time making ready to embark at Nieuport. Meanwhile, Don Alvaro de Bazan, Marquis of Santa Cruz, would, by the spring, have gathered together at Lisbon a fleet strong enough to hold Elizabeth's at bay and destroy it if necessary. The fleet would cover the crossing and protect the Army's line of supply and communication. Once he reached England, having crossed in a flotilla of barges, Parma would be able to count on the Catholic nobility rallying to him and on the combined forces of the Irish and the Scots. The King sent William Semple over with 42,000 escudos to distribute among potential local fifth columns.

For financial support in his crusade, the Defender of the Faith quite naturally turned to Christ's Vicar on Earth, to Pope Sixtus V, who had been urging him to act since the day of his investiture, and who declared himself ready to aid the undertaking of the leading soldier of Catholicism in every possible way (except one, that is, as I discovered very early on in my research).

Pius V had already excommunicated Elizabeth in 1570 in his papal bull *Regnans in Excelsis*, in which the queen was declared a heretic and a persecutor of true religion and was deprived of 'her pretended right to the throne.' Subsequently Gregory XIII had promised plenary absolution to William Parry, the man picked to assassinate Elizabeth, if his mission were successful. The blundering fool failed and got himself arrested, as did at least two more of Rome's hired assassins, both before and after him. Sixtus V had, in his turn, confirmed Philip's hereditary claims to the English throne. Philip repeatedly assured him that he had quite enough crowns as it was, and that the English one would be for his daughter; that his aim was not to enlarge his empire but purely to defend the true faith.

As soon as Philip had drawn up a plan for his military offensive, Sixtus V launched his psychological offensive. He issued a new bull,

informing all Christians that Elizabeth was 'a heretic and a schismatic
. . . twice excommunicated . . . illegitimate . . . conceived and
born of an incestuous adultery'; that she had 'usurped the throne in
violation of the law . . .'; that she had committed 'many serious
offences, outrages, extortions and breaches of the law against the poor
and innocent population of the Two Kingdoms . . .' that she was
therefore incapable of governing and not worthy to live. 'Therefore,'
the Bull went on, 'his Holiness renews the sentence of excommunication and relieves her once more of all royal rank . . . and releases her
subjects from every sort of subjection, oath and other forms of allegiance . . .'

To all who set off on this crusade the Pope granted plenary indulgence, absolution, remission of sins, apostolic blessing, and everything
else.

The ready? Ah, yes, ready money—but of course. Count Olivarez,
the Spanish Ambassador in Rome, who was besieging the Pope with
his demands, had suggested an advance of two million ducats. After
close consideration Sixtus had talked vaguely of 200,000 on account
plus a further 100,000 when the army landed, another 100,000 in six
months and 200,000 a year for the duration of the war. Olivarez had
strict instructions not to take charity and he made this clear to the Pope.
But Philip, having made his resolution, was prepared to compromise.
He reduced his demand to a million and a half ducats. The Pope
promised a million.

A promise is a promise, he had sworn to the Ambassador in the
names of various saints. 'The day the first Spanish soldier sets foot on
English soil, I, Sixtus V, will give the King of Spain one million gold
ducats.' An advance? Patience, my son, patience. A loan, meanwhile?
Out of the question, what's said is said. And on 8 August the Ambassador rebuffed yet again, wrote, sheepishly, to the King 'His Holiness
remained intractable *como un diamante* . . . His Holiness would rather
have his guts torn from him than money. I am getting nowhere.'

3

The Marquis of Santa Cruz

I have read every single one of the countless missives that were sent
out every day via galloping couriers from the Escurial—to get together
at Lisbon and Cadiz, as soon as possible, ships, men and provisions
from all over the kingdom. To all those in positions of responsibility,
Philip had stipulated absolute secrecy. If it was impossible to conceal
the enterprise itself, it was possible to maintain a degree, of uncertainty around its objective. 'The house must be ablaze,' he wrote,
'before anyone even knows where the lightning will strike.'

But Elizabeth had been expecting that particular lightning to
strike her roof for some time. Any lingering doubts that she may have
had were soon dispelled by one of Sir Francis Walsyngham's spies,
who learnt of the existence of a letter from Philip to the Pope. It was
purchased from a Venetian priest who had himself acquired it from
one of the Gentlemen of His Holiness's Bedchamber. While the Pope
was sleeping the key to his secret closet was abstracted from his purse,
the letter found and copied. It was conclusive.

To gain time to get her defences and fleet in better order, Elizabeth
loudly protested her desire for peace and got the ex king of Denmark to
suggest a meeting to Philip so as to 'avoid a battle.' Philip protested
his own heartfelt desire for peace equally loudly and immediately
accepted the suggestion of a meeting. Once they had agreed on it in
principle, it was decided that it should take place at Bourbourg, near
Calais. Elizabeth sent a delegation headed by Sir James Croft. Philip
ordered Parma to send the chancellor Frederick Perrenot, an old hand
in tricky matters of diplomacy.

While the coastal defences of the whole of England, the Isle of Wight,
the Thames and approaches to London were hurriedly strengthened,
Drake convinced the Queen that the thing to do was to nip the invasion
in the bud. She must let him attack Cadiz. That, he felt sure, would be
the main centre of the Spanish preparations. The Queen charged him
to do it in one written order, and forbade him in another, which she
had delivered to Plymouth nine days after he had left. She was careful
to keep a copy of it to show Philip, who would be requiring an explanation.

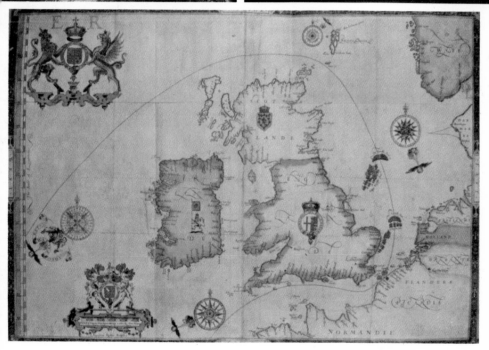

Above left: *Phillip II (From the portrait by Titian in the Prado, Madrid.)* Above right: *Elizabeth I (From a miniature by Hilliard in the Victoria and Albert Museum, London.)* Below: *Having failed to make the planned rendezvous with Parma and his army, the Most Fortunate Armada sailed back to Spain via Scotland and Ireland. (From a contemporary engraving by Robert Adams.)*

At midnight on 26 October, 1588, the Girona *broke her back on Lacada Point. (Artist's impression of the shipwreck. From an original painting by Kenneth Riley. Copyright 1969 National Geographic Magazine Washington DC. Reproduced by special permission.)*

Above: *A Galleass of the Armada.* (*From a contemporary cartoon for a set of tapestries in the National Maritime Museum, Greenwich.*) Below: *Spaniard Rock. In the foreground the Chimney Rocks, on the right Lacada Point, where the* Girona *perished. As seen from the top of the cliff.*

The arrival of *El Draque*, the Dragon of the Apocalypse, spread panic in Cadiz. He captured six good ships and burned eighteen more, including Santa Cruz's personal galleon. He landed more or less where he chose in Portugal, then cruised off Cape St Vincent, where he sunk or captured sixty tuna fishing boats. What was far more serious, though, he burned forty coasting vessels loaded with staves for casks, barrels, hogsheads, butts, pipes and tuns, forty cargo loads of seasoned wood staves, that the Armada would badly need for storing water and wine and keeping provisions. Drake raised the blockade only to go out and meet the *San Felipe*, an enormous Portuguese carrack on her way back from Goa, her holds packed with spices, silks and ivory and her coffers brimming with gold, silver and exotic jewels. He captured her after a brief skirmish, bringing his booty up to a total of £115,000, of which his own share was £17,000 and Her Majesty's £40,000 (in the Queen's written order, the only paragraph that was absolutely clear and unambiguous was the one establishing the Crown's share of the booty). Drake could boast on his return of having 'singed the King of Spain's beard'. He had completely upset preparations for the fleet for months. It was principally because of his action that the Armada would not be ready in 1587.

On other fronts things were going rather better for Spain. That summer, Parma made sure of his rear by capturing Sluys from the Dutch, after an epic siege. All the time he was pretending to negotiate, he was having a new canal dug between Sluys and Nieuport to protect his lines of communication from storms and the Sea Beggars. He was having the whole of the forest of Waas cut down to build another 100 troop barges, 40 flyboats and 2 small, 200-ton galleons.

Meanwhile in Paris, Mendoza was plotting day and night, supporting the Holy League and Mary's relatives, the Guises, against Henry III. Daily more divided and bloodless, France would never risk invading Flanders while Parma was fighting in England.

For four years, Santa Cruz had in vain been urging Philip to act. Suddenly, in September 1587, when he was no longer prepared for it, when he no longer believed in it, when he was actually in the Azores escorting the plate fleet, the King wrote to him, 'As soon as you return and the Neapolitan galleys and Andalusian victuallers have joined you, you will sail for the Cape of Margate and the Thames. Your task will be to support Parma. That the enemy will be taken by surprise is assured, and by the Grace of God for whom we toil you will have calm seas and favourable winds.'

Santa Cruz was dumbfounded, protesting that the situation had completely changed. Drake had doubled his forces. The storm had loosened the timbers of many of his ships. It would be utterly reckless. Philip gave him three weeks to make ready—Santa Cruz begged for five. Philip argued that with the Italian reinforcements, the Prince of Parma had 30,000 men ready and waiting in Flanders, and few would be left if action was delayed to the spring. He ordered Santa Cruz to depart. Santa Cruz complained that he had asked for 50 galleons, but had only 13 together with 4 galleasses and 60 old 'tubs' that were not even water-tight. He had neither enough armaments nor enough ordnance, and hardly any auxiliary small craft.

Philip, in December, again pressed him to leave immediately, whether the Armada was ready or not, and to rendezvous with Parma. Santa Cruz reported that he was leaving, but that he had word from England that fortifications had been erected all round the coast, militia troops were being recruited, and that already Drake was waiting for them with a strong and well-equipped fleet. Philip had heard so too. Santa Cruz was to wait, carry on preparations, and be ready by 15 February.

Santa Cruz worked on through the winter without a moment's respite, bombarded by letters from the King full of reproaches and curt instructions to make ready his great enterprise. He was galled that the Duke of Parma should have been given precedence over him. The King was told of this, and begged him to state once and for all whether he was willing to sail under those conditions or whether he preferred to remain where he was, in which case he would still have to see to all the necessary preparations.

Don Alonzo de Leiva, Philip's favourite, former Captain General of the galleys of Naples, and former Captain General of the Milanese cavalry, declared publicly that 'it might be a good idea to send someone to Lisbon to spur the old Marquis on.' The King sent the Count of Fuentes to inspect the fleet and the preparations. His Council of War, sensing that the wind was changing, lined itself up behind the King.

Santa Cruz knew that he was the object of intrigue, that he was being slandered at court. He was sixty-two. At the beginning of February he had to take to his bed. By the 9th he was dead. It was said in Lisbon that what had killed him were the King's 'continual and unreasonable demands', that he had died of 'overwork, shame and grief,' and that he was 'universally mourned, by captains and soldiers alike—it was in him that all hope of success had been vested.'

4
His Excellency The Duke of Medina Sidonia

The day Philip learned that Santa Cruz was ill, he summoned his secretary and had him write to Don Alonso Perez de Guzman a letter marked 'top secret', in which he commanded him to take over from the Marquis and ordered him to set off immediately. Known like the most prestigious of his illustrious ancestors as *el Bueno*, he was thirty-eight, a Knight of the Order of the Golden Fleece, Marquis of Cazaza in Africa, twelfth Señor and fifth Marquis of Sanlucar de Barramaeda, ninth Count of Niebla and seventh Duke of Medina Sidonia. In other words he owned half of Andalusia. 'Short, stocky, with a thin, friendly face . . . rather bow legged . . .', his friends said of him that he was 'the best horseman in Spain, the best at the sport of canes, the best rejaneador . . . that he had killed with his lance the most savage bulls.' At the age of twenty-two, after an engagement lasting six years and by special dispensation from the Pope, he had married Dona Ana de Silva Mendoza, then aged ten and a half. The marriage was consummated that very night; as Medina Sidonia's biographer explains, 'The Duchess's judgement and discretion more than made up for any disadvantage that her age might have had for the marriage.' At the age of thirty-one he was awarded by Philip the Order of the Golden Fleece, the highest order of knighthood, normally restricted to reigning monarchs and princes of the blood royal.

The Duke was not an ambitious man. He liked a peaceful, quiet life and the calm of his orange groves. When he was offered the post of Governor of Milan, he was profuse in his apologies. He couldn't possibly go . . . a matter of his health . . . the health of his wife. So he carried on shooting quail and looking after his vast estates.

The Marquis's illness and the King's letter vexed him deeply. On 16 February, Sidonia took up his pen. 'I must first kiss His Majesty's hands and the royal feet for having deigned to consider me for so great a task . . .' To the most powerful king in the world, who was offering him the most glorious post at the head of the most important enterprise of his reign, the Spanish grandee, noblest of all the nobles, continued, 'but my health is not up to such a voyage. . . . On the rare occasions when I have been at sea I have been seasick, and moreover I catch cold easily.'

The head of the most powerful family in all Spain, in lands, privileges and riches, the man whose personal fortune was reputed to be even greater than the King's, went on:

> Besides, I am in such dire financial straits that every time I come to Madrid I have to borrow money . . . my estate has debts of 900,000 ducats. I should be unable to contribute so much as a *real* to the enterprise. It would not be right for me to accept, for I have no experience of seafaring or of war . . . and even if I had, it would mean going into it blind, throwing myself into this expedition totally unprepared, and not knowing the first thing about it . . . besides which His Majesty will find a man most fit to serve him in this voyage in the person of the Adelantado Major [governor] of Castile a man of great experience . . . and His Majesty can be confident that the Adelantado will have God's help behind him, for he is a very good Christian. . . . I humbly beg His Majesty not to entrust me with a task of which I should give a bad account, for I know nothing and understand nothing about it, I have not health for the sea and no money to put into it. . . . May God preserve and keep the Most Catholic Person of Your Majesty.

On the 18th the King signed his official appointment. He had him advised of it the same day and commanded him to leave for Lisbon—immediately.

It was said in Spain at the time—how accurately I do not know: these are rumours and gossip reported by a Dominican monk, Fray Juan de la Victoria—that the Duchess had urged her husband to refuse the appointment. According to certain of her lady friends, she is supposed to have said, 'Ladies, I know the Duke can keep up appearances in his own house and in places where he is not too well known, but it pains me to think that now he will be shown up for what he is, and will lose his reputation.'

The Duke did not reply to the royal command until the 29th. He was still at home.

> . . . since Your Majesty, notwithstanding my frank admissions, orders me to serve him, my conscience is clear. I shall do so . . . may the Lord help your Majesty in your good intentions, and since what is to be done is for Him, I hope that in His goodness He will do so. . . . I should appreciate it if Your Majesty could have me informed and instructed on everything that pertains to this expedition and on how to act in all things . . . and that a decision should be made as to what needs to be done. I remain Your Majesty's most humble servant . . . and I pray Your Majesty to permit Francisco Duarte, who is very experienced in matters of seafaring, to sail with me.

From the King to the Duke, 11 March:—

Duke of Medina Sidonia, Cousin, my Captain General of the Ocean Sea and of the coast of Andalusia . . . I thank you for the good will with which, setting aside all difficulties, you have decided to depart and serve me in this expedition. . . . I am certain that you will enjoy every success . . . that there is no reason for you to worry, and if you should die in this expedition I shall take care of your children.

Meticulously, the Duke put his affairs in order, stepped sadly into his carriage and took the road to Lisbon, through his orange groves.

At Lisbon, he states, he found chaos. He had barely arrived before he buried himself in Santa Cruz's papers. He listened to what everyone had to tell him and looked around him. He assembled a general staff. He surrounded himself with sailors, soldiers, artillerymen, strategists, advisors. The picture was gloomy: too few ships, and those too small and in bad condition; too few cannon, and those with only half the range of English guns; insufficient powder and shot; shortage of provisions and water; far too few soldiers, experienced mariners or qualified gunners; and not enough money. Some companies were owed sixteen pays, arrears which could not be made up. For the time being, Sidonia did not mention any of this to the King, who, basing his impressions on his correspondence with Santa Cruz, had written to Sidonia on 7 March assuring him that everything was ready at Lisbon, that there was nothing more to be done. 'You will be able,' wrote Philip, 'to embark the infantry before the 20th, and, weather permitting, and with God's help, you should sail on the 24th or 25th at the latest.'

The old Marquis of Santa Cruz had originally asked for 510 ships. It was asking the impossible of Philip, as Philip was asking the impossible of Santa Cruz in ordering him to sail on such short notice. One way or another, the Marquis had managed to swell the numbers of his fighting fleet, until it mustered 65 ships and 16,500 men. The Duke increased the numbers further still.

On 19 March he went personally to look over the fleet. On the basis of this inspection he informed the King that everyone was ready. There were just one or two carpentry and joinery jobs that needed doing. He was going to have stronger bow and stern castles built, and the decks reinforced to give better protection to the crew in bad weather and in battle. A few ships were too old and would have to be left behind. Cargoes could be better divided between the vessels, the artillery shared out, and the Andalusian fleet still lacked its full complement, and so on. . . . The galleasses would be finished and ready by the end of the week.

Then, from letter to letter, little by little, I watched this optimism fade. The Duke paints a blacker and blacker picture of a situation that he sees as more and more serious.

> Everyone is either deserting or about to desert . . . the soldiers are barefoot, few of them have clothes . . . there are many who haven't been paid for a year now. There aren't more than 10,000 men left, more like 9,000. . . . We haven't enough seasoned mariners. . . . The money is melting away.

5
'*You Will Sail with 200,000 Ducats*'

On 20 March the King dictated a seven-page letter (of particular interest to me) to Sidonia, ordering him to review his troops and embark them, and giving instructions that the Armada should be ready to sail by the end of the month and not a day later. In addition to clothes and relief already provided, Philip gave Sidonia permission to give every member of the expedition two month's pay, 'which will send them all off in good spirits . . . it would be well to give them only one pay before embarking and the other when they are on board in their ships . . . and once they are on board, you will make sure that no one leaves again.'

What followed interested me still more:

One pay for the entire Armada . . . mariners and soldiers . . . amounts to 116,000 ducats of ten reals a month, two pays to 232,000 ducats. . . . The Paymaster has in his possession 433,878 ducats of ten reals, which leaves 200,000 to take with you in the Armada. You will permit no one to touch this sum for any reason whatsoever, but will make sure that it is taken on board intact.

200,000 ducats! Even spread over ten *capitanas*, there was enough there to make a treasure hunter's mouth water. Being first and foremost an archaeologist, I merely made a mental note of it, and went on reading.

On 26 March the Duke, who was becoming increasingly reticent, wrote again to the King; 'Your Majesty was told that the Armada was ready to leave at two days' notice. When I arrived I found a very different state of affairs.' The Duke's letter crossed one from the King, in which he was adamant in his insistence. 'Seeing that you have now checked with your own eyes that everything is virtually ready, you will embark the infantry, if you have not already done so. . . . You will be ready to sail on April 5th, or 6th at the latest and earlier if possible. . . .'

In defiance of orders, Medina Sidonia was calmly having every rotten timber replaced, hulls recaulked, and sails and rigging carefully checked and renewed where necessary. So it was not until 2 April that the Captain General informed the King that the general inspection had taken place and that the troops were ready to be embarked. On the question of money, he wrote:

> Even if we give our men only two pays, there will be no money left to take along with us, and the mariners are in no mood to be satisfied with so little considering how much they are owed. As it is extremely difficult to get good work from discontented and underpaid men, I beg Your Majesty to be pleased to send us a decent sum, if possible by special courier or riders.

Meanwhile the Duke had received detailed orders:

> Since victories are in the hands of God, to give and to take away as he sees fit, and since your cause is so preculiarly His as to assure you of His help and favour, if this is not undeserved by sinfulness, great care must be taken that none is committed in this fleet, and in particular that no blasphemy is uttered, under pain of the most severe punishment to be carried out publicly, in order that the chastisement for having tolerated such blasphemy may not descend upon all.
>
> On receipt of my orders, you will leave immediately for the English Channel. You will sail up the Channel as far as Cape Margate, where you will rendezvous with my nephew, the Duke of Parma and Piacenza, in order to cover his crossing.
>
> You will send him regular reports of your progress. You will prearrange certain meeting points in the event of the Armada's being scattered by a storm, say Vigo, Corunna and the Scilly Islands. Once in the Channel you will not seek battle with Drake, unless you find his forces divided and are able to get the weather gauge of him . . . rather, you will sail on in good order to your rendezvous with Parma.
>
> Do not fail to let every man know that the enemy has the advantage in artillery and with his superior firepower will try to fight at long range. The aim of our men must, on the contrary, be to bring the enemy to close quarters and grapple with him. . . . You will also be sure that following the victory our fleet does not scatter in persuit of booty . . . and you will have to economise as best as you can all the money there is in the Armada.
>
> Once the troops carried by the Armada have been landed, they will be entrusted to Don Alonzo de Leiva, my Captain General of the Milanese Light Cavalry, who will command them until the arrival of the Duke, my nephew, to whom he will then turn over his command.
>
> [Done at Madrid, April 1st, 1588, I, the King.]

Medina Sidonia replied to the King on 11 April:

> I humbly kiss Your Majesty's hands for doing me the honour of placing such trust in me. . . . I will serve him to the fullest extent of my powers, my only bitter regret being that they are not greater, so that I might devote them all to the service of God and Your Majesty. But I put my trust in the Divine Mercy . . . for the conduct of this mission which is so

truly His that no one can be doubtful of victory. . . . Once again I must impress on Your Majesty the seriousness of our shortage of money. While I know that Your Majesty will already have given the order, I beseech him yet again to have some sent immediately, if he has not already done so. This alone is holding up our departure. Until it arrives, I have decided to send a special courier to Your Majesty every day for no other purpose than to request it. To conclude, may God perserve and keep Your Most Catholic Majesty. . . .

On 4 April, tired of the Duke's endless promises, the captains, *alfereces*, officers, sergeants and veteran soldiers, who were still waiting vainly for their pay, threatened to go home. Sidonia wrote to the King, that the most experienced and valuable of his men might leave, and that he would be unable to stop them. Again he pleaded for more money.

By the time I got to this letter I too was beginning to beseech His Majesty, 'Come now, Sire, a bit of generosity. Zounds, Sire, you're not going to have me find the wrecks empty!' My wishes were granted in a letter from Philip giving Sidonia 20,000 ducats to cover his personal expenses in the Armada . . . these 20,000 ducats to be deducted from what was left over from the 232,000 set aside for the two pays. But, if Philip had decided to ignore his demands for money and thought to shut him up by a personal favour, the Duke was in no mood to read between the lines. He turned a deaf ear, thanked him kindly and went on to say he was greatly troubled by the shortage of powder, again stressing the need for funds. Still more dispatches flew back and forth, and once more the Duke emphasised:

Departure is proceededing with all possible haste. If the money for which I have sent Your Majesty a special courier, and the Indies galleons which I expect from Cadiz at any moment, were to arrive, I could leave here within a day. . . . But without money the Armada cannot sail.

37

6
The Most Fortunate Fleet

While the Duke stubbornly continued to wait, the organising and strengthening of the fleet progressed gradually. But each day passed in port meant fresh inroads into the coffers and into the provisions. It was costing the King 30,000 ducats a day simply to keep the fleet in port.

The Captain General had ordered that the oldest provisions be served up first, but the meat that had been salted down in October was green and putrid in April. The biscuits were crawling with worms. And every day the list of deserters grew longer, in spite of the guards. Every day, too, though it had not yet reached catastrophic proportions, the hospitals and the local cemetery became just a little more crowded, thanks to dysentery.

On 25 April, St Mark's Day, the sun shone brightly in a deep blue sky. With great pomp the Captain General of the Most Fortunate Armada proceeded to the Cathedral of Lisbon, to take from the High Altar the sacred banner of the crusade.

After which, standard or no standard, Medina Sidonia still went on waiting for his cash. It was not until dawn on 9 May, with all hope gone and every ruse exhausted, that he finally gave the order for departure.

They manned the capstans and weighed anchor. The Tagus was filled with sail.

'Like a town on the march,' the ships sailed down towards Belem under their white and red canvas—the red crosses of war against the white of purity. The galleys and launches helped manoeuvre the galleons, their aftercastles gleaming under a new coat of paint. Pennants and flags fluttered at all masts. On the decks corslets, breastplates and morions glistened in the sun. Gold-embroidered doublets and velvet cloaks shimmered on the poops. Gold chains sparkled and white hat feathers quivered gracefully in the wind.

His Excellency the Duke of Medina Sidonia was himself on the *San Martín*, a galleon of 1,000 tons (Spanish), flagship of the squadron of Portugal. With him he had his confessor, his spiritual advisor and sixty servants.

38

At the mouth of the Tagus the fleet encountered a strong head wind. The harbour pilots shook their heads. Any attempt at crossing the bar was out of the question. The vessels dropped anchor and waited. Men huddled in the lower decks, while the storm sent an icy wind howling through the badly fitted gunports and hatchways. 'December weather', declared the pilots, and the Duke wrote, 'The weather is preventing the Armada from coming out, . . . but as it is God who sends the weather, this must fit in with his designs.'

The Duke took advantage of the delay to draw up his orders to the fleet and have them passed from ship to ship:

First and foremost, it must be clearly understood by all, from the highest to the lowest, that the principal aim of His Majesty is the service of God. . . . No one, therefore, must sail without confessing and communicating in true repentance for his sins. Similarly, to utter any oath or to take in vain the name of Our Lord, or of Our Lady or of the Saints is forbidden on pain of the most severe punishments and stoppage of wine. . . .

Gambling is a prohibited, forbidden game in particular and especially at night.

It is well known what inconvenience and offence to God is caused by the presence of public or private women. I therefore forbid that any be taken on board.

Every morning, according to custom, the ships' boys will say the morning salutation at the foot of the mainmast, and at vespers they will say the Ave Maria, sometimes the Salve Regina and, on Saturdays at least, the litany as well.

Brawls and other disgraceful activities . . . will be prohibited and no one is to wear a dagger . . . there will be no private feuds. . . .

Each captain had already received detailed sailing instructions. Signals and methods of communication had been agreed for the fleet. A rendezvous point had been fixed. At sea, in battle or in case of fire, every man knew what he had to do. The Duke placed particular emphasis on the importance of cleanliness and personal hygiene. Each squadron had been allotted its quota of the most experienced pilots, Spanish, French, Dutch and English, with a knowledge of the Channel. Each one of them had been given the latest maps and pilot books, which marked all the ports and landmarks, depths, tides, currents and principal shoals from the Scilly Islands to Dover.

Each captain, in turn, did the same on his own ship, allocating to every man his place on board—on the aftercastle, on the main companionway, in the mizzen crow's nest—and his precise role in battle. Monks, valets, barbers and 'other non-combatants' were assigned the duties of stopping leaks and putting out fires.

Once this was done, they waited for a favourable wind, and while they waited nature began to have her way again. The Duke's stringency, a reflection of the King's, had banned all 'public and private' women from the fleet, which meant that the 'camp followers' had to charter themselves a special ship, in which they sailed behind the Armada. This ship does not feature in the official inventory made before the departure from Lisbon, but there are several references to it in contemporary documents. Furthermore, an English list notes the presence of a 'German woman accompanied by her husband, a gunner', on the *San Salvador* (later captured in the Channel half burnt out).

For seventeen days they waited. Still the wind blew from the wrong quarter. They took advantage of the delay to take on beans, rice, and oil in place of the rotten meat that was already being thrown overboard.

Amused idlers swarmed on the shore from which the roadstead 'seemed covered by a forest of masts'. The *San Martín* was one of the tallest galleons in the Armada, and from up on the aftercastle the Duke had an even better view. He had reason to be proud, for none had ever seen a larger fleet or a mightier expedition.

At the time, however, no one ever called the Armada invincible. While planning the fleet in 1586, Santa Cruz had christened it 'Felicissima Armada', literally 'The Most Fortunate War Fleet' or 'The Most Fortunate Fleet'. Sidonia used the same name or called it simply 'the Armada'. English official documents refer to 'The Spanish Armada' or 'The Spanish Fleet'. Never did the King, or the Duke or any squadron commander, officer, councillor, secretary or courtier, any Spanish chronicler or historian of the period, ever describe it as invincible. Philip was too well aware that *Dios da y quita la Victoria comoquiere*. Who then gave it the name that was ironically to stick for ever? Perhaps a group of drunks brawling round a table in a Lisbon bawdy house? Or some obscure hidalgo raring for a fight? The English pamphleteers, who were the first to put the word 'invincible' into print? Or the Pope, from whom they claimed to have had the adjective?

Meanwhile the Duke sent the King his 'Report of all that is going in this Armada,' a detailed, official inventory of ships, troops, and cannon. It lists 130 ships, 65 galleons, or large merchantmen converted into warships, 25 hulks carrying stores and horses, 19 *pataches*, 13 *zabras* (small, swift frigates from the Bay of Biscay), 4 galleys and 4 galleasses, including the *Girona*. At the gunports were 2,431 pieces of ordnance, 1,497 bronze and 934 iron, and there were 123,790 rounds of shot, or roughly 50 per gun. In the ships were 30,696 men (this figure is almost certainly exaggerated by 20 per cent); 8,000 seamen and gunners; 2,100 rowers, convicts, prisoners, slaves (or volunteers)—the *benevoglie* or *buenas boyas*; 19,000 soldiers, musketeers, arquebusiers and pikemen; and 1,545 volunteers, including 300 gentlemen adventurers, noblemen, hidalgos and caballeros along with their valets; German, Irish, English and Scottish captains; ships' surgeons and other non-combatants, and 180 priests and monks, medicants and others. (See pages 62 and 67.)

The Captain General of the Ocean Sea was personally commanding the ten galleons and two *zabras* of the squadron of Portugal. The man who was called 'the Premier Sailor of Spain', Juan Martinez de Recalde, Knight of Santiago, was second-in-command of the Armada, and Captain General of the Biscayan squadron (ten ships and four *pataches*). His personal pennant flew on the *capitana Santa Ana*. A squadron captain general for sixteen years, he had served in the West Indies and in the plate fleets. He had been Santa Cruz's right hand man. He was said to have the heart of a lion.

The fourteen galleons and *naos* of Castile, with the two *pataches* that completed the squadron, were commanded by Don Diego Flores de Valdes. He had twenty years of transatlantic voyaging behind him and was a brilliant sailor, highly regarded as a technician in matters of navigation and nautical construction; but he was said to be an overambitious man, jealous and quarrelsome. Whether or not this was true, he was hated and despised by all and sundry. Philip made him Chief of Staff to the Duke, an appointment that was as mystifying to contemporary observers and to historians as that of Medina Sidonia. In the words of one commentator, 'If Medina Sidonia was incapable of commanding, nobody was willing to take orders from Diego Flores.' He therefore transferred to Sidonia's flagship, the *San Martin*, shortly after sailing, and remained in that ship throughout the campaign.

Don Pedro de Valdez, a cousin and sworn enemy of Diego Flores, was Captain General of the Armada of Andalsuia, consisting of ten merchantmen and one *patache*. A knight of Santiago and also trained in the plate fleets, he had distinguished himself fighting in Portugal, in the Azores, and at Ferrol, where he was seriously wounded. In the Armada, he had made himself an energetic advocate of long-range artillery.

Another squadron, that of Guipuzcoa, consisting of ten ships and two *pataches*, was commanded by Don Miguel de Oquendo. Known as 'La Gloria de la Armada,' Don Miguel was regarded as a fearless hero. A proud and hauty warrior, his exploits were retailed in every port in Spain. He was considered to be the finest sailor in Spain, second only to Recalde.

The squadron of the Levant—this term denoting Barcelona and the Italian ports—numbered ten good ships under the command of Don Martin de Bertendona, a competent sailor and a brave soldier. His squadron included the *rata Sancta Maria Encoronada*, an 820-ton carrack

41

carrying 35 cannon, 335 soldiers, and 84 seamen and officers. (See page 103.) It was in this ship that Alonza de Leiva, together with at least one of his brothers and almost all the noblemen in the expedition, had taken passage. As the leader who would command in the battle once the troops had been landed, Don Alonzo bore the title of Commander in Chief of the Army of the Armada.

Stores, reserve arms and ammunition, field artillery and gun carriages; camp, earthwork and siege material; wagons, mules, horses and grooms, were all carried in twenty-five hulks—heavy, unarmed, or only lightly armed merchantmen. Juan Gomez de Medina had received this inglorious command.

Each squadron had a few *pataches*, frigates or *zabras* for reconnoitering and scouting, taking prisoners and carrying orders and pilots from squadron to squadron. In addition, twenty-two of these small ships made up a separate squadron of their own, the squadron of *pataches*, commanded by Don Antonio Hurtado, from his flagship *La Nuestra Señora del Pilar de Saragoza*, a small galleon.

Don Diego Medrano commanded the four galleys of Portugal.

Lastly, Don Hugo de Moncada, in the *capitana San Lorenzo*, led the galleasses of Naples, four huge and formidable engines of war, each bristling with fifty cannons. Great things were expected of them, particularly in calm weather, when their free movement would give them a clear advantage over the English galleons. The four galleasses were the *San Lorenzo* (*capitana*), *Zuñiga* (*patrona*), *Napolitana* and *Girona*. A galleass was a cross between a galley and a galleon, manned by 300 rowers and 3–400 soldiers and sailors. (See pages 28 and 67.) Moncada, a Catalan of very noble birth, was a dyed-in-the-wool galley man, one of that old aristocracy of the sea. In battle he was known to be the bravest of the brave. He was also known to be haughty and lacking in self-control.

7

Don Alonzo Martinez De Leiva

One thing struck me above all others. It was clear that of all the lords gathered at Lisbon, of all the knights and all the great captains, the best loved and the most admired was Don Alonzo Martinez de Leiva. He was constantly referred to, and always it was 'El Buen Alonzo de Leiva', or 'Don Alonzo himself'. The historian Antonio de Herrera wrote in 1612, *La segunda persona qui vui en el Armada, despues del Duque . . . era Don Alonzo de Leiva.* The Duke would consult 'all the generals *and* Alonzo de Leiva'. He seems to have embodied for his period every noble and military quality. 'As one knew he would', Spaniards said when he excelled in battle, 'as one might have expected from such a leader', when he proved himself indestructible in adversity.

I have failed to find a portrait of him, but chroniclers of the period are unanimous in picturing him as a young cavalier *sans peur et sans reproche.* He could not possibly have been anything but gay, young, handsome, and flamboyant, whether at court or on the battlefield.

Members of the crew later questioned by the English described him as 'tall and slender, of a whitely complexion, of a flaxen and smooth hair, of behaviour mild and temperate, of speech good and deliberate, greatly reverenced not only by his own men but generally of all the whole company.' 'Don Alonzo was a whitely man with an Abram beard,' reads the record of the examination of Jorge de Venerey, a Cretan sailor.

He was the King's favourite and the idol of the nobility and people alike. His wife, daughter of the Count of Corunna, had born him many sons.

Don Alonzo had begun his military career as lieutenant to his father, the celebrated Don Sancho. He fought bravely in the War of Grenada and in all the battles of the period. In Italy at the time when Don Juan of Austria was having trouble confronting the Flemish rebels, he took it upon himself to raise a company of young gentlemen adventurers, appointing himself as their captain, Don Diego Hurtade de Mendoza as lieutenant and his brother, Don Sancho, as sergeant major. All of the 400 soldiers in this company were either one-time

43

captains or unemployed ensigns. With this company, its numbers swelled by valets and men who joined along the way, he marched to the Netherlands. There the courage he inspired in his men changed the course of the campaign. The company gained a glorious reputation. The rebels crushed, Don Alonzo made his way back to Italy.

Next becoming Captain General of the Sicilian Galleys, he led them to victory in the conquest of Portugal in 1580. In naval operations he demonstrated the same personal courage and judgment as his father. The King appointed Don Alonzo Captain General of the Milanese cavalry at a salary of 300 escudos a month, but he resigned his commission in 1587 to join the Enterprise of England.

De Leiva then held the distinguished titles of Knight of Santiago and Commander of Alcuescar. He had hoped that he would be the man chosen by the King to lead the Enterprise of England. Soon after arriving in Lisbon, as we have seen, he is said to have started the rumour that Santa Cruz was deliberately creating difficulties and delays because he was jealous and offended at not having been given command of the invasion army as well as the Armada, rather than Parma. Rumours like this and other slanderous gossip broke the old Marquis's heart and almost certainly hastened his death. Don Alonzo, *joven de condicion asaz ferviente*, who really loved and respected the Marquis, must have found his death painful.

De Leiva was naturally included in the General Staff together with Don Francisco de Bobadilla, the Maestro de Campo General, and the other great military leaders.

In June 1587 the King sent De Leiva to Cadiz to inspect the state of the ships, after which he was to go back up to Lisbon to report the progress of preparations there. In July he was patrolling the Algarve coast with a squadron of galleys, and in November we find his name on a list of noblemen receiving an *ayuda ee costa*.

A little later the Venetian ambassador in Paris, in a report to the Doge, wrote, '. . . Don Alonso de Leiva's name has been mentioned in connection with Armada's high command . . . but he is too reckless. . . .'

If he really did hope to command the Armada, he did not miss it by much. Before the fleet sailed, Sidonia received an envelope from the King, marked 'secret' and, 'to be opened only in the event of the Captain General's death—to be given back to me otherwise, unopened, on return'. Inside was a second envelope addressed to Don Alonzo Marintez de Leiva and inside that, this letter, now in the Archivo General de Simancas:

. . . I have resolved . . . in consideration of possible eventualities . . . to appoint a man of valour, courage and experience . . . to succeed the

Don Alonzo Martinez De Leiva

Duke. . . . Having complete confidence in you, Don Alonzo Martinez de Leiva, my Captain General of the Milanes' Cavalry, by reason of the importance and quality of your past services and of the fact that you fulfil all the requirements necessary for such a position, I have chosen you. I appoint you henceforth Captain General of the said Armada . . . I, the King. . . .

Don Alonzo entertained the Duke on board the *rata* in Lisbon. Again at Belem he received him in grand style, with musical accompaniment, at his table sumptuously set with silver plate and cutlery and gold-plated candelabra (which I found four centuries later). Sixty sons and nephews of the most noble families in Spain surrounded him, eager for battle and glory. They had deemed it a point of honour to serve under no one but him. No wonder the grandees of the kingdom would have entrusted their heirs, the hopes of their families, to none other than Don Alonzo.

8
'I Have Set Sail at Last . . .'

On 27 May the wind began to shift. Next day the *San Martín* crossed the bar. It took two whole days for the fleet to sail out. On the 30th Sidonia wrote to the King:

> I have set sail at last, and am now looking for the current which I am told will take us North. . . . I did not mean to be the one to have to tell Your Majesty how well I have served him in all this, nor about the problems . . . but I humbly beg Your Majesty not to forget my children, my wretched children who I have had to leave behind, with my house and my calm and peaceful life, in order to serve him with the same love and disinterest that I have always shown. Indeed it is high time he made some gesture of thanks, bestowed some honour on those who have left their homes as I have. Once more, with the humility and obedience that I owe to Him, I beg Our Lord to keep him and give him many more years of life. From my galleon, May 30th, three leagues out to sea. The Duke of Medina Sidonia.

The wind was north-north-west, and it wasn't long before it reached gale force, sweeping first the hulks, and then the rest of the fleet southward.

On 1 June they sighted Cape St Vincent, and at this rate they would soon sight Africa. Philip was advised of the situation and took immediate measures: he ordered solemn and continuous processions throughout his kingdoms, with orations, fasts, alms and penances, and many hours of prayer. His Hieronymite monks were relieved of all other duties. In Madrid, Our Lady of Atocha was paraded for three days on end.

And so God was pleased that this delay should be only a short one. The wind shifted and shifted again. The ships had to tack laboriously, beating to windward, until 9 June, when the wind finally veered to south-south-west. They did not sight Cape Finisterre until the 14th, where they expected to meet some victuallers. 'A large part of the provisions have been thrown overboard, being rotten and spoilt,' Medina Sidonia had written in a dispatch to the King. 'They would have been useless, only infecting the men and making them ill. I humbly beg Your Majesty to send victuallers to meet us with provisions, particularly meat and fish.'

They waited in vain. On the 15th the fleet sheltered in the lee of the Sisarga Islands, eight leagues from Corunna. The Duke sent a *patache* into Corunna with orders to requisition all vessels in the port, load them with provisions, and return with them as quickly as possible.

18 June, and still nothing to be seen. Sidonia sent the galleys for news. The *capitana* was getting the same complaint from several ships; in the barrels of unseasoned wood (Drake had burnt all the good, seasoned staves) the water was turning stinking and green. The men who had drunk it had fallen sick with 'gastric fevers'.

'Tomorrow', wrote the Duke on 18 June, in his daily letter to the King, 'if the wind still holds from south-south-east, I shall sail on, in spite of the serious shortage of provisions. . . .'

Barely had the Captain General handed his letter to the master of a *zabra* to take it to Corunna, when a storm was seen to be threatening. The Duke called the squadron commanders to a council with the most experienced of the mariners. The council decided simply to stay where they were and see how the weather turned out. On 19 June the wind had freshened, the sea was a little rougher. The Duke hurried into Corunna for shelter.

As for the rest, those that were near the *capitana* followed her: thirty-eight ships and a few *pataches* sailing in her wake. Others, being downwind, were unable to get in by nightfall. The remainder, having had no orders or signal, and being too far away to see the Duke's manoeuvre, continued to cruise off the coast.

19 June. From the Duke to the King,

> We waited in vain for provisions. In view of the storminess of the weather and the serious shortage of water and supplies, I sailed into Corunna with part of the Armada. The rest remained outside the roadstead when night fell and prevented them from coming in. They will come in tomorrow, God willing, and I will do my utmost to be finished here in two days. I shall water, drop off the contagiously sick, and set sail again forthwith.

A violent storm broke that night, and on the 20th when the Duke awoke, there was not a sail to be seen on the horizon. He was missing over half his fleet. He drank his chocolate, sat down, played thoughtfully with his pen. A tricky situation: the Captain General himself had actually taken shelter *before* the storm, when in his written instructions he had warned all his captains, on pain of death for treason and confiscation of their properties, against leaving the *capitana*'s wake to shelter in any Spanish port. He had already had the wit to bring the storm forward a day. He had to make what capital he could out of this, and gloss over the fact that in his haste he had failed to give the fleet any signal, and that, contrary to the King's orders, he had fixed only one rendezvous point for the fleet, in the Scilly Islands, in the event of their being scattered by a storm. He wrote on 19 June:

> I thought that the rest of the Armada would join me in port the next morning, but alas . . . storm during the night . . . squalls the like of which have never been seen before. . . . And it was a stroke of luck that the whole Armada was not caught out to sea, especially the galleys, which would without doubt, have been lost. . . . And the fleet would have been completely scattered. Days and days would have been wasted getting it together again; in fact it must have been God's will that part of the Armada came in here; like this, the others will know that this is where they are to come to revictual. The weather is already showing signs of improvement, so they should be here in two or three days. . . .

On Tuesday, 21 June, a messenger arrived at full gallop from Vivero with the news: 'De Leiva is in our port with ten ships.' The *rata's* rigging was damaged, quite apart from which she had lost four anchors in Sisargas roadstead. A second rider shortly arrived from Gijon, where there were two galleasses 'in bad shape'; one of them was the *Girona*, needing 'both tillers, her rigging and her prow repaired, her decks and hull recaulked, and her soaked biscuit supply [4 cwt] dried out.' That afternoon, although it was still rough, the pinnaces set out in search of the missing ships. They passed Recalde on his way back to the fleet with two galleons and eight other ships.

On the same day Sidonia again wrote to the King:

> Recalde has lost his mainmast. We have taken on fish, meat and bacon, as well as water, and although I am not at all well, I am seeing to everything as best I can. It distresses me more than Your Majesty can ever know to think, that for all my care, I was nonetheless forced to come in here with most of the Armada still outside, but God be praised. . . . It is thanks to His great mercy that I did come in here. . . . Seamen and soldiers are under close watch . . . no one will desert. . . . Many of the men are sick.

When the Armada first sailed, the King rather optimistically had started to send his letters for Sidonia to Flanders. A royal letter of 26 June in answer to the Duke's letter of the 19th, betrays his feelings at having to lower his sights.

> I want to be certain that you will leave port on the appointed day, without fail. . . . I am expecting you to justify the trust I have put in you. . . . I am sending a copy of this letter to Flanders, since you should have left before this reaches you.

These were the harshest words the King ever had for the Duke, and by the very next letter, he had softened again.

> Indeed it was the hand of God that guided you into Corunna where it will be easier for the rest of the fleet to join you than it would have been at sea. You will find it easier too to revictual there and to carry out any repairs. . . . Do not be so distressed about it. . . . In addition to the supplies I am sending you biscuit, oil, vinegar, wine and tuna fish in hulks from Lisbon.

Two very fast, oared *pataches* had left for the Scilly Islands to bring back any ships which might have obeyed their official orders and sailed to the rendezvous. But by the 24th the Duke, frantic with worry, was still without news of twenty-three vessels (including two galleasses) carrying between them 8,449 men.

9
An Honourable Agreement, Perhaps?

If the situation really was as bad as the Duke now maintained, it cannot have been encouraging: dysentery and scurvy, damaged ships, leaks, broken masts, lost sails, uneatable provisions, water gone sour because of the unseasoned wood (Drake, always Drake!) and the weather was 'still as bad as December' with:

> showers and continuous squalls seriously hindering the taking on of fresh provisions. . . . I am particularly concerned and troubled by this because it is so extraordinary for the end of June, especially when you consider that everything that is being done here is being done in God's cause, and after all those prayers, too. . . . But no doubt this must, for some reason, fit in better with His cause; and this brings me to tell your Majesty something that I have been putting off for some time.

It is 24 June. From the galleon *San Martin* the Duke writes his King the most amazing letter. It is of prime importance because it is largely on this document that history has judged Medina Sidonia. Some modern historians used words like 'courageous, intelligent, lucid, honest' to describe this letter. It required of its writer, writes Garrett Mattingly, 'moral courage of a kind . . . unusual in that century'. Others, Spanish historians in particular (with the exception of the Duke of Maura) see in it nothing but cowardice, defeatism, an attempt at desertion.

> What I am about to say is not an expression of my own personal wishes. I am not looking for any last minute excuse. Your Majesty is well aware of my determination and zealous desire to serve him . . . but this is what my allegiance to Your Majesty, my duty and my conscience force me to say. . . .

The Captain General goes on to recall in detail his initial refusal and misgivings. He paints a blacker picture than ever of the whole saga of the preparations and the events leading up to the present situation—sick crews whose condition can only deteriorate; provisions spoiled and insufficient, barely two months' supplies; the fleet split up and badly damaged, and no way, that he can see, of repairing it or making the necessary replacements without completely depleting the Indies and Flanders. He claims that the fleet is far inferior in strength to the enemy's, asking the King to judge for himself how the enterprise has started off, and when so much depends on its success. Sidonia reminds him of the consequences of failure and repeats again and again, *ad nauseam* such warnings as:

> Inferior forces, inexperienced crews, officers of which not one, I must in all conscience tell Your Majesty, is up to his position . . . and Your Majesty must not let anyone deceive him on this matter. I have observed it myself and know that it is true.
>
> The Prince of Parma's army is also too small, even if we could support them. As things are we can do nothing for them. . . . Is this really the way to go about attacking such a powerful kingdom, and one with so many allies?
>
> I felt it necessary to bring all this to Your Majesty's notice, that he might decide . . . in view of the present situation . . . whether it might not after all be better to try to reach some honourable agreement with the enemy.

Whether Philip choked with rage, or whether he remained icily unmoved, I cannot say. I have found no account that gives the slightest hint of his inner reaction. He replied once more, obstinately,

> My letters of June 26th and July 1st will have already made my intention clear to you, which is not to withdraw from the Enterprise, but to complete what has been started, overcoming all obstacles. . . . You must send me a daily courier and hold yourself in readiness to get under sail the very day you receive orders from me.

A few days earlier, the Duke of Parma, for his part, had sent Philip an equally defeatist communiqué. The landing was beginning to be *aventurado* he wrote on 30 May. His army had rotted on its feet under the damp and cold campaign tents; the numbers of sick and dead increased every week; they were consuming more provisions and more gold than he could lay his hands on. In short, he too was now suggesting turning the Bourbourg farce into genuine negotiations. (It is most unfair to Sidonia that no one ever considered holding this piece of advice against Parma.)

Alexander Farnese was considered by friends and enemies alike the greatest tactician and finest military leader of the century. But at this stage nothing could move the Defender of the Faith. To encourage Sidonia he at last got around to the question of money. But alas, not in the way the Duke had hoped(nor I—I saw yet another slice of my prospective fortune slipping into the money bags of Galician market gardeners and victuallers).

You can spend the money you have left on fresh supplies. There can be no better way of using it than providing health for our men . . . and take care this time with the new provisions that they keep properly, and do not let yourself be cheated as you have been in the past. The information you sent me from Lisbon about provisions gave me an entirely false impression, since belied by the facts . . . and the same goes for the water. . . .

Indeed, the taste of fresh meat and vegetables did restore the sailors to health, and ashore the five hundred who were sick were regaining their strength. The Archbishop of Santiago had set up a hospital that was working wonders.

Sidonia wrote:

I have posted guards at all the landing stages and on all the roads by which the men might try to escape. . . . Water, which has been my biggest worry, is being loaded as carefully as possible. I have twenty-six coopers working day and night to repair the casks that were completely wrecked in the storm. I hope, God willing, that all will be ready for us to sail this Saturday or Sunday. I have continued to give the men fresh meat, but not bread as there is not enough even for the sick. . . . Only nine have died, thanks be to God.

Another letter from the Duke is dated 26 June. Now all is rosy. What has happened is that the King's early letters have arrived, and from their firm tone Sidonia already has a pretty good idea what kind of response his peacemaking suggestions will elicit.

I kiss Your Majesty's hands for the grace he has shown me in his recent letters. They have brought some consolation for all the worries, and not unfounded ones, I have had as a result of this storm. . . .

That said, the Duke reported that all the ships had returned to the northern ports, with not a single one missing. For the rest, he would supervise the repairs in person, being more anxious than anyone to hasten their departure.

The whole of the Armada had in fact now returned. Alferez Esquivel, who had gone in his pinnace to the Scilly Islands to look for the missing vessels, had found them on the 30th. Nine were at the rendezvous: Don Juan Gomez de Medina's *capitana*, and most of the other hulks, the *Trinidad Valencera*, the Duke of Florence's galleon and the 'women's hulk' (Urca de las Mujeres).

Gomez de Medina was no more enthusiastic than any of the other generals concerning the Duke's unexpected show of initiative. As soon as he got back he wrote personally to the King to say that 'it had simply never crossed my mind that the flagship might have taken shelter in the port, because it would have been so much better, both as far as the

King was concerned and for many other reasons, to do otherwise'. Following the Duke's express instructions, he had made for the Scilly Islands. There he had captured a hulk that the English had taken from some merchants. They had waited there several days, when a small boat had spotted them. They had not been able to capture it (it was a merchantman with a cargo of salt which had hurried off to raise the alert). He had exchanged several broadsides with an English squadron come to reconnoitre them. He had captured several small ships and obtained information about the enemy squadrons. Then, when a *patache* arrived from the Duke, he had returned to Corunna.

If Philip read correctly between the lines of this letter, dated 6 July, he must have understood something like this: What I did without any difficulty and according to orders with the worst of our ships, the whole of the Armada could have done too. The storm was not as bad as all that. Sailing before the wind rather than against it would have saved all that damage. If Your Majesty's Armada had had a leader it would be in the English Channel by now.

It was personal letters like that from the Duke's subordinates that finally persuaded the King to send his private secretary, Don Andres de Alba, to 'assist him in his work . . . to supervise preparations and attend the council'. From that day forward, miraculously, the problems began to iron themselves out.

On 12 July, the King had sent definite orders:

It is my wish that you leave port and start your voyage, the day you receive this letter, without so much as an hour's delay, and even if it means leaving some twelve or fifteen ships behind. . . .

On 13 July, the Duke wrote, 'I hope and trust that God will permit me to set sail with the Armada on Saturday the 16th or Sunday at the latest.' On 14 July: 'Everything is ready, but the sea is like a millpond.' On 13 July:

By the grace of God, excepting contrary orders from Your Majesty, and weather permitting, I hope to be able to sail tomorrow morning or the day after at the latest. . . . To enable every man to take communion and not be deprived of this spiritual and physical benefit, I have ordered all the father confessors in the Armada to land on a small island in the port and have had tent and altars put up for the occasion. And I have given orders that the island be well guarded. It has all gone so well, I am told that more than 8,000 have already taken communion and confessed. This represents such riches, that I rate it the most precious jewel I am taking with me in the whole Armada. Everything is in far better shape than when we left Lisbon and everyone on board is leaving in good spirit.

Then on 19 July, 'since the 16th the Armada has been waiting only for a favourable wind on which to sail out.' And on the 20th, with the weather still uncertain, the Duke summoned a meeting of the Council. He was undecided. Alonzo de Leiva took the floor, advising that they should sail with all possible dispatch. Admirals and pilots were divided in their opinions. They finally agreed to wait until a favourable wind was well established before setting out.

The wind held long enough to get the fleet out of harbour on the 22nd, only to leave it, a few hours later, drifting still within sight of the coast, sails flapping. The wind shifted northward and the Duke talked of returning to Corunna, then it dropped and they anchored three leagues out.

During the night of the 23rd the wind freshened at last from the south-east. The Duke fired a shot as the signal that he was weighing anchor. Two hours later another shot rang out: the *Zuniga*'s rudder hinges were broken and she could no longer steer. The rest of the day was taken up waiting for them to be repaired, as the Duke explained to the King in his letter of 23 July.

After that, silence.

10
'*Drake is Captured!*'

On 24 July 1588 Philip received from Galicia the news that he had been waiting for, week after week, for nearly a year: the Armada had disappeared over the horizon.

In his last letter, the Duke had enclosed his 'report of ships, seamen (*gente de mar*), soldiers (*soldados*), admirals, His Majesty's colonels (*maestros de campos*), artillerists, doctors and officers of justice, priests and others . . . leaving this port of Corunna on 23rd inst.' There were now 131 ships carrying 24,607 soldiers and seamen; 1,338 generals, colonels, captains and officers; 1,549 volunteers, gentlemen adventurers, artillery officers; about 800 ecclesiastics, valets and servants. The Duke therefore had nearly 28,000 men in his command. This new report was to be confidential, so this inventory of troops can be taken as accurate. The latest delay had lasted thirty-two days, not two as originally announced, but now the crusade really was setting out, stronger, better supplied and better equipped than ever.

Health on board was good and morale was at its highest for the good reason that the men were now eating every day—some days even eating their fill. The daily rations included $1\frac{1}{2}$ lb of biscuits, 3/10 pint of wine and 2 gal of water (solely for drinking and cooking). In addition to this they had 6 oz of bacon and 2 oz of rice on Sundays and Thursdays, 6 oz of bone and 3 oz of beans or dried peas on Mondays and Wednesdays; and on Tuesdays, Fridays and Saturdays, 6 oz of tuna with oil and vinegar or dried cod or octopus, or failing that 5 sardines and 3 oz of chick-peas.

If the written orders of Francisco Duarte, the chief victualling officer, were actually obeyed (which seems highly improbable), the rations should have been

> calculated according to the list of troops aboard and handed to each man in person, in the presence of the ship's clerk, who would make a note of it in his books . . . and if anyone dies or changes ships his ration will be deleted from the lists. . . . And if, on certain days, because of bad weather or shortage of supplies, half rations only are given, or even no rations at all, this will not be made up the following day. . . .

55

Once the Armada had sailed, people up and down the country in convents, churches and chapels redoubled their prayers.

On the King's orders, Count Olivarez sought another audience with the Pope. The expedition, he told him, was now under way. The expenses were astronomical. And they would get higher. It was the Holy See which had desired that the crusade take place, and it was on the Holy See now that its success would depend. Parma was short of money, the troops were getting restless: it was impossible to wait any longer.

Nothing would move Sixtus V—his word was final—and the Ambassador was forced to take up his pen again on 19 August and report to his sovereign:

I shall not mention the question of money again to His Holiness. It only irritates him. He turns his back on me at the table and chatters away with less sense than a two-year-old. . . . He has neither charity, breeding nor intelligence. His behaviour is generally put down to his anxiety at seeing the time fast approaching when his ducats will be torn from his heart.

Olivarez was speaking the truth. The Pope had declared to the Venetian Ambassador: 'Philip II's ships are worthless. . . . For every step forward in Flanders they take two back.' The story he told the French Ambassador was that '20,000 men had died in the Armada while it was being made ready in Lisbon. . . . 28 ships had been lost through sheer incompetence.' Medina Sidonia was no better 'than a fool'.

For several days the Escurial had no word of the Armada.

The King waited. On 1 August his private secretary came running with a dispatch from Paris. To Philip in his dark retreat, with its spartan furnishing of leather and oak, where he now spent all his time, Ambassador Mendoza wrote that the Armada had been sighted in the English Channel.

Several letters arrived on 3 August. A large Spanish ship had anchored in the bay of La Hougue.

During the days that followed a shower of letters arrived from everywhere. Gunfire was heard in the Channel for a whole day; the Spanish had landed in England; the Armada had been decimated and was fleeing towards the North Sea with Drake in pursuit; Sidonia had taken Drake prisoner. Rumour followed rumour, and Mendoza immediately relayed every one. Occasionally he took the precaution of adding, 'This news has not been confirmed; it would be a mistake to form an opinion too hastily.'

'*Drake is Captured!*'

On 7 June a 'reliable' agent wrote to him from Rouen:

> I learn from the skippers of certain fishing barks returning from New-foundland, who passed the fleets, that there was an encounter between Drake and Medina Sidonia off the Isle of Wight. The Spanish took the weather gauge from the English and after 24 hours of hellish fighting, they had sunk fifteen English galleons and captured many more, taking countless prisoners. The galleasses were a great success. The same reports are substantiated from Dieppe by some other Newfoundland skippers. . . . A Breton fisherman saw it all: it was a galleass that dismasted Drake's ship with the first broadside and sank it with the second.

According to another source, Drake, wounded in the cheek, threw himself into a launch to escape and fled the battle. This time Mendoza sent the news to the Escurial and to Rome, bursting with delight. He sang out victory all over Paris and had a bonfire built in the embassy courtyard.

On 11 August came confirmation that the Armada had reached Calais, and that Parma was there to meet it. As soon as he heard this the King wrote to the Duke, on 18 August:

> Don Bernadino de Mendoza has sent news from Rouen that God has given you victory, that you succeeded in taking the weather gauge from Drake, that you have sunk fifteen enemy ships, including their flagship, and that the rest have fled to Dover. . . . I trust in God that this is so. . . . I assume that you will by now have gone on to meet my nephew the Duke. With the enemy in the grip of fear and our own men in high spirits we can place our hope in God that more victories will follow. . . . By the grace of God I expect a fair outcome in this cause which is so particularly his. . . . I await confirmation of this.

There was more to come. Dispatch after dispatch. The enemy fleet was burning, it was sinking ever faster. The time had come for Mendoza to put his reports in some sort of order:

On 10 August, he reported, the Armada had in fact sunk seventeen enemy ships. It was in the legs that Drake was wounded, by a cannon ball. On 14 August at 'the battel of New-Castle', thirty ships were captured or sunk. On 20 August, forty English ships were sunk, including the English flagship and Drake's. Drake, wounded again, this time in the cheek, had got away in a launch. In short, as a simple piece of mental arithmetic would show, the enemy fleet no longer existed.

And Olivarez learned on 28 August that the Armada was in the Channel, there had been three days of gunfire, victory was theirs. Straightway he obtained a special audience with the Pope. He asked him to say a thanksgiving *Te Deum* and to have the Vatican illuminated. And, while they were on the subject, as Parma's army must by now be in England, how about paying over the first half million of the first instalment?

Sixtus replied that he saw no reason to do any more than he was committed to . . . that he would not be pushed and that he would do nothing until the fate of the Armada was known for certain. . . .

When Olivarez went back with more news of victory to the Vatican —'Drake is dead or captured'—he was being less truthful and the Pope was even more sceptical. For other reports, highly alarming ones, were reaching Rome from all over Europe. 'Drake is victorious; the Armada is either fleeing or destroyed.'

The King of France, too, had received different reports. And when Mendoza requested an audience at Chartres to ask that a thanksgiving *Te Deum* be sung all over the kingdom, the King informed him of them, personally. The old ambassador was badly out of favour at court. The power of his King, and his direct interference in French internal affairs, which he did not even take the trouble to disguise, had earned him deep and widespread hatred. Henry's only reply to his requests was to hand him a letter from Calais. The Governor, Monsieur Gourdan, had indeed seen the Armada anchoring under the city walls. Their sails and rigging were all in shreds, and during Sunday night English fire-ships had put them to flight. The following morning the well ordered English fleet had set sail in pursuit. A galleass had run aground at the foot of the castle.

'It is clear', said Don Bernardino, 'that we have received differing accounts. . . .' He took his leave and returned to Paris. 'What about the bonfire', asked his second secretary, 'can we light the bonfire?' 'Wait', said Mendoza.

These vague rumours and fragmented reports went on for another week. The galleass that had run aground was the *San Lorenzo*; the Governor of Calais was willing to return her guns. The La Hougue ship was the *Santa Ana*, Recalde's *capitana*. Mendoza knew that there were 50,000 of the King's ducats on board. He took immediate measures for their safety. A merchant ship from one of the Hansa ports had sailed for hours without seeing a single sail, but in the sea she had sighted hundreds of horses and mules. The English had captured two galleons, the Dutch two more. One English ship had actually been seen sinking. A reconnaissance pinnace sent out by the Duke of Parma had sighted the entire English fleet in flight. De Leiva had just captured the English flagship and fifty other ships. There was confirmation from Antwerp that Drake had had a leg blown off by a cannon ball. The *Ark Royal* had surrendered. More news from Dieppe: the entire English fleet, apart from twenty ships, had been either captured or sunk. It was after a general skirmish off the coast of Scotland on 13 August that Drake had been captured trying to board the *San Martin*.

Having annihilated the enemy, the Duke had taken shelter in a Scottish port in order to carry out repairs and take on water. He was just waiting for the right wind to return to the Channel. England was in a state of panic.

All over Europe, the moment they were received, either by letter or via some traveller, these reports were printed, translated, copied. Pamphlets appeared everywhere, each one more tenditious than the last, and basing their stories on one another's.

By now Mendoza was convinced. He lit his bonfire and wrote to Philip that Drake had been taken prisoner by Sidonia while trying to board the *San Martin*. He hadn't actually had confirmation of this from the Duke himself, but everyone said it was so and it seemed to be highly probable.

The news spread from the Escurial to every castle and village in Spain, where families were waiting for word of sons, nephews, husbands. The narrow streets were illuminated and *gaitas*, tambourines and guitars called people to the fiesta. A victory announcement was published in Madrid, and a second edition quickly produced in Seville.

Once more Olivarez called on the Pope. In his pocket he had an exuberant letter from Mendoza. But he looked worried. From the north were coming the most distressing rumours: two Spanish galleons run aground on the coast of Holland, Don Diego Pimentel captured, and a copy of the minutes of his examination circulated. Spanish banners in St Paul's Cathedral. A pamphlet entitled 'A pack of Spanish lyes' arrived in Rome. Paragraph by paragraph it refuted the victory announcement published in Madrid and Seville on the basis of Mendoza's report.

Philip II finally learned the truth from Parma's letters, which contained a precise account, up until 10 August, of a disaster. The Armada was fatally stricken, demoralised, short of powder, shot and courage. It was fleeing. There was not a hope of a landing in England now. He was going to strike camp and withdraw from Dunkirk.

Since Parma neglected to inform Mendoza of any of this (Mendoza later vilified him, blaming him for the whole disaster), it was from England that the truth first reached the Spanish embassy in Paris. The first news came in a pamphlet, which was translated on arrival, entitled 'Journal of all that passed between the armies of Spain and England, from July 28th to August 11th, 1588', and then in a second document whose very title sent a chill to the old ambassador's heart. It was 'Certain advertisements out of Ireland concerning the losses and distressed happened to the Spanish Navy upon the West coasts of Ireland. . . .'

Out of Ireland! God! Shipwrecks, massacres, disasters, epidemics, famine—the news from Ireland was too dreadful. No, it was impossible! It was English propaganda! And on 29 September Mendoza wrote once more to Philip: 'The fleet has reformed in the Shetlands and Orkneys. It has taken on fresh provisions, and is now heading for the coast of Flanders, reinforced by twelve captured English galleons, and several Dutch.'

When Philip received this report, a bundle of letters from Alexander Farnese had already been lying on his desk for three weeks. They asserted that Parma had struck camp at Dunkirk, that his unpaid troops had mutinied, that the Armada was somewhere between Scotland and Norway. Also on Philip's desk was a journal of Prince d'Ascoli which had been sent from Calais, and dispatches from Juan de Manrique, one of the Duke's men, putting the blame for all the catastrophes, present and future, on Parma, who had been 'nowhere near ready'. The King had on his desk the *diario*, or journal, of Medina Sidonia, in the Duke s own hand, brought to him in a fast *patache* by Don Balthazar de Zuñiga. And before Philip also lay messages from Santander and the northern ports, where the Duke had arrived with a handful of ghost ships, their decks littered with dying men.

These documents still exist, and one can still see in the margin the toll of lost ships totted up day by day in the King's own anxious hand. In the margin of Mendoza's last victorious communiqué Philip has scrawled: 'Nothing of this is true; he really ought to be told.'

Wrote Count Olivarez:

Judging by His Holiness's attitude these last few days one would hardly credit him with the sort of apostolic zeal for the suppression of heresy and the salvation of souls that his position should demand. . . . When it seemed that victory was ours he softened his tone and was more courteous . . . once the truth was known he turned haughty and arrogant . . . and treated me like a slave. Anyone would think that our present misfortune had not come about through his fault, and in the service of God. His ill will and that of the cardinals is such that under the circumstances it is positively heretical.

LA FELI
CISSIMA AR-
MADA QVE ELREY
DON FELIPE NVESTRO
Señor mandó juntar enel puerto
de la Ciudad de Lisboa enel
Reyno de Portu-
gal.

*El Año de mil y quinientos y
ochenta y ocho.*

HECHA POR
Pedro de Paz
Salas.

ᏋᏋ S V M A R I O ᏋᏋ
GENERAL DE TODA
EL ARMADA.

	Numero dNauios	Toneladas	Géte dguerra.	Géte dmar	Numero dtodos.	Pieças de artilleria.	Peloteria.	Poluora	Plomo qui tales.	Cuerda qui tales.
¶ Armada de Galeones de Portugal.	12.	7.737.	3.330.	1.293.	4623.	347.	18450.	789.	186.	150
¶ Armada de Vizcaya, de que es General Iuan Martinez de Ricalde.	14	6567.	1.937.	863.	2800	238.	11.900.	477.	140.	87
¶ Galeones de la Armada de Castilla.	16	8714.	2.458..	1.719.	4171.	384.	23040.	710	290.	309
¶ Armada de naues del Andaluzia.	11.	8.762.	2.325.	780.	3.105.	240.	10.200.	415.	63.	119
¶ Armada de naos de la Prouincia de Guipuscua.	14.	6.991.	1992.	616.	2.608.	247.	12.150.	518.	139.	109
¶ Armada de naos leuantiscas.	10.	7.705.	2.780.	767.	3523.	280.	14000.	584.	177.	141
¶ Armada de Vrcas.	23.	10271.	3121.	608.	3729.	384	19.200.	258.	142.	215
¶ Pataches y zabras.	22.	1.221.	479.	574.	1093	91.	4550.	66.	20.	13
¶ Galeaças de Napo	4.		873.	468.	1.341.	200.	10.000.	498.	61.	88
¶ Galeras.	4		362.	362.	20.	1200.	60.	20.	20.
	130	57.868.	19295.	8050.	27365.	2.431	123790.	4.575.	1.232.	1.151

Gente de remo.

En las Galeaças.	1.200.
En las Galeras.	888.
	2.088.

De mas de la dicha poluora se lleua de respecto para si se ofreciere alguna bateria 600. qs. **600.**

POr manera que ay en la dicha armada, segun parece por este sumario, ciento y treynta nauios, que tienen cincuenta y siete mil ochocientas y sessenta y ocho toneladas, y dizinueue mil dozientos y nouenta y cinco soldados de Infanteria, y ocho mil y cincuenta y dos hombres de mar, que todos hazen, veyntisiete mil trezientas y setenta y cinco personas, y dos mil y ochenta y ocho remeros, y dos mil y quatrocientas y treynta y vna pieças de artilleria, las mil quatrocientas y nouenta y siete de bronce, de todas suertes en que ay muchos cañones, y medios cañones, culebrinas, y medias culebrinas, y cañones pedreros, y las ncuecientas y treynta y quatro restantes de hierro colado de todos caliuos, y ciento y veyntitres mil cinto y nouenta balas para ellas, y cinco mil ciento y setenta y cinco quintales de poluora, y mil y dozientos y treynta y ocho de plomo, y mil ciento y cincuenta y vn quintales de cuerda: y los generos de los nauios son en esta manera.

A 9

Previous page: *Frontispiece of the 'General Inventory of the Most Fortunate Fleet', printed in Lisbon 1588 for Pedro de Paz Salas.*

Above: *In the summary of the Inventory: 10 squadrons, 130 ships, 30,000 men.*

The most formidable engine of war in those days was the galleass. This contemporary Dutch engraving is supposed to be of an Armada galleass in the Channel. It is highly inaccurate. What Van Luyck has in fact depicted here (and very approximately at that) is a Mediterranean Venetian galleass, not a real Atlantic one, which was not simply a large galley, but a cross between a galleon and a galley.

The Armada in the crescent formation that it adopted in the Channel, with two galleasses at each point. The English, having sailed round them to both sides, have succeeded in taking the wind. The Lord Admiral of England has sent his pinnace, the Disdain, *to bear his personal challenge to the Captain*

General, the Duke of Medina Sidonia. (From an engraving by John Pine, copied in 1739 from a set of tapestries made at the time for the Lord Admiral Lord Howard of Effingham, by Francis Speirrig. Speirrig used Cornelis de Vroom's designs made from Howard's own sketches.)

The San Salvador was destroyed by fire following an explosion. The English subsequently captured two vessels, both of which had already been damaged. Otherwise they wisely avoided boarding, preferring to take advantage of the longer range of their artillery and the greater mobility of their new galleons.

Above: *The 'Gente de Guerra'. Sixteenth century Spanish captains, pikemen and arquebusiers. (From an engraving by Theodore de Bry.)* Below: *One of the Armada's four genuine galleasses. Could it be the Girona? The illustration (from an engraving by John Pine) is almost certainly accurate: as a patron the Lord Admiral was not an easy man to please.*

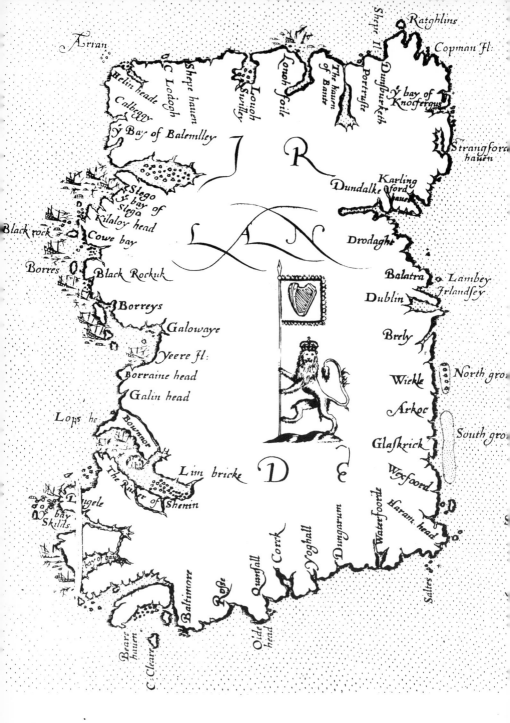

A contemporary map drawn by Robert Adams showing ships of the Armada wrecked on the Irish coast. The only one not marked is the Girona. She was the last to go down.

I I

The Armada Takes up a Crescent Formation

What had in fact happened?

At 4 o'clock in the afternoon of Friday, 29 July, land had been sighted from the crow's nest of the *San Martin*. Towards 7 pm, when they were three leagues from the Lizard they struck their sails for the Armada to assemble and take up its formation. Sidonia wrote:

> First sight of land was from this galleon. I hoisted at the main the banner bearing the image of Christ cruicified with the Virgin to one side of Him and Mary Magdalen to the other. I ordered three shots to be fired, as a signal to every man to make his prayer.

This letter, like those that followed, did not reach the King until the end of September.

Since the 22nd, the Duke had made regular entries in his 'Journal of the Enterprise of England , his *diario*. On 30 July he noted that several smoke signals had been observed on the mainland and that during the night, while they were sailing up the Channel, alarm beacons had been sighted signalling from headland to headland.

At a council of war on 30 July, Oquendo took the floor, arguing that it would be madness to advance any further until they knew whether Farnese was ready. There wasn't another friendly port in front of them where they could wait for him, and if the wind held from the present quarter they wouldn't have another chance to turn back. De Leiva and Pedro de Valdez spoke next. They urged the Duke to attack Plymouth. There, they believed, they would have *El Draque* trapped, his ships isolated and faced with the difficulty of beating out against the wind. But the Duke hesitated and decided against it. After the council he sat down at his desk and wrote to the King: 'I propose to sail in good order as far as the Isle of Wight, where I shall stay at anchor until I receive word from the Duke of Parma as to the state of readiness of his fleet and army.' He does not mention the contrary opinions that have been voiced.

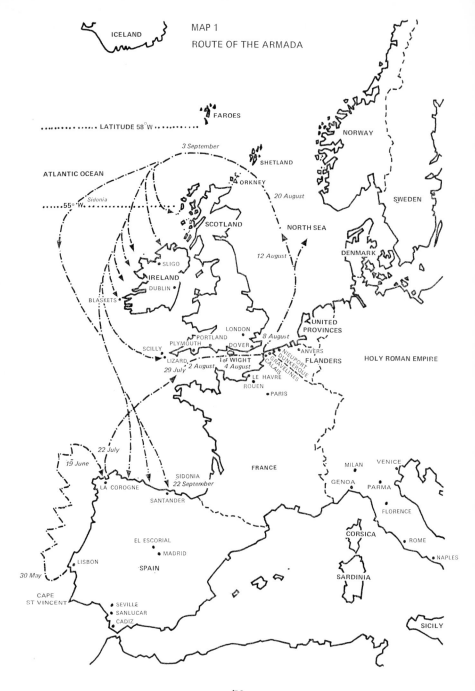

MAP 1

ROUTE OF THE ARMADA

That evening they learned from some captured fishermen that there are sixty ships at Plymouth, but that they have started to sail out. Drake had in fact started to beat out of Plymouth on the night of the 29th with the ebb tide. By the afternoon of the 30th most of the galleons were already up with the Eddystone.

That same evening, through the haze of the setting sun, Lord Howard of Effingham, Earl of Nottingham and Lord Admiral of England, had his first glimpse of the largest fleet he had ever seen in his life. It spanned the whole horizon a few leagues to westward and to windward of him.

The *San Martin*'s lookout had sighted white sails picked out by the setting sun and reported a fleet standing out for the open Channel, hard ahead, with the wind abeam. Then as darkness finally fell, the lookout still seemed to have seen a few sails inshore of them.

At moonrise the wind freshened again, blowing from west-south-west. Somewhat perplexed, Sidonia issued orders to heave to, so as not to risk losing the weather gauge to the enemy overnight. The wind then veered to west nor'west.

The first light of dawn revealed eighty ships astern of the Armada, to seaward and to windward of them. This was the main body of the English fleet commanded by Howard and his Vice-Admiral, Sir Francis Drake. Inshore of the Spanish ships were eleven other English vessels, tacking about, sailing upwind to get astern of the Spaniards (they were the last to leave Plymouth and arrived too late to round the van of the Armada). Three of them, three huge galleons, were already exchanging the first broadsides with the Biscayans of Recalde's rear-guard.

Stunned by their incredible speed and manoeuvrability, the Spanish gazed paralysed, as the eleven enemy ships, tack after tack, beat up close to the wind, gained the wind and the rear of the Spanish fleet, joining the rest of the English vessels which during the night had made a wide sweep round the front of the Armada.

Howard had been successful. As long as the wind held he would be able to attack how, when and where he chose. He had the added advantage that the best of the Spanish ships, having been placed in the foremost positions, were now right in the rear. 'The advantage of time and place in all martial actions is half a victory, which being lost is irrecoverable.' Drake had written to the Queen in the spring of that year.

The Most Fortunate Fleet had entered the Channel in perfect formation, like an army on the march. Bertendona's squadron of the Levant and the galleasses made up the vanguard. Sidonia was behind with the galleons of Portugal, then the squadron of Castile followed by the hulks, protected to each side by the Andalusian and

Guipuscoan squadrons. Recalde and his Biscayans formed the rear-guard. *Pataches* and *zabras* acted as scouts, dispatch carriers and flank guards.

Sidonia had retired to bed late and risen early. From the forecastle of the flagship, the *San Martín*, he gloomily observed the successful junction of the English squadrons less than six miles in his wake.

The Duke ordered a signal to be fired. Promptly every ship came about, shortened or made sail. The vanguard became the starboard wing, on the side nearer France, the rear-guard became the port wing, on the English side. The manoeuvre was complete. With two galleasses at each point the Armada formed a threatening crescent, majestically sweeping across seven miles of horizon. The English were impressed by the perfection of the manoeuvre. It was a classic formation for an army in the field, but disconcerting to encounter at sea. (See pages 64–5.)

The Duke and his council had planned it well in advance. In a letter to the King dated 28 May, the Duke had written:

> If Drake is at Plymouth waiting for me to sail past so that he can attack from the rear, while the fleet they have sent against Parma attacks from ahead, I shall be able to confront both at once. Either one of the wings of my crescent, supported by the reinforcement that I will send in and two galleasses covered by four of the largest ships, will easily be able to attack one of the enemy fleets. I, meanwhile, will make a frontal attack on the other fleet, with the capitana, the other galleons and the two other galleasses.

However, contrary to his expressed intentions, and without being threatened by any frontal assault, the Duke had placed two galleasses at each wing of his formation. Contemporary engravings made after Howard's sketches confirm this. Furthermore, according to the plan, enemy ships pursuing the crescent in a following wind, would be able, lest they should lose the weather gauge, to attack only the protruding wings, where Sidonia would have stationed the strongest ships. Any vessels rash enough to penetrate into the middle of the crescent would see it closing in on them and would find themselves the central target of the entire Spanish fire. If the others came to their aid, a general mélée would arise with the hand to hand combat that the Spanish, outnumbering the English in manpower by five to one, wanted to precipitate as much as the English wanted to avoid it. Such at least were the formation the Duke had hoped to maintain and the results he expected of it.

On the English side Howard and Drake divided their fleet into two columns. Their agreed tactics were to avoid a direct confrontation with such a formidable enemy. If the Spanish showed signs of attacking they would flee, otherwise they would follow at a safe distance, ready to launch a joint attack on any straggler and destroy it in the cross-fire of their long-range culverins. If there were no stragglers, they would try to engage the last ship at the rearmost point, the one, that is, which the others, forced to put back against the wind, would have the greatest difficulty in rescuing. Here it was that the first attempt would be made.

Following the rules of chivalry, unchanged since the Middle Ages, the Lord Admiral of England sent his defiance to the Captain General of the Ocean Sea, using his personal pinnace as a herald of arms. The *Disdain*, commanded by Captain James Bradbury, left the fleet and sped alone towards what he assumed to be the *capitana*. It was in fact the *rata Sancta Maria Encoronada*. When she was within a cable's length of her, the *Disdain* took aim and discharged a minute cannon ball from her small gun into the hull of the enormous carrack.

The gauntlet was down. The pinnace bobbed lightly back over the waves to the fleet, vainly pursued by the *rata's* fire. Howard of Effingham ordered insignia, pennants and standards to be hoisted. His officers ordered gunports to be opened, guns loaded and fuses recharged. Leading his ships in single file behind his *Ark Royal*, Howard attacked the Spanish vanguard (the right wing). The *rata*, which he still believed to be the *capitana*, turned to meet him, followed by Martin de Bertendona's *Regazona* and the entire squadron of Levant. De Leiva tried to close, but failed. The English ships dodged and the *rata* was too heavy too follow. With the wind abeam, the two ships fired at each other from a distance.

Meanwhile Drake in the *Revenge*, Frobisher in the *Triumph*, and Hawkins in the *Victory* sailed their squadrons towards the rear-guard (the left wing). The first fire thundered from the English ships, the first cannon balls whistled through the air, the first skulls were shattered, the first blood flowed on the decks. The merchant captains of several Biscayans were scared out of their wits: they were all ordinary working men, vine growers, tapsters, tuna fishermen, pressed into the navy and dubbed for the occasion soldiers or sailors. Several captains abandoned their wing positions and fled, ploughing into the main body of the Armada, like sheep into the heart of the flock.

Don Juan Martinez de Recalde, the Armada's second in command, turned about and headed, alone, towards the advancing enemy. Seven English ships levelled their fire at him. Don Diego Pimentel, in the *Gran Grin*, hastened to his rescue. For two hours the two of them endured the *fuego horroroso* of the enemy culverins. Bravely they returned the fire, but the enemy ships kept a safe distance of over 300 yards, a wise tactic according to the English, cowardly according to the Spanish. Spanish cannon, demi-cannon and perriers were dangerous at 150 yards, fatal at 80 yards, at 300 yards virtually ineffective.

The strength of the Royal Navy lay in her new galleons. They were absolutely the latest thing: they had lower forecastles, rode lower in the water and were narrower and longer than the ships of the first half of the century, which gave them a greater ease of manoeuvre and enabled them to carry more guns each side.

Recalde's *San Juan* was now under fire from eight ships. Seven men had been blown to smithereens by English gunfire. Her gunports had already spewed out the blood of thirty-one wounded men. Her mizzen had been hit twice by cannonballs, and her rigging was in bad shape. De Leiva attempted to engage Drake, trying to manoeuvre his heavy carrack, but the wind blew him off before he could get alongside.

Now the Duke himself came to his aid. The *San Martín* and the *San Mateo* had turned about and rounded the fleet to westward with the galleons of Portugal. The galleasses were rowing hard. Seeing this, the Lord Admiral broke off the action. 'We durst not adventure to put in among them,' he wrote, 'their fleet being so strong', and added that he thought it wiser to await the arrival of the forty ships still at Plymouth before advancing further. Henry Whyte, a volunteer on the *Mary Rose*, thought his prudence excessive and considered that their first onset had been 'more coldly done than became the value of our nation and the credit of the English navy'. Drake was sufficiently impressed to write, 'As far as we perceive, they are determined to sell their lives with blows.'*

On the Spanish side, the personal intervention of the Duke fired the hearts of his men, and even of his generals who had been somewhat reluctant to take up what was essentially a defensive formation, when they had the advantage in numbers. Having got his men out of trouble around 1 or 2 o'clock in the afternoon, the Duke tried until 5 o'clock to engage battle again. He lined his fleet up roughly into four columns and tacked towards the enemy. He was unsuccessful. 'Those enemy ships were so amazingly nimble. . . .'

---

* The historian Garrett Mattingly makes the unsubstantiated supposition that Recalde intended by his manoeuvre and in defiance of orders, to force the Duke to come to his aid, in order to precipitate a general hand to hand mêlée. And that, Mattingly goes on to suppose, is why he ordered his squadron not to follow him.

12

Fire in the Powder Room

The Duke gave up. At a signal from him the Armada, now in total disorder, begun to reform into its crescent. In the muddled confusion of ships, the *Santa Catalina*, clumsily steered, rammed the *capitana* of Pedro de Valdez's Andalusians and wrenched off her spritsail yard and bowsprit. Badly unbalanced, the ship lay across the wind. Before there was time to shorten sail, a strong gust brought down her mizzen mast with all its rigging, and her mainyard. The *Nuestra Señora del Rosario*, broken timbers everywhere and her rigging hopelessly entangled, was utterly paralysed.

Valdez fired four shots for help. The Duke stood over to the *Rosario* in answer to his call. Hardly had he gone about when a blinding ball of fire burst into the dusk. A moment later a shattering explosion echoed across the waves, and a heavy red and black cloud mushroomed up above the *San Salvador*. The whole of her poop was ablaze. Once more the *San Martín* went about to bring help.

On board the *San Salvador* were the Vice-Admiral of the Guipuscoan squadron and the paymaster-general, Juan de la Huerta, together with a sizeable part of the Armada treasure, 'divided up as a precautionary measure'. When the Duke approached, a terrible spectacle confronted him. The explosion had blown away two decks and the stern castle. The long, regular, piercing howls of men burnt to the bone rose above the roar of the flames and with the wind came the sickening stench of burnt flesh and hair. The whole powder magazine had blown up. (See page 66.)

It was almost certainly an accident, although subsequently at least half a dozen versions of the story grew up, all different and all highly coloured, putting the explosion down to sabotage or personal revenge on the part of a gunner, German, Dutch, English or French according to the version, flogged by Captain Priego. It will be recalled that there was actually a German gunner on board with his wife, and this was doubtless the starting point for the most melodramatic account of all, in which the cuckolded husband chose this way of revenging himself on the seducing captain.

A rescue operation soon began. Two pinnaces hooked the prow of

75

the ship to tug her into the wind so that the flames could not blow forward. Rescuers climbed aboard from the *pataches*, to help survivors fight the fire and to take off the wounded. They had a difficult task. A squally wind was coming up and the swell was getting heavier. The decks were slippery with blood, and it was almost impossible to keep one's balance. Dismembered bodies lay in little heaps, arms or a leg ending in a molten foot hang from the shroud ratlines. A charred head rolled from one side of the deck to the other.

Naked bodies, charred bodies, striped with gashes of red, 'giving off a regular rattle', were taken off to the two hospital ships. Some of them, when they were picked up, lost a limb; or their skin fell away or their flesh, leaving nothing but bones in their rescuers' hands. The number of dead and wounded came to two hundred. According to the Duke's reckoning another fifty were drowned jumping overboard to escape the furnace.

Once the fire was under control the Duke gave two galleasses orders to tow the hull of the *San Salvador* over to the hulks, according to the evening's entry in his *diario*. His final instructions were to 'transfer the coffers without delay onto a seaworthy ship', then (and we must take his word for it) he stood across to the *Rosario*.

During this time Pedro de Valdez's ship has been trailing behind the rest of the Armada under foresail and main topgallants. A gust of wind carried off her unsupported mainmast as well and now she was motionless.

According to his own account, 'The Duke signalled to the whole fleet to heave to and wait while he stood across to the *Rosario* and tried to pass a hawser.' According to an officer of the *San Marcos*: '. . . She fired four shots but no-one went to her rescue. There was a hard wind blowing, a heavy swell, and the English were hard behind. We abandoned her at vespers, following a signal shot from the Duke.'

Jorge Manrique, one of the Duke's men recorded that: '. . . the Armada carried on its way leaving her astern in full view of the enemy . . ., and in the words of one of the *Rosario's* passengers, 'The Duke went on his way, abandoning her to the enemy, who were still following, three miles astern.' Don Pedro de Valdez himself was to later write to the King:

> Unable to make the necessary repairs, I sent someone to inform the Duke and fired . . . four shots to signal our distress to the rest of the Armada.. . . The Duke was close enough to see quite clearly what sort of difficulties I was in and to come to my aid . . . but he did nothing of the sort! He seemed to have forgotten that we were servants of Your Majesty and in his command! He fired a shot to reform the Armada and sailed on leaving me in distress, and the enemy only a quarter of a league astern of me.

It does indeed seem that the Duke's first reaction was, instinctively, to go to Don Pedro's rescue, but Diego Flores, his Chief of Staff and principal adviser, argued hotly to the effect that night was falling and the weather was deteriorating badly. If the Captain General delayed any longer, by the morning the Armada would be hopelessly scattered and at the mercy of the enemy. It was not right to imperil the entire fleet for the sake of one ship. Medina Sidonia yielded, but not before he sent his personal *patache* over to the *Rosario* to take off the King's treasure and bring it back safely to his own galleon. Boiling with rage, Valdez replied that since he was risking his own life and so many noblemen and hildagos, surely a little bit of gold might be risked too and he sent the *patache* back, empty. He did however allow Fray Bernardo de Gongora to make a getaway in the *patache*, as well as four English Catholics, who would have risked hanging for high treason had they been captured. According to the Duke:

> I then ordered Captain Ojedo to go to Don Pedro de Valdez's rescue with his nao and four pataches. . . . I saw them reach the Rosario [it seems that the Duke was the only person who did] and did not leave until I had made quite sure for myself that two other vessels and a galleon had received my orders to accompany them.

Whatever the truth of the matter is, whether the convoy was in fact never sent, whether it was recalled or simply gave up, by 9 pm Don Pedro was alone on the sea.

The Captain General had listened to the voice of reason. And he had been wrong. For the Castilians there could be no excuse for what he had done. He had abandoned to the enemy a subordinate, a commander who was loved and respected by everyone. In so doing he had forfeited his honour and earned the undying contempt of his captains. The squadron commanders took it as a mortal affront. Not one of them ever spoke to Diego Flores again. The Commander in Chief had also undermined his men's morale. 'If that's the way a *caballero* like that is abandoned, what kind of help can the likes of us expect?' they are said to have asked themselves.

The bitter hatred that Diego Flores felt for his cousin Don Pedro was common knowledge. Only recently the two men had once more violently disagreed in the council. It was openly suggested that Diego Flores had used this as a means of personal revenge.

By that very night angry reproaches had already reached the Duke's ear. Perhaps that was why when he wrote up his *diario* he specifically stated, 'Diego Flores then said to me' and again, 'so, following his advice. . . .'

13
'The Enemy showed Don Pedro more Mercy than We did Ourselves'

At a council meeting that evening the English decided on their battle order. Sidonia might try to shelter in Tor Bay or land on the Isle of Wight, or possibly at Weymouth. Every eventuality should be foreseen. But how could any of these moves be prevented if they restricted themselves to following him rather than blocking his path?

All the squadron commanders were there. At the end of the day none of them had tried to take the two crippled Spanish ships. For sailors who were by tradition pirates rather than military men, the rewards were tempting. But, no, in the interests of the nation such lust for booty must be controlled. Howard brought this up once again in the council. At the end of the meeting the Lord Admiral entrusted Drake with the task of maintaining contact with the Armada, and leading the whole fleet behind the great poop-lantern of the *Revenge*. Howard was in effect doing Drake the remarkable honour of yielding him the position that was properly his own.

When it was dark Drake put out his lantern, headed due north with two of his ships, the *White Bear* and the *Mary Rose*, and disappeared into the night. Once he was out of sight he went about again, due west, and sailed back up the fleet.

Howard was roused and informed that the Vice-Admiral's lantern was nowhere to be seen. Deeply puzzled, he had topgallants hoisted to go and find out what had happened. He pressed on through the night. At daybreak, no Drake.

Dawn on 1 August found Drake and his two accomplices alongside the *Rosario*. He took her without firing a single shot. Don Pedro, hopelessly isolated, had agreed, in exchange for honourable pledges, to surrender his indefensible ship to the three English vessels.

Drake rejoined the fleet in the afternoon with his prize, the Lord Admiral asked for a detailed account of his expedition. Why had he put out the lantern when he had been ordered to keep it alight to guide the rest of the fleet behind him? Why had he not maintained contact with the enemy?

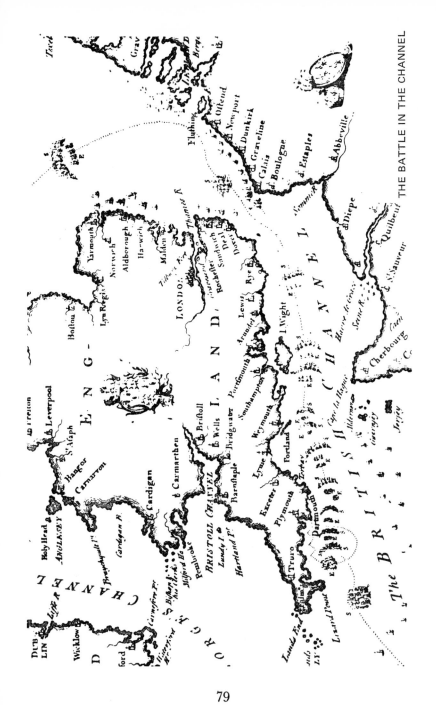

79

Drake explained that at nightfall they thought they sighted sails to port, between them and the coast, passing to windward of them. He immediately suspected the Spanish of trying to manoeuvre round them, to steal the wind and surround the fleet. So, he followed them to see what was afoot. He put the lantern out so that the enemy wouldn't know they were being followed. The enemy ships turned out to be some passing German hulks, Hansa merchantmen, an easy mistake to make . . . how odd that no one else saw them! But of course it was very dark. He had come across the *Rosario* by chance, sheer chance.

Sir Martin Frobisher later commented to one of Drake's officers, that Drake had been trying to do them out of their share of the fifteen thousand ducats (*sic*). They would get it back or have his blood. Really, his trickeries were becoming quite intolerable. Drake's booty that day in fact amounted to 55,000 of his Most Catholic Majesty's gold ducats, a ship with forty-six cannon, the ransom of a squadron commander and of several noblemen, and an armful of gold-plated swords with richly encrusted pommels, intended for the English Catholic nobility. He allowed his men to loot cabins and baggage, all except that of Don Pedro (whom Drake entertained royally at his own table, inviting him to watch the remainder of the battle, until Howard pointed out the impropriety of this, quite apart from the potential danger). From the Duke's men, who showed approval of their leader in what they wrote but criticised him sharply in private, this later elicited the comment that 'the enemy showed Don Pedro more mercy than we did ourselves'. Towed to Dartmouth, the *Rosario* was looted from truck to keelson, long before the local magistrates arrived to affix the seals.

That night, 31 July to 1 August, the Captain General of the Ocean Sea slept badly. He had two things on his mind. The points of the Spanish crescent were too vulnerable, and the rear-guard generally too weak. The first English attack had shown this up, when Sidonia had been forced to send back reinforcements from the van, a lengthy manoeuvre and a tricky one against the wind. Clearly it was in the rear that the next blows would come. The Duke turned his quarter moon into a plum, with the hulks as the kernel. Taking advantage of the calmer sea and a light breeze, rearguard and vanguard linked to form a single rear strengthened by the galleasses and four galleons of Portugal. There were altogether forty of the best Spanish vessels, under the command of Alonzo de Leiva until Recalde had completed his repairs. The English would now find themselves confronted by a solid wall.

His second problem was that discipline and fighting spirit had been seriously lacking in those ships not commanded by a Grandee of Spain, a nobleman, a hidalgo or a knight. This had been obvious when fifteen ships had fled leaving Recalde virtually stranded. In order to tighten up on discipline the Duke had gallows put up at the yardarms of several *pataches*. Aboard each one he placed a *capitano de campo* (ie a military attorney) and a hangman. These *pataches* were to relay to all sergeant majors (provost marshals) written orders for improving conduct. They were to have 'any captain who left his position in the new formation hanged by the neck, publicly dishonoured and deprived of his property'. The Spanish historian, Duro, is profoundly critical of this action, describing it as 'a pointless act of severity, ill adapted either to raise moral or to calm the restiveness'. But Antonio de Herrera says that 'The Armada lacked the discipline vital for manoeuvres to be efficiently carried out. . . .'

Towards 11 o'clock the Duke received a message from the *San Salvador* that she was no longer seaworthy and was going down. Sidonia ordered the silver and the crew taken off, and the ship scuttled. He adds in his *diario* that this was done; but it was not. Her captain was badly wounded and the survivors more than anxious to get out of that hellhole. They took off the treasure—whether they took it all or only part of it no one knows—but in any case I made another little mental note on the subject, and later, for greater certainty, transferred it to my little red notebook. Luis de Miranda wrote: '. . . orders were to take off the King's money . . . there were 50,000 or 60,000 ducats on board but only a small amount was removed'. 'There were many on board suffering from wounds and burns whom it was not possible to save,' reported the purser, Pedro Coco Calderon. 'The ship was abandoned in full view of the English,' noted Don Jorge Manrique. 'She was taken by the enemy in full view of the Armada . . .' is a comment in the diary of one of the *Zuñiga*'s crew. When John Hawkins and Lord Thomas Howard climbed aboard the charred wreck, they found fifty wretched men lying on deck horribly burnt and in the most pitiful condition. 'The stink in the ship was so unsavoury and the sight within board so ugly' that they were quickly forced to retire. But there was still some precious shot there and there were even a few barrels of powder left. Having been towed into an English harbour, the *San Salvador*, like the *Rosario* before her, was thoroughly looked over by fishermen and locals, long before any officials arrived on the scene. There is one rather obscure reference in their report to the effect that 'this very night some inkling came unto us that a chest of great weight should be found in the fore-peak of the ship'.

Taking advantage of the lull, supply ships had sailed from the south coast to revictual the English with biscuit, salted meat and sour beer, together with assorted cannon balls and powder 'mixed with a certain amount of sawdust, for they had had to scrape the bottom of the barrels'.

14
De Leiva Enters the Fray

The sea had been quite calm all night. But at dawn on 2 August, a
light squall sent a ripple through the huge Burgundy crosses on the
Sancta Maria Encoronada's limp sails. This flurry of wind was blowing
from the north-east. Was the Armada at last going to be mistress of her
tactics?

It must have been God who had ordained that wind for the good
of His cause. Alonzo de Leiva lost no time in sending the Captain
General a message, begging him to take advantage of it and give battle.
He suggested attacking right away with the galleasses to the fore. His
messenger, Oquendo's and Recalde's almost collided on the *capitana*'s
gangway ladder. They were all bearing the same petition.

Don Alonzo sighted some enemy ships sailing as close to the wind
as possible. They were trying to work inshore to get the weather gauge,
between the coast and the Armada. His messenger returned with the
Duke's orders. They were to attack.

As the two squadrons drew level with Portland Bill, the Armada
went about at the tip of the peninsula. With the Levant squadron
Bertendona and De Leiva bore down on Howard's flagship. Diego
Henriques, Diego Pimentel, Oquendo and Mejia follow with the
whole Armada's striking force. The *San Martín* was there too, with the
galleons of Portugal. But the English ships moved fast. They beat up
close to the wind. To the Spaniards it seemed that they would dodge
about at will, that their culverins rang out relentlessly three times as
fast as the Spanish guns. Even with the wind in their favour the
Spanish failed to grapple and board.

An English ship caught fire, but the blaze was quickly put out. A
lucky shot sank one of their smallest vessels, the *Pleasure*. Hugo de
Moncada sent his galleasses in against Frobisher's squadron. It was
they who worked inshore that morning to steal the new wind.

Howard saw the approaching danger, tried to join Frobisher, but
failed. Don Hugo attacked the *Triumph*, which he found at anchor.
She was the biggest vessel in either fleet, and flying Sir Martin Frobisher's own pennant. At the approach of the galleasses Frobisher cut
his cable, manoeuvred round and fired on the rowers, shooting to kill.

His cannonballs left gaping holes in the ranks of the galley slaves. Once their ranks were broken and their rowing rhythm lost, the oars became crossed and tangled. Compelled to hoist their sails, the heavy galleasses lost their one advantage, which was their free movement. The *Triumph* and five merchantmen managed to hold them at a distance.

The guns had been thundering away since 5 o'clock, when towards midday the wind suddenly veered southwards, from north-east, to south-west. The land breeze of the morning was replaced by a sea breeze. Drake knew his Channel. Anticipating this change, he had left the battle, and with fifty ships in the wake of the *Revenge* he had sailed out to sea. The Armada in the heat of the chase had scattered once more.

The wind changed and Drake was in position. At full tilt he bore down before the wind. Suddenly he loomed out of a cloud of acrid smoke that had blown like a screen across the sea. The moment he saw Drake approaching, Sidonia recalled his galleasses and centred his attack on Drake. Frobisher was saved. Howard and all the others also took advantage of the situation to overpower isolated Spanish ships. The prime target was the *San Martin*. One after another she suffered the salvos of the *Ark Royal* and six other enemy ships. The flagship received five hundred hits (according to Medina Sidonia) and lost fifty men. The Duke stood in the aftercastle and with Diego Flore's assistance calmly directed the firing and the manoeuvre, which the ship's captain, Marolin de Juan, carried out with the precision of a naval exercise. No enemy ship dared to approach the enormous galleon closely, as she steadily spat fire from her gunports. But Recalde was being closed in on again. His Portuguese galleons had rejoined him at last, and the Duke must go with them to get Recalde out of trouble. So he broke off what was a pretty aimless battle. The Armada took up its plum formation again and sailed on eastward.

From dawn until 5 o'clock that evening, 'nothing could be heard from the shore but a continuous roll, that kept every man in a state of extreme anxiety'. The two fleets did actually exchange more than 4,000 shots that day, according to the Duke's *diario*, approximately one shot every ten seconds. The action had left the Spanish with fifty dead and more than sixty wounded, though it is not clear whether these figures refer to the whole Armada, or only to the *capitana*. But if the casualty figures on the Spanish side are vague, on the English side they were nonexistent. Captains would conceal deaths among their men in order to go on collecting their pay. The smaller shot had riddled the sails with holes, cut through halyards and stays, and brought down masts and yards. But neither the Protestant roundshot fired at long range out of prudence, or the Catholic balls fired at long range in desperation, had succeeded in piercing any hulls, nor, in the final analysis, had the balance of power been altered. The two fleets reforming on the evening of the battle, had spent their powder for nothing.

The action started up again on the morning of 3 August when De Leiva's rear-guard became involved in a hot skirmish with some English vessels. Recalde, with the galleasses bringing up the rear, joined in the action. The enemy seemed to be about to give battle. Once more the gunfire started up, as furiously as the previous day, slowing down only during the course of the day as the guns overheated, and the gunners had to try to cool them down by wrapping them in sheets soaked in vinegar and water.

Finding themselves short of powder and ball, the English finally retired, or, according to the Spaniards, fled. That evening the Duke reckoned that a further 5,000 shots had been fired. Sixty corpses were thrown without ceremony overboard, and the hospital hulks took in a further seventy wounded. Sidonia noted too that he had counted 140 enemy sail that evening. Then, closing his *diario*, he wrote two letters. The first was to the Duke of Parma, to whom he wrote nearly every day, to keep him up-to-date and to urge him on. The second was to the King. ' . . . I intend to take the Isle of Wight and occupy the port. This will be my base when we join forces.' Having done this, he went to bed.

That same night the English were deciding on a change of tactics. They were dividing themselves up into four squadrons, under Howard, Drake, Hawkins and Frobisher.

The first light of dawn on Thursday, 4 August, showed the English two Spanish stragglers in an empty sea. John Hawkins had himself towed towards them. They were the hulk *Santa Ana* (not the *capitana Santa Ana* that Recalde had abandoned because of extensive damage) and one of the galleons of Portugal, the *San Luis*. Lowering their sail, three galleasses immediately set off under oar to their rescue, followed at a distance by several galleons and De Leiva's carrack. The galleasses arrived alone to find themselves surrounded, in an extremely perilous situation, under a hail of iron and lead. The *Girona* lost her poop lantern, the *San Lorenzo* lost her figureheads. The *Zuniga*'s hull was holed at the water level, and she had to move clear, listing badly. Aiming as before into the oars, the enemy fired their shot in among the rowers. And as before the thwarts were soon jammed with bodies (it was impossible to throw them overboard quickly enough because of their chains) and wounded men screaming in agony. There were seven men slaving at each oar, four pulling and three pushing. All it needed was for one man to collapse at the feet of the others, covering the planks with a gory mess of blood and guts, and they were all entangled. And it only needed one oar to stop for those immediately next to it to get caught up too. When one side of the vessel was without a certain number of oars, any manoeuvre became impossible. And if they hoisted their sails the galleasses completely lost their mobility. The galleasses demonstrated in the English Channel that, far from combining the advantages of the galley with those of the galleon as had been anticipated, they combined nothing but the disadvantages of both, once they were outclassed in firepower.

Recalde was first to the rescue. Then, as the fleets came abeam of the Isle of Wight, the other galleons joined them. The wind veered from south-south-west to west-south-west. Now, with the wind abeam, the Armada could manoeuvre. It was the Feast of St Domingo de Guzman that day and the Duke, a regular worshipper of his, decided to give battle again. He broke out the royal standard and had pennants and banners hoisted at all mast-heads. It seemed as if this time the English were going to let the Spanish get near. Quite soon separate groups here and there began to exchange fire in some confusion. Under fire from the Spanish perriers the 'English flagship' (wrongly identified by the Duke—English documents prove that it was in fact the damaged *Triumph*) was cut off at one moment from the rest of the squadron, and caught on a lee shore, seemed in serious danger. The Duke saw her strike the flag, fire two shots for help and try to get away from the battle towed by her boats. The *San Martín* was ideally placed to dispatch her. The Duke hesitated. That moment was crucial. Alonzo de Leiva offered up a silent prayer. He saw it as their chance to snatch victory. If the flagship had been engaged the rest of the English fleet would have had to come to her aid. At last there would have been some hand-to-hand fighting.

Still the Duke hesitated. That, at any rate, was what the Spanish captains claimed when they later heaped abuse on him at court. The crack shots had already been ordered to the crows' nests, the arquebusiers had taken their positions, arms loaded and matches already smoking. The boarding parties were at their posts, grappling hooks at the ready.

But the Duke waited, and the English galleon moved off.

She must have slipped away by moving cleverly from an unfavourable local current into a neighbouring countercurrent. She was also helped by nine launches sent in to the rescue under the Duke's very eyes. De Leiva, Oquendo, Recalde and all the generals, indignant with rage, let loose a flood of sarcastic comments. Fray Juan de Victoria later wrote (from hearsay, it is true) that once De Leiva was within hail of the *San Martín*, he hurled across a flood of abuse, of which the least offensive was: 'God's body, His Majesty has given us a man to command us at sea who looks as if he wouldn't know how to walk on dry land.' The friar reported that when Oquendo's ship in turn came abreast of the *San Martín*, Oquendo shouted for the Duke and all his Andalucians to hear: 'Go on then, chickens! Get to your fishing nets, and go fish for tuna if you don't want to fight!' (The monopoly of tuna-fishing rights was a long-standing privilege of the Dukes of Medina Sidonia, as well as being the traditional pursuit of Andalusian sailor-fishermen). He then shouted to the soldiers on board that the best thing they could do would be to throw the Duke's counsellor, Diego Flores, overboard, after which they might be able to get down to fighting a war. 'The Duke took Oquendo to court for this insult', continues the good priest. 'He sent the records to the King, who read them and just smiled sadly.'

Elsewhere, amidst general confusion, the battle continued. Both sides were blinded by the acrid black smoke that drifted up in thick clouds. A new wind came up, giving the advantage to the English. The Duke discharged a piece and continued on his course. The rest of the Armada following in good order . . . the enemy a long way astern. They were heading now for the Straits of Dover. That day about 3,000 shot had been fired. Two men had been killed on the *San Martín*, and a shot had cut the main throat halyard. Throughout the Armada fifty Spanish bodies were consigned to the waves. There were seventy wounded.

The Spaniards from the North despised the Andalusians as much as the Castilians loathed the Portuguese and the Catalans the Basques. Abused from all sides, Medina Sidonia threatened a few men around him with sentences of death. He wrote up for the King his own account of the day's event.

> The capitana and the vice-flagship were gaining on her [*Triumph*] so fast that the rest of the enemy sailed to the rescue. This time we felt quite sure that we would succeed in boarding, the only way we can win a victory.

In the words of Alonso Vanegas of the *San Martín*, who was writing a eulogy of the Duke to which he added something daily: 'We had her almost within musket range when nine launches towed her off, snatching her so swiftly from our grasp, it was quite miraculous.'

So the Duke and his Andalusians were writing up their reports. And meanwhile, instead of lying in the roads of the Isle of Wight, which is what the King had told Sidonia to do, what had been agreed at the council, and also what the Duke had just written to the King that he intended to do, the Armada sailed on up the Channel. If the prevailing winds held, this meant that the fleet was now proceeding without any chance of turning back and without a single port along the way in which to shelter, and it was still not known whether Parma was ready or not.

Why? Sidonia gives not the slightest hint. Very hastily and vaguely he wrote, '. . . Given that we no longer had the advantage of the weather for our planned attack, the Duke proceeded on his way.' (The Duke consistently refers to himself in the third person.) English records are no more informative. And yet if the Spaniards did not, as planned, sail up the Solent, which is the way into the roads of the Isle of Wight, it can only have been because the English prevented them from doing so. And they must have managed this thanks to their perfect knowledge of the changing winds, and of the complex interplay of local tidal currents, of eddies, and dangerous shoals.

The success of this manoeuvre represented a major victory for Howard. The Armada had not landed or put into port on the south coast of England. The Spanish were, it is true, still making for their rendezvous, and there was still the Thames. But there Howard would have the added reinforcements of John Seymour's ships and the Dover squadron.

15
'*The Hellburners of Antwerp!*'

Friday, 5 August, the sea was like a mill pond and the fleets, both in good order, drifted slowly two miles apart. On both sides there were broken timbers to be repaired. Carpenters, able seamen and master sailmakers were busy on board. Divers were nailing lead plates to the hulls and inside the flooded holds to stop leaks. Soldiers, rowers and seamen slept.

In his daily letter to Farnese, the Duke asked for supplies of bullets, powder, and 4 lb, 6 lb and 10 lb balls of which they were running short; they also needed more biscuit, and if possible forty or fifty fly-boats and small craft, easily manoeuvrable, in which Sidonia intended to launch his floating army against the enemy galleons. Farnese had none of these things. Had he had any small, seaworthy boats, Justin of Nassau and the Sea Beggars, who were lying in wait for him, would have sunk them immediately they left harbour.

Meanwhile, the English, revictualled by launches from the Cinque Ports, were spending the day loading provisions, powder and shot and augmenting their crews.

At sunset the wind freshened a little and the Armada continued on its course to Calais.

At dawn on the 6th, the Duke summoned another meeting of the council. He had decided to anchor at Calais and send word to Farnese to join him there from Dunkirk and Nieuport, these two places, as it seemed to him, not being too far away. The majority of squadron commanders were not at all of the same opinion. The anchorage seemed to them exceedingly dangerous. They were worried about the nearness of the enemy, and most important, they reckoned it impossible that the Flanders army could reach Calais in unarmed, flat-bottomed barges. Recalde and De Leiva advised anchoring further on at Cape Margate, which had several advantages, quite apart from being the place specifically designated in the King's instructions. Oquendo said quite bluntly that if the Armada anchored at Calais 'she was lost'. But the pilots thought that if they went on before the south-west wind, the currents would force the Armada into the North Sea and it would be extremely difficult to get back into the Channel again.

The Duke gave orders to drop two anchors because of the force of the tidal currents. The English fleet anchored too, smartly enough not to lose the weather gauge. The Duke lost no time in sending Captain Heredia to pay a courtesy visit to the Governor of Calais.

In the evening Lord Henry Seymour's squadron and Sir William Wynter's joined Howard. The Armada was surrounded by Howard and Drake to the west, to the north by a section of the fleet anchored between Dover and Sandwich (they were to arrive the following day) and to the east by Justin of Nassau's forty ships, making in all 230 vessels.

Night fell, bringing with it a mood of anxiety. 'We were greatly afraid of a disaster and had a strong premonition that some dastardly trick would be played by that diabolical race of men', wrote Captain Louis de Miranda. The night was quite peaceful however. On Sunday morning the Duke sent his victualling officer ashore for supplies.

Captain Rodrigo Tello arrived back from Dunkirk with a letter from Farnese, promising that in six days everything would be ready for a sortie. Tello himself was less optimistic. The soldiers, he said, had not even begun to embark. The Duke hurriedly sent his secretary to Farnese to urge him to make haste. When the secretary saw for himself the stage things had reached, he estimated that it would be more than a fortnight before the embarkation was completed. Parma replied that embarkation was to begin at once. He ordered his soldiers to embark in 'barges, constructed in such a way that any boarder who jumped onto them immediately landed in the water. Fourteen thousand men were embarked in one day, so tightly crammed that they looked more like sacks of wheat squashed into the holds'.

At sunset the look-outs reported much coming and going by launches in the English fleet, and sinister looking preparations going on. The threat was obvious. In that position, lying at anchor, the Armada was the perfect target for an attack by fireships. It was a text-book situation. Captain Serrano was ordered to take up a position to windward of the fleet with eight pinnaces all equipped with grappling irons and butts. If they saw a fireship approaching they were to tow it ashore at right angles to the wind and standing in to the current. All officers in command ordered a double watch and left their ship's boats in the water similarly equipped. No one can have slept much that night.

Soon after midnight a cry rang out, and quickly spread from ship to ship, louder and louder: 'Fireships'! Eight blazing vessels, swiftly propelled by the wind and the tide, were bearing down like a wall of flame on the Armada in lines two pike lengths' apart.

Serrano's pinnaces were to be seen rowing hard in the direction of the danger. There was an explosion on board one of the ships, and the cry changed. 'The hellburners of Antwerp! The hellburners of Antwerp!'

That particular cry resurrected old fears. In the siege of Antwerp three years earlier, infernal delayed-action machines drifting on the Scheldt had killed more than a thousand Spaniards. One had wounded Parma himself, who like everyone else had been taken completely by surprise by Frederico Giambelli's diabolical invention. The Italian engineer had had the idea of filling a small boat with gunpowder, then packing the compressed powder round the sides and top, with solid layers of bricks or heavy stones. A well-concealed slow fuse, or occasionally a clockwork timing mechanism, set off the charge. The force of the explosion was devastating, and a rain of falling shrapnel crippled anyone who had not already been knocked out by the blast.

The Duke ordered cables to be cut at once. Oquendo, who was standing by at the time, begged him to withdraw his order and pleaded with him to send more pinnaces with boathooks and grapnels to help Serrano divert the fireships onto the beach, or at least to wait until they had tried. The Duke's idea was to cut their cables, move out of the path of the fireships and then recover their previous positions. Oquendo assured him that such a manoeuvre was utterly impracticable, at dead of night with so many ships so close together and with the wind and current as they were. To no effect. The order went out. Most of the ships cut their cables and hoisted their sails, all at once, and in such confusion that several of them rammed each other and were damaged. Some were seen to be drifting, hopelessly entangled, in the direction of Dunkirk. The fireships, which carried only faggots, pitch and tar, sailed on through the empty roads, their guns overheated by the fire, going off at random, until finally they burned themselves out on the beach. They had not directly inflicted any damage at all.

The *capitana* discharged a piece and reanchored. A few nearby ships did likewise, but at dawn on 8 August, when the Duke looked for his fleet, it was scattered all the way from Calais to Gravelines. Though they had not set light to one single vessel Howard's fireships had succeeded in shattering the Armada's formation and had caused its scattered ships to leave their best anchors at the bottom of the sea. All told, Medina Sidonia had with him two galleons and eight *pataches*. He weighed anchor and stood across to where the main body of his fleet lay.

First light showed the English how the enemy was scattered. At the head of their columns, Drake and Seymour went straight into the attack. They directed their fire first on three detached ships at arquebus range, which they systematically pounded with their overwhelmingly superior firepower. Far away to the north, Spanish admirals and vice-admirals were trying one after another to beat up to windward, and one after another they were caught by the enemy. This battle royal stretched from Calais as far as the eye could see. From 8 am to 3 pm, with seventeen enemy ships to port and seven to starboard, 'frequently within musket range and sometimes within arquebus range', Medina Sidonia stood at his post without a moment's respite, receiving and returning broadside after broadside, 'as furiously as one might imagine' . . . 'That evening the gunners were exhausted, having stuck to their guns and not taken a morsel to eat.' So wrote Captain Vanegas and Pedro Coco Calderon.

16

From Calais to Gravelines

During the night of 7–8 August, the *capitana San Lorenzo* collided with the *rata* in all the confusion. The two ships managed to disentangle themselves, but in the course of the manoeuvre the galleass's rudder fouled itself on a cable (probably belonging to one of the anchors that had been abandoned) and both gudgeons were snapped clean off. Don Hugo was rudderless. Dawn found him all alone. With the enemy closing fast, he tried to row into Calais and shelter under the guns of the castle, by arrangement with the Governor, while he repaired the damages. But Don Hugo had no French pilot. He was crossing the bar in a heavy swell when the galleass was swept onto a shoal. The ebbing tide soon caused her to heel over with her starboard battery pointing to the sky and her port battery leaning hard over into the sea. The *capitana* of the galleasses was 'the finest ship in the Armada', an incomparable prize. She was almost certainly carrying more gold and more silver plate than any other vessel except the *San Martín*. Forgetting the plans that had been decided on at the previous day's council, the Lord Admiral—who ought to have led the first attack on the scattered enemy fleet, before Drake, second in charge, and Seymour third—lay to with his entire squadron and sent his officers 'to have their pillage of her'. Though unable to use his cannon, Moncada put up a manly resistance. His arquebusiers went up to the castles and gave the first English boats a hot reception. His small calibre perriers and esmerils, loaded with small shot, beat back fifteen longboats crammed with musketeers. But Don Hugo fell, both eyes blown away by a musket ball. The first to get away were the galley slaves, Turkish and Berber convicts. They swam ashore, followed by Italian artillery-men and sailors. Two captains, Luis Macian and Francisco de Torres were fatally wounded. Man by man the defenders were shot down, until the last survivors hung a white handkershief on a rapier and surrendered the ship to the English.

Fifty men lay dead in the English boats, awash with blood slopping about in the bottom. The 200 uninjured assailants scaled the sides of the galleasses and rushed in after the booty. The chapel of St Lawrence was sacked, just like the cabins: the baggage was gutted. Officers and

Out of 1300 men, 5 survived the shipwreck. The local chieftain, James McDonnell, provided shelter for them at Dunluce Castle. He extended his rescue operation to salvaging the contents of the dead men's pockets and also collecting a considerable treasure from out of the part of the wreck left on the rocks. He used it the following year to rebuild and modernise his castle.

Having systematically explored the whole area, our first task was to draw up a trigonometrical plan, on which we plotted the exact position of every object before moving it.

men squabbled over 'fourteen coffers of most noble spoils'. They divide up between themselves the treasure of the squadron of Naples. (22,000 of the King's gold ducats, according to the historians Ubaldino and Steinitz—50,000 ducats according to Lediard.) Candlesticks, silver and gold plate, crystal, the officers' jewels, including Don Hugo de Moncada's Malta cross, his gold chains, and his insignia of the Order of Santiago. They stripped the sailors and tore chains and jewels from the dead men. None of the loot ever left the pockets into which it was stuffed. Officially, '. . . there was no treasure on board at all, other than a very few things . . .', according to the account of Captain Richard Thomson, one of the pillagers.

The Governor of Calais sent out his cousin and a few other gentlemen in a boat to congratulate the victors on their success, to assure them that he wholeheartedly agreed to their taking their hard-won booty, and to remind them that the vessel herself, with her guns, was lying aground on a stretch of coastline that falls under his jurisdiction, and that they were therefore his by right. It would be quite out of order for them to try to tow her away, and besides the castle cannon are levelled directly on her. Thomson answered politely and hastened back to his pillage. Then, '. . . some of our rude men . . . fell to spoiling the Frenchmen, taking away their rings and jewels . . .'.

Furious, the Governor's cousin went ashore and made straight for the castle. The Calais cannon opened fire and the English lost another twenty men killed or drowned, in a matter of minutes. They beat a hasty retreat, leaving the ship and her guns for Monsieur Gourdan. But they did carry off three captains, in the hope of some ransom money. Howard and his squadron then returned to the battle.

While most of the Armada were struggling against a strong northwest wind that was driving them onto the Dunkirk banks, off Gravelines eleven ships were bearing for hours the brunt of the fire of more than 100 enemy ships. Throughout the whole day barely forty Spanish vessels managed to position themselves to fire. The cannonade had begun at 8 am. The more manoeuvrable English galleons sailed swiftly past, their decks empty, only a pike's length from the Spanish carracks and great ships, their decks packed with soldiers whose courage was useless. The English would fire one broadside, circle to come in and fire the other, and then come in again, reloading three times in the time it took the Spanish or Italians to load once. It was not until 3 o'clock in the afternoon that the main body of the Armada arrived to help. The English hurriedly retired, not being over-anxious to engage in too equal a fight. Outnumbering the Spanish by one hundred to eleven, they had neither sunk nor captured a single ship. Neither had they allowed the enemy to board, although he had tried to do so a dozen times or more. The *capitana*, one of the eleven, had been

95

'the shield for the whole Armada', said the Duke, 'allowing it to extricate itself from the danger'.

The *San Martín* had been holed all over. She had received 107 direct hits, 'enough to bring down a mountain', wrote Alonzo Vanegas. Her divers worked until nightfall to stop the leaks with pitch, tow and lead plates. The English shot had dismounted three guns, pierced her aftercastle, killed twelve men and wounded 120.

The *San Marco*'s pumps could hardly keep down the water. It was rising hopelessly fast, too, in the bilges of the *San Juan de Sicilia*. The *Neustra Señora de Begona* had suffered badly. The *San Felipe* was listing to port. The *San Mateo* and the Biscayan *San Juan* were straggling, their decks awash with blood, and leaving a red wake. They had both received the successive broadsides of a whole English firing line. Their hulls were riddled with holes, their rigging was torn to shreds, their sails were like sieves. The *Maria Juan*, her decks awash, sent out repeated distress signals. Suddenly she sank like a stone, taking down 300 men, all hanging in her tops and in the ratlines.

The cannonade had cost the Spanish in all 600 men killed and 800 wounded. The wounded were taken off in *pataches* to the hospital ships as soon as the enemy retired. The English had not lost a ship, nor more than twenty men.

17
'Only God Could Save Us!'

At dusk the long hammering of the cannonade died down, but as silence fell over the water, a new danger loomed. Over on the horizon, to the east northeast, surf was breaking on the Zeeland Banks in heavy rollers, dirty and foaming. The northwest wind was freshening.

'Not a man among us slept that night', wrote Fray de la Torre. 'All we could do was wait for the moment when we would be hurled into the shoals.'

On the morning of 9 August rain was falling. The Duke wrote that he tried to get the Armada to take up its battle formation again, but that at least twenty of his captains ignored the signal and ran on eastwards instead of lying to and awaiting the enemy. The *capitana* had in company three galleasses, Recalde's galleons, De Leiva's squadron and two other vessels. In all, 109 English ships were visible, standing in the eye of the wind, but some way off. The swell was rising, the wind blowing fresh from the northwest. Sailing as close-hauled as they could, the Spanish ships, driven by the wind and the current, were drifting helplessly into the Zeeland Banks. Already the sea about them was brown with roiled-up sand. They had left their bower anchors behind at Calais and the kedges would never hold in the shifting sand bottom.

The Duke was no longer capable of any reaction. At dawn, it is said, when he was within hail of Oquendo, he had shouted across from the forecastle, in full hearing of two crews, 'Señor Oquendo, Señor Oquendo, we are lost! What are we to do?' Don Miguel shouted back angrily that he should ask Diego Flores . . . as for me, I intend to fight and die like a man.' It was the view of the pilots that 'in the present situation not a ship could be saved except by a miracle. . . . They would all run aground on the shoals and be pounded to pieces by the surf. It was only a matter of hours. . . .' The English must have shared this view. They turned back and beat windward to get away from the Armada and from the trap into which it was being pushed. As the minutes passed, the leadsmen's cries grew more alarmed. The *Trinidad Escala* had six fathoms of water under her keel, the *patrona* of the galleasses less than five. 'It was the most fearful day in the world,

97

for every man had lost all hope and waited only for death,' wrote Luis de Miranda.

'The Duke's officers,' wrote Calderon, 'gathered round him, beseeching him with tears in their eyes to take a pinnace and save himself and the Holy Banner from certain capture. The Duke refused and sent them back to their posts. . . .' But later it was put about at court that the Sidonia had 'offered a pilot 5,000 ducats to get him ashore safely in his pinnace, but the pilot refused . . .'.

The men on the ships most immediately threatened, confessed, took communion and prepared to die. Then at the very last minute, the leadsmen standing in the chains of the *capitana*, which drew four fathoms, had called six. 'It pleased God to change the wind to west-southwest which enabled the Armada to sail full North, without one ship having been damaged', wrote Calderon.

The miracle had happened. Now the Armada was standing away into deep water, its sails filled by a fair breeze. At 11 o'clock the ships started to reform. That evening Sidonia wrote in his *diario*, 'Only God could save us.'

Not all, however, were saved. The Captain General had to leave to the Dutch two crippled ships, the *San Mateo* and the *San Felipe*.

The Lord Admiral summoned his council. They reckoned up their losses. Hawkins reported little damage and Fenner only slight losses. The council considered their reserves of powder, which like their reserves of match and fuse, shot, victuals and beer, were virtually exhausted. Howard decided to send Seymour's and Wynter's squadrons to cruise off the Thames so as to block Parma if he risked coming out. Meanwhile the main body of the fleet, on empty stomachs and with their cannon reduced to impotence, would follow the Armada and prevent them from making a landing or even putting in along the east coast, or in Scotland, if that seemed to be their intention.

The Captain General, too, was holding a council, having summoned all the generals and Alonzo de Leiva to the flagship.

On balance, things looked black. The Duke lingered over the score: eight ships lost, including some of the best, and all the others damaged and making water. Almost all were short of shot. One man in five was dead, wounded or sick. And then there was the wind that was stopping them going back into the Channel for the rendezvous that they had failed to make. And still Parma was not ready. Would it not be wiser to go back via the North Sea? What did everyone think?

De Leiva gave his views:

You all know how I have given battle, I have now no more than thirty cannon ball, my ship is riddled with small shot, and pierced in several places. She is taking in water badly. But I do not consider any of this sufficient reason not to do my duty. I am not in favour of entering the North Sea.

Recalde suggested that they cruise locally for a few days, until the wind changed, and then return to Calais. An Andalusian captain declared that the time had passed for demonstrations of personal bravery. What they must consider now was what would be in the best interests of His Majesty. What if the enemy were to press hard upon them for three days, what would they do without any ammunition? De Leiva rejoined with a proposal that they sail to Norway for fresh supplies. The Duke objected to all these views. If the whole Armada spent the winter in enemy waters, and the English fleet was not destroyed, the coast of Spain would be without any defence. In the end all were agreed that they should return to the Channel as soon as the weather permitted. In his *diario* the Duke (who did not keep a record of council discussions) translated this as, 'The Council then unanimously agreed to return to the Channel, weather permitting. And if not, to go back to Spain via the North Sea. . . .' Then, making sure that he was covered, he continued:

> In matters of warfare I have in all things bowed to the opinion of Don Francisco de Bobadilla, a man of considerable experience, both at sea and on land, and in everything connected with the fleet and the sea. I have always bowed, too, to the opinion of Diego Flores de Valdez, the veteran amongst us, and to that of the two advisers appointed by His Majesty who were on the capitana.

On 10 August a steady sou'wester was blowing. They passed Dogger Bank on the 11th. On the 12th the English closed several times, but withdrew again as soon as the rearguard turned to face them. Howard feared that Sidonia might be seeking an anchorage where he could make good his defects and return to the battle. When he saw that the Armada had passed the Firth of Forth without showing any sign of attempting a landing, he realised that Sidonia was fleeing. The enemy fleet was returning to Spain by the northern route. (See page 25.)

Towards midday the Lord Admiral of England turned for home, leaving behind a pinnace and a caravel to shadow the enemy as far as the Orkneys and Shetlands.

The rendezvous had been missed. Philip's dream was turning to dust.

18
750 Leagues of Stormy Seas

That same day the Duke made the retreat official by handing out sailing orders to each ship's captain for the return of the fleet to Spain. The English later found a copy on a ship wrecked off the Irish coast.

> The course that is to be followed first is to the north-northeast, up to the latitude of $61\frac{1}{2}°$; you will take great care lest you fall upon the Island of Ireland, for fear of the harm that may befall you upon that coast. Then parting from these islands and rounding the Cape in $61\frac{1}{2}°$ you will run west-southwest until you are in latitude $58°$ and then southwest until $53°$; then south-southeast to Cape Finisterre and so you will procure your entrance into Corunna.

Purser Coco Calderon's reply to two captains who were uneasy about this circumnavigation, was that 'The return journey will indeed be one of the most difficult and arduous ever, for we shall have to sail round England, Scotland and Ireland through 750 leagues of stormy seas, virtually unknown to us. . . .' He might have added that no one had a chart or sailing directions for the route to be covered and that few of the pilots had ever been there before. And he was unaware of the fact that the charts of Ireland that some of the pilots had in their heads were dangerously inaccurate.

On the 13th rations were cut to half a pound of biscuits each, a pint of water and half a pint of wine. Most of the barrels had the worm in them (Drake again!); the staves had shrunk and warped, and the water had leaked, leaving only a couple of inches of slime at the bottom. The wine had soured in the butts.

The Duke ordered all horses and mules to be thrown overboard, in order not to have to water them. There were many hungry men who would have been only too happy to eat horse flesh, but orders were orders.

The first to desert had been some pressganged Dutch sailors who had gone over to the enemy. Then, once the English fleet was out of sight, the captains of two merchantmen chartered in the Hansa ports, sailed off home by night.

On 15 August, the Feast of the Assumption, three Scottish fishing boats were captured and their seamen held to serve as pilots.

Freezing fog on the 17th made it impossible to see from one ship to another. 'In latitude 62° it is not warm. I am shivering, for I left my coat behind on Pedro de Valdez's ship when by a miracle I managed to escape,' wrote de Gongora. It was very cold indeed for August. The negroes were the first to succumb and then it was the Andalusians and Sicilians who were suffering the most. Many men died of cold, for they were practically naked having sold what coverings they had for food or gambled them away. When the fog lifted there were several ships missing. The fleet did not wait for them. Then the wind changed. . . .

'We have decided to avoid the Norway Channel. Instead we shall sail between the Scottish Isles to shorten our journey, and also because we are suffering from a serious shortage of supplies,' wrote Sidonia to King Philip. In fact their course lay between Fair Isle and the Orkneys.

On 20 August, having rounded the Orkneys without mishap, the Duke sent Don Balthazar de Zuñiga on ahead in a fast *patache* to bring the King news of the disaster and to take him his *diario*.

Sick and morose, the Duke shut himself away from the rest of the world, handing over the command to Bobadilla, for many would have refused by now to take orders from Diego Florez. On 3 September, abeam of the Hebrides, he wrote to the King in an attempt to justify his failure.

It has pleased God to ordain things otherwise than we had hoped. This enterprise was fervently commended to Him, so it must be that what has happened was the right thing for Him and for Your Majesty. . . . The Armada was in such bad shape, that I considered the best way I could serve Your Majesty was by saving what was left of it, though it meant risking it in this long journey in such a latitude. Our best ships had no shot, and we had already seen how little could be expected of the rest. The Queen's fleet had shown itself vastly superior in battle, in tactics, in the range of its artillery, and in its manoeuvrability. So following the advice of the generals and of Your Majesty's appointed advisers, we set off on this course. We were driven to it also by the weather. The wind held first from the south then later from the south-west [the Duke seems to forget that the enemy sailed back to England on the same wind]. Since the 21st we have had four nights of storms, and seventeen ships have disappeared out of sight, including De Leiva's and Recalde's as well as some other important ones. . . . Today at latitude 58° we counted 95 ships. . . . 3,000 of the men are sick, not counting the large number of wounded, and many are dying.

Elsewhere, on the other ships, the situation was worse. Scurvied or doubled up with typhoid or food poisoning, the men '. . . were dying of a fine and malignant pestilence, and if any man fell sick only a miracle could save him.' Their stomachs empty and their throats dry, the sick lay one on top of another across sodden mattresses. In the bottom of the ships a fetid liquid stinking of excrement and vomit slopped about, floating with dead cockroaches and drowned, bloated rats. Rain and waves came through the gaping planks in the decks, streaming between the timbers and pouring out of the smashed gun-ports.

The *San Martín*, under the skilful guidance of her chief pilot, took only fifteen days to cover the 1500-mile return journey. For a ship 'whose mainmast was so badly damaged that it could no longer carry its canvas' this was not bad going. The heavy weather conditions made it impossible to take any astrolabe measurement of the height of the sun at midday, or even to see the North Star at night. The pilots were navigating by guesswork, not knowing where the current was taking them, and at the whim of the squalls, which often turned into storms. One such storm blew up on the 16th, 'the day we all thought to die'.

The Duke had enjoined everyone to avoid Ireland, 'for fear of the harm that may befall you upon that coast'. But for many captains, shortage of supplies left no alternative. Whatever the risk, they had to find food and drink and this meant that they had to land. Others, because of mistakes by their pilots, found cliffs suddenly looming across their bows where they had been expecting only the open seas.

Alonzo Martinez de Leiva sailed in a Genoese carrack, the rata Sancta Maria Encoronada, *taking with him all the young men of gentle birth in the fleet. (From an engraving by Breughel.) The ship ran aground in Blacksod Bay (in the background). Don Alonzo led all his men carrying their valuables and small arms safely ashore. They fortified themselves in Fahy Castle (Doona).*

With their personal belongings and their flags they put to sea again in the hulk Duquessa Santa Ana. (From an engraving by Breughel.) Driven north by the wind, they were forced to anchor in Loughross More Bay. The anchor dragged and they tried in vain to find a mooring on the rocky promontory (right). She ran aground on the sand (left of the photograph) in a storm.

ce more Don Alonzo led his people ashore, carrying their money and jewellery, and this time, an iron
nnon. They entrenched themselves in a ruined castle on an island in Kiltoorish Lake. I found the
non where de Leiva left it a few weeks later when he set off overland to Killybegs. There he put to sea
 the third time in the Girona taking with him the crews of all three ships along with their valuables.

llowing page: *in 1967, after 600 hours' research in the archives of five countries and an hour's
diving, I found the remains of the Girona. First a lead ingot, then two bronze cannon.*

Above: *Port na Spaniagh. The local name perpetuates the memory of the tragedy.* Below: *Four hundred years of storms had piled up most of the treasure into one cave.*

Photographer Marc Jasinski. He developed his own lenses and special corrective optical devices to work in the murky waters of the Atlantic.

After twelve years of repeated failures, I have at last found gold under the sea.

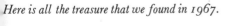

Here is all the treasure that we found in 1967.

Above: *1968: we were back in force with all the necessary equipment.*

Below: *Left to right: the author, Louis Gorsse, Maurice Vidal, Francis Dumont. Behind the Asahi Pentax, Marc Jasinski.*

19
The Return of the Armada

Tossed by the play of wind and waves, the bones of the old ships groaned pitifully. The ribs warped, splitting the sides and cracking the caulking. Day and night the steady creaking of the pumps never stopped.

By 18 September only sixty ships remained in the *capitana*'s wake. Then such a storm blew up that the Duke was left with a company of eleven.

On the 21st the *San Martín* sighted land one league away. It was Santander.

The galleon sailed up to the harbour bar, but had to wait until the following day's tide to enter. The Duke boarded the first launch to arrive and went ashore as fast as he could. 'I am so ill after twenty-five days of dysentery and fever that I am quite weakened and utterly indisposed,' he wrote. The Captain General was abandoning his fleet. his ship, his crew and his sick men. He was leaving behind, too, the Holy Banner that he had solemnly sworn, on the altar of Lisbon Cathedral, to defend with his life and personally return to the King. Shortly afterwards the wind freshened and carried the *San Martín* on. Diego Flores put her into Laredo.

Sidonia wrote to the King:

> The trials and miseries that we have suffered cannot be described. On one of the ships that put in here the crew had gone for fourteen days without a drop of water. On the capitana 180 died of disease, and the rest of the crew are seriously afflicted with contagious diseases and typhoid in particular. So many of my servants have died that I am left with only two. May the Lord be praised for all that he has ordained. . . . And now we are in even worse danger, for in a week nothing will be left of our meagre remains of biscuit and wine. May it please Your Majesty to send some money as soon as possible. We have not a maravedis between us. Oquendo has all the treasure with him . . . 55,000 escudos. . . . As for myself I have neither the health nor the head to cope with anything at all.

During the next few weeks sixty-five vessels put into the northern Spanish ports. One sank in harbour as soon as it arrived, another blew up, yet another ran aground at Laredo, because there was not a man on board with enough strength left to lower the sails or to cast anchor. Most of the ships were beyond repair. They were broken up for timber and firewood.

The Duke had set himself up in some comfort ashore, sufficiently far away from the men who were still on board, suffering variously from bronchitis, typhoid or dysentery. By 27 September he found himself so weak that he could neither hold a pen nor even move. He had to dictate this letter to the King's secretary:

> My health is not restored. I am good for nothing . . . and as for seafaring, never, for any reason whatsoever, or in any way at all, will I involve myself in it again, if it costs me my head. Even that would be preferable to me than failing properly to fulfil a mission about which I neither know nor understand anything and in which I am forced to turn for advice to men whose designs I know not. . . .

And he ended by begging the King, in the name of God, to be pleased to permit him to return home to San Lucar forthwith and without a moment's delay. Meanwhile, aboard their ships, Oquendo and Recalde were dying.

Medina Sidonia had returned 'white haired, having set out with a shock of raven black hair'. Shame and sickness had reduced him utterly. He passed whole days delirious with fever. Philip realised this. He wrote to him:

> I am distressed to learn that your ill health continues and since you say that it is necessary for your convalescence that you return to your estate to recover and regain your strength, since you are so insistent about it, I will agree to it as soon as you have made arrangements for the care of the sick . . . and you will leave orders that as soon as he arrives Alonzo de Leiva is to be appointed Commander in Chief . . . and you will make sure that everyone knows help is on the way and that any who tries to escape meanwhile will be severely punished. And you will make sure, too, that I am kept daily informed of developments.

The King was indeed kept informed. On 23 November Juan de Cardona reported:

> On every ship three or four men die each day. For 26 days the men have eaten nothing but mouldy chickpeas, with half a pint of water a day. Most of the men are naked or in rags and soaked to the skin, day and night. . . . The ships they are living in are filled with stench and wretchedness . . . 1,000 sick men in Santander alone. . . . Of our 18,000 soldiers, there are 5,000 alive now in our Galician ports.

De Leiva still had not returned, so it was Don Garcia de Villejo who took over from the Duke in Santander. On 30 September he wrote that the Duke had left that day, saying that he had no instructions to give. The state in which Sidonia left things compelled Garcia to tell the King what he thought of all this. Don Garcia did not mince his words, and he concluded: 'the Armada has ceased to exist'.

As soon as he had the royal permission safely in his pocket, the Duke had himself taken to his carriage. The leather blinds were pulled and he headed south with his men and 'twelve mules loaded with silver and ducats'. Insults and abuse followed him wherever he went. He was flagrantly reviled and greatly dishonoured. Children stoned him at Medina de Campo and at Salamanca.

There were after all 9,000 dead, 60 ships had been lost, and 1,400 million reals scattered to the winds. The whole of Spain was in mourning, Philip had to issue a special edict limiting the period of mourning to thirty days and restricting it to the immediate families of the men who had been lost. What was needed was someone to blame, a scapegoat. The finger pointed to one man above all others, a man hated equally by all and sundry; Diego Flores, of course. As the Duke was no longer good for anything, it was Flores who had been given the task of organising rescue operations in all northern ports and taking everything in hand. Just as soon as someone was found to replace him, he was dragged from Santander to Burgos castle, and there he was imprisoned. He stayed there fifteen months.

Sententious historians, particularly Spanish ones, have attributed any number of highly inspired historic pronouncements to the King on hearing the awful truth. In fact Philip said nothing. He shut himself away with his confessor. It was gossiped that he never got over it, nor ever regained his health; that he seldom went out again; that from that moment on he began to talk to himself. If none ever pierced the secrets of his soul, the front which Philip chose to present to the world appears in this letter of 13 October.

> Most Reverend Archbishop of our Council, we all know how unpredictable the sea is; the fate of the Armada bears witness to this . . . and we know, too, how we are bound to render thanks to God for all that He is pleased to do and for His mercy. I have therefore rendered up thanks to Him, for when one considers the storms and perils that this Armada encountered it would have been reasonable to have feared for it a fate worse than the one it met. I attribute this to your prayers and special orations, which can nevertheless now be discontinued.

The victorious English seamen had also returned. 'Most of our sailors are now seriously ill and some die every day. It is a veritable epidemic. It is reckoned that men newly recruited are infected the first day and dead by the second. Which means that many of our ships no longer have enough men even to weigh anchor. . . . Whole crews sicken each day,' wrote Hawkins to Burghley.

Typhus, scurvy, furunculosis, blood-poisoning, scabies, vermin, dysentery—officers and men alike put it all down to the 'bad beer'. The beer was sour indeed, and as Howard had once said, 'for my own part I know not which way to deal with the mariners to make them rest content with sour beer'. Neither can the diseases have been unconnected with conditions on board.

On the 18th Elizabeth received the following letter from Drake: 'We left the Spanish army so far to the north that they will no longer be able to make it back either to Scotland or to England. . . . Three days later a heavy storm . . . must have done them the greatest damage. . . .' Immediately the miserly Queen gave orders effectively to disband everyone, return the freighted ships and send her detailed accounts with all vouchers. Her privy councillors had the greatest difficulty in persuading her that the danger was not yet averted. As Howard wrote, it was still possible that the Armada would reform in Norway, Denmark or the Orkneys and return to rendezvous with Parma. To please the Queen the Lord Treasurer suggested that it might be possible now to economise on the pay of those who had been killed in battle or discharged, and to use this money to pay the others what they were owed. With great firmness, John Hawkins reminded him that in all justice and equity the dead men's pay belonged to their widows and their dependents.

As soon as news reached London that the Armada had rounded the Orkneys, the Queen prevailed. Crews were demobilised, but without pay. They were to be seen wandering the streets of Margate, Dover, Harwich and Rochester, starving, penniless and begging. They slept in the gutters, or after Howard had taken things in hand, on the bare earth in barns and hovels. It was the Lord Admiral who wrote, 'It would grieve any man's heart to see them that have served so valiantly to die so miserably.' It was he too who paid them, out of his own pocket.

20
'But Where is De Leiva?'

Half the Armada had not returned. Worst of all, Alonzo de Leiva and his noble company had not returned. In every palace in Spain a husband was awaited, a son or a nephew. Day and night families scanned the horizon in every Galician, Asturian and Biscayan port. Envoys ran to meet every ship they sighted, inquiring anxiously, 'Don Alonzo? Where is Don Alonzo?' The answer was always the same. The *rata* had been lost from sight 'following a very heavy storm, that lasted from 2 o'clock in the afternoon until 10 o'clock the next morning'.

This was the storm of 10 September, one that had also wrought havoc on the Irish mainland. That day, according to a letter of Edward Whyte's, 'there blew a most extreme wind and cruel storm, the like thereof has not been seen or heard a long time'. This storm and that of 20 September cost the life of nearly 3,000 Spaniards.

Philip learned nothing more of De Leiva from the copy he received in the Escurial of 'Certain advertisements out of Ireland concerning the losses and distresses happened to the Spanish Navy upon the West Coast of Ireland. . . .' In twelve quarto pages he found only one reference. Emmanuel Fremoza, a seaman off the *San Juan* of Portugal, captured and questioned in Ireland, had apparently given some rather confused information which was summed up as follows:

> But he saith, there was a great Prince, an Italian, that was a Chief Man in a great Argosy, very well furnished, who, before their coming to the English Coast, did very often banquet the Duke and the other great men of the Navy. This Argosy was called the Ratte. He saith he did not perceive if this ship were in this fleet, the day before, the said tempest or not . . . but he saith, this being a famous ship, it was often demanded if she were in their company, and it was answered that she was.

It was around 58° N that De Leiva had lost contact with the fleet. With her poorly repaired mainstays his ship could no longer carry even half her canvas. The storm reopened old wounds. Through the holes in her hull, patched up with lead and tow after the battle, and through the gaps between her timbers, she was taking more water than the crew could pump out, though they worked day and night.

Alonzo de Leiva had personally supervised the victualling, and though there was rationing on board, no one was starving. They were resisting sickness better than crews elsewhere in the fleet. They were, however, running short of fresh water.

Don Alonzo considered that his carrack would never reach Spain, so he set sail for the coast, counting on the Irishmen aboard to get him safely into port and to make sure he got help from the Catholic princes. Maurice Fitzgerald, son of the 'late arch-traitor Fitzmaurice' as the English called him (in other words, the hero of the Resistance), was on board, as were several Irish pilots, various monks and shavelings, and the Bishop of Killaloe. Maurice Fitzgerald never saw his homeland again; he died forty leagues out at sea.

On 17 September the *Santa Maria Encoronada* entered Blacksod Bay, north of Achill Island (County Mayo) and found an anchorage northwest of Fahy. There with due ceremony Fitzgerald's remains were cast to the waves in a cypress wood coffin. (See page 103.)

Stealing each other's lands, wives and livestock, and then massacring each other over them, was a traditional pursuit of Irish chieftains. Their other main activity, for the last four hundred years (since 1167, to be precise, when Henry II had sent over the vanguard of colonisers) was fighting the English invader. Dublin fell in 1170. It was to remain English for 750 years. Year after year, in spite of continual wars, countless coalitions, countless revolts and massacres, countless violated treaties and broken promises, countless defeats and countless victories, the English colonisers went on establishing themselves in town after town and in county after county. Using cold steel and a carefully organised state of permanent famine, they drove out or exterminated the native Gaelic population.

On the accession of the Tudors the English administration already had a firm hold on most of Leinster (the southwest quarter of the island) and partial control of the west. The north was still free.

Henry VIII established a Church of Ireland and put himself at the head of it, and then declared himself King of Ireland, a fictitious kingdom, legitimised by the Pope in 1555 for Henry's daughter, Mary Tudor.

The better to secure this new throne, Mary had as many title deeds as were necessary drawn up for the crown and everywhere set up English and Welsh 'planters' who coolly turned out the legal (according to Irish law) occupants. Plantation became a regular policy in 1556. It was pursued by Elizabeth (and those who came after her) who sent in large reinforcements of Protestant colonists.

To govern this kingdom, the English monarchy appointed a local Lord Deputy, responsible to the Privy Council in London, from whom he received his instructions. In 1588 the post of Lord Deputy, based at

Dublin Castle, was held by Sir William Fitzwilliam, ex-Treasurer at War, ex-Lord Justice, and now a sick old man. Like everyone else in Ireland, he knew nothing at that stage of the outcome of the Enterprise of England, but he did feel threatened because Spain had always been the ultimate hope of the Irish Catholic resistance. The Irish waited for the King of Spain's armies to land much as they might have awaited the Messiah.

Spanish ships had already arrived once, bearing the papal banner, and Don Martinez de Recalde had landed his troops. But there were too few of them—600 badly equipped men. They had been surrounded and captured at Smerwick before any of the armed Irish could reach them. The English had massacred their prisoners down to the last man.

And now rumours were rife in London and Dublin. According to some spies, one section of the Armada was going to take Ireland; according to others the whole fleet was coming to winter there before launching an assault on England in the spring.

The task of the Lord Deputy had been becoming increasingly difficult over the last twenty years. The old Gaelic chieftains were permanently in a state of revolt against English tyranny, but now there was the added problem of the 'Old English'. These were the descendants of the early British settlers who were now being threatened by a new wave of adventurers like Sir Peter Carew and Sir Walter Raleigh, Protestant speculators protected by Elizabeth. James Fitzmaurice was leading this second rebellion, which had the support of the nationals. Having crushed the uprising, the English had gone on systematically to burn or massacre the wives, children and families of the men they had killed on the battlefield. Scorched earth was all that was left of Munster. In 1583 the last remaining strongholds of resistance were destroyed in another blood bath. And now rumour had it that the young Maurice Fitzgerald, the rebel's own son, was in the Armada.

Towards the middle of September 'great ships' were sighted off the West coast of Ireland. Driving their horses for all they were worth, messengers were arriving from 'O'Dogherty Land', from the coast of Donegal, from Sligo, Galway and the mouth of the Shannon, in fact from all round the coast, with the same news. A state of panic overtook the local officials. The Lord Deputy could not sleep for worry. Was this the Armada come from the Channel? Had it not been defeated after all, not sunk, not destroyed? Or was this another invasion fleet, attacking on a second front?

Seven ships had been sighted at Carrigfoyle. In a mad panic, the Mayor of Limerick hurriedly wrote to the Council that seven squadrons had been sighted. Twenty-four men had landed at Tralee. Fitzwilliam informed London of the arrival of twenty-four galleons.

117

The Governor of Connaught, Sir Richard Byngham, an old soldier who had at various times fought both with and against the Spanish, sent for powder, lead and match. He also thought it 'very convenient to levy a band of footmen of this country people . . . to prevent their going away to the enemy . . . them being idle men . . .'. There were grave doubts as to whether the country would be true to the English or not.

These doubts were not entirely unfounded. The Lord Deputy did not conceal from the Privy Council the fact that they had 'neither men, money, nor munitions to answer these extraordinary services' . . . nor that 'there are not 750 foot in bands in the whole realm. . . . We cannot imprest the few soldiers for the shoeing of their horses. . . . We look rather to be overrun by the Spaniards than otherwise'. The Queen immediately issued orders for 700 soldiers to be levied in England and vessels armed to send them to him.

Then little by little the authorities began to find out what sort of state these 'great ships' were in, and how dying men littered their decks. The twenty-four men who had landed at Tralee were some of Medina Sidonia's men who had survived the wreck of a small frigate. Half dead already, they begged for mercy, promised ransoms, pleaded for their lives. Sir Edward Denny had every one of them put to the sword. 'Fear and weakness could not afford to be magnanimous,' wrote the English historian, Froude, much later.

Recalde anchored by Dingle Bay, the most sacred spot of the Catholic resistance, the very spot where eight years earlier the ill-fated liberation forces had landed. All that was left on board on the *almiranta* were '25 pipes of wine, and very little bread, and no water, but what they brought out of Spain, which stinketh marvellously; and their flesh meat they cannot eat, their drouth is so great.' On the 15th, the Admiral sent his launch ashore with the eight strongest men in the ship. Just to look at these fleshless sailors, at their wretched appearance, and to listen to their appalling stories, spoke volumes on the state of the King's fleet. The Catholic cause was losing . . . definitely losing. The soldiers of the Crusade asked for water and the Irish threw them into prison, seized their boats, and not long afterward cut their throats. Recalde set sail again, with 100 sick men (out of 500). Four or five were dying every day of hunger and thirst.

The *Nuestra Señora de la Rosa*, in her turn, came in by Dingle in Blaskets Sound. On board, out of 700 men, 200 were still on their feet. They cast the last anchor. It dragged in the changing tide, and the galleon was thrown onto a hidden reef and split open. She went down leaving only one survivor.

The seven Spanish ships anchored in the mouth of the Shannon sent their boats in to fetch water at Kilrush, flying a white flag at the

With our metal detector, we were able to spot artifacts hidden under sand and pebbles. Later we went through it grain by grain, using a high-pressure water jet, connected to a surface pump, to remove sterile fresh deposits.

It was Marc who found the anchor under a camouflage of seaweed and a crust of assorted marine life. We used a large lifting balloon to float it and towed it to Port Ballintrae.

prow. There were no English troops at Kilrush, but 400 years of informing and massacres had bred fear of repression, and it prevailed there
too The authorities refused the Spanish permission to land.
They pleaded for a 'barrel of water against one of wine' or as much
gold as they wanted. They offered the Sheriff of Clare a great ship
complete with rigging and guns, in exchange for being allowed to fill
their cask. The Sheriff refused all their offers. The galleass *Zuñiga*
tried to land a few tottering men by force, but they were repelled
empty-handed. There was nothing for it but to set out to sea again,
into the storm.

At Galway harbour, Don Luis de Cordoba put ashore a party of
shivering skeletons. They were immediately taken prisoner, before his
very eyes. Don Luis offered to give himself up in exchange for a promise
of safety for his companions. The Mayor accepted on condition that
they first hand over their arms. But while this was going on the towns-
people were already throwing themselves onto the first prisoners,
tearing off their gold chains, their doublets and their shirts. 'Weigh
anchor', ordered Cordoba, 'we're leaving.' The seamen collapsed at
the capstan. The Mayor sent out fishermen to take the ship, and had
the noblemen and mariners taken to the castle. They were so weak
'they could not swallow what food they were given, but vomited it
straight away.' Don Luis was spared in the hope of a ransom. The
others were shot or hanged along with some hundreds of other survivors taken in County Clare and Connemara.

Don Pedro de Mendoza, leaving his fast sinking ship, put ashore at
Clare Island, carrying his treasure chests. The storm of the 20th finally
put an end to his galleon and to those who were still struggling to
repair the damage and pump her out. The local chieftain, Dowdarra
O'Maillie, massacred all 100 of them and seized their very considerable
treasure, before Don Pedro could lay hands on his curraghs (light
boats of leather stretched over a wooden frame).

One galleon ran aground on the sand near Burrishole. Two hundred
Spaniards were thrown onto the sand by the waves, shivering and
exhausted. The local Irish rushed up and battered them to death for
the sake of their shirts and their boots.

And false rumours too were rife in the country. Medina Sidonia was
reported shipwrecked. The Duke of Ormond issued immediate orders
that Sidonia be carefully guarded but not put in irons and that he be
allowed to ride his own horse. Another rumour had it that he had died
in the great ship that had set out from Torane. Elsewhere they had
found the dead body of Recalde, then the body of Prince Ascoli.

The storm of 20th threw three Spanish ships onto the sand between
Sligo and Ballyshannon and pounded them to pieces. 'When I was at
Sligo, I numbered on one strand of less than five miles in length, 1,100
dead bodies of men which the sea had driven upon the shore. The

country people told me the like was in other places, though not to the like number,' wrote Fenton to Burghley. Fitzwilliam, too, went to see the bay where some of those ships were wrecked;

> and where, as I heard, lay not long before, twelve or thirteen hundred of the dead bodies. I rode along upon that strand near two miles but left behind me a long mile or more and then turned off from the shore leaving before me a mile and better; in both which places they said they had seen it, there lay as great store of the timber of wrecked ships as was in that place which myself had viewed being in my opinion more than would have built five of the greatest ships that I ever saw.

In the letters that were reaching Dublin from all around the coast, one finds the same story repeated time and again until October: Two ships lost with a 1,000 men; 140 Spaniards came ashore and were cut down with sabres; 300 Spaniards landed and were rightly put to the sword—and so on, day after day. Those were the orders. Feeding the mariners would have been expensive, and once back on their feet they would have constituted a dangerous threat.

The danger averted, Fitzwilliam countermanded the troops promised by the Queen. 'Since it hath pleased God by His hand upon the rocks to drown the greater and better sort of them [the Spaniards] I will, with his favour, be His soldier for the despatching of those ragges which yet remain. . . .'

Sir George Carew, Master of Ordnance in Ireland, estimated on 28 September that 3,000 Spaniards who came to land by swimming were slain, besides 2,000 drowned between Lough Foyle and the Dingle. Fenton was inclined to reckon 16 ships lost and 5,394 drowned, killed or captured. Richard Byngham put the figure at 4,600 drowned and claimed to have been personally responsible for hanging or cutting the throats of 1,100 survivors. On mature reflection he subsequently modified his estimate: 15 or 16 ships and 6–7,000 dead, of whom 7–800 were killed either by him or by his brother. Thus he reported to the Lord Deputy, and continued, clearly rather pleased with himself: 'having made a clean dispatch of them, both in town and country, we rested Sunday all day, giving praise and thanks to Almighty God for Her Majesty's most happy success and deliverance from her dangerous enemies.

As for the Irish peasants, they had brained or battered to death between 2,000 and 3,000 and stripped and robbed many more. A certain Nicholas Kahane, reporting to the Mayor of Limerick on the 22nd, desires him 'to content this bearer of 40 tescons for by much ado I could get him to go there, for all men be about those ships that be lost. . . . I will never have none to send Your Worship if that you do not consider this boy'. And a survivor of one of the Sligo wrecks wrote:

Whenever one of our men set foot on the shore, two hundred savages and other enemies surrounded him, stripped him naked, ill-treating him and wounding him without pity. . . . I passed many Spaniards stark naked and shivering with the cold. . . . There were more than six hundred dead bodies cast up by the sea which the crows and wolves would devour pitilessly. . . . It is the custom of these savages to live like wild beasts. . . . There is neither order nor justice in this country. . . .

Edward Whyte writes, 'They were so miserably distressed coming to land that one man, named Melaghlin M'Cabbe killed 80 with his gallowglass axe.'* Fitzwilliam could write jubilantly: 'Don Luis de Cordoba (he was a prisoner) blames the Irish for letting the Spaniards range up and down the country after they had stripped them of their apparel and robbed them of their money and jewels.' And he concluded, on the basis of the evidence that he had, that sixteen of the fifty-nine ships sighted had been lost and that 8,000 Spaniards had met their death on the North and West coasts. This calculation did not include either the prisoners at Dingle, nor those ships that were lost at sea and whose crews had the good fortune simply to drown, nor did it include the 1,300 dead still to come on the *Girona* or those in a hospital ship that sank later on the Devon coast. (See page 68.)

---

* The Gallowglasses were champion fighters grouped together in special units.

21

Alonzo De Leiva's First Shipwreck

Don Alonzo, in the *rata*, had anchored in Blacksod Bay and sent Giovanni Avancini ashore with fourteen men to fetch water and parley with the locals. This was MacWilliam country and the local

MAP 2

THE THREE SHIPWRECKS OF DON ALONZO DE LEIVA

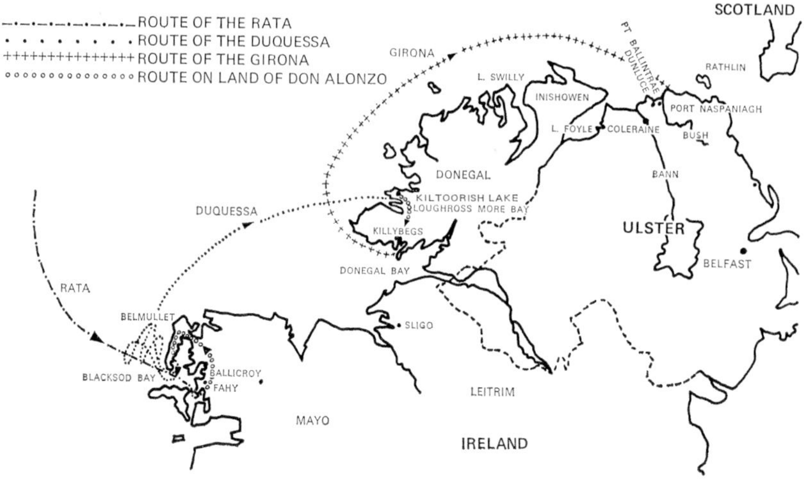

—·—·—·—·—·—·— ROUTE OF THE RATA
· · · · · · · · ROUTE OF THE DUQUESSA
+++++++++++++++ ROUTE OF THE GIRONA
○○○○○○○○○○○○○○ ROUTE ON LAND OF DON ALONZO

industry was piracy. It was not long before they encountered the leader of a small gang, Richard Burke, known as the 'Devil's Hook' or the 'Devil's Son'. He stripped them bare and kept them prisoner.

Bryan na Murtha O'Rourke of Breffni was the guiding spirit of Irish resistance in Connaught. As soon as he heard what had happened, he came to their rescue, and apologised profusely. Not long afterward Governor Byngham, who complained that he could never get O'Rourke to pay the 'Queen's rent' reported on 10 October that

'. . . Certain Spaniards, being stript were relieved by Sir Brian O'Rourke, apparelled and new furnished with weapons.' When the patrol did not return, the captain of the *rata*, Francisco Vidal, sent some seamen ashore astride empty barrels to rescue the launch. The following day a storm broke from the West.

The *rata* or carrack was a characteristic Mediterranean merchant-man. A huge, pot-bellied tub, out of which rose the high, solid walls of the square fore and aftercastles. The design had not changed since the fifteenth century, when the Genoese carracks first plied the seas to and from the Hansa ports. To convert the *rata* into a warship, thirty-five gunports had been opened in her sides and the heaviest available guns placed in them. A floating fortress of that sort was impossible to take by boarding, but it was incapable of sailing into the wind and was difficult to manoeuvre in battle as it was to anchor. Being without any shelter, the carrack, whose high castles presented such an area to the wind, quickly dragged her anchor, struck bottom and ran firmly aground on a gently sloping beach.

Perfected over the years, the English intelligence system was highly efficient. As early as the 22nd Edward Whyte, a member of the Council of Connaught, was writing to his brother, Stephen, an alderman in Limerick that there was a ship of 900 tons, 'cast upon the sands at Ballycrouhie; 13 of their gentlemen are taken, the rest . . . to the number of 400 are come to land and fortify at Ballycrouhie'. He meant near Ballycroy, which is inland. More precisely it was at Doona.

Once the storm died down Don Alonzo had in fact gone ashore with all his men, in good order. He fired the wreck and crossed the beach to a small fortress close to the water's edge. There he entrenched himself.

Nearly four hundred years later I followed in his footsteps along this path, a moving pilgrimage. I had seen Blacksod Bay for the first time under a sky that managed to be blue and white and grey all at once. Here was the Ireland of the picture postcards: a lake edged with golden sand, gleaming pebbles and all around lush fields cut across by dry stone walls, and everywhere sheep grazed the lush green grass. I revisited the bay in September and then another year in October, under the same stormy squalls that must have frozen Don Alonzo and his noble young company, in the same torrential rain that covered the peat bogs under heavy floods. I followed his steps from the beach, where the great ship left her bones, to Doona (Fahy) Castle; only one corner of a tower and bits of a wall are left now, and a local peasant has leaned his pigsty against it. I stood dreaming for a long time as I ran my hand over the stones where he had perhaps put his.

De Leiva did not stay long at Doona. Just before the storm he had sighted another Spanish ship coming in to land. She had gone further north, to a sheltered cove of the vast bay, and anchored 'at Pollilly by Torane' (now Tirawn), in fact in Elly Cove, a very safe anchorage.

They must have had some fishermen aboard who knew the coast well (a 1572 report to the Queen mentions a Spanish fishing fleet, 600 strong around the South and West coasts of Ireland as well as several permanent establishments). De Leiva made contact. It was the *Duquessa Santa Ana*, a 900-ton hulk from the Andalusian squadron, having 23 guns and carrying 280 soldiers and 77 sailors.

The Governor of Connaught was a busy man. Byngham was virtually living in the saddle, riding up and down the coast from castle to castle on the lookout for any information, and writing letter after letter to Walsingham to keep him up to date. On 24 September, Sir Richard learned from a local official by the name of Comerford that '. . . the 600 Spaniards who were at Ballycrauhie were conveyed to the castle of Torane, a very strong place, and there joined with 800 more who came out of another great ship which lay at anchor in the road of Torane . . .' De Leiva had just joined the captain of the *Duquessa*, Don Pedro Mares, and his crew on the Mullet Peninsula. Together they were now occupying a castle in Elly Cove.

It was in the summary of the examination of a sailor of the *Duquessa*, which was later abandoned, that I found details of these events. It ran as follows:

> The examination of James Machary of the Cross (within the County of Tipperary) taken before the Lord Deputy—He said he was imprest at Lisbon and put into a Flemish hulk called St Ann. . . . After the fight in the Narrow Seas, she fell upon the coast of Ireland in a Haven . . . where they found a great ship called the Rat in which was Don Alonso de Leva and . . . above 700 men. After she perished, Don Alonso and all his company were received into the hulk of St Ann with all the goods they had in the ship of any value, as plate, apparel, money, jewels, weapons and armour, leaving behind them victual, ordnance and much other stuff which the hulk was not able to carry away.

It seemed quite clear to the 'Devil's Son' and his acolytes, that they had a natural right to this 'stuff which the hulk was not able to carry away'. Gerald Comerford, who was keeping an eye on the ship anchored at Pollilly, had other ideas. He had not even received any orders, but he was a good civil servant and he did not doubt that there was every good reason why the rightful place for the Spanish spoils was in Her Majesty's coffers. So he put an armed guard on the half burnt wreck of the *rata*. By 23 September he had grown somewhat weary of this and had to admit to Byngham:

> The Ship that is here aground is well stored of great pieces and other munition, wine and oil and many other things under water. Here are

no boats able to come by them, neither is it possible to take anything of great value out of the same as yet. . . . But James Blake, Ferriegh McTyrrell, Richard Iccoggy, MoylMory M'Ranyll, Marcus Roe M'-Tyriell and Thomas Burke M'Niabbe took out of the wreck a boat full of treasure, cloth of gold, velvet etc. . . . I pray your Lordship that if they be taken they may be put up safe and not bailed . . . as we wish to charge them with disloyalty for they have disobeyed commandments given them in writing and beaten and wounded our people.

Byngham was more concerned about what Don Alonzo was intending to do. What if he was planning to conquer the province himself with his 1,500 men? What if the local Irish were to join him? He certainly did not rush to attack them, but he did ask the Lord Deputy for two bands of foot soldiers to help him take Torane castle and oppose the enemy in all future enterprises. Byngham had asked the Lord Deputy for reinforcements sufficiently often to know that he ran no risk of getting them, or of having to encounter any able-bodied Spanish soldiers. His messenger set off at a gallop and had been gone barely two hours when Comerford sent him word that: 'The ship that was at Pollilly, by Torane, has sailed . . . towards the south-west . . . taking the company that was wrecked . . . with bags and baggage. . . .' Behind them the Spanish left a much relieved Governor and a tradition that is still alive today.

On 11 October the Governor wrote to the Lord Deputy:

And touching the ordnance and other munitions lost here, all diligence shall be used to save as much as may be for Her Majesty's use, but the great ship at Ballycro . . . is now all broken in pieces and the ordnance and everything else utterly lost I fear me. Treasure and great wealth hath been taken no doubt, but that by such unworthy persons as it will hardly be ever any thereoff come by at all.

In Blacksod Bay, some local peasants pointed out to me the spot where the carcass of the 'great ship from Spain' had gradually buried itself in the sand. As late as 1900 people were still taking timbers from it at the low spring tides, and in 1906 the Chief Inspector of Irish Fisheries recorded that 'he had secured one of her frame timbers of Italian oak, burnt off at one end . . .'

22

De Leiva's Second
Shipwreck

Leaving the bay, the *Duquessa Santa Ana* had been badly shaken in the
heavy swell. Hulks such as the *Duquessa* were the direct descendants of
that medieval vessel, the *nao*: transport ships of enormous capacity,
high of freeboard and shallow in draught, with a rounded bow and a
high, narrow poop. These ships were slow and unwieldy to manoeuvre.
(See page 104.) For two days and two nights the *Duquessa Santa
Ana* had to tack from Inishkea to Erris Head, rolling badly and
making hardly any headway. On the 27th Byngham learned from
Comerford that 'one of the great ships which lay before Torane was
driven back with a contrary wind, but afterwards put to sea again'.

Out in the open sea again, the *Duquessa* met repeatedly shifting
winds. They had to run northwards for a whole night, and then do so
again, 'in which course by a contrary wind they were driven back
upon M'Sweeney Ne Doe's country to a place called Lougherris,
where failing to anchor, there fell a great storm which broke in sunder
all their cables'. So reported James Machary.

Juan De Nova and Francisco De Barja, two seamen from the *Trinidad Valencera*, later gave further details as related to them by one of the
survivors. Rearranging these details in the only order that makes
sense according to the map, it appears that the force of the current
caused the cable of the hulk's only anchor to part. They managed to
pass a mooring line ashore and make it fast to a rock. The current,
however, drove the vessel aground, and seeing what condition she was
in, all hands decided to go ashore, taking with them some food, some
ammunition, and a piece of ordnance.

Carrying their jewel boxes under their arms, De Leiva and his young
noblemen waded in to a beach on the north coast of Loughros More
Bay, near Rossbeg, with some 800 men. (Tradition thereabouts has it
that until the last century, at very low tide and when the sea was
particularly clear, one could still make out the timbers of the hull
coming just level with the sand.) They climbed onto a sand-dune and
from there they saw O'Boyle Island, rising sheer out of the middle of
Kiltoorish Lake, and on the island a castle built of large flat stones.
(See page 105.) There, near the ship, they camped for the space of

eight or nine days. Don Alonzo sent Father James ne Dowrough, an Irish monk, with a message for the local chieftain McSweeney ne Doe, one of O'Neil's vassals, who welcomed them most warmly. News of this soon reached Walsingham in London.

The Lord Deputy organised a new expedition to oust them. His spies, who were acting as double agents, lost no time in informing McSweeney who, in turn, informed Don Alonzo. Meanwhile the Spanish had discovered that the galleass *Girona* was at anchor further down the coast and they went to find her. De Leiva was carried in a sedan-chair. Before he landed, his leg was injured by the capstan of the ship so badly that he was able neither to walk nor ride.

A galleass! It must have been Heaven sent! The four galleasses of the Neapolitan squadron were renowned throughout the Armada. During the battle they had always been in the thick of every action, more conspicuous for the courage of their men, as it turned out, than for their success. They had not managed to repeat their earlier victorious intervention at Lepanto. With eighteen oars on each side and a rather slender hull, with two castles, and a very high freeboard, they were a cross between a galley and a galleon. They were decked vessels about 150 ft long with three fixed masts, carrying square sails on foremast and mainmast and a gaff-rigged lateen on the mizzen. 'The galleasses,' writes the historian Leti, 'were strikingly beautiful and ornate, with their cabins, towers, chapels and pulpits.' We know that there were carved figures on the castles, the prow and the sides and large ornate lanterns above the stern. The officers had their quarters in the aftercastle, where there was either a tent or a sumptuously decorated cabin, and hung inside with velvet or tapestries, and lit by stained-glass windows, with a large lantern in the ceiling. Pennants and banners fluttered at all points. In port dinner was taken on board to musical accompaniment. The table plate, candlesticks, knives and forks were gold-plated. The officers were bedecked with chains and jewels; their evening dress was a velvet doublet and satin breeches. Things were different for the galley slaves, and the soldiers; they dressed at their own expense as best they could, when they happened to be paid.

There are a number of contemporary engravings of Armada galleasses. Some show fantasy ships, while others simply depict large galleys. There does however exist a set of engravings by John Pine, which give what is probably an accurate portrayal of vessels such as the *Girona* and the other galleasses. These engravings, made in 1739, are an exact copy of the famous tapestries that hung in the House of Lords until the fire of 1834. (See pages 28 and 67.) The tapestries were made by Francis Spiernig around 1589 (for a fee of £1,628) from cartoons by Cornelis de Vroom, an outstanding painter of naval subjects, who worked from the original plans and sketches that Lord Howard of Effingham had given him. It was the Lord Admiral himself who commissioned the tapestries. He later sold them to James I, and they were already hanging at Westminster in 1650. For such a client de Vroom would certainly have paid great attention to the likeness. (His fee was 100 gold crowns.)

When she left Lisbon, the *Girona* carried a crew of 121—22 officers, 2 mates, 39 gunners, 10 helmsmen, 27 able seamen, 21 sailors and ship's boys. There were 244 rowers: 161 convicts, 15 slaves and 68 volunteers (*bonevoglies*). The captains, Gonzalo Beltran and Antonio de Silva, had embarked their companies, 76 men and 110 men respectively—arquebusiers and pikemen.

The ordnance consisted of 50 bronze pieces: 6 cannon, 2 demi-cannon, 4 demi-culverins, 8 periers, 6 sakers, 4 demi-sakers and 20 esmerils, and the ammunition of 400 50-lb balls, 400 35-lb balls, 400 25-lb balls, 316 16-lb balls, 450 15-lb balls, 400 12-lb balls, 1,200 6-lb balls, 800 4-lb balls, 2,000 3-lb balls and 1,000 1-lb balls, plus 800 stone balls, adding up to a total of 8,166 rounds.

When the *Girona* left Naples she had 200 quintals* of gunpowder, 3 quintals of refined powder for use in the touch-holes, 12 quintals of match, and 30 quintals of lead for casting more cannon balls in England. At Lisbon they took on a further 208 quintals† of powder and 65 of match.

The provisions consisted of 750 *bizcoches*, 100 butts of wine, 62·5 quintals of bacon and the same amount of cheese, 60 barrels of tuna fish, 40 barrels of sardines, and 15 quintals of rice, as well as beans and dried vegetables, raisins, oil, vinegar, sugar, salt and semolina.

A ship as powerful as the *Girona* inspired confidence in those who sailed in her.‡

When he set out to join the *Girona*, De Leiva left behind the piece of artillery mentioned by the two seamen, De Nova and De Boja. In 1968, I found it. Nothing remained of its wooden carriage, and it sat directly on the ground, on the very edge of the southeast slope of O'Boyle Island, forty paces from the castle ruins and still levelled on the narrow strip of land that leads to the island. It is a falcon, a small, cast-iron gun, wider at the breech with the reinforcement shrunk on there, and with a long, conical cascabel button.

The gun is typical of the period. (Identical pieces have been found recently in Bermuda on a wreck of 1595.) I photographed it, measured

---

* One quintal = 100 Neapolitan pounds. One Neapolitan pound = 891 grams.
† These were Castilian quintals each of 46 kilograms.
‡ See Appendix II for further details on galleasses.

it, and drew up an exact plan. No other iron cannon from the Invincible Armada was then known to exist anywhere in the world, and for 400 years this irreplaceable relic had been rusting away in the salt spray and slowly disintegrating, in the very spot where De Leiva left it. Shortly after I revealed the existence of this cannon by publishing a photograph of it in the *National Geographic Magazine*, it was bought from the local farmer and taken away. (See Appendix III for a plan of the gun.)

Carried at the head of his small army, Don Alonzo followed the coast, cutting across rivers and peat bogs. Some of McSweeney's envoys guided them from Ardara southwards along the pass leading directly through the valleys to Killybegs. Nowadays the T72/road follows the same route except that it avoids the old, stony, winding stretches where the four men carrying De Leiva in his makeshift chair must more than once have stumbled.

23
De Leiva's Third Shipwreck

This stony path followed the Stragar valley across McSweeney ne Bannagh's fief and led straight to Killybegs, a very safe harbour in McSwyne's bay, on the North side of Donegal Bay. The Spanish sailors knew the locality well; fishing smacks and merchant ships often put in there.

There were Spanish sailors over the whole area. They gave De Leiva a triumphant reception. Apart from the *Girona*, one of the four galleasses of the squadron of Naples and two other small ships had arrived at almost the same time. One ran onto the rocks just outside the harbour and as the other seemed in imminent danger of sinking, her crew had run her aground in the port.

Under its soft grey light, Killybegs still retains much of its old charm. A little way away from the modern jetty where the trawlers moor, I found the old, worn, stone quays, now lying above the high water mark. I do not know if they really were there in Don Alonzo's time, but the gulls crying plaintively as they circled over me must have circled in much the same way over his tent. Dotted around in the black sludge of the disused docks I could see the carcasses of wooden ships sinking from view. . . . Under that compost of old rope, dead seaweed and rotting fish, could one of those skeletons have been the second of the smaller Spanish vessels—perhaps the deepest of all?

Carpenters were busy taking timbers and iron fittings off the beached vessel. They would use her steering gear and rigging to repair the *Girona*, which was in poor shape and rudderless. McSweeney helped by lending them his boats and giving them a pinnace to break up the timbers. He also managed to get together some victuals of sorts for them.

It was not long before all this reached the ears of the Lord Deputy:

The Spaniards from the two ships wrecked off M'Sweeney Banagh's country have joined those in M'Sweeney ne Doe's; M'Sweeney fears to hunger his country; The Spaniards are buying garrons and mares for food; The Spaniards in M'Sweeney ne Doe's country have repaired one ship.

And James Machary later testified that Don Alonzo and all his company encamped twelve to fourteen days, in which time the galleass was finished and made ready for the sea as well as she could be. De Leiva knew that the Lord Deputy was preparing to move against them. It was nearly a month now since Don Alonzo had moved ashore and time was short. He had been thinking. Before setting sail again there were two decisions he had to make—where to go, and who to take with him.

First, where to go? To try to get back to Spain would be mad. The head wind was still holding and showed no signs of changing. Winter was coming and the ship was not in any fit state to withstand a week of bad weather, let alone two or three. So Don Alonzo issued orders to return by Cape Clear, 'thinking that like that they might reach Scotland, where they would find help'. Cape Clear was a fantasy. The Spanish were ill-informed and had inaccurate maps, and this was a figment of their imagination. What they thought they were referring to was the westernmost point of Ireland. Actually they called virtually every single headland in the island, Cape Clear one after another. In this case 'Cape Clear' must have referred to the Bloody Foreland.

The West of Scotland was Catholic. The nobility there had close links with France and the Guises. During the whole episode of the Armada the young King James had remained irreproachably neutral. He listened impartially to his Catholic lords. The Duke of Parma had sent them 13,000 crowns in May, care of the Earl of Morton and Colonel Semple, in order that they should occupy a Scottish port and prepare to invade England when the time came. With the same grace he greeted Elizabeth's promises in August: if he stayed out of it he would get a pension of £5,000 a year, a dukedom in England, and enough to support a guard of more than 50 gentlemen and another of 100 foot and 100 cavalry. And was he not, besides, Her Majesty's sole heir as Burghley tactfully reminded him. Her Majesty was, after all, not getting any younger. And then finally James put on a good face for the papal emissaries who arrived with welcome ducats. The bishops let it be understood that all things considered, the Vatican had no desire to see Philip reigning over too many states. The English throne, Catholic once more, would be James's. So wasn't it time he got down to opening up a second front in the North?

Once victory seemed to be in the bag, James rushed to the aid of the Queen and his undying loyalty to the Protestant cause became quite apparent. At that point, however, promises of pensions, dukedoms and guards went right out of Elizabeth's mind. When he did eventually become James I of England, although officially a Protestant, many felt that he behaved as a protector of Catholicism.

De Leiva well knew that even though Mary Stuart's son had been brought up in the Protestant faith, deep down he may have been Catholic. That, at least, was what was said in Spain, in France and in Rome, a theory which seemed to be confirmed by the aid which he generously provided for the Spanish survivors sent to him from Ireland. Under his protection many hundreds of them were fed and housed before being repatriated via Flanders or France.

Who should De Leiva take with him? It was physically impossible to fit five ships' crews into one. The Lord Deputy's estimate had him take his own company 'being near 1,200, and all as may be with greatest reason thought choice men and of best account for birth and service, went aboard her, who together with the galleasses company being at the point of 700 or 800'. The Lord Deputy had got his figures wrong. Apart from a few passengers, the *Girona* must have carried 186 soldiers, 121 sailors and 244 rowers, a total of 551 men, not 700 or 800. Fitzwilliam's estimate that Don Alonso's 'company' was of 1,200 men seems similarly exaggerated. In the official inventory of the Most Fortunate Armada, I found the exact figures for the *rata* (419 men), the *Duquessa* (357) and the *Girona* (307 plus 244) and one can reckon on another 100 for the crews of the two small ships lost at Killybegs—a total of 1,427 men to begin with. Taking off say 10 per cent for those killed in action, and another 10 per cent for those dead from disease (epidemics had not in fact taken too great a toll on any of these ships), that leaves 1,157 for crews and soldiers. Adding, say, 305 passengers for the *rata* (noblemen and gentlemen adventurers with their servants, pilots, Irish Catholics, monks, barbers, surgeons, etc.) and 30 or so passengers for each of the other large vessels (losses were negligible among this privileged group) the total comes to about 1,540 men. Of those, according to various accounts, De Leiva embarked 800, 1,100, 1,300, 1,500, more than 1,500, or 1,800. He left few, if any, Spaniards behind; but English accounts made it clear that those left ashore soon became wretched beggars.

There was one possible solution to the problem of how many shipped with Don Alonso. Fitzwilliam learnt that de Leiva had written 'two several letters sent away by special men to Spain'. Two letters? One must have been to the King, the other to his family, perhaps. Either the letter to the King never arrived—I found no trace of it—or else it is lying, yellowed with age, having gone astray, in a dusty bundle of uncatalogued letters, lost for ever in the miles of stacks in the National Archives at Simancas or the archives of the Academie de la Historia in Madrid, or God knows where. I did not go through the family archives of the Castille Martinez De Leivas, so I do not know whether the letter to his family, if that is what it was, ever arrived, but I would give a good month of my life to lay hands on it.

Meanwhile I am inclined (and here I am in agreement with the survivors of the third shipwreck) to put at 1,300 the number of men who left Killybegs harbour in the *Girona*, just before dawn on 26 October 1588.

There is no doubt that Don Alonzo had loaded the galleass well over the safety margin, but did he really have any option? The Spaniards gave McSweeney at their departure twelve butts of sack wine and to one Murrouch Oge M'Murrough I Vayell, four butts. 'The McSweeneys and their vassals have received a substantial supply of Spanish muskets and calivers', wrote one Henry Duke. 'McSweeney killed 40 of the best Spaniards as soon as the rest were gone a-shipboard,' reported William Taaffe to Richard Byngham. An economy measure, no doubt! And this is what a neighbouring landowner, Sir John O'Dogherty, had to say about it when he wrote complaining to the Lord Deputy on 3 November: 'McSweeney having subsisted the 3,000 Spaniards till his country is consumed, directs them now for hate into this country to lie upon it and consume it.' The last days of the Spaniards sojourn cannot have been comfortable.

The days went by, a week, ten days. Where was the galleass? Not a word from Scotland, not a word in Dublin, or in London, or in Spain.

It was not until 5 November, a Saturday and late at night, that the first news began to percolate through to the Lord Deputy in Dublin Castle. He was awakened to read it. Henry Duke had learned from a spy sent up to the North that on:

> the 16th [26th]* of this instant October, the said galley departed from the said harbour [Killybegs] with as many of the Spaniards as she could carry and sailing along the coast towards the Out Isles of Scotland whither they were then bound, struck against the rock of Bunboys where both ship and men perished, save only five who hardly got to shore: three of which five men came the next day being the 17th [27th] in company with Sorley Boy McDonnell unto O'Neil's home at Strabane where they certified of their late shipwreck. . . . This rock of Bunboys is hard by Sorley Boy's house.

This 'house' was in fact Dunluce Castle, a veritable eagle's nest, occupied by his son James. McDonnell lived at Dunanyme, near Ballycastle. (See page 93.)

Sorley Boy McDonnell ruled over northeast Ulster. His Norwegian ancestor, who had settled in Scotland in the twelfth century, was called Sumar Lidi, the summer marauder. Just like the bear, sleeping

---

* The 16th according to the English Calendar (the old Julian Calendar still in use despite Gregory XIII's reforms in 1582). In 1588 it was 10 days behind the Gregorian Calendar (which we still use). All dates on English documents are therefore ten days behind those on Spanish documents. Throughout the text I have referred all dates to the new calendar.

in winter and plundering in the summer, the Vikings used to spend the winter in port and the summer looting. Having driven out of Argyll the Norwegians who had preceded him, Sumar Lidi had himself renamed Somerled, or Somhairle Duidhe, which later became Sorley Boy.

Sorley Boy was a rebel who could not be put down. Thirteen years earlier, in the course of a peacemaking expedition, the Earl of Essex had ordered the massacre of McDonnell's wife and youngest sons, along with 600 other women and children who had taken refuge on Rathlin Island, either in the castle, in the caves, or in some hideaway. Sorley Boy was powerless, because Sir Francis Drake had sunk his 'galleys' (in fact they were only smacks). He could only stand and watch the flames shooting up from the castle.

Hardly had the Lord Deputy returned to his bed when the following confirmation arrived. 'The Spanish ship which arrived in Tirconnell with the McSweeney was on Friday the 18th [28th] of this present month descried over against Dunluce and by rough weather was perished so that there were driven to the land, being drowned, the number of 260 persons, with certain butts of wine' which Sorley Boy hath taken up for his use.'

And how about De Leiva? Not a word of him. There were some survivors, but how many? Five, they said, but was it true? Don Alonzo, was he well and truly drowned? It was not confirmed. The Privy Council was concerned. With De Leiva alive the whole of Ireland was in peril. 'Further where it pleased your Lordship', wrote Fitzwilliam to the Privy Council, 'that I should make an inquiry whether Don Alonzo de Leva (*sic*) were drowned. . . .' The inquiry would be a perilous one. Secret agents in the pay of the English who dared to go and spy on Sorley Boy, did not always come back. His men were all 'bad types'; one could expect no good of them.

Another whole month passed bringing nothing but rumours. Captain George Thornton, of HMS *Popinjay*, one of the Queen's galleons—the only one, as it happened, stationed on the west coast of Ireland—declared 'that as he passed the Rathlins and Skirrys with her Majesty's ship, it was constantly affirmed by a gunner saved out of the galleass who yet remaineth with Sorley Boy McDonnell that Alonzo de Leva was drowned'. This was not enough to reassure Secretary Walsingham.

It was, indeed nothing more than a rumour, and not the last. In January 1589, a letter from France delivered to the depths of the Escurial brought with it a new glimmer of hope. Ambassador Mendoza wrote to Philip, 'There are reports from Scotland that Don Alonzo De Leiva has landed 2,000 men in Ireland, in Mac Win land, and that the local population has risen in support of him.' The news had been not far off the truth, but it was two months out of date.

Previous page: *We had to shift several hundred boulders in order to excavate underneath them. The biggest weighed over 8 tons. It took the whole team to move it. Over the months a kind of telepathy developed among the divers. We worked together tying wire slings around the boulders, shackling them in place, inflating the lifting balloons to shift them—three pairs of hands moved, or so it seemed, by one mind. Seldom did we feel the slightest need for sign language.* Above: *The perrier balls and arquebus shot roll in the sand for the last time.*

Philip knew by now just how much faith to put in Don Bernadino's 'good news' and each day that passed without any definite information prepared him a little more for the worst. Nonetheless he scratched a note to his secretary in the margin of the letter, 'Find out what province [part of Ireland] he means, and let me know.'

On the very same day Mendoza's letter was written, 27 December, the Armada's chief navigator, Marolin de Juan, who had been left behind in Calais was writing to Mendoza from Le Havre that Don Alonzo was drowned, and all the nobles with him. He wrote:

> Some Scottish ships arrived here yesterday with 32 Spanish soldiers and a few sailors from the Armada, who were shipwrecked on the coast of Ireland. . . . They were on the Venetian ship *la Valencera* . . . Don Alonzo De Leiva, with his ship's crew and the *Santa Ana*'s, embarked in the galleass *Girona*, which had sheltered in some port somewhere. No sooner had she set sail for Spain than she was overtaken by a violent storm, which broke her rudder and threw her at midnight upon the rocks. . . . Of the 1,300 men aboard, nine managed to save themselves, and it was these men who told the story to the soldiers who are come here.'

(That is, to the *Valencera*'s soldiers, whom they met at Dunluce Castle, where James McDonnell was sheltering them until they could be repatriated.)

The old ambassador was overcome with grief. He was nearly blind now, racked with every sort of illness, and in such bad favour at court that every week he begged Philip to accept his resignation. He sent the letter on to Philip with no comment.

Later in a letter dated 21 January, he reported: 'A sailor passing by the spot where Don Alonzo was lost with 1,300 men recognised many of the bodies strewn along the coast. He took 300 ducats out of the belt of one of them.'

For Don Alonzo, 'who had with him all the nobles in the expedition', all Spain went into mourning. And it was said that 'the King minded his loss more bitterly than that of all the rest of the fleet'.

8

PART TWO

GOLD UNDER THE SEAWEED

O lord, methought what pain it was to drown,
What dreadful noise of waters in mine ears,
What sights of ugly death within mine eyes!
Methought I saw a thousand fearful wrecks;
A thousand men that fishes gnawed upon,
Wedges of gold, great anchors, heaps of pearl,
Inestimable stones, unvalued jewels,
All scattered in the bottom of the sea!
Some lay in dead mens' skulls, and in the holes
Where eyes did once inhabit, there were crept,
As 'twere in scorn of eyes, reflecting gems,
That wooed the slimy bottom of the deep,
And mocked the dead bones, that lay scattered by.

(William Shakespeare, *Richard III*, I. iv.)

24
A Three-Star Wreck

In 1952 I discovered Rieseberg, the American fiction writer, and his unblushing accounts of imaginary battles with giant squid, octopus and sharks, staunch protectors of those ocean treasures that he unfailingly brought back, by the chest load, from his expeditions in what he called the South Seas. His books enjoyed phenomenal success and went through many editions. I didn't believe a word of his stories, needless to say, but I had found my vocation.

I was nineteen, a student of politics in Brusssls and I had recently developed two great passions, for deep sea diving and historical research. As I put Rieseberg's book down, I filled in my first index card. Today my card indexes take up a whole room.

My first wreck hunt, in 1954, took me to Vigo Bay in the Spanish province of Galicia. I was looking for the lost galleons of the 1702 Plate Fleet. *Les Épaves de l'Or* (Paris, 1958) is an account of this expedition. It is only with considerable effort that I manage to keep a straight face nowadays when I refer to it as an 'early work'. I wrote then:

> I felt sure that there were wrecks loaded with gold, that I had at my disposal the means of seeing them, touching them. I could imagine no more fascinating or enjoyable way of spending my life than looking for treasure, and maybe even finding it. Wherever else life might take me, I would always think the place I really want to be is Vigo, on my galleons.

And so I set off, giving up everything else, dropping out of university and the preordained future that it promised and that I no longer wanted. After two years of failure, in a highflown, lyrical rapture I concluded:

> But I can see gold, gold under the mud, the fabulous gold of the Americas, lying under fifty feet of slime and fifty feet of water waiting to be found, the gold that one day will glisten under the sun in the palm of my hand.

I became a professional diver. In 1964, after a few more treasure hunts and a few more failures, I could still write, in the introduction to *Le Livre des Trésors Perdu*, (Paris, 1964):

Treasures of The Armada

I had not the slightest wish to invent responsibilities for myself, in the way that "they" did, only to have to spend the rest of my life coping with them ("they" were all the little cogs in the vast machine). I did not want to "make a career" and I wanted nothing to do with their so-called "experience" if it was going to turn me into one of them. They could keep their "realistic view of things" which prevented them from seeing the only true reality in the world: sea and coconut palms. I wanted to look for treasure, to live under the sea, a free man, an animal capable of thinking straight, unlike all the others, someone who could live his own life, not in his little cell in the beehive but the master of his own destiny.

I read these lines again in 1967. By then I was living in London. I had had other experiences. I had been a spelunken and a cave diver and I had spent three whole years doing experimental deep sea diving. And yet as I reread them I could find little to change in them. By then, of course, I had emerged from my treasure hunter's cocoon and spread my wings as an underwater archaeologist (an amateur one and self-taught—there are hardly any others). The prospect of the *Girona*'s cargo of gold held less meaning for me now than the weight of history in her. But apart from replacing the words 'treasures' by 'historical wrecks', I wouldn't change a word. I decided to devote myself completely, for just as long as it might take, to finding the *Girona*.

Why the *Girona*? Because, in my Renaissance file, under *Spain: British territorial waters*, the *Girona*'s index card sported three stars in the top right-hand corner.

It was at Bayona in Vigo Bay that I first heard her mentioned. I had returned there in 1958 for a third expedition, which was to last six months. This time we were operating an underwater magnetometer. During the winter storm, John Potter, who was leading this expedition, was writing a master work on wrecks. I had contributed to some of the chapters. Numb with cold, for the wind was whistling through his flat, rattling the windows, he handed me the second revised and corrected draft of his manuscript. Immediately my imagination was caught by the story of the *Girona*. My blood was up! Battles, storms, five crews, the noblest, richest, bravest men in the whole fleet, jammed with all their treasures into one ship. Three wrecks in succession! At least a 1,000 dead! This was what tragedy was made of, what romance was made of. This was what treasures were made of.

The *Girona* had me in her grasp. John Potter tried to put me on my guard and quoted Conrad. 'There is no way to escape from a treasure, once it fastens itself upon your mind.' The warning came too late.

I started on my research, right there in Spain. But, alas, I was pressed for time and could not do very much there. I pursued it at greater length in Brussels, in the Bibliothèque Royale, which has a wealth of old Spanish publications; then in the Archives Nationales

144

in Paris, where they have the whole of Ambassador Mendoza's corre-
spondence with Philip II on microfilm, and then in Holland, where
there is not very much. In all this represented about 200 hours' work.
But although the *Armada: general* file got fatter as I looked at it, the
Girona file remained slim. I was finding few worthwhile references.
Meanwhile my job took me for a year to Colombia, then back to
Brussels, where it left me little spare time; then, for over two years, to
America. Finally I went to London. I boarded the plane carrying
under my arm the *Girona* file, thick with dust. Ocean Systems, Inc
(affiliated with Union Carbide), an American industrial diving and
underwater engineering company, had put me in charge of their
London office. I had first joined them with Edwin A. Link and
the 'Man in Sea' team after our record dive in the Bahamas in 1964
(two days and two nights living and working 430 ft beneath the sea).
   Now, if, back in 1588, someone who actually knew had happened
to note down on some scrap of paper the exact spot where the *Girona*
was wrecked, that piece of paper would almost certainly be in London.
   Drilling was beginning on all the off-shore rigs in the North Sea gas
and oil-fields and I was occupied full time by my professional commitments. Nonetheless I made it a rule for myself to set aside three
evenings a week, from 6 pm to 9 pm, which I would spend under the
blue and gold dome of the British Museum Reading Room, or in the
rotunda of the Public Record Office Reading Room. In the space of a
year and a half I must have put in about 600 hours' work. I believe that
everything, still extant, ever written in England or Ireland on the
Armada and its wrecks must have passed through my hands. I discovered that there was another Armada wreck, the *Nuestra Señora de la
Rosa*, which went down off the Blaskets (the south-west tip of Ireland),
that also deserved one or two stars. So I was conducting my research
campaign on two fronts. It wasn't long before I was tempted to award
the *Nuestra Señora* two stars and give the *Girona* a fourth.
   But where in Heaven's name was this ship, the *Girona?* It was
becoming less and less clear. The more information I collected, the
more contradictions I found . . . unless, of course my own theory,
which had struck me out of the blue right at the start, was the right
one after all. . . .
   Calling a halt to all this paper work, I decided that the time had
come to go and take a look. This involved at least one team mate, a
boat, a motor, a compressor, cylinders and two cars to put it all in.
It was the Belgian photographer, Marc Jasinski, my companion in
countless dives and caving expeditions who would, once more, be my
team mate. (See page 109.)

25
The Girona *in the* Archives

'But surely,' argued Marc, 'other divers must have been there and looked before us.'

'Not many, and always in the wrong spots.'

'And they found nothing?'

'Nothing, as far as I know. But it wasn't entirely their fault. They put too much trust in the historians. Look.' And I passed him a summary I had drawn up. 'Look where these famous Armada historians made them dive.'

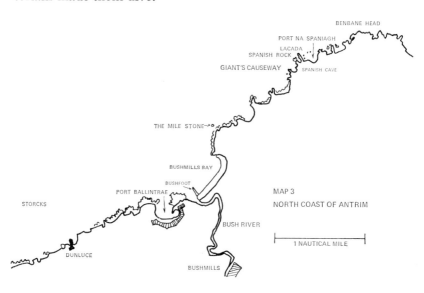

'Wait,' said Marc, 'show me the Admirality chart first.'

It was Number 2798, Rathlin Island to Lough Foyle, the north coast of Ulster, the English part of Ireland, the Six Counties. There was Portrush and the Skerries, Dunluce Castle to the East and opposite some isolated rocks, the Storks. There was a beacon on them now. Further east we could see Port Ballintrae and then Bushmills Bay,

146

the estuary of the Bush River. The chart showed a long stretch of beach, then the coast became rocky again, cliff, the Giant's Causeway and then . . .

'What's the Giant's Causeway? Some tourist spot?'

'Yes, apparently it's very fine, a solidified lava flow. It fissured as it cooled into a sort of honeycomb, because the lava all contracted evenly. The fissures went right through from top to bottom, and each hexagon eventually became a column. Then, still going eastwards, we have a few bays, some more cliffs, and there—see those two little points with a bay to one side? Well, pass me the other map now. No, not that one. The Ordnance Survey map, six inches to the mile. Yes, that's the one. I just got it. Sheet three of County Antrim. Right, see this little point here?'

'But it's called Spaniard Rock,' exclaimed Marc, suddenly excited, 'and Spaniard Cove and . . . Port na Spaniagh—well, well, how about that.' (See pages 28 and 108.)

'Indeed, and that's not all. Look at that, Lacada Point. That's no Irish name, is it?'

I was mistaken, as it happened. Mr C. Trench has since been kind enough to point out to me that Lacada is in fact, on the contrary, a Gaelic name, Leac fhada, meaning long stone, or long promontory. But, as yet comfortably confident in my ignorance, I went on to explain, 'It could be the name of a survivor, couldn't it? Maybe that was where they found Juan or Miguel Lacada, the next morning, soaked to the skin.'

'But, Robert, if that is so, then we haven't got far to look.'

'Right, but read my summary of statements of Armada historians all the same.'

It ran as follows:

De Bavia: . . . She was so tossed by the weather that she was lost. . . . Five or six mariners managed to swim ashore.

Hadfield: Girona struck a submerged rock near the Giant's Causeway and went down in the deep sea off Dunluce. . . .

Hardy: . . . went down west of the Giant's Causeway. She was wrecked on the rock of Bunboys . . . [but elsewhere] . . . the bay is smaller than Port Ballintrae where the *Girona* foundered. . . .

Kilfeather: . . . driven ashore at Dunluce . . . at a point known ever since as Port na Spaniagh.

Laughton: . . . near the Giant's Causeway, at Spaniard Rock.

Mattingly: . . . near the Giant's Causeway. . . .

McKee: . . . struck a submerged rock . . . in sight of Dunluce Castle. . . . Under the high cliff topped by the sombre castle of Dunluce. . . .

Lewis: hit the rock of Bunboys. . . .

Froude: . . . They struck upon a rock off Dunluce. . . .

Duro: . . . They hit Dunluce rock . . . [but elsewhere] . . . the storm split her again in the canal and she sank. . . .

'What is the rock of Bunboys?'

'That bit was easy. It's spelt Bunbois or Bon Boys but on the sixteenth-century maps I've seen, the River Bush is called Boys river, and the Irish-English glossary in the Pilot Book, says that Bun means estuary, so the rock of the Boy's Bun is the rock of the Bush estuary. It's called Bushfoot now on the Ordnance Survey map.'

Marc handed me back my summary, saying we wouldn't stand much chance of finding the wreck with his lot. But these were all historians of the Armada in general. As far as they are concerned it is just one tiny detail. Weren't there any local historians or experts?

There was one in particular, the Reverend Spotswood Green, who gave a paper to the Royal Geographic Society on Armada wrecks in Ireland. He is considered the leading authority on the subject and for the most part his work is remarkable, but he above all had been responsible for sending our predecessors off on the wrong track. Just think, here was this chap, this most excellent fellow, who in 1894 knew that there was a Port na Spaniagh and a Spanish Rock and yet, God bless him, he wrote this: 'It is hard to doubt tradition that has fixed a name to a place. . . . Taking all things into account, I incline to the conclusion that the remains of the *Girona* lie off the mouth of the Bush River near Port Ballintrae. . . .'

'But what if he was right after all?' Marc argued.

'No, I don't think so. I've got another theory. I'll tell you. But there's more. Another nineteenth-century expert, Hugh Allingham of the Royal Irish Academy, achieved a really remarkable feat. By completely mixing up the entire history of the shipwrecks and of De Leiva he managed to cram into two and a half pages no less than eleven mistakes and major untruths. I'll spare you the details. He ended up by getting so lost in his four wrecked ships and all the other ships he added on, that in order to tie up his paper he was forced to invent still another wreck. It's in the *Ulster Journal of Archaeology*, 1897. He sinks another ship, name unknown, on Bunboys rock, to which he assigns nine survivors and three cannon salvaged, as against five survivors and some wine butts for the *Girona*.'

'Right,' said Marc, 'then we'll have to forget that. How about eyewitnesses? What do they have to say?'

Unfortunately I had to tell him that there was not a single eyewitness account. I'd thought at first that Sorley Boy McDonnell or his son, or some clerk in their household must have left some notes, somewhere, on what was after all the event of the century for them. One might have found there the exact spot of the shipwreck and details of what they managed to salvage. Nothing doing. Not even a hint of a line of even the briefest account.* Then I thought of Spanish sources. What the survivors had to say.

'How many were there in fact?' demanded Marc.

'I don't know. Some say none, some five, others nine, eleven, thirteen. It depends what document you read. They had incidentally no contact whatsoever with the English. No point in looking at English records except for vague, garbled accounts. The men they did tell their story to were some other survivors, from the *Trinidad Valencera*, whom they met at James McDonnell's, at Dunluce Castle. Here, listen. "Sorley Boy received them most kindly and kept them for twenty days, having masses said for them. . . . He obtained some boats . . . eighty soldiers embarked to go to an island off Scotland; the others waited there for the boats to come back. Meanwhile the Governor in Dublin had learned that this gentleman had taken in some Spaniards, and sent him word in the name of the Queen not to embark one more man, on pain of death and confiscation of all his property, and to surrender those that were still in his house. He answered that he would rather forfeit all his property and his wife's and his childrens' rather than sell the blood of a Christian man . . . and when the boats returned he embarked the others, etc., etc. . . ." It's rather strange, really, because just before this he had sworn on oath of allegiance to the Queen and kissed her slipper in effigy at Dublin Castle. In short, you can see that in twenty days the survivors had ample time to go over every detail of what happened to the *Girona*. They told the story to two mariners in particular from the *Valencera*, Juan de Nova and Francisco de Borja. And when these two old salts reached Calais, via Scotland, they were questioned by Marolin de Juan, the Armada's chief navigator, who had got left behind ashore after taking a message to Parma. Marolin de Juan sent the King a summary of their story, before having an official record of their testimony drawn up. From Calais this record was sent to Ambassador Mendoza in Paris, enclosed in a letter from Marolin dated 21 January 1589. The Ambassador forwarded it to the King. And from the Escurial this document finally ended up in the Spanish National Archives in Simanca, where it is today.'

'Okay, okay. That's all very well. But where's the wreck?'

'Oh, that. Marolin de Juan just says that according to them, the *Girona* ran aground on the rocks at midnight.'

---

* The Earl of Antrim, Randall McDonnell, direct descendant of Sorley Boy, later confirmed that his family had never kept any proper archives. He himself has no relics of his long family history in his castle at Glenarm, apart from two iron chests of uncertain date.

'And how about the *Girona* survivors? Did they go back to Spain?' Some of them had returned. Some, including a gunner, were still at Dunluce a year later, but others, I discovered, got back to Corunna as early as February 1589. Marc made the point that they must have been questioned directly, and they must have had a pretty good idea what rock it was they were clinging onto till dawn, or what beach it was they tramped along. What had happened to their testimony? I couldn't find any trace of it. And I'd looked for anything that might have been written from Ireland, Scotland, Flanders or France, from anywhere along the return route, in effect, and still I found nothing. Then I gave up. When it came to the point, all there was to work on was hearsay and some guesswork based on hearsay. Marc wanted to know about the guesswork too.

The most meaningful deduction one could draw was this: if the natives managed to salvage the cannon, that must indicate that the *Girona* actually ran aground, on the coast, or else sank in shallow water, definitely not more than 30 ft deep. One could make other guesses but one could set too much store by them. Duro, for example, published an account, for which he doesn't quote a source, which says that the *Girona* was wrecked because of the current. It would seem that Don Alonzo drew the pilots' attention to the fact that the current was driving them hard toward land, but that they wouldn't listen to him and that was why they went on the rocks. One could check that one out on the spot by making a study of the currents. It would give one a probable area of study. But in fact the only major currents in the vicinity of the wreck appear to be tidal ones, parallel to the coast. The story was, I thought, spurious. That was the second hypothesis. There are more details in de Nova and de Borja's testimony which do not feature in Marolin de Juan's initial summary of their account, but only in their detailed testimony. They only confuse the issue:

When they arrived between the Spanish sea (Atlantic) and the Scottish isle, there was a good wind blowing to get them back to Spain. The pilot said to Don Alonzo that if he gave his permission they could go about and in five days they would be in Spain. Don Alonzo replied if he was sure the good weather would hold he had his permission. But the pilot was wrong in thinking that the wind was established. It veered round, throwing them onto the Island of Hibernia (the Latin name for Ireland). They hit a submerged rock and the galleass broke into pieces. More than 1,300 men drowned. Only nine seamen managed to save themselves, of whom one made this declaration.

'On the Island of Hibernia, that's a bit vague', Marc commented as he finished reading the account, 'but if she did hit a submerged rock, that makes it somewhat easier to find than having to go over the whole coast. There can't be that many.'

I explained my fourth hypothesis. The rock can't have been far out to sea: 260 bodies were washed ashore with the wine butts. Only this story upset all the others, because we now had a ship going from east to west instead of west to east. It all sounded suspicious anyway, for De Leiva had almost reached his objective, and he knew it. If it had been light he would already have sighted the Western Isles. He knew too that he didn't have anything like enough provisions on board to feed 1300 men for five or possibly ten days, and that his ship was not sufficiently seaworthy. And besides, from the time he set out, say before dawn on the 26th to the time of the shipwreck at midnight, 100 nautical miles further on, twenty hours had passed. With a good following wind, the *Girona* could do five knots and twenty hours would be about right to cover 100 miles, but it wouldn't be anything like long enough to get all the way to the Isles, bearing in mind that the wind dropped, then changed, and then, that they doubtless waited a while until the new wind seemed properly established, before working back to the west.

'But you said that James McDonnell salvaged some stuff right away. The English must have learnt of it, otherwise we wouldn't know about it ourselves, since the Irish didn't write anything down.'

'Yes, "some butts of wine". The Lord Deputy heard about them. In theory he should have claimed them for the Queen. In fact, more likely kept them for himself. He was said to be a bit of a rogue. He had declared that "the Spanish wrecks belong to the Queen as waifs . . ." "Waif" is a fairly cloudy legal term, quite vague, meaning roughly a piece of abandoned property the owners of which came ashore alive. But Fitzwilliam didn't risk claiming them from Sorley Boy. And then in December he found out something else and wrote to London: "And further I hear that three fair pieces of brass, which lie within view between rocks at Bunboys where Don Alonzo was drowned, will also be recovered".'

'Aha,' said Marc in a satisfied tone of voice. 'So it was at Bunboys. And not deep.'

As usual he was one jump ahead of me, but first I wanted him to read what Captain Cuellar wrote when he too arrived at Dunluce, in 1589, from the west coat where he had been shipwrecked, 'I went into the huts of some savages that were there and learned from them of the terrible sufferings of our people who were drowned there. I was shown many jewels and valuables that had belonged to them. This caused me great sorrow. . . .'

They'd robbed the 260 bodies thrown up on the beach, on the day after the wreck, of that there could be no doubt. But more than that,

James must have taken the lion's share of the treasure for himself, either then or during the summer of 1589. George Hill had written 'Every Spanish ship carried aboard two exceedingly strong iron chests. . . .' This was sheer invention. Previously Hill even went so far as to specify that one was for gold and the other for silver, and that the McDonnells probably did not take any of the gold or silver (Hill was the family historian, so the picture had to be an edifying one). He also claimed that the two coffers are still preserved and in the possession of the Antrim family. Hill doesn't give his source, and there is no mention of these two chests in any other document. Personally I thought he'd invented them so as to provide a pedigree for two chests that he had seen in the castle. But that was neither here nor there. What was certain was that James must have found—either in the wreck or the dead men's pockets—a very considerable fortune. I'd read in a history of Dunluce, that starting in 1590, the original square keep was rebuilt and greatly enlarged. James even decorated the entrance with a turreted Scottish baronial portal. Where else could this new fortune have come from—in 1590?

If McDonnell had left anything for us, it must be at Port na Spaniagh, and for two reasons. Firstly, everyone else had looked at Bunboys, but I was convinced that the Irish lied at the time. There they were quietly salvaging cannon, gold and silver. They would never have talked to an Englishman or to some stranger who looked like a spy, unless it was to send him off on the wrong track. They had known the English long enough to be pretty sure that they would claim the lot. The text of the Lord Deputy's commission to his subordinates is clear enough on this point:

> Whereas the distressed fleet of the Spaniards, by tempest and contrary winds, through the providence of God, have been driven upon this coast, and many of them wrecked in several places, where is to be thought hath not only been much treasure cast away, now subject to the spoil of the country people, but also great store of ordnance, munitions, armours, and other goods of several kinds . . . we authorise you to make inquiry by all good means . . . to take all hulls of ships, stores, treasure, etc. . . . into your hands and to apprehend and execute all Spaniards found there of what quality soever. Torture may be used in prosecuting this inquiry.

The McDonnells must have known about that order and they wouldn't have taken any chances.

'So you think that all the early reports, where they give Bunboys as the place where the shipwreck occurred, are deliberately misleading?' Marc asked.

'I'm certain of it. And that's not all. On reflection Sorley Boy must have decided he hadn't lied enough. The Bush estuary was still too near the actual spot. He probably tried to improve his story because in December 1588, Carew received further details. He informed the Queen of them on the 13th: "Don Alonzo De Leiva . . . being again driven back upon the northern coast in Ulster and from thence putting to sea again, are sithence, as I hear say, cast away about the isles going for Scotland. . . .' They lied, and quite rightly too. In the following year, the same George Carew was already looking for cannon on the west coast.'

'With any success?'

'Hardly. In 1588 the Lord Deputy wrote that only three small pieces remained of the Spanish gun. But the next summer, when the weather was calmer and warmer, he commissioned Carew to see what more was worth salvaging on the Munster coast.'

They must have used a diving bell in these salvage operations, with the whole paraphernalia of hooks and hawsers and nooses to grab the cannon from the bell. That was the method used on the Tobermory wreck and on the *Wasa*. And then they would have had lifting jacks between two boats, like the ones they used around that time in the Cadaques operation—pulley blocks and so on.

But Carew was a poor supervisor. That summer he was in the midst of his honeymoon. He wasn't the slightest bit interested in the *Girona*. All in all, he only raised some dozen cannon. Fitzwilliam was sympathetic and did not press him too hard. Soon it was autumn, and the time for a thorough search had passed. As a result none of the misleading reports were disproved.

I had another argument, too, in favour of Port na Spaniagh. The only place names that appear on sixteenth-century maps of Ireland between Portrush and Rathlin Island are Dunluce and the Bush River. Obviously these would have been the only meaningful names a spy or a civil servant could quote to his superiors. There were virtually no paths along the coast. The cliffs were inaccessible. So even if the Irish had been truthful, they couldn't have pointed to the exact spot. All they could say was that the wreck was 'near the river Boys' or else that it was 'near Dunluce'. This was where I thought the nineteenth-century historians made their mistake, and similarly the divers who believed them; they took these two names literally. They dived immediately under Dunluce and at Bushfoot, without thinking. And then, one day in 1904, the man from the Ordnance Survey, come to do his surveys, asked the locals for the names of places roundabout so as to draw up the first edition of that map we had with us. The old fishermen he asked didn't see any reason to lie any more. The tradition had been handed down among them for fifteen generations, and they told him: 'That, sir, that's Port na Spaniagh.' Like Schlieman when he was looking for Troy, I set more store by local tradition than on all the so-called experts. Everywhere I have found that the old fishermen are right, when official hydrographic charts and serious historians are way off the mark.

I had the good fortune to be the one to find some of the most beautiful jewels, like this delicately engraved salamander.

Left: *Bit by bit, Louis pieced together underwater this cross of Knight of Malta. From the motif the angles of the cross which a features in his family coat of arms established that it must have longed to the Girona's capta Don Fabricio Spinola.*

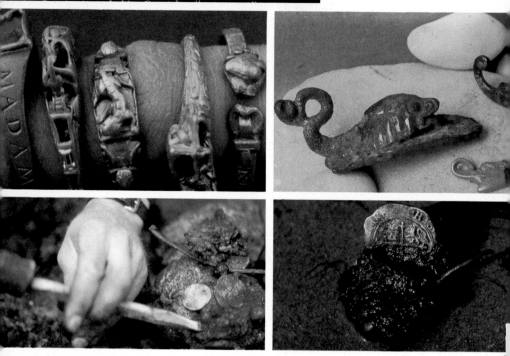

Centre: *We found twelve gold rings, also four dolphins; in front: a combined tooth and ear pick, an instrument in common use at the time.* Below: *For a month we did nothing but break up and raise large chunks of the natural black magma, encrusted in the crevices of the sea bed. This was where the treasure was.*

26
1967: I Find the Wreck

June 1967. We left London first thing in the morning. At 12 pm the following day we were drawing up by the Atlantic. It was wild and stormy. It had been drizzling when we set out from London, in the Midlands it had been raining properly, it had poured cats and dogs in Scotland and over the Irish Sea it had come down in buckets. Now that we were in Ireland it seemed that the heavens had opened.

Marc unfolded an oilskin. He opened his door. A gust of wind slammed it shut again. There was no question of going out to sea today. Bent double under the squalls, we floundered across to the Giant's Causeway. Judging by the number of souvenir stalls it seemed that tourists must come in their droves on days when it wasn't pouring with rain. Further along was a sheep track swept by a stream.

We walked some distance. Port na Spaniagh is out of this world. An amphitheatre of 400 ft high cliffs, sheer and terrifying. The wind howled round our ears. Beside the cliffs sea birds hovered, circling ceaselessly in one spot and their raucous cries, endlessly modulated, echoed into infinity. The rock was black—the cliffs were black, with gashes of red where men have cut out paths. Occasional patches of green pasture were specked with nimble white sheep. Mounds of fallen debris were piled up at the bottom to form a chaotic mass of boulders where the beach ought to have been. All the floating wrecks from miles around end up here.

Below us, the green ocean showed its power. The breakers' rippling backs heaved as the approached they shore, and broke on Lacada Point, sending fountains of milky spray rocketing up to the sky. In front of Spaniards' Cave flakes of foam flew up, spinning in the air like flights of yellow butterflies.

Neither of us spoke. The wildness of the spot made a deep impression on me. It's a place that calls for death, cries out for tragedy. It's too much. A film set. Nature has overdone it. I could see the great ship being pounded to pieces down there by the waves that never stop. Her sides crack, and men are thrown out onto the black rocks, snatched up by the breakers, hurled down again, smashed, broken up like old puppets.

Marc turns to me after a long silence. 'What can be left of the wreck after 400 years of this?'

When we got back, Marc went into a tourist shop and bought a one and threepenny guide book to the Giant's Causeway. He flicked through it. Suddenly he roared with laughter.

'How much of your precious youth have you spent poring over Armada achives? How many hours altogether? Six hundred? More like eight, probably? There was an easier way, old man. Here. Try this next time.'

And this was what I read: 'In 1588 . . . the galleass *Girona* was wrecked at a little cove, near the Giant's Causeway, still called Port na Spaniagh.'

It was easy enough to laugh then, but if I'd just read it there in that one and threepenny guide like everyone else, I'd have done exactly what everyone else has done before. I'd have shrugged my shoulders and gone about finding some more serious source.

* * *

The next day there were gale force winds.

Apart from Portrush there is not another proper port on the whole coast, only small coves with little or no shelter from the open sea. To get into them you have to know how to wind your way between the reefs. The fishermen use these coves whenever the weather begins to look a bit threatening, winching their boats up the beach on rollers. We had reconnoitred all of them on foot, with a map, before deciding on Port Ballintrae for our base. We managed to assemble the boat between two storms.

For this first exploratory expedition we had with us only the very lightest of equipment: a small inflatable dinghy with an eighteen horse-power Johnson, four double-cylinder aqualungs and a small high-pressure air-compressor. With our wet suits, photographic equipment and our bits and pieces, it all fitted into two cars.

We inflated the dinghy, and as it was still very rough, went to have a look at Dunluce. Sir John Perrot, Lord Deputy in 1584, gave a good description of it in a letter that he wrote to the Privy Council while he was besieging it.

I set up camp with the whole company in front of Dunluce, the best fortified spot in the kingdom. It is built on an overhanging rock and cut off from the mainland by a natural trench; the only access to it is by a narrow rocky bridge, which also has a deep cleft in it. . . .

It was exactly as he had described it. A fairy-tale castle, perched like an eagle's nest on a sea-swept rock promontory. There are caves there, which we looked at, that were once lived in by early troglodyte Christians.

Around the thirteenth century a square fort was built, which later fell into the hands of the clan McQuillan. A rival clan, the McDonnells, wanted it for themselves. They tried to appropriate it first by a peaceful alliance and later by more forceful means. At the battle of Bun na Mairge they virtually exterminated the McQuillans. But a few survived, including some of the more powerful members of the clan. The McDonnells invited them to a picnic at Minehill, to celebrate their reconciliation. To create a more friendly atmosphere and foster better relations between the two families, they placed them alternately in the seating. Beside each McQuillan sat a McDonnell. At the end of their feast, when they had all eaten and drunk their fill, the bards in their long, coloured robes began to sing, accompanying themselves on the harp. At a given signal every McDonnell turned swiftly to his left, plunging his dagger deep into the heart of the McQuillan beside him. The castle was theirs.

Sir John Perrot captured it in 1584. He left a garrison and a high constable there to guard it in the name of the Queen. He had hardly turned his back when Sorley Boy McDonnell retook the castle by force, hanging the English constable by the neck from the highest wall. Sorley Boy installed his son in it, and it was he who was living there in 1588.

From the castle windows, one can see the Western Isles; James McDonnell was well placed to organise the evacuation of Spanish survivors.

The atmosphere in these ruins is heavy with history, fascinating for those who are as steeped in it as I am. I have often been back to look at the Scottish baronial door and the new additions that James McDonnell built after 1588, with what I cannot help thinking of as 'my' money, taken from 'my' wreck, in 'my' coffers.

About 200 yards from the castle is the old church of Dunluce, where the *Girona* survivors went to pray and offer their thanksgivings to God. James McDonnell had a special weekday Mass said for them there. Now all that is left of it are four walls overgrown with ivy and honeysuckle. All around and inside the tombs have collapsed. Some have quite disappeared in the long grass. One after another we scrutinised the tombstones. Tradition has it that the bodies that were thrown up onto the beach from the galleass were buried here. But there must have been hundreds of bodies. How could they have been carried so far? Loading them onto a boat and then onto carts would have involved more than thirty journeys, considerable expense, and at least a week's work. In any case how could so many bodies have been laid to rest in such a small area? We found no sign of any Spanish graves. The earliest date on any stone was 1630. There were some older ones, even more worn and pocked by sea spray and salt air, on which the dates were no longer visible. But the names on those were Irish. Don Alonzo and his companions must, I think, have been buried in Port na Spaniagh itself, straight in the earth under the boulders. On 27 June the sun managed to break through between showers, and in this new light the watery landscape seemed suddenly to become vaster, bursting into colour as it broke out of its coccoon of rain. As the countryside awoke so something in us awoke with it.

The fishermen shook their heads as they watched our absurd little boat heading out towards the open sea, riding wave after wave of the incoming swell from Iceland. Immediately we left the port we were right out in the open. Marc steered towards the one-mile stone at the other end of Bushmills Bay. From there to Spaniard Rock are jagged cliffs, marked out by the Chimney Rocks, hexagonal columns of solidified lava, which rise dizzily on the edge of the abyss.

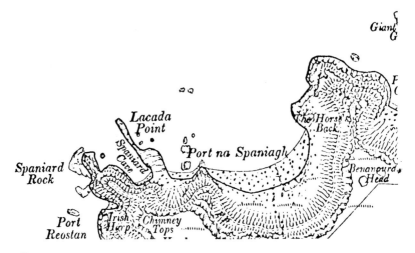

Seen from the sea Port na Spaniagh looks even more sinister. What if the engine broke down? There one would be, utterly defenceless against the raging sea, infinitesimal at the bottom of those soaring cliffs; 1,300 men were drowned there! A myriad of clichés come to mind. Dante, Villehardouin, Shakespeare . . . .

'Abandon hope, all ye who anchor here,' Marc called into the wind as he dropped the dinghy's grappling anchor next to the reefs, those two bared teeth in the middle of Port na Spaniagh. 'How reckless is he,' I said, 'who places between himself and death the thickness of a diving suit.' I put on flippers, face mask, gloves and lead belt and

160

worked out what bearing to follow under water. I toppled backwards and Marc went on declaiming for the benefit of the seagulls:

'O Lord, methought what pain it was to drown,
What dreadful noise of waters in mine ears,
What sights of ugly death within mine eyes!'

I dived and silence was all around me. I felt the biting cold on my face, cutting right through my sinuses. I went down slowly, following the anchor line. Everywhere, greys, greens, browns. Moving at one knot, the tide was pulling westwards. The grappling anchor had caught on a sea tangle, a long glistening stem, fixed to the rock by a large tendril and ending above my head in a huge brown front. I wedged the grapple between two rocks and waited for a while to get used to the cold.

If Port na Spaniagh had been the first to get its Spanish name, and the rocks and the neighbouring cave had been named after it, that would mean that the *Girona* was in the bay. If, on the other hand, the rock had been named first, we should have to look there. I decided to start in Port na Spaniagh, exploring the two reefs, which are covered at high tide and could so easily foul an incoming ship.

Guided by my compass, I reached the base of the twin reefs. The sediment stirred up by the stormy weather had not yet settled. Swimming in this pea soup it was impossible to see further than four yards in front of me at the most. I swam round and round one reef and then the other, but found nothing. The sea bed here is rocky and chaotic, but following my bearings I worked along parallel lines from north to south—still nothing. Then I moved in a hard southwesterly direction towards Lacada Point, moving very slowly, trying to see the sea bed through the algae, which sway ceaselessly in the swell, rather as one watches the road through moving windscreen wipers.

When you are looking for 400-year-old wrecks, it doesn't do to take Shakespeare too literally. Intent on finding gems reflecting in '. . . dead men's skulls, and in the holes. Where eyes did once inhabit . . .', it's all too easy to swim on without noticing some faint reddish protuberance which would betray the whereabouts of the caked remains of a cannon ball, not quite buried by the sea.

I stopped in a cleft in the rock and moved three stones to stir up the sand—still nothing. My depth gauge needle had moved up from 30 to 20 ft. Suddenly a cliff barred my way. Where was I! It must be the east face of Lacada Point. The cliff ran along the edge of a vast platform leading to an enormous rock. A white shape caught my eye. Ah! I went closer. A lead ingot.

In a flash I remembered something I read, sitting under the blue

and gold dome of the British Museum Reading Room, avidly devour-
ing the story of a man called Boyle, who discovered another Armada
wreck in Donegal at the end of the eighteenth century. 'With several
other good swimmers and expert divers . . .' he found apart from a
few gold pieces and some bronze cannon, 'a piece of lead which he
supposed to be ballast, a yard long, triangular, the sides being pointed
towards the ends, getting thick in the middle'. My ingot fitted the
description perfectly. Arching my back, I heaved it over, and there
stamped on the upper face were five Jerusalem crosses.

I had found the wreck. I closed my eyes, and felt my mouth, frozen
with cold, turn up into a smile. The elation I felt was calm, a slow but
very deep joy, a feeling of relief almost. (See pages 106–7.)

So, we had won the first round. Now for the second. I swam on,
ferreting about in a long corridor which led me straight to a large
verdigris-coloured cylinder. A bronze cannon. It lay crossways, protruding between stones, about two feet longer than my armspan, its
calibre—four fingers, a little over three inches. A demi-saker. There
was nothing else around. An underwater shelf inclines sharply down
to Lacada Point. If the ship ran onto this, everything would have rolled
down to the bottom of it. I followed the tortuous slope all the way
down. There, lying in an oblong crevice, I found another bronze
cannon. But what a strange shape it was. Box-like with a barrel
coming out of it. Of course, a breechloading piece! The breech blocks*
must be somewhere near. I couldn't take my eyes off this unique object.
A Spanish Armada gun. There wasn't a museum in the world that
had one, not even a cannon ball, not even a nail.

Lying just beside it were the powder chambers—two, three, four,
five of them. A chalky crust, impregnated with copper oxide, had
soldered some of them to the rock. Others were loose, and two were of a
large calibre. Perhaps they belong to one of the guns Sorley Boy fished
up? There were lead ingots everywhere, twelve at least, and some
thick rectangular plates. It all tallied with the inventory drawn up
before the departure from Lisbon. There were holes and marks on the
plates that must have been left by the round-headed, square nails that
were used to fix them. The nails must have been made of iron, for
nothing was left of them. Shapeless lumps had fused to the rock and
filled up the fissures. Cannon balls were everywhere, and traces of
rust on the sea bed, round stains, where shot had succumbed to the

---

* That is to say the powder chamber (*recamaras* or *servidores*) loaded in advance,
then half screwed into place and secured by hammering in a wooden wedge.
When a shot had been fired, one man changed the chamber, while another cleaned
the barrel and a third put in the shot. By this method it was possible to fire up to
three shots a minute.

combined effects of corrosion and erosion. From between two stones, I picked up a copper coin. Enough, it was time to make my way back.

I was smiling so broadly when I caught hold of the dinghy that I dropped my mouthpiece from between my teeth. 'I've found it, Marc,' I said. But he had guessed as much already from my face.

27

380 Years After

The following day the wind was up before us, blowing from the south while we ate our porridge. It changed, as we dressed, to south-west, and by the time we left the port a strong west sou'wester was blowing. After ten minutes of switchbacking over the waves, the wind had swept in so much spray that we had taken six inches of water. We had to turn back, bailing all the way.

It was the beginning of three days of really bad weather. A stiff west wind blew without a break.

To allay our impatience we went back to Port na Spaniagh by the coastal path. Rabbits were out playing all over the slope. Using clods of fallen earth for stepping stones, we climbed down to the spot where the Spanish bodies were thrown up by the sea. Today buoys, cork floats and tons of driftwood are still tossed ashore just like those drowned men. The whole bay is white and thick, cakes of foam form between the stones. We found bones everywhere. The remains of the shipwreck victims? No. Dead sheep, probably.

By 1 July the sea was calm and we were able to dive again. When I first saw the cannon it had been quite clear. After three days of storms it was half buried under huge stones. I took Marc to photograph it, and showed him the ingot. While he was focusing his camera, I picked up a flat, round, grey pebble. 'What a laugh,' I thought, 'I'll make him think it's a piece of eight.' I examined it. Just an ordinary pebble. I turned it over. It *was* a piece of eight. A silver piece of eight. No doubt about it. There was the cross, the Jerusalem cross, almost worn away, but it was there all right. I waved my arms about with excitement and pushed the piece of eight under Marc's nose. I watched his expression, sure that he was saying to himself, 'Ha, ha. What a joke. He's trying to make me think it's a piece of eight.' I showed him the cross. He took my hand and shook it, ceremoniously, mumbling congratulations into his mouthpiece. There in the same place, by the entrance to a large cave, was another, lying flat on the pebbles, just waiting for me to come along and find it.

We went back up to change cylinders. The silver coins were Spanish and, like the cannons, they were of the right period. The amount of lead and the number of cannon balls proved that the wreck was that of a warship. Was it an Armada wreck? According to the documents the only one on the north coast of Ulster was the *Girona*. It remained to be proved.

That the cannon had got half buried like that in three days, shows how thoroughly the seabed here is stirred up in bad weather. Storms, real ones, must send small stones flying, roll large ones around and generally turn the whole seafloor upside down. Heavy wreck débris, anything made of metal, for example, must have collected on the solid rock bed under a layer of light sediment.

I spent the whole of this dive digging around the first ingot, in front of a huge boulder. I shifted three stones. There was a cannon ball, encrusted with that brown magma of iron oxide and chalky deposits, typical of the gangue that all cannon balls secrete under water over the centuries. I dug down further, to find more cannon balls and then just like that, a piece of eight, firmly wedged. It had not rolled around at all. The silver is very well preserved. The arms of Spain are clearly visible, a capital T with a small o underneath: it was minted at Toledo. I slipped it into my glove and then, oh . . . gold . . . it's gold. My pulse raced. Yes, a little gold ring, there between two stones, all shining. I had to take off my glove to get at it, not noticing the cold. At last, after twelve years of laughable attempts, after twelve years of monotonous failure, I have found gold under the sea. There, shining in the palm of my hand. Enough. Into my glove with it and on with the job. Here were some lead plates from the lining of the hull, a green marble egg with a hole through it. What on earth could that be? And then, more. A little fragment of gold chain, six gold links shaped like flattened figures of eight, entwined together, of the most exquisite delicacy. Where could the rest of it be? I would have to look further, to dig right down to the bottom. But how? I didn't have the right tools. And besides, I'd run out of air.

Meanwhile Marc was reconnoitring Spaniard Rock and the little cove in front of Spaniard Cave. Nothing there. As he described it, the sea bed there was quite smooth, flayed by underwater erosion: giant's kettles, devils cauldrons—a real lesson in geology. Then further out, some way away from Lacada Point, he found an anchor. A big one, 'one Jasinksi armspan plus one foot from fluke to fluke'. It was heavily eroded, missing its shank and one fluke, hidden under a mesh of fine algae. 'A less experienced eye', he added, 'less acute, less sharp than mine, might easily have missed it.'

And now what were we to do? That evening, sitting by the fire, we made a plan. What could we possibly do, just the two of us, without any proper equipment, and with a find like that on our hands? We had seen two cannon. There must have been fifty. If we had found pieces of eight as easily as that lying on the surface, there must have been ten or a hundred times as many buried further down. And if there were silver coins, it followed that there must be gold ones. In the 1580s the Americas were producing ten pounds of silver for every one of gold, and the proportion of coins in circulation was roughly the same. So for every ten pieces of eight, we should find one gold escudo. Only there was no getting away from the fact that there were 3,000 or 4,000 cubic feet of chalk, sand, gravel and rocks to be meticulously sorted through. To get at them we would have to move mountains or break them up. We would have to shift the boulders on top of the sediment. And there were boulders of every shape and size, some as small as a pumpkin others as big as carriages. It would mean at least two years' work, and two years' work by a large professional team of experts, at that.

This was the first Armada wreck found since Boyle found his. What Boyle did with his 'pretty made and pretty shaped bronze guns' was to bring them to white heat over a peat fire and then break them up (a wandering tinker had suggested this method to him). He sold 'three cartloads of brass at $4\frac{1}{2}$d a pound'. The gold coins that Boyle found have disappeared, made into rings, perhaps, for they do say roundabout that there isn't anywhere else that the family fortune could have come from. My plans were quite different. I wanted this to be the first Armada wreck to be properly excavated and scientifically studied.

What we wanted to do was not the sort of thing one can do just like that. And in any case it was 1 July. We both had our professional commitments. It would be autumn by the time we had the thing set up. There was only one answer. Wait.

We decided to come back fully prepared the following year. From now until then we must keep the secret to ourselves, for there is in England no legal provision by which my rights as finder could be protected in my absence. We must offer prayers to Poseidon, night and morning, that no other divers would find our wreck. *Dura lex, sed lex.* Before leaving, we must replace all our odds and ends of treasure, piece by piece, at the back of the cave.

28
A Two-Star Wreck

Back in London, I began, on reflection to have certain reservations. The *Girona* deserves three stars. There's no doubt about that. But the *Nuestra Señora* has two, and so have many other Armada ships that left their bones along the coast of Ireland. Before rushing into this perhaps we should, after all, go and have a look at the other wrecks. I went through my notes once more, and picked out two other tempting wrecks and some groups of wrecks.

In September Marc and I were on our way to Eire. Besides our light equipment, I took along a magnetometer this time. It's a detecting instrument that reacts to any disturbance in the magnetic field caused by a foreign magnetic mass, twenty or thirty iron cannon, for example, or an anchor, or a few tons of iron shot. We spent five days at the first site. Very promising. . . . But definitely less so than the *Girona*. That wreck would have to be left for another expedition. The next group of wrecks proved to present trickier problems than had appeared on paper. To be reconsidered.

Without any feelings of regret we now made for the *Nuestra Señora de la Rosa*. She was the one that sank like a stone between the Blaskets and the Kerry coast, on the very south-west point of Ireland. To get there we had to drive right down the west coast of this beautiful country. Its very poverty has made it one of the few parts of Western Europe to have maintained a real identity.

23 September. Our cylinders were full of air and we, likewise, were full of ourselves. The sun shone. The sea was like a mill pond. Marc was driving, and between the 'oohs' and 'aahs' and the 'did you see thats' at the fantastic landscape, he asked why I had given the wreck two stars. I said, 'She's the *Rosa* isn't she, and an *almiranta*. She was the Guipuzcoan flagship.' I argued that the King's gold was divided among all the squadrons on the *capitanas* and *almirantes*. They were the only ships that had *contadores* and *pagadores* on board, officers entitled to sign cargo on and off, and therefore, to hand out the King's money, on orders from the squadron commander or from the admiral. I didn't know exactly how much royal gold there was on board. In theory Medina Sidonia was supposed to be taking 200,000 ducats. There was

a lot of money talk in his letters to the King. I had been over his expenditure letter by letter; in the end he did take most of it with him. What wasn't at all clear, was why the Pagador General of the Armada, one Juan de la Huerta, swore on oath that he left Lisbon with 430,690,091 maravedis. It was possible that this represented the total funds, for fleet and army together, but I didn't know where it came from.

Marc asked, 'How much does that number of maravedis equal?'

'About 1,148,240 ducats. But there were expenses at Corunna. All that was left would have been on the *almirantes* and the *capitanas*.'

'But, Robert, the *Girona* was neither a *capitana* nor an *almiranta*.'

I explained that of course she wasn't. There wasn't any treasure on the *Girona*, not official chests, anyway. All we could hope to find there was the money that noblemen and gentlemen adventurers would have had on them, as well as their jewels, no doubt, and then whatever the five crews might have had in their pockets. Just before sailing they had received two months pay. The Duke received 3,500 escudos a month, plus expenses; his 'Ayuda de Costa', a Maestro de Campo, got 500; a cavalry general, like Alonzo de Leiva, 300; a captain in the Guards, 100 escudos; a ship's captain got 100 too; a doctor, 30; an alguacil, 24; soldiers and seamen must have got between 4 and 10, depending on their length of service and seniority.

On the other hand the treasure of the *Santa Maria de la Rosa* was down in black and white. The sole survivor swore to the English: 'In silver there are in her 50,000 ducats; in gold as much more: more rich apparel and plate, and cups of gold.' That's what he is quoted as saying in *Certain advertisements* . . ., a contemporary propaganda pamphlet, in which a translation of his evidence was published. Only his evidence is taken up again in other pamphlets and in them it becomes 15,000 silver ducats and 15,000 gold, and then in his second examination, he mentions only 'three chests full of money'.

'Do these sort of amounts seem at all realistic to you?' asked Marc.

The answer was yes. Killjoy historians have pointed out that this sole survivor, a Genoese, called Giovanni de Manona, was in no position to know what he was talking about, because he was only the pilot's son, and that in any case his evidence is full of errors. But all the same, the *Rosa* was an *almiranta*, and all the *almirantes* and *capitanas* I knew about, whether they were lost, captured or got back to Spain, were carrying a sizeable treasure. And then, quite apart from the treasure, this was a fascinating wreck, because she went down in deep water, at least 100 ft, which meant that she could have remained fairly intact.

'Yes, okay. But to get back to this treasure. How much do you reckon?'

I had made a note of all that was on the other flagships, and had the figures with me. The treasure on the *Rosa* must have been roughly the same:

Santa Ana, capitana of the Biscayans, ran aground at le Havre, 50,000 crowns of ten reals, deposited in safe hands in France.

San Lorenzo, capitana of the galleasses, looted by the English—nothing, according to them, but according to the historians, 50,000 or 22,000 escudos.

Nuestra Señora del Rosario, capitana of the Andalusians, 52,000 escudos, or 25,300 or 22,000 according to whose evidence you take, a Spaniard's or an Englishman's—not counting Pedro de Valdez's own money, say 4000 reals—or his silver. This was all Drake's loot.

San Salvador, vice *almiranta* of the Guipuzcoans, captured in the Channel, said to have then contained a chest, but it disappeared.

Oquendo's *capitana*, another *Santa Ana*, the Guipuzcoan flagship, as it happens: 55,000 escudos, brought back to Spain.

Apart from the fact that somewhere Juan de la Huerta mentions the sum of 4,000,000 maravedis on one ship, possibly the *San Salvador*—this was all that was known.

'But, Robert, this is really something. I mean to say, it's a fortune.'

Marc was right, it was a fortune on paper, at any rate. The ship went down in the presence of an eyewitness, Marcos de Aramburu, who was just a few cables away on the *San Juan Bautista*. He gave all the details. All one had to do was to dive along the dotted line, still on paper, of course. Then Spotswood Green, the good Reverend, who we mentioned before, constructed a theory that seems to stand up. He thought that the ship struck Stromboli reef and went down at the foot of it, to the southeast in view of the tide, and according to the map, about 90–100 ft down.

'The wreck must have held together then?'

'Yes, apart from the wood, it should all be there. And as well as the treasure, you know, there were 50 field cannon on board, and bronze ones at that, if the pilot's son knew what he was talking about.'

'But it's a dream come true!'

'Isn't it? For independent archaeologists, not living off handouts from some committee or commission or ministry, it really is a dream come true. A dig that pays for itself. I always have thought that profitability wasn't necessarily synonymous with badly carried out excavations, and that a loss doesn't necessarily imply scientific accuracy.'

'Quite, poverty is no virtue. But how about some lunch?'

We had just arrived in Limerick. Before sitting down to lunch I bought a local newspaper, the *Evening Press*. Splashed across the front page was an enormous headline:

Treasures of The Armada

'After a four-year search amateur divers claim they have discovered the wreck of a flagship from the Spanish Armada off the County Kerry coast; the discovery could be worth at least a million pounds. Mr Sidney Wignall, 44, has declared. . . .'

Somehow we weren't hungry any more. I had already experienced that sensation, like the time that some other divers found the wreck of the *De Liefde* in the Shetlands, and the wreck of the *St Gerans* off Mauritius, the *Chameau* off Nova Scotia and any amount of other treasures ships—wrecks I had spent hours diligently studying and carefully indexing when I should have been out looking for them. This time, too, it was not the lucky divers I felt sore about. I felt like hitting myself.

Sidney Wignall, leader of the expedition, that found the *Nuestro Señora*, deserved to have us take our hats off to him. He had been searching for six years. First he had looked for the *Girona* and failed. This time he deserved to succeed. We drank his health in large dry sherries in a pub in the main street in Limerick and wished him all the luck in the world.

For us, then, it would have to be the *Girona*. On the way back we made a long list of all the equipment we would need to take. On reading through it I realised we had left something out: a lorry to load it all on.

On the equipment side, our friend from Marseilles, Henri Delauze, founder and president of COMEX, and pioneer of experimental and industrial diving, was to be our patron. He was going to lend us the lorry, ready filled. On the diving side we needed more men, real professionals. On the money side the question was how best to spend the few cents I had managed to bleed out of my publishers during the last ten years. The National Geographic Society in Washington D.C. to which I had contributed for some time, had promised a small extra sum. And then above all we would need time. My Managing Director was willing to release me from professional commitments in my London office for the summer. Finally we would need an Armada expert. I undertook to become one.

But for the whole of that winter I knew I wouldn't be able to open *The Times* in the morning without getting into a cold sweat.

29
1968: Topography of a Shipwreck

On 27 April 1968, three overloaded vehicles drew up in front of the Manor Guest House, Port Ballintrae.

In the Peugeot van were 2 Zodiac inflatable dinghies (Mark 5 and Mark 3), 2 outboard motors (50 and 35 hp), 2 compressors (8 and 10 cubic metres/hr), a powerful force-pump, 12 double air tanks, 6 sets of diving equipment, 9 crates and 11 sacks filled with accessories and tools; and 2 French divers.

In the Opel station wagon, were cases filled with photographic equipment, cameras, underwater camera housings, sacks of lenses, underwater lights, flashbulbs, a small compressor, a metal detector, cylinders, carboys of acid and chemicals, drawing and topographical material, and two Belgian divers.

In the Alpine and its trailer, two sets of diving equipment, a low pressure compressor for two hookahs, rolls of Admiralty charts, crates of documents and photocopies, cases of reference books (histories of ordnance and navigation, books on naval construction, numismatics, preservation and treatment of artifacts, and so on) files, and the leader of the expedition.

But expeditions, like wars, are won by men first, equipment second.

Marc Jasinski was to be with us for two months. Marc is one of the best underwater (and underground for that matter) photographers in Europe. He is a chemistry graduate, so as well as his cameras he was going to take charge of the preservation of underwater finds.

He had brought with him Francis Dumont, known as Jules, designer and architectural student, veteran speleologist and novice diver. He was to take charge of all charts, plans and sketches.

Henri Delauze, our friend from Marseilles, patron of the expedition, had picked the two other members of the team from among the top French professional divers.

Maurice Vidal, 33, with fifteen years in the French Navy; comes from Cannes and could talk the hind legs off a donkey. To shut him up you'd have to knock him out, which wouldn't be easy. He is an instructor in unarmed combat, a frogman-trooper, commando, instructor in demolition-sabotage, and a combat diver. He developed these skills mostly in Algeria and in Indochina, and returned the mildest, most peaceloving man imaginable. From the Navy he went into professional diving.

Louis Gorsse, native of Auvergne, but now living in Toulon, is as taciturn as Maurice is verbose. He spent three and a half years in the Navy doing what must be the nastiest of all jobs, underwater explosive disposal. It didn't put him off, though, and immediately afterwards he became a professional diver, specialising first of all in public works, and later in the most arduous branch of the profession, off-shore oil rigs. His qualifications, like Maurice's, are many and varied.

Come the evening the boats are already inflated, the cylinders were filled and we were ready to go. (See page 110.)

On 28 April, we set out. The sea was calm but swept by hail and sleet. We were shivering by the time we got to Port na Spaniagh and the sight of those rocks, blacker even than usual, chilled us to the marrow.

First of all I wanted to draw up a precise plan of all the wreck remains. Underwater archaeologists excavating Roman and Greek wrecks in the Mediterranean, on an even mud bed, in deep water, use the classic methods of land archaeology. A grid of metal squares placed on the sea bed serves as the basis for all measurements and general reference. Colour stereophotographs are taken systematically at every stage of the excavation, followed by careful layering in each square which enables them to locate every object precisely in three dimensions. Later they can plot on their chart the exact layout of the cargo and of the ship herself. But here there isn't a ship any more, nor any cargo. All there is here is an irregular chaos of cliffs and crevices with shallow basins here and there filled with pebbles, coarse sand and enormous boulders all over the place; between these we could get as lost as ants in a pile of gravel. Laying out a metal grid here would be about as easy as it would be on the top of Milan Cathedral. And besides it would be utterly useless. The first square we put down wouldn't last three days, and even if the square itself stayed put, even before the ink had dried on our chart, everything in it would have been tossed about and scattered into the next square and the next. Every movement of the ocean upsets the seabed, fills up holes, covering and uncovering cannon at random.

Of the actual ship which must have split on the rock, nothing will have survived. Of that we can be certain. Only the whereabouts of heavy objects will be able to tell us anything of how the *Girona* met her end. Her anchor, cannon, ingots and cannon balls have not moved far. They have just rolled down as far as the first ledge. Everything else has been swept along like dead leaves in a tornado, resting one day here, another somewhere else.

Above: *Spanish (left) and Neapolitan (right) copper coins.*

Below: *Hilts and handles of various swords, daggers, pocket and other knives.*

Above: *We found the remains of 45 forks (left—the handles) an important discovery because until now it had been thought that the fork was not in common use at that time.* Centre: *A silver perfume phial (right) with its crystal dipper with which to dab the moustache with when the wind blew from the direction of the galley slaves. Silver whistle (left) belonging to one of the five ships' captains drowned in the Girona. Originally used for giving orders, this type of whistle eventually became the actual insignia of office.* Below: *Silver candlesticks and a silver chair decoration.*

Left: *Perhaps an inkwell lid. Could it have been Don Alonzo's?*

Below and right: *Fragments of gold plate and engraved silver. On one of them is either a hallmark, or, more probably, the owner's initials (unidentified).*

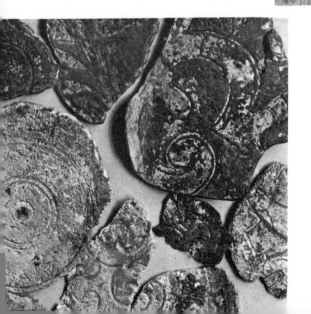

Above: *Religious medallions and silver lions.* Centre: *A link of an elaborately worked gold chain, set with rubies and pearls, and a ring belonging to a Canon of the Holy Sepulchre or to a Jesuit father.* Below: *Bronze buckles, bronze shoe and chair nails and a bronze pin.*

So to draw up our chart we must use the simpler method of bearings and measurements taken from set control points.

I started by stretching a red rope between the first and second cannon. The rope was marked out in metres and zigzags to link the two pieces to the most obvious points. Another rope ran from the cave to the first ingot. These formed the backbone of our plan. Meanwhile they provided guidelines for Louis and Maurice, who were doing an exploratory dive to get to know the area and the local diving conditions.

Back in the cave I reclaimed our embryo treasure. It had stayed put. Then just casually in passing, I turned over a stone and there was a handful of silver fragments, a gold link, a silver half escudo and two more pieces of eight for the evening's inventory.

The thing that really worried me was the weather. Already by the next day it was beginning to deteriorate. Visibility was down to arm's length. No question of being able to make a start on the systematic circular exploration that I had planned. It was impossible even to find one's way around, and there wasn't a hope of being able to work on Lacada Point, where Marc had meant to finish setting out the buoys. I made one attempt to go and take a look, but the surf enveloped me and somersaulted me into a vertical cleft. I made my way back to the dinghy only to have Louis point out Maurice to me. He had strayed out to sea and was heading eastwards; already he was no more than a tiny speck, swept swiftly along the surface by the irresistible tidal current.

Having recovered Vidal, we returned to the harbour.

And there we were to stay for three days. My room faced the sea. At night the wind from Greenland would rush in through the badly fitting window, streak under my frozen nose and then dart out under the door on its way to the Azores.

In the morning, I could tell just by listening what the weather was like. If I heard the thunder of waves breaking on the beach, there was nothing for it but to resign myself to going back to sleep.

On 2 May it was the silence that woke me. The sea had calmed. We could go on with setting out the buoys. Taking advantage of the crevices, Marc and Francis laid out white ropes marked off in metres, to north and south, perpendicular to the red rope. They numbered the intersections. These would serve as a general grid for the chart of the area. Louis and I worked as a team, plotting every object and control point with distance and bearings. For a simple triangulation I took bearings using a fixed wheel with degrees marked on its rim, while he stretched a tape to the selected control points. To fill in the details Marc would systematically photograph it all from top to bottom. (See page 94.)

177

We had worked hard. We deserved a little treat as a reward. We would go on a treasure hunt. Immediate success: some gold coins.

Louis and Maurice brought back the first ones, two pieces of four escudos, bearing the shield of arms, and above, the crown of Aragon, and therein lies the whole history of Spain. There isn't a mark on them, not a sign of wear. 'Extremely fine', certainly 'very fine'. As well as these they had found two dozen or so pieces of eight reals, some badly worn pieces of four, some exquisitely engraved gold buttons, a heap of broken silver forks, and assorted artifacts and tiny fragments. The pace was set for such finds. It would not slacken and it wouldn't be long before the 'treasure site' chart was covered with symbols and arrows.

We decided to split up like that every day, one team plotting charts, another surveying, and the third out hunting for treasure.

But barely were our measuring lines in place when the sea got up again. By the time we were able to go back, the red rope, a half-inch nylon climbing rope, had snapped right through and tangled itself up into a cat's cradle, and the white ropes were snaking about in the seaweed like overcooked spaghetti.

We had to start again. And it was not always possible to work in the shallows of Lacada Point where we began before. Louis tried once or twice at the beginning, but in the swell it took both hands just to stay in one place and one couldn't work with one's teeth: they were already taken up with the mouthpiece. There was nothing for it but to give up.

There was nothing we could do about it, so on bad days we all concentrated on the treasure in front of the cave, where it's deeper and somewhat more sheltered. I had already found several engraved gold medallions there, or rather empty settings, all missing their central cameo miniature or cabochon. Doggedly, I searched everywhere, but never did I find a single one. They were lighter than the gold and would have been swept away like dead leaves. One finds these same jewels in portraits of the period, sewn onto a hat, or a doublet, or occasionally worn on a bracelet.

I found a gold coin. I kissed it. My first gold coin, my very first.

Fifteen years I had been looking for that coin, fifteen years I had waited to bestow that kiss and it was not the dry kiss of a miser. It was not the metal I was kissing, nor what it could buy. What I was kissing was the symbol, the dream come true.

For a long while I just looked at it. Then I found a second one. In less than an hour I had filled my jam jar with gold and silver, not only that but a mustard pot, a pickle jar and a band-aid tin as well. Finally I was stuffing things into my left glove.

How we needed that glimmer of gold between the pebbles to keep us warm! After a few hours on the sea bed the cold started to drill its way into one's sinuses. One's neck went rigid; it paralysed one's muscles. The pain was excrutiating. We were used to letting our feet get paralysed, to letting our calves go rigid. When it got to the point when one's knees wouldn't bend then it was time to get back while one still could.

We tried everything. Francis wore three neoprene suits one on top of the other. Maurice wore three layers of woollen underwear under a dry suit and Louis a dry suit over neoprene. I myself had to give up dry suits, because the sleeves cut into my wrists so badly that they drew blood. I finally found the best thing to be a new Piel wet suit, which is cellular and designed to maintain a constant thickness. A little bottle of compressed air with a reducing valve reinflates it at depth.

In the evenings we took the cold with us in our bones from the sea back to the shore. We took it into dinner with us, and then to bed. It lingered in the marrow of our bones until the next morning, and finally left us just as we began to dress for a new dive.

30

Treasure Cave

We lived by the rhythm of the sea. Our daily life was utterly dictated by the whims of her temper, her anger and her moments of tranquillity. Her anger confined us to the harbour, her periods of tranquillity sent us to work. There were days when we dived blind, when the water was so dense that one could not see one's hand at the end of one's arm. We would get lost in the places that we knew the best. Huge black masses would hurl towards us, veering off only at the last minute, or else the darkness around us would quite suddenly intensify. We did not know it but we were nothing more than the playthings of the swell which was throwing us at a rock or sweeping us into a cave.

On days like that we would come ashore in the evening, pitching and rolling like drunks, and later, even lying in bed, we would still feel the sea rocking us.

Diving keeps one's hands busy but it leaves the mind free. As I humped my stones around I let my mind wander happily. At last there was nowhere else I would rather be, nothing I would rather be doing. After all these years I was living out my dream. When I got up that morning I felt shattered already. I would go to bed more dead beat still. Hardly time to eat or sleep. That's how I like it. What I really enjoy is the discomfort, the exhaustion, the biting cold, the wretchedness of sea-sickness and the agonising need for a pee.

Under my hand something yellow moved and cut short my soliloquy. A gold coin? No, a shell. It's so easy to be fooled. Let's have a good look. It'll teach me a lesson. I won't get caught like that again. *Santiago y a ellos!* I am away on a crusade. *Santiago y Cierra España!* It's not a shell. It's a gold medallion, with the cross of St James on it. It's the insignia of an order of knighthood, could it be the Order of Santiago? Then it must be Don Alonzo's. I wave my arms about in excitement, talk to myself. But no. On the other side there is a saint beautifully engraved, but he has neither a shell nor a staff. It can't be St James. Keep calm, now. Let's examine this cross. Well, yes . . . no, it's not the military order of St James of the Sword. There's no blade and there's no pommel. The ends of the arms are shaped like fleurs-de-lis.

On the reverse, the saint's side, a tree. What saint can that be the symbol of, a tree? A new bit of research for the winter.

The floor of the cave was covered in a dense amalgam of round stones, shot and conglomerated remains—so was the floor in front of it, with a thick layer of pebbles on top.

'Have you seen this?' I said very learnedly to the others when I came up. 'Highly significant. Typical Spanish ballast. I found exactly the same sort of thing in Vigo, in some 1702 wrecks.'

'Really', said Maurice sarcastically. 'How interesting. I wonder why they put a whetstone in their ballast and a pair of dividers?' And he pulled both these things out of his jam jar.

Louis was not much more impressed than Maurice. He turned out his little green bag. 'But what are all these gold coins doing then, in the middle of this "significant ballast"?'

My theory was getting a bit shaky. It finally collapsed the next day when I lifted up one end of a splendid gold chain and found that it went right down into the black magma and came out again on the other side. My 'significant ballast' was in fact natural concretion. Rust from the cannon balls, gunpowder, chalky deposits, empty shells and sand had petrified with time and now covered most of the remains of the wreck.

Should we try to remove this husk underwater? Dangerous. There was always the risk of breakage. It would in any case have been a lengthy business. So for the first month our work consisted of shifting great chunks of the sea bed out of their honeycomb of solid rock, raising them and loading them aboard, heaving and sweating and straining our backs. Once ashore, and taking every possible precaution, we spent every evening breaking up the concretion, pebble by pebble. From out of this vile magma came escudos and reals, maravedis and ducats, copper buckles, little gold chains, broken pots, lead bullets, leather straps, fragments of cartridges, knives, spoons and forks.

It was there in the cave that the swell had collected the bulk of the débris. Every morning at breakfast, in between the porridge and the eggs and bacon, I would say: 'Francis, Maurice, Louis, Marc, listen! No more risks in the cave. Better to leave a few coins behind than one of us.' (See page 108.)

The cave, so-called, was in fact two enormous slabs held up by a few pillars in the middle and some large round stones in front.

The left-hand side was a regular gold mine, the right a silver mine. We shovelled out tons of stones and gravel by the bucket load before painstakingly raking over the bottom. Our efforts created a sort of funnel effect in the cave. In rough weather the water would surge in through the enlarged opening and spray out of the little holes at the back, like a turbine. Gravel flew everywhere and stones rolled around.

The ground swell would knock one over if one let it, so one had to work clinging on, with the hoses of one's regulator flapping and bubbles of air escaping in horizontal dotted lines.

We had already jacked out one supporting stone, to clear the way for a large chunk of magma. Now we were setting to work on the pillars, Maurice on one side and me on the other. The pillars were built up of stones tightly packed and 'cemented' together. The natural concretion supported the stones, the stones supported the pillars and the pillars the roof, all two hundred tons of it. We were working right there underneath it at the very back. If the roof had given way we would have been squashed flat as two pancakes. But in among the stones that held up the 200 tons of the 'Rock of Damocles' was a silver candlestick in perfect condition. I could touch it, but it was jammed—only by the little stone that rested on the stone that held the one that supported the other . . . and so on. The trouble was that only the day before I had broken down two other pillars that happened to be on top of some silver phials—could they have been for the apothecaries' potions?—and uncovered a regular vein of pieces of eight. At arms' length, with one eye on the way out and the other on the ceiling, I slipped my crowbar under the stone. Should I push it? I did. The rock moved. Suddenly I was out in the open. What on earth had happened? What was I doing outside? Reflex action? What had that noise been? There had been a sound of stones rolling. Something must have collapsed in the other part of the cave. But Maurice was outside too. He must have set the stone rolling, the idiot. 'Look here, Maurice, come off it.' I made angry signs and snarled into my mouthpiece. 'You're crazy.' I pointed at the massive roof, and mimed—collapse—pancake. After all, I had said it again that very morning! He didn't look impressed. 'How about you, then? I saw you.' He pointed at his eye, at me then at my crowbar. Maurice's sign language is remarkably eloquent. I quickly grasped what he was trying to say. If one of us was a stupid ass, a blundering oaf, an elephant in a china shop, it certainly wasn't him. He had been watching me. He had seen it all. I was a public menace. *He* had been very methodically removing a few tiny pebbles, here and there, of no structural significance whatever. On his side there were still three pillars. Three. He held up three fingers. There was no denying it. But wait a minute. How come he got out in such a hurry too?

Next day I had my candlestick, but the stones I had removed had revealed, in a gaping hole at the base of the pillar, the dull sheen of another. The other half of the pair. I had to have the pair. The following day I had it, but then I spotted a real gem, a brilliant gold object, the biggest yet. A piece of table plate, it must be. A plate? A meat dish? A fruit bowl? A bath? Perhaps we could try shoring up the whole cave somehow. A long job though. Let me see. If this stone moves, then it means it is not holding anything up. That one is a bit trickier. But see how it shines. I am blinded by the reflection of my torch light. An hour later I have the great jewel in my hands. It's a large saucepan handle. Copper. But behind it . . . behind it I can see a long section of the little figure of eight chain, so fine and delicate, disappearing under the base of the last pillar. . . .

The cave is still there, scraped down to the last wrinkle of the last crevice of the last cranny. And no one left any bones behind. The slab is hanging there suspended in thin air, defying gravity, a monument to our temerity.

31
'Is the Minister of Defence Aware?'

The people of Port Ballintrae are the nicest in the world. Week after week, our two compressors, lined up like guns in the harbour, back-fired for four hours a day, battering their eardrums, spoiling their quayside walks, ruining weekends for the whole village, upsetting their holidays and disturbing their convalescences. Anywhere else than in Ireland we would have had stones thrown at us, insults heaped upon us. We would have been asked to go and do our compressing else-where. Petitions would have been got up and we'd have been accused of disturbing the peace.

But here, the local people used to just put their heads to one side, smile good morning to us and raise their voices slightly to say in our ear: 'Pretty awful weather again today, eh?'

The people of Port Ballintrae are also exceedingly discreet. There we were, diving every single day at the same spot, which just happened to be called Port na Spaniagh, and where—though, of course no one believed it—according to local tradition, there lay the wreck of a large Spanish ship. It must be a coincidence . . . but all the same . . . every evening we used to bring back huge sacks, dripping wet, and immediately stuff them into the lorry and everyday a large metal trunk used to go from the lorry to the boat and back again. More coincidences. The fishermen and anyone else who happened to be standing around would discuss yesterday's weather with us, today's inclemency, tomorrow's probable meteorological conditions, and then they might ask one or two general questions, just to be polite and friendly. Louis would reply, with a gentle smile: 'I wonder, could you say it in Auvergnat?' And Maurice would answer: 'Sorri, mi not spik ingliche.' I would try to be a bit more precise myself. 'Ah, yes. Didn't I tell you? We're doing a general geological survey of the sea bed, of the volcanic system around Giant's Causeway. Fascinating examples of eruptive cristallography, you know, resistance of lava to marine erosion. All that sort of thing . . . we're making a film about it.' And our Irish friends would keep a straight face and comment non-chalantly. 'Yes indeed, how very interesting. Of course that's what it is.' They looked forward to seeing our eruptive, volcanic underwater film one day; in fact they could hardly wait . . . and they would change the subject. 'And what about lobsters? Do you see many lobsters down there?'

Every day we used to ask our perfectly delightful hostess, Mrs McConaghie, for more empty jam jars, more pickle jars. (Some of us, you see, were rather clumsy and kept breaking them.) Right from the start she must have found it the most natural thing in the world for geological film makers to want. She remained quite unsurprised by it. Not once did Mrs McConaghie even begin to inquire or seem in the least bit puzzled.

With the help of a Belfast solicitor, I had taken certain precautions to ensure the full rights of the expedition in case of any incidents. I had spent days on end in London examining the minutiae of British law concerning the recovery of wreck and sunken ships. A very well informed lawyer had pointed out to me that English law establishes, by a clear and indisputable precedent, that any salvor who is working uninterruptedly on a wreck that he has discovered and buoyed becomes the sole 'salvor in possession'. In the case of the *Girona*, the 'salvor in possession' was me, which meant that I was allowed to fend off any potential rival who might be tempted along by the rumours or the wiff of gold.

So that everything should be in order we had anchored a large red plastic buoy near the cave (not too near, one couldn't be too careful) by a steel rope. It read:

NOTICE TO ALL DIVERS

ALL SUNKEN OBJECTS WITHIN A RADIUS OF 400 YARDS ROUND THIS BUOY ARE UNDER AN ARCHAEOLOGICAL SURVEY BEING CARRIED OUT BY MR. ROBERT STÉNUIT AS EXCLUSIVE SALVOR. IT IS STRICTLY FORBIDDEN TO TAMPER WITH ANY SUNKEN OBJECTS IN ANY WAY WHATSOEVER. IMMEDIATE ACTION WILL BE TAKEN IN COURT AGAINST TRESPASSERS.

I had also informed the Coleraine Receiver of Wreck of what we were doing and had promised to let him have a complete inventory of finds every two weeks. The Receiver of Wreck is a civil servant in the Department of Customs and Excise, part of the Board of Trade. It is his job to see that 'wreck', properly so called, is placed in the Queen's bond to be sold by the Crown, with a fee to the salvor if no claimant comes forward within one year. Legally, what we were bringing up from the cave was not 'wreck', however.

Our legal position was watertight, but we still felt that with a little discretion and a few white lies we might improve our chances of being spared angry set-tos with other divers, and that would be in everybody's best interest.

The day came, however, when we had to abandon our policy of discretion. We had finished marking out the first section with buoys, and our next job was to raise the gun to uncover what lay underneath, so as to complete our chart. Louis fastened a lifting bag to the small breech-loading piece. Maurice opened a cylinder under it. The rubber filled out, expanding like a frightened blow-fish. The gun quivered, bucked and then, very slowly, moved up to the surface under the fat black bag which was spitting out silvery bubbles. And there, waiting for us in the hollow imprint left by the cannon, was a sounding lead.

I made a chain with Louis to shift the blocks in the fissure where it had been lying. Lying among the stones and shapeless cakes of rust and remains of cannon balls were two very simple bronze pestles. Were they apothecaries' pestles, or were they powder pestles? Gunpowder used to be carried in barrels ready made up in large quantities (five parts saltpetre to one of good willow or alder wood charcoal, and one of refined sulphur). But the so-called fine-corned powder was not always fine enough. It contained more saltpetre and was used as a fuse (a trail of 'fine-corn' worked quicker than cotton match steeped in saltpetre) as well as for small arms, muskets, arquebuses and pistols. Perfectionists used to make their own powder according to their personal recipes.

We had previously found, not far from there, two flat mortars, plain bronze slabs, hollowed out on top, where the various ingredients would have been carefully ground up—bronze on bronze so as to avoid any risk of sparks. Musketeers used to steep the mixture in brandy to make it blend better, and then sieve it when it was dry.

I think, in fact, that these are powder pestles and not for medicines.

Elsewhere, at the bottom of a round hole full of silver and cannon balls, I found a superbly decorated apothecary's pestle, a much nobler instrument altogether, in quite another class. Scattered next to it lay fragments of an old crucible mortar, such as one still sees in the shop fronts of old-fashioned chemists.

But back to the cannon. All that was left to do was to secure it properly and tug the whole lot—balloon and all, very slowly—back to Port Ballintrae, now that the tide was pulling with us. Everything went without a hitch, but inevitably our manoeuvres were conspicuous. The secret was out. As four of us carried the small cannon to the van, the whole population seemed to converge on the harbour, on foot, on bicycles or in cars. They all wanted to get a look, to touch it, to know all about it. One inquisitive local nearly got his nose caught as the van doors closed behind the gun. From the harbour, the news flew from pub to pub and then, mysteriously, from newspaper office to broadcasting studio. The following day we were besieged by the press.

But these journalists didn't speak French . . . my English was a little imprecise . . . and of course an old diver's hearing is not as sharp as it might be. A wreck? What wreck? Had they heard something about a wreck? But tell me where. Oh, I see. We were supposed to have found one? Oh, you know what wrecks are like. Big place, the sea. The Armada? Just a moment, now. Just remind me, who was this fellow Yarmada? A cannon? You know what they are like round here, they'd say anything. Why are we still diving at Port na Spaniagh for the second year? Seems a bit odd? Does it? Well, yes, thank you, our survey is going very well. But the wreck? The gold? Chained skeletons of galley slaves? A film, yes a kind of underwater film. As for the rest, I'm afraid we have an exclusive contract with the *National Geographic Magazine*, very strict. . . . I can't tell you any more about the geology. I am so sorry . . . thank you again for your interest.

The following day, back at their typewriters, these journalists were tapping out their stories. 'Mystery hangs on cannon barrel found off Antrim coast . . . a team of mystery divers are believed to have located the wreck of one of the ill-fated Spanish Armada warships . . . they are reluctant to comment on the matter', and so on.

Then the television crews put to sea in a hired boat, cameras levelled. How had they found out about it? Once more I had to explain that yes, indeed, there was that cannon; but no, it was not possible to film it. A question of contracts, that was all. Treasure? You mean historical treasure? Why, indeed, yes, some cannon balls of the greatest archaeological interest, stone and iron ones. Gold? But my dear chaps, that's the kind of things you see in the movies. A man doesn't take his safe with him when he goes to war. The *Girona* was, after all, a warship, not one of those galleons from the Americas, packed with jewels and pearls, or with gold and silver ingots. No, no. Only the *capitanas* and the *almirantes* were carrying any of the King's treasure. (That at least was true.)

The programme was broadcast on 24 May, but was fortunately interrupted by a wildcat strike of company technicians. Ha, they said, another cunning move by the mystery divers to tighten the web of silence they have spun round themselves.

One thing did rather worry me. In a recent press conference the public relations officer of the Belfast branch of a big English diving club had made a public announcement of the club's future plans. I read the hand-out in a Coleraine newspaper (*The Northern Constitution*, 18 May), which I picked up quite by chance:

Members of the . . . club are searching for the remains of a Spanish galleon, the *Girona*. . . . We will be diving in three different spots . . . where we have been told the galleon went down. The hunt could take years. Until now we have been hiring local fishing boats with echo sounding equipment. . . . Diviners have been helpful in finding wrecks in other parts of the world and we were wondering if any local diviner would give us suggestions as to the possible location of the *Girona*.

If they were intending to use echo sounding equipment and a diviner to look for a 400-year-old wreck under a chaotic bed of rock, I could well believe that their search might take them years. I did feel, however, that I ought to inform the club of our discovery and invite their members to come and look at what we were doing. So I got my solicitor to send a letter to the chairman saying that I was the finder and 'salvor in possession' of the *Girona* and ready to stand up for my rights. I ended by expressing my warm desire that the club committee would accept our invitation to come and make an observatory dive around the remains of the wreck. The following Sunday the pirates attacked.

On 26 May, twelve of them arrived, twelve divers from Belfast, armed with jemmies and ice axes, housebreakers' sacks and lifting balloons.

There they were, in the harbour dressing beside their cars. They did not announce themselves. They did not introduce themselves. They ignored us. I inquired whether they had received my letter. No answer.

'Careful', I warned them. 'Don't touch anything. We are in the middle of plotting a chart of the wreck, and besides I am "salvor in possession", and have sole rights over it. You will see our marker buoy; it makes it quite clear.' They look at each other, then at me, but say nothing. I warn the boat-keeper who is taking them out. 'Take care, a boat used for illegal purposes can be siezed. If anything happens in the vicinity of the wreck, in the eyes of the law you are an accomplice.'

'Come, along now', he says, 'what will you be thinking of. These gentlemen are going out to look for an outboard motor that was lost last year, and a few lobster pots of mine that have got caught on the bottom. . . .' And off he went, making straight for Port na Spaniagh.

A man from Port Ballintrae who went with them, and has since become a good friend of ours, told me in detail what happened. They had taken with them an extra specially clear sighted diviner-soothsayer-clairvoyant. He was standing on the prow, eyes fixed on the horizon, using both hands to hold his copper wire dowsing stick. He turned to the boatman. 'Think of something.' 'Gold', said the mariner. The dowsing stick writhed and twisted. From the way he carried on you would have thought the poor soothsayer could hardly keep a grip on it. It went on like that the whole journey. It could only be a gold mine.

We left after them, but soon overtook them and were the first to anchor above the cave. We had all agreed, whatever happened, they would not take anything away.

Team after team, they came, weighed down with all their apparatus and searched for hours, all over the place, but nowhere near the wreck. Then one group found the end of one of our lines and followed it to the cave, only to come face to face with our guard. One look at Louis was enough. Bolt upright, motionless, arms crossed, chin set for battle and with an icy glint in his eye, he was about as welcoming as a prison door. Four marauders turned sharply to starboard and made themselves scarce, further out to sea.

Meanwhile their hired boat had gone back to Port Ballintrae to pick up the next batch. They climbed up onto a small rock to wait for it. On this very same rock where they saw nothing, immediately under where their feet had been, we later found forty gold coins and a little heap of jewels. I really must tell them one day.

And now the next team arrived. They too found one of our lines and followed it to the breech blocks. 'Tankards, apparently', was how they described them afterwards to the press. This time I swam above them, watching them, without being noticed. Then at the very tip of Lacada point I saw the last one stop. He picked up a small square lead plate, and stuffed it swiftly into his bag. Not only was this stealing, but that piece wasn't even plotted on our chart yet. What really shocked me was having our excavation programme upset like this. We had put too much hard work into it to stand for some irresponsible gang coming along like this and messing up our results.

The souvenir hunter moves on again. I dive down and swim up to him, tapping him lightly on the shoulder. He turns, as though he's just had his foot bitten by a shark. I point to his sack and shake my head. I turn it upside down. The lead falls out. Suddenly I am surrounded. Someone is shaking me from behind. They are all waving their arms about. One of them is trying to pull off my flippers. I kick but he hangs on. I get free and go up to the surface. Four heads bob up. I protest. 'I warned you that you had no right to take anything at all off this wreck.' They threaten me, they remind me in no uncertain terms that we are 'only foreigners' and that we 'better be careful'. And now the abuse starts. What right have I got to take the law into my own hands? And what about that cannon? I had no right to take that either.

Our Zodiac comes up. Louis leaps out to the rescue. Francis is ready to join him. Six divers jump out of the enemy boat and advance like skirmishers. Only the invaders can't forget the fact that they are members of a club. A committee meeting is clearly called for. So in the middle of the ocean motions are proposed, amendments suggested. They vote, and decide, by the required majority, on a retreat. The minutes are taken and they leave, empty-handed. We can get back to work.

A police car was waiting for us when we returned to the harbour. Apparently one of the divers from the city had complained about our 'violence' (not that he had anything to show for it). An extremely polite and rather embarrassed policeman asked us whether we could spare him a few minutes, once we were dressed and warmed up, unless, of course it would be more convenient another day. The club secretary was overcome with confusion and utterly charming. She apologised profusely. No, my letter hadn't arrived (which was true. My solicitor in Belfast hadn't posted it yet). 'What an unfortunate misunderstanding. And when I think, she added, 'that we dived there only seven or eight weeks ago and didn't see a thing. . . .'

Of course it had all been nothing more than a misunderstanding. The club's Belfast Chairman told the press that the divers in question were a group of members acting quite independently. The official club dive for that Sunday had been held somewhere completely different (which was true). Summoning an extraordinary meeting of the committee, the club called upon its members not to dive at Port na Spaniagh any more, while the legal situation remained unclear. When I started legal proceedings before the Supreme Court of Northern Ireland to insure the protection of our expedition, four of the divers made it their business to assure me, either by telephone, in writing or in person, that they hadn't touched a thing. It was the others. Personally they found the whole affair deeply shocking.

The incident upset me all the more in that the club, at national level, has an outstanding record in the diving world for courtesy and responsibility. For many years I have had some very good friends among its founder members.

But such epic battles are rare in the quiet little village of Port Ballintrae and the next day the BBC broadcast an account of it. It was both detailed and objective. But according to Radio Belfast: 'Belfast divers were rammed when they attempted to take some things off the wreck.' (The prow of an inflatable dinghy is about as lethal a weapon as a beach ball.) For the big London dailies it was a godsend. Better than the Loch Ness monster! Front page headlines: 'Storm on the Sea Bed as Rival Divers Clash' (*Daily Mail*); 'Deep Sea Fight Over Wreck' (*Daily Express*); 'Spanish Treasure Ship Divers in Under Sea Clash' (*Daily Mirror*).

The incident took place on 26 May and I spent the whole of the following week in Belfast in the marble passages of the Law Courts. This time I was diving into the mysteries of British procedure. By the following weekend a bewigged judge, had clearly reaffirmed our rights.

There is good evidence that Mr Sténuit is indeed the exclusive salvor in possession. . . . Any person who has taken any object from the wreck, has not acted legally. . . . . All underwater swimmers and archaeologists should abstain from taking any object on the bottom of the sea in the vicinity of the wreck of the galleass *Girona*. (Mr Justice Lowry, Supreme Court of Judicature of Northern Ireland, May 31.)

But on 30 May, in the House of Commons in London, the Hon. member for North Antrim was asking the Minister of Defence the following questions:

Is the Minister of Defence aware that a wreck at Port na Spaniagh, County of Antrim, ownership of which is vested in his Department, is being damaged and looted by foreign frogmen, and what steps is he taking to deal with this situation?

The M.P. had clearly got his information from Belfast. The Minister replied:

Ownership of this wreck is not vested in the Ministry of Defence and the prevention of looting of such wrecks is not a Ministry of Defence responsibility. . . . It is the responsibility of the Board of Trade.

But meanwhile, some of the good folk of Port Ballintrae, who knew us well and had been shocked by the incident, had taken it upon themselves to telephone their Member of Parliament in London in the middle of the night to explain to him exactly what had happened. The question had already been tabled and it was too late to change the text, but the following day in his comments to the press after the House had risen, the Honourable Member, who now, at last, knew what he was talking about, put the record straight, showing a truly British sense of justice and fair play.

As far as I know, there is no one who claims ownership of the galleon and as the Belgian team of frogmen have kept in close touch with the Receiver of Wreck at Coleraine, they are completely within the law. The Belgians, I understand, are highly skilled underwater archaeologists and we are very fortunate that men like these should have come to North Antrim to investigate the possible galleon. . . . I have had to word my question in a particular way to get it on the Order Paper in the House, but I am casting no reflection whatever on the divers.

That was the last of the stormy visits.

32
Gold Under the Algae

It was getting on for the middle of May. The sun was shining and in the space of a week the algae had blossomed into life.

They were everywhere, always moving, dense as a field of sugar cane. They engulfed us, drove us mad. One couldn't talk of a sea bed any more, just thousands of these fluid rubbery tentacles. Paralysed, trapped, swallowed up, enraged, you cut through twenty, forty, a hundred. They didn't move. You pushed them out of the way, in a moment they were back. You could carry them right away and by tomorrow the current would have brought them back and filled up the hole you had just dug.

June. Living at the bottom of the ocean, we didn't see the sun even when it shone. But we had our own barometer: the turned up nose of our most loyal supporter, 4-year-old Wee John McConaghie. Red and peeling already, it told us all we needed to know about the weather. Wee John, the youngest son of our hosts at Port Ballintrae, came down to the harbour every morning to cast off for us, and every evening he was at his post to supervise unloading.

There was often a land breeze now, which brought with it a strong smell of cows. The sea was calmer. We could actually stand up in the Zodiacs to put on our equipment. The fishermen said 'You're lucky. It's the best spring we've had for twenty years.' The water was warmer too, and now we could dive comfortably for five or six hours a day. Our chart was beginning to take shape. For weeks we had been working on it and now we had put a name to each section of the site: the canyon, the corridor, the mound, the basin and so on. The 'esplanade', for example, was actually a basin 100 ft by 50 ft opening out in front of the cave. On the solid rock bed lay a layer of pebbles, stones and rocks of every size, ranging in depth from 1 ft to 10 ft. At first we screened those pebbles with great care, moving them systematically from one section to the next, exposing the solid rock underneath. In this shifting gravel, we found nothing but perfectly round white perrier balls, of beautiful chalky stone. All the metal objects had collected, like nuggets in a riverbed, in the fissures of the rock. Pounded by 400 years of storms, any jewels here had been shattered to smithereens. The sea had bent gold rings, torn stones from their

Above: *Medallion of an unidentified Knight of Alcantara. The cross was originally covered with green enamel. The pear tree and the fountain identify the saint San Julian del Pereiro. The Knights of Alcantara were once known as the Knights of St Julian of the Pear Tree.*

Below: *I identified three of the Caesars. They are almost certainly Byzantine emperors. Left: Stauracius (unless of course it's Julius Caesar). Centre: Michael I Rhangabe (no possible doubt). Right: The younger Constantine (Constantine II) or possibly Vespasian.*

The treasure grew and grew.

Spanish gold coins: one, two and four escudos from the reign of Philip II.

*er, Charles V on a Neapolitan gold ducat.

Son, Philip II on a Neapolitan escudo.

Rare Neapolitan gold escudo from the reign of Charles V and his mother Joan the Mad.

A very rare Neapolitan gold ducat from the reign of Charles V.

Portuguese gold coin: a St Vincent from the reign of John III.

Above: *Ducats, half ducats, testons and silver carlins from the Kingdom of the Two Sicilies.*

Below: *Silver coins of Spain or the Americas, of 2, 4 and 8 reoles.*

settings and miniatures from their frames; unlinked precious chains; smashed goblets and tankards, leaving only the handles and knobs of the covers (the thickest parts) intact; and crumpled the silver plate. Lead musket balls lay flattened between stones. Small, heavy things, on the other hand, like gold coins, soon sorted themselves out from all the rest and found a sheltered spot at the bottom of a crevice. They remained there undamaged and were still perfectly intact when we found them.

The upper strata here proved to be sterile, so we could shift them without further ado. In the inflatable dinghy a self-powered water pump roared, much to the annoyance of the seagulls, which had to strain to make themselves heard above it in the wind. Attached to it was a 100 ft-long hose, which plunged down into the sea ending in a nozzle, like a fire extinguisher. Using both hands, wedging himself in position with feet and knees, the diver had to try to hang on to it, helped by a lead weight holding down the nozzle. In spite of that, because of the powerful backthrust, it threatened at any moment to turn the hose into an epileptic sea serpent. We had a Galeazzi non-recoil nozzle, an ingenious system which drives some of the jet of water backwards to counteract the backthrust of the main jet. But the wastage of power is considerable and with the small pump which is all we had room for in our tiny boat, we could ill afford it. So the only answer was to hang on for all we were worth.

The high-pressure water jet itself is invisible, but it stirs the sand up in huge dark swirls; pebbles are sent flying, stones jump and roll around, scaling the slopes. One diver can move mountains. The feeling of power is tremendous. But as soon as one reaches solid rock one has to stop and begin sifting through very carefully, by hand, every tiny wrinkle on the sea bed. Here the pieces of eight were worn and smooth, the forks prongless, the ewers and meat dishes were in pieces. Only the gold had remained intact. Because of its weight it fell straight down away from the danger of erosion, and it is not susceptible to chemical corrosion. The escudos that lay waiting for us to find them were shining and bright. Three-quarters hidden in a crevice, they had that same cheeky look about them that a collar stud has when one finds it in its proper place in a drawer after looking for it under every bit of furniture.

It stayed light now until 11 pm. The glistening sea tangles were full of sap, thick as one's arm and taller than a fully-grown man. Their brown thalluses, their fronds and their long velvety strap leaves were themselves covered with the purplish red algae that spread everywhere, all over the red rock and over the grey and black boulders. The interplay of colours on the sea-bed dancing in the sunlight never ceased to be a delight.

The holiday makers had arrived, and in the evening they crowded round the boat-filled harbour to count the gold ingots and the silver. 'I do wonder', said Maurice 'what on earth they find to do in other years, when there aren't any frogmen.' One might ask what they find to talk about too, those years. Already the most fantastic rumours were going around concerning what we are doing.

According to them, we have, very discreetly, exported to the United States enough gold to replenish Fort Knox. An American photographer is supposed to be slipping the 'little stuff' over. A local telephone call warned the customs of this, but, alas, too late. Another story is that a customs officer, an accomplice of the divers, that is, was stopped at the border with Eire and found to have jewels and gold coins in the back of his car.*

The teacher in the village school set her little class 'The Frogmen' as a composition subject. She showed us the results. There was no doubt in the minds of the local children. We had found 200 tons of gold ingots, as well as several solid gold cannon. For their parents even that was not enough. We had also, it seems, found some silver pistols, in perfect condition.

Nonetheless it is true that with our joke boats, our navvies' tools and a few rubber bags, those of us who followed behind the photographic team, were everyday bringing up the sort of treasure one reads about in story books. I had found in the cave a marvellous chased gold salamander, winged, with every scale engraved and encrusted with rubies. A few feet away Louis found a strange gold fragment, a point, apparently off some star shaped jewel, with a fleur-de-lis shaped link to hang it from, and a double gold ring to thread a ribbon through. Two days later, a bit further along, he had spotted, with his practised eye, a straight edge on the side of a little black ball, about the size of an apple and made of that magma that clogged everything up. Carefully he scratched the edge. Under the black, it was gold.

That evening I plunged the ball into a dilute solution of acetic acid. The next morning there was some black liquid in the jar and a slightly pocked gold Malta cross. With the star-shaped fragment the jewel was

---

* In fact everything we found on the expedition was noted down the very same day on the official inventory for the Receiver of Wreck, and then deposited in a safe in a Belfast bank, or, where necessary, given immediate preservation treatment. This was carried out either in the house where we were staying or in the preservation laboratory in Belfast, founded jointly by Queen's University and the Ulster Museum. Our experience has shown that honesty in an activity like ours elicits one of two responses in conversation: incredulity or piteous contempt. The most common response is of the wink, nudge, and conspiratorial smile type, accompanied by asides like: 'Why, naturally, but you pocketed some for yourself on the quiet, I hope' —a remark which gives an interesting hint to what the behaviour of the interlocutor would have been in our place.

complete, except for the end of one of its eight points. I knew I could count on Louis, and by the end of the week he had the last piece. This fragment still had traces of the white enamel on it that originally covered both faces of the cross.

By that stage, we had twelve gold coins on the inventory (one, two and four Spanish escudos, and scudi from the Two Sicilies). In my wildest dreams I had visions of the day when I would find another twelve all by myself. The time I found fifteen all in one day I enjoyed a minor triumph. I paid for it the next day, when Maurice found twenty and I found only a bronze bootnail. And to tell the whole truth I must admit that modesty was not the only reason why my triumph that day was so minor, or why afterwards I took care never to mention the fifteen-coin day again.

The moment I surfaced, I rushed to have Louis photograph me, first in black and white and then in colour, hands full of gold. And then to make it look more natural, I tried spilling the coins like manna from one hand to the other. One of the fifteen coins, a four escudo piece from Seville, spilled so realistically it jumped out of my right hand onto the back of the dinghy and then—splash—into the water.

Rarely in my life have I felt so abashed. I broke off the photographic session there and then. I gave Louis the coins (or maybe he snatched them out of my hands immediately, to put them away somewhere safe —that's the sort of detail I prefer not to remember), and I dived down again. I never did recover that fifteenth coin.

As the weeks went by we widened our area of research. I now realised that the sea must have scattered the wreck debris over an enormous area, for wherever we looked, our luck seemed to follow us. Ten or twelve gold-coin days were standard now. On 12 July we celebrated our hundredth gold coin, and by then we already had 500 silver ones on the inventory.

And that was not all. As a child I had pinned up on my wall a reproduction of the frontispiece of *The Mariner's Mirror*, published in 1583. It showed a pilot in a greatcoat holding a sounding lead, and on either side of him an astrolabe and a pair of dividers. This picture of my childhood was recreated for me again, in colour this time, the day I found an astrolabe lying slightly askew on the sea-bed, and again when Maurice brought up the identical bronze dividers, scarcely bent, and Francis found the sounding lead. (See page 258–9.)

One day, at the far end of the site, on Lacada Point, sticking out from under a protective coating of black magma, harder than stone, made of rusted cannon balls, kitchen debris (animal bones, charcoal, broken pots) and cartridges, and cemented again by the gunpowder, I spotted a small piece of wood. 'Part of an oar', I motioned to Maurice. He came and looked. 'No', he waved, putting an imaginary gun to his shoulder. The next day, after three hours work with a hammer and a chisel, I had uncovered 6 in of a musket stock. On the third day, having worked my fingers sore to get through that dense mass, I could see the chamber. All that was left of the barrel was a grey paste sticking to the wood and to the rock. It was disintegrating before my very eyes with every movement of the swell. The firing piece had gone down loaded. I found the round lead ball still in the breech. Working at the rate I was, it took me the rest of the week to finish digging it out. Then, firing piece in hand, I swam up and in pantomime fired a victory salvo into the air.

At the same spot, I found a scrap of black velvet in the magma, a bit of doublet perhaps, and some leather thongs. And then one day I came across the most fragile object of all, the most unexpected: a delicate hexagonal point, made of rock crystal, about two inches long, set in a little silver top. And suddenly everything fell into place. The countless rounded silver phials that we had been finding bits of everywhere, had not as I thought originally contained apothecaries' remedies, but scent. (See page 174.) Every nobleman, every hidalgo must have had one. When the wind brought to their nostrils the suffocating stench of 244 rowers, living in a shirt and chained night and day to their places, they would pass the crystal dippers, loaded with scent, under their curled moustaches. (Another explanation has been suggested to me by an English expert: because of its strange optical qualities, rock crystal was thought to have certain magical powers. It might have been some sort of charm to hang on a chain.)

And finally, amid the kitchen remains, I found an absolutely unique relic, unhoped for, incredible, perfectly preserved, in the dense gangue that must have encrusted it from the very first, protecting it from erosion and from all contact with oxygen. In a mass of magma, made of broken crockery, charcoal and one bird's feather and in mint condition, I found the only Armada plumstone in the world.

33
The Summer of the Century

The summer was drawing to a close. The tourists were leaving, and there were six divers who were beginning to feel a little lonely.

Only Wee John McConaghie stuck loyally to his post. 'The best summer of the century', they said. Even the hotel keepers agreed. There never was a summer like it in Ireland, not in living memory. The barometer needle never moved from set fair. The sea was limpid. Never did we feel the least bit cold. Once more the scene under water had quite changed. A new layer of white algae had started to grow on top of the red ones that were already covering the brown algae.

We raised the anchor under a huge black balloon, and the second cannon. While Francis was measuring it before drawing up his plan of it (see Appendix III), I remembered what Carew wrote to the Lord Deputy in 1589. 'Yet those pieces that be under the water I presume are there still. . . .' Well, yes, Sir George, you were quite right. (See page 120.)

Like other objects that sank to the bottom, the lead too escaped the notice of the Scottish captain hired by Sorley Boy to harvest the crop of shipwreck. We raised a ton and a half of lead in the form of ingots or plates. It was not ballast, as Boyle had thought. At that time Spanish ships were ballasted with round stones, taken from river banks. The lead was raw material for casting musket shot and arquebus balls. Most of the ingots had Roman numerals stamped on them, or crosses potent. These markings did not relate to the weight, for ingots of equal weight were stamped differently. Perhaps they indicated for which ships' companies the ingots were earmarked.* One of them had on it the monogram of St Peter, a P inside an E, forming a key. Could that one have been cast for a Vatican galley?

Every evening, after work, I made a tour of the site to check on the others' progress for the daily report.

Francis's flippers could be seen from way off, flapping about at the end of his long legs among the fronds. He was working head down on

---

* In a letter to the King from Lisbon, the Duke wrote: 'The lead ingots have been distributed . . . 30 quintals to each of the five regiments.'

Lacada Point. He must have been waist deep in a narrow pot hole, feeling his way around. From the knees down he was hidden in a fine sand cloud. I spotted two sword pommels in his jam jar, finely decorated with plaited copper wire. The pommels were wooden ones, typical of the sixteenth century. All the rest, blade, hilt guard, and hand shield would have been made of iron. Nothing was left of them. He emerged for a moment from his sand cloud to drop three gold links into his jar. We found one or more of these links virtually every day throughout our three excavation seasons. The heavy chain that they made up had been scattered by the sea over some 1000 sq ft. And yet elsewhere Maurice found far more fragile chains still intact.

Maurice had said to me: 'If you come over to my corner today, you won't know where you are. You won't recognise it. I've practically built a motorway.' It was true. Five- and six-ton boulders had been bound with three steel bands and raised under bunches of lifting balloons, leaving behind a wide avenue. Maurice was nowhere to be seen. His air cylinder was lying on the bottom, with a long rubber hose running out of it. I followed it, looking for the other end of the demand valve and for the man who had it in his teeth. A bit further on I saw bubbles percolating up from under a large flat stone. Maurice was probably crawling about busily under there, torch in hand, in pursuit of the missing rubies from the fragile, intricate baroque pendant, of which as yet he had found only fragments, mixed up with various rings and Neapolitan gold ducats bearing Philip's profile.

It was Maurice's first dive for a fortnight. He had been out of action with a dislocated finger and a crushed left hand. This was the story as he told it to me.

'I had just rolled back my stone, you know, the big four-ton one. Underneath there was another five or six hundred-pound one. It moved. Great! I thought I could roll it out of the way. I was just pushing it upwards, to get it over a ridge, when—crash! My support slipped. Down it came. Right on my hand. It hurt. Everything was spinning. I'm going to faint, I thought. I'm going to drown. Drown. Was I scared! When I came to, I found myself pinned to the bottom, caught by my left hand. What was I to do? The first thing you think of is your air. How much longer did I have? Then I remembered that I could still reach the crow bar with my right hand. I managed to stretch out my arm, grab hold of it and slip it under the boulder. I pushed as hard as I could and managed to release my hand. But when I took my glove off later in the boat it was not a pretty sight.'

Louis was currently working east of the red line rock, in a vast expanse of stones and sand. He moved with calm and precision, but he moved with great power. With his parachutes, his bucket and shovel, and his tireless left hand sweeping the sand up like a windmill sail, he sifted through 30 cubic feet each day. In the green bag where he put all his finds, there was a diamond ring—there must originally have been ten stones in it, but only two were left—a little solitaire ruby in a gold setting, two two-escudo pieces, some silver goblet handles, a few shapeless bits of copper and some fragments of gilded table plate.

Marc had laid aside his cameras and was now on the lookout for lead. Gold and precious stones had little attraction for Marc. His thing was lead bullets. That was all he ever found. But he found them everywhere. One could not risk leaving an empty container lying around. The next thing one knew it was full of lead. Little bullets, big bullets, round ones, flat ones, musket balls, arquebus shot, pistol bullets and case shot—he did not miss one. He stopped only to feed large fat pink worms that he found under stones our our familiar fish. The fish had found himself a girl friend; quite a bit smaller, pink with brown marbly streaks, pretty though. Now there were two of them, following us wherever we went, gulping down the assorted prey—larvae, worms, and other creatures—that we disturbed as we went. Marc was going over everything again, checking our work with a specially designed metal detector. He would reprimand us for every little forgotten fragment. 'For the archaeologist,' he would say, quite rightly, 'a piece of a lead bullet is just as important as a chest full of doubloons.'

For all of us the remains of the wreck were strangely evocative. The gold summoned up figures of long dead hidalgos as clearly as if we had stolen the ducats from their half open purses. The silver crucifix that Francis found, all eroded and covered with a black patina, astonishingly simple and modern in style, carried with it a strong whiff of the mendicant friar who wore it. We could see it hanging from the girdle of his rough robe, beating against his legs as he strode up and down the deck of the galleass. The copper, pewter and lead medallions, mass-produced, bearing images of the Virgin Mary, Christ or the Holy Family, medallions bought on some pilgrimage, told us of the death of the galley slave who must have clutched them in the palm of his hand, as he murmured a silent prayer and his irons and chains dragged him down to the bottom, with only his ragged shirt for a shroud.

Since the day I first met them in Florida, I have been in love with dolphins, man's cousins returned to the sea. Like all divers I am deeply envious of their perfect adaptation to this world where I can never be more than a tolerated intruder. I have studied them, fascinated, and it was with much pleasure that I once wrote a book to their greater glory.* The day Francis brought up with great ceremony a gold-plated dolphin that he had just found, I felt a real pang of

---

* *Dolphin, Cousin to Man.* (New York and London 1968)

temptation. My collection, after all . . . I have porcelain dolphins, ceramic dolphins, copper ones, stone ones and any number of others. But a sixteenth-century Armada dolphin . . . a dolphin with an upturned tail, on a base of waves, with two big round eyes, a dolphin that must have formed part of the decoration of the base of a table clock, like the one I had once admired in the Jewellery Room in the Victoria and Albert Museum in London—that would be the jewel of my humble collection.

And how about the other one? The little silver one that looked like a tadpole or an inverted comma, and which must have been a cup handle or the knob of a lid? And the gold dolphin? The gold dolphin whose nose was a tooth pick and whose tail was an ear pick—an instrument in common use at the time. (The American treasure hunter, Kip Wagner, found among the remains of the *capitana* of the 1715 *Flota* in Florida, a gold oriental jewel on a gold chain made of 2,176 flower-shaped links, which combined the functions of whistle, insignia of office, tooth pick and ear pick.)

And the dragon dolphin, wrapped around a silver naval pea-whistle, forming a ring to hang it from? That whistle must have been the insignia of office of one of the five ships' captains drowned on the *Girona*. Whistles of this type had been in use in all fleets since the thirteenth century; originally for giving orders, they subsequently became the actual insignia of office. (See page 156.)

It was at night particularly that temptation really needled me. I visualised the little showcase that would house my enriched collection, the right plinths, the angle of lighting, and then, finally, with a heavy heart, I put the complete fortnightly inventory in the post for the Receiver of Wreck, with no omissions.

One day Maurice and I went to take a sounding quite some way from Lacada Point, in a little cove where I reckoned any drifting bodies would have been piled up by the swell.

The sea was like oil. The sun—all things being relative—positively tropical. Not a ripple on the water, not a breath of wind. The rocky shore is almost vertical here. There would be no chance of finding a foothold here in bad weather, especially at the end of October, when there aren't even any algae to hang on to. Further along the shore is nothing but a mass of rocks. Any survivors who came anywhere near would have had their heads cracked open on them by the waves. The thick layer of foam that lies on the water when it's rough would have suffocated anyone who tried to swim away. At the foot of the vertical rock stretches a long stone-paved corridor. Recently, when I was doing an exploratory dive there, I found one of those veined marble eggs, pierced through from end to end (what they were for remains a mystery). It was clearly visible among the stones. I had found one like it earlier in front of the cave, where we later found hundreds of coins and dozens of jewels.

It was not very deep, only about 14 ft of water. It was possible to work there only when it was absolutely calm—the Zodiac bobbing about overhead. Yet another advantage of these extremely seaworthy and stable dinghies is that one can take them anywhere. Where a wooden boat would be smashed into a hundred pieces and a steel frame would bend and burst its rivets, this sort bounces off the rocks unharmed, like a football. The pump was on board and Francis was on duty, keeping an eye on it.

Maurice wedged himself in between two rocks and set to work clearing the corridor. Almost immediately he found a gold ring. Excitedly, he swam over to show it to me. It is bent and the setting is empty but one can still read the inscription: MADAME DE CHAMPAGNEY MDXXIIII. Our first dated find! What an excitement! But wait—1524 . . . 88 minus 24 equals 64. Whoever the beauty was who gave this ring, she gave it 64 years before the Armada sailed. So it can't have been her lover who was wearing it, unless he was well into his eighties and most exceptionally faithful to his first love. (See page 264.)

Already the name fascinated me. I swore to search until I knew every detail of the family history. I must know who it was that wore the ring at Port na Spaniagh on 26 October 1588. And why. And whether Madame de Champagney was dark or fair, pretty or ugly.

I left my hole to go and work with Maurice. He held the hose and looked in the direction of the jet, watching the fan of flying stones. I looked from on top. It was a worthwhile precaution: he spotted a four escudo piece that I missed as it flew up, and stopped to pick it up. An hour later, it was I who saw a gold ring rolling among the pebbles, which he hadn't seen from where he was standing. It was intact. The setting was an exquisite little salamander, gracefully coiled into an S shape. Another salamander! Could it have any connection with the first one? Did one of the noble lords on board have a salamander in his coat of arms? (See page 155.)

For three hours we watched the water jet carve its way through the stones. We moved the whole floor of the corridor in one direction, and the next day we went over it all over again in the opposite direction, just to make quite sure. But there was nothing more.

The following day it was still like a mill pond. Francis and Maurice took advantage of it to empty out all the potholes and crevices at the top of Lacada Point. You had to be a diviner even to spot them because they were all full to the brim and cemented over by rock-coloured stones camouflaged by algae. They found some earthenware pots, a fragment of window glass, a few scattered links, a gold chain, some spherical buttons, and then, under a protective layer of bullets, a complete pewter plate.

I had found myself a vast basin some way off from Lacada Point, full of pebbles, dead algae and vegetable debris. It was only logical to assume that in a basin such as this fifty bodies at least must have piled up, along with all their money and their jewels. We were going to pick their pockets.

As soon as Louis turned the hose on the pebbles he stirred up an inky black mushroom cloud of mud. Suspended vegetable compost made the water so dense we could hardly see further than 6 in ahead. With my nose to the jet, I kept my eyes skinned for the glint of gold, at the same time pricking up my ears for the dull clunk of a gold coin. We worked in strips and progress was slow. As soon as we had passed, the ever shifting stones filled the basin again. Nothing. Nothing at all. If there were fifty bodies here, then they must have been paupers' bodies.

The most beautiful jewels of all came to light during the last few days. Our finds were beginning to be more and more spaced out. We didn't talk about it but we were beginning to feel that the end was in sight. Still I wondered whether we had actually exhausted the lode, or whether we had done no more than skim the top of the cream. And thinking forward to the next season, I made some rapid soundings everywhere we hadn't already covered.

In the spring Louis had found two oval, baroque medallions in finely worked gold, topped by a triton with a long seaweed moustache, and enamelled emerald green and purplish red. One had been in front of the cave, the other nearly 50 yds away. From both of them the central stone was missing.

Then, just as I was coming to the end of a series of soundings in a virgin area, on the sand and gravel that I was scooping from under an unsteady rock—there, new and shining, was a lapis lazuli cameo of a Roman emperor in profile, wearing a crown of laurels, set in one of Louis's gold medallions and framed by eight perfect pearls.

Under the same stone, after an hour's feverish work, breathing out as hard as I could so as to squeeze further under, I caught hold of another one. I felt sure that there must be more. I was using my hand to sweep little heaps of gravel towards me. Then, like a poker player who fans his cards open as slowly as possible, I spread out the little pile, grain by grain, storing up the suspense for as long as possible. To get to the back, I had to go right inside, twisting like an eel. The edge of the face plate of my mask jammed when I pushed my head forward. It filled with water. I had to screw up my face to unstick the bottom edge and blow into it through my nose to empty it as it filled. But I had gained 6 in and, stretching my arm out of joint to scrape the last corner, I felt the pearls of a third jewel under my finger tips.

For some time I stayed quite still, looking at them lying there on a pink rock. Each profile was different. The likenesses must have been copied from classical models. Could they be the twelve Caesars of Suetonius's history? It really is true: the sea-bed is without doubt the richest museum in the world.

Louis and I spent the next few days eagerly turning over every stone around there. I found a sixth jewel, intact and with not a scratch on it. Louis, meanwhile, followed my example and had edged himself in to work in a narrow crevice, between two large boulders leaning one against the other. When he found his air was getting low and decided to go up, he had to come out backwards. His cylinder jammed. Trapped, he couldn't get out, couldn't move. His knife was strapped to his left calf. He stretched to reach it but failed—he tried again. By twisting both his wrist and his knee he managed to inch them closer together. He gripped the handle of his knife with his fingertips, and feeling his way, tried to find the cylinder straps behind his back. He hacked away at everything he could reach. Snap! He released the cylinder. It swung round. He was free. He backed out and swam calmly up, carrying the air tank.

He went back there the next day and raised the rock under one of our bunches of balloons. The seventh Caesar was waiting underneath for him. And then, quite by chance, a few days later, some way away from there, he came across an eighth medallion, without its central cameo. My question was answered. The next year we should have four more Caesars still to find.

It was the end of September. The harbour was completely deserted. Even Wee John had abandoned us. For two days we saw him walking smartly up and down practising carrying his satchel. Now he had gone to school.

It was back to school for us, too. We let the air out of the dinghies. I counted the cannon balls again, photographed the jewels, the chains and the buttons, cleaned the black crust off the last of our 140 gold coins, our 600 silver coins and 60 copper ones. We said our goodbyes and were on the road again.

It was libraries that led me to the treasure and now the treasure was sending me back to them. That winter, in Brussels, I must clear up all the mysteries.

Who was she, this Madame de Champagney, who must have already been a great-grandmother in 1588? What was the significance of these two salamanders, and the order of knighthood, if it is one? Which order, whose, and who was the Knight of Malta? On the cameos, who's who? I thought I had recognised Julius Caesar, and the one who looked like Mussolini might be Vespasian. But how about the others? Who made them, in what workshop? I knew nothing about glyptics. I would have to start from scratch. Which Renaissance goldsmith engraved the medallions and our marvellous jewels, and where, in what town, what country? For what patron and what fee? And the saint's profile—or is it a Pope—on a large lead plaque? And the church on the other side, what church is that?

And the young mistress, who with one hand gave her ring and her heart, while with the other she unclasped her belt, was she fair or dark? Who did she mourn? And after the tears, was she quickly consoled or did she die of a broken heart?

And these thousands of fragments of silver? How on earth could one fit the puzzle together? And what were the two guns called, exactly? Those lead things of all sizes, shaped like truncated pyramids, with a round hole through them, that we found everywhere, what could they have been for? And the pierced marble eggs? And what other vital questions were there that I hadn't even thought of asking yet?

34
Madame de Champagney

'Madame de Champagney 1524.' Engraved in fine capitals in gold, that name more than any other was going round and round in my head. I thought about it all the way back. It was a large man's ring, much too big for my finger, obviously made to be worn, clearly visible, over a glove. But who wore it and for whose fair eyes? I could hardly wait to get back and race off to the Bibliothèque Royale.

From the archives to the sea and back again, I had to complete the circuit. I was determined to, because it is this fundamental interaction between the library and the ocean, between the intellectual effort of research and the physical exertions of diving, that has always given me the total physical and mental satisfaction that comes only with total exhaustion.

The first thing I found out was that there were three villages in Franche Comté called Champagney. One was in Haute Saône: in the fifteenth and sixteenth centuries the lordship of the manor belonged to the Abbots of Lure. To the Abbots? No Madame, then. What about the others? The second was in the Jura (in the Dôle region) and the third in the Doubs region, near Besançon.

In 1588, the lordship of this Champagney belonged to the diplomat Frédéric Perrenot—well, there's an old friend, who was Chancellor to Charles V, King's major domo under Philip II, Governor of Antwerp, then Head of the Finance Committee in Flanders. But he sided with the people against Philip II and was exiled by him to Franche Comté, where he ended his days in deepest gloom. Born 1536, died 1602. He was Count of Champagney and Baron of Renaix.

So he didn't die in the Armada. In any case he was no fighting man, and can have had nothing to do with it, since he was the man who in 1588 was leading the Spanish delegation at the Bourbourg Peace Conference. His Madame de Champagney was a very rich widow, Constance de Berchem. He had married her thanks to the good offices of the Duke of Alba. Constance was not born in 1524, so the ring must have been a family heirloom.

From incomplete family trees in various general or universal (but invariably contradictory) biographies, I set myself to work tracing back through this whole complex family history. Finding this was a step in the right direction: 'His brother Jérome died in 1554, from a gunshot wound received at Montreuil and left him the estate of Champagney in Franche Comté, of which he took the name.' This brother Jérome, the heir to the title, was indeed born in 1524. The ring, then? Was it not a present from the happy mother to her husband on the occasion of the birth of this son, who was to inherit the maternal land? And so if our Madame de Champagney was the proud mother, what was *her* name?

A few more hours spent leafing through fat, worn, leather bound volumes, and I had my answer. Jérome was the son of Nicolas Perrenot (1486–1550) and Nicolasa or Nicole Bonvalot, daughter of Jacques Bonvalot, citizen of Besançon, and Lord of the Manor of Champagney. She was renowned for her beauty from Burgundy to the Netherlands. It was she who brought the title as her dowry to her husband, Nicolas Perrenot, Chancellor, Guard of the Seals, Minister of Charles V and already Lord of the Manors of Granvelle, Chantennay, Cantecroix and other places.

On the death of his Chancellor, Charles V wrote to Philip: 'My son, I am deeply grieved at the death of Granvelle, for we have lost, you and I, a loyal and trusted friend.' Nicole had born him eleven children, six daughters and five sons. The eldest was Antoine, the famous Cardinal de Granvelle (1517–1586), patron of the arts and a highly cultured man. He was successively Bishop of Arras, Councillor to Margaret of Parma, Inquisitor in Flanders, Cardinal, Archbishop of Malines, Viceroy in Naples, and Philip II's Prime Minister in Spain. Jérome, born in 1524, was their third son and sixth child. After Antoine came Thomas and Jérome, then Charles and Frédéric. As for the daughters, they are not considered worthy to be included in the biographies.

I now knew who my 'Madame de Champagney' was and I knew the possible reason for her gift to her husband of a ring engraved with her name and set with a fine, large stone. If it wasn't for the birth of their third son, it might have been to mark their tenth wedding anniversary. Although the date of Nicole and Nicolas's marriage is not known, we do know that their second child, Antoine, was born in 1517. If he was conceived in 1516, the first Marguerite was probably conceived in 1515, so the marriage could well have taken place in 1514.

Now I wanted to know on whose hand the ring reached Port na Spaniagh. I waded about for a bit and then the answer came to me in a flash. It was in Antonio de Herrera. In fact, it was in the third part of his *General History of the World*, published in Madrid in 1612. He devotes six pages to a complete list of important participants, taken from Zuñita: 'It is only right to name the men of quality who accompanied [the Armada], following in this the detailed account of the chronicler, Geronymo de Zuñita. . . .'

de Antonio de Herrera.

de Orgaz, don Tomas Perrenoto, fobrino del Cardenal Granuela, don Diego Odorio, fobrino del Marques de Aftorga, don Ramon La-

nando de Quefada, de Vb Fernando de Ricalde Nevi Iladolid, Ruygomez de Il Cuellar, don Melchior Pi

Reading through his endless list, I found, at the top of page 97 (lib. IIII, capitulo IIII), this name: Don Tomas Perrenoto Sobrino del Cardenal Granvela. . . . The Cardinal's nephew! Nicole Bonvalot's grandson. Finding this name in the Reading Room of the Bibliothèque Royale, I found at the same time a fresh pleasure, an echo of that which I had already experienced under the Atlantic when I first found the ring. The mystery was solved.

All the same, I still had to make quite sure, to cross-check. The young Don Tomas had sailed, I knew that, but on which ship? I soon unearthed another list (published by Duro) which gave his name among the passengers on the *rata*. Perfect. He had left on the right ship. But he might have disembarked on the way, or changed ships as so many others did—Prince Ascoli, for example, Marolin de Juan, Recalde. . . .

Did he ever get to Blacksod Bay? Yes. James Machary, the Irish sailor who was left behind at Killybegs, mentions him in his account to the English of the *rata's* passengers arriving on his ship (the *Duquessa Santa Ana*).

A great ship called the *Rat* of 1000 tons or more in which was Don Alonzo de Leva and an Earl called Count de Paris [de Paredes] . . . also a gentleman named Don Tomaso de Gran Bello [de Granvelle], a man much favoured with the King, of great revenue and a natural Spaniard born; with divers good Captains and other gallant gentlemen. . . .

Perfect, all was well as far as Lough Ross More Bay. Don Tomas had indeed re-embarked on the *Duquessa*. But what if he had been left ashore at Killybegs? This time it was a letter from a survivor of another wreck (de Cuellar) written from Antwerp in 1589 (and already quoted) that held the answer. In describing his arrival at Dunluce, from whence he intended to reach Scotland, he goes into some detail:

I travelled across the mountains and uninhabited regions and suffered much hardship, as God knows, then after twenty days' journey I reached the place where Don Alonzo de Leiva, the Conde de Paredes and Don Tomas de Granvela had perished, with many other gentlemen whose names would fill a score of pages. . . .

I too felt that I had arrived.

I wrote to the Library at Besançon for a portrait of Tomas and one of our Madame de Champagney. With great courtesy, the librarian, Madame Paris, sent me a copy of the complete family tree drawn up by General Jean Tiburce de Mesmay. She went into even greater detail:

> Your discovery is most interesting. The records doi n fact contain mention of Cardinal de Granvelle's nephew, who met his death in this disaster at the age of 22. It was Jean Thomas Perrenot, Lord of the Manor of Maîche, son of Thomas Perrenot, not Jérome, Lord of the Manor of Chantonnay and other places. Curiously enough, he does not feature in the most complete of the printed family trees, but in one or two manuscript documents. . . . His grandmother was indeed Nicole Bonvalot. . . . Unfortunately, although there are quite a few portraits of the Cardinal and of his father, here in the library we have neither of the two people in whom you are more especially interested. According to one scholar: "the portraits of all Chancellor Perrenot's descendants, have perished, in their dozens; leaving both history and art the poorer." There is, however, a famous portrait of Nicole Bonvalot by Titian, painted in 1584, now apparently in the United States.

I never did find this painting, in spite of lengthy researches. But what I did find at Besançon was a portrait (painted at the same time also by Titian) of her husband the Chancellor. Alas, although he is wearing a ring, it is not ours.

Jean Thomas, born in 1566, cannot have had a very clear memory of his grandmother, who died when he was only four years old, but there is no doubt that it was her ring that he was wearing when the suffocating yellow foam of Port na Spaniagh flooded his lungs, when the stormy waves beat him unconscious and drowned him at the foot of those black rocks.

*　　*　　*

We had also found two gold salamanders, one a ring setting, the other a pendant (43 mm long, 33 mm wide, 5–6 mm thick, weight 19 grams). Who did they belong to, and why salamanders?

It did cross my mind that it might be a charge from the coat of arms of one of the dead men. We had found the salamander ring right beside young Thomas's. It might have belonged to him as well, and the three gold and three silver coins that we found nearby might have been the small change from his pockets. Champagney, Granvelle,

Chantonnay—in none of their coats of arms does one find anything but gules lions, spread eagles issuant and boars' heads. As for the Lords of the Manor of Maîche, they did not bear arms.

Working from Zuñita and all other lists and mentions of passengers on the three ill-fated vessels, I drew up a complete list of all those who might have been in the *Girona*. To make doubly sure, I added all those who took more than one servant with them. But, however hard I looked at their shields in the illustrated armorials, I could not find so much as the smallest salamander twisting anywhere among them. I tried working backwards from a classification by heraldic charges, but not one of the families with a salamander was represented in the Armada. One of the salamanders had wings, so I thought I would look under dragon. Still no luck.

So? An English expert has pointed out that salamanders were frequently carried as a charm against fire. Legend has it that salamanders can extinguish flames and live in fire. The salamander is the Cabalistic spirit of fire, and in coats of arms it is almost always shown surrounded by flames. (Francis I had it on in his shield to symbolise his ardour in love.)

Ours may well have been mere charms, or perhaps I was looking for something that just was not there to be found. Salamanders were also a fashionable Renaissance motif, and ours may simply have been decorative, like the scrolls and flowers on some of the other jewels, like the dolphins or the grimacing old men on some of the forks.

35
'Fabricio Spinola, Captn.'

Now for the Malta Cross. Who had that belonged to, but first, was it actually a Malta Cross? An English Knight of Malta, who, like all his friends in the Order, was fascinated by our find, had his doubts.

I applied myself to the study of military orders of knighthood and learned that in the sixteenth century there were sixteen active orders. Only three, apart from the Order of Malta, had as insignia the eight-pointed cross of St Stephen. The eight points symbolise the eight beatitudes mentioned in the Gospels (Matthew, V, 1–12) and, by extension, perfect happiness. The four arms stand for the four virtues: prudence, temperance, fortitude and justice.

There was the French Order of the Holy Ghost, set up by Henry III in 1578 to replace the declining Order of St Michael, but their white enamelled cross was pommelly. It had little apples or balls at its points and was cantoned (i.e. decorated between the arms of the cross) with lilies; in the centre it had a dove. All one hundred members of the Order had to be French.

Then there was the Tuscan Order of St Stephen, founded in 1562 by Cosimo de Medici to combat pirates and defend the Catholic faith, but that cross was enamelled in red, edged in gold (while ours still had traces of white enamelling) and was cantoned with crowns and lilies.

And thirdly, there was the cross of the military Order of St Lazarus of Jerusalem, founded by the Crusaders in the twelfth century, originally to help lepers. It became a military order a century later. Their cross was an eight-pointed one, with lilies between the arms, but the Order had hardly developed outside France, England and Austria, and was in any case declining fast by the sixteenth century.

There could be no doubt, then: our cross (diameter 62 mm, width from point to point 20 mm, weight 37 grams) must have belonged to a Knight of Malta. But which one? (See page 156.)

The only Knight of Malta mentioned in the countless documents on the Armada is Hugo de Moncada, the Captain General of the Squadron of the Galleasses of Naples, killed at Calais on the *capitana San Lorenzo*. An engraving reproduced in a number of books actually shows a Hugo de Moncada with the white, eight-pointed cross on his breastplate. I think this engraving is in fact of a different Hugo de Moncada, the one who was first Captain General of the Ocean Sea and who was killed at Genoa in 1528. Not that our Moncada was not also a Knight of Malta; this much is clearly borne out by documents of the period.

But his cross could never have been on the *Girona*, because after Calais there was absolutely no contact between the survivors of the *San Lorenzo* and the rest of the Armada. Don Hugo's cross must have disappeared in the pillaging after the ship had run aground, probably finding its way into the pocket of one of Lord Howard of Effingham's officers, unless one of his servants managed to take it to France with him when he fled.

I went back over the list of noblemen who sailed in the *rata*, the *Duquessa* and the *Girona*, delving into their lives, going through their genealogies. I set off on many a long journey through families, over the centuries and across continents. The conquistadores took me to Chile, to Peru, to Colombia and Florida—a paleologue to Byzantium. Admirals took me across the seven seas. But while many of them must have been knights of one military order or another, I found no definite mention of the fact.

I then followed up each of the references. I re-read all the other lists and in particular the most complete, Geronymo de Zuñita's list of all the nobility and gentry.

This time I found six knights of St John.

Besides Hugo de Moncada, there were Gomez Perez de las Marinas and Francisco del Corral, both passengers in the galleon *San Martín*, who in all probability returned with her to port; there was Don Christobal de Torres Osorio, of whom no more is said than that 'he died on the voyage'; there was Lope de Vega, twenty-six and as yet neither a playwright nor famous; and there was Diego, Marquez de Medina. None of them, alas, as far as is known, ended their voyage on the *Girona*.

What was I to do now? Should I perhaps make a closer study of the Order itself? And its connections with Philip II? Yes. Maybe I would find a lead there.

Like the Knights Templar and the Order of Teutonic Knights, the Sovereign Order of St John Hospitaller of Jerusalem was born out of the Crusades. It retained its original character until the Renaissance.

The Order started as a Benedictine hospital, established around 1070 in Jerusalem, initially for travellers from Amalfi, and later for all pilgrims. The Brotherhood was established in a hospital adjoining a church dedicated to St John the Baptist, from which the Order derived its name.

In 1113, His Holiness Pope Paschal III took the Order and their possessions under his protection in exchange for services rendered to the Crusaders. Unlike the Knights Templar, a military order, the Order of Knights Hospitallers devoted themselves primarily to medical research, to the training of surgeons and doctors, and to the building and equipping of hospitals in Jerusalem and at other stopping points along the pilgrimage routes. It was because they were frequently called upon to defend the pilgrims against the Saracens that their order became, perforce, a military one.

In 1291, Palestine fell and the Order moved to Cyprus, and from there, in 1310, to Rhodes, where the Knights became Christianity's foremost sailors and its most redoubtable corsairs. The Order then became known as the Knights of Rhodes. It was an international order. The Knights had to prove noble birth for at least four generations. The Order was ruled over by an elected Grand Master who presided over the Sagro Consiglio, the Supreme Council.

The Knights were 'of the nine Tongues', the Venerable Tongues of Auvergne, Provence, France, Aragon, Castile, Portugal, England, Germany and Italy. The Order also included Chaplains of Obedience, ecclesiastics, who were the real hospitallers, and serving brothers who were soldiers and were required merely to be 'respectable'. The titles of Magistral Knight and Knight of Grace, given by the Grand Master, were only honorary ones. All knights and serving brothers took vows of chastity and obedience and, in theory, the Order paid direct allegiance to the Pope, but only in theory. The Knights were allowed to fight only against Moslems and not against Christian princes.

The sea power of the Knights of St John and their great fighting strength was a source of some concern to the Barbary Turks and the Ottomans. Sulieman the Magnificent began his reign by besieging Rhodes, and in 1522, after a lengthy siege, the Knights were expelled from the island. They left with the honours of war. In 1530 Charles V, who saw in them the most solid rampart of his kingdoms of Naples and Sicily, gave them Malta, where they established themselves. The Order was renamed the Sovereign Order of Malta, and was known as the 'Maritime Marshalsea of Europe' because of its persistent privateering, and the fact that in all encounters between Christians and Moslems, the Knight's galleys were always in the front line.

The Order had maintained close links with Spain, to whom it owed its territory. But when it came to the ultimate ordeal, the great siege of 1565, during which they were besieged for several months by Sulieman's 30,000 Janissaries and soldiers, commanded by Dragut and Mustapha, it seemed to the Grand Master, Jean Parisot de la Valette, that the calculated delay on the part of the Viceroy of Naples, Don

Garcia of Toledo, in sending help, was tantamount to betrayal. Perhaps what Philip II had really wanted was to leave the Turks and the Christians to wipe each other out so that he should be able to reclaim the island for himself? From then on the Order turned towards France. Nonetheless at Lepanto (1571), the greatest victory of Philip II's reign, the Order's galleys were up with the Spanish and the Venetians in the heat of the battle.

In 1588, the Grand Master was Hugues de Loubens de Verdalle, of the Venerable Langue of Languedoc. The Order as such took no part in the Enterprise of England. The English might be heretics, and their Queen excommunicated, but they were not Moslems. The Order had lost its Langue of England after Henry VIII's Reformation and his anti-papist activities. In 1583 Henry had sent the Grand Master, Jean d'Omedes, an unacceptable ultimatum. Two years later he had dictated an Act of Parliament whereby all the confiscated possessions of the Order and all its property reverted to the Crown. Mary Tudor had quickly restored the Order in 1553, and Elizabeth, once crowned, had suppressed it again, equally quickly. But the Knights of the Venerable Langues of Castile, Aragon, Portugal and Italy, having once fulfilled their duties to the Order (one year of the 'Convent', which meant service at sea, followed by three years in the galleys and, finally, two years residence ashore), could choose to go into the reserve and return to their families. They would be summoned only if the Order was in peril, as it was, for example, in 1565. While 'under pain of losing their habit' they were forbidden to bear arms against a Christian prince, they could not as individuals refuse to fight wherever they were summoned to do so by their King.

I must have gone through ten or a dozen histories of the Order of Malta, and I found countless knights, but not a single one more who had definitely sailed in the Armada. The exercise had been a pleasant one, but futile.

For a long time I had been wondering whether contemporary portraits might not have something to offer, those sixteenth-century paintings in which the grandees of the period never failed to don any and every medallion they were entitled to wear. If, by some stroke of luck, I were to find a cross identical to ours, perhaps then I would have my answer. My task was made easier from the very beginning by the fact that a great many sixteenth-century knights are shown wearing a simple cross with no decoration in the angles between the arms (those, for example, painted by Giorgione, Bassano, Carravaggio), so ours would be that much easier to spot. The rule was that knights were forbidden to decorate their crosses with any motif or personal symbol, but by this time no one took much notice of such rules. Several Grand Masters inveighed against 'the knights who decorated their crosses with diamonds', wrote Mlle Claire Eliane Engel, the eminent historian of the Order in a personal letter to me, 'clear proof that it must have been general practise'.

A portrait by Paolo Farinatti in the Louvre (sometimes attributed to Titian) shows a 'Knight of Italy', red haired and bearded, whose cross is cantoned with long petals. A sixteenth-century cross in the Musée de la Légion d'Honneur in Paris has fleurs-de-lis between the arms. A portrait of Lope de Vega shows him wearing a similar one. Later crosses are almost always personalised.

It was by ferreting about in museum catalogues that I found, or rather, thought I found, our cross. It was on a ribbon, entwined in a gold chain, around the neck of Don Fernando de Toledo, natural son of the Duke of Alba and Military Commander in Flanders (portrait by Antonio Moro, in the Imperial Gallery in Vienna). I examined the cross under a magnifying glass. It looked very like ours, but painting is not photography. The angle decorations could equally well have been rather loosely painted fleurs-de-lis, whereas on our cross they were thorns, shaped like cloves, with a tiny, finely engraved grenade at the end, clearly separated from the point. Struts in right angled segments, reinforcing the arms of the cross to form a circle, join the thorns and give them from a distance the appearance of four fleurs-de-lis.

In any case, Fernando de Toledo, who was also a Knight of Alcantara, was not in the Armada. There was one Don Francisco De Toledo among the passengers, but he disembarked from the *San Felipe* at Nieuport when she ran aground, and four de Toledos of minor importance, a Don Garcia, Don Juan, Don Pedro and a Don Alonzo. Another false trail—Fernando's brothers were called Federico and Fadrique.

I had almost given up hope, when another letter from Mlle Engel finally put me on the right track. 'It is very difficult,' she wrote, 'to get any documentation on the sixteenth century. Del Pozzo . . . gives an incomplete list . . . of Knights of the Langue of Italy. Among Italian Knights Vertot mentions only some Spinolas from Genoa.' Spinolas . . . wait a minute! Hadn't I seen the name Spinola somewhere before?

In 1967, I had looked at a copy of Pedro de Paz Salas's General Inventory of the Felicissima Armada (Lisbon, 9 May 1588) in the British Museum. It is a particularly interesting copy in that it belonged to Lord Burghley. Burghley, whose information was always good, and quick, had been among the first in England to get hold of a copy of the inventory. In his *Annals*, Stow records that he noticed on it several notes in Burghley's own hand, made shortly after the defeat, giving details of which captains had been captured or killed and which ships had been sunk. Fortunately I had had these pages photocopied at the Museum. I looked them up. On the left of the page next to the name *Girona* Burghley had written: 'perished on the coast of Ireland', and on the right he had written: 'Fabricio Spinola Captn.'

¶ Las quatro Galeaças de Napoles que eſtan a cargo de Don Hugo de Moncada.

Toneladas.	Nauios.	Géte d guerra.	Géte de mar.	Numero de todospemo.	Piezas de artillería.	Pelote-ria.	Poluora	Plomo.	Cuerda.
La galeaça capitana nombra.la S.Lorejo. Luis h... capi...									
Iuã Perez de Coayfa	144 118 262	161.	114.	386.	300.	50.	2500.	132.	16. 24
Galeaça Patrona. Hernãdo de quefada	116								
Andres Verdugo.	62 178	178.	112.	290.	320.	50.	2500.	118.	16. 24
Galeaça Girona. Gonçalo Beltran.	75								
De Antonio de Sylua galeaça Napolitana	94 169 161	169.	110.	283.	300.	50.	2500.	130.	15. 24

The command of a galleass was, traditionally, the preserve of officers of noble birth (eligible therefore for the Order of Malta) who swore on their lives 'not to flee before 25 enemy galleys and not to refuse battle with them'. If Fabricio Spinola was a Knight of Malta, I was doing more than just getting warm, I was burning.

The Spinolas (originally Spinula) were one of the biggest families in Genoa. They had made their fortune in trade with the Levant, and then turned to public life, as early as the twelfth century. The first politician was Guido Spinola, Consul of Genoa. After him came several captains and generals. Once the wealth and influence of the family were well established, they gave thirteen cardinals to the Church and to the Republic countless ambassadors, consuls, doges and magistrates, as well as 127 senators. By the fifteenth century one finds the family's increasingly illustrious name linked with every important event. During Philip's reign the most famous members of the family were without doubt Fredericu and Ambrogio, two brothers who distinguished themselves in the service of Spain by raising, at their own expense, a galley fleet and an army 'more powerful than any that a king could have provided for himself'.

Aubert de la Mire, the famous polymath, has written, among many others, two works of particular interest here: *Origine des Chevaliers et Ordres Militaires* and *Gentis Spinulae Illustrium Elogia*. As I set out on this new track, I told myself that if I didn't find Fabricio there, there would be nothing for it but to give up. Fabricio wasn't there. There were sixty-seven Spinolas and any number of Fernandus, Fredericus, and Franciscus, Knights of Santiago, Alcantara and Calatrava, but not a word about our man. But the list was very incomplete, giving only the principal heads of families; Fabricio might have died in his prime, before holding any important public office or earning any entitlement to immortality.

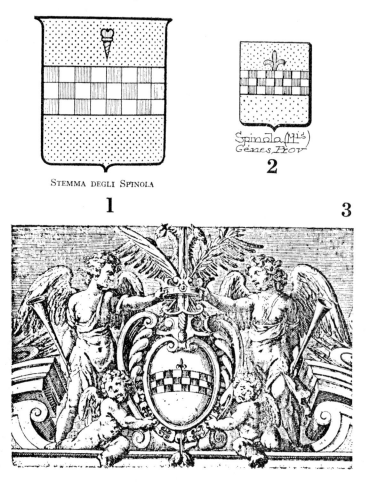

STEMMA DEGLI SPINOLA

1

2

3

Following Mademoiselle Engel's advice, I made it my job to plough once more through both volumes of del Pozzo *Historia della Sacra Religione Militare di San Giovanni . . . 1571–1688*. It is a remarkable work, extremely detailed. Alas, it disposed of the 'ill-fated attempt at

Above and left: *In this gold reliquary, which opens like a book, one of the passengers, possibly the Bishop of Killaloe, kept his Agnus Dei.*

Below: *A Neapolitan gold ducat, bearing the effigy of Charles I of Spain and the Kingdom of the Two Sicilies, and V of the Holy Roman Empire.*

The Treasures of the Armada.

A lapis lazuli cameo in an enamelled setting of chased gold and pearls, bearing the profile of a Roman Emperor (sixteenth century Italian). We found eleven of them. The twelfth is still under the sea.

invasion' in only three lines and mentioned a grand total of two knights of the name of Spinola in the seventeenth century.

The Abbé de Vertot in *The History of the Knights of Malta*, written in 1776, lists thirty Spinolas under the Venerable Langue of Italy, between 1416 and 1702. Ah, at last! This time, amongst all those, I must find my man. Alas, among the Italians, only ten, going by the dates when they were received (from 1562 to 1583) could have been of the right age to be in the Armada and not one of them was called Fabricio. As for the Venerable Langue of Castile, only one knight, received in 1588, would not have been anachronistic and he had the bad taste to be called Francisco Spinola de Covaccio.

Still there was no cause for despair. Vertot's list is notoriously incomplete, he admits it himself. I had to steel myself once more to setting off on the heraldry tack. Maybe the Spinolas had a salamander in their coat of arms.

Very early on the Spinolas had shown signs of pretensions to nobility and had acquired titles on the basis of a genealogical table. According to Joseph Lefèvre in *Spinola et la Belgique* it was 'drawn up possibly at their instigation and expense, which claimed to show their ascendance and alliances back as far as the eleventh century. One might be forgiven for being a little sceptical at the prospect of these trees, growing just a bit too high into the air'.

Once more I opened the illustrated books of heraldry and there, on the arms of the Spinolas of Genoa, I found straight away the motif that was between the arms of our cross. There could be no doubt about it. This time it was the real thing. It was a fesse chequy silver and gules, a thorn gules in pale in the middle of the fesse. On the Spinola's original coat of arms the thorn (*spina* in Italian) is shown on its own. It is quite clearly a thorn, with its separate grenade shaped head. On later coats of arms, it became half thorn, half fleur-de-lis. On the arms of Philip Charles Francis Spinola, carved in marble at the top of his mausoleum in the Eglise de la Chapelle in Brussels, where I went to look at them, the hybrid thorn has given way to a full blown fleur-de-lis. Our cross shows it at the intermediate stage.

Captain Fabricio Spinola, forgotten by Vertot, unless Burghley or his spies simply got his Christian name wrong, must indeed have been a Knight of Malta. It was he, without doubt, who lost his cross, personalised with a charge from his own arms, in the wreck of his ship.

36
The Unknown Knight

The medallion* that I had foolishly assumed to belong to a Knight of Santiago (De Leiva's!)—wishful thinking—turned out on closer inspection to be nothing short of a tiny marvel. On the obverse each arms of the cross ended in a fleur-de-lis. The decorated frame had been a little twisted in the course of time, and the enamel that must have covered the surface was missing (for the cross is cloisonné, meaning that round the outline is a raised frame, which would have contained the enamel). Under the cross is a simple gold plaque backed by another, with a fine engraving on the obverse of a bearded, long-haired saint with a halo and dressed in rags. He is walking through a ravine. On his right are a tree and a waterfall. On his left is what looks like a small basket, perhaps, or a boat that he is pointing at, or carrying, and in it is the stylised head of an animal. The rest of the basket is hidden by the crushed frame. It must have been hung on a ribbon by a tiny soldered ring that we found a few weeks later, not far away. (See page 193.)

At that time there were three military orders of knighthood in Spain: the Orders of Santiago, Alcantara and Calatrava, all dating back to the twelfth century.

The Marquis de Casa Valdez, who is the present Secretary of the Real Consejo de las Ordenes Militares de Santiago, Calatrava, Alcantara y Montesa (and whose help in my research was as generous as it was valuable) wondered whether our medallion was not simply a decorative jewel, imitating the cross of an order of knighthood, quite a common occurrence:

> The Knight's habit . . . was a very large cape with the cross of the Order either embroidered or sewn on and a tunic with a cross on the breast, worn short in battle with a helmet, mail coat, knight's sword and belt, a costume probably very similar to the one worn at the time of the Crusades. . . . These orders, being religious and military, the equipment of a knight did not include jewels, either for war or for the church.

---

* Size of medallion: oval 27.5 × 23 mm, 4.5 mm thick, weight 14 grams.

This was true in the early days, when the knights, poor and chaste, virtuously devoted every day of their lives to serving the order according to their vows. But, by the sixteenth century knighthood had become mainly honorary, and because of the rich commands that could be obtained it was, above all, a good financial proposition. 'The Grandees preferred to be received in it [the Order of Santiago] than in the Order of the Golden Fleece, because they hoped thereby to obtain for themselves commands and other not inconsiderable privileges.' The rule, which required that no jewels be worn in view of the vows of poverty that had been taken, had fallen into disuse and the knights had as little respect for it as they had for the rule of chastity (abrogated long before in any case for those married by the Pope).

One only needs to look at the portraits of the period: Juan Martinez de Recalde in a well known painting is shown wearing the insignia of a Knight of Santiago, very similar to ours; so is Pedro de Valdez; Miguel de Oquendo wears a slightly different one; so do the Marquis de Santa Cruz and the Governor of the Netherlands; Luis de Requesens wears his on a gold chain, Gonzalo Chacon is wearing the Cross of Alcantara without a medallion. I have also seen a jewel of a Knight of the Order of Calatrava very like ours but studded with stones, and also several Orders of Santiago set with rubies, amethysts and white topazes in the Jewellery Room at the Victoria and Albert Museum.

So at the time of the Armada, it was not unusual for knights to wear such jewels. (I was to learn later that it was Pope Benedict XIII, in 1411, who gave the knights permission to lay aside the hood and scapular of the Cistercians for the cross with fleurs-de-lis of either vert or gules.) Two questions remained: which order, and which knight?

Most of the literature on the history of military orders of knighthood is in Latin. I was going to have to brush mine up a bit if I was going to identify ours. The task was all the more agreeable in that the subject is fascinating in itself. It is not by chance that knights feature so prominently in folklore, like princes in fairy stories.

It was clear from the start that Santiago must be ruled out. The knights of this Order wore the cross of Santiago el Mayor, Santiago Apostol, or St James of the Sword. The cross was a flory fitchy, the ends of the upper arms having the shape of a stylised lily, the lower arm forming a sword point, the pommel ending in an inverted heart. The flory cross that featured on the sacred banner of Santiago in the thirteenth century had long ago fallen into disuse.

That left Calatrava and Alcantara. The crosses of these two Orders are flory crosses identical to ours. The only difference between them is the colour: green for Alcantara, red for Calatrava.* The enamel on ours had disappeared without trace.

Fortunately there was still the saint engraved on the reverse, with what must have been his characteristic attributes, the tree, the waterfall and the dog basket. That was the direction in which I was going to have to look. What else could I do but make another detailed study of the lives of the saints on one front, and on the other, of the history of the two Orders.

In all the research I had done on Calatrava, I had come up with only one knight who sailed in the Armada: Don Gonzalo de Eraso, a passenger on the galleon *San Martín*. I was sure there must have been others.

The Order of Calatrava dates back to the wars against the Almohades, who, in the twelfth century, still held the southern part of Spain. A certain Raymond Serrat, from Saint Gaudens, a Cistercian, Abbot of Fitero (an abbey that he had established in Navarre), founded the Order to defend a town against the Moors. The town had previously been abandoned by the Templars as indefensible. It was called Kalaat Rawah. King Alfonso VII gave the Abbot the town but only on condition that he defend it. With his friend Fray Diego Velazquez, the Abbot set about populating it. By distributing land to anyone who swore to defend it, he managed to attract some 20,000 people within its walls and in the surrounding countryside. In this way he built up a semi-military, semi-religious militia of 'Knights of Calatrava'. Alexander III gave the Order official recognition in 1164. They wore a white mantle with a crimson cross (the red cross of war) having fleurs-de-lis (for purity) at the ends of the arms. The Abbot was canonised after his death (in Toledo in 1163) and made San Raimundo de Fitero. Ah! I had found a saint. But was he the right one?

I set out to find all the portraits, statues and medallions of St Raymond that I could dig out of the very best hagiographies. Heaven is full of St Raymonds, but there are three important ones, including Serrat. Nowhere, however, was this holy man depicted in rags, nor with a tree, nor with any animal.

---

* In the Jewellery Room at the Victoria and Albert Museum in London, I also saw two seventeenth and eighteenth century jewels with crosses similar to ours, marked 'Insignia of a Familiar of the Inquisition' and 'Insignia of the Inquisition'. The Familiars of the Inquisition were lay auxiliaries recruited for their energetic devotion to the cause. According to the experts they wore 'antique crosses bordered with gold thread'. 'Antique crosses' in this context means nothing in particular. If one chooses to take it as meaning 'flory cross', the fact still remains that the arms of the London crosses are enamelled lengthways half white, half black. Our cross lacked the central vertical cloison that would have been necessary for the jeweller to lay two different enamels. The second cross, mounted in gold on an aquamarine the size of a pigeon's egg, seems more like an ornamental jewel.

I then followed up the fact of Serrat being a Cistercian: the original rule of the Order of Calatrava was that of the Abbey of Cîteaux, founded by *Saint* Benedict and made famous by *Saint* Bernard. Another dead end! Neither of these two saints had any connection with a tree.

As for the arms of the Order, they, for some unfathomable reason, are two hobbles, two lengths of rope with a buckle at each end. So, how about the arms of Alcantara?

On the shield of Alcantara was . . . a pear tree. In 1156, the town of Alcantara (El Kantarah) was also threatened by the Moors. In order to defend it two gentlemen of Salamanca, Don Suero Fernandez Barrientes and his brother, Don Gomez, founded a military order, also under the rule of St Benedict. On the advice of a hermit named Arnaud, held in high esteem locally by reason of his piety, they built the Order's first home, a fortified priory on the edge of Rio Coa (in the diocese of Ciudad Rodrigo, on the Portuguese border) immediately next to the hermitage. The hermitage was dedicated to St Julian, Bishop of Le Mans, and because his little chapel was set in a grove of pear trees, it was known as the Hermitage of St Julian of the Pear Tree. Because it was there that the Order was started, the knights were also known as 'Caballeros de San Julian del Pereiro' (*pereiro* being Portuguese for pear-tree). In his *diario*, Medina Sidonia refers to the Knight, Don Diego Tellez Henriquez, son of the Grand Commander of Alcantara, as 'El del Peral', or knight of the pear orchard, to distinguish him from the other five Henriquezes (including two Diegos) in the Armada.

The Maestre-General of the Order remained there until 1252, when the Order was temporarily amalgamated with the Order of Calatrava. In 1411 Benedict XIII granted permission for the knights to wear the green silk flory cross on their breasts. Later their medallion was a gold cross enamelled in green on a green ribbon. By the time of the Armada, the Order had thirty-seven commands and fifty-three bourgs, either taken from the Moors, acquired in some other way, or given to them. Their power and their wealth, in fact the power and wealth of all three orders, made for unending conflicts between the grand masters, the Church and the King. Finally the King of Spain took over the three orders, making himself Grand Master.

According to the most detailed histories, 'they took for their arms a pear tree, with exposed roots and bare branches on a gold field'. The pear tree on our medallion is in full leaf and its trunk disappears deep into the earth.

But, in fact, although one does frequently find such a tree on the arms of the Order (for example in the frontispiece of *Diffiniciones de la Orde y Cavalleria de Alcantara*, Madrid (1569), one also often finds a perfectly ordinary tree (in the frontispiece of the *Cronica de las Tres Ordenes*, by Francisco de Rades, printed in Toledo in 1572, for example, or in the frontispiece of the *Historia de las Ordenes Militares*, by Francisco Carro de Torres, published in Madrid in 1629).

Clearly the tree pointed to the saint being St Julian of the Pear Tree. But how about the animal? And the fountain?

Heaven be praised! Heaven had forty-five St Julians! Forty-five unless any had been left out of the *Biblioteca Sanctorum*, forty-five among whom reigns the most indescribable confusion. The one worshipped by the hermit, Arnaud, was St Julian, first Bishop of Le Mans in the fourth century. There are thousands of details recorded about his life, all edifying, all invented long after the event by his falsifying biographer, whose one aim was to bring fame and fortune to the diocese of Le Mans, for his own personal advancement. But the best known characteristics attributed to him, which I discovered from a more reliable source, are that he preached the Gospel to the Gauls (along with sixty-nine other disciples of the Apostles), that he went to Rome to find some relics that caused several miracles to happen (could the animal in the basket have something to do with the things he brought back from Rome?), and, above all, that, one day, he miraculously caused a fountain to spring out of the earth. It is said that the springing forth of this fountain brought about the conversion of a very large number of princes indeed, along with their subjects.

It converted me, anyway, that fountain playing on the left of the saint on the medallion. As far as I am concerned the saint is San Julian de Pereiro, Bishop of Le Mans, and it is without much doubt the medallion of a Knight of Alcantara.

With positively pious devotion I worked until I could hardly see, trying to pin a name on the medallion. Whom had it belonged to? I did not succeed. I discovered only two Knights of Alcantara in the whole Armada. Neither one of them perished with the *Girona*. The first was Don Diego Tellez Henriques, son of the Grand Commander of the Order, whom the Duke referred to as 'El del Peral.' Captain Francisco de Cuellar says that he buried him, with his own hands, on the beach at Stredegagh (near Sligo) after 'the Irish savages' had slaughtered him for his ducats and his clothes. The second was Don Henrique de Guzman, Marquis of Pobar, but Carro de Torres says that he served in the Enterprise of England and 'having returned' continued his career.

One Diego De Leiva, who sailed with Don Alonzo in the *rata* with a company of 145 soldiers, might have been a brother of his. They were drowned together, but nowhere, alas, is there any mention of his being a knight of any Order whatsoever. Another brother, Don Pedro De Leiva, Knight of Alcantara, and General of the Galleys of Sicily and of Spain, served from childhood with his father, Don Sancho, and with his elder brother, Don Alonzo, as lieutenant of his galley squadrons. He was involved in several actions in Barbary and was a great sailor, recognised as such by his contemporaries. But Carro de Torres, who always (or almost always) says which knights were involved in the Enterprise of England, does not say whether or not Don Pedro was, or, if he was, how he died. As a final blow, although the chronicler Zuñita mentions in his list of *caballeros aventureros* in the Armada, apart from Don Diego, a Juan De Leiva, and, in his list of captains, an Antonio De Leiva, nowhere does he mention anyone by the name of Pedro De Leiva.

So, was Don Pedro there, unnoticed? It would take too great a stretch of the imagination to believe that.

If one stretches a point, and translates *caballero* as knight (caballero means noble in general, and knight is only one special meaning of the word), and if one stretches another point and receives this knight into the Order of Alcantara, and if one stretches a third point and decides that this Juan was also Don Alonzo's brother, then one could conclude that he was sailing at his side and the problem is solved. But that's a bit too much stretching for my taste.

I spent the whole winter searching, buried deep in my papers, and then in the spring I gave it up. The Knight of Alcantara, drowned at Port na Spaniagh, must forever remain 'the unknown knight'.

37
1969: We Return to Port na Spaniagh

We returned to Port na Spaniagh in April, with the sand-martins.

The gulls and seamews, ever spiralling up and down by the black cliffs, greeted us once more with their raucous cries. We were very curious at the first dive. What would we find this time? Would the winter storms have churned over the sea bed, demolished the cave and destroyed all our efforts by mixing excavated sediments with virgin deposits? Or would they have revealed some golden pavements or lines of cannon—or Shakespearian skulls, their eye sockets stuffed with diamonds?

I was bubbling over with impatience. The temperature of the water brought me rudely to my senses. Hell, it was even icier than last year, 6°C according to the thermometer. Other than that, nothing had changed. All our holes had been filled up again, but with stuff that we had already excavated. I need not have feared for my eyes. There was no dazzling display of newly uncovered jewels.

We wanted to take advantage of the early part of the season, while the algae were still small and thinly scattered, to make a systematic exploration in the bay of Port na Spaniagh itself. As Louis had pointed out to me in 1968, we had after all found only signs of a ship having gone down, not the remains of a complete vessel.

'There were fifty guns on the *Girona*, weren't there?' he demanded. 'Well, we've found two. Where are the rest?'

Sorley Boy fished out three in 1589, or, to be more precise, that Scottish captain fished them out for him. Maybe the captain made a deal with him, half and half: three cannon for the noble lord and three for himself, in exchange for services rendered. But even allowing for that, it still left forty-two or forty-five cannon unaccounted for. The English never came to get them, so where were they? Perhaps the galleass broke in two on Lacada Point. One half might have drifted off with the rest of the cannon and the bulk of the treasure, somewhere in Port na Spaniagh.

So Louis thought, but I doubted it, because all the lead stores from the ship were on Lacada Point. In fact there was actually more than there should be if we were to believe the inventories, and then there were so many cannon balls.

'But what about the rest of the stuff?' Louis argued. 'On a ship that size there must have been millions of things. Where are they?'

'Disintegrated!' I told him. 'Look, here are the inventories. Supplies, for example. What the sailors didn't eat will have been eaten by the sea. Biscuits, bacon, tuna fish, sardines, semolina, sugar, salt . . . you can't imagine any of that being left. Look at the small arms: arquebuses, muskets, halberds, pikes, half-pikes, partisans. De Leiva left a lot behind at Killybegs and the rest wouldn't have lasted two years on the sea bed. What else? Corslets—same thing. What else? Gunpowder, water and wine butts? Sorley Boy drank his way through some of them, the rest are long gone. Other than that, there would have been wooden mugs and bowls for the sailors, jugs and dishes for handing out rations in, leather water bottles, lamps, lanterns, candles, match, oil for the lamps, cow hides and tow for repairing shot holes and damaged caulking, cuir bouilli buckets for the gunners' powder, steelyards. . . .'

'But we did find one steelyard. Remember? The lead weight backed with a bronze plaque?'

I admitted there might be some left. But as I turned over page after page of the inventory—sacks an sacks of canvas, rope, siege equipment, carpenters', sailmakers' and caulkers' tools, galley slaves' irons and chains—I was sure there couldn't be much left of any of that.

Louis persisted. 'How about the musket? That was still there, wasn't it?'

He was right, we must go and look to make quite certain.

In order to go and look, we had to mark out the area. First we laid a line from east to west, fixed at intervals, right across the bay and then, day by day, we worked our way along equi-distant lines to north and south. Much to our surprise we found the algae already tall and dense, at the height of the previous summer, and already covered with little pink algae. That slowed down our search somewhat, but in fact, apart from some bits of modern rubbish, we found nothing. So what was not on the sea bed must have been thrown ashore. Back in 1588, the MacDonnell clan must only have needed to bend down to reap the harvest of the wreck, and the following year the Scottish captain must have just dabbled his toes in the water.

Louis was still shaking his head. 'But where have those forty-five cannon got to, then?'

I thought I knew where they were. There were 6 cannon on board, 2 demi-cannon, 4 demi-culverins, 8 perriers, 6 sakers, 4 demi-sakers, 20 esmerils and then another 40 mascolos (they were more like arquebuses than cannon). The 40 mascolos De Leiva gave to McSweeney before leaving Killybegs. There is a letter in my files from a certain Henry Duke informing the English of this. We found two small guns, and Sorley Boy raised at least three. In 1597 Sir John Chichester, who was then Governor, wrote:

> The McDonnells have planted three pieces of ordinance, half cannon and culverin which were had out of one of the Spanish ships coming upon that coast after our fight with them at sea in 1588. I have demanded the said pieces. . . but they have utterly refused to deliver them.. . . .

The names he gives to the pieces are almost certainly inaccurate. Firstly there were no culverins on board, and secondly it doesn't tally with the breech loading cannon that we found the blocks for on Lacada Point.

It's always possible the Scottish captain kept that one for himself. But in any case that was the only description of cannon recovered that I'd found, apart from a rather vague letter from someone called Lady Agnes Campbell, who wrote asking Sorley Boy for 'a large piece of Spanish artillery', in December, 1589.

But where were these cannon now? A mystery! Hill, who wrote the history of the McDonnell family says: 'The cannon subsequently appear to have been sent to Scotland, perhaps as early as August, 1589, and perhaps mounted on the McDonnell stronghold of Dunstaffnage Castle. . . .' He's wrong, about the date anyway, since Lady Campbell was asking for one of them in December and Governor Chichester was still after them in 1597. These cannon were a source of bad luck to everyone—to De Leiva, to James McDonnell and finally to Chichester as well. There was trouble in November 1597 between the Earl of Carrickfergus and James over some stolen livestock—one might almost say that the whole of Irish history then was made out of small battles over a couple of stolen cows. To cut a long story short, Chichester got mixed up in it and accused James McDonnell of treason in having fortified Dunluce with cannon from the galleass. He attacked. And won. James counterattacked, reinforced by some of the Scottish McDonnells. He imprisoned Chichester and cut off his head. The Lord Deputy appointed Chichester's brother in his place, in spite of James's protests, and in 1601, the brother, Sir Arthur, had James poisoned in his castle. At least everyone suspected him, although it could have been Burghley himself, who was trying to get O'Neill poisoned at the same time.

'Yes, yes,' Louis went on, 'but have you actually been to look at Dunstaffnage?'

We hadn't because our friend John McLennan lent me a book, published in 1860, called *Castellated Architecture of Scotland*, which contains the following statement:

Three beautiful Spanish pieces, relics of the Armada, were seen on the ruined walls of Dunstaffnage as recently as twenty years ago. . . . There are also openings in the walls for said guns. . . .

But the castle was currently undergoing restoration. It had been going on for years. I had written to the local schoolmaster, who answered that the cannon were not on show at the moment. They had been put away for safe keeping until the restoration work was completed. According to him the most serious book on Dunstaffnage is the one by W. Douglas Simpson, which said nothing about *three* cannon. He had enclosed a copy of a passage from the book mentioning two old cannon, one very rusty iron one, said to have been dredged up from the sea-bed not far from the castle; the other, a bronze one, 6 ft 6 in long, 3¾ in calibre, with the usual dolphin decorations, and engraved round the breech ASVERVUS ROSTER ME FECIT AMSTELREDAM. That one is supposed to have come off the Tobermory wreck. A false trail, in short.

'It's absolutely classic!' said Louis. 'There can't be a single iron chest or cannon in the whole country that's not called "Armada chest" or something to that effect. But there isn't a clue as to where those forty-five missing cannon are.'

'No,' I said, 'but don't forget that De Leiva embarked 1300 men at Killybegs, 700 more than the normal crew of 600, and in a patched up ship at that. Reckoning say 140 lb a head, 700 men equals about 49 tons of human flesh. Forty-five cannon, taking an average weight, come to about the same—49 tons. So, in order to embark 49 tons of Spaniards, he must have had to throw overboard 49 tons of bronze. Quite simple. . . .'

'Well, then if they are at Killybegs, what are we waiting for?'

'It's big, you know, Killybegs roads. They could be anywhere, and wherever they are they would be in deep mud. Each time I've been there, I've asked the local fishermen about them, but no one knows anything. There have, in fact, recently been some big dredging operations there; it seems that they found nothing at all.'

38
Archimedes, or How We Resort to Extreme Measures

This year Louis and Maurice had brought along with them a young French diver, Patrick Couture, to reinforce the team. It was not long before he began to make out very well. Francis was still with us and the Belgian speleologist, Bob Destreille, the bravest cave diver I know, was to join us shortly. Marc was coming a little later, just long enough to make a short underwater colour film for television, using an underwater camera of his own design, with special corrective lenses. His assistant, young André Fassotte, was going to stay with the team until the end of the season. Altogether there would be eight of us.

We were also better equipped to move the hundreds of tons of rock under which we were once more going to dig. I did not want to use explosives for fear of destroying the very things that we were looking for. We had a hydraulic jack capable of lifting the twenty-ton monsters a few inches at a time. If the jack gave way, the sea bed shook with the impact. Fortunately these monsters were few and far between. I didn't like to see divers edging under huge boulders, precariously propped up by our makeshift scaffoldings of small rocks, in place of pillars.

Apart from the monsters, there were any number of six to eight-ton rocks. Last year we could not have touched these 'big guns', but this time I had had special air bags made to lift two and four tons each.

We had drawn up a list. For those of us who had hovered greedily around, sniffing and scratching as far as our arms would stretch, each boulder still remaining in a fertile excavated area obviously promised great riches.

We each had our own boulders, ours as it were, by right. Considering their position and the wealth of artifacts that had been found around them, they ought to have been covering rivers of diamonds and bucket loads of pearls or, at the very least, Alonzo De Leiva's gold plate. To avoid fighting over the largest bags we had to work according to a rota. Under the first rock, in the middle of the canyon, Louis found a sizeable piece of a musket ball, under the second a whole lead bullet, under the third nothing, under the fourth another rock, and under the fifth a perrier ball. Under the sixth he found a lead ingot, two whole arquebus balls, and a large piece of the weighted underside of an astrolabe.

That was important, for I had, collected in various plastic bags, five or six very worn sections of a bronze circle that might have belonged to a broken astrolabe, or indeed almost anything. . . . But now the jigsaw was beginning to take shape. We had our second astrolabe, the world its twenty-eighth. By 1966, Lieutenant Commander David Waters, Director of the Department of Navigation and Astronomy at the National Maritime Museum in Greenwich, and the world expert on astrolabes, had indexed, measured, weighed and written up twenty-one, six of which were found in wrecks. Ours seemed to be identical to Waters's Numbers 9 and 10. Since, he has studied a few more, including two from the sea-bed, and a twenty-sixth was found recently in Bermuda on a Portuguese wreck of 1580–1589.

The mariner's astrolabe was what made ocean navigation possible. The instrument enabled one to measure the height of the sun or the pole star above the horizon and work out what latitude the ship was in. It was the successor to the armillary sphere, used by the Greeks for many astronomical measurements, and the planispheric astrolabe that Arab astronomers and medieval astrologers used to foretell the movement of the heavenly bodies in order to know whether the time was right for embarking on a war, a journey or a marriage. The Portuguese navigators first used them at sea in the fifteenth century (the earliest time they are mentioned, according to Waters, is in 1481).

The instrument consisted of an evenly balanced brass circle suspended by a ring, and provided with a rotatable alidade or a diametrical rule with sights, turning within a circle of degrees, for measuring the altitudes of stars or sun. (See page 259.)

In 1673, at a time when the astrolabe was already being superseded by Davis's quadrant, which consists of a quarter of an astrolabe much enlarged, and by the cross-staff or Jacob's staff, an ecclesiastic, Abbot Denis, was instructing the pilots of Dieppe in the art of navigation:

> . . . Navigation walks on two feet, latitude and longitude. . . . to work out the latitude with an astrolabe, one must first take note of the roll of the ship and choose the spot where there is the least movement, near the mainmast. Then, slipping the ring over one's finger, one allows the astrolabe to hang free, lowering and raising the alidade until the rays of the sun align with the holes in the middle of the pinules.

In order to measure the height of the Pole Star at night, one lined the star up through the pinules by holding the instrument to one's eye, which one would never have been able to do in the case of the sun, without being blinded.

In new territory also, our methodical search led us this year to areas where we needed to use the large lifting balloons as often as previously we had used our crowbars.

In calm weather, the operation was a very simple one. One slipped a steel sling around the rock to be shifted, if its shape lent itself to such treatment (rocks with a concave middle were ideal, but alas, very rare). If the rock was round or egg-shaped, the only thing to do was to spin a whole web of cable round it. One then shackled the sling onto the lifting bag and inflated it with an aqualung tank. As the cable tightened, the rock would buck, waddle about a bit, hesitate and then go up, helped on its way by Archimedes, slowly at first, and then quicker and quicker until finally the balloon reached the surface. All that remained then was to tow the whole lot to an area that had already been excavated, and to sink the rock by pushing the deflater valve.

The weather on the north coast of Ireland might have been tropical in 1968 (the best summer of the century), but throughout the summer of 1969 it was absolutely normal, that is absolutely frightful. For weeks on end we kicked our heels in port. Northwest gales followed one after another. If it wasn't that, some distant storm around Iceland would be sending over a mountainous swell.

A swell complicates everything. First of all, one can hardly see, because one is having to swim in a soup of stirred-up vegetable waste. Secondly, one must use one hand to hang on, to stay anywhere near the rock that is to be strapped. Strapping up a rock one-handed is not all that easy—try it! Then you have to try to pull or push the empty balloons from the boat to the rock, and nylon-lined neoprene balloons are heavy and extremely large. The sea pulls them forward, backward or anywhere that takes her fancy. You go and get help. With three of you pushing and pulling you eventually manage it. Out of breath, exhausted, pulse racing, finally you tighten up the last shackle of the last link. You ram the inflater tubes under the mouth of the first balloon, open the valve, and then try to get a look at what is happening, whenever the swell carries you anywhere near. As soon as it begins to lighten, the rock goes quite mad. The coming and going of the waves drags the balloons, tearing out the tube, or else throwing eight tons of granite in your face, only to snatch it back a moment later. At this point your main concern is to avoid being squashed to a pulp. And yet you have to keep an eye on what is happening. But how can you possibly be expected to see anything, when the crazy rock is raising thick clouds of sand, when perspiration is running stinging into your eyes, and when with every other wave an algae frond sticks onto the face plate of your mask? The swell comes again, snatching at your hand hold, throwing you onto a jagged rock which catches the buckle of your lead belt. There you are, coming and going, holding the inflation cylinder under one arm, and with the other wrapped round a bit of seaweed while you fix your belt, with one eye on the buckle and the other on the rocky mass that is still hammering away at the sea bed, thudding dully like a rumbling earthquake.

Often, if the swell is persistent, it will shake the rock about long enough to split the steel cable with one cunning swipe against the jagged edge of a nearby rock, or else slip your careful arrangement of ropes. In that split second when your mask isn't obscured by seaweed, you get a brief glimpse of a bunch of balloons rising up to the surface like so many flares. Otherwise, if the cables hold, and the rock rises, you follow, towed by your uncontrollable team until you decide to sink it, or rather until you are left with no alternative other than being thrown ashore with it or dragged out to sea.

It was just such an exercise that earned Francis his only rest of the season, a long convalescence at home nursing a bandaged hand and two crushed fingers.

One always finds something bigger than oneself. There were some super-monsters that were absolutely unassailable. When we couldn't lift them, we had to dig under them and crawl, and then, once underneath we would gradually undermine the supporting pillars, as a perfect fool would.

On 21 June, I was, as usual, doing something I ought not to have been, rather nervously chipping away at the support of a thirty-ton rock, under which I was following a trail of Neapolitan silver ducats in 'very fine' condition. I came out for a minute to fetch a bigger crowbar. Just as I got outside the trap, it collapsed. The slab literally brushed my flippers as it crashed down seven feet. When I had gathered my wits about me again, I saw just next to me a huge crab, unscathed, but lying on its back, being swept from side to side by the swell, dead but not crushed. Clearly it had died of shock. I have often wondered whether such a case of a crustacean being overcome by a heart attack might not open up a whole new field of marine biology.

*   *   *

All divers know from experience that whenever some gawper you meet by the harbour opens his mouth, it's always to ask the same question: 'What about sharks? Aren't you scared of sharks?' The Port Ballintrae summer visitors were no exception to the rule.

Our friends the salmon fishermen told us stories of having caught sharks in their nets, but we never caught sight of one. Once, way out to sea, we spotted a school of about a hundred killer whales. You could spot them easily by their large, black, tapering bodies, their pointed dorsal fin and large white patches. They moved forward in a group (like porpoises) from east to west and took not the slightest notice of us.

It was rather disappointing in a way. Days passed, then weeks, then months. The cameras were loaded. Already in my mind I had the plan for a chapter headed: 'We Grapple with the Maneaters'—and still nothing. The closest thing we met to a shark were some frightened little dogfish, no longer than your arm. It was disappointing, because after all there is *always* a shark scene in *real* treasure hunts, in the films and on television. Really we are doing it all wrong. No palm trees, no three-masted topsail schooner, no wreck, lying, sails torn, listing slightly, on the very edge of a reef, no captain's cabin door creaking open to reveal the chest and the regulation octopus, no typhoon, no traitors and no sensuous blondes in bikinis (two at least to keep up the psychological intrigue), not even the flash of knives at the sharing out.

Sadly we realise that we are the jobbing treasure hunters, the face-less figures with horny hands, the grey men. We are the artisans, with our coal shovels and pickle jars. Our work consists of shifting stones, under the quiet gaze of the cod, or sweeping sand with our hands for six hours a day, frozen to the marrow, and dying to pee in our neoprene pants. Last year we did have the pirates—a lucky break! Without that, who would have taken us seriously?

At the beginning of June we enjoyed another moment of glory. The *National Geographic Magazine* gave over thirty colour pages to my article. The first copy to arrive in Belfast, at the Public Library, was stolen three-quarters of an hour after being placed on the shelves, and the one in Queen's University half an hour later. The local press was busy paraphrasing the article. The typographers in the composing room had dug out the biggest type they could find from the back of their drawers—it had probably been lying there since V-E Day—to print GOLD right across the front page. The television people remembered us again, and once more there was the daily influx of curious visitors in the harbour and along the cliff path. But the pirates did not return. There was nothing to see this year. We were a disappointment to the tourists. By Sunday evening it was clear that the family parties were sorry they had come.

We had got a routine going. In theory it went something like this: up at 8 am, breakfast at the Manor Guest House at 8.30 am for all, that is, except the one whose turn it was to refill the tanks. He went straight off to the compressor to finish filling the cylinders he hadn't managed to get done the previous evening. At 9 am, start loading; Francis brings the Zodiac round to the quay, we clamber aboard, squeezing in behind the parachutes, cylinders, sacks, weights, pump and everything else. . . . Louis meanwhile goes to fill up the petrol tanks. We dress: undergarments, first suit, second suit. Some last-minute preparations, then leave the harbour around 10.30 am. At 11 am anchor at Lacada Point, on two grapples. By 11.15 am or thereabouts we tumble into the water. Three hours' work on the sea-bed, long enough to get through one pair of cylinders (2 cubic metre tanks inflated to 200 kg), fifteen minutes on board, time for a cigarette while we change cylinders, followed by another three hours on the sea-bed, with a second pair of cylinders. Half an hour for the return journey. if the weather is calm. If not, we have to take a more roundabout route to avoid the dangerous 'one mile stone' where the swell and counter-currents stir the sea up until it is like a witch's cauldron. At 6 pm, go ashore. An hour to unload, swallow a cup of hot coffee, and undress. Ten minutes wait outside the bathroom door and then three minutes under a hot shower with the rest of the team drumming at the door. By 7.15 pm we are all showered and dry. For some of us, two hours' work breaking up the magma that we have brought back. Someone else must spend three hours filling cylinders. Maurice will spend the time repairing an engine or a compressor. The lucky ones get off lightly, cooking crabs and lobsters. For all of us there are some skilled gluing jobs to be done, mending the knees in our diving suits. And for me, finally, two or three hours at my desk, writing up the daily report, classifying what we have found, making a detailed inventory of all the objects, cleaning them in acid or carrying out the first stages of the preservation treatment, and sending off, posthaste, our most urgent administrative correspondence. At 10 pm or 10.30 we sit down to a supper of lobster, grilled salmon, or a leg of lamb, and at 11.30 pm Francis brings in the coffee and we roll out the green baize, put the bottle of Old Bushmills in the middle of the table, and lay out the bundles of notes. Louis shuffles the cards and the poker game gets under way.

At last one collapses into bed and then one tells oneself that under-water archaeology truly is a complete sport. And the proof is that one aches all over. One aches from having carried cylinders and motors, one aches from having pushed stones around like a human bulldozer, from having dug craters and built hills, shovelled sand and cleared it, one aches from having swum too much, from having towed enormous parachutes, pulled anchors or heaved aboard 120-lb lead ingots.

The sea does not recognise weekends. Every season we lost between 12 lb and 16 lb each in weight. Right from the start we decided to rest only when the weather was bad, so when it kept consistently calm for two weeks on end, or as once happened for six weeks, we all suffered strained backs, aching limbs, slipped discs or palpitations.

Two or three times, frozen, cold-ridden and dead tired, I did give up in calm weather after only one dive. The guilt that I felt in the evening was infinitely worse than the agony of diving again, and I didn't soon repeat the experiment.

When the bad weather did come, Maurice would announce: 'Equipment maintenance', or 'Dinghy cleaning'. Some of us would set to with scrubbing brushes, others with paint brushes and Francis, usually, would be given his own special task: his job was counting, weighing, measuring and carefully classifying, one by one, all our lead bullets, including crushed ones, half ones and even quarter ones. He would also weigh and measure stone cannon balls and iron ones, then sort them out, checking them off, according to calibre, against the *Girona*'s 8,166 balls for use with her fifty firing pieces of eight different types.

I would take our thousands of fragments of silver, pewter, bronze and pottery out of their boxes, spread them out on a table and sort them into little plastic bags, trying to fit the jigsaw together, or at least work out exactly how many different artifacts our various fragments must have made upon 26 October 1588, at midnight. How many gold-plated goblets, silver plates and forks, how many meat dishes, how many pewter pots and silver candlesticks, how many glazed clay bowls?

If the bad weather persisted I would get out my Nikon and go on with the photographic inventory of artifacts, or else I would make a trip to Belfast to take the jewels and gold coins to the bank and deliver the most fragile objects to the preservation laboratory for treatment.

The preservation laboratory, which operates under the combined auspices of Queen's University and the Ulster Museum, was of tremendous help to us. The Museum Curator, Mr W. A. Seaby, the keeper, Lawrence N. W. Flanagan, had offered to help of their own accord, and Stephen Rees Jones, Director of the Laboratory, showed himself willing to put himself to any amount of trouble to solve the preservation problems posed by the thousands of impossible objects we would bring him, in the most daunting condition. Anything made of metal, other than gold or lead, that has spent a long period of time in the sea, requires very delicate preservation, as does anything made from an organic material (such as bone, leather or wood). Otherwise, as soon as they come into contact with the air, they are swiftly and totally destroyed. An iron cannon ball, for example, just out of its gangue of oxide and sand, looks as good as new, black and perfectly round. Once exposed to the air, it turns brown in a matter of minutes, red in an hour, and after a few days the changes in temperature and humidity in the atmosphere cause it to crack and scale, and sweat great drops of brown liquid. After two weeks it begins to erupt in blisters and the whole of its outer layer flakes off. After another month or two all that will be left of the ball will be a shapeless little mound of rust. The same process occurs over a longer period with iron cannons and anchors.

Protected from erosion and borers by mud and sand, a wooden pulley block or figurehead may have remained in perfect condition. But without treatment the fibres of the wood will contract as it dries out. It will warp and crack, lose its shape and finally disappear to nothing. As the water seeps out, the destroyed cells of the wood collapse completely if they are left unsupported (briefly the treatment consists in replacing the water in the wood with polyethylene glycol to keep the fibres in shape). This is why bringing things like this up from a wreck, as souvenir hunting divers sometimes do, without having made any provisions for treating them, is effectively to destroy them. We took great care never to expose anything fragile that we found to the air. Depending on the object, we would either keep it under water, or else we would put the first stage of the treatment into operation immediately, ourselves.

For small objects, straightforward cleaning did not pose any problems. I did it myself in the evenings. My bedroom was cluttered with pots, filled with brownish, blue, green, murky liquids, bubbling away and filling the air with noxious smells and acrid fumes that used to make my eyes smart all night long. This was to dissolve the chalky encrustations or the black gangue that clogged some of the jewels.

But chemical, electro-chemical, or electrolytic preservation methods are long and complex. They require daily attention by a team of experts and a perfectly equipped laboratory. It had taken Stephen the whole winter to save some of the cannon balls, the anchor and about a hundred other metal objects. His masterpiece was the musket. He had let it stew over a long period, then rinsed it to remove the salt, and dehydrated it in alcohol before steeping it at heat in polyethylene glycol. The butt and stock of the gun were now like new. One could count the strokes made by the plane; the ramrod slipped in its hole better than on the night of the shipwreck. He returned to us in equally pristine condition the sycamore and soft wood (according to Queen's University botanists) sword pommels; a large lime-wood knife handle still bound with its original string; a penknife handle with copper flower-shaped rivets, carved from some exotic hardwood; a dagger handle, intricately decorated with plaited copper wire and its leather sheath; as well as a few oak and alder wood splinters of the galleass herself.

His assistants had patiently straightened out the pewter plates. They had glued the earthenware pots and the glazed plates together. They had rubbed the original animal oil back into the leather sandal straps and boot soles and made them supple once more, ready for wear.

By treating them with various complicated solutions, Stephen had also succeeded in saving the two bronze cannons, which were exuding a sort of white froth and threatening to lose their surface layer. This cleaning process had revealed a coat of arms embossed on one of the two firing pieces. The arms were clearly visible but undecipherable. They had weathered too many storms and suffered too much battering by stones and rocks. On the little breech loading cannon, I thought I recognised the arms of Spain. The four quarterings were there and the collar round it was certainly a Golden Fleece one. The breech blocks (*servidores*) had been given the same treatment, and inside Stephen had found intact the cotton match, the plug of powder and the poplar wood stopper. (See page 263.) We had also found two dozen miniature iron cannon balls (4·3 cm calibre), so we were ready to fire. (See Appendix III for plan of the guns.)

It had taken lengthy correspondence on my part with sixteenth-century artillery experts, and many visits to museums and long research in books, to identify the gun (164·3 cm long, calibre 4·5 cm). The support pivot that held the trunnions was made of cast iron and had disappeared along with the *rabisa* (a 2-ft long stem that one rested on one's shoulder to aim) and the wooden chocks, or *cuñas* (put in through holes in the side to lock the powder chamber—the *servidor* or *recamara*—tightly).

I had called it quite incorrectly a 'falconete' because of its overall similarity to a fifteenth-century falconet. I had even toyed with the idea that it might be a 'pasavolante'. Finally, and without being quite sure of my ground yet, I decided 'esmeril'. (See page 262.) I had lost one illusion along the way. Having been interested in antique Spanish naval ordnance for fifteen years, I had thought I knew something about it. My advice to those who share that illusion is never to open the masterly *Armada Guns*, by the late Professor Michael Lewis. They will need to do no more than flick quickly through it and the damage will be done. Not only will they realise right from the start that they know nothing about the subject, they will also realise that they never will know anything about it, unless like the author himself, they spend the best years of their lives going through all the contemporary literature, making an individual study of every gun in every museum, and taking apart every logbook, letter and list as well as the inventories of every fleet of every nation. Worse still, they will learn that the artillerists of the sixteenth century, who wrote treatises extending to many volumes, purely theoretical and full of mistakes, knew little or nothing about it either. First of all, the arts of building cannon, serving, laying and firing them were closely guarded secrets. Secondly, the technical vocabularly, dimensions and calibres, units of weights and measure, the whole terminology in fact, were subject to infinite variations. In the same way as happened with the names of ship types, for example, guns that were quite different in length, calibre, weight and appearance, would at different times and in different countries, or sometimes even at the same time and in the same country, be called by same names. (In the *Girona* inventory there were only eight named types of cannon, but we found shot for guns of at least eleven different calibres.)

Artillery first appeared in Spain in the fourteenth century. It developed rapidly in the fifteenth—which is when one finds it for the first time in ships—but it was not until the seventeenth century that Philip III first tried to standardise somewhat the manufacture of pieces of ordnance. Under Philip II, total anarchy still reigned in this area. The diversity of names used was infinite. It was not until I found (in Arantegui, the great Spanish expert) the following reference to some documents of 1547 in the National Archives in Simancas, that I found the answer to my particular problem: 'An octagonal esmeril [like ours], which fires a shot of $\frac{1}{2}$ lb [approximately the weight of ours], with the same weight of powder [about the weight of powder we found in our breech blocks] . . . 38 calibres long from vent to muzzle [ours was about 36 calibres].' And: 'an octagonal esmeril firing 4-ounce shot [Ufano mentions 15-ounce shot for another esmeril] 24 calibres long.'

In 1587 Santa Cruz requested 'esmerils with two *servidores* each' for the galleasses. We found six of them. Spanish experts define the esmeril as 'a piece of light artillery, in use from the end of the fifteenth century to the first half of the seventeenth, falling somewhere between the *ribadoquin* and the musketoon, 38 calibres long'. Professor Lewis describes it as a small-calibre, short-range mankiller, breech loading and mounted on a universal joint pivot, used especially for defending a vessel in case of boarding by the enemy. F. F. Olesa Muñido concludes from his own research that 'it is a gun varying considerably in appearance, calibre and weight.'

But what finally disposed of any hesitation I might have had, was this providential quote from Lt. Col. Arantegui: 'Esmerils, like all other small guns, varied so much in weight and dimensions, that one could say that their features were whatever one wanted them to be.'

As for the other powder chambers, the big ones, that we found on Lacada Point without their guns, they belonged, I think to what the Marquis de Santa Cruz referred to in his inventories as a 'large esmeril'.

The other cannon—no possible doubt here—is a demi-saker. It has a calibre of 7·6 cm and is 234 cm long, or about 31 calibres (the expert, Lechuga, gives 32 calibres).

A demi-saker? Bronze? Once I had identified it, it began to remind me of something, that cannon. I dug about in the confusion of my files and out of the bale marked 'artillery' I pulled a note, scribbled down long ago in Madrid. 'In 1588, to arm the galleasses, the Duke of Medina Sidonia lent the Armada seven bronze demi-sakers from his personal arsenal at San Lucar.' Those would not have been naval guns. Now, in the centre of our demi-saker were some quite distinct rectangular slots (one on top, in front of the vent, and two on the sides) and some protruding supports on either side of the vent. That could have been where the tangent scale and plumb line sights were fixed to measure the angle of firing (these sorts of instruments were many and varied). Such a piece of equipment would obviously have been used only on land, not on a ship that was always moving.

We had raised from a galleass a bronze demi-saker that was not a piece of naval ordnance (the Associate Curator of the Madrid Naval Museum confirmed this for me). Could it have been one of the seven pieces lent by the Duke himself? If only the arms were clearer! (See page 263.)

39
A Bottle for Every Ten Gold Coins

Someone tapped me lightly on the shin.

I was digging in a deep cave, a long way under an enormous boulder, lying on the rock, flat on my stomach, my air cylinders scraping against the roof. I crawled out backwards.

I turned round: it was Louis. He was beaming. Behind his mask his eyes were shining. He was smiling broadly into his beard, and round his neck hung an enormous gold chain, three rows of gold chain—miles of gold chain.

The season had got off to rather a slow start. The inventories for the end of April and May were not remarkable, lists of fragments, nothing more. The first gold coin, a four escudo piece, did not come up until 11 May. It was Louis who found it. Then in June, Louis had a period of quite incredible luck. While the rest of us would work away staunchly in our corners and after five hours come up with one tiny, badly worn coin, he would be filling his bottomless green bag with a positive ballast of ducats and two-escudo pieces in perfect condition, plus twice as many pieces of eight and a few odd jewels, just for good measure.

Two miles from Port Ballintrae, the Irish distill the best whisky in the world. During the lean days I had made a rash promise and thereby set a precedent: for every ten gold coins I would give the lucky diver a bottle of Old Bushmills.

It must be said that whisky is as necessary for divers on land as air is under water. It is a well established tradition in Ireland, and I had only been following the example of my predecessor, Sir George Carew, Master of the Ordnance, who used the same device in June 1589 to fire the enthusiasm of his men, when he was trying to raise some Spanish cannon off the West Coast. He gives a very good explanation for it in a letter to the Lord Deputy, dated 1 July:

> Yesterday we fastened our haullsers to a cannon of battery or basalyke as we supposed by the length, for they lie at four fathoms and a half of water, which was so huge that it broke our cables. Our diver was nearly drowned, but Irish aqua vitae hath such virtue as I hope of his recovery.

Irish divers have not lost their faith in the old therapy and it is probably to that that they owe their resistance to the cold. Our friend John McLennan, for example, usually dives in a short neoprene suit, with bare arms, bare hands, bare legs and bare feet. Just to look at him, perfectly happy on the sea-bed in such a state of undress, is enough to make one shiver. I must admit though, he is a special case. John does actually make Old Bushmills whisky. . . .

Anyway, by the time June came round, my rash promise was leading me into financial ruin and the rest of the team was falling into a drunken stupor. The day Louis came looking for me under the sea, wearing his triple gold necklace, I honestly saw the spectre of delirium tremens hovering in the algae.

His chain was as thick as a man's finger, 2·5 metres long and intact. Not one of its oval links had so much as a scratch on it. It was so heavy (1·8 kg) that we couldn't help thinking of how some poor, rich nobleman must have been dragged down head first to the bottom under the weight of it.

In contemporary accounts, Spanish survivors often mention the chains that the English took from around their necks (sometimes they took the skin too). The English make markedly less mention of them in the minutes of their examinations of prisoners, for not all of them went through the official channels which would have taken them to Her Majesty's chests. Among the questions laid down by the Lord Deputy for local authorities to ask Spanish prisoners before they cut their throats was 'whether any . . . have any chain, jewels or money of theirs in custody and who they be.' The question features in all the prescribed forms of examination without exception, and one David Gwyn, an interpreter who was said to have perjured himself and appropriated some gold chains taken from the Spaniards, found himself in very bad trouble.

One George Wadloke wrote to the Mayor of Waterford reporting that sixteen survivors had come ashore from a Spanish vessel run aground on the sand, wearing their gold chains around their necks. Medina Sidonia presented the Governor of Calais with a chain and noted the fact in his *diario*. Such chains were promised to French pilots, engaged in action in the Channel. They also came in handy for bribing traitors: in the autumn of 1588, in an attempt to buy off the English defence in Bergen Op Zoom, Parma promised Colonel Grimston 7,000 crowns, plus a gold chain for each officer.

In their portraits Renaissance gentlemen are invariably shown wearing such chains, which served as a necktie and an outward demonstration of wealth. A chain was also useful as the modern equivalent of the travellers' cheque: If he found himself short of cash a gentleman had only to open up a link with his teeth to pay for a horse, a meal or a girl.

Today, with a few exceptions, these chains have disappeared. Their value lay in the weight of the metal rather than in the workmanship and with changing fashions they were usually melted down. I knew of only one or two museums which still had examples. This is what made the ones found in wrecks absolutely priceless. (See page 257.)

The sea is unpredictable. Next to the large chain, Louis had found another (76 cm long), amazingly fine and light, a continuous chain, made in such a way—God alone knows how—that each of the flat links passed through three others: to cut it, one would have to cut not one but four links. This fragile masterpiece was all twisted, but complete, while other chains we found (a total of eight) had their links scattered all over the sea-bed. In 1967, for instance, as previously mentioned, the first gold object I found in front of the case was a round link from a particular chain from which we kept finding more and more links every day for three summers, all over the site. They were everywhere, some open, some closed. By the end of 1968 we had 136 links, of five grams each, found either singly or in lengths of two, three, or six. The chain then measured four feet. The following year it had grown to almost six feet. This chain is a plain one, identical to the one King Philip is shown wearing in an engraving done when he was nineteen, and similar to other portraits painted by Rubens in some famous portraits. I often wondered if it was actually possible that the sea should break a chain open and scatter such heavy, small objects so widely. Could not the owner have lost his chain, bit by bit, playing dice? And was it not more likely the links had been scattered along with the rest of the dead winners' possessions? But other small chains, like the figure-of-eight one, far too fine for anyone to have even thought of breaking them up, were scattered in the same way. . . . One splendidly worked, originally studded with pearls and other precious stones, had been similarly dispersed. (See page 176.)

On the two-gold-chain day, Louis also found thirty gold pieces, but by that time we weren't even bothering to mention the escudos. Every day Louis used to find his dozen regularly, some days more. It had become an accepted pattern. When he came up we would ask: 'And what else have you found?'

What else? One day it was a gold signet ring, a large seal engraved with the letters IHS. (See page 176.) IHS is the classical monogram for IHEOUS (Jesus in Greek). The H is stamped with a cross and underlined with a strange symbol: a nail from the cross and a sort of bracket, instead of the usual three nails. It was probably a Jesuit father's ring. Ignatius Loyola adopted the sigma IHS in 1541 in his seal as General of the Society of Jesus and it subsequently became the emblem of the institution (he is shown, in a famous portrait, wearing the same sigma on his breastplate). Alternatively the ring might have belonged to a

249

Canon of the Order of the Holy Sepulchre, the religious order founded in Spain in the twelfth century, not the military order of knighthood of the same name. The nuns of the Order still wear the same seal, with the bracket instead of the nails.

Another day Louis fished up a Portuguese gold coin, the only one in the inventory, minted in the reign of John III (1521–1557). On the reverse it had St Vincent with palm and ship and the inscription: 'Zelator Fidei usque ad Mortem'; on the obverse were the crowned arms of Portugal and 'Johannus III REX POTV ET AL' (King of Portugal and Algarbe).

Another day it was a handful of gold buttons, little balls 0·5–1·5 cm in diameter, engraved with stylised flowers and geometrical designs, with a ring to sew them on by. They were just like the ones seen on doublets in Spanish and Flemish portraits of the period. What amused me considerably was finding those same Spanish buttons, which we picked up by the dozen, on Sir Francis Drake's doublet and slashed sleeves in an engraving by Joss de Hondt. Did he get his off his prisoners' clothes?

And finally, another day, it was a gold book!

I was lifting myself on board and I saw that everyone was smiling. I knew what it meant. Louis had done it again? Of course! My eyes went straight to his little green bag and there was a block of gold. A block, exquisitely chased with flowers and scrolls. I took it in my hand—a little bible on a small double chain. It has a thick binding. On the cover, a saint, finely engraved, holds a staff in one hand and a book in the other. The engraved figure is framed by small pillars and a pediment. It must be St John the Baptist, for on closer inspection I can just see that the staff ends in a cross (half hidden by the frame) and has a banner on it. The oriflamme cross and the Holy Book (and often, but not always, a lamb, the Lamb of God) are the attributes of St John the Baptist in all religious iconography. The back cover, moulded into a now empty recess, must have contained a relic. The next day, a couple of yards away, Louis found the gold frame, like the one on the front cover, that must have held the protective crystal in place. The reliquary (43 × 32 × 9 mm) opened like a real book, but the clasp had jammed when the cover got crushed by stones. We should have to wait until the evening to find out what marvels it contained.

That evening, very carefully, using jewellers tools, I removed the gold wire that had held the book closed for four hundred years and very slowly opened it. Inside lay neither diamonds nor emeralds, but a broken gold ring and two little columns with a hinge at the bottom (perhaps the broken pieces of some other jewel). Most important of all were five little round containers, five gold cylinders, fixed to the back cover. Two of them still contained a little tablet of red wax, all shrivelled up. What could they be? Pills? Incense? Poison? But there weren't any Borgias aboard. Some cosmetic concentrate? Rhinoceros horn aphrodisiacs, perhaps? In order to get the mystery cleared up, I sent off one of the wax-based tablets to the Chemistry Department of Queen's University in Belfast. The results of the analysis took some time to come through. At last I heard from the experts. In their opinion it was without any doubt 'a tablet made from some wax-based substance'. (See page 221.)

Two months' later, after millions of viewers had seen the little book on British television, during a special fifty minute colour programme, I got my answer. It arrived from Miss Margaret Cronin along with an avalanche of other letters full of fantastic suggestions. The tablets were *Agnus Dei*.

Agnus Dei had been made in Rome since the ninth century, with the wax from the previous year's Easter candles, mixed with holy oil (the wax symbolised Christ's virgin flesh). They were votive objects, supposed to have miraculous, protective qualities, and were often worn hung round the neck. A highly complex ritual, modified several times over the centuries, accompanied each stage of their manufacture. In the sixteenth century there were specialist monks in Rome who made them in advance. On one side they stamped the image of the paschal lamb, the ancient symbol of Christ, the Lamb of God; of innocence; and of St John the Baptist, God's servant, innocently suffering for his people. It was obvious that the image of St John would appear on a box made to hold *Agnus Dei*. The lamb stamped on the tablets carried a cross or a flag. On the reverse the monks impressed the image of a saint, or the name or arms of the reigning Pope. Nothing of that was visible any more on our red tablets, all cracked and shrivelled, and also somewhat smaller than usual.

The Pope would bless them all together, on the Wednesday of Holy Week in the first year of his reign and then every seven years after that. He dipped them in a mixture of holy water and oil over which he had said a few prayers. The distribution took place the following Saturday. During the Mass, after the *Agnus Dei*, the Pope would place packets of the wax tablets in the upturned mitres of bishops and cardinals who had come to receive them. The dignitaries of the Church, in their turn, would distribute them to those of their friends and acquaintances who in one way or another had shown themselves worthy of such a signal favour.

The counterfeiting of *Agnus Dei* was severely prohibited, and several Bulls were published forbidding the decoration or painting of them. These miraculous amulets were thought to protect their lucky owner from all evil forces, and particularly from fire and flood. Many examples are quoted of fires and serious floods being stopped in their tracks by an *Angus Dei*. They also protected pregnant women from the perils of childbirth, and one of their prime functions was the protection of sailors from plague and storm.

At the time of the Armada, Queen Elizabeth had forbidden by law the importing of '*Agnus Dei* and other popish trumperies' into England.

The custom in Rome was that one was given, at the same time as the *Agnus Dei*, a little instruction book, a printed leaflet listing the amulets' many qualities. I wondered whether it was such a leaflet that was kept, carefully folded, in the deep recess in the back cover of our gold reliquary book. I also wondered about the fact that there were five gold containers in the box. Was it usual for an ordinary Catholic to carry not one but several *Agnus Dei*? Might the reliquary not have belonged to a bishop who had received his small supply in Rome and was parsimoniously distributing them (he still had two left out of five)? In which case it could possibly have belonged to the Bishop of Killaloe, who sailed with Don Alonzo on the *rata*.

Following Louis, I had my own period of plenty. I began by finding, around a small protruding rock, the ship's silver—gold plated, engraved and decorated, but smashed to smithereens. It made a silver jigsaw puzzle: broken knives and forks; fragments of dishes; plate or goblet rims; jug handles, samovar feet, chest hinges; ewer spouts, broken pieces of statuettes; bits of fruit or sugar bowls; candlesticks, flasks, inkpots or sauce boats. Then I struck a vein of four-escudo pieces that produced some six to twelve coins a day, as well as some small medallion or other, usually an empty frame, as a daily bonus. Some of these frames were originally parts of bracelets, others would have been badges, or held jewels sewn onto ribbons or doublets. Almost all of them had lost their central cameo, their miniature or their semi-precious stone. With exceptional luck, André found a pair of them intact, still set with bright pearls and a little central ruby. Bob found a very large one, but empty. Apart from that bad luck dogged this tireless giant. Every day he moved underwater mountains, only to find nothing but half a lead bullet or a highly suspect bone. For a long time Francis shared his bad luck, while Maurice, a specialist since last year on Neapolitan ducats and scudis, used to bring back Charles V as a Roman Emperor one day, and Philip II the next, crowned, bare-headed, or wreathed in laurels.

My record for 1969 was to be 17 gold coins in one day of six hours' work on the sea-bed. I am the first to admit that compared to Maurice's twenty, and Louis' thirty coins, seventeen is not much. But this time, I am pleased to report, no unfortunate incidents occurred while the coins were in my hands, and, even though they were photographed, I did bring all seventeen ashore.

40
A History Lesson Under the Ocean

We found in all 405 gold coins, 756 silver and 115 copper coins, minted in six different countries—Spain, Portugal, the Kingdom of the Two Sicilies, the Republic of Genoa, Mexico and Peru; in eight different reigns—the Catholic Kings, Joan the Mad, Charles V and Philip II of Spain; Manuel I, John III and Sebastian of Portugal, and an unidentified doge of Genoa. They were struck in fourteen different mints: Seville, Toledo, Segovia, Madrid, Burgos, Cuenca, Granada, Corunna, Valladolid, Mexico, Lima, Potosi, Lisbon and Genoa, and were of sixty different denominations. (See pages 195–6.)

This seemingly extraordinary variety is easily explained. We did not bring up the contents of an official chest, but money that belonged to the many passengers who had come from far and wide to join the crusade. Some of the coins are very rare, two or three possibly previously unknown, and most of them at least 'very fine'. Some of them contain variations, anomalies, spelling mistakes, or inverted dates, such as to make the most sophisticated of numismatists jump from their seats.

As far as we are concerned they are quite simply beautiful objects that we love to look at and touch again and again, beautiful objects that set our minds wandering each time we see them, for as we found them, one by one, thirty feet under water, each one of those 1,276 coins gave us a fascinating history lesson.

Spain, united for the first time in the marriage of Isabella of Castile and Ferdinand of Aragon in 1469, became officially one nation ten years later. In 1492 the last territories were recaptured from the Moors. From the reign of the Catholic Kings, we found pieces of four and pieces of eight, bearing the yoke and the bundle of arrows intertwined, symbols of Ferdinand's and Isabella's respective states, and the arms of Spain (Castile, Leon, Aragon, Catalonia and the Balearic Islands) over the arms of Granada, marking the recent conquest of Granada and the end of the *Reconquista*. These coins would probably have been already 100 years old when the *Girona* went down.

Charles I of Spain (Charles V of the Holy Roman Empire) began his reign with his mother, Joan the Mad (widow of Archduke Philip of

Austria) as Regent. We had about ten ducats from that period, found by Maurice, inscribed: CAROLUS ET JOHANA HISPANIARUM REGES ET SICILIAE. Charles was also King of the Two Sicilies, whose capital was Naples. It was at the mint in Naples that all our gold ducats and silver half ducats were struck, carrying his effigy as Holy Roman Emperor, wearing a Roman breastplate. These are inscribed CAROLUS V RO. IMP and on the reverse R. HISPAN.UTRIUS SICIL. (Charles V Emperor of the Romans, King of all the Spains and of the Two Sicilies). It was Naples that had armed the *Girona* and the three other galleasses of the squadron for Charles's son, her King, Philip II.

We have almost every coin of Philip's reign: one, two and four gold escudos, struck in almost every mint in Spain; one, two, four and eight silver reals (the famous pieces of eight); unfortunately we are still missing the half and quarter reals.

The Kings of Spain were also rulers of the West Indies and of the Americas. One look at the coins we found was sufficient to remind us of this fact: PHILIPPUS DEI GRATIA HISPANIARUM ET INDIARUM REX. Philip, like his father before him, had money minted in America. Many of our silver coins, pieces of eight, of four and of two, bear the stamp of Mexico, Lima or Potósi (then in northern Peru, now in Bolivia). Some Mexican coins have the device PLUS ULTRA inscribed on a scroll stretched between two columns, Hercules' columns, representing the Straits of Gibraltar, against a background of waves. The ancients believed that the world ended at the Pillars of Hercules, and that beyond them lay nothing—*nil plus ultra*. Under the aegis of the Catholic Kings, Don Cristobal Colon proved that this was not so. The Spaniards were proud to recall it. *Plus ultra*—their empire stretched far beyond them.

In his youth Philip took as his second wife the Queen of England, Mary Tudor. We found ducats dating from this period, bearing the name of Philip II, King of England, King of France and Naples, Prince of Spain, King of France (because of Calais, England's last stronghold and the last vestige of her claims in France). When the Queen, his wife, died childless in 1558, the King Consort lost all claims to the English throne. Identical half ducats say simply: 'Philip II, by the Grace of God, King of Aragon and the Two Sicilies.' Thus we know that the coins were minted after 1558.

Because the fleet assembled in Lisbon and there were some Portuguese units on board (Portugal had come under Philip's rule in 1580), we can explain why we found any number of Portuguese gold, silver and copper coins.

My acquaintance with numismatics is restricted to a limited period, from the sixteenth to the nineteenth century, of Spanish and colonial issues. I therefore had the greatest difficulty, and consequently the greatest pleasure, in identifying some partially effaced Neapolitan and Portuguese pieces. I would never have managed it without the help of Professor Michael Dolley, a brilliant and ebullient Irish numismatist, and Mr Wilfred A. Seaby, Director of the Ulster Museum in Belfast, whose reputation as a numismatist is worldwide and who was kind enough to allow me the run of his library.

But the coin that really stumped me was a small silver one that Louis found all by himself. On the reverse was a castle and a palm tree and the legend: DUX ET GUBER . . . illegible . . . ENU . . . illegible . . . and on the obverse was a cross, somewhere between a St George's cross and a Lusitanian cross and the inscription CONRADUS REX RO . . . illegible . . . A . . . illegible.

A king, who was also duke *and* governor? Why didn't they throw in mayor for good measure? Who on earth could it be? I dug about in the history books and came across several highly improbable Conrads: a thirteenth-century Duke of Mazovia in Prussia; a Conrad von Jungingen and another von Wettin, who ruled over some obscure little states on the borders of Germany and Poland; and then some more who at least had the merit of being kings. A tenth-century Conrad I of Franconia; an eleventh-century Conrad II; a Conrad III of Hohenstauffen, who went to the Second Crusade; and a Conrad IV of Germany who died in 1254. But we were way off. In the sixteenth century there wasn't the ghost of a Conrad to be found in the whole of Europe. Perhaps there was a collector of old coins on the *Girona*?

And then one evening, the Spanish Consul in Belfast introduced me to Professor Dolley. In the course of conversation I described our mystery coin to him. Dolley leapt out of his chair, exclaiming 'I know, I know.' He fell back, then sprung up again and immediately began to explain very fast and in great detail, that the coin was Genoese, probably contemporary with the Armada. It was a 'genovino', minted sometime between 1527 and 1557, modelled on a much older coin which had inspired such confidence in merchants and bankers all over Italy and the rest of Europe that it went on being minted until the eighteenth century. The Conrad in question had long been forgotten (in much the same way as Maria Theresa Austrian thalers are still minted in Vienna for the Yemen, where they are legal tender).

The Conradus in question, continued Professor Dolley, was probably Conrad II, son of Conrad I, who acceded to the throne of France after extinction of the Carolingians in 911. He was himself Emperor of the Franconians and had conquered Italy, where in 1027 he was crowned in Milan with the iron crown of the Kings of Lombardy. It was there too that he won the right to the title of King of the Romans, and Doge (Dux) and Governor of the ancient Roman province of Liguna, now the Republic of Genoa. This type of coin is famous in both gold and silver. Dolley showed me a picture of it, marked 'very rare'. Complete, the inscription reads: CONRADUS REX ROMA AS + DUX ET GUBER RIPV. GEN.

The cameos, too, were proving something of an enigma. The previous year we had found eight very fine gold jewels, set with pearls, six of which still contained a lapis lazuli cameo, each bearing the profile of a different Roman Emperor wearing a laurel crown. This year Francis had been set to do nothing else for a month but look for the others. In May he found the ninth jewel. In September, Louis and André brought up the tenth and the eleventh. I think I know where the twelfth is—the last, maybe—but the equinoctial storms put us off and we left it behind.

I had assumed from the start that what we had there were the twelve Caesars. But in that case, who was who? The emperors celebrated by Suetonius in his *Lives of the Twelve Caesars*, were the twelve first: Julius Caesar, then Augustus, Tiberius, Caligula, Claudius, Nero, Galba, Otto, Vitellius, Vespasian, Titus and Domitian. Being the best known, these are the ones who have been portrayed most often by sculptors, miniaturists, engravers and the makers of cameos and medals, frequently using coins for the likenesses. With such a widespread iconography they ought to have been easy to recognise. In fact, the more portraits of Roman emperors I studied the more obvious it became to me that the special qualities of Renaissance artists, lay more in their powers of imagination and ease of style than in their concern for a good likeness of a Roman coin. Our cameos were not Roman but Renaissance ones and almost certainly Italian (or Spanish of Italian influence), like the jewels in which they were set. The experts were all agreed on that point. That they were all from the one workshop was obvious from the uniformity of medium and technique and also from the hair styles—the laurel crowns were identical. Glyptics, the art of eroding on hard stones, at which the Romans and the Egyptians excelled, had been enjoying a revival for 100 years already by the time of the Armada. This was due mainly to the patronage of the Medicis and Leo X. The best known artists of the sixteenth century (whose work, however, lacked the quality of the cameos produced in the studios of the previous century) were Domenico dei Camei and Valerio Vincentino (died 1546), who was particularly famous for his cameos depicting gods, mythological scenes, and emperors in the classical style. He might well have made ours.

My task was made that much more difficult by the fact that three of the profiles, while one could not deny that they were noble and pure, were utterly anonymous. Augustus, Tiberius, Domitian, one could give them any name one liked; they were interchangeable. I

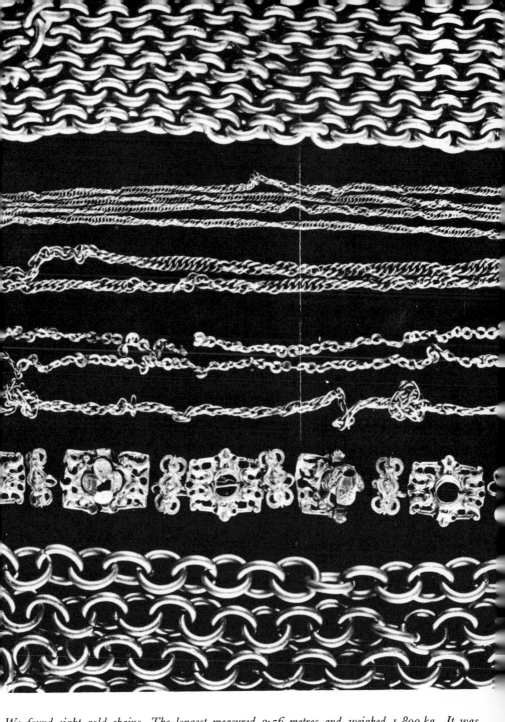

We found eight gold chains. The longest measured 2·56 metres and weighed 1,800 kg. It was absolutely intact.

Above: *As a child I often used to dream of the frontispiece of* The Mariner's Mirror. *Opposite (above):* I was thrilled when I found those very same instruments on the sea bed: the sounding lead, nautical dividers and astrolabes. Below (left): *An astrolabe being used to measure the height of the sun and calculate the latitude.* (right): *A sixteenth century astrolabe, possibly Spanish, in the National Maritime Museum, Greenwich. It is similar to ours, although ours are unfortunately in very bad condition.*

The whole team (minus Marc—still behind the camera). Left to right Louis Gorsse, Maurice Vidal, Patrick Couture, André Fassotte, Francis Dumont, and the author.

Above and opposite (top): *Maurice raised the esmeril. We did what James McDonnell did in 1589 with the three cannon he took off the wreck, and carried ours on to the walls of Dunluce Castle. (The stone cannon balls do not belong to the esmeril.)*

*ht: The 'servidores' or breech blocks still had
.de their cartridges of powder, poplar wood
per, and cotton match. We had also found the
mall iron balls, so we were ready to fire.*

*ow: a demi-saker, possibly one of the guns that
dina Sidonia provided for the galleasses from
his own arsenal.*

The ring setting: a tiny hand holding a heart and an open belt clasp.

The inscription: 'I have nothing more to g... thee'.

Madam de Champagney 1524. I found that she was the grandmother of Jean Thomas Perrenot who drowned in the Girona wearing this very ring.

could, therefore, work only from the three faces with clearly defined features, which were easily identifiable. I immediately recognised, or so I thought, Julius Caesar, with his hollow cheeks and aquiline nose turning down to meet his hooked chin, and, possibly, Vitellius (or Vespasian) in the fat man with the double chin.

But it was the eleventh cameo that brought my theory crashing down. It was a young face, unusual, with a squashed boxer's nose, thick lips (the upper protruding above the lower) and a rounded chin with a deep dimple. That could not possibly be one of the twelve Caesars. But then, who was it?

It was a Renaissance piece so I looked through contemporary iconographies for portraits of figures considered important at the time—those same portraits that sixteenth-century cameo makers would have copied. And almost immediately I found my young Caesar with the boxer's nose. In a work dated 1544, 'Icones Imperatorum' by Jacobus Micylus, was a detailed engraving clearly showing every detail of his profile. It was Michael I, Rhangabe, crowned Emperor of the Romans in Byzantium in 811, when he was still very young. Within two years, as a result of his weakness and countless capitulations, he had become an object of ridicule. He abdicated and went to live out the last thirty-five years of his life in a monastery.

And what about the others? Were they just any old emperors, picked out at random from the twelve Caesars and others, or were they all Byzantine Caesars? By the time I had finished I was inclined to think that they were in fact all Byzantine emperors, for the one that I had originally called Julius Caesar was as like as two peas to Stauratius, who reigned for a short time in 811 just before Michael I, and my Vitellius/Vespasian could well have been Constantine the Younger (Constantine II) who after the death of Constantine I in 337 reigned jointly with Constantius for a short while.

And if in fact they were the Emperors of Constantinople, might the cameos not have belonged to Manuel Paleologus, a direct descendant of their successors, who, I knew, was on the expedition? What more appropriate for the victory Te Deum in London than that he should be wearing the portraits of his ancestors in a necklace on his breast? (See pages 222–4.)

41
Six Thousand Hours on the Sea Bed

September was drawing to a close. The faded algae were frayed like flags the evening after a battle.

Repeated gales finally drove us away for good. It was high time. The straps on our cylinders were covered with little green algae and shell-fish were thriving on our flippers. Our engines and compressors were giving up the ghost, the inflatable dinghies began to leak like sieves. Francis's knees had come through his two diving suits.

I handed Louis my second cylinder to inflate one last parachute. I wanted to feast my eyes one last time on the spot where I was leaving behind a little of my soul. It was raining. The clouds were low. I sat dreaming in the Zodiac as it rocked in the swell, anchored between the two grapples.

I now knew everything that I wanted to know. I had proved what was just a guess. I had found the remains of a ship. It contained Spanish cannon, coins and seals from all over the Spanish Empire, and Spanish lead ingots. The name of the site perpetuates the tradition that it was a Spanish ship. The ship was connected in one way or another with Naples; the number of coins that we found from the Two Sicilies proves that. She sank at the end of the sixteenth century—the coins stop at Philip II and the last date is 1585. It was not a merchant ship; she was carrying too much shot and too much lead, plates, and ingots, for that. And besides the Spanish never traded with northern Ireland. Therefore she must have been a Spanish warship. She must have come from the Armada. A great many Spanish and English documents contain accounts of the loss of the *Girona* somewhere in this area—none mentions any other Armada ship lost off Ulster. Spanish and English documents talk of jewels, gold and silver found on bodies and in the remains of the ship. We found 47 gold jewels, 8 chains, 1,256 coins, 2 insignia of knighthood, and any amount of gold table plate and silver, proof that there must have been many rich men aboard, and several noblemen. None of the ships lost, other than the *Girona* had a significantly large crew aboard. No other ship lost off Ireland would have contained cannon balls corresponding exactly to the *Girona*'s. And, finally, no other ship would have gone down with

Captain Spinola's Order of Malta, or a ring belonging to Nicole de Champagney's grandson, drowned in the *Girona* and mourned on the spot by Captain Cuellar.

I watched the waves breaking off Lacada Point, 50 yds to the northwest. They catch on a reef there, a submerged mound, rising up in some 40 ft of water. At low tide the top of it is only about 12 ft below the surface. It was actually at the foot of this that Marc found the anchor and I found the astrolabe. It all seems clear.

That stormy night in October 1588, the *Girona* struck the top of the reef, or maybe she just rolled over it, caught athwartships by a breaker. As soon as the Spanish realised that they were about to go on the rocks they dropped anchor. It was near midnight. The pilot was standing on the deck holding his astrolabe at the ready, waiting for a break in the cloud to take a sighting on a star. As the galleass rolled his astrolabe slipped into the sea.

Between the reef and Lacada Point, I found the remains of a smaller anchor. Did they try to launch a boat? Did it capsize, losing its anchor?

The vessel had begun to turn round on herself, but the next moment she was being broken apart on Lacada Point. From her gaping hull spilled cannon balls and lead ingots along with all the kitchen equipment. A section of the hull, weighed down by the lead plates that had been nailed to it, stayed where it was. Some of the cannon were left high and dry, others rolled down the underwater slope until they reached the flat. Men came tumbling out of her, only to be drowned within minutes, scattered, thrown onto the cliffs or carried out to sea by the tide. Wave upon wave cast up onto the rock fragments of the dead ship and men with bulging pockets (and perhaps with their caskets, on which James McDonnell will have got his hands). The aftercastle broke away from the shattered hull and drifted eastwards. The Captain's cabin emptied out its treasures and its passengers, sprinkling the sea-bed with coins, jewels and a thousand more ephemeral things. It finally came up against a blind rock to the east of Lacada Point, crashed and split itself open underwater, disgorging its silver plate.

Another part of the *Girona* was carried along the west side of Lacada Point, leaving behind it a trail of perrier balls which we found, and men, whose possessions we also recovered. From there the swirling currents drove it onto a reef to the west of Spaniard Cave. It ended by running into the foot of it, together with all its cannon balls, ballast and debris. This was almost certainly part of the prow, containing the crew's quarters. We found only small coins there.

For 380 years, the sea churned it all up. Then along we came to undo what she had done.

And so the divers surfaced for the last time. I hoisted the neoprene lifting bags aboard. Maurice brought back the crowbars, the worn out shovels and the dented buckets.

For the last time we weighed the grappling anchors. As we headed into the swell the black sky broke, and the sun cast warm streaks of colour across the cliffs. On the rocky teeth of the reefs, spreadeagled, totem-like cormorants took advantage of the warmth and stretched out their wings to dry.

No one spoke. We were proud of our 6,000 hours of work underwater. The sea-bed we excavated is now gutted, broken up, over-turned and unrecognisable. The rock, scraped to the quick for ten whole months, is gouged with deep wounds. The sea hid her secret well, but with patience we learned all her ruses, one by one, and snatched from her all she had been keeping to herself for 400 years.

Of course we did not cover every square inch. There are still a few gold coins scattered around at Port na Spaniagh and one or two can-non balls buried under stones and sand. But less and less of them, further and further apart, more and more difficult to find. We would not return to Port na Spaniagh. We had done a good job. We have fulfilled, maybe even surpassed, all reasonable expectations. Our consciences were clear.

The legal problems raised by my discoveries were without precedent and incredibly complicated. The artifacts recovered have no clear legal status and no owner. I am only the possessor of them.

My own wish was that rather than going under the hammer to the highest bidder and straight into the glass cases of a few American or Swiss millionaires, the entire collection from the finest jewel down to the humblest cannon ball, should remain intact in a maritime or archaeological museum. There it could be permanently displayed with contemporary documents and together with our maps, charts and photographs that tell the complete story of those three long, marvel-lous years of work. After years of delays and negotiations with the Crown, I was to succeed. The Ulster Museum, Northern Ireland National Museum, was officially designated to house the collection, and the 'Girona Rooms' were opened on 22 June, 1972.

And now, the most difficult part still remained to be done: from some 12,000 artifacts: jewels, coins, utensils, ship's remains, arms, shot, instruments, pot shards and other fragments, I must extract every bit of information they can still yield—about the galleass and her passengers, about life aboard, about the technical skills and the art of the period, and having done that I must publish it all.

After that we will all set off together to a new wreck.

One day, in the cave, I was trying to release the winged golden sala-mander from between three large stones. It was encrusted with rubies and engraved down to the tiniest scale. I did not want to scratch it. I

thought I had been working at it for three quarters of an hour. When
I had to go on to reserve, I realised that I had been there three hours,
but at last I was holding the salamander in the palm of my hand, quite
beautiful, and firmly set on its feet. Then, almost imperceptibly he
beat his wings and wriggled. He looked up at me with his little dragon's
eye, his turned up nose, and curled back his lip, showing his teeth. I
smiled back at him and that day I knew that I was still a child and I
swore to myself that I would remain a child for the rest of my life, that
I would never stop enjoying the pastimes and simple delights of childhood. For I knew then that I was making good use of my life, every
moment of it, because I knew that I was happy.

ALONZO MARTINEZ DE LEIVA

'Our' Don Alonzo Martinez De Leiva must not be confused with:

—Don Sancho De Leiva, his father, Knight of Santiago, famous general of galleys and Viceroy of Naples.

—Don Sancho De Leiva, his brother, Knight of Santiago, who was not on the expedition.

—Don Pedro De Leiva, his younger brother, Knight of Alcantara, who served with his father and with his brother, Alonzo. No one knows whether he was on the expedition or not.

—Don Diego De Leiva (perhaps another brother) who sailed on the *rata* also, with his company of 145 soldiers (Tercio of Andalusia).

—Captain Antonio De Leiva, who had a company of 134 Castilians in the Armada.

—Don Francisco De Leiva, ex-admiral of the Plate Fleets, who was *cabo*, second in command of the squadron of Levant.

—Don Juan De Leyva, described simply as a 'knight adventurer'.

—Don Antonio Luis De Leiva, Prince of Ascoli, said to be the bastard son of Philip II, who sailed in the *San Martin* and who should not be confused with

—Don Antonio De Leiva, famous for his defense of Pavia against Francis I, favourite general of Charles V and first Prince of Ascoli (1480–1536). He was the uncle of Don Sancho, 'our' De Leiva's father.

There were two houses of De Leiva (or De Leyva; both spellings were used), the Castile one and the Murcia one. 'Our' Don Alonzo was 'Señor de la Casa De Leiva de Rioja' (Castile). His arms were sinoples, a tower with three open turrets or fretty gules, bordered gules charged with thirteen stars, three on the chief, four on the point, and three on each flank, one above another.

APPENDIX II

THE GALLEASS

The name galleass was applied to large war galleys, in particular Venetian ones, but the real galleass was a large square-rigged vessel, a cross between a galley and a great ship, with an iron-covered beak. It was thought by its designers to combine the advantages of the two types of vessel, the free movement of the one with the firepower and solid bulk of the other.

Vittore Fausto built the first galleass in Venice in 1529, but at that stage it was no more than a large galley with lateen sails.

At the battle of Lepanto (1571) six Venetian galleasses, in the vanguard of the Christian galleys, destroyed the Turkish formation with the fire from their heavy prow batteries and managed to upset the enemy with their broadside perriers. Those particular galleasses, built by Francis Bressano, carried sixty pieces of ordnance—lombards, cannon, demi-cannon, culverins and perriers—in three heavy prow batteries and two poop batteries, the perriers between the thwarts, somewhat hindering their manoeuvring. In the shelter of the castles were musketeers and arquebusiers. Those galleasses were 172 ft long by 22 ft wide. There were between thirteen and sixteen oars on each side. Chained to each of the twenty-six to thirty-two thwarts and protected by the upper deck, six to ten galley slaves pushed or pulled them, using grips fixed to the shafts. Two more oars reinforced the stern rudder.

In 1587, Santa Cruz had requested six for the Armada. He was expecting great things of them. And yet even at Lepanto the galleys had had to tow the galleasses into the battle and then position them for firing.

While the Venetian galleasses, Mediterranean vessels, were more like galleys than great ships, the ones that Bazan wanted for the Atlantic were closer to the great ship than to the galley.

There were never very many galleasses. The Channel encounters proved that in practise they combined the disadvantages of the galleys with those of the galleons, rather than their advantages. In normal conditions they moved under sail, using their oars only in absolutely calm, mill pond conditions. Even then, as soon as they were outclassed in fire power, the rowers became too vulnerable for the vessels to retain any worthwhile degree of mobility.

PLAN OF ORDNANCE SALVAGED

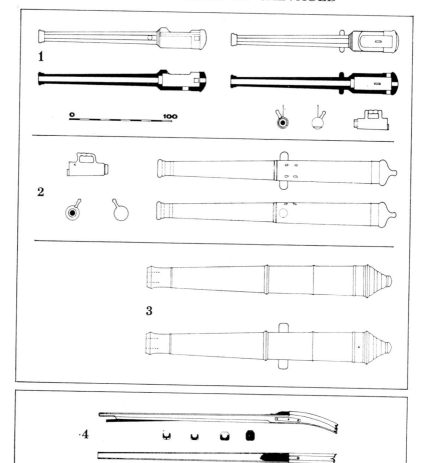

1. Esmeril with its *recamaras* (*Girona*, bronze)
2. Demi-saker with a missing part (*Girona*, bronze)
3. Falcon recovered from the small island in Kiltoorish
   Lake (*Daquessa Santa Ana*, Iron)
4. Musket (*Girona*)

Family tree of the de Granvelles, showing the relation between Madame de Champagney and Don Tomas Perrenoto.

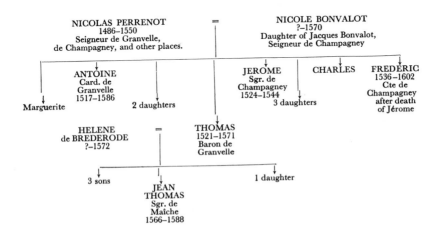

SUMMARY INVENTORY OF ARTIFACTS SALVAGED: 1967–1969

Coins

Gold: 405
Silver: 756
Copper: 115

Jewellery

Important gold jewels: 35
Gold rings: 12
Gold chains: 8
Gold-plated chains: 1 (fragment)
Silver crucifixes: 2 (1 gold-plated)
plus several fragments

Medallions

Holy (made to be worn): 6
Round: 2

Nautical Instruments

Nautical dividers: 5
Astrolabes: 2
Sounding leads: 3
Unidentified: 1 (fragment)
Hour-glasses: 2 (doubtful, fragments of support)

Armaments

Bronze cannon: 2 (+ powder chamber of a third)
Small arms: 1 musket (stock only)
         2 flint locks (fragments)
         3 unidentified (fragments)
Sidearms: Swords or daggers: 4 (hilts only)

V. Summary inventory of artifacts salvaged 1967–1969

Shot

Iron cannon balls: 61
Stone balls: 127
Lead bullets: 1865

Lead

Ingots: 17 + 7 fragments
Plates: 23 + 3 fragments
Parts of Pulley blocks (square truncated pyramids, with a round central hole for the
   shaft): 32
Seals: 17
Steelyard weight: 1
Thin fragments of hull linings: several

Silver

Debris and fragments of
   Forks: 48
   Spoons: 22
   Ladles: 2
   Plates: 71 (one gold-plated)
   Small plates: 3
   Dishes: 41
   Gold-plated or decorated dishes: 10
   Sauce boats: 1
   Assorted spouts: 39
   Phials: 17
   Flasks: 4
   Bowls: 31
   Gold-plated or decorated bowls: 7
   Goblets and tankards: 27
   Covered pots: 27
   Candle snuffer: 1
   Sugar basin: 1
   Inkwells: 3 (doubtful)
   Candlesticks: 36
   Unidentified objects, moulded, gold-plated and chased: 26
   Chair decorations (?): 2
   Hilt-guard: 1
   plus many unidentified fragments

Pewter

Vases: 2
Bowls: 7

Dishes: 2
Soup plates: 3
Plates: 16
Small plate: 1
Capsules (?): 3
Pots: 2
Pots with handles: 2
Candlestick: 1
Jugs (or pitchers): 3
Hinge: 1

Bronze

Unidentified instruments: 11
Belt or strap buckles: 4
Feet from caskets, dishes, etc.: 3
Rod: 1
Decorated artifacts set on four feet: 1
Casket on bronze feet: 1
Crucible: 1
Powder pestles: 2
Powder mortars: 2
Apothecary's pestle: 1
Nails: 19
Pins: 2

Copper

Dishes: 2
Circular container: 1
Cooking pot: 1
Knobs of cooking pot lids: 4
Cooking pot handles: 10
Feet off kitchen pots: 19
Stems and rods: 19
Unidentified hooks: 13
Unidentified tools and instruments: 7 (fragments)
Blade: 1
Ring: 1
Handle: 1 (from a knife or fork?)
plus many unidentified fragments

Pottery

Large pot with handle: 1
Other pots: 5

V. Summary inventory of artifacts salvaged 1967–1969

Small pot with spout: 1
Flat-bottomed vases: 2
Glazed pots: black: 3
           green: 8
           grey: 2
           yellow: 2
           white: 2
Decorated bowls: 4

Marble

Unidentified objects: egg-shaped, pierced from end to end: 4

Various

Knife: 1 (handle only)
Pen knives: 3 (handles and handle decorations)
Whetstone: 2
Rope: 3 bits
Sinkers: 13
Leather objects: straps: 2
                sole: 1
                Unidentified: 1
Glass bottle: 1 (fragment)
Window pane: 1 (bevelled corner fragment)
Bone: fragments (kitchen debris)
Anchor: 1
Anvil: 1
Small anchor: 1 (from a launch?)

Index

Index

Mary, Queen of Scots, 21, 133
Mary Rose, 74, 78
Mary Tudor, 116, 217, 254
M'Cabbe, Melaghlin, 123
McConaghie, John, 192, 201, 207
McConaghie, Mrs, 185
McDonnell, James, 135, 139, 149, 151, 152, 159, 234, 267
McDonnell, Randall (Earl of Antrim), 149n
McDonnell, Sorley Boy, 135, 136, 149, 152, 153, 159, 162, 201, 232, 233, 234
McLennan, John, 234, 248
McSweeney ne Bannagh, 132
McSweeney ne Doe, 128, 129, 131, 132, 135, 233
Medina, Don Juan Gomez de, 42, 52
Medina, Diego, Marquez de, 215
Medina Sidonia, Duke of, 13, 31–41, 44, 46–57, 59, 60, 71, 72, 74, 74n, 75–8, 80, 81, 83–91, 97–102, 111–13, 118, 121, 167, 169, 201n, 229, 246, 248
Medrano, Don Diego, 42
Mendoza, Don Bernardino de, 19, 21, 29, 56, 57, 58, 59, 60, 136, 139, 145, 149, 150
Mendoza, Don Pedro de, 121
Miranda, Captain Louis de, 81, 89, 98
Moncada, Don Hugo de, 42, 82, 92, 214–5

Napolitana (galleas), 42
National Geographic Magazine, 131, 187, 240
National Maritime Museum, Greenwich, 237
Nova, Juan de, 128, 130, 149, 150
Nuestra Señora de Begona, 96
Nuestra Señora de la Rosa (Guipuzcoan *almiranta*), 118, 145, 167, 170
Nuestra Señora del Pilar de Saragoza, 42
Nuestra Señora del Rosario, (Andalusian *capitana*), 75, 76, 77, 78, 80, 81, 169

Ocean Systems Inc, 145
O'Dogherty, Sir John, 135
Olivarez, Count, 23, 56, 57, 58, 59, 60
O'Maillie, Dowdarra, 121
Oquendo, Don Miguel de, 41, 69, 82, 86, 88, 90, 97, 112, 227
Ormond, Duke of, 121
O'Rourke, Bryan na Murtha, 124
Osorio, Don Cristobal de Torres, 215
Paleologus, Manuel, 265

Parma and Piacenza, Duke of, 22, 24, 29, 30, 36, 51, 57, 58, 59, 60, 69, 72, 84, 86, 88, 89, 98, 114, 133, 248
Patrona, the (of the galleases), *see Zuniga*
Perrenot, Frédéric (Comte de Champagney), 24, 209, 273
Perrenot, Jean Thomas (grandson of Mme de Champagney), 211, 212, 267, 273
Perrenot, Jérome, 210, 273
Perrenot, Nicolas, 210, 273
Perrot, Sir John, 158, 159
Philip II, 13, 18, 19, 20, 21, 24, 29, 30, 31, 32, 33, 35, 36, 37, 48, 49, 50, 51, 52, 53, 55, 56, 57, 58, 59, 60, 69, 72, 76, 84, 86, 99, 101, 111, 112, 113, 115, 133, 134, 136, 139, 145, 150, 201n, 217, 219, 245, 249, 252, 253, 254
Pimental, Don Diego, 59, 73, 82
Pius V, Pope, 22
Pleasure, 82
Plymouth, 69, 71, 72, 74
Pollilly, 125, 126, 127
Popinjay, 136
Port Ballintrae, 171, 184, 186, 188, 192, 239, 247
Port na Spaniagh, 147, 148, 152, 153, 154, 157, 160, 161, 172, 184, 186, 188, 190, 191, 205, 210, 231, 232, 268
Potter, John, 144
Preservation Laboratory, Ulster Museum, 242
Priego, Captain, 75

Queen's University, Belfast, 242, 243, 251

Rata, the, *see Sancta Maria Encoronada*
Recalde, Juan Martinez de, 41, 48, 58, 71, 72, 73, 74, 74n, 80, 82, 83, 84, 85, 88, 97, 99, 101, 112, 117, 118, 121, 211, 227
Receiver of Wreck, Coleraine, 185, 191, 198n
Rees Jones, Stephen, 242, 243, 244
Regazona, 73
Revenge, 73, 78, 83

Sancta Maria Encoronada (the *rata*), 41, 45, 48, 73, 82, 92, 115, 116, 124, 125, 126, 134, 211, 215, 231, 252
San Felipe, 29, 96, 98
San Juan, 74, 96, 115
San Juan Batista, 169